MW01620821

Jasper Johns GRAY

James Rondeau & Douglas Druick

With contributions by Mark Pascale,
Richard Shiff, Barbara Rose, and
Kelly Keegan and Kristin Lister,
and an interview with the artist by
Nan Rosenthal

Jasper Johns
GRAY

THE ART INSTITUTE OF CHICAGO
YALE UNIVERSITY PRESS, New Haven and London

generously provided by the Harris Family Foundation in memory of Bette and Neison Harris.

In New York, the exhibition is made possible by United Technologies Corporation.

The project is also supported by an award from the National Endowment for the Arts, which believes a great nation deserves great art. An indemnity is provided by the Federal Council on the Arts and the Humanities.

First edition
Printed in Germany
Library of Congress Control Number: 2007933996
ISBN 978-0-300-11949-7 (cloth)
ISBN 978-0-86559-224-7 (paper)

Susan F. Rossen, Executiv

Edited by Robert V. Sharp
and Elizabeth Stepina, Sp

Production by Sarah E. G
Associate Director, and C
Production Coordinator

Photography research by
Photography Editor

Designed and typeset by
Fold Four, Inc., Milwauke

Separations by Professio
Rockford, Illinois

Printed in Germany by C

Details

Page 17: *Jubilee* (cat. no.
Page 18: *0 through 9* (cat.
Page 19: *Good Time Char*
Page 20: *The Dutch Wives*
Page 21: *Tracing* (cat. no.
Page 174: *Within* (cat. no.

Contents

Exhibition Sponsors

The exhibition in Chicago is made possible by
Kenneth and Anne Griffin.

Major funding is generously provided by
the Harris Family Foundation
in memory of Bette and Neison Harris.

In the hope that visitors and readers will glean a new appreciation and enriched understanding of an extraordinary artist who has been before the public for over fifty years, we are pleased to be able to mount this exhibition on Jasper Johns and issue this accompanying catalogue. The logistical challenges that went into organizing the exhibition were substantial, as were the research and scholarship that inform the catalogue. Such projects can not be undertaken without significant benefaction from the museum's patrons and friends. On behalf of the Trustees of The Art Institute of Chicago, I want to gratefully acknowledge the support and confidence of Kenneth and Anne Griffin and the Harris Family Foundation in underwriting the organization of this exemplary exhibition and the publication of this handsome catalogue.

Thomas J. Pritzker
Chairman of the Board of Trustees
The Art Institute of Chicago

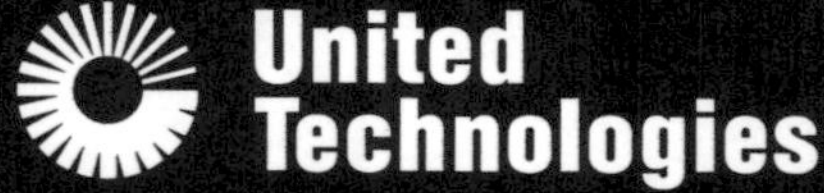

The French poet André Gide once remarked, "The color of truth is gray." Perhaps the same thought has motivated Jasper Johns's lifelong use of gray, his favorite color. He has captured each of his motifs in varying shades of gray and in a range of media, seeking to discover whether gray is a color or, as he has suggested, the absence of it.

United Technologies Corporation is pleased to sponsor this first ever retrospective of Johns's works in shades of gray. This is comparably a constant design theme for us. The absence of noise and vibration, perfect reliability, and minimizing energy use with more efficient performance characterize all that we do, whether in elevators (Otis) or air conditioning (Carrier) or aircraft engines (Pratt & Whitney). Making UTC products disappear in their footprint while still performing their service could be said to be our own "shades of gray."

UTC's first sponsorship of a Metropolitan Museum of Art exhibition was in 1982, and we are glad to be returning with this exhibition as we have often in the interim. Special thanks to the Metropolitan Museum's curatorial and administrative staff for bringing this remarkable show to New York.

George David
Chairman and Chief Executive Officer

Louis Chênevert
President and Chief Operating Officer

Directors' Foreword

Without question, Jasper Johns is one of the greatest artists of our era. For fifty years his paintings, drawings, sculptures, and prints have attracted intelligent criticism and high praise, in equal measure. From Johns's first solo exhibition at Leo Castelli's gallery in 1958, Alfred H. Barr bought three paintings for The Museum of Modern Art, New York; a fourth was acquired by Philip Johnson at Barr's urging and given to the museum fifteen years later. The paintings' apparent subjects included the soon to be familiar Johnsian motifs of stenciled numbers, a target, and the American flag; images and icons that would later lead some critics to misinterpret Johns's paintings as pictures referencing the banal world of commercial products and the popular media as a means of criticizing, even subverting it. But Johns's art was never that straightforward. Indeed, it was always more ambiguous and deeply resonant with references to the psychology of perception, philosophical inquiry, poetry, and the history of painting.

In interview after interview Johns has been disarmingly literal in his responses to questions and in his remarks about his works. On the one hand, his sketchbook notes include statements that appear to reduce painting to a set of simple operations, of making marks free of other, more sophisticated intentions. Yet we know his paintings work on levels other than that. His earliest target was surmounted with plaster casts of human body parts, suggesting perhaps the fragmentation of the self. The next painting was accompanied by plaster casts of faces cut off at eye level, as if to invite meditation on blindness as a measure of failure in the world of the visual. We can not know if Johns intended these thoughtful responses to his pictures — only that his art encourages them: "I personally would like to keep the painting in a state of 'shunning statement,' so that one is left with the fact that one can experience individually as one pleases; that is, not to focus the attention in one way, but to leave the situation as a kind of actual thing, so that the experience of it is variable."

Given that Johns's early paintings are nuanced in gesture, straightforward in imagery, and limited in their range of colors, one might imagine that they would deflect further inquiry. Nothing could be farther from the truth. Yet, one aspect of his work that has not attracted serious attention until now is his use of gray, throughout his career, in all media. It is the contribution of this exhibition and this catalogue to focus our attention on how Johns has used this color in his art over the years, from his earliest work to his most recent, in ways seemingly direct and in other ways indirect and highly evocative.

At The Art Institute of Chicago we are grateful to James Rondeau, the Frances and Thomas Dittmer Curator and Chair of the Department of Contemporary Art, and to Douglas Druick, the Searle Curator of Medieval through Modern European Painting and Sculpture, and the Prince Trust Curator of Prints and Drawings, and Chair of those respective departments, for their conception of the exhibition and its accompanying catalogue, and for the impressive scholarship that they have brought to bear on Johns's career. We express our thanks as well to Mark Pascale, Associate Curator of Prints and Drawings at the Art Institute, and to Nan Rosenthal, Senior Consultant for Nineteenth-Century, Modern, and Contemporary Art at The Metropolitan Museum of Art, New York, for their part in shaping the exhibition's content and for their lasting contributions to this catalogue. We are also grateful to the many lenders, private and institutional, who have entrusted us with the care of their works during the course of this exhibition. We know how difficult it is to part with things one derives such daily pleasure from, even if only for a few months. That they have agreed to part with these works is testament to their regard for the importance of the artist, the originality of the exhibition's subject, and the role of museums in bringing a large and diverse public before works of art of the very highest quality.

We also acknowledge the generous funders who have made possible the organization of this exhibition and the publication of its scholarship, Kenneth and Anne Griffin. Major support was also received from the Harris Family Foundation, and, for the presentation at the Metropolitan Museum, from United Technologies Corporation.

Our greatest debt of gratitude is of course to the artist himself, for the art that he has made over five decades and for his generosity in lending so many important works from his own collection. No artist is more trusting of serious curatorial effort than Jasper Johns. And we thank him very much indeed.

James Cuno
President & Eloise W. Martin Director
The Art Institute of Chicago

Philippe de Montebello
Director
The Metropolitan Museum of Art, New York

Acknowledgments

We would like to express our gratitude to Jasper Johns. The idea for this exhibition, which grew out of two acquisitions of his work for the collection of the Art Institute of Chicago—*Untitled*, 2001, and *Near the Lagoon*, 2002–03—has, from the outset, enjoyed the artist's crucial and active support. We deeply appreciate his gracious and ready engagement during our regular visits to the studio over the last four years. Not only has he been critical to the evolution of the exhibition's concept, he is also its principal lender. Sarah Taggart, Administrative Assistant to Jasper Johns, has been invaluable in every aspect of the organizational process, tirelessly sharing information and responding to our seemingly endless queries with characteristic professionalism and thoughtfulness.

No exhibition of this scale and ambition can take place without generous loans from private collectors and public institutions. We are profoundly indebted to all lenders, listed on a page following these acknowledgments, for entrusting us to care for, and hopefully elucidate, these precious objects.

We express our appreciation to numerous individuals for their assistance with loans from private collections: Stefano Basilico, Neal Benezra, Carol Borah, Calvin Brown, Marjorie Cohn, Harry Cooper, Magdalena Dabrowski, Jodi Deichmiller, Anthony Dorment, Lily Dorment, Geena Dygas, James Elliot, Vicki Gambill, Laura Giles, Helyn Goldenberg, Michelle Gonçalves, Joan Gonzalez, Jeannine Guido, Anthony Grant, Gina C. Guy, Emily Hankle, Sandy Heller, Joanne Heyler, Katherine Hinds, Susan Hirschfeld, Antonio Homem, Brad Hudson, Alexia Hughes, Johanna Humbert, Erin Hyde, Lauren Jaeger, Bonnie Jordan, Lynn Kearcher, Margo Leavin, Thomas Lentz, Peggy Letts, Arabella Makari, Ann Marcus, Giovanni Massimo Martino, Jessica Mastro, Rachel Mauro, Maureen McCormick, Trina McKeever, James Meyer, Sharon Monahan, Maria Naula, Lana Nelson, Kelly Parady, Laura Paulson, Jeanette Preston, Margaret Rosenbaum, Whitney Rugg, Paula Sasso, Chloé Schon, Piers Secunda, David Sturtevant, David White, Lanya White, Queenie Wong, Charles Wylie, Annemarie and Gianfranco Verna, Mary Zlot.

Among institutional lenders, we are grateful to these colleagues: Brian T. Allen, Juliann McDonough, Denise Johnson, James Sousa at the Addison Gallery of American Art, Phillips Academy, Andover; Doreen Bolger, Jay Fisher, Darsie Alexander, Melanie Harwood, Sarah Sellers, Mandy Bartram, Brianna Bedigan at the Baltimore Museum of Art; Jeffrey Fleming, Rose Wood, Mickey Koch at the Des Moines Art Center; Olga Viso, Kerry Brougher, Kristen Hileman, Barbara Freund, Keri Towler, Lee Stalworth, Amy Snyder, Bruce Day at the Hirshhorn Museum and Sculpture Garden, Smithsonian Institution; Bernhard Mendes Burghi, Roland Wetzel, Janine Guntern, Charlotte Gutzwiller, Sara De Bernardis at the Kunstmuseum Basel; Armin Zweite, Anette Kruszynski, Katharina Nettekoven, Katja Winterpagt, Dagmar Kurtz at the Kunstsammlung Nordrhein-Westfalen; Jeremy Strick, Paul Schimmel, Ann Goldstein, Robert Hollister, Karen Hanus, George Davis, Elma O'Donoghue at the Los Angeles Museum of Contemporary Art; Josef Helfenstein, Franklin Sirmans, Anne Adams, Judy Kwon at the Menil Collection; Robert Fitzpatrick, Elizabeth Smith, Francesco Bonami, Jennifer Draffen, Jude Palmese at the Museum of Contemporary Art, Chicago; Glenn Lowry, John Elderfield, Cornelia Butler, Cora Rosevear, Kathy Curry, John Prochilo, Erik Landsberg, Karl Buchberg, Mattias Herold at the Museum of Modern Art, New York; Minoru Ohata, Hiroko Inazuka at the Museum of Modern Art, Toyama; Edelbert Köb, Dr. Sophie Hasser at the Museum Moderner Kunst Stiftung Ludwig, Vienna; Earl A. Powell III, Alan Shestack, Jeffrey Weiss, Molly Donovan, Judith Brodie, Charles

Ritchie, Carlotta Owens, Ruth Fine, Alicia Thomas, Michelle Fondas, Marcie Hocking, Stephanie Belt, Barbara Wood at the National Gallery of Art, Washington; Shuji Takashina, Hideyuki Yanagisawa, Chikako Takaoka, Sara Durt at the Ohara Museum of Art; Anne d'Harnoncourt, Michael Taylor, Carlos Basualdo, Shannon Schuler, Ashley Carey, Emily Hage, Holly Frisbee at the Philadelphia Museum of Art; Michael Rush, Raphaela Platow, Kimberly Dorazewski at the Rose Art Museum, Brandeis University; Michael Brand, Thomas Allen, Alex Nyerges, John Ravenal, Mary Sullivan, Katherine Wetzel, Susie Rock at the Virginia Museum of Fine Arts; Kathy Halbreich, Philippe Vergne, Joan Rothfuss, Gwen Bitz, Joseph King, Heather Scanlan, Pamela Caserta, Cameron Wittig at the Walker Art Center; Adam Weinberg, Donna DeSalvo, Carter Foster, Abigail Hoover, Anita Duquette, Claire Gerhard at the Whitney Museum of American Art.

We owe a special debt of thanks to Matthew Marks, who was key to the early planning for the exhibition and has been an on-going resource. He and the staff of the Matthew Marks Gallery were tremendously helpful in a variety of capacities, most especially in helping us to locate works of art in private collections.

It has been our great pleasure to work with the distinguished guest contributors to this publication: Richard Shiff, Effie Marie Cain Regents Chair in Art, Director of the Center for the Study of Modernism, University of Texas at Austin; Barbara Rose, Independent Scholar; Nan Rosenthal, Senior Consultant, Department of Nineteenth-Century, Modern, and Contemporary Art at the Metropolitan Museum of Art. Each is an established Johns scholar, and, having learned from their previous work, we are fortunate to have had their participation. At the Art Institute of Chicago, fellow authors Mark Pascale, Associate Curator of Prints and Drawings, Kristin Lister, Conservator of Painting, and Kelly Keegan, Assistant Conservator of Painting, have enriched our understanding of the topic through their original research and writing.

Research for this publication has been advanced by the expertise of many. Foremost, we acknowledge with great appreciation the scholarship of Roberta Bernstein, Professor of Art History, State University of New York at Albany. Her knowledge of Jasper Johns's work is as comprehensive as her generosity in sharing it. We thank her for her conscientious readings and sage counsel. Many other experts, archivists, writers, educators, and administrators answered our queries with patience and insight: Theodore Barber, Ann Brandwein, Robin Copp, Roberta VH. Copp, Brenda Danilowitz, Gene Gaddis, Bill Goldston, Michelle Harvey, Judith Hastings, Fred Horowitz, Jonathan Katz, Raimond Livasgani, Katy Martin, Sina Najafi, Esther Sprague, Lilian Tone.

The research for the project naturally involved the careful examination of objects, aided by conservation professionals around the country. In this regard, we owe particular thanks to Brad Epley, Joe Fronek, Franca Franciolli, Kelley Loftus, Liz Lunning, Werner Müller, Rachel Mustalish, Martin Bansbach, Samantha Rippner, Cheryle Robertson, Paul Pfister, Yosi Pozeilov, Carol Sawyer, Bruce Suffield, Jim Wright.

For other support, we thank Cliff Ackley, Barbara Baruch, Michael Brandweis, Cristopher Canizares, Tommaso Corvi-Mora, Igor DaCosta, Sandi di Andrea, Spencer Finch, Gaylen Gerber, Cornelia Grassi, Eric Johnson, Judith Russi Kirshner, Kasper König, Peter Marzio, James Meyer, Yutaka Mino, Muriel Kallis Steinberg Newman, Alfred Pacquement, Eugenia Petrova, Paul and Stacy Polydoran, Barbaralee Diamonstein Spielvogel, Michael and Judy Steinhardt, Barry Walker, Billie Milam Weisman, Peter Zegers.

This exhibition, initiated and organized by the Art Institute of Chicago, has benefited from our collaboration with colleagues at the Metropolitan Museum of Art. Philippe de Montebello, Director, and Gary Tinterow, Engelhard Curator in Charge of the Department of Nineteenth-Century, Modern, and Contemporary Art, responded enthusiastically to the idea for the exhibition early on, and have been stalwart supporters throughout. It has been stimulating to work with Nan Rosenthal, whose efforts have been assisted by Nora Burnett and Ian Alteveer. Nan's relationship with Johns's work, and her informed opinions about his practice, have enhanced our project in meaningful ways. Also deserving of thanks are Mahrukh Tarapor, Associate Director for Exhibitions and Director for International Affairs, and Linda Sylling, Manager for Special Exhibitions, Gallery Installations, and Design.

At the Art Institute of Chicago, the project has benefited from extraordinary support, beginning with the initial encouragement of James N. Wood, who was instrumental in working with the artist to acquire *Near the Lagoon*, the last in a long line of major purchases that he oversaw for this museum as director. Since his arrival in 2004, James Cuno, the current President and Eloise W. Martin Director—and himself a Johns scholar—has been unstintingly enthusiastic in his embrace of the exhibition and related programming. Their contributions have been critical, as has that of Dorothy Schroeder, Vice President for Exhibitions and Museum Administration. Special thanks are due as well to Patricia Woodworth, Julie Getzels, Meredith Mack, Mary Jane Drews, Maria Simon, Jeanne Ladd.

In the Department of Contemporary Art, Maureen Pskowski, Exhibitions Manager, deserves particular recognition. With her meticulous organizational skills, unfailing composure, and astute attention to detail, the contributions she has made to the multifaceted organization of this exhibition are incalculable. Essential as well has been the participation of Jesse Feiman, Research Assistant, who has been singularly devoted in his efforts to help us come to terms with the vast Johns's literature. Further, we gratefully acknowledge Lisa Dorin, Nora Riccio, Kristin Brockman, Colleen Thorne, Rae Riffel. Nicholas Barron oversaw the installation of the exhibition with care and finesse. In the Departments of Prints and Drawings and Medieval to Modern European Painting and Sculpture, we wish to thank Suzanne McCullagh and Matt Stolle, as well as Geri Banik, whose tireless devotion to the often-complicated issues of travel and scheduling merits individual mention.

The museum's Ryerson and Burnham Libraries, under the direction of Jack Brown, together with Bart Ryckbosch, Mary Woolever, Amy Ballmer, Melanie Emerson, significantly fostered our research efforts. We would also like to acknowledge the important contributions of those who, on our behalf, accessed these resources the most, our interns and volunteers: Tom Barron, Anne Roberts, Eileen Jeng, Hilary Coe Smith, Kim Baskin, Suzanna Rudofsky, Kathleen McGovern, Emma Bee Bernstein, Jenny Gheith.

From the inception of the project, conservation research, examination, and issues of presentation have been crucial elements. In addition to Kristin Lister and Kelly Keegan, whose work is published here, we would like to recognize our Art Institute colleagues Frank Zuccari, Harriet Stratis, Allison Langley, Francesca Casadio, Barbara Hall, Kirk Vuillemot, Charles Pietraszewski, Chris Conniff-O'Shea, Gwenäelle Gautier, Inge Fiedler, Anikó Bezúr.

The present volume is the result of exceptional efforts by the staff of the Publications Department, headed by Susan Rossen. Robert V. Sharp deftly led the extensive editorial enterprise with the excellent collaboration of Elizabeth Stepina. We thankfully acknowledge our indebtedness to both of them for their extremely diligent oversight and many valued suggestions. Former colleague Britt Salvesen was an invaluable reader, and both of our essays were further improved as a result of her insights. Sarah Guernsey, aided by Carolyn Heidrich and Joseph Mohan, has been indefatigable in her expert supervision of and dedication to the quality of the catalogue's design and production. We also acknowledge the assistance of Kate Kotan and Emily Clary. A fundamental goal was to realize a plate section that would do justice to the richness and diversity of Johns's grays. To this end, we engaged Jamie Stukenberg of Professional Graphics, Inc., to digitally capture every work in the exhibition with an eye toward accuracy and consistency. In this Jim Szyskowski ably assisted him in his many travels in the US and abroad. Pat Goley and Kirsti Monsen-Kellogg at Professional Graphics were also indispensable. Moreover, the willingness of our lenders and their respective curators, collection managers, registrars, imaging specialists, and assistants to accommodate our requests for the new photography has been remarkable. The book was beautifully designed by Roy Brooks, the principal of Fold Four, Inc., Milwaukee, Wisconsin; he showed remarkable creativity, sensitivity, and patience during a demanding process. We thank them all.

For the design and construction of the installation at the Art Institute, the wall texts and labels, and the multitude of exhibition-related material and outreach, we thank Bernice Chu, Joe Cochand, Lyn Delliquadri, Jeff Wonderland, Carrie Heinonen, Erin Hogan, Chai Lee, Ginny Voedisch, Troy Klyber, Robert Eskridge. The registrarial team, led by Mary Solt with Debra Purden and Angie Morrow, has, as usual, provided exceptional coordination of the many and complex loans and attendant shipping arrangements. The exhibition benefited from a partial indemnification from the Federal Council on the Arts and Humanities. We recognize the support of Alice Wheilihan of the National Endowment for the Arts. We are also grateful to Paul Gray, Susan Lorence, Jacqueline Tran for their assistance with the application process.

Finally, we add our sincere thanks to Kenneth and Anne Griffin, and King and Caryn Harris for their commitment to Jasper Johns's work and their generous sponsorship of the exhibition. It has been our great privilege to realize *Jasper Johns: Gray*.

James Rondeau

Frances and Thomas Dittmer Curator and Chair, Department of Contemporary Art

Douglas Druick

Prince Trust Curator and Chair, Department of Prints and Drawings

Searle Curator and Chair, Department of Medieval through Modern European Painting and Sculpture

Lenders to the Exhibition

Addison Gallery of American Art, Phillips Academy, Andover, Massachusetts
The Art Institute of Chicago
The Baltimore Museum of Art
Barbara Bluhm-Kaul
The Eli and Edythe L. Broad Collection
Barbara Bertozzi Castelli
Jean-Christophe Castelli
Steven A. Cohen
Michael Crichton
Des Moines Art Center
Barney A. Ebsworth
Stefan Edlis and H. Gael Neeson
Fogg Art Museum, Harvard University Art Museums, Cambridge, Massachusetts
Gail and Tony Ganz
Kate Ganz
Lenore and Bernard Greenberg
Kenneth and Anne Griffin
Hirshhorn Museum and Sculpture Garden, Smithsonian Institution, Washington, D.C.
The Marguerite and Robert Hoffman Collection
Jasper Johns
Kunstmuseum Basel
Kunstsammlung Nordrhein-Westfalen, Düsseldorf
Lady Belle Partnership
Mark Lancaster
Tom Levine
Ludwig Collection, Aachen
Martin Z. Margulies
The Menil Collection, Houston
Robert and Jane Meyerhoff Collection
Museum of Contemporary Art, Chicago
The Museum of Contemporary Art, Los Angeles
The Museum of Modern Art, New York
The Museum of Modern Art, Toyama
Museum Moderner Kunst Stiftung Ludwig, Vienna
National Gallery of Art, Washington
Nerman Collection, Kansas City
Ohara Museum of Art
Philadelphia Museum of Art
Judith Racht and Irving Stenn, Jr.
Robert Rauschenberg Collection
Robert Rauschenberg Foundation Collection
The Rose Art Museum, Brandeis University, Waltham, Massachusetts
The San Francisco Museum of Modern Art
Mr. and Mrs. Andrew Saul
Richard Serra and Clara Weyergraf-Serra
Sonnabend Collection
Stenn Family Collection
Virginia Museum of Fine Arts, Richmond
Walker Art Center, Minneapolis
Whitney Museum of American Art, New York

And other private collectors who wish to remain anonymous

Note to the Reader

Throughout this volume, all works reproduced are by Jasper Johns, unless otherwise stated.

PHOTOGRAPHY OF WORKS IN THE EXHIBITION

Given the nature of this exhibition — which is to examine the rich variety of gray media used by Jasper Johns across his entire career — the Art Institute of Chicago, as the organizing institution, undertook the perhaps unprecedented task of having every work in the show photographed by the same photographer, using the same lighting and digital equipment, regardless of whether the work is held by a museum, foundation, or private collection. This work was undertaken between September 2006 and July 2007, throughout the United States and Europe, by Jamie Stukenberg of Professional Graphics, Inc., Rockford, Illinois. The two works in Japanese collections were photographed by Taku Saiki of Tokyo.

CATALOGUE OF THE EXHIBITION

In the catalogue of the works in the exhibition (pp. 175–313), for all published works (whether lithographs or intaglios) the second line of the entry records the name of the publisher and the date of issue. Thus, the notation *ULAE, 1960* would indicate that a print was published in that year by Universal Limited Art Editions, West Islip, New York.

Paper types or manufacturers, where known, are indicated in parentheses at the end of the media line. In addition, two abbreviations have been used: *wmk.*, watermark, and *bls.*, blind stamp.

All prints included in the exhibition are editioned works or artist's proofs of final editioned works, unless otherwise identified as a *trial proof* or *working proof*.

Works that are included in the 1994 volume *The Prints of Jasper Johns, 1960–1993: A Catalogue Raisonné*, published by Universal Limited Art Editions, have been identified on a separate line with their respective number following the designation *ULAE/Johns cat. raisonné*. These numbers are also included for the trial or working proofs produced in advance of the editioned state.

In the designation of media, *plastic* has been used as a general term to designate Mylar or other similar polyester sheets.

All dimensions for paintings in the Catenary series are given with their maximum sizes, i.e., with hinged side wings extended.

BIBLIOGRAPHY

Short-form (i.e, author date) citations used in the endnotes for each essay are given in full in the Selected Bibliography (pp. 314–17). Citations given in full in the endnotes are not included in the bibliography.

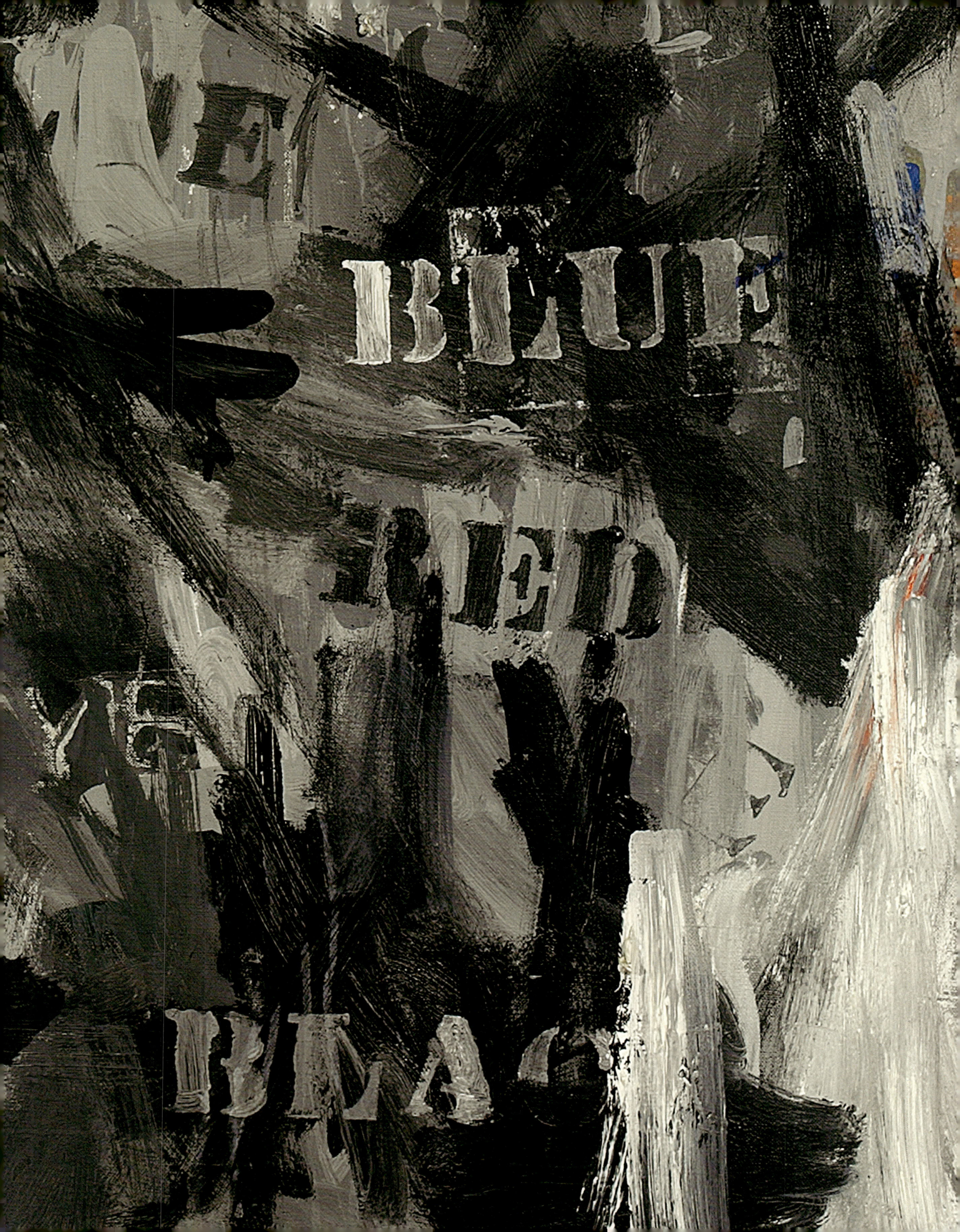
BLUE
RED

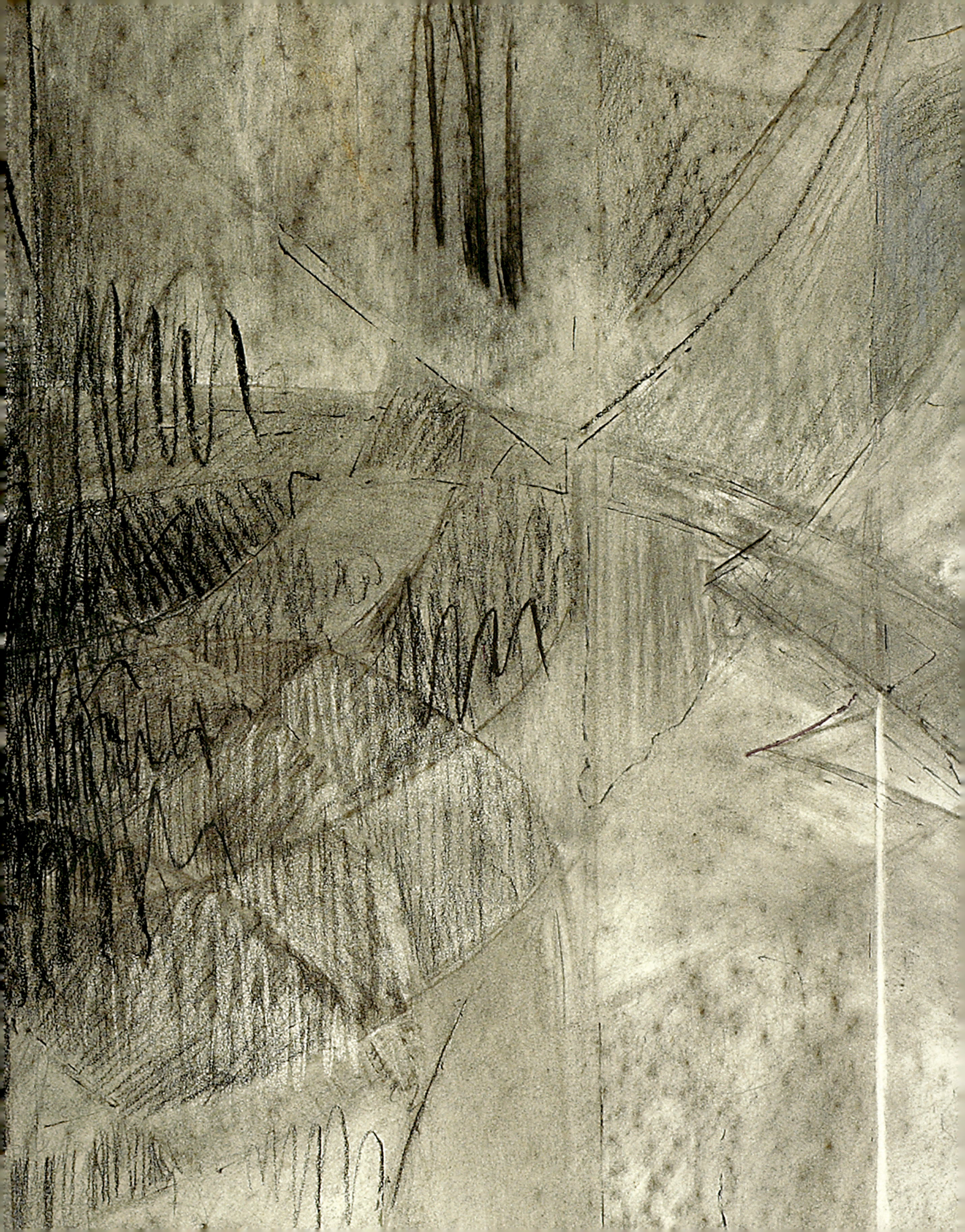

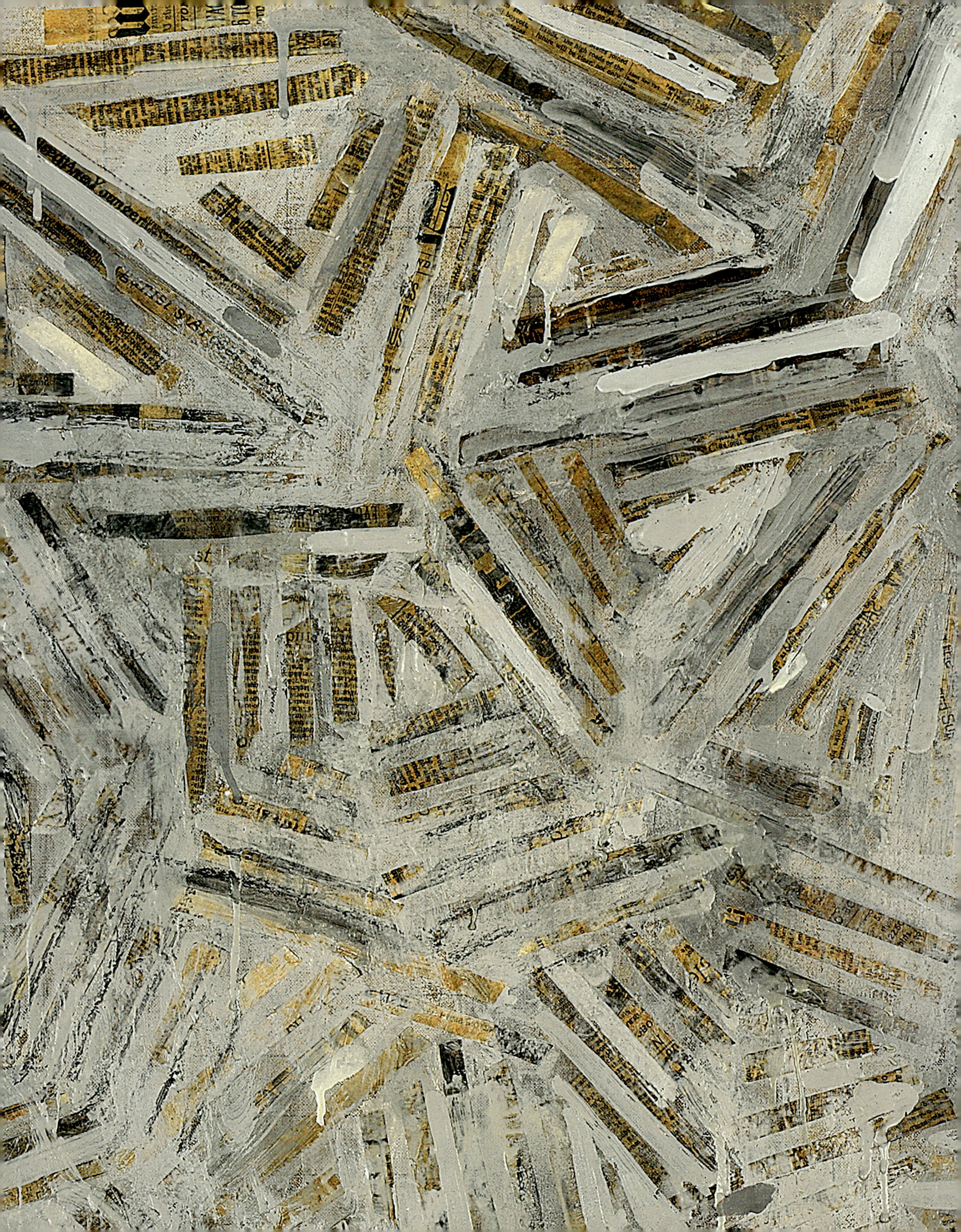

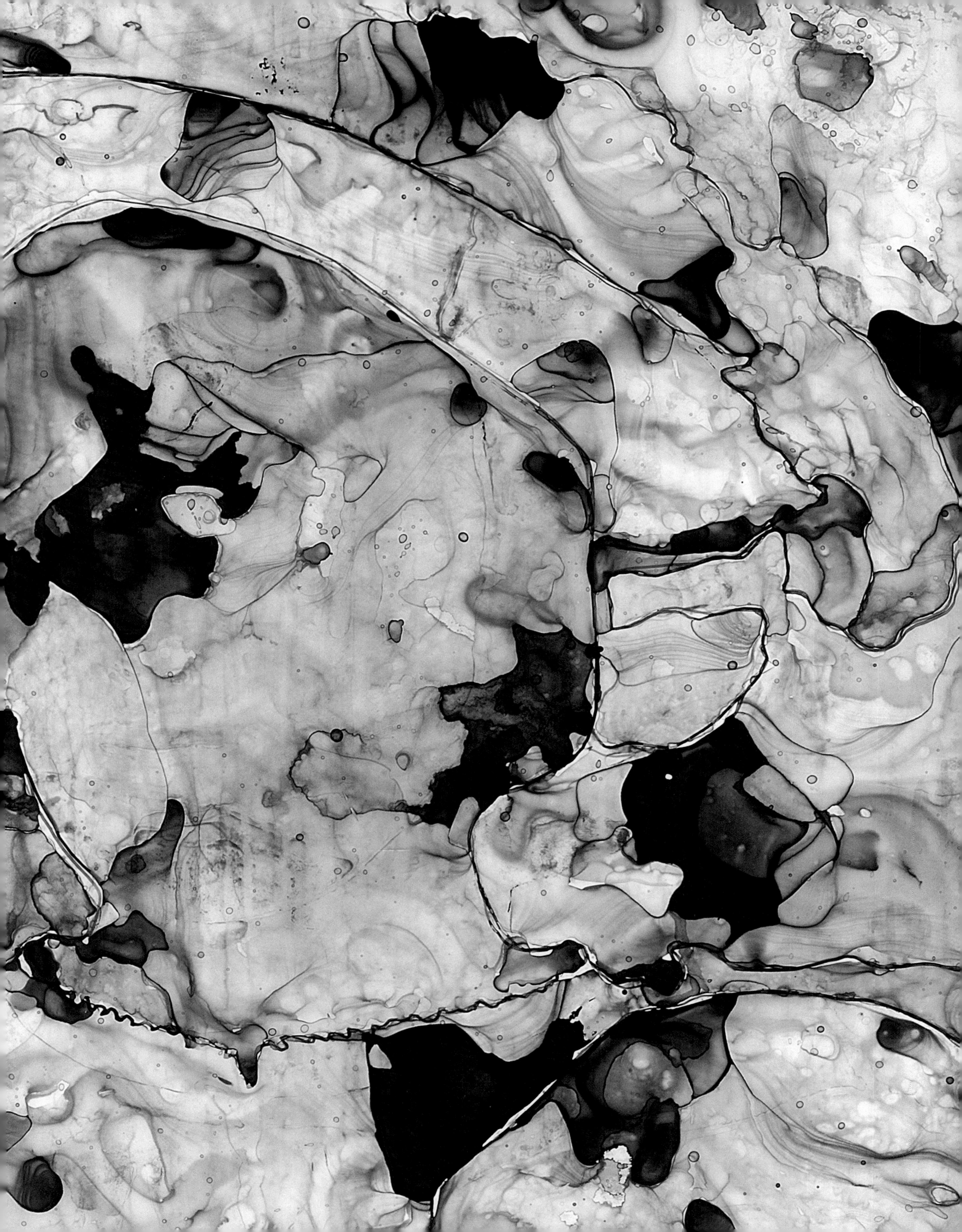

Jasper Johns
Gray

JAMES RONDEAU

For Johns gray alone has always offered so great a potential as to be almost inexhaustible by itself. His neutral paintings always exploit a certain chromatic undertone, and touches of color usually resonate through the grays. . . . This kind of close exploration of a subtle and restricted range in search of the most abundant and commodious discoveries, as we have seen so often, exactly suits Johns, and one can imagine why he hesitated for a while to move out into the larger realm of color.[1]

THE PRODUCTION OF MEANING IN THE WORK OF JASPER JOHNS, it has been argued, derives from a commitment to subject matter, a selection of medium and support, an incorporation of language on the surface or as title, the determination of compositional strategies (including the use of collage materials and objects), an approach to mark making, and the application of color.[2] Often his preferences are made manifest through essentially additive processes. Motifs and images, allusions and associations accrue over time through strategies of accumulation, repetition, and quotation. His decisions may be reasoned or intuitive, conscious or unconscious, justified or arbitrary; or they may reflect a simultaneous combination of motivations known and unknown to either the artist or a viewer or both. At other times, effect is achieved through a more determined, subtractive process, distilled as a language of forms, gestures, and objects in the absence of color. The insightful critic Max Kozloff acknowledged in 1968: "Especially after 1959, a Johns painting is a series of cancellations as much as it is a sequence of additions."[3] *Jasper Johns: Gray* isolates a certain kind of multivalent intentionality, arguing that the formal refusal of color must be understood to be its own affirmative category, a decisive act of limiting coexistent with a principled conviction to conceive and execute work in composites of black and white, or mixed color: gray. In Johns's art, gray is certainly not an unconscious or unreasoned decision, but a consequence of purposive and deliberate actions. Jean-Paul Sartre, in a passage appropriate for this consideration of Johns, once described the existential condition of man in the following way: "Not at all free not to choose: he is implicated, he must wager; abstention is a choice."[4]

The first use of the word "gray" in a picture by Jasper Johns occurs in the watershed oil painting *False Start* (1959; cat. no. 1), where it appears three times, surrounded by words naming but not labeling colors: red, yellow, blue, orange, green, violet, white, gray, and black. The designations—which were not intended to match the colors used to depict each word but in some cases do—have been stenciled onto the canvas. The technique, indebted to select Cubist precedents, proved to be hugely generative for Johns. The terms are oriented in a riot of variously opposing horizontal, vertical, and diagonal directions—angles that correspond in a general way to the overlapping brushstrokes. In places the letters are partially obscured, hidden underneath paint or cropped by the edge of the canvas.[5] The layering suggests a pictorial depth, albeit a shallow one; concerns of flatness and surface are almost equally valued. Overall, the apparently random arrangement and repetition releases a legibility calculated by both choice and accident, in the same way that certain snippets of words and phrases from embedded newsprint are allowed to surface in examples of Johns's encaustic paintings made before and after *False Start*. The picture, alive with a nervous energy, demarcates a major verge in Johns's art.[6]

Laden with thoughtful incident, *False Start* is both a form of closure and a new beginning. While such pronouncements never quite hold, given a chronology of making that does not allow for hard and fast delineations of either continuity or change, *False Start* signifies a shift, the implications of which will preoccupy the artist for decades. To begin with, the picture carries the first title Johns used that does not describe an obvious aspect of the work.[7] This departure from strictly literal nominal precedents is significant, belying an ambitiously complicated agenda. There is, more importantly, a change in the way this work is painted. The encaustics of 1954–59, largely based on found or predetermined signs such as flags, targets, alphabets, and numerals, exhibit a regular, contained facture; as such, they offered an alternative to the visual and critical rhetoric surrounding performance, gesture, and emotion endemic to New York School Action painting. This model, best exemplified in the work of Jackson Pollock and Willem de Kooning, expressed subjectivity through brushwork, spontaneity of form, and often, the temperature of "hot" colors. *False Start,* executed in oil, marks a departure from Johns's near-exclusive use of encaustic since his first surviving works of 1954. Oil paint allows a freer handling of the medium, naturally producing an attendant change in Johns's brushwork. The picture evidences flares of color, marks that curator and noted Johns scholar Kirk Varnedoe dubbed "rocket-burst patches."[8] These strokes—for which Johns coined the term "brushmarking" in a 1965 interview—are still determined and controlled, offering an overt, almost programmatic, cancellation of improvisational expressionism. (Johns will return to encaustic, of course, but his handling of this medium will correspond more closely to a style of application developed in the oils of 1959.) By embracing a painterly, if self-conscious, mode of application and simultaneously setting color at odds with language, *False Start* dismantles the expressive use of both gesture and color. The result is contradiction, a complete discordance between perceptual and linguistic cues.[9]

False Start effectively establishes a critical distance between Johns's subjectivity and his use of color. The strategy is intuitively indebted to the Austrian philosopher Ludwig Wittgenstein, although it is hardly a case of direct borrowing, as Johns perhaps did not begin a systematic study of Wittgenstein's writings until after 1960. In the *Philosophical Investigations* (1953), Wittgenstein wrote:

> Does it make sense to say that people generally agree in their judgments of color? What would it be like for them not to? One man would say a flower was red which another called blue and so on. But what right should we have to call these words "red" and "blue" our "color words"? How would they learn to use these words? And is the language-game which they learn still such as we call the use of "names of color"? There are evidently differences of degree here.[10]

Johns, pioneering his own philosophical inquiry, severed the parallel corollaries between painting and identity.

> I have attempted to develop my thinking in such a way that the work I have done is not me—not to confuse my feelings with what I produced. I didn't want my work to be an exposure of my feelings. Abstract Expressionism was so lively—personal identity and painting were more or less the same, and I tried to operate the same way. But I found I couldn't do anything that would be identical to my feelings. So I worked in such a way that I could say that it's not me. That accounts for the separation.[11]

The freedoms explored in *False Start* are not particularly the conventional ones afforded by color. Rather, the painting can only be understood as a conceptualization of color based on the concrete dissonances of perception and fact—what Kozloff qualified as "perhaps the most intellectualized formulation of color in this century."[12] Thought replaces action, to be sure, but the color "thoughts" of *False Start* are not fully realized until they are expressed alternatively through absence.

Immediately following *False Start*, Johns made a closely related oil painting in black, white, and gray, *Jubilee* (1959; cat. no. 2). By any superficial accounting, the picture is simply a grisaille copy of *False Start*.[13] But the more sedate, ironically titled *Jubilee* is not a version of the former; it is a transformative elaboration. *Jubilee* is slightly smaller (a subtle clue), and while the strategic vocabulary of words and painterly gesture is the same, neither the choice and application of color words (stenciled in thick paint) nor the deployment of brushstrokes faithfully follows their color precedent. *Jubilee* has all of the energy of *False Start* but none of the heat. Warm and cool grays mix with blacks and whites on top of brief passages of red, green, and blue. (A fragment of textile—the single visible collage element—measuring 14.5 × 6.5 cm is barely hidden along the right edge of the canvas underneath streaking layers of black and gray paint. This piece of fabric supports seven chalky red horizontal stripes. Immediately adjacent are small smudges of vibrant ultramarine and the word "blue" in gray paint. Together, these elements amount to a schematic suggestion of a flag, a buried, self-referential trademark.)[14] If *False Start* succeeds in divorcing gesture, color, and emotionalism, *Jubilee* must be understood as an emphatic reiteration, underscoring the differences between thinking *in* color and thinking *without* color. It is a point that evidently mattered to Johns. The next year, the artist realized a black-and-white-and-gray pastel rendering on paper of the brushwork and lettering of *False Start*, now, following *Jubilee*, similarly drained of color. An act of quiet differentiation, *From False Start* (1960; cat. no. 3) reprises the irony of the colorless *Jubilee* without imitating its composition.[15] Grisaille stands vividly alone.

Thirty-five years later, the artist returned to the relationship between the two compositions, again asserting the independence of the *Jubilee* composition by restating its autonomy from even a colorless version of *False Start*. The as-yet-unpublished drawing *Jubilee* (1962 and 1994; cat. no. 6) is a pastel executed in black, white, and gray (with hints of purple, red, green, and yellow) over *False Start II* (1962; cat. no. 4), a black-and-white lithograph after the painting. (Johns made both black-and-white and color lithographic printings of *False Start*. The color lithograph is entitled *False Start I* [see fig. 7 in the essay by Mark Pascale in this volume].) The 1962/1994 *Jubilee* pastel obliterates the language and the mark making of *False Start II* beneath, replacing it with a rough facsimile of the eponymous painting. By drawing directly on top of the lithograph, Johns avowed the sovereign status of the *Jubilee* composition, proving that it is not just a "gray" version but rather a careful metamorphosis, a related but unique endeavor. *Jubilee* (1962 and 1994) marks the third time the *False Start* composition has been altered not *through* but *in* grisaille. In this instance, however, the *Jubilee* composition is declared on top of an existing grisaille. The accumulated gestures chart a course of modification from color to black-and-white-and-gray in painting, from color painting to black-and-white-and-gray drawing, from color painting to black-and-white-and-gray lithography, and, finally, from black-and-white-and-gray lithography to black-and-white-and-gray drawing. *Jubilee* (1962 and 1994) is, then, a particularly insistent maneuver.

In 1965, speaking of *False Start* and *Jubilee*, Johns, who rarely qualifies his works, asserted the importance of the two source paintings:

> I had worked for a long time with red, yellow, and blue—the colors—usually restricted to geometric areas, very well defined. When painting was moving away from such well defined areas, this idea occurred to me of using the color names instead of the colors I had been using. . . . I liked it that the words had a meaning. I liked it that the letters had a concrete characteristic. I liked it that those objects—the letters—appeared in the context of this arbitrary, suggestive painting. I liked it that the meaning of the words either denied or coincided in the color paintings, denied the actual experience or reaffirmed the actual experience of the color sensation. It seemed to me, at that point, that those paintings . . . were an accomplishment in ambiguity that previous paintings had not reached.[16]

The aura of ambiguity has also been extended to Johns's now-legendary titles for these two works, which have yet to be fully parsed for their potential meanings—both ironic and sincere. Taking full advantage of the only reliable language attached to these paintings, Johns established the colorful and apparently celebratory painting as the "false start," a disqualifying, preemptive exercise; the real cause for jubilation was, counterintuitively, gray.

Gray

Although possibly a curious claim in other contexts, Johns's valorization of his own "accomplishment in ambiguity" is perfectly congruent with his larger stated and unstated aims. His art is a reverie of unremitting irresolution—schematic, familiar, occasionally candid expressions, shrouded in fog. To borrow the artist's own useful description of the art of Marcel Duchamp, it operates in a visual field where "language, thought, and vision act upon one another."[17] Johns is widely recognized for over fifty years of rigorously inventive, impeccably executed objects. An internal compass has, by all accounts, guided him on an independent and wildly influential course in postwar American art. Not only is he credited with forging a generative set of propositions that advanced painting beyond the rhetorical endgames of Abstract Expressionism, but he is also recognized as a progenitor of Pop Art and, in his reductive, literalist, and antiillusionist modes, as the catalyst for much Minimal and Conceptual art. The complexities of his evolution deny easy summary, but Johns's methodological consistency permits some general observations. Nearly every work of art he has made—paintings, drawings, and prints—derives from found or otherwise predetermined, two-dimensional sources: flags, targets, numbers, letters, plans, maps, stencils, patterns, and tracings. Often these subjects are arrived at involuntarily through fortuitous chance encounters, unforeseen events, and provocative suggestions. Once he has taken them up, however, motifs are not fixed in temporally distinct series, but instead appear, flourish, recede, and return, over decades. Johns paints with short strokes and small daubs, a vocabulary of repeatable yet highly individuated and easily identifiable marks, which also include ironically controlled drips and splats. His approach to color is similarly schematized. Johns works almost exclusively with the three primary colors (red, yellow, and blue) and their immediate secondaries (green, orange, violet), as well as in black, white, and gray. The artist's palette is as "found" and prelimited as the schema for signs like a flag or a target.

> It all began with my painting a picture of an American flag. Using this design took care of a great deal for me because I didn't have to design it.

> So I went on to similar things like the targets—things the mind already knows. That gave me room to work on other levels. For instance, I have always thought of a painting as a surface, *painting it in one color made this very clear.*[18]

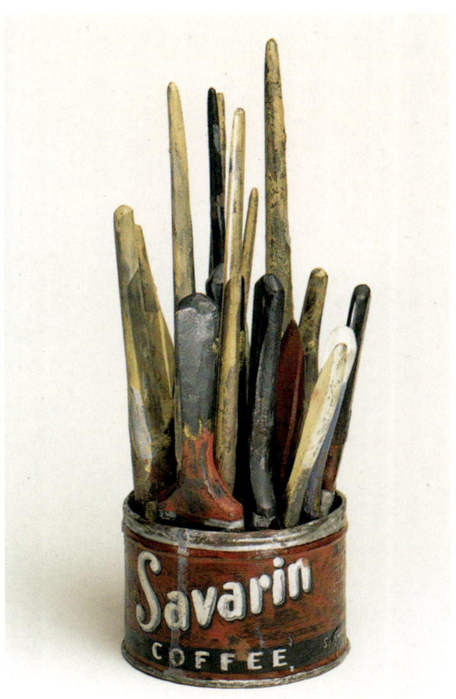

Fig. 1. *Painted Bronze*, 1960. Painted bronze; h.: 34.3 cm (13 ½ in.), d.: 20.3 cm (8 in.). Collection of the artist.

Achromatic, monochromatic, or near-monochromatic work—across a spectrum of media but especially in painting—has been absolutely central to Johns's enterprise from the very beginning.[19] Although the artist is rarely considered in relation to monochrome art, single-color experimentations have figured prominently in his production since 1955, and within that important subset of the oeuvre, the majority are gray. This exhibition, in fact, marks the first full consideration of a topic that has been hiding in plain sight for over fifty years.[20] *Jasper Johns: Gray*, while encompassing monochromatic abstraction, aims to address a related, more inclusive practice: the creation of both abstract and representational images imbued with the formal and conceptual associations of a single color.[21]

Gray is Johns's favorite color.[22] In *Painted Bronze* (1960; **FIG. 1**) a facsimile of the artist's painting tools at rest and arguably a self-portrait,[23] nearly all of the seventeen brush handles evidence gray paint. Across the span of his creative work, deliberate uses of gray media—oil paint, acrylic paint, encaustic, collage, Sculp-metal, aluminum, lead, silver, graphite, graphite wash, carborundum, metallic powder, charcoal, pastel, watercolor, and ink—have brought forth paintings, sculptures, drawings, lithographs, screenprints, etchings, aquatints, and monotypes that convey a singular and unparalleled preoccupation with this color. Johns works with a range of gray: warm to cool, light to dark, stringent to lush, closed to expansive. His handling of gray allows an evenness of expression, monochromatic but never monotonous. As it has been realized by the artist in various media, gray cannot be considered a single color, but rather must be understood in plural terms. Johns's grays encompass a nearly infinite zone of differentiated hues and values, always rich in medium tones, deployed within a range of finite physical materializations. (Owing to the difficulty of capturing such nuances of shade and atmosphere in commercial reproduction, this is a fact little understood without a direct and comparative experience of the works.) Ultimately, a study of gray encourages a useful appreciation of the artist as a tonalist rather than, more strictly speaking, a colorist.[24]

Johns is less interested in images than he is in working form and surface.[25] His paintings are built rather than performed. Feelings yield to tactility; representation cedes to effect. Contrary to much speculative criticism, the image is rarely the true subject of Johns's work; it is rather an armature on which the artist hangs ideas. From flags, targets, and crosshatches to his most recent reprisals of flagstones, Johns attends to the outline of particular forms, "followed rather faithfully, but not entirely faithfully, and filled in with some variation of color and texture."[26] This is the essence of his art: not seriality per se, but insistent processes of calibrated sameness and change. As early as 1964, in the catalogue essay for Johns's first one-person museum exhibition in New York, curator Alan Solomon wrote presciently: "His essential position, which may at first seem complex and unfamiliar, turns out to be quite uncomplicated and lucid. It has built into it infinite possibilities of variation, which account for the ultimate diversity of his production."[27] The artist has described his methodology in these terms: "With a slight re-emphasis of elements, one finds that one can behave very differently toward it [an image], see it in a different way."[28] For over fifty years, gray has been such a clarifying element. Throughout, gray functions as an apparently impartial hue, an adaptable uniform that reveals form without attendant costumes of color.

Structured modes of repetition—every so often verging on obsessive fixation—remain a key feature of Johns's work. His use of gray, as a specific category of endeavor, is an integral component of his essential strategy of limiting possibilities, closing down on extraneous choices or unnecessary decisions. Within the artist's larger body of work, the gray pictures constitute an independent idiom of remarkable objective consistency that supplies an endless subjective variety of interpretations. Every major motif or serial exploration generates at least one but usually many gray versions. There are paintings that are gray and that are not undertaken in other guises; paintings that begin with color and later occasion gray distillations; and paintings that begin in gray and later merit color treatments. Johns's most famous statement is: "Take an object, do something to it. Do something else to it."[29] For an artist who prizes contradiction, the dictum is also superbly meaningful when inverted. In other words, Johns can also be found doing the same thing to different objects (or themes) over and over. His early sketchbook records the following:

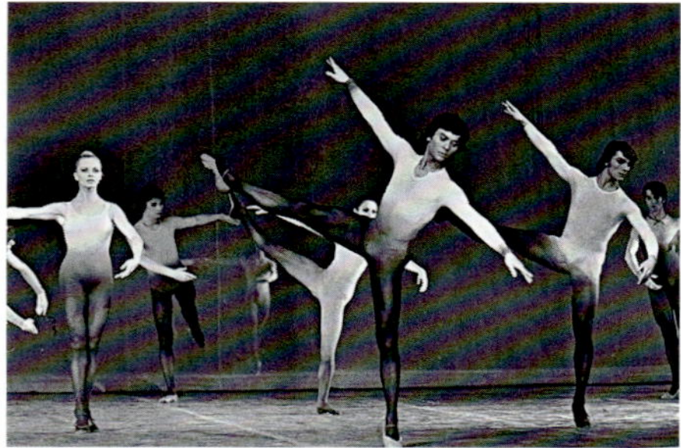

Fig. 2. Performance of Merce Cunningham's *Un Jour ou Deux* (1973), with set design by Johns.

> One thing working one way
> Another " " another "
> One thing working different ways
> at different times.[30]

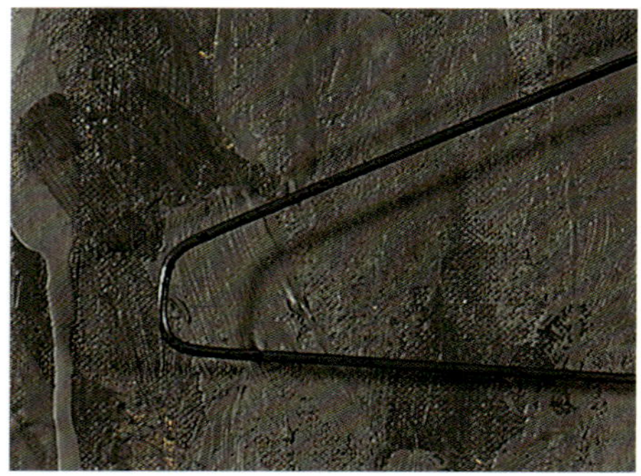

Fig. 3. Detail of the shadow in *Coat Hanger* (cat. no. 16).

The use of gray—or, more precisely, the conversion of something into or from gray—is part of this practice. In choosing to articulate gray versions of nearly every key pictorial theme, Johns encourages comparisons across, not just within, related bodies of work. Gray allows the artist to pose allied questions within disparate fields of inquiry, to see something and then to resee it differently. If painting is a language, as Johns, descended from Wittgenstein, has often suggested, then gray can be inflected much like a noun, verb, or adjective. More accurately, gray is all pervasive, like syntax. Gray exists in Johns's work not just as color, but also as idea, condition, and material—a thing in and of itself. "I like to repeat an image in another medium," he has said, "to observe the play between the two: the image and the medium."[31] A composite of many media, gray ultimately emerges as its own medium.

At times, a more theoretical or conjectural grayness operates on varying levels of legibility. A brief foray into the artist's work in the arena of performance is instructive in this regard.[32] In 1973 Johns designed the sets and costumes for *Un Jour ou Deux*, a ballet choreographed by Merce Cunningham, with music by John Cage, for the Paris Opera. The performance was structured by a set consisting of two scrims painted with a gray scale, dark to light, from left to right. The dance started with the downstage scrim lit, and thus opaque. As lights went on behind it, revealing the dancers, that scrim was raised. The second scrim was halfway upstage, and the dancers performed on both sides of the gray planes of varying degrees of translucence (FIG. 2). There was no other color present on stage. The twenty-six dancers were attired in costumes dyed in shades of dark to light gray.[33] The layered effect was one of movement in a gray field, a choreography of shadows. Similarly, in painting, gray can exert its influence as a ghostly presence. Beginning with *Coat Hanger* (1959; cat. no. 16) and *No* (1961; cat. no. 91) and continuing through the recent Catenary paintings (1997–2003; cat. nos. 128–35), gray literally draws itself onto Johns's paintings in the form of transitory shadows made by objects affixed to the surface (FIG. 3).[34] At other times, as in the suite of works around the Seasons (1985–87; see cat. nos. 119–21), a shadow rendered in gray tones emerges as an overt subject.

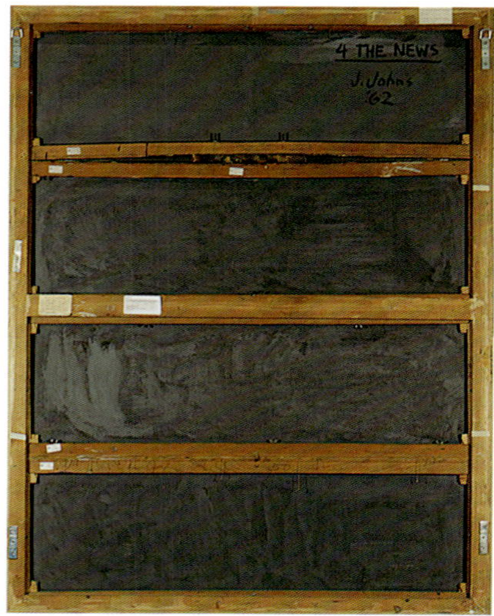

Fig. 4. Verso of *4 the News* (cat. no. 94).

Gray is also implicated in related acts of secretion or dissimulation. Johns has produced paintings—*4 the News* (1962; cat. no. 94) and *Between the Clock and the Bed* (1982–83; cat. no. 115), for example—the backs of which are covered in gray paint, never to be seen by the casual viewer (FIG. 4). Gray can be within as well, selectively added to spectrum colors to mute the overall appearance of a picture, or gray fields can exist underneath color.[35] The artist

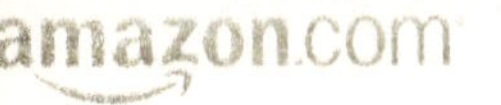

Billing Address:
Martha Kropf
418 Brookes Walk
Woodstock, GA 30188
United States

Shipping Address:
Martha Kropf
418 Brookes Walk
Woodstock, GA 30188-5185
United States

SDCX2yvqYR

Returns Are Easy!
Visit http://www.amazon.com/returns to return any item -including gifts- in unopened or original condition within 30 days for a full refund (other restrictions apply)

Your order of December 12, 2007 (Order ID:104 – 3817923 – 4464218)

Qty	Item	Item Price	Total
	IN THIS SHIPMENT		
1	**Jasper Johns: Gray (Art Institute of Chicago)** 0300119496 0300119496 0300119496 Hardcover	$40.95	$40.95
1	**Sean Scully: Retrospective** 0500093385 0500093385 0500093385 Hardcover	$40.95	$40.95
1	**Black Paintings: Robert Rauschenberg, Ad Reinhardt, Mark** 3775718605 3775718605 3775718605 Hardcover	$37.80	$37.80

SubTotal	$119.70
Shipping & Handling	$5.22
Promotional Certificate	– $5.22
Order Total	$119.70
Paid via Visa	$119.70
Balance due	$0.00

This shipment completes your order.

3807 (3 of 3)

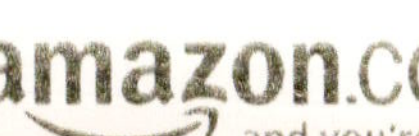

240/DCX2yvqYR/-3 of 3-//CP/econ-us/3729817/1220-04.00/1220-02.50/sp080493807/1-1 Z3

p27 oil paint
acrylic "
encaustic
collage
sculp - metal
aluminum
lead
silver
graphite
graphite wash
carborundum
metallic powder
charcoal
pastel
water color
ink

Study of grey - tonalist rather than colorist

infinite possibilities of variation

stated in 1963: "There are many, many strokes and everything is built up on a very simple frame but there is a great deal of work in it, and the work tends to correct what lies underneath constantly."[36] When Johns was making *Three Flags* (1958; Whitney Museum of American Art, New York), a painting in which three red, white, and blue flags are stacked on three, successively smaller canvases, one on top of the other, he faced a charged dilemma.

> I remember having a kind of moral conflict about whether to paint the covered portions, because the idea of doing work which will be covered, and is therefore not a part of the necessary information about the picture—that idea conflicts with the teasing quality of the picture, which suggests that you have done it. I solved it by telling myself that I was doing the painting for myself, and *I* knew that I hadn't painted it.[37]

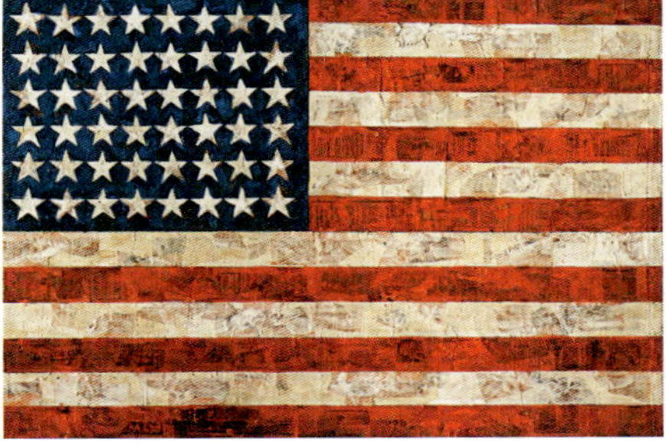

Fig. 5. *Flag*, 1954–55. Encaustic, oil, and collage on fabric mounted on plywood; 107.3 × 154 cm (42 ¼ × 60 ⅝ in.). The Museum of Modern Art, New York, gift of Philip Johnson in honor of Alfred H. Barr, Jr.

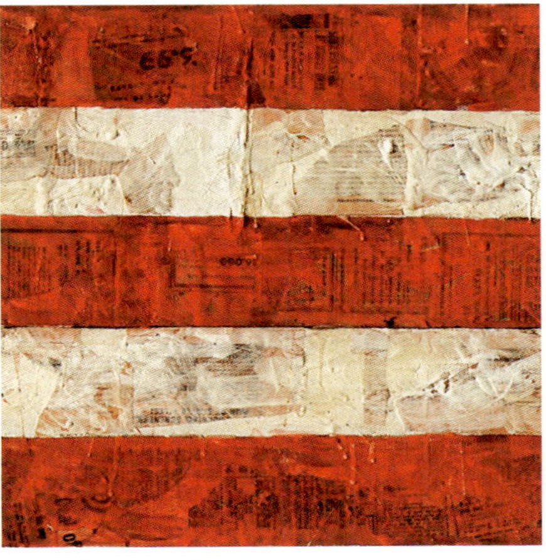

Fig. 6. Detail of newspaper collage in *Flag* (fig. 5).

In fact, the artist did paint the concealed areas: he painted them gray.[38] Here the flag serves as field and object, figure and ground, and a hidden gray territory undergirds its image. Similarly, gray can also function as a surface to receive color as an afterimage. In *Flags* (see fig. 16 in the essay by Douglas Druick in this volume) gray structures an optical game: two painted flags lie within a gray field; the lower one is a lighter gray, while the upper flag is painted in complementary colors; the stars and white lines in black, the background of the stars in orange, and the red lines in green. If one stares at the upper flag, then shifts attention to the gray flag, red, white, and blue appear as an afterimage. Gray, in other words, plays host to the intangible.[39] This game of perception is constitutive of Johns's larger interest in the superimposition of one image or object upon another (see the essay by Douglas Druick in this volume). In both *Three Flags* and *Flags* the use of gray was, for Johns, somehow a necessary decision. (Art historian Leo Steinberg argued that Johns acknowledged no difference between necessity and subjective preference.)[40] To be sure, every object he makes has an unseen interiority *because of the way it was made*, and it is this ontology—not the image itself—that is so often the subject of and the source for investigations of meaning in his pictures.

The corpus of much of Johns's most iconic early production—in black, white, and gray, as well as in color—has gray in its bloodstream. In key works from *Flag* (**FIGS. 5–6**) forward, Johns used newspaper collage—dipping scraps of newspaper (as well as strips of cloth) into molten, pigmented wax and fixing these pieces to the surface before the wax cooled and hardened. (The practice was predominant in Johns's early work, and he has employed it selectively since that time.) He was effectively embalming newspaper shreds, the most fragile of daily ephemera, in encaustic, one of the most ancient of media. Kozloff was the first to wonder whether if what was underneath was not somehow the most important element in the work.

> Physically speaking . . . this [newsprint] would be a *hidden* collage. But one is entitled to ask whether, pictorially, the "paint" is not itself the collage element, affirming the newsprint ground (although concealed behind this layer is still another surface, the actual canvas). If it is true that Johns has reversed the normal constituents of the collage process, then surely he has done the same with its play on reality. The "real" is whatever is underneath, partially withheld from sight. Art reticently covers up or shields life, instead of assimilating and triumphing over it as in traditional collage.[41]

The predominantly gray *Newspaper* (1957; cat. no. 8), in which a double-page spread of a daily is thinly concealed under gray encaustic, is perhaps the most didactic acknowledgment of the use of the news as art material. Explicitly signaled here, the composite tonalities of newsprint and ink embed a notional grayness into every object they are a part of, independent of any added pigmentation.[42] Discussing his own use of newspaper collage in the early 1950s, artist Robert Rauschenberg, from whom Johns adapted the technique, first noted the poetic, if at times latent, symbolic language. Newspaper strips, he observed, provided a rough texture and activated the surface so that "even the first stroke in the painting had its own unique position in a gray map of words."[43]

Surprisingly, focused discussions of gray have been largely absent from the copious body of mostly hagiographic critical literature on the artist.[44] It is interesting to note, however, that certain critics generally skeptical of Johns have singled out gray works for praise. The poet John Ashbery, reviewing Johns's one-person exhibition at the Galerie Ileana Sonnabend (in the rented space of the Galerie Marcelle Dupuis), Paris, in 1962, discussed "recent gray paintings such as *Ruler with Gray*": "The later ones are in fact exclusively occupied with gray—what it is, where it comes from, how it both begins and ends light. It puts a livid sheen everywhere, starting speculations and containing them in a blanket disapproval that is like the darkest of daytime skies." Ashbery concluded this less-than-laudatory review by calling Johns "the white, or the gray, hope of American painting."[45] Dore Ashton, in an otherwise ungenerous review of 1963, noted: "It is in the dark-gray-to-white scale within which Johns' instinct for intriguing conundrum is best expressed."[46] A year later, Fairfield Porter wrote: "It is this breadth and this banality, a banality extending to the grayness and the monotonous textures, which saves his paintings from preciosity and gives them their wholeness."[47] In his landmark treatise "After Abstract Expressionism," published in 1962, Clement Greenberg, the titan of mid-century American art criticism, rehearsed the various strands of abstraction following the canons of Synthetic Cubism, "which meant cleanly marked contours, closed and more or less regular shapes, and flat color."[48] For Greenberg, Johns was, strictly speaking, a representational artist, and he therefore remained highly ambivalent about his work. What enlivened the critic's relationship to Johns's paintings was "largely in the area of the formal or plastic."[49] In this arena, he perceived a curious sort of inversion:

> Everything that usually serves representation and illusion is left to serve nothing but itself, that is abstraction; while everything that usually serves the abstract or decorative—flatness, bare outlines, all-over or symmetrical design—is put to the service of representation. And the more explicit this contradiction is made, the more effective in every sense the picture tends to be. When the image is too obscured the paint surface is liable to become less pointedly superfluous; conversely, when the image is left too prominent it is liable to reduce the whole picture to a mere image. . . . *The effect of a Johns picture is also weakened, often, when it is done in bright colors instead of neutral ones like black and gray, for these, being the shading hues* par excellence, *are just those that become the most exhibitedly and poignantly superfluous when applied to ineluctably flat images.*[50]

Greenberg, who was invested in Johns's art mostly in terms of its abstract tensions, privileged the access gray afforded to purer types of form.

Admittedly, a great deal of Johns's work does not involve any gray at all, and gray has occurred with varying degrees of frequency, and with significant changes in tone and mood, over the course of the nearly six decades that have composed Johns's career to date. Achromatic and monochromatic pictures are disproportionately prominent in his work of the 1950s and early 1960s.

First, the narrow range of his palette seems to register neutrality; subsequently, certain readings posit it as a corollary to emotional states, elegiac and melancholic. Johns's handling of color matured from the 1970s onward, but gray continued to foil its uses in remarkable ways. As seen in this exhibition, gray returned in a dramatic and self-conscious manner with the Catenary pictures (1997–2003), absorbing more than a decade of biographical data, and literally and metaphorically bridging the early and late works. Key recent paintings and prints are gray (2005–07). Despite important differences over time, Johns's grays are united by a prevailing "family resemblance," a term Wittgenstein used to characterize similarities while accommodating differences. In all of its endless varieties, gray has been and remains an inexorable, recurring presence.

Definitions and Associations

Painting with Ruler and "Gray" (FIG. 7) contains the word "gray" on a found object, a wooden slat onto which the word had been stamped in gray ink. Johns mounted the slat in the manner of a vertical stretcher bar over an expressively rendered surface. (Two years later, he restaged the fortuitous, stenciling "gray" onto a similarly mounted slat in *Device* [1962; cat. no. 93].) In the first title, the use of "gray" calls attention to the inclusion of the word as a found-object component of the still life. The quotation marks also problematize the word's meaning—almost as though it were a reference to something borrowed from the outside world that could be fixed to the canvas but otherwise not pinned down.

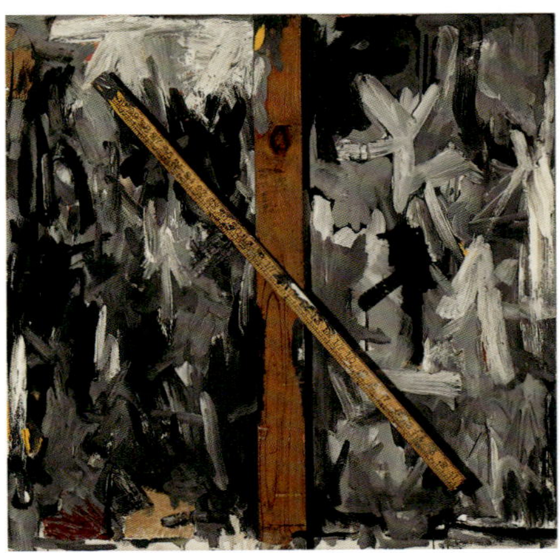

Fig. 7. *Painting with Ruler and "Gray,"* 1960. Oil and collage on canvas with objects; 81.3 × 81.3 cm (32 × 32 in.). Frederick R. Weisman Art Foundation, Los Angeles.

As a word, gray is not difficult to define, but the complexity of its application belies the simple statement of what it is. According to the most basic citation in the *Oxford English Dictionary*, gray is "the color intermediate between black and white, or composed of a mixture of black and white with little or no positive hue."[51] Black, white, and gray, which are not present in the spectrum, are achromatic colors. Generally speaking, the mixture of black and white in equal portions produces middle gray, the center of the gray scale. Naturally, there are endless variations between the absolute poles of black and white, so that any color darker than white and lighter than black, which does not give an independent impression of color, is defined as gray. Mixing the three primaries—yellow, red, blue—also produces various shades of gray. As any two complementary colors contain all three primaries, gray is also the result of mixing any two complementary colors. For example, mixing red and green (yellow and blue) in certain proportions produces colorless gray. The same effect will be produced by blending blue and orange (yellow and red), or yellow and violet (red and blue). When these two colors are adjacent, they heighten each other; mixed, they cancel each other out. Gray will always appear to be tinged with the complement of an adjacent color. For example, next to red, it looks greenish gray; next to green, that same gray would look reddish gray, and so forth: next to violet, yellowish gray, next to yellow, violet-gray. Finally, a saturated color can be diluted by mixing into it blacks and whites together to produce a tonal range of grayed colors.

Gray is also a valuable descriptive term of remarkable plasticity, and can be used to characterize ambience—a mood lacking cheer or brightness in outlook, style, or essence—or, more literally, atmosphere—qualities of light in the sky or sea resulting from an absence of direct illumination by the sun. The word can denote related emotional valences lacking hope—dismal, gloomy, sad, depressing, bleak, or despairing—or designate a quality of being—prosaic, ordinary, dull, or uninteresting—and is often suggestive of anonymity. Following such usages, gray can convey an intermediate position, condition, or character, whether used in the place of black, for example, to reference a loss of power limited to partial sectors of a grid ("gray out"), or to conjure a zone of ambiguity ("gray area"). In symbolic terms, gray is the color of ashes and is associated with death and mourning. Art historian Molly Teasdale Smith speculated that in France and surrounding countries in the fourteenth and early fifteenth centuries ecclesiastical decorations in gray monochrome—of various types ranging from vestments to hangings and panel paintings, many of which no longer exist today—were used in chapels during the penitential season of Lent.[52] Artist Vasily Kandinsky, in his treatise "Concerning the Spiritual in Art," defined gray as silent: "In gray there is no possibility of movement because gray consists of two colors that have no active force, for they stand the one in motionless discord, the other in motionless negation, even of discord, like an endless wall, a bottomless pit."[53] Such established associations with grayness, dating back centuries, remain firmly embedded in the popular consciousness of the twenty-first century.[54]

This range of denotative and connotative associations coalesces around Johns's work in gray. In general terms, throughout the chronological span of the work (in both abstract and representational paintings), shared formal properties of gray operate in particular ways that isolate and distill larger aspects of Johns's entire project—dispassion, ideation, abstraction, tactility, ambiguity, concealment, neutrality.

As age-old arguments go, color plays to the senses and emotions; the lack of color, to the mind.[55] The use of gray in particular is linked to notions of personal temperament and psychology. Assuredly, gray indexes modes of sublimation. The rigorous Johns scholar Roberta Bernstein once recalled: "In a conversation, [on] November 15, 1974, [Johns] said that he heard about psychological tests showing that people who prefer gray are more emotionally repressed than people who prefer other colors."[56] Refuting emotionalism, Johns's use of gray, more than any other set of choices, embodies the most conceptual of his expressions. Painterly sensuousness thrives, but the lack of color allows for a fuller presence of ideation. Gray enhances Johns's cultivation of the cool, the detached, the dispassionate stance, allowing the ascetic cerebration of his paintings to come to the fore. In a foundational statement, Johns maintained:

> I used gray encaustic to avoid the color situation. The encaustic paintings were done in gray because to me this suggested a different kind of literal quality that was unmoved and unmovable by coloration and thus *avoided all of the emotional and dramatic quality of color.*[57]

For centuries, thinkers as diverse and accomplished as Johann Wolfgang von Goethe and Georg Wilhelm Friedrich Hegel have characterized theory as gray. Hegel, for example, wrote:

> When philosophy paints its grey in grey, then has a shape of life grown old. By philosophy's grey in grey it cannot be rejuvenated but only understood. The owl of Minerva spreads it wings only with the falling of the dusk.[58]

Gray is, quite literally, the look of thought: according to color studies conducted by the German psychologist David Katz in the 1930s, "subjective visual gray" is the term used to describe the filmy, shadowy color we see when our eyes are closed.[59] Vija Celmins, whose rejection of color derives, in part, from her exposure to Johns's gray work, commented: "I start the art in my head. . . . and [prefer] to work in a kind of intuitive, half-blind way, maybe in a kind of 'gray room'. . . . It's like applying your brainpower to the painting."[60] Leo Steinberg, who said of Johns's early work, "Seeing them becomes thinking," is joined in his assessment by two artists.[61] Bruce Nauman has spoken of the intellectual qualities in Johns's art: "I loved de Kooning's work but Johns was the first artist to put some intellectual distance between himself and the physical act of making a painting,"[62] and Robert Morris recently made explicit the link between the idea-driven art that Nauman describes and grayness: "Thought is not colored. Color adds nothing to thought. Thought is black, white, and gray."[63]

Throughout Johns's career, gray versions of existing leitmotifs amplify a sense of abstraction. Gray defamiliarizes well-known representations by counteracting associative meanings engendered by the illusionism of color, and it operates in the service of flatness, as the monochromatic compositions all but eliminate figure-ground distinctions. If the initial re-creation or appropriation of an emblem from the larger culture into painting—whether an early target or a later tracing—is an act of displacement of an already elusive image or object, gray painting, like a black-and-white photograph, compounds the act by not providing a full record of the real. Of the early work, Johns stated: "I was concerned with the invisibility those images had acquired, and the idea of knowing an image rather than just seeing it out of the corner of your eye. I wanted to make the flags and targets very concrete, to see them as objects."[64] But he has also conceded: "The flag images exist at different levels of recognizability. Some are in red, white, and blue, and are easy to see. There's a gray one that I think is difficult to determine as a flag" (see *Gray Flag*, 1957; cat. no. 23).[65] This holds true not only among the various motifs but also comparatively across the spectrum of imagery. Art historian Rosalind Krauss has written about the radical leveling of the concept of genre.[66] Johns, who has worked with and through still life, landscape, figuration, and pure abstraction, uses gray to elide the distinctions afforded by certain generic conventions.

Gray isolates touch. During the 1960s, Johns thought of copying Paul Cézanne's *The Bather* (c. 1885; the Museum of Modern Art, New York; see fig. 8 in the essay by Richard Shiff in this volume) in gray, but he did not want to work directly from the painting nor could he find reproductions large enough to realize the idea.[67] Yet his aspiration correlates with his desire to isolate the pure facts of touch in order to perceive and understand the physicality of paint. Encaustic allowed the artist to add discrete, sculptural strokes of paint, choosing to maintain or to obliterate them depending on the use of heat.

> It was very simple. I wanted to show what had gone before in a picture, and what was done after. But if you put on a heavy brushstroke in paint, and then add another stroke, the second stroke smears the first unless the paint is dry. And paint takes too long to dry. I didn't know what to do. Then someone suggested wax. It worked very well; as soon as the wax was cool I could put on another stroke and it would not alter the first.[68]

Layers of accrued meaning could, if chosen, be maintained. The quality of an encaustic surface could also be achieved, or simulated, in oil, a peculiar skill in which Johns has developed real expertise. Paintings limited to a grisaille palette—in encaustic as well as in oil and the rare acrylic—emphasize the tactility of surface, the almost sculptural quality of application. Other gray media, such as Sculp-metal, a hard-drying material that can be applied like paint, allow Johns to focus on tactility.[69] In gray, touch becomes both form and image.

Mediating between the extremes of black and white, gray connotes ambiguity, a purposive indeterminacy of meaning.[70] Johns has elaborated the well-worn role of gray to convey such a sentiment: "It is the gray zone between two extremes that I'm interested in.... You can have a certain view of a thing at one time and a different view of it at another. This phenomenon interests me."[71]

The very "in-betweenness" or irresolution of gray is its principal characteristic. Within a larger oeuvre in which fixed meanings are eschewed, doubt is vigorously cultivated.[72] Johns, who has long avoided direct explanations of what things are or what they mean, once stated in an interview:

> Intention involves such a small fragment of our consciousness and of our mind and of our life. I think a painting should include more experience than simple intended statement. I personally would like to keep the painting in a state of "shunning statement," so that one is left with the fact that one can experience individually as one pleases; that is not to focus the attention in one way, but to leave the situation as a kind of actual thing, so that the experience of it is variable.

When interviewer David Sylvester then responded, "In other words, if your painting says something that could be pinned down, what it says is that nothing can be pinned down, that nothing is pure, that nothing is simple," Johns replied: "I don't like saying that it says that. I would like it to *be* that."[73]

Conditions of *being*, in Johns's art, it turns out, are often predicated on games of hiding. Gray, suggestive of concealing or veiling, provides a certain kind of cover. In his oft-cited notes for the "Spy/Watchman," Johns described two characters, one ordinary and obvious, the other clandestine: the watchman, who looks openly but takes away no information, and the spy, who looks covertly, watching the watchman.[74] As the central, effectively omniscient protagonist of his own art, Johns is more spy than watchman. Within an analogous dynamic of art making, knowledge and attendant actions must be revealed and simultaneously shrouded. Gray can function as a field of obfuscation. This is the essence of Johns's refusal of meaning, his way of distancing himself from the necessity of interpretation:

> Say that you have an idea. Well, one can then defend and separate that idea from all the other ideas which one has ever heard of or perhaps with all the techniques which one has heard of and make the idea less clear. And that whole range from precision to imprecision to disappearance interests me. A large part of my work has been involved in this.[75]

On the most basic level, Johns's practice struggles to embrace objectivity over subjectivity. He wrote the following, sometime in the late 1960s:

> The idea of background
> (and background music)
> idea of neutrality. . .[76]

Gray is the background music of neutrality. But that neutrality is for Johns a form of intentionality. In 1963 he wrote:

> Judd spoke of a "neutral"
> surface but what is meant? Neutrality
> must involve some relationship (to other ways of painting, thinking?)
> He would have to include these in his work
> to establish the neutrality of that surface. He also used "'non" or "not"
> expressive
> this is an early problem
> a negative solution or
> expression of new sense
> which can help one into

what one has not known
"Neutral" expresses an intention.[77]

Ultimately, Johns decided, "the painting remains indifferent."[78] There is no better expression of this willed resistance than gray. At one point in the sketchbooks, Johns spoke of an object that might possess a "Physical and Metaphysical Obstinacy."[79] The stance teases nihilism. "I was interested in the kind of nuance, modulation, play between thinking, seeing, saying, and nothing."[80]

Monochromism

Monochrome is the term applied to a work of art predominantly of a single color or tone. In the twentieth century, it is a genre originally associated with the emergence of radically reductive painting among the Russian avant-garde, namely in the extremist propositions of Kazimir Malevich and Aleksandr Rodchenko, and subsequently almost exclusively associated with "nonobjective" painting, a label coined by Rodchenko in reference to his own *Non-Objective Painting no. 80 (Black on Black)* (**FIG. 8**). In an exhibition at the 0.10 Gallery in St. Petersburg in 1915, Malevich presented paintings of colored geometric shapes against white grounds along with his *Black Square* (1915; Tret'yakov Gallery, Moscow), arguably his first Suprematist painting. This provocation was further refined in his white-on-white paintings, such as *Suprematist Composition: White on White* (**FIG. 9**). Following closely on Malevich's formal reductivism, Rodchenko, the first artist to pursue the use of single color on a single plane, exhibited in 1921 a series of three monotone red, yellow, and blue panels entitled *Last Painting* (1921; A. Rodchenko and V. Stepanova Archive, Moscow). For Malevich the triumph of this moment was tied particularly to the absence of color. "I have torn through the blue lampshade of colour limitations," Malevich wrote in 1919, "and come out into the white; after me, comrade aviators sail into the chasm—I have set up the semaphores of Suprematism."[81] In spite or perhaps partly because of such bombastic claims, these advances in the art of painting proved to be endgame propositions, stranded and tangled in the ideological battleground of Soviet Russia. Both Malevich and Rodchenko abandoned painting after 1921. In the first half of the twentieth century, the genre of monochrome existed in relative degrees of isolation. True monochromes were rare, but near-monochromatic experiments can be found in the exactly contemporaneous developments of the de Stijl group in Holland, as artists like Theo van Doesburg and Piet Mondrian, after working through Cubism, abandoned naturalistic references in favor of a regimented, geometric abstract vocabulary of line and color limited to the primaries and black and, occasionally, gray (see **FIGS. 10** and **17**).[82]

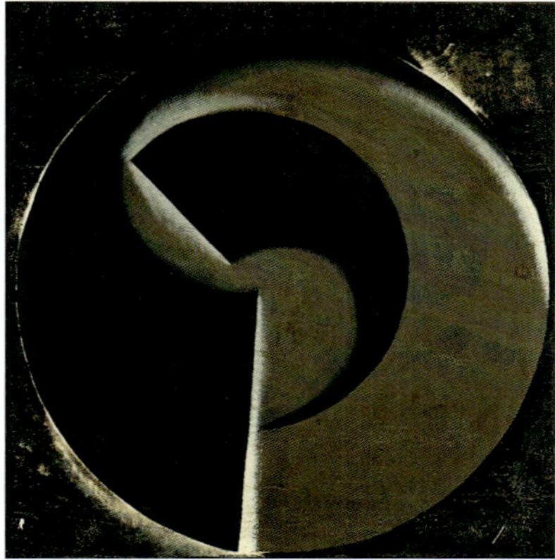

Fig. 8. Aleksandr Rodchenko. *Non-Objective Painting no. 80 (Black on Black)*, 1918. Oil on canvas; 81.9 × 79.4 cm (32 ¼ × 31 ¼ in.). The Museum of Modern Art, New York, gift of the artist, through Jay Leyda.

Fig. 9. Kazimir Malevich. *Suprematist Composition: White on White*, 1918. Oil on canvas; 79.4 × 79.4 cm (31 ¼ × 31 ¼ in.). The Museum of Modern Art, New York, acquisition confirmed in 1999 by agreement with the Estate of Kazimir Malevich and made possible with funds from the Mrs. John Hay Whitney Bequest (by exchange).

Mondrian was of course a figure of significant renown and presence among artists in New York from the time of his arrival in 1940 until his death in 1944. His reductive impulses and those of others helped shape the intellectual and creative climate Johns first became aware of when he entered the crucible of the New York art world in 1948. Johns has said that he "never really saw paintings" until he came to New York;[83] it is safe to assume that the impact of what he found there during his earliest formative years was profound. Such influences must be understood in emphatic terms because Johns is essentially self-taught. His three distinct attempts to study art formally—both in South Carolina and in New York—all ended prematurely. An extraordinarily accomplished autodidact, Johns would have been particularly attuned to what was going on around him, learning from artists who were being shown

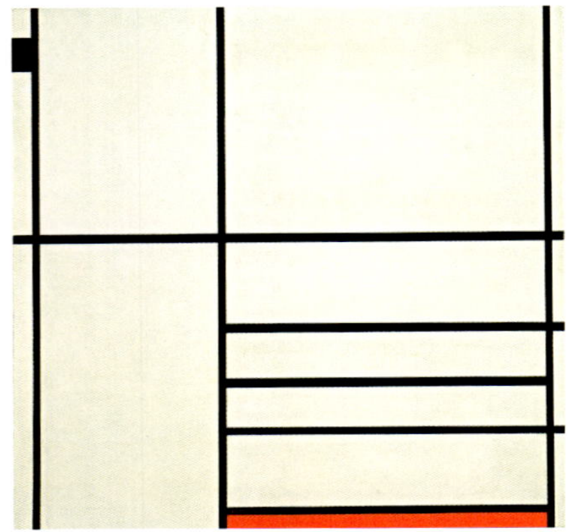

Fig. 10. Piet Mondrian. *Composition en Blanc, Noir, et Rouge*, 1936. Oil on canvas; 102.2 × 104.1 cm (40 ¼ × 41 in.). The Museum of Modern Art, New York. © 2007 Mondrian/Holtzman Trust c/o HCR International, Warrenton, Virginia.

in museums and, importantly, commercial galleries. (Johns came to know many of these artists personally and, in some cases, would later acquire their work for himself.) Such a notion is confirmed by Johns's teacher at the University of South Carolina, Catharine Rembert: "He left for New York because he wanted to study more art, and because he had exhausted what USC had to offer."[84] It is not possible to track wholly and exactly what Johns saw, and what impact, if any, a given exhibition or body of work might have had on the young artist. In New York in the late 1940s, however, exhibitions were centered around only a few museum programs showing recent art and a handful of galleries, notably those of Charles Egan, Samuel Kootz, Betty Parsons, and Sidney Janis. Given the size of the art world, it would have been next to impossible not to absorb general trends in new painting. (Johns left New York in May 1951 for Army service, although he did visit the city on a number of occasions when on leave. He returned in the summer of 1953. Many of the influential galleries—such as Betty Parsons and Sidney Janis, both at 15 East 57th Street—were located only steps from Johns's job as a night-shift clerk at Marboro Books. Presumably his hours enabled him to see exhibitions during the day. Between 1952 and 1954, Johns was also making art, although almost none of the works from this period survive.)

It is useful to isolate potentially stimulating or provocative examples of the art that were available to a young artist in New York in these definitive, transitional years. What was happening there that Johns would have been able to absorb or reject? Certainly, monochromatic or near-monochromatic explorations were taking hold in New York in the late 1940s and early 1950s, the precise moment between Johns's arrival and the real beginning of his own work as an artist in 1954. It is not an overstatement to suggest that the emergence of his creative self-awareness was coextant with the flowering of chromatically and compositionally restricted practices in New York. Indeed the mid-century point in American art was a watershed moment for the monochrome.[85] Often, however, single-color work meant the absence of color; specifically, there was a widespread fascination with black and white among the New York School artists.[86] Abstract Expressionism, by far both the dominant style and controlling logic of the moment, often embraced a palette restricted to achromatic polarities.

A direct line can be drawn to connect the young Jasper Johns to the philosophy of Hans Hofmann, who had been the teacher of Johns's teacher Catharine Rembert. Hofmann showed his work in almost annual solo exhibitions at Samuel Kootz Gallery throughout the late 1940s and 1950s. At this moment, he was the presiding dean of abstract art in America, the most tangible link in New York to the trajectories of modern European painting. He was at the height of his powers and influence, however, as a teacher more than as an artist in his own right.[87] (Hofmann ran his own art school in New York between 1934 and 1958.) Drawing on an incredibly wide range of sources and influences, from School of Paris to German metaphysics, Hofmann sought to promulgate his version of the fundamental mechanics of pictorial construction. "The ability to simplify means to eliminate the unnecessary so that the necessary may speak."[88] This edict attributed to Hofmann—expressed in language strikingly similar to Johns's own statements a few years later—is emblematic of prevailing attitudes toward painting; the comment sets the stage, so to speak, for Johns. A cursory overview of the moment Johns first began seeing new art is revealing.

Johns entered the orbit of the art world in the immediate wake of Willem de Kooning's hugely influential solo exhibition at the Charles Egan Gallery (April 12–30, 1948), where the artist presented ten works from his series of linear black-and-white abstractions begun in 1946. For many of

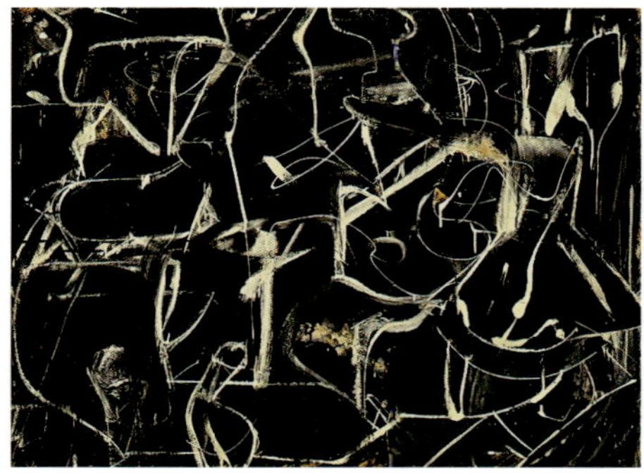

Fig. 11. Willem de Kooning. *Untitled*, 1948–49. Oil and enamel on paper mounted on composition board; 91.4 × 123.8 cm (36 × 48 ¾ in.). The Art Institute of Chicago, Mary and Earle Ludgin Collection, 1981.260.

Fig. 12. Clyfford Still. *Untitled*, 1951–52, PH-247. Oil on canvas; 301.8 × 396.2 cm (118 ¾ × 156 in.). The Art Institute of Chicago, Wirt D. Walker Fund; gift of John Stephan, 1962.906.

Fig. 13. Barnett Newman. *The Voice*, 1950. Egg tempura and enamel on canvas; 244.1 × 268 cm (96 ⅛ × 105 ½ in.). The Museum of Modern Art, New York, the Sidney and Harriet Janis Collection.

these de Kooning used commercial enamel paints. Some incorporate explicit alphabetic signs (*Zurich*, 1947; Hirshhorn Museum and Sculpture Garden, Washington), while others hint at language by means of the calligraphic qualities of lyric line (**FIG. 11**). While Johns did not see the exhibition, the Egan Gallery show generated enormous interest in the artist community and was lavishly praised by Clement Greenberg in *The Nation*. These pictures established de Kooning's reputation, for the first time, among a wider audience. Jackson Pollock, whose work was well known to Johns from as early as 1949, also made a number of paintings limited to black and white the previous year. In fact, his 1948 solo exhibition at Betty Parsons was predominantly black and white.[89] For his fifth solo exhibition at Parsons in the late fall of 1951, this time called *Black and White Paintings*, Pollock exhibited twenty-one paintings, all but one made with black paint on raw canvas. In the fall of 1950, Franz Kline presented his first show of black-and-white paintings of isolated, enlarged gestures at Egan. Robert Motherwell, who began his predominantly black *Elegy to the Spanish Republic* series in 1949 (they remained almost exclusively black and white until 1974), exhibited these works at the Samuel Kootz Gallery in several exhibitions between 1950 and 1953. Clyfford Still, who moved to New York City in 1950, presented his work in regular solo exhibitions, first with Peggy Guggenheim's Art of this Century Gallery in 1946, and subsequently in three solo exhibitions at Parsons between 1947 and 1951. Although his paintings only rarely qualify as pure monochrome, the essential building blocks of his mature art are epic fields of heavily textured, single color, offset by jagged patches of contrast. Still had begun making nearly all-black paintings as early as 1944 (*Painting 1944–N*; the Museum of Modern Art, New York). Much of his work of the early 1950s was more aggressively monochromatic, and, often, aggressively black (**FIG. 12**). (After a burst of visibility following his 1951 Parsons exhibition, Still would not show again regularly in New York.)

Johns encountered Barnett Newman's paintings as early as 1951. Like Still, Newman presented his work at Parsons in the formative years of 1950 and 1951, and only infrequently thereafter.[90] Newman's "pure idea" of a single color interrupted by one or more vertical stripes or "zips" is best evidenced by his breakthrough painting, *Onement I* (1948; the Museum of Modern Art, New York). Subsequently, his works commonly contain no more than two variations on a single hue. (At the time of Newman's first solo exhibition at Parsons, the artist was nearly unknown if not outright neglected.) He presented eleven largely monochromatic works in earthy tones of red, brown, green, and orange, including one canvas, later called *The Promise* (1950; Whitney Museum of American Art, New York), painted black with two vertical zips, one in white, the other in bluish gray. The second one-person show, which Johns certainly saw, opened in April 1951 and evidenced a more restrained palette. The exhibition was announced by an all-white invitation, white-ink lettering stamped on white cardboard.[91] Carrying through on the card's achromatic suggestions, the gallery was dominated by the saturated red zones of the monumental *Vir Heroicus Sublimis* (1950–51; the Museum of Modern Art, New York), but it also included two large paintings in white: one, later titled *The Voice* (**FIG. 13**), with one off-white stripe measured at 2.4 × 2.7 meters; a second, later called *The Name II* (1950; National Gallery of Art, Washington), with four stripes in off-white, was of the same dimensions though opposite in orientation.[92]

During Johns's first years in New York, then, the rhetoric of black and white would have inevitably and decisively filtered his absorption of current Abstract Expressionist painting. The pervasiveness of black-and-white work in New York extended to select presentations of European modernism, which Johns was also seeing for the first time. Key group exhibitions—such as *Black or White: Paintings by European and American Artists* at Kootz in 1950

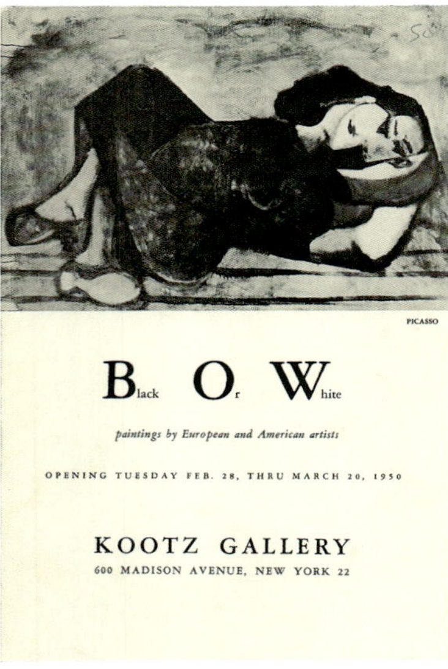

Fig. 14. Cover of exhibition brochure for *Black or White: Paintings by European and American Artists*, at Samuel Kootz Gallery, New York, 1950.

Fig. 15. Robert Rauschenberg. *White Painting (Three Panel)*, 1951. Oil on canvas; 182.9 × 274.3 cm (72 × 108 in.). San Francisco Museum of Modern Art, purchased through a gift of Phyllis Wattis.

(see **FIG. 14**) and *Ivory and Black in Modern Painting* at Pierre Matisse Gallery in 1951—including the work of Georges Braque, Jean Dubuffet, Juan Gris, Henri Matisse, Pablo Picasso, Mondrian, Yves Tanguy, and others, reflected the preponderant influence of achromatic ventures, and might well have also shaped a young artist's understanding of established formal concerns abroad.

By early 1954 Johns retreated into an intensely close relationship with fellow artist Robert Rauschenberg; each became the primary influence on the other. That summer, Johns left his job and his proximity to the galleries, and by his own definition, began to work in earnest as an artist. During this period the two men closely observed, shaped, and even sometimes made each other's work. Johns's immersion in a dialectic of influence was total. Of that time he has said: "Bob was the first person I knew who was a real artist. Everything was arranged to accommodate that fact."[93] Through Rauschenberg, Johns would have become even more acutely aware of the theoretical and material possibilities of a conceptually determined monochromism.[94] When the two met, Rauschenberg was already working with a restricted palette, in distinct color episodes. He, too, had attended Newman's show at Parsons in 1951, which immediately preceded his own solo debut at that same gallery.[95] Early that year Rauschenberg had limited his canvases to "matte and enamel blacks, white, and white with dirt rubbed into it to make rough-textured gray tones that could not be duplicated."[96] At Black Mountain College in the fall of 1951, he had produced all-white paintings whose radically empty surfaces John Cage famously referred to as "airports for lights, shadows, and particles" (**FIG. 15**).[97] In the summer of 1952, Rauschenberg returned to black paintings, and beginning in 1953, he started a series exploring the opposite, the least austere color: red. He described the moment in their careers in the following way:

> Jasper was just beginning as an artist, too. Even though our ideas were very far apart, the thing we had in common was that we were not in the Abstract Expressionist movement.... So we really did not have to fight to be off by ourselves.... Our isolation was forced on us through our differences and attitudes.... during that period Jasper and I didn't much get along with other artists—not by choice but by esthetics.[98]

Having taken stock of painting at a very particular moment in time, before withdrawing into a more closed dialogue with Rauschenberg—still formative in both affirmative and negative respects—Johns would have certainly understood the prevailing politics of color choice.

Searching his way forward, Johns would have been geared to avoid any sustained use of black and white. Describing his own potential effect on younger artists, Newman opined: "I think [my influence] is precisely because I have not insisted on a dogmatic situation. Somehow what I've done has, I think, inspired...other people to free themselves of these conventions."[99] This was exactly the case with Johns. Independence from prevailing modes was the essential goal he and Rauschenberg shared. Beginning with his first mature art works in 1954, Johns undertook a systematic dismantling of the rhetoric of Abstract Expressionism. As Harold Rosenberg acknowledged in 1977: "Johns's cold-blooded rearrangements of the ingredients of America's passionate postwar abstract art amount to a double parody."[100] Johns refused to accept a condition of art making predicated on polarities—emotional, chromatic, and otherwise—and pioneered a form of painting based on the recognizable and the dispassionate. He always reacts against readily available formal models, maintaining that exposure to certain precedents forces him to work in contrary ways:

> That is to say when I look at another artist's work I automatically think, "That's what I should avoid in my own painting." When, by chance, my work reminds me of someone else's—I don't know, it can be an idea, a gesture, the placement of an object—I immediately distance myself, to escape from that situation.[101]

Seeing or sensing the dominant, expressive rhetoric of black and white, Johns reacted against the strictness. In 1969 he would articulate his rejection in more specific terms: "The encaustic paintings were done in gray because to me this suggested a different kind of literal quality... *Black and white is very leading. It tells you what to say or do.*"[102] Johns will always reject such pointedness. Indeed, he actively shuns prescriptive statements. Refusing the import of expressionist gesture was also profoundly linked to refusing the leading qualities of black and white. "You react against your surroundings to carry out something else."[103] This "something else" was, among other things, an embrace of gray as a distinct, even oppositional, idea.

Within larger critical frameworks of art at mid-century, there has been a tendency to abridge the distinctions between black and white as separate from the uses of gray. A benchmark in this elision was the 1964 exhibition *Black, White, and Grey* at the Wadsworth Atheneum, Hartford, organized by curator Samuel Wagstaff. Sometimes called the first minimal show,[104] it included two to three works each by the painters and sculptors represented (including works on paper). In addition to Johns, the diverse roster included Robert Moskowitz, Roy Lichtenstein, Ad Reinhardt, Anne Truitt, Tony Smith, Ellsworth Kelly, Cy Twombly, Agnes Martin, Robert Morris, Frank Stella, and Andy Warhol. Its short, one-month run stands in disproportionate contrast to its legend and influence. Wagstaff, confessing a sort of curatorial disingenuousness, declared in an essay in *Artnews*:

> Quite arbitrarily, all the works selected are black, white, or grey, so chosen in an attempt to keep the viewer from being distracted by the emotionalism of color. In this way the degree of severity between artists, which varies greatly, should be easier to see as well as the degree of difference within the work of each artist himself.... If no single aesthetic blankets all of these artists, a tendency, an affinity, does give them a nodding rapport.... One is left uneasy... in front of much of this painting, with an embarrassing freedom.[105]

In unpublished sources, Wagstaff elaborated on "the sparse aesthetic," heralding the new art, which had "no subject, no emotion (showing), no handwriting, brushwork, space, or attempt to please or ingratiate."[106] Johns was represented with the gray *Canvas* (1956; cat. no. 7) and the gray *Newspaper* (1957; cat. no. 8), among other works, while other artists were represented with either all black or all white objects.[107]

Art historian James Meyer has wisely questioned the central assumption of the exhibition—that is, the equal treatment of black, white, and gray. He noted that black held near-mystical associations for artists such as Newman and Smith, and was avoided by younger artists for that very reason, while white was overloaded with allusions, not the least of which was its modernist imputation of "purity" and transcendence. It was perhaps gray that most clearly conveyed the "flat" feeling Wagstaff sought. Johns and Morris preferred gray, Meyer observed, because it appeared the most anonymous, the least personal color. He recalled Wagstaff's remark: "One thinks of Juan Gris, who changed his name to 'John Gray' so as to be as anonymous as possible." Meyer concluded: "Gray was more appropriate to a 'conceptual' art; it stimulated

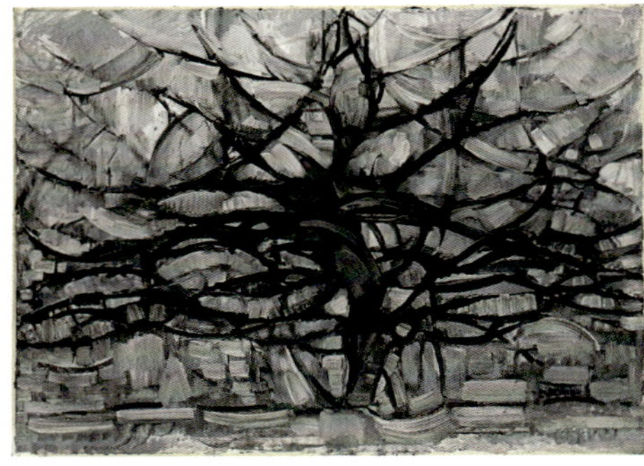

Fig. 16. Piet Mondrian. *The Grey Tree*, 1911. Oil on canvas; 78.5 × 107.5 cm (30 7/8 × 42 3/8 in.). Gemeentemuseum, The Hague. © 2007 Mondrian/Holtzman Trust c/o HCR International, Warrenton, Virginia.

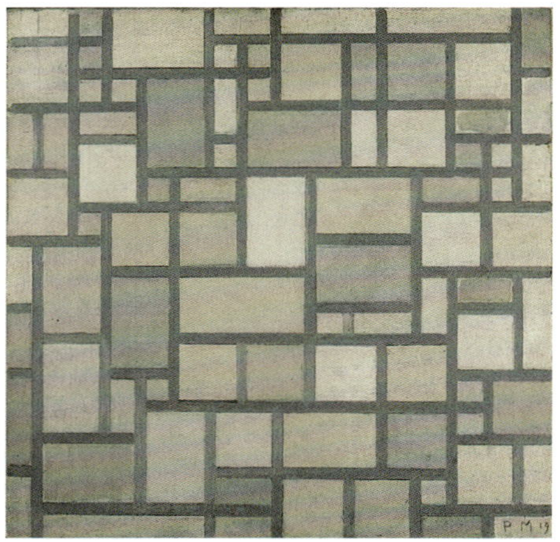

Fig. 17. Piet Mondrian. *Composition with Grid 7*, 1919. Oil on canvas; 48.5 × 48.5 cm (19 1/8 × 19 1/8 in.). Kunstmuseum Basel. © 2007 Mondrian/Holtzman Trust c/o HCR International, Warrenton, Virginia.

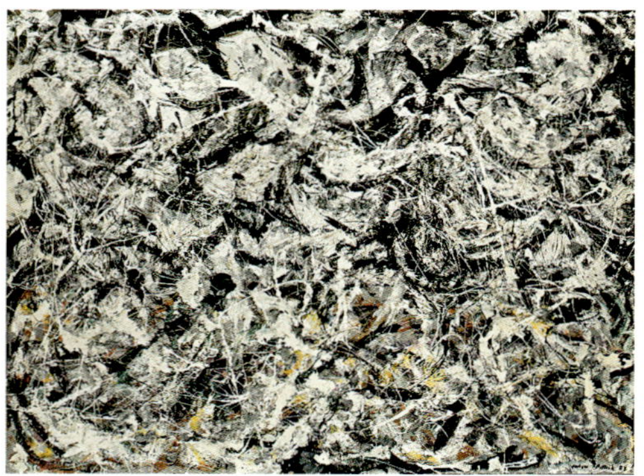

Fig. 18. Jackson Pollock. *Greyed Rainbow*, 1953. Oil on canvas; 182.9 × 244.5 cm (72 × 96 1/8 in.). The Art Institute of Chicago, gift of Society for Contemporary American Art, 1955.494.

vision the least. Perceptually inert, it did not occlude the presentation of ideas."[108]

What might Johns have been aware of that would have contributed to his understanding of the use of gray in art? Again, such a question does not necessarily invite documented instances of direct exposure and influence—although in some unverifiable cases it almost certainly must—but is rather an issue of understanding the parameters and permissions of a focused commitment to the restriction of color afforded by available examples of both nonobjective and representational monochrome art. Unlike black and white, gray was not especially visible during Johns's formative years 1948–54, nor was the use of gray compatible with the prevailing modes of expressionist painting. Indeed, it was in many ways inimical to the demands of the genre. (Consider, for example, that Eugène Delacroix cautioned, "Gray is the enemy of all painting.")[109] Johns would have recognized then—as he did throughout his career—a path untaken.

Yet gray was not invisible either. Mondrian's gray works were available to Johns in New York through a series of solo shows at Sidney Janis between October 1949 and November 1957. The October 1949 exhibition included *The Tree A* (1913; Tate Gallery, London); a February 1951 exhibition included all gray works such as *Gray Tree* (FIG. 16) and *Composition with Grid 7* (FIG. 17); and a November 1953 exhibition, *Composition Trees II* (1912–13; Gemeentemuseum, The Hague). Additionally, Johns would surely have seen Pollock's *Ocean Greyness* (1953; Solomon R. Guggenheim Museum, New York) and *Greyed Rainbow* (FIG. 18) in Pollock's solo exhibition at Janis in 1954. Both paintings offer titular and formal meditations on grayness. Among the last great purely abstract paintings Pollock made before his death in 1956, *Greyed Rainbow* is predominantly black, white, gray, and silver. Underneath the complex, labyrinthine skeins of paint in the bottom third of the canvas, however, Pollock thinly concealed orange, yellow, green, blue, and violet. The title of the work presumably refers to these "grayed" sections of hidden color—a lesson not easily lost on Johns (see section on gray and color, below). Clyfford Still had also made at least one major, mostly gray work in 1948–49 (*Untitled 1949*; Private collection), which Johns might easily have seen at Parsons. Ad Reinhardt was also showing regularly at Parsons; Johns might have seen his *Abstract Painting—Grey* (FIG. 19). In the mid-1950s, he would also have been aware of a no-longer-extant body of gray work—six to eight paintings on cloth with white chalk over cool, dark gray grounds—by Cy Twombly, who himself had been working almost exclusively in black and white since 1952. The largest of these works, *Panorama*, was shown at Stable Gallery (January 2–19, 1957). But Johns would most definitely have seen all of these works because they were photographed, and almost certainly painted, in Rauschenberg's Fulton Street studio in late 1954 or early 1955.[110] Johns was then living on Pearl Street, one block from Rauschenberg, and he was a frequent visitor.) These examples, perhaps enough to stimulate thought, were scattered across an uncrowded playing field.

Importantly, the specific impulse to gray was stronger outside of the realm of nonobjective painting. In the history of twentieth-century art, a monochromatic palette in representational work dates back to Analytic Cubist pictures of 1907–12, as both Picasso and Braque, working closely together during those years, limited themselves to neutral, earthy hues of tan, gray, and brown, "a recondite atmosphere of cerebration and analysis."[111] This legacy was extended, in a very particular manner, by René Magritte. The Belgian Surrealist started to make his so-called "stone" or "petrification" paintings in 1950—again, exactly synchronous with Johns's first serious exposure to contemporary art and its attendant critical discourses. In these paintings,

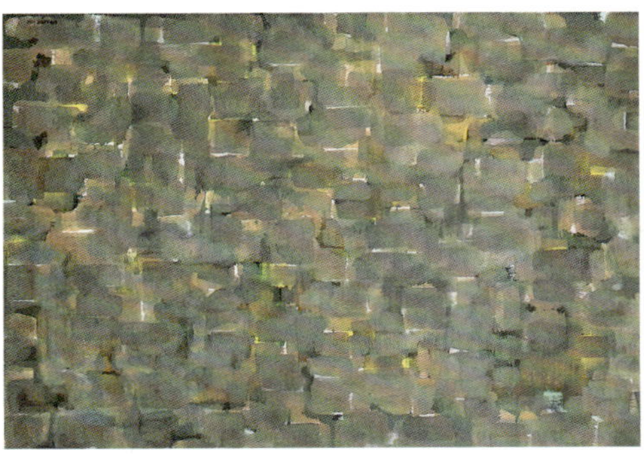

Fig. 19. Ad Reinhardt. *Abstract Painting–Grey*, 1950. Oil on canvas; 77.5 × 102.9 cm (30 ½ × 40 ½ in.). The Metropolitan Museum of Art, New York, gift of Henry Geldzahler, 1976.

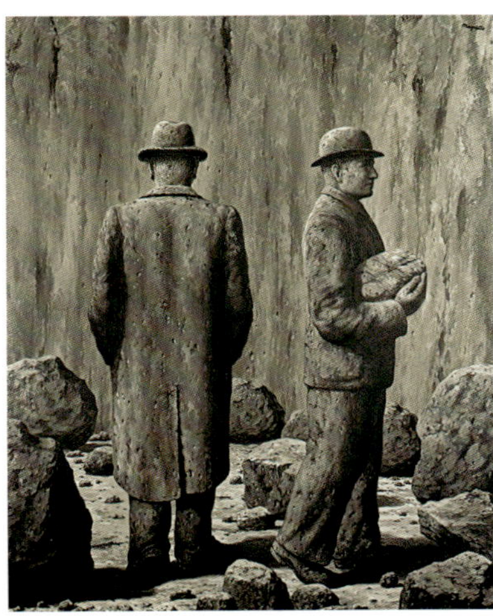

Fig. 20. René Magritte. *The Song of the Violet*, 1951. Oil on canvas; 100 × 80 cm (39 ⅜ × 31 ½ in.). Private collection.

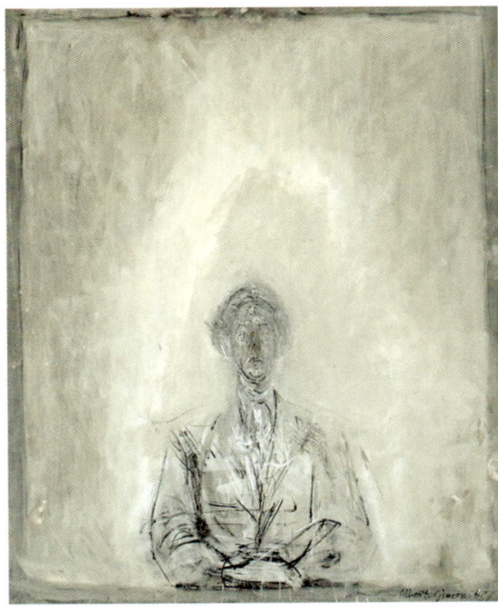

Fig. 21. Alberto Giacometti. *Portrait of Isaku Yanaihara*, 1956. Oil on canvas; 81.3 × 65.1 cm (32 × 25 ⅝ in.). The Art Institute of Chicago, gift of Silvain and Arma Wyler, 1959.11.

typified by a work such as *The Song of the Violet* (**FIG. 20**), all animate and inanimate things are rendered in a cool gray palette, as if they had been turned to stone.[112] Magritte, happy for the pretext to engage in grisaille, worked frequently in this mode through 1952, and then, occasionally, until the end of his career. Johns first saw Magritte's work at Janis in March 1954, an exhibition that presented work made between 1928 and 1930, and therefore included no petrification paintings. Nonetheless, one can speculate whether a curious artist like Johns, who admired (and later collected) Magritte's art, would have remained wholly unaware of the dominant mode of Magritte's then-current undertaking.

In a similarly speculative vein, one must also contend with the legacy of Alberto Giacometti and the potential impact of his work on Johns's young imagination. Again, the work was readily available in New York during the crucible years. In 1948 Pierre Matisse Gallery presented, with some fanfare, Giacometti's first solo exhibition in New York since 1934, and then opened another in 1950. The 1948 show included more than thirty sculptures and two major paintings, *Portrait of the Artist's Mother* (1937; Private collection) and *Apple on a Side Board* (1937; Private collection), both composed with monochromatic passages of browns, beiges, and red-browns, along with a number of drawings. The November 1950 exhibition contained six oils, among them *Annette on a Chariot* (1950; Private collection), also rendered in grays, reds, and browns. (Giacometti's paintings were also seen in a number of group shows at Pierre Matisse's and Sidney Janis's galleries between 1948 and 1956.) Giacometti's paintings, particularly after 1952, consist mostly of single figures in interior settings, closely aligned to the practice of drawing and deeply indebted in their figurative imagery to his sculptures. They are predominantly grisaille, a definition here inclusive of grays, beiges, and browns. This focus freed Giacometti to concentrate, like Johns, on "other things"; indeed, these quasi-programmatic works disclose nascently conceptual aspects. Giacometti produced paintings in which the actively defined gray expanses threaten the tense, solitary figures. Often, the artist would quickly render a portrait, paint over the area with gray, and begin again. In fact, his use of gray was connected to an existential crisis. Giacometti focused on a series of painted portraits of a friend, the Japanese professor of philosophy Isaku Yanaihara (himself steeped in existential theory), between 1956 and 1961 (**FIG. 21**). Here is curator Valerie J. Fletcher's description of Giacometti's attempt to paint his friend:

> Because Giacometti often hesitated and agonized for weeks and months over each portrait, the assured and exuberant strokes that characterized the earlier paintings increasingly succumbed to the miasma of gray space. This process had begun earlier, but it became overwhelming in the fall of 1956, when he experienced an artistic crisis while painting the first portrait of Isaku Yanaihara.... The crisis took the form of an inability to capture Yanaihara's visage on canvas, which intensified Giacometti's already chronic anxieties. Rather than precipitating a radical stylistic change (as he later claimed), this experience resulted in a compulsive reworking of each composition and more undefined gray areas.[113]

Johns would have likely encountered these paintings in an exhibition of Giacometti's work at the Galerie Maeght (May 27–June 20, 1961) in Paris during his visit to the city in the summer of 1961. This show featured over twenty gray paintings, including six versions of the Yanaihara paintings. According to Fletcher, no less an authority than Sartre viewed these works as quintessential talismans in the existentialist struggle between being and nothingness,

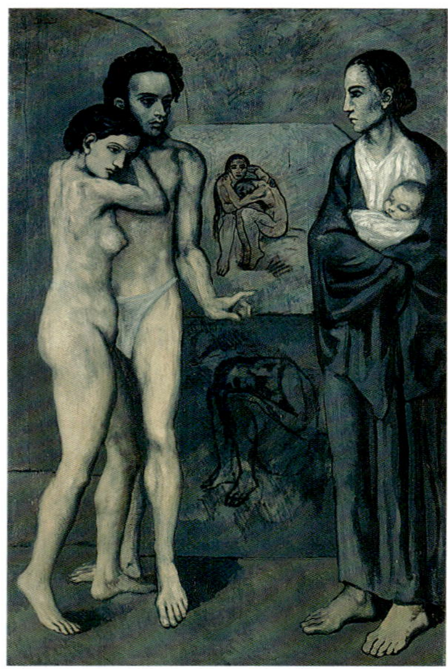

Fig. 22. Pablo Picasso. *La Vie*, 1903. Oil on canvas; 196.5 × 129.2 cm (77 3/8 × 50 7/8 in.). Cleveland Museum of Art, Gift of the Hanna Fund, 1945.24.

Fig. 23. Yves Klein. *IKB 79*, 1959. Acrylic on fabric and wood; 139.7 × 119.7 cm (55 × 47 1/8 in.). Tate Liverpool.

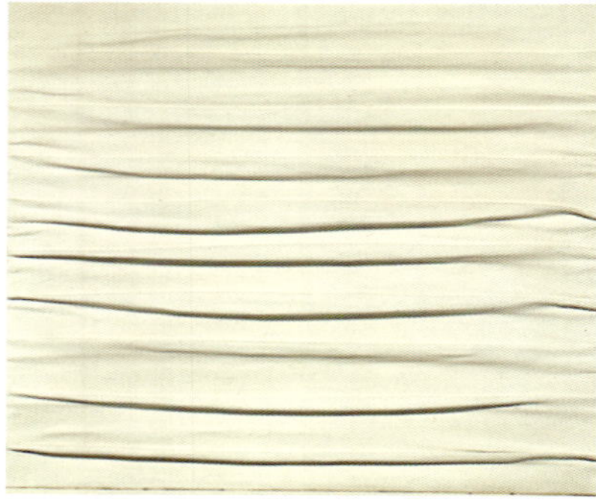

Fig. 24. Piero Manzoni. *Achrome*, 1957–58. Kaolin on folded canvas; 44.4 × 54 cm (17 1/2 × 21 1/4 in.). The Art Institute of Chicago, restricted and promised gift of Anstiss and Ronald Krueck Fund for Contemporary Art, 2000.309.

claiming that the painter "would like us to see the seated [figure] he has just painted through layers of emptiness. . . . Nothing enfolds him, nothing supports him, nothing contains him: he *appears*, isolated in the immense frame of the void."[114] Giacometti concurred, emphasizing the role of gray in his vision:

> When I see everything in gray and in this gray all the colors I experience and thus want to reproduce, then why should I use any other color? I've tried it, because I never intended to paint only . . . with gray. As I was working . . . one color after the other dropped out, and what remained? Gray! Gray! Gray! My experience is that the color that I feel, that I see, that I want to reproduce . . . means life itself to me.[115]

An understanding of Giacometti's art is, most certainly, bound to his use of gray. Johns would have known this, or, at the least, been aware of the precedents—both historical and contemporaneous—for such prevailing single-color associations.

Throughout the history of art, certain artists have been strongly identified with a particular color at certain moments in time. Picasso's practice at the turn of the century provides the best-known examples of paintings built around single colors or hues. In 1901–04, during his Blue Period—typified by *La Vie* (**FIG. 22**)—his imagery focused on outcasts, beggars, and invalided prostitutes, and the overall mood is one of despair. By the end of 1904 both the color schemes and subject matter of Picasso's paintings brightened. He turned to representations of saltimbanques, harlequins, and clowns dominated by earthy, pinkish tints. The paintings of 1904–06 are less strictly focused on the use of a single hue, although they have coalesced in the art historical imagination as his Rose Period, exemplified by a painting such as *Nude Boy* (1906; State Russian Museum, St. Petersburg). As a student in South Carolina, Johns was certainly aware of Picasso and would have known the iconic works of these periods, if only in reproduction. After arriving in New York, however, Johns encountered his art relatively early on, recalling: "I remember the first Picasso I ever saw, the first real Picasso, I could not believe is was a Picasso. I thought it was the ugliest thing I'd ever seen. I'd been used to the light coming in from color slides: I didn't realize I would have to revise my notions of what painting was."[116] An aspect of this revision would have been a reckoning with "color periods."

Historical notions of "color periods" in European art, fused with the reductive impulses in American art around 1950, provided a concentrated, fertile, and suggestive sphere of influence. It is within this context that Johns first confronted more radicalized monochromatic propositions from Europe. The pioneer in this regard was Yves Klein, whose practice encompassed painting, installation, performance, and actions. Johns met Klein in Paris in June 1961 and would have likely seen his work that year when Leo Castelli presented Klein's first and only New York solo show. Klein's breakthrough exhibition occurred in 1956 with *Yves: Propositions monochromes* at Galerie Colette Allendy in Paris: twenty monochrome canvases, each a different shade of red, purple, orange, yellow, and blue. The French critic Pierre Restany, in his speech at the opening of the exhibition, described Klein's paintings as "single-color proposals." Klein's commitment to the monochrome was cemented through his discovery of a suitable binding material of ether and petroleum extracts that could retain the intense brilliancy of granular color pigment. Klein focused on his favorite color, blue, calling the new substance IKB (International Klein Blue), which he also used as the title of his blue pictures (**FIG. 23**). From this moment on, IKB was the color with which he most readily identified; it corresponded perfectly to his ideas of the aesthetic of the immaterial and to the attainment of spiritual values and cosmological sensibility.[117] Klein's proposals were immediately influential. Italian artist Piero Manzoni, for example, discovered Klein in early 1957, and began to execute his two-dimensional work exclusively in white from that year until his death in 1963. Dubbing his paintings *Achromes*, Manzoni used gesso that had been scratched, scored, cut, or pleated, and other materials such as kaolin, cotton, and even bread (**FIG. 24**). Artists like Klein and Manzoni firmly established the idea in the postwar European imagination of artists whose very identities revolved around a forged association with a single color.

Monochromism is also related to the Minimalist proposals of the 1960s in the United States. Most of these examples must be seen as independent from even speculative questions of earliest influences, as Johns's commitment to gray predates—although it might have been reinforced by—the advanced art of the 1960s. These endeavors, however, both known and unknown to Johns, provide a comparative context for understanding the monochromatic aspects of his practice. At key moments, select American artists became attached to and associated with certain colors and their attendant formal properties. By 1960 Ad Reinhardt, who began making all-red and all-blue paintings in 1951–52, had committed himself exclusively to black. The 1950s had been for him a process of gradually moving nearer and nearer to the absence of color. "There is something wrong, irresponsible, and mindless about color," Reinhardt said, "something impossible to control. Control and rationality are part of any morality."[118] Robert Ryman, who admired Reinhardt's experiments, similarly began to reject color around 1958. By the early 1960s, Ryman began to produce predominantly white paintings (**FIG. 25**). Such choices were not limited to painting, as the work of three sculptors in the 1960s would demonstrate: Sol LeWitt, who embraced white; Robert Morris, who turned to gray; and Donald Judd, cadmium red.

Fig. 25. Robert Ryman. *Untitled*, 1959. Oil on cotton canvas; 110.5 × 110.5 cm (43 ½ × 43 ½ in.). Private collection.

Painting as Object, Object as Painting

"I have always considered myself a very literal artist."[119]

Distilling relations of thought and sight, Johns uses art as a form of philosophy; the subject of his painting is the very condition of painting itself. His use of the medium is always self-reflexive to one degree or another, representing a meditation on the nature of the material, the subject matter, the object, or particularly in later work, the painter himself. A group of very early gray paintings is concerned with understanding the nature of paint as a sign and its opposite, sign as paint, especially in relation to the nature of canvas as object and its opposite, object as canvas. This interaction sets in motion a series of maneuvers, generative and lasting, in which gray is a leading protagonist in a painterly drama of revealing and concealing.

Gray first emerged in this context as an encompassing, if ostensibly neutral, mode of abstract rendition. In a 1965 interview, the artist stated:

> The canvas is object, the paint is object, and object is object. Once the canvas can be taken to have any kind of spatial meaning, then an object can be taken to have that meaning within the canvas.[120]

Johns's initial forays into abstraction were gray and were executed concurrently with his first flags, targets, alphabets, and numbers between 1956 and 1959. These gray works, carrying (with one exception) the most literally descriptive titles, are vehicles for the presentation of objects—in the form of the actual canvas itself or of objects conjoined to the surface—in lieu of iconic, representational imagery.[121] (The emphasis on paintings as object coincides with Johns's principal foray into object making as sculpture, 1958–61.) In these works, the artist used gray to establish a uniform equity between the qualities of flat surfaces, front and back, and those of dimensional objects, whether real or implied. Souvenirs of the everyday, derived from common studio or household inventory, they famously include a stretched canvas, a drawer, a ball, a newspaper, and a coat hanger, among other items. Drafted into pictorial service, these items confer a concrete, three-dimensional status onto an otherwise two-dimensional ground.[122] In this context, gray emerges as a means of accomplishing one of the most basic aspects of his enterprise: the struggle to "seek direct, nonillusionistic ways of mediating between a fully dimensional world and a flat plane."[123]

As distinct from the artist's contemporaneous explorations of signs and symbols, these encaustic works—among them, *Canvas* (1956; cat. no. 7), *Drawer* (1957; cat. no. 9), *Gray Rectangles* (1957; cat. no. 10), *The* (1957; cat. no. 11), *Tennyson* (1958; cat. no. 12), *Gray Painting with Ball* (1958; cat. no. 15), *Coat Hanger* (1959; cat. no. 16)—do not incorporate newspaper collage.[124] Resisting the addition of another material layer, Johns deployed gray encaustic, by and large, in a direct, unmediated relationship between various surfaces; here "paint as object" meets "canvas as object" meets "object as object." (*Newspaper* [1957; cat. no. 8] establishes the clear, conceptual difference in the use of this specific material. Almost didactically, Johns isolated a whole newspaper sheet as an object in direct dialogue with canvas and paint, a pointed departure from his use of torn fragments incorporated within the encaustic medium itself.)[125] The application of paint, as in other works of this moment, is characterized by short strokes and daubs, alternately energetic and flat, achieving an uncanny balance between expressive and distancing, what one observer called "repressed expressionism."[126] For Johns the choice of gray for these decisive, early paintings advanced the cause of literalism most explicitly because it avoided the distraction of emotion.

> I used gray encaustic to avoid the color situation. The encaustic paintings were done in gray because to me this suggested a different kind of literal quality that was unmoved or unmovable by coloration and thus avoided all the emotional and dramatic quality of color. Black and white is very leading. It tells you what to say or do. *The gray encaustic paintings seemed to me to allow the literal qualities of the painting to predominate over any of the others.*[127]

Canvas (1956) is among the first gray monochromes. The work is made from two conjoined canvases painted in encaustic, the smaller one affixed in the center, facedown against the flat surface of the larger in order to showcase its usually concealed back and stretcher. The subject, obviously enough, is the material fact or "objectness" of canvas. Indeed, one of the consequences of Johns's holistic consideration of painting as object is the leveling of the conventional hierarchies attending recto and verso:

> My use of objects comes out of, originally, thinking of the painting as an object and considering the materialistic aspect of painting: seeing that painting was paint on canvas, and then by extension seeing that it occupied a space and sat on the wall, and all that, and then, if those elements seemed to be necessary to what I was doing. And so I thought to use this idea and *extend the kind of physicality by bringing what is usually concealed behind the painting in front of the painting*. . . . And maybe you can exaggerate that.[128]

It was the first of many times over more than fifty years that the artist has inverted verso and recto. Johns's enduring fascination with the back of a painting is encapsulated in an amusing anecdote the artist related in 1966:

> In 1950 or [19]51, a painter whom I admired said that he was to have an exhibition of eight or ten canvases which were turned face to the wall in the kitchen where we were talking. He said that the works were very new and good, and that he would not show them to anyone before the scheduled exhibition. When he left the room, another friend looked at the fronts of the canvases and found that they had not been painted.[129]

Parodying the impulse to secrecy, Johns's story suggests that what is hidden is often just another form of blankness. This body of early gray work, then, aims to present the fundamental dichotomies of painting: front and back, surface and object, image and abstraction, revealed and concealed. Johns resolved these variously rivaling elements with the use of allover gray, establishing a compelling visual and intellectual equity between competing polarities. A form of cancellation, the use of gray ultimately reinforces a sense of painting as lacuna. Ultimately, for Johns, revealing can become another way of concealing.

This tension is further articulated in both *Drawer* (1957) and *Coat Hanger* (1959). Unlike other gray encaustics of this period, *Drawer*, a particularly energetic, almost slap-dash display of Johns's cautiously expressive brushworks, reads as a light gray, with an overall frosty blue cast. In fact, the surface holds three blended grays—alternately cool and warm—and touches of white. The title derives from a rectangular piece of wood, painted in the same combination of grays with the same handling, mounted in an opening cut into the lower center of the canvas.[130] Two simple knobs create the illusion of a front panel of a drawer, suggesting that painting may be a receptacle for objects and not simply images.[131] Advancing the arguments proposed by *Canvas*, *Drawer* portrays an object that is itself a container, whose very function is to store or conceal. Significantly, the drawer sits flush on the edge of the opening, but the very small gap at the top suggests the weight of its pretended contents. A theoretical work, *Drawer* imagines painting to comprise something hidden or embedded.[132] The lesser-known *Coat Hanger* also conjures a repository of stored personal possessions—a closet. (This painting also introduces notions of suspension, the fluid interaction of a hanging object and its shadow.)[133] Scaled to a head-and-shoulders portrait format, the work suggests both presence and absence—of the shirt or jacket and the figure such articles require.

Fig. 26. Detail of *Tennyson* (cat. no. 12).

Tennyson (1958) is an epic meditation on the formal, philosophical questions raised by the earlier *Canvas*, as well as a singularly personal expression of the relationship between gray media and questions of concealment. (The recondite role color plays in this work is discussed later in this essay.) This large vertical painting is dominated by dense, mottled gray encaustic brushwork and canvas collage. It is constructed of two narrow stretchers bolted together on the verso. An unstretched canvas, used here by Johns for the first time, is drawn up and over much of the surface, folded back and painted in the same tonality and massaging facture as the stretched canvas beneath. This complex construction produces six planar surfaces, four of which are hidden from view. The strictly formal explorations of canvas on canvas are heightened by the complex suggestion of mystery and compounded by the strangely evocative title.[134] The word TENNYSON, executed in thin roman letters, sits on top of the margin created by the unpainted bottom edge (**FIG. 26**). The painting is exceptional in its suggestive citation of the quintessential, once widely read, Victorian poet Alfred, Lord Tennyson.

Johns's naming of a painting for a specific individual warrants a brief, focused digression. On one level, the use of a melancholic gray in combination with the reference to the poet seems obvious enough: certain lines of Tennyson's poetry offer sufficiently redolent associations of grief and isolation that are seemingly compatible in tone and mood. "The long mechanic pacings to and fro / The set, gray life, and apathetic end" from "Love and Duty" (1842) is but one example. Such games of referential discovery, while tempting, are ultimately beside the point—if we believe the painting to be something more complex than a reminiscent illustration of isolated stanzas. Reading the painting through the lens of Tennyson, however, does warrant the mention of a striking biographical anecdote. In 1874 Lord Tennyson, then sixty-five years old, recounted an episode from his childhood:

> A kind of waking trance (this for lack of a better word) I have frequently had . . . when I have been all alone. This has often come upon me through repeating my own name to myself silently, till all at once . . . the intensity of the consciousness of individuality . . . seemed to dissolve and fade away into boundless being—and this not a confused state but the clearest of the clearest, the surest of the surest, utterly beyond words.[135]

The story suggests an extreme moment of self-knowledge attained through repeated, solitary references to one's own presence in the world. This notion of affirmation by means of a knowing naming feels entirely congruent with a painting that declares itself—counterintuitively, revealing not obscuring—by covering itself *with* painting. Both the narrative and the object evidence a shared interest in self-reflexivity.

No mention of Tennyson can avoid a consideration of the poem that earned him the title of poet laureate in 1850 only a few months after its publication and that proved to be one of the best-loved and most widely celebrated works of the Victorian era, *In Memoriam A.H.H.* This long elegy, which he composed over a period of seventeen years following the death at the age of twenty-two of his closest friend, Arthur Henry Hallam, is certainly the record of Tennyson's struggle to reconcile his love for Hallam and the loneliness and joylessness he endured during an extended period of mourning with his belief in a divinity and his hold on the meaning of life. Considerable speculation has surrounded the nature of Tennyson's friendship with Hallam during their years at Cambridge and two trips to the Continent they made together. Suffice it to say that Hallam's death from a cerebral hemorrhage during an excursion he made without Tennyson left the latter devastated and despairing.[136] The example for many readers—as it might have been for Johns—was the profound message of the preciousness of relationships and the fragility of love, platonic or otherwise, between men.

Another comparably tender—if equally unsupported—interpretation can also be offered. The structure of the painting suggests a bed made for a couple.[137] The two vertical canvases, each 186.7 × 61.3 cm, are scaled to the size of an adult body. Separate but joined together, they stand in for two figures resting side-by-side. The collaged canvas is folded over like a sheet, proportionally enveloping the canvas in the way a bedspread would—just enough to cover two bodies to the shoulder. The exposed top section of canvas, equally divided in half, reads as two pillows. (The suggestion of two pillows is buttressed by the second drawing made after the painting. As opposed to his treatment of the top quarter of the sheet in the ink on paper version [1958; Private collection], Johns's mark making on the second drawing, a pastel [1959; cat. no. 13], lends a clear sense of volume to the forms.) The painting may be Johns's own, wildly restrained response to Rauschenberg's *Bed* (**FIG. 27**),

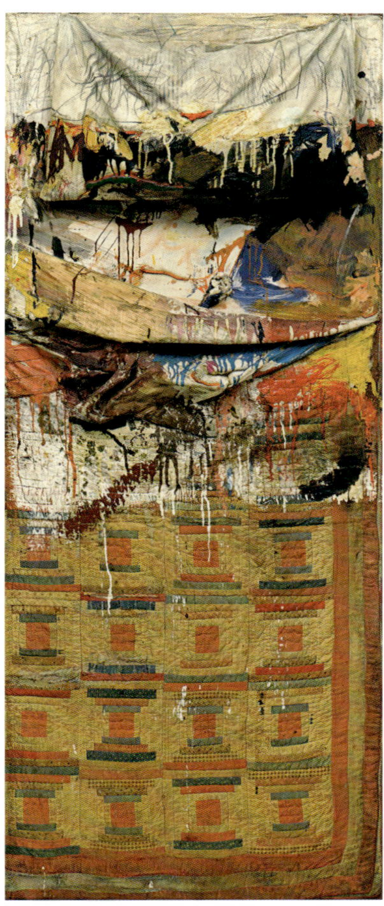

Fig. 27. Robert Rauschenberg. *Bed*, 1955. Combine painting: oil and pencil on pillow, quilt, and sheet; 192.4 × 80 × 20.3 cm (75 ¾ × 31 ½ × 8 in.). The Museum of Modern Art, New York, gift of Leo Castelli in honor of Alfred H. Barr, Jr.

a landmark Combine painting made two years earlier—the year the artists began living in the same building on Pearl Street.[138] Rauschenberg's construction measures 192.4 × 80 × 20.3 cm—strikingly similar to the size of the individual panels of *Tennyson* and equivalent to the scale of a single bed—and is likewise covered with paint and bedding, in this case, an actual quilt. Many have interpreted Rauschenberg's choice of this patterned bedcover, which reads as a surrogate for abstract, geometric painting, as a comment on Johns's own work at a moment when the dialogue between the two artists was singularly consuming. Perhaps secreted within Johns's adoption of Tennyson is his own version of *Bed*, painstakingly controlled and concealing where the Rauschenberg was a catastrophic release of color and gesture, double where the other was single. In this context Michael Crichton's observations on the differences between the two artists are useful:

> Rauschenberg was voluble and outgoing where Johns was reserved; Rauschenberg was explosively energetic where Johns was patient and deliberate; Rauschenberg was hectic where Johns was elegant and precise; Rauschenberg was exasperating and shocking where Johns never desired to shock.[139]

There could not be a better description of the differences between the two paintings, or a better foil for contemplating the use of gray. Indulging such a speculative analysis does not, of course, obviate the need to explicate Johns's summoning of Tennyson. Perhaps, if the artist is not behaving as uncharacteristically as one might suppose in his use of such a reference, other analyses notwithstanding, the title of the painting also could be read as formal trope, deciphered as code. Along the bottom edge, the eight letters of TENNYSON are divided equally, four on the left half of the canvas, four on the right. In the center, straddling the divide, are the letters NY—the abbreviation of the city to which Johns and Rauschenberg both emigrated from the South, the city in which both were living when the work was made. Gray, the color of the Confederacy, signals their shared point of origin.

Independent of such conjectural interpretations, what remains most significant about these works is the unifying treatment given to all surfaces by the gray medium; it collapses distinctions between figure and ground, surface and support, image and object. These early encaustic paintings set a practical foundation—elaborated and modified over time in both formal and conceptual terms—for Johns's use of gray throughout his career.

"The Mood Changes," Selectively

The artist is frequently in a position of doing more or less or different from his intentions, I think. . . . I don't think you find out anything about the artist. I think you find out what use you have for things. I don't see anything else to find out. Because the attitude toward painting from any particular time and the use of it vary from minute to minute. And you can't think that it's going to be a static representation of anything. Our verbal language changes in the same way. You use a word one day and then the next day it means something else and then eventually it's gone.[140]

The year 1961 was a watershed in Johns's art. Among other things, he enjoyed his first trip to France, and his first retrospective exhibition, at the Columbia Museum of Art in his native South Carolina. In January he purchased a beach house on Edisto Island, South Carolina, and began to spend notable portions of his time outside of New York City. The house was isolated, the island sparsely inhabited. Some of the works Johns produced in Edisto understandably evidence a melancholic engagement with the sea, and with the intense emotionality of the poetry of Frank O'Hara and Hart Crane. Johns will later allow that his departure from New York working conditions, especially in terms of Edisto's proximity to the water and the quality of light there, affected the texture and color of the work. Importantly, 1961 was also the year Johns's relationship with Rauschenberg dissolved.[141]

Much of the work of this period is gray. Johns himself has acknowledged the attendant changes in his art. In 1970, while arranging a chronological listing of his works, he commented, "the mood changes," when he got to 1961.[142] The notion of a shift was given further weight and authority by Roberta Bernstein, who noted the evidence of emotional crisis in Johns's art and life:

> For Johns, gray is a neutral color which gives the painting a more literal or objective quality than any other color. But like blue, gray is associated with sadness (or gloominess) and Johns often used gray to suggest a mood of sadness (coldness, emotional withdrawal), especially in his 1961 paintings like *No* and *Water Freezes*. The result of using a cool or neutral color to suggest an emotional condition is that the emotionalism is perceived as repressed and hidden rather than openly revealed.[143]

For the 1996 survey exhibition on Johns organized by the Museum of Modern Art, curator Kirk Varnedoe rehearsed a similar argument.

> Between *Thermometer* of 1959 and *Water Freezes* of 1961, a new emotional tone intervened in Johns's work, chill, dark, and bleak. Titles of negation, melancholy, or bitterness (*No*, *Liar*, *In Memory of My Feelings—Frank O'Hara*) underlined the altered mood. . . . Gray, formerly the guise of impassive neutrality, became an expressive cast of gloom and morbidity.[144]

Such apparent critical consensus notwithstanding, this biographical thesis—"the mood changes"—does not fully account for the role of gray in the work of this period. There is, certainly, a dominance of expressively (and negatively) titled, achromatic and monochromatic pictures in the early 1960s, a time of significant change in the artist's life, and there are a host of works that equate grayness and sadness. But the rather prosaic and limited associations of gray with such moods, while valid up to a point, have resulted in a simplifying homogenization of the meanings of Johns's use of this color. An understanding of the fullness and importance of gray in his art before and well after the early 1960s is essential; then, the flurry of gray pictures during the Edisto years is less anomalous and therefore not exclusively dependent on biographical readings. To be sure, "the mood changes," selectively; concurrently, it is important to allow biographical readings, selectively.[145]

The notion of Johns working in lonely isolation in his Edisto retreat,[146] while perhaps sanctionable at times, is misleading. A notable group of predominantly gray works of 1961—*Water Freezes* (cat. no. 86), *Liar* (cat. no. 87), *In Memory of My Feelings—Frank O'Hara* (cat. no. 85), *No* (cat. no. 91), *Painting Bitten by a Man* (cat. no. 90), *Disappearance II* (cat. no. 88), *Good Time Charley* (cat. no. 92)—were, in fact, made in New York. Throughout this period Johns was alternating between South Carolina and the studio at Front Street in New York, beginning to work on more than one picture simultaneously. Because gray sustains multiple valences, it is important to consider individual expressions, not to rely on a blanket categorization of gray during this period. At times gray remains matter-of-fact. In 1962, working at Front Street, Johns returned his attention to the gray *0–9* (1959–62; cat. no. 65) in acrylic paint with the numbers arranged in two rows, 0 to 4 and 5 to 9. Four years previously, he had made *0–9* (1958; Private collection) in white encaustic and collage, and a year later, a version in red, yellow, and blue encaustic (1959; Museum Ludwig, Cologne). The gray canvas is the third and final version and in its place in a somewhat mechanical, formulaic succession must be understood as a challenge to any categorical assumptions regarding the artist's use of gray. (See also the color *0 through 9* [1960; Private collection, Atherton, California] in comparison to *0 through 9* [1961; cat. no. 61].) Doubtless there are gray pictures that correspond to, or are intended to evoke, feelings of anger and sadness; at the same time, there are others that evince levity. Thus, the matrix can only be regarded as complex.

Few pictures in Johns's oeuvre are tougher than *Disappearance II* (1961), an aggressively nasty, uningratiating painting. It was made toward the end of the year, following after some delay a related work of 1960 of the same theme and title (*Disappearance I,* 1960; Private collection). (The artist had originally proposed making four "disappearance" paintings; only two were completed.) For this construction, Johns folded a raw, trimmed canvas into a scrubby, scrappy, diamond-shaped quatrefoil and mounted the origami-like form on top of an existing, stretched canvas. On one side, the cuts are clean, almost elegant; on the other, the tears are irregular, even brutal. Of the eleven surfaces (counting the fronts and backs of each area of support), only five are visible. Applied in a streaking fashion, the oils are somber shades of gray—here pushed as far toward black as Johns's grays allow—with touches of an odd, grapey purple and orange. The artist's typical brushstrokes—including his trademark squiggles—are present, but they are largely cancelled out or hazed over. In a painting about the dynamics of over and under, much of the brushwork is concerned with reinforcing the confusion between the two. Tarpaper-like patches of canvas nullify the presence of the paint strokes, which are unable to compete with the dimensionality of the canvas collage. (In the various areas where the collaged canvas lifts, scrapes of white, black, and purple paint are visible beneath. Once again Johns set gray and color in dialogue in order to hint at a secret life, to structure a dynamic of concealment.) The overall appearance is one of determined obstinacy.

With this dry, irregular surface, which feels even burned or scorched, Johns seems to be processing the work of artists such as Antoni Tàpies or Lucio Fontana.[147] Yet the picture is closely linked to Johns's own formal, pre-1961 concerns, specifically to the use of canvas collage in *Tennyson* (1958; cat. no. 12). Kozloff described it accurately:

> Encouraged to penetrate behind the plane, the eye is shown that that plane is merely physical. . . . Illusionism is devaluated, and abstraction is contradicted, by a device which reveals the inevitable artificiality of pictorial depth. A further refinement on this "undeception" occurs in *Disappearance II*, where the pasted plane is folded back over itself to make a quatrefoil envelope that has received the same stroking as the background. In this instance, the front and back of a surface, verso and recto, are demonstrated to be, for all practical purposes, identical.[148]

Kozloff was right to draw out the relationship between the two compositions. *Disappearance II* is most certainly a mean reworking of *Tennyson*, a transformation of the lyrical examination of "painting as object"—even allowing for a potentially personal subtext—into an equally formal, yet more expressively cloaked, drama of denial and refusal. Close reading discloses an irrefutable connection: on a 1967 graphite wash and gouache on paper also titled *Tennyson* (cat. no. 14), Johns made a clearly discernible diamond-shaped pattern by deliberately creasing the sheet, thereby grafting the form of the *Disappearance* paintings onto a graphic variant of the *Tennyson* motif. Assuredly, then, *Disappearance II* underscores the relativity of mood. Here, as elsewhere, Johns used one gray painting to engage with formal tropes of his own invention in another gray painting. To greater and lesser degrees, such actions thicken the plot, abating access to aspects of personal biography, dissembling the transient phenomena of mood and emotion.

The uniquely paradigmatic corollary between grayness and sentiment in the work of the early 1960s is *In Memory of My Feelings—Frank O'Hara* (1961), a provocatively brooding oil painting made of two canvases attached together along the vertical axis with two brass hinges. (The paintings are hinged backward, precluding the possibility of movement.) A fork and spoon hang from an unraveled coat hanger, which is attached to a screw eye penetrating through the left canvas. The title and Johns's signature run along the bottom edge, crossing both canvases. The upper-left quadrant is executed in a very thin oil wash over a white ground. The lower half of the left panel and the entire right panel are painted heavily in Johns's trademark gestural style.[149] The predominant gray covers over and incorporates color—red, yellow, blue, purple, and orange. Ample visual evidence on the surface suggests that the painting was quite colorful in a previous iteration. (Johns reused part of an unfinished painting for this work.)

Frank O'Hara was a curator of painting and sculpture at the Museum of Modern Art, New York (1960–66), as well as a poet, playwright, critic, and a friend of Johns's from the late 1950s onward. Part of the title of the painting is borrowed from one of O'Hara's best-known poems, an elegiac recounting of the pain of lost love, written in 1956. Johns's brushstrokes practically adumbrate the words DEAD MAN along the bottom of the right panel (the largest D appears on the far-right edge of the left panel). The stenciled words are repeated in three superimposed layers, the built-up edges of the middle version being the most plainly visible. More striking still is the buried image of a skull in the upper right, revealed by X-ray studies and now suggested only through its hard-to-discern pentimenti. Both marks presumably belong to the earlier, now mostly obscured, composition beneath *In Memory of My Feelings*. Remarkably, the work reads as a memorial for its eponymous dedicatee, who died in an accident on Fire Island five years *after* the work was made. A note in Johns's sketchbook, which Cage cited in his 1964 essay on the artist, partially explains the coincidence of these uncannily predictive associations: "A Dead Man. Take a skull. Cover it in paint. Rub it against canvas. Skull against canvas."[150]

In Memory of My Feelings—Frank O'Hara is as much about the poet as it is about Johns. Arguably, the work is an exercise in self-abnegation. The words that compose the phrase "In Memory of My Feelings" are stenciled in gray letters, with the exception of "of" and "my," which are left unpainted—white on white. These ghost letters minimize the presence of the possessive pronoun, intimating a reluctance on Johns's part to totally occupy the first-person voice. The shape and composition of *In Memory of My Feelings—Frank O'Hara* clearly suggest a flag, for Johns an unmistakable reference to self. A horizontal black line, drawn in charcoal across a wet wash of paint, helps to define a zone in the upper-left quadrant of the painting. This demarcation calls out the relationship of the distinct fields of stars and stripes. (The upper-left portion is even slightly larger than the lower-left portion, consistent with the composition of a flag.) As he had hinted at in *Jubilee* (1959; cat. no. 2), Johns again obscured the form of the flag—the most charged emblem of his own accomplishments—underneath a morass of gray. In fact, the application of thin oil in the upper left was most likely done by rubbing a cloth over the stretched canvas, a gesture that persuasively bolsters the sense of the stars being "wiped away." The result is a symbolic form of renunciation consonant with the emotional, nearly maudlin, tenor of O'Hara's poem, the last lines of which read:

> I have forgotten my loves, and chiefly that one, the cancerous
> statue which my body could no longer contain,
> against my will
> against my love
> become art,
> I could not change it into history
> and so remember it,
> and *I have lost what is always and everywhere*
> *present, the scene of my selves*, the occasion of these rules,
> *which I myself and singly now must kill*
> and save the serpent in their midst.[151]

Even here, in this expressly stygian account, gray must be understood in relative terms, as previous exhibition contexts heighten or restrain potential readings. The lachrymose overtones of *In Memory of My Feelings—Frank O'Hara*, for example, were underscored when the work was first exhibited in a group show at Castelli (December 8, 1961–January 10, 1962) in which Johns presented only four paintings, all of them gray, on a single wall: *In Memory of My Feelings—Frank O'Hara*, *No*, *Liar*, and *Good Time Charley* (**FIG. 28**). Here the intoned, blank neutrality and self-reflexivity of earlier gray works were replaced by heated, accusatory, and outwardly directed speech related to personal betrayal. The title *Good Time Charley* suggests an affable, convivial fellow who prizes the amusements of the moment over loyalty, friendship, or love; *No* is an edict of refusal;[152] *Liar*, an accusation of perfidy. These three paintings, together with the O'Hara references to lost love, present a clear, coherent narrative inflected by melancholy, anger, and heartbreak. A year later, in Johns's solo show at Castelli (January 12–February 7, 1963), *In Memory of My Feelings—Frank O'Hara* was presented in a sufficiently different context (**FIG. 29**). On a wall next to *Slow Field* (1962; Moderna Museet, Stockholm), the painting was double-hung above *4 the News* (1962; cat. no. 94); the two newer paintings return to a detached, analytical mode. The emotionalism of gray, and the content suggested by the reference to Frank O'Hara in particular, were substantially modulated.[153]

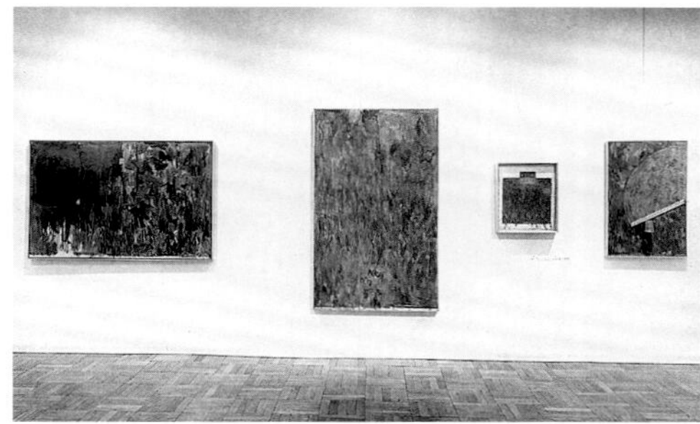

Fig. 28. Installation view of the 1961–62 group exhibition at Leo Castelli featuring (from left to right): *In Memory of My Feelings–Frank O'Hara*, *No*, *Liar*, and *Good Time Charley*.

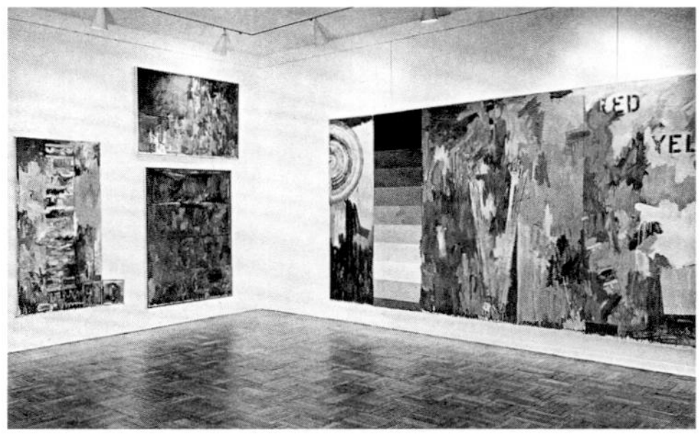

Fig. 29. Installation view of Johns's 1963 solo exhibition at Leo Castelli.

Throughout this period, Johns was using gray to very different ends. The lesser-known, infrequently exhibited *Portrait—Viola Farber* (1961; cat. no. 96) is, as Bernstein has pointed out, a version of *In Memory of My Feelings—Frank O'Hara*.[154] Both are horizontal rectangles of approximately the same size, painted gray, with the same elements: a spoon and fork, wire and hinges, and words. Most emphatically, both canvases are portraits of artists who were also friends of Johns's.[155] The fact that one work is in oil and the other is in encaustic lends credence to the notion that they are, in a fashion, alternate versions of each other. The crucial difference between the works is that *Viola Farber* never accrued the obviously sad connotations of *Frank O'Hara*. Farber was a founding member and leading dancer with Merce Cunningham Dance Company from 1953 to 1965, and later, a noted choreographer. Apart from the painting's title, the overt reference to Farber is limited to her name, printed twice, in superimposed lettering of different sizes across the bottom of the canvas. In a maneuver reminiscent of *Canvas* (1956; cat. no. 7), Johns

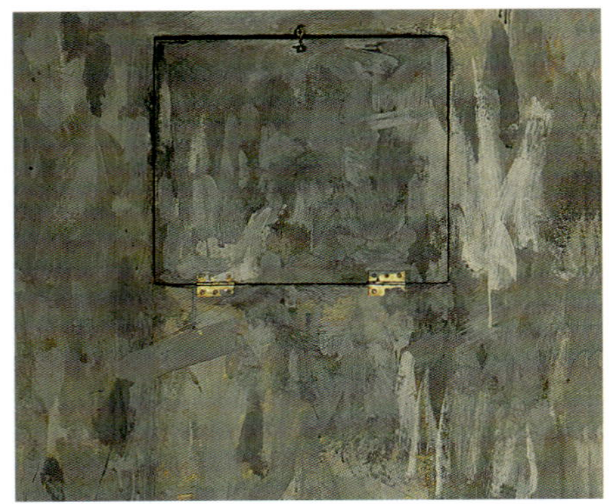

Fig. 30. Detail of *Portrait–Viola Farber* (cat. no. 96), with the panel closed.

inset a small rectangular, stretched canvas — the recto and verso of which have been painted in the same grays — in the upper-right portion of the composition. Hinged at the bottom, this small panel can be open, revealing the wall behind, or closed and secured with a hook, so that it is flush with the larger canvas. Just beneath the bottom edge of the smaller canvas when it is unhooked, Johns affixed a bent spoon on the left and a bent fork on the right, projecting outward. They are connected by a taut rubber band (**FIG. 30**). In marked contrast to their first, portentous appearance in *Frank O'Hara*, Farber's fork and spoon — here unburdened by proximity to a densely poetic subtext — feel good-humored, almost comic.

Portrait — Viola Farber is a playful piece. Farber was born in Germany and her last name shares the German root word for color (*Farbe*). In that linguistic context, her first name, Viola, also suggests a play on words, as it is the Latin root of violet (a color used at times as an undertone in Johns's gray paintings), and doubles as the word for a musical instrument. Harkening back to one of Johns's earliest extant pieces, *Construction with Toy Piano* (1954; Kunstmuseum Basel), the painting is itself actually a crude instrument: when the rubber band is plucked, the sound does approximate a note. Johns has recalled showing Farber how the work could make music and Farber's delighted, quizzical response: "But can it eat?"[156] Finally, more than playful, *Portrait — Viola Farber* suggests a knowing self-consciousness on Johns's part about his own, perhaps occasionally over-determined, use of gray. The small inset monochrome within the larger gray painting — alternately present or absent — places Johns's gray under wry scrutiny. This embedded reference, a form of self-quotation, attests, perhaps, to the artist's awareness of the possibilities of overemphasizing the symbolic status of a single color.

Color and Material Translations: Flags

The flag images exist at different levels of recognizability. Some are in red, white, and blue and are easy to see. There's a gray one that I think is difficult to determine as a flag.[157]

The flag, a subject matter Johns turned to for his breakthrough painting, is a recurring motif, deployed in complex and materially varied ways over decades. Throughout his career, the form of the flag has provided a composition that has freed Johns to explore its nature as sign and image in painting, sculpture, drawing, lithography, etching, and screenprinting. As Bernstein has aptly pointed out, it must be "regarded as more. . . [than] an initial statement."[158] It is not, as is often assumed, limited to the early red-white-and-blue encaustics and their various reappraisals. Johns has made approximately thirty Flag paintings and fifty Flag drawings since the mid-1950s, and he continued to use the motif at least through the 1990s (see *Flag*, 1994; cat. no. 37). In addition to red, white, and blue single flags, he has produced single flags set within larger fields, multiple flags set within a single field, and backward or vertical flags. Notably, of the eleven known monochrome Flag paintings, seven are gray.[159]

Gray shadows the origins of Johns's relationship to the flag. Both Johns and his father were named for Sergeant William Jasper, a South Carolinian who lost his life while saving a flag in battle.[160] He died in October 1779 in Savannah, Georgia, together with another soldier defending the colors, a lieutenant named Grey.[161] This is, perhaps, merely a bit of fascinating trivia, but it can be added to the lore that surrounds accounts of Johns's first use of the flag. The artist initially described the origins of the flag as intuitive; yet by 1964 he was insisting that the idea to paint the stars and stripes came to him in a dream, about which, when questioned, he replied: "I don't know that it was in color."[162] (It may be that Johns does not have a strong memory for color; his grandmother Evaline Wilson Johns was an amateur artist and porcelain painter, and her work offered her grandson his earliest exposure to art. He has stated with respect to her porcelain: "I don't remember any use of color, but there may have been some.")[163] His first painting of the subject, *Flag* (see **FIG. 5**), quite literally resurrects the dream by incorporating bed sheets as a support for the image. The linens remain, imbedded, as a displaced site or unconscious text within the painting, a material reminder of the apparently colorless flag of his dream.

From the beginning, there has been a "call and response" quality to the relationship between gray and color flags. *Flag*, painted with red, white, and blue, was followed three years later by a smaller, single, horizontal painting of the motif in gray encaustic, *Gray Flag* (1957; cat. no. 23). With Johns one of the best ways to confirm a point of speculative analysis is to test if the inverse is also true. Indeed it is. In 1959 he painted *Two Flags* (cat. no. 24), a composition of two stacked horizontal flags in gray acrylic paint. (Gray seemingly offered Johns an appropriate opportunity to work in acrylic, a medium he rarely uses because of a basic dislike for the available range of color.) This distillation was followed three years later by *Two Flags* (1962; Collection of Irma and Norman Braman), a larger, two-panel red, white, and blue oil of stacked horizontals. The pattern, so to speak, continued. *Two Flags* (1973; Private collection) is a double vertical arrangement of the flag inverted. Four years later, Johns completed *Two Flags* (1973–77; Private collection), a duplicative composition of almost the same size, using oil on paper over canvas, in gray. (*Flag*, 1971 [cat. no. 29], a single, inverted, vertical flag in gray encaustic with collage, the first gray encaustic flag with newspaper collage, seems to have no exact equivalent color version.)[164] Invested readings of these various rejoinders, while telling, are assuredly limited. Johns's uses of grays are neither didactic nor precisely dialectic; rather, less tactical, partially intuitive exercises in accrual and modification trump strictly comparative or oppositional operations.

Monochrome or colorless renderings of the flag diminish its pictorial presence and heighten its abstract qualities. The literary historian Philip Fisher, writing of *White Flag* (1955; see fig. 2 in the essay by Douglas Druick in this volume), addressed the question of legibility in the monochrome.

> The spirit of a flag hovers over the painting much like our fantasy of a vaporous ghost in a room. Where is the red, white, and blue that "has to be there" if this is to be an American flag? Where are the sharply contrasted red and white stripes, the distinct, countable white stars? . . . . It would be more accurate to say that this is a painting done at the site of a flag in the way that a suburban housing tract can be built where a farm used to be.[165]

If whiteness, or grayness, mitigates the "flagness" of the flag imagery, so too does the act of repetition. When first considered, acts of repetition might seem to affirm the subject of "flag" by demonstrating its inexhaustible fascination. In fact, the contrary is more likely; repeating the image affirms the "thingness" of the work of art at the expense of its ostensible subject, the flag: "To paint a flag is to efface it. The more it is represented, the less it is." Each new iteration, Fisher argued, "calls attention to itself and consequently away from the flag."[166] This effect is compounded, not only within painting, but also with each different material incarnation.

Gray is a material condition that endlessly effaces "flagness" by demonstrating the possibilities of its physical multiplicity. As Kozloff observed of Johns's work, "Color is something out of which the substance forms itself . . . rather than something externally conferred upon it."[167] Johns himself most certainly regards color as material:

> I only try to find a way to leap from one material to another. . . . I said leap between materials, but to be exact, such leaps also occur between colors. When I used white and gray, there was a leap between them. . . . I felt the difference between materials.[168]

No other color and no other image in Johns's oeuvre allows for the diversity of physical interpolation as gray allows in the Flag motif—gray is expressed in encaustic, oil, acrylic, pencil, graphite wash, lithography, silkscreen, ink on plastic, carborundum wash, Sculp-metal, lead, and silver.[169] The nearly endless reiterations, however, do not, for Johns, aspire to the level of the transformative. "Transformation," the artist has stated, "is in the head. If you have one thing and make another thing, there is no transformation, but there are two things. I don't think you would mistake one for the other."[170] The changes remain autonomous, owing to their emphatically material diversity. In the case of the now-iconic image of the flag that began its life as enamel paint on a bed sheet, the artist quickly abandoned this course of action because the combination of medium and support was too flimsy; he switched to encaustic for its more solid qualities. In Johns's revisions of the flag—particularly with gray media—a related series of transubstantiations occur.[171]

Over time various media facilitate a set of physical migrations from liquid to solid, solid to liquid, and back again. Artist Robert Smithson speculated on "the climate of sight" that changes "from wet to dry and from dry to wet in one's mental weather."[172] In Johns's work with the Flags, this narrative begins with paintings such as the encaustic *Gray Flag* (1957; cat. no. 23) and the acrylic *Two Flags* (1959). Literalizing the abstract, objectlike qualities of the flag, the paintings become flat sculptures. *Flag* (1960; cat. no. 34), for example, is made of Sculp-metal and collage. Sculp-metal dries to a light matte gray and can be burnished to variously dull or lustrous finishes. (In 1987 the artist will use a moulage of the 1960 Sculp-metal to cast the object in a highly reflective silver; see cat. no. 36.) In 1969 Johns issued an edition with Gemini G.E.L. in lead (cat. no. 35), a material that indirectly references painting, as it was once a fairly common constituent of both red and white pigments. On its own, this malleable metal is bluish white when freshly cut, but tarnishes to a dull gray when exposed to air. By 1985 Johns's experiments with ink on plastic—a combination he prized precisely because of the difficulty of controlling this medium on this support—contributed somewhat belatedly to his treatment of the flag. *Two Flags* (1985; cat. no. 33) is executed on a frosted plastic sheet, which offers little resistance and allows for almost no absorption. The result is a totally liquid drawing. Here, the form of the flag, arrived at without apparent benefit of any underdrawing, emerges from wet-on-wet passages of pooled, puddled, and evaporated ink. A large handprint, presumably the artist's own, dominates the lower-right corner. The drawing registers his fleeting touch directly, without the enhancement of another medium, as a mark of wetness. Johns seems to have been emphasizing the importance of his hand, even in a format that does not respond to its control or direction. Touch, so central to discussions of his use of encaustic medium, persists as index. Seeing this ink on plastic drawing of a flag in the context of its colorless precedents, one can nearly imagine it as an alternate interpretation of the surface of *Gray Flag* (1957)—a watery skin momentarily rippled by contact, which, seconds later, will return to stillness, its ability to reflect an image intact restored.

Gray and Color

I was working on a colored numbers painting. When I worked on it for longer than a minute, the entire painting would turn gray to me. I couldn't see any of the colors, and I would have to stop. . . . I mentioned this to Duchamp. He said, perhaps you have physiological need.[173]

For Johns, gray is always in dialogue with color.[174] Color is regarded as fundamental to the art of painting. At times, however, color achieves a particular kind of importance by means of abrogation. When Johns was asked his opinion of the idea for a survey exhibition of gray works, his initial response was that "it's not so much about gray as it is about the absence of color."[175]

For many years Johns insisted that he was not a great colorist. His close friend John Cage, confirming the artist's own, arguably modest assertions, addressed him directly in his 1964 essay: "You are the only painter I know who can't tell one color from another."[176] Kozloff, speaking of Johns's use of color, wrote: "It does not 'convey' anything but rather seems to act as a container into which nothing has been put."[177] As has been established, when Johns takes up color, he most often embraces the restrictions afforded by the predetermined "found" palette of the three primaries and their immediate secondaries. Admittedly, an improvisational or otherwise extemporized use of color was never his strong suit.[178] Even as late as 1982, for example, the putrid, candy colors—ribbon pinks, chalky teals, lemon yellows, and lime greens—evident in a painting like *Usuyuki* (1982; Sezon Museum of Modern Art, Japan) suggest a failure to control color when his palette is not fully schematized. An amusing and revealing anecdote regarding Johns's abilities as a colorist concerns Josef Albers, arguably the most famous color theorist of the twentieth century. The German-born Albers established one of the first courses on the relativity of color shortly after arriving at Black Mountain College in 1933.[179] Albers's teaching explored "the tonal possibilities of colors, their relativity, their interaction and influence on each other, cold and warmth, light intensity, color intensity, psychical and spatial effects."[180] Thomas Hess claims Johns told him the following story:

> In Hawaii, [Johns] bumped into a friend who had been a student of Albers and who had a copy of an Albers test on color with him—some 100 questions for artists and students. He gave it to Johns while they were sunning themselves on the beach. Some time later, Johns saw Albers and told him: 'Mr. Albers, I took your color test and got all the answers wrong.' Albers beamed. 'Dot's vunderful,' he exclaimed, 'you got 100 percent!'[181]

Johns, who met Albers only once, in 1964, and admired him, owns one work by the artist, appropriately, a gray-scale painting on glass titled *In the Water* (1931).[182]

Charles Baudelaire once observed that "great colorists know how to get an effect of color with a black suit, a white necktie, and a gray background."[183] An heir to the masters conjured by Baudelaire, Johns has repeatedly demonstrated his virtuosity with the gray scale, exploiting in his paintings an achromatic richness and variety few would think possible. Furthermore, some of Johns's most exquisitely nuanced uses of color appear in gray pictures. Poet and critic David Shapiro has celebrated Johns's "rainbow of grays."[184] Indeed the artist takes full advantage of a seemingly infinite range of mixed grays—alternately blended with gradations of black and white, or at other times with warm ochers or cold violets, and so on. His use of color to modify gray can also be found in Johns's work with sets and costumes for Merce Cunningham. *Exchange* is a performance the artist designed in 1978. As he had for the design of *Un Jour ou Deux* (1973), Johns designed a painted gray scale as a backdrop. The costumes were also dyed in graduated gray tones, some warm, some cold. Unlike the earlier example, in which no color was present on stage, some of these costumes had very small patches of exceptionally subtle colored details at the wrists and ankles. These areas were separately dyed—red, orange, yellow, green, blue, and violet—none of the colors bright, all barely noticeable alongside the gray.[185] Again, such gestures have clear corollaries in painting. *Map* (1962; cat. no. 39), *0 through 9* (1961; cat. no. 61), and *Céline* (1978; cat. no. 110) are among the most chromatically elegant and refined uses of color in Johns's oeuvre. Somewhat counterintuitively, the handling of color in many of the gray pictures conveys a strong sense of the uncomplicated pleasures associated with painterly pursuits.

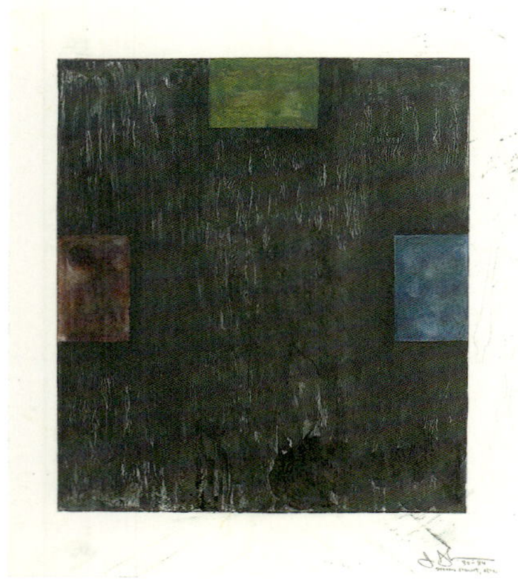

Fig. 31. *Untitled*, 1980–84. Graphite wash and acrylic on paper collaged onto plastic; 41.3 × 36.8 cm (16 ¼ × 14 ½ in.). Collection of Werner H. Kramarsky.

Yet a conceptual armature almost always anchors Johns's practice. From the earliest moments of his career through to the present, he has deployed gray in a careful formal and intellectual dialogue with the three primary colors that have always been the essential building blocks of his art. A particularly revealing example of Johns's thinking in this regard is *Untitled* (FIG. 31), a compellingly anomalous graphite wash and acrylic collage. This little-known work seems odd for a number of reasons, most especially because the sheet captured Johns's attention at least twice over the course of a four-year period and because it does not correspond to any known painting. Three very thin, tissuelike pieces of paper were painted with acrylic red, yellow, and blue. These delicate monochromes were fixed to a square field of modulated graphite wash on plastic, which was then cut and laid down on a larger sheet with scattered marks suggestive of a fragment of another, unfinished drawing.[186] The resistant surface did not absorb the rich, dark grays of the graphite wash; rather, they read through the saturated primaries of the three color blocks, compromising the clarity and purity of their hues. The drawing—again, corresponding to no known painting—is an isolated signpost. A piece of purely visual thinking, the sheet evidences the studied, willful nature of the mutually dependent, overlapping relationships between gray and the primaries.[187]

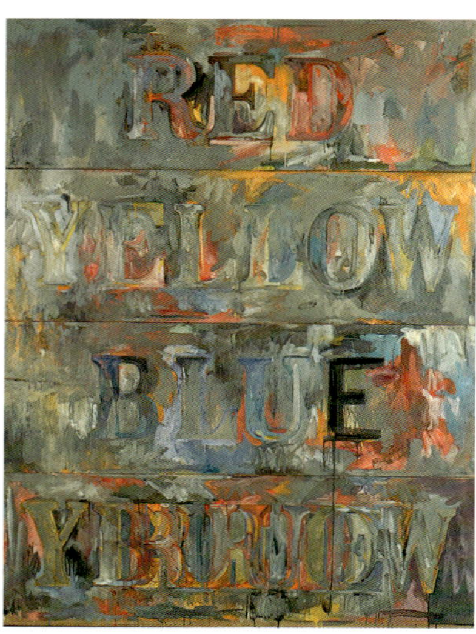

Fig. 32. *By the Sea*, 1961. Encaustic on canvas (four panels); 182.9 × 138.4 cm (72 × 54 ½ in.). Private collection.

For decades Johns has engineered a complex deployment of gray over and under color. Most commonly he uses fields and washes of gray media to conceal the primaries. *Gray Rectangles* (1957; cat. no. 10) is a large gray monochrome with three smaller gray canvases, underpainted from left to right in red, yellow, blue, and inset flush at regular intervals on a horizontal axis in the lower third of the larger canvas. Trace elements of color are visible at the margins of each inserted object. (The paintings within the painting call attention to the depth and construction of the object.) The controlled red, yellow, and blue drips—some seemingly deliberately composed as clues, others evidence of a less-controlled painterly incident—hint at the presence of the primary colors hidden in this moody gray painting. *Tennyson* (1958; cat. no. 12) similarly intimates the placement of primaries underneath fields of gray. The principal support (the conjoined canvases) and the top, visible surface of the folded canvas collage are underpainted with intense, saturated blues, both light and dark, and then very heavily overpainted with warm and cool grays—to the point that almost all traces of color beneath are obliterated. The folded gray canvas conceals a bright red monochromatic field, visible at the fold and along the seams of the collage. Along the bottom edge, the stenciled letters are underpainted with yellow. Careful looking, aided by magnification, reveals that the very word "Tennyson," apparently gray on gray, sits on a glowing yellow on red below a curtain of blue.[188] *Near the Lagoon* (2002–03; cat. no. 135), formally speaking, the closest known relative to *Tennyson*, is also significantly underpainted and subtly overpainted with subdued red, yellow, and blue; rather than overtly concealing these hues, however, Johns used a much thinner covering of gray strokes through which colored underlayers glow. He even integrated the three colors on the top layers, at times precisely working in red, yellow, and blue in areas that correspond to passages of the same colors below. (See the essay by conservators Kelly Keegan and Kristin Lister in this volume, p. 169.) Most recently, in 2005, the artist turned to a brightly colored, unfinished Crosshatch painting from 1983. In this case the colors include but are not limited to the primaries. For some reason, perhaps because the color veered out of control, the painting had stalled and Johns abandoned the canvas—as he had done with the colorful composition beneath *In Memory of My Feelings—Frank O'Hara* (1961; cat. no. 85). Returning to it more than twenty years later, the artist resolved the composition by painting over it, covering the crosshatches with a monochrome rendering of the flagstone motif in gray oil. The new painting is suggestively titled *Within* (1983 and 2005; cat. no. 136), calling direct attention to the now largely concealed content of the painting.

Since *Jubilee* (1959; cat. no. 2) the actual words "Red, Yellow, Blue" have often been submerged under layers of gray paint. Mixing the three primary colors produces gray. This action is illustrated for the first and only time in *By the Sea* (FIG. 32). The painting comprises four conjoined horizontal panels stacked vertically: from the top, RED appears in the first, YELLOW in the second, BLUE in the third. In the fourth, bottom panel, the three words are superimposed, metaphorically and literally mixed. The overall appearance is one of muddied grays. (The strategy will be reprised in the 1980s, when gray is added to primaries to create muted or grayed color tones, as in *Untitled* (*Red, Yellow, Blue*) [FIG. 33]). Such a constituent interrelationship of gray with the primaries is further suggested in *Diver* (FIG. 34), in which a gray scale makes its first appearance in Johns's art, alongside expressively rendered and schematically stenciled RED, YELLOW, BLUE. This is made most explicit in *Periscope (Hart Crane)* (1963; cat. no. 103), an extension of *Jubilee*, in which the obliteration of color, an act of both cerebration and painterly extravagance, is now combined with the full apotheosis of elegy. In this painting color comes undone, suggested by the occasional backward and upside-down application of the stenciled letters that name but do not represent colors. Johns rubbed thin black and dark gray paint across the surface most likely with a cloth, allowing the washes to run and drip down the surface, falling in between superimposed stenciled letters. Philip Fisher described the painting—an homage to the suicidal leap and death by drowning of poet Hart Crane—as a funeral for RED YELLOW BLUE[189]—a watery gray grave for color. For the first time, Johns substituted his own arm for the wooden slat device—reaching out, in presumed desperation, from the sea, here expressed as a swirling eddy of grays.

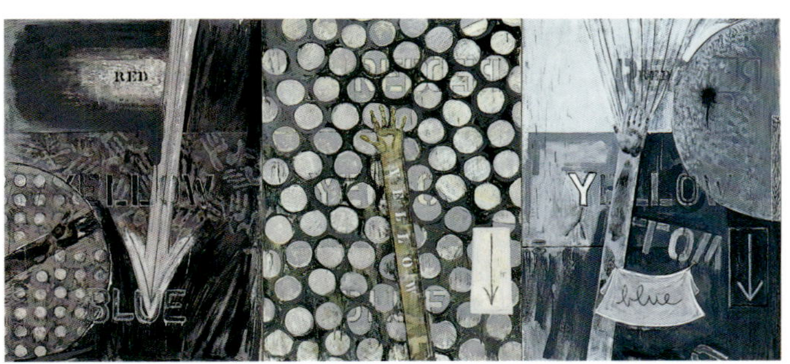

Fig. 33. *Untitled (Red, Yellow, Blue)*, 1984. Encaustic on canvas (three panels); 140.3 × 300.9 cm (55 ¼ × 118 ½ in.). Museum of Fine Arts, Houston, gift of the Brown Foundation, Inc.

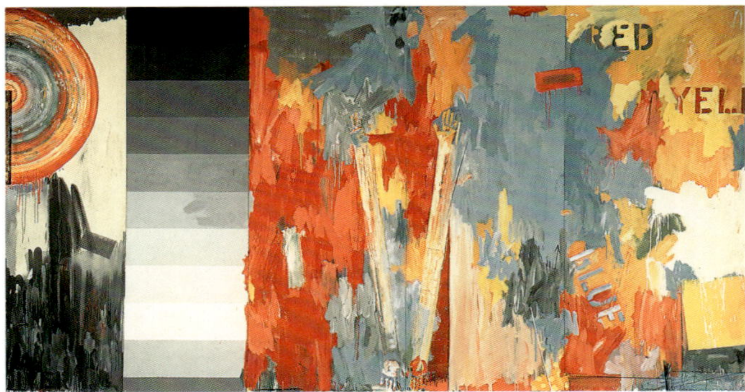

Fig. 34. *Diver*, 1962. Oil on canvas with objects (five panels); 228.6 × 431.8 cm (90 × 170 in.). Collection of Irma and Norman Braman.

The expunction of color in favor of gray has multiple valences. Consider the fate of the single largest (and only irregularly shaped) work of Johns's career to date, the 4.6 × 9.1-meter *Map* (*Based on Buckminster Fuller's Dymaxion Air Ocean World*) (FIG. 35), which the artist made for *American Painting Now* at the United States Pavilion at Expo 67 in Montreal. The twenty-two-panel painting was first exhibited vertically (although in subsequent years, the painting has generally been presented horizontally) in the twenty-story-high geodesic dome designed by the visionary architect Buckminster Fuller to house the

US Pavilion. The source of the painting is Fuller's world map, first published in 1943, which divided the surface of the earth into twenty-two pieces—predominantly equilateral triangles—in an effort to render the shapes and relative sizes of the Earth's land masses without the distortions introduced by other orthographic projections. In conceiving this homage, Johns largely borrowed from Fuller's color system, which followed, by gradations of the spectrum, the climatic zones of the earth, mostly in oranges, yellows, and greens, with blue for the ocean. Johns had painted the work in sections (in David Whitney's 3.7 meter wide studio on Canal Street) and never obtained a space to see the whole map assembled before it was installed. When he finally saw the work in Montreal, he was dissatisfied.

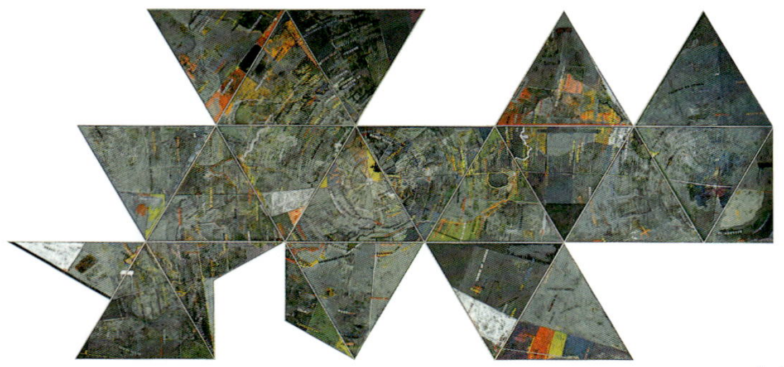

Fig. 35. *Map (Based on Buckminster Fuller's Dymaxion Air Ocean World)*, 1967–71. Encaustic and collage on canvas (twenty-two parts); 500.1 × 1000.1 cm (196 7/8 × 393 11/16 in.). Museum Ludwig, Cologne.

> I didn't like it. It just looked like a map to me. When I got the painting back—by then I had moved into a very large space down on Houston Street.... I could have it all together, and look at it as one thing. I completely repainted it.[190]

The faithful transcription of Fuller's colors had prevented the map from attaining a sufficient degree of abstraction. Consider David Shapiro's pointed observations:

> The first version looked like a blowup of Fuller's schema: an image divided into clear information of areas and place names, with no sense of being a painting, colors representing what they represent by means of a color key. It lacked Johns's usual quality of doubt and of casting into shadow the idea of identity or unity.[191]

Johns himself agreed and he completely remade the work in 1970–71.[192] Shapiro described the resulting changes as "adventurous, all embracing revisions," used to "tactfully disguise the former system of color.... He did not merely make local color revisions but spent much time getting rid of the initial system of color—*secreting* the original as much as concealing."[193] The application of color, where it still exists, became arbitrary rather than systematic. More importantly, Johns transformed the Fuller map by turning it gray, relying once again, perhaps, on the instincts that led him to make his very first Map painting, this one of the United States (1960; cat. no. 38), in gray (see the essay by Barbara Rose in this volume, pp. 143–44).

Crosshatch

A distinct arrangement of hatched marks first appeared in 1972 on the far-left canvas of *Untitled* (1972; Museum Ludwig, Cologne). Johns has frequently recounted glimpsing the pattern on a passing car.

> I only saw it for a second, but knew immediately that I was going to use it. It had all the qualities that interest me—literalness, repetitiveness, an obsessive quality, order with dumbness, and the possibility of a complete lack of meaning.[194]

The image, remembered and applied repeatedly, became the dominant motif in painting from 1973 to 1982. The design is commonly called crosshatch, although in Johns's paintings the lines rarely cross. Indeed, crosshatching is traditionally a graphic method of adding depth and volume, or it is used to convey the illusion of light in space. Johns's marks emphasize flatness.

Gray is not a dominant mode during this period. The majority of the Crosshatch canvases are in color. Nevertheless, these must be understood as an extension of Johns's larger critique of expressionist models of painting—an enterprise for which gray had been foundational in his early thinking. *Scent* (1973–74; Museum Ludwig, Aachen)—the title, shared by one of the last works of Jackson Pollock, was adopted by Johns almost as if to suggest that he was taking up the cause of abstraction where Pollock left off—was the first picture conceived and executed as an allover crosshatching motif; it is articulated in strong, bright tones of green, orange, and purple. With this and other Crosshatch works, Johns forged a new model of painterly abstraction using a schema that is ordered but not strictly geometric or reductive, gestural without being emotive. The origins of Johns's embrace of such mark making—mistakenly regarded by many at the time as an endeavor inconsistent with his previous achievements—can be traced to early revisions of prevailing modes of painting first seen in *False Start* and *Jubilee*. In these works, as in the Crosshatch pieces, Johns engineered a dialogue between apparently expressive modes, color or otherwise, and a more conceptual approach.

The Dutch Wives (1975; cat. no. 108) is arguably the best and most beautiful example of Johns's use of gray in crosshatching. The two vertical encaustic and collage panels are, like conjoined twins, linked but separated by a shared feature, the center divider of the double frame. Two strong, black lines, made with a dry medium (perhaps pastel), are drawn left of center in the right panel. The paintings are predominantly gray with exceptionally subtle touches of red, blue, purple, orange, and green in the right panel. A red outline, also drawn in dry medium, highlights a trademark "splatter" and "drip" shot to the right of center in the right panel. The two panels suggest coupling, and the application of the paint documents repetitive, manual gestures. Given the painting's title, in addition, allusions to sex and masturbation are plausible.[195] A collage of cut newsprint (along with a few instances of wove paper) establishes the crosshatching pattern, arrayed over a drawn pencil grid occasionally evident on the unprimed canvas (**FIG. 36**). The application of gray encaustic in discrete, methodical gestures closely follows the linear, directional rhythms established by the collage. What is unusual about this work is that the patterns are not reversed mirror images of one another but in almost every case, nearly identical copies.[196] The patterning is the same, and it is composed of precisely matching fragments of newsprint, which Johns carefully exposed in some areas to allow for the confirmation of his exactitude.[197] (Johns applied the heat used to bind the encaustic medium to the canvas in different ways, obliterating some marks while preserving others. The surface of the right panel, while maintaining the overall consistency of the underlying newspaper collage, is considerably more melted than the left.)

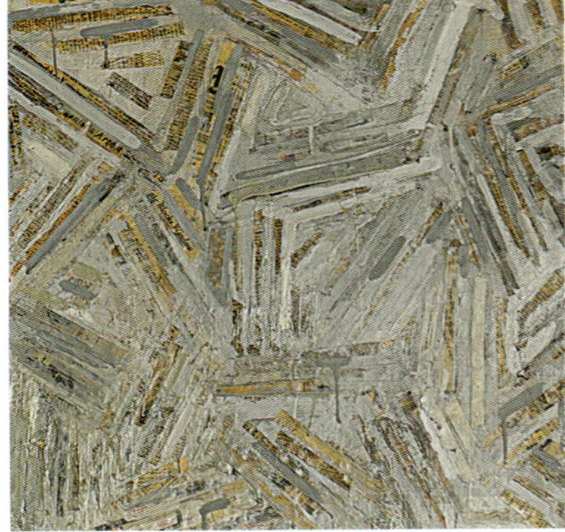

Fig. 36. Detail of *The Dutch Wives* (cat. no. 108).

What is most interesting here is that the gray values are established, or denoted, in almost equal measure by the newspaper and paint. Johns selectively applied the paint to allow newsprint images to show through. On one canvas, a gray mark is established in paint, while its double on the other canvas is expressed by the halftone fields of newspaper ink. Critic Trevor Winkfield's description of Johns's early work seems applicable to the *Dutch Wives* as well: paintings "bedecked with petrified wax, evoking troops of nerves circulating beneath, as though the paintings' real lives, as ever, took place out of sight."[198]

In 1980, a full eight years after his first use of crosshatching, Johns received a postcard reproduction of Edvard Munch's *Between the Clock and the Bed* (1940–42; Munch Museum, Oslo). In this late self-portrait, Munch, near death, depicted himself in his bedroom, standing in front of the open door to his studio; the bright red and dark blue pattern of the bedspread is rendered in a fashion markedly similar to Johns's crosshatches. As is often the case with Johns and questions of influence, the revelation of precedent is both engaging and distancing. The series of works inspired by *Between the Clock and the Bed* announced the beginning of the end of the motif. Between 1980 and 1982, Johns, inspired by the Munch, made several drawings, followed by two large paintings, first one in encaustic and then one in oil, isolating the theme in relation to the source, previously unknown to him. In the two works, both of which are conjoined three-panel paintings of the same size, color plays an important role. (A glowing orange section marks the spot occupied by Munch in his self-portrait. Secondary colors appear to be layered over primary colors, an effect most visible in the lower-right section of each canvas.) The upper half of the right canvas of the oil includes a screened image of his black-and-white 1979–80 *Usuyuki* screenprint. The inclusion foreshadows the draining of color from, and a subsequent terminus of, the crosshatch motif. This oil was followed by two related, black-and-white works: a charcoal and pastel on paper (*Between the Clock and the Bed*, 1982; Private collection, New York) and an ink on plastic (*Between the Clock and the Bed*, 1982; Collection of Aldo Crommelynck). Nearing the end of the series, these drawings reveal Johns thinking in motif, not in color. (An illustration of the progressive draining of color within the context of the crosshatch can be found in the three independent *Tantric Detail* paintings [1980–81; cat. nos. 111–13]. The most intense use of primary color can be found on the left side of the first completed canvas, while the right side of the third canvas fades out to white on white.)

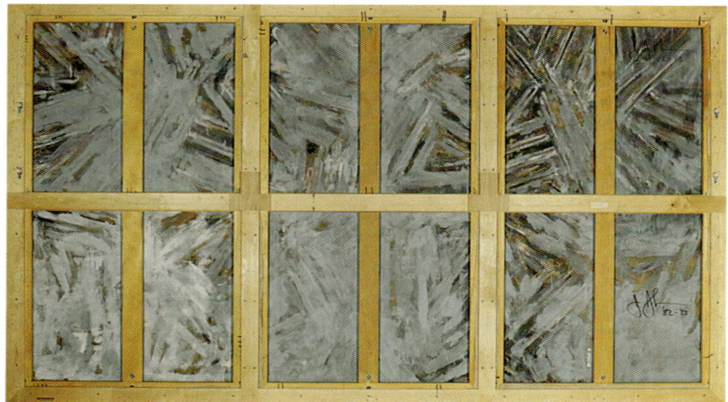

Fig. 37. Verso of *Between the Clock and the Bed* (cat. no. 115).

The previous paintings and related drawings culminate in 1982–83 in an authoritative, monumental grisaille painting, the last major independent articulation of the Crosshatch motif in painting as of this writing.[199] *Between the Clock and the Bed* (cat. no. 115) is composed of three joined, unprimed, medium-weight canvases, each individually stretched and stapled. The compositional strokes appear to glide across these seams, and in reality are a combination of continuous and discontinuous brushmarks, the latter of which are designed to appear unbroken in order to provide even coverage of the support across the seam. Johns incorporated touches of red, blue, green, ocher, pink, purple, and yellow, but the painting is predominantly gray.

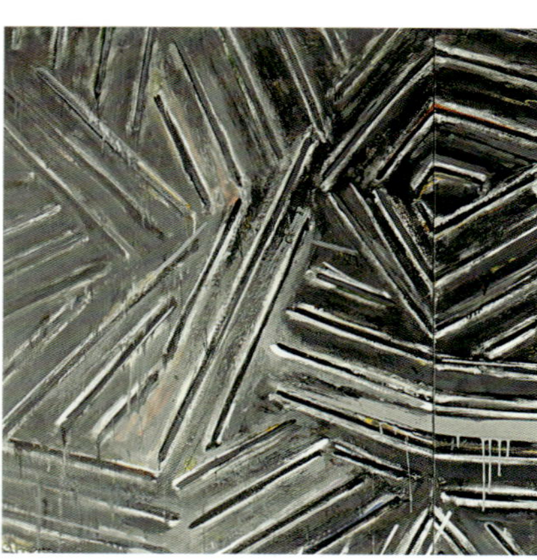

Fig. 38. Detail of *Between the Clock and the Bed* (cat. no. 115).

In fact, *Between the Clock and the Bed* is gray—front and back. The painting process began with a monochromatic outline of the chief compositional strokes in mid-tone gray encaustic, leaving a few inches along the bottom unpainted. Apparently the artist applied a great deal of heat to the work after this initial stage; this, combined with the subsequent heat used in the encaustic process, triggered an osmosis of sorts, causing most of the paint from the outlining of the composition to pass through the unprimed canvas to the back, so that it now appears almost as if the artist applied paint to the verso (FIG. 37). From the front, these areas where most of the paint has penetrated through have the appearance of slightly grayed canvas, with paint entirely absent from some upper parts of the fabric weave and visible only in the interstices. The next layers of encaustic include more varied grays, thick strokes often superimposed on the middle gray. The top layer of paint is distinguished by linear black strokes mostly juxtaposed with white (FIG. 38). Overall, the black and white lines, along with the few traces of color, remain alternately distinct and merged. Under the heat of the encaustic process, certain of them seem to dissolve into a blur of molten, grayed hues. Through heat, absorption, blending, and attendant optical effects, the painting, quite literally, embodies grayness. For whatever reasons, Johns chose to end his extended treatment of the Crosshatch motif—which was most often effectuated in color paintings—with this distillation in gray.

The Break with Abstraction

In my early work, I tried to hide my personality, my psychological state, my emotions. This was partly to do with my feelings about myself and partly to do with my feelings about painting at the time. I sort of stuck to my guns for a while, but eventually it seemed like a losing battle. Finally, one must simply drop the reserve. I think some of the changes in my work relate to that.[200]

With the conclusion of the Crosshatch paintings, Johns's art changed radically and unexpectedly. Although one must remain wary of categorical simplifications, the principal shift is from the abstraction of the Crosshatch paintings to a new representational style.[201] After nine years of an almost singular focus, there occurred a sudden burst of newly refractory motifs derived both from art historical sources as well as from the artist's own personal history. Having been banished for decades, perspectival space and some degree of pictorial depth returned with *In the Studio* (1982; Collection of the artist).[202] From this picture forward, Johns resumed, in a new way, the task of painting images and objects as they appear in life. This evolution, while admittedly major, has often been misunderstood as a total reinvention, even as apostasy. Essentially, however, Johns still relied on readymade, largely flat, schematic structures as the compositional basis for his imagery.

The first of Johns's art historical appropriations in his work of this period, the likeness of two armored soldiers from Matthias Grünewald's *Isenheim Altarpiece* (1512–16; see figs. 3–4 in the essay by Richard Shiff in this volume), comes from colorless source material. In the summer of 1980, shortly after Johns had received the Munch postcard, Wolfgang Wittrock, a Düsseldorf-based dealer of modern drawings, sent him a copy of the portfolio *Grünewalds Isenheimer Altar in neun und verzig Aufnahmen*, a 1919 Munich publication featuring numerous black-and-white photographic plates of the then-newly-restored multipanel painting. Although Johns had visited Colmar, France, to see the work in 1976 (and would again in 1990), the grisaille facsimiles disclosed less-obvious facets of the composition—most especially, its patterning:

> Looking at [the reproduced details] I thought how moving it would be to extract the abstract quality of the work, its patterning, from the figurative meaning. So I started making these tracings. Some became illegible in terms of the figuration, while in others I could not get rid of the figure. But in all of them I was trying to uncover something else in the work, some other kind of meaning.[203]

The excavation of imagery—or, more precisely, of structure and form—from Grünewald's *Altarpiece* haunted Johns's art for more than a decade. Following two major, sequentially executed paintings—*In the Studio* and *Perilous Night* (1982; National Gallery of Art, Washington)—the new mode coalesced, with serial concentration, in a group of pictures begun in 1983 that have been dubbed the "bathtub-eye view" paintings.[204] In these works, Johns rendered the bathroom wall and door in his home in Stony Point, New York, as they appeared from the artist's perspective while soaking in the tub.[205]

Racing Thoughts (1984; cat. no. 116), arguably the definitive work from the series, is a grisaille executed in oil and based on a color encaustic of the same title and general composition created a year earlier (FIG. 39). In terms of composition and surface treatment, both paintings play on notions of adding, subtracting, layering, and connecting. Every image or object depicted was a personal possession in Johns's studio or home: on the left, the wood-grain pattern is meshed with a compositional device from Johns's 1983 encaustic painting *Untitled* (Private collection), a barely legible, upside-down tracing of a demon from the *Temptation of St. Anthony* panel of Grünewald's *Altarpiece*; tacked next to his beige-yellow, faintly striped pants on the back of the door is a small portrait of Johns's dealer, Leo Castelli based on a puzzle Johns was given; at the right, held up with masking tape next to Barnett Newman's print *Untitled* (1961), the artist depicted a decal made after Leonardo's *Mona Lisa* (Johns had secreted a small image of the painting, largely concealed by brushwork in *Figure 2* [1962; cat. no. 79]); at the far right hangs a warning for avalanches in German, French, and English featuring a skull and crossbones; below, the top of a laundry hamper supports a vase commemorating the Silver Jubilee of Queen Elizabeth II (the form is created by the negative space between her profile and that of her husband, Prince Philip), and a ceramic pot by early-twentieth-century artist George Ohr. *Racing Thoughts* is a conceptual collage, a veritable self-portrait, its elements not unlike items posted on a bulletin board. The enterprise is analogous to Johns's incorporation of household and studio objects in certain paintings of the late 1950s and 1960s or, as emblems of the everyday, to the newspaper fragments embedded in many encaustic paintings.[206] In each of these instances, Johns assimilated the objects, images, and texts around him into his art. (The act of painting suggests a desire to fix, or contain, the limitless chain of potential associative meanings. In the early 1980s, Johns told a psychologist friend that, while trying to sleep, fragments of disconnected images and thoughts filled his mind. The friend identified his condition as a phenomenon known as "racing thoughts," a diagnosis that relieved Johns.)

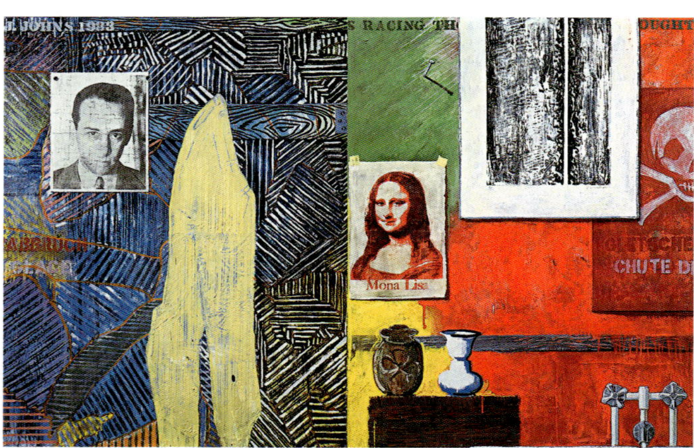

Fig. 39. *Racing Thoughts*, 1983. Encaustic and collage on canvas; 121.9 × 190.8 cm (48 × 75 ⅛ in.). Whitney Museum of American Art, New York, purchase, with fund from the Burroughs Wellcome Purchase Fund; Leo Castelli; the Wilford P. and Rose J. Cohen Purchase Fund; the Julia B. Engel Purchase Fund; the Equitable Life Assurance Society of the United States Purchase Fund; the Sondra and Charles Gilman, Jr. Foundation, Inc.; S. Sidney Kahn; the Lauder Foundation, Leonard and Evelyn Lauder Fund; the Sara Roby Foundation; and the Painting and Sculpture Committee.

The point of all of the plangently self-referential imagery is not so much what it means, but how it is represented. The color and grisaille versions are a play of opposites — not for the first time, Johns explored the differences inherent in creating two nearly identical versions of the same work in alternate media and palette. The artist seems to exploit the general "feel" of each medium *through* palette: the brighter colors of the Whitney Museum's 1983 *Racing Thoughts* (FIG. 39) appear diffuse, the great depth and translucence intrinsic to encaustic preventing the work from looking excessively garish. (Johns's use of color began, at this point in his career, to be less schematic. He moved beyond the "found palette" of the primaries and secondaries; the result, here and in much of the work of this moment, is a sense of color without control.) With the 1984 version, Johns's choice of a more somber palette dominated by gray reinforced the more opaque nature of oil paint; even though it is painted in thinner layers in many areas, the work feels heavier than its encaustic counterpart. The dialogue between two distinct modes is reinforced by the inclusion of the Grünewald and Newman quotations, which exemplify two extremely different kinds of art making.[207] One model is figurative, narrative, and expressive; the other abstract, theoretical, and restrained. Free of the conventional associations of color, grisaille allowed Johns to think the picture differently, to work in a different medium, and to achieve different results with the same subject matter. The color version, which Judith Goldman called "a cheerful rebus,"[208] was succeeded by a work of impassive constraint. The use of gray relieved, even ameliorated, some of the dense, often dolorous, and endlessly self-referential and art historically referential content of these pictures. It is a clarifying pronouncement.

Racing Thoughts, like earlier works such as *Fool's House* (1962; cat. no. 95) and *Field Painting* (1963–64; Collection of the artist), brings together objects and images with both explicit and implicit references to self and place. In a series of four paintings collectively referred to as the Seasons (1985–86), the accumulation of related imagery serves a narrative intent: Johns assembled artifacts and seasonal symbols—rain, a nesting bird, a broken tree branch, a snowman—to represent the epochs of his life, from "the bloom of spring to the cold, gray deprivation of winter."[209] The compositional and iconographic conceits of the cycle derive from, among other sources, Picasso's *Minotaur Moving His House* (1936; Private collection), a painting that imagines a half-man, half-beast surrogate for the artist pulling a cart loaded with symbolically charged examples of his own belongings and a horse giving birth.[210] An allegory of the cycles of life, Johns's four paintings—made around the time of his moving to a new house—illustrate four seasons, four times of day, four ages of man, in four different locations.

While Johns appears as a gray figure in all four paintings, only *Winter* (1986; cat. no. 121) is predominantly gray. In this picture, Johns's use of gray is determined and consuming. He uses gray to cover over and mingle with touches of dull, earthy reds, yellows, and browns. Every star, for example, was painted with a bright yellow and then painted over in pale gray. Where each turn of the rope had been established in a dull yellow, Johns went back in and covered over all but one torque of the cord with gray (**FIG. 40**). A pale gray wash covers an intermittent, frosty tone of purple in large areas of the bricks surrounding the figure. Functioning by now as a form of signature, a bright, primary red and white pattern below Johns's shadow is the edge of an element from his own double-flag painting (easily identifiable in *Summer* [1985; the Museum of Modern Art, New York]) and it is one of the only moments of unsuppressed color.

The dominant motif is that of the shadow, which Johns also borrowed from Picasso, whose painting *The Shadow* (1953; Musée Picasso, Paris) shows the artist, here in the form of his own shadow, in his bedroom (as in the Munch self-portrait) in melancholy contemplation. Johns eschewed the bedroom for the similarly complex psychosexual dynamics of the studio, each shadow depicting floors of bricks, tiles, or boards corresponding to one or another of his studios in four different residences.[211] For this rare self-portrait, the artist pictured himself as a transparent gray shadow. (It is not the first time Johns himself appeared in gray. He emerged in similarly spectral form in charcoal in *Study for "Skin I"* [1962; cat. no. 97], *Study for "Skin II"* [1962; cat. no. 98], *Skin I* [1973; cat. no. 99], and *Skin* [1975; cat. no. 101].) Johns worked from a tracing of his shadow that he asked a friend, the painter Julian Lethbridge, to draw. Cast over his possessions and his own art, Johns's shadow qualifies as the first full figure to appear in his art.[212] Judith Goldman judged it to be "an inelegant debut. He stands alone—bulky, ungainly, an off-balance mass of gray."[213] The shadow also stages a pun on the formal language of painting: Johns's "figure" is on the "ground." The representation does not, however, correspond to the rules of perspective. In each of the four paintings, the legs of the shadow are less defined than the upper body; it is the opposite effect one sees with a real shadow in which the feet and legs are most sharply defined because they are closest to the ground. Johns seems to have consciously subtracted his own presence from the shadow.[214]

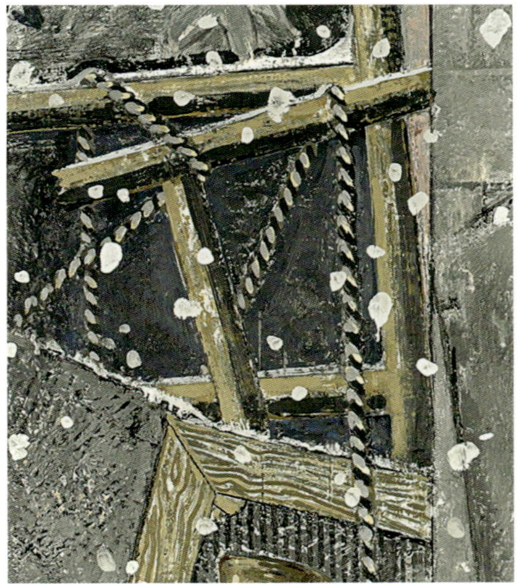

Fig. 40. Detail of *Winter* (cat. no. 121).

Winter is a carefully measured and constructed painting. The work is divided in half along a vertical axis, with Johns's shadow against the bricks on the right side and the free-floating associative icons—including the pots by George Orr, a snowman, and the Minotaur's ladder—on the left. (Adjacent renderings of horizontal and vertical planes result in a spatially disjunctive composition.) The left side is further divided by the "device" circle with the hand, like the arm of a clock, extended downward.[215] The painting is structurally divided into sections by the use of canvas collage—a fact not previously noted. Johns began *Winter* by covering the stretched canvas with two separate pieces of additional canvas to create a slight vertical seam through the middle of the right portion, thereby dividing this half into quarters. Aside from the space of this largely concealed seam, the two collage pieces cover the underlying canvas completely from top to bottom (wrapping around the stretcher, and side to side). The interstice runs through the figure's right leg and left ear, literally dividing him along the same axis that compositionally splits the figure in *Fall* (1986; Collection of the artist).[216] In *Winter*, Johns filled in the cleft, already partially hidden by the demarcations of the mortar of the bricks, with daubs and swaths of gray paint—metaphorically healing the rift, which is now only partially visible as an indented line.

In Johns's *Winter*, the ostensible subject is climate and weather—specifically, snow. (For *Water Freezes*, 1961 [cat. no. 86], Johns also used cold gray tonalities to describe a condition associated with seasonal chill.) The entire composition is dotted with thick hits of white impasto suggesting snowfall. His longstanding interest in the Japanese word *usuyuki*, which designates both thin snow and a type of ephemeral beauty, is particularly evident in a collage drawing, *Winter* (1985; cat. no. 119), made, somewhat unusually, in advance of the painting, in which the snow is rendered with small bits of tissuelike paper affixed to the surface.[217] The 1986 painting enacts a droll link between the depiction of snow (as snowflakes and as snowman) and Johns's encaustic process: both necessarily involve melting. The right side of the painting, particularly the figure, has been subjected to repeated heating. The snowman on the left side has also been painted, selectively liquefied with heat, and then partially repainted. The left corner of the ladder was melted, as well. These effacing gestures suggest a certain vulnerability. Snow, frozen and melted, also morphs into a representation of wounds. Some of the white daubs of paint on the figure, which elsewhere seem to signify only flakes, are covered in oozing black encaustic (**FIG. 41**), so that they resemble sores or pustules similar to those of the afflicted demon suffering from St. Anthony's Fire in the lower-left corner of the *Temptation of St. Anthony* in the *Isenheim Altarpiece*. Such a dermatological reading is reinforced by the fact that the fault line made by the canvas collage can be considered akin to an old, weathered scar.[218] Notions of a fragile body are appropriate for the theme; chromatically, gray signifies old age. In all of the Seasons paintings, an arrow indicates the inevitable trajectory that the palm will follow over the course of the seasons, until in *Winter,* the seasonal and climatic equivalent of death, "it points toward the nadir, the grave."[219] Although it is the second painting on the theme of the four seasons, it feels like the last. When Johns first exhibited the Seasons at Castelli (January 31–March 7, 1987), the arrangement encouraged a linear reading beginning with *Spring* (1986; Robert and Jane Meyerhoff Collection, Phoenix, Maryland) and ending with *Winter*. Again, gray serves in a position of finality.[220]

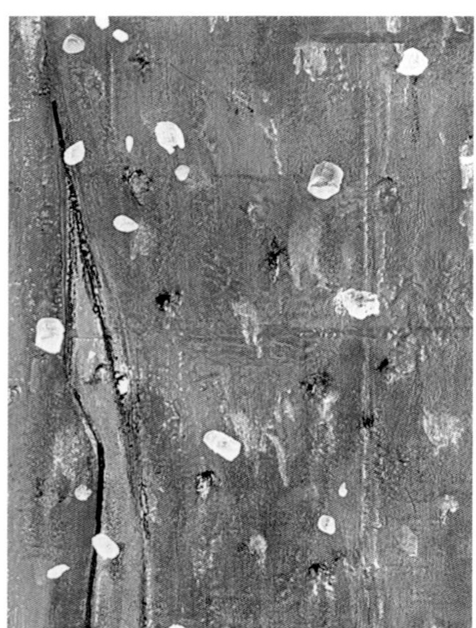

Fig. 41. Detail of *Winter* (cat. no. 121).

The cycle of the Seasons was conceived in response to Wallace Stevens's 1921 poem *The Snow Man*, even though *Summer* (1985), the first painting of the series, was inspired by Picasso's paintings and was intended as an independent work. The poem depicts a bleak and cold world:

> One must have a mind of winter
> To regard the frost and the boughs
> Of the pine-trees crusted with snow;

And have been cold a long time
To behold the junipers shagged with ice,
The spruces rough in the distant glitter

Of the January sun; and not to think
Of any misery in the sound of the wind,
In the sound of a few leaves,

Which is the sound of the land
Full of the same wind
That is blowing in the same bare place

For the listener, who listens in the snow,
And, nothing himself, beholds
Nothing that is not there and the nothing that is.

Having described this poem as embodying Stevens's "ultimate vision of unadorned reality," scholar A. Walton Litz was quick to note that it "is not a poem of negation, as has often been claimed, but an affirmation of primary reality."[221] The listener who can accept the barrenness of the winter landscape and understand that he is "nothing himself" is not a "man without imagination," in Litz's words, but quite to the contrary, one who is ready to build upon his "transforming imagination."[222]

Catenary

The Catenary works (1997–2003), one of Johns's largest, self-contained series to date, comprise eighty paintings, drawings, and prints. With this endeavor, Johns announced his emphatic, purposeful return to working with gray. Of the nineteen paintings in the series, sixteen are predominantly gray. (Underscoring the conceptual relationship of gray to color, Johns executed one work, *Untitled* [2003; Private collection], in white and one, *Study for Merce* [2002; Private collection], in red, yellow, and blue; the drawing for the latter [2002; Collection of the artist] shows the three primary bands over a field of gray acrylic.) The shared motif in every work is the catenary, from the Latin *catena* (chain). The word, most often used in reference to the engineering of suspension bridges, describes the curve imposed by the force of gravity on a string suspended freely from two points. In this series Johns combined both actual string, attached to the canvas or its supports, and depictions of the form, registered graphically or indexically on various surfaces.

The paintings eloquently recall the artist's now-iconic oil and encaustic works of the late 1950s and 1960s. Of further interest, Johns might have also been recalling, consciously or not, the hanging parachute strings in Rauschenberg's *Untitled* (**FIG. 42**)—a painting Johns owned for many years—which create six catenaries, or catenary-like forms in the bottom right of the Combine. It is instructive to note that Johns began the series in the immediate wake of his 1996 retrospective exhibition at the Museum of Modern Art, a project that surveyed his work over more than forty years and required him to confront and scrutinize his past in an unprecedented way. The Catenary series can be understood in this sense as a self-conscious examination of specific aspects of his practice. Since the early 1960s, Johns had affixed objects to the surfaces of his paintings in an ongoing search for non-illusionistic ways of mediating between the flat plane of the picture and a fully dimensional world.[223] Reinforcing an understanding of continuity, albeit delayed and elliptical, the

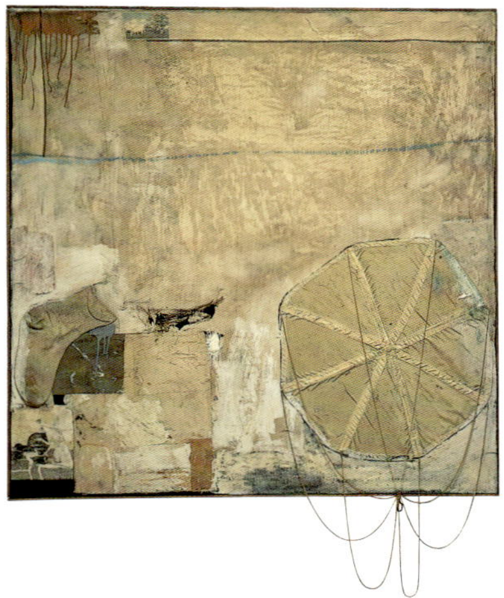

Fig. 42. Robert Rauschenberg. *Untitled*, c. 1955. Oil, house paint, paper, fabric, and printed reproductions, with sock and parachute on canvas; 172.7 × 139.7 cm (68 × 55 in.). Stefan T. Edlis Collection.

formal device in this series denotes a concept of linking or bridging. The first painting, made without the intention of inaugurating a series and before Johns was aware of the word "catenary," is called *Bridge* (1997; cat. no. 128).[224] The title acknowledges the trope of connection and harkens back to Hart Crane and his ode to the Brooklyn Bridge.[225] The summoning of Crane is not an isolated reoccurrence. The catenary device also speaks to Johns's abiding interests in suspension, and in the use of the picture plane to carry an object and its corollaries (whether depicted as line or shadow or both): the surface beneath a string may show an actual shadow, in addition to painted ones, or appear as a rut, as if the string had been embedded there and later pulled out. These notions were, of course, first convincingly assayed as early as 1959 in *Coat Hanger* (cat. no. 16), and later in other works such as *Voice* (1964–67; cat. no. 106) and *Passage II* (1966; Tehran Museum of Art).[226] The list goes on: Johns will ultimately use the catenary to return to a full exploration of canvas as collage, and the hidden role of underpainted, primary color. In this regard, the specter of *Tennyson* (1958; cat. no. 12) and *Disappearance II* (1961; cat. no. 88) is unavoidable. The Catenary series—attempting to show from a single vantage point, the work's front, side, and back, here suggested by the cord as hanging device—complicates the visual rhetoric of verso and recto, recalling *Canvas* (1956; cat. no. 7) and *Portrait—Viola Farber* (1961; cat. no. 96). Finally, these works explore the delimiting functions of stretchers—whether in drawings, by representing them in trompe l'oeil fashion, or in paintings, by affixing pieces of wood to the edges. Such tactics necessarily summon *Device* (1962; cat. no. 93). All of these dialogues, across decades, rely upon gray.

With the Catenary paintings—a grandly ambitious series that is dazzling in its sheer scope, variety, and subtlety—Johns returned to gray as a means of clarifying not only his palette but also his very approach to painting. Clarification, in this regard, does not imply simplification; rather, Johns's ability to pare down what had become a surfeit of images and devices in favor of a more rigorously abstract praxis arguably enriches an understanding of his art. "Jasper Johns's paintings," art historian Scott Rothkopf wrote, obliquely if diplomatically, in 2005, "had become too full." After a detailed litany of the referential signs, symbols, and images contained within the artist's summarizing opus *Untitled* (1992–95; cat. no. 127)—itemized as if to acknowledge the picture's almost absurd density—Rothkopf succinctly noted, "And then Johns wiped the slate clean."[227]

There are three major works in the series—*Bridge* (1997), *Catenary* (*I Call to the Grave*) (1998; cat. no. 129), and *Near the Lagoon* (2002–03; cat. no. 135)—each made on canvases measuring almost 3 × 2.1 meters, although the first two works are oriented horizontally. (These paintings have a special affinity for one another: they were made to hang on the same wall in Johns's home on the Caribbean island of St. Martin.) The first, *Bridge*, carries forward imagery from earlier pronouncements: the outlines of the tacked handkerchief, likely borrowed from Picasso's 1938 etching *Weeping Woman*; a photographic screenprint of a spiral form in the galaxy taken from a textbook; a diagram of the Big Dipper (Ursa Major); and the colorful diamond pattern readily associated with Picasso's harlequins. As the series progresses, gray seems metaphorically and literally to absorb, and eventually eliminate, the imagery. *Catenary* (*I Call to the Grave*) is radically simplified; gray encroaches from left to right across the surface of the canvas, not unlike an ink spill, eventually covering part of an already grayed-down harlequin pattern (**FIG. 43**). The relationship of gray paint to Johns's sustained depictions of *faux bois* frame structures again signals his concretizing of the "painting as object." Beginning on the upper-left side of *Bridge*, as Rothkopf has noted, strokes of gray progressively transgress the theoretical boundary separating illusion from the core reality of paint (**FIG. 44**).

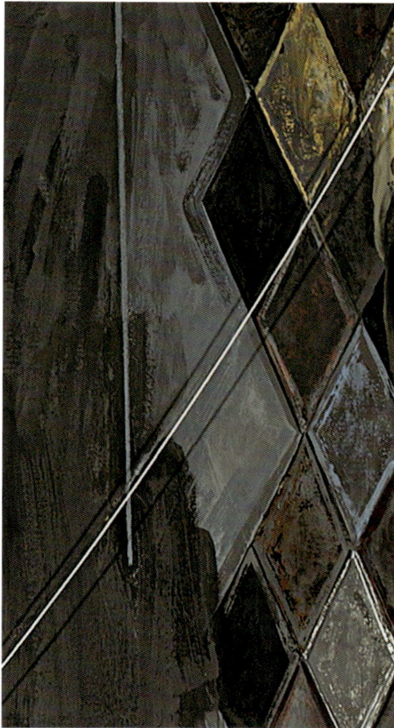

Fig. 43. Detail of harlequin pattern in *Catenary (I Call to the Grave)* (cat. no. 129).

Fig. 44. Detail of upper-left corner of *Bridge* (cat. no. 128).

The outward seepage of gray continues on two sides of *Untitled* (1997; Private collection) and on three sides of *Untitled* (*Halloween*) (1998; Collection of Marguerite and Robert Hoffman), both of which presage the demise of the illusion in *Catenary* (*I Call to the Grave*), in which the gray strokes cover only traces of wood-grain effects underneath.[228] By 2002 *Near the Lagoon* announces a monumental return to pure, gray monochrome abstraction. The energy and thrust of the series, it can be argued, advances from full to empty, from nominally representational to abstract, with a consuming, vibrant, tonally rich gray as the principal agent of change.[229] In all cases, Johns was mining his own history as well as the broader history of art—but in far more oblique ways than before.

Near the Lagoon (2002–03), a picture as epic and elegant as any in Johns's corpus, is the largest and the last work to be completed in the catenary series. A summary statement, the painting restages and closes, for the moment, Johns's involvement with a work by the quintessential early modernist painter Édouard Manet. In 1999, in response to a request from the National Gallery, London, to make a work of art in dialogue with an object in the Gallery's collection for the exhibition *Encounters: New Art from Old* (June 14–September 17, 2000), Johns chose the fragmentary version of Manet's *The Execution of Maximilian* (1867–68). The history of Manet's depictions of Maximilian's death—three large paintings, an oil sketch, and a lithograph—has been well examined, most recently in *Manet and the Execution of Maximilian* (the Museum of Modern Art, New York, November 5, 2006–January 29, 2007) and the accompanying catalogue by curator John Elderfield. The object of Johns's fascination is Manet's second painting, the only one not to have survived intact. In poor condition at the time of the artist's death, the canvas was cut into pieces by his heirs and sold off individually. In the 1890s, Manet's friend and fellow artist Edgar Degas purchased four of the unstretched fragments and reassembled them—in a manner approximately corresponding to their original placement—on one stretched canvas, the same size as the lost original. The National Gallery acquired the reconstituted work in 1918. (The pieces were subsequently disassembled and framed separately at the museum and were only restored to a single support in 1992.) The arrangement, exposing large parts of the underlying canvas, signals the missing fragments—most notably, the emperor—as much as it preserves the originals. Johns's opening salvo was a comparably small, gray encaustic painting, *Catenary* (*Manet-Degas*) (1999; Private collection), made up of four patches of canvas collage, similarly, if not exactly, scaled to the fragments of the source painting.[230] (Curiously, Johns wavered on his decision to send the work to the London exhibition, questioning the appropriateness of a gray painting for an essentially "celebratory show.")[231]

Returning to the structural conceit of the Manet-Degas composition in 2002, Johns mounted four blank canvas fragments onto a 3 × 2.1 meter support canvas, a surface only slightly larger than the one used by Degas, basically preserving the proportions of Degas's construction but reorienting the canvases vertically. (See the essay by Kelly Keegan and Kristin Lister in this volume.) *Near the Lagoon* thus begs the question of Johns's relationship to Manet's composition and Degas's reconstruction. The simplest answer may be Johns's admiration for Manet and in particular, for this painting, the central feature of which, not incidentally, is a group of men in gray uniforms casting darker gray shadows on a light gray ground. Beyond an appreciation of Manet's palette, Johns would have been drawn into aspects of his process. Manet was an artist known for his, at times rigorous, commitment to reworking his pictures. Describing Manet's radical methods of editing of his work—methods that included the use of a knife to remove a section of finished canvas—art historian Theodore Reff has written that "cutting was merely the most extreme component of a creative process that habitually included scraping down, washing out, and painting over."[232] Acts of concealment and erasure are, to say the least, of interest to Johns. He might well have admired some of Manet's own compositional gambits, chief among them here the presence of a hidden soldier—standing behind the cluster of five men, revealed only by his raised sword. In the London reconstruction, both intention and chance therefore resulted in the absence of two protagonists: one of the assassins and one of the assassinated. The themes of Manet's picture, particularly its reckoning with a narrative of betrayal and mortality, are not unfamiliar to Johns. More to the point, the work is exceptionally unusual in its attempt to represent the very moment of death.[233] Its present status as a collage of fragments, rescued by an act of fraternal devotion, would have obvious formal appeal and emotional resonance. Finally, Degas's salvaging of Manet's painting conveys the beginnings of an artistic chain reaction of creative reworkings, homage, and eulogy that extended to, or was extended by, Johns. The device of the catenary, for this reason, provides a fully appropriate metaphor for Johns's various points of connected engagement.

Other, more classically oriented art historical references abound in *Near the Lagoon*. Primary among these is the suggestion of veiling, or the folds of classical drapery. In the fall of 1987, Johns had seen the *Veil of Saint Veronica* (c. 1635–40; Nationalmuseum, Stockholm) and *Saint Serapion* (1628; Wadsworth Atheneum, Hartford), two works that present virtuouso treatments of suspended, draping fabrics, on view in a retrospective exhibition of the work of Francisco de Zurbarán at the Metropolitan Museum of Art in New York (September 22–December 13, 1987).[234] The Spanish master must have made a powerful impression on Johns, for at that time he made a number of works, such as *Untitled* (**FIG. 45**), combining in an increasingly ponderous manner references to Grünewald, Picasso, an anonymous drawing by a schizophrenic child, and other well-used favorites, rendered as if they were images transferred onto pieces of draping fabric tacked to the plane of the picture. These folds predict by more than ten years the cascading ones suggested in *Near the Lagoon*. This effect is perhaps most evident in the graphite, acrylic, and watercolor study *Untitled* (2001; cat. no. 132), in which Johns took pains to depict the multiple shadows cast by the string on the ground of the painting, which appears as a field of draped, linenlike fabric. Such depictions are often associated, in the context of historical painting, with religious art; these overtones are heightened by the painting's formal, structural relationship to a multipanel painted altarpiece, an art form for which Johns's admiration is well-known. The hinged, movable side panels of *Near the Lagoon*, partially painted gray, pointedly recall the sides and tops of medieval altarpieces. As cited earlier, Molly Teasdale Smith traced the very development of the winged, stationary altarpiece, with shutters that can be closed over the interior sculptures or paintings, to the practice in parts of late-medieval Europe of concealing church ornament during Lent. Another principal Lenten decoration was the use of gray monochrome, from vestments to hangings to panel paintings (see the essay by Douglas Druick in this volume, p. 82). Indeed some extant grisaille panels dating from the 1440s in Flanders and France originated on the exterior wings of altarpieces and were visible only when the panels were closed. Thus, the very existence of multipanel altarpieces is tied to similarly motivated uses of gray.[235]

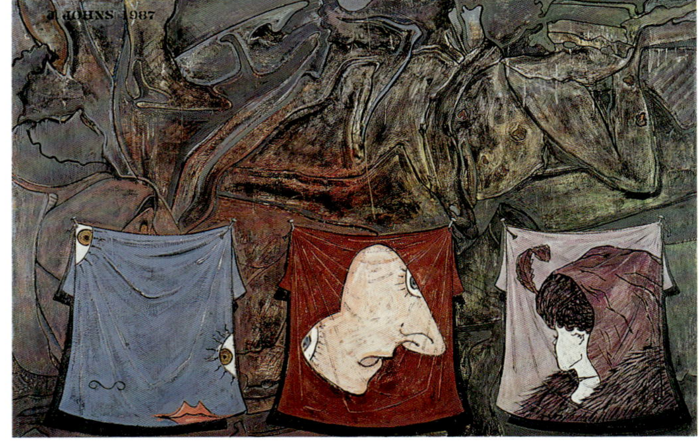

Fig. 45. *Untitled*, 1987. Encaustic and collage on canvas; 127 × 190.5 cm (50 × 75 in.). Robert and Jane Meyerhoff Collection, Phoenix, Maryland.

Although overtly connected to his own history and to the history of art, Johns's gray emerges in a new way. The grays of *Near the Lagoon* are not the same grays as those in *Tennyson*. They are lighter and more open, integrated with rather than strictly opposed to color. Like *Tennyson*, *Near the Lagoon* has an atmospheric title evocative of life outside the picture, thus breaking from the preceding, related works that, by and large, bear the most literal, descriptive titles. But where the grays of *Tennyson* are heavy, opaque, and loaded with possible references, the treatment of *Near the Lagoon*, while equally clever, is diaphanous and transparent. The picture was painted in Johns's studio in St. Martin, where it was first installed on a wall adjacent to windows with a view of the bright blue waters outside, the strong tropical sun igniting the luminescence of the wax, breezes off the lagoon animating the play of string and shadow.[236] The dirgelike aspects of gray, conjured as recently as the parenthetical references to the Book of Job in *Catenary (I Call to the Grave)*,[237] seem finally to dissolve in a play of open-ended virtuosity. In 1964 John Cage had noted:

> Finally, with nothing in it to grasp, the work is weather, an atmosphere that is heavy rather than light (something he knows and regrets); in oscillation with it we tend toward our ultimate place: zero, gray disinterest.[238]

While Cage was not wrong, nearly forty years later the weather had changed; the atmosphere had become lighter (which it might have been, at least sometimes, long before). Cage's equation of gray with disinterest notwithstanding, one is in fact encouraged to keep watching, monitoring Johns's persistent climatic, material, and conceptual variations. Throughout, gray will doubtless remain a cynosure.

Recent Work

Some of Johns's most recent work, following the closure of the Catenary paintings, while lacking the cohesion of an overriding concern, is unified by his continuing, if selective, use of gray. Two of these paintings fittingly conjure the spirit of Samuel Beckett. In both Johns returned to an earlier motif, the flagstones that he had first glimpsed from a passing car on a wall in Harlem in 1967 and explored in works such as *Harlem Light* (1967; Private collection) and *Wall Piece* (1968; Collection of the artist). An independent gray articulation of this pattern materialized only in 2005. *Within* (1983 and 2005; cat. no. 136), as discussed above, was painted on top of an unfinished Crosshatch painting from 1983, perhaps the very last canvas in the series (FIG. 46). Johns had executed a side-by-side combination of the two motifs in *End Paper* (1976; the Museum of Modern Art, New York), a two-panel oil painting in which the left panel was covered with crosshatches and the right panel was covered with flagstones. The title of the painting and all subsequent combinations of the two motifs (including *Céline* [1978; cat. no. 110]) were, in part, inspired by Johns's collaboration with Beckett on *Foirades/Fizzles* (1976), a folio of five texts by Beckett and thirty-three etchings by Johns. Looking at the crosshatch and flagstone patterns as they are arrayed, Beckett commented to Johns: "Here you move all directions, but no matter where you turn you come against this wall."[239] In fact, the very first painting to render the stones in gray is actually called *Beckett* (2005; cat. no. 138), two panels made of oil and encaustic, respectively.[240] Like Beckett's writing, however, the painting encourages uncertainty: Johns worked the encaustic in such a way that it mimics the appearance of a surface made with oil, and, conversely, applied oil paint in a manner that visually approximates the look and feel of encaustic.

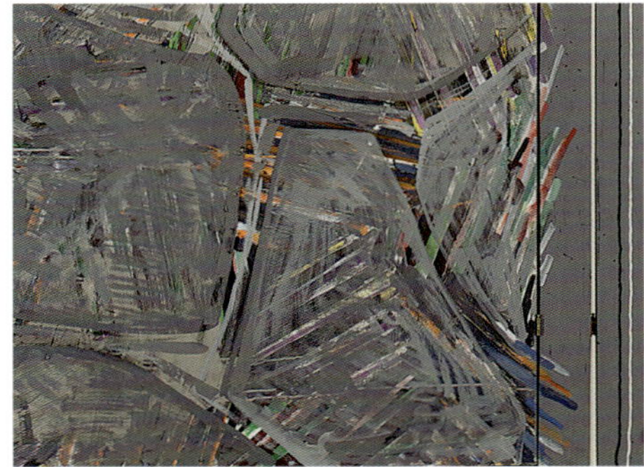

Fig. 46. Detail of *Within* (cat. no. 136).

Johns has maintained a long-standing interest in Beckett, traceable, perhaps, to Frank O'Hara's advice in 1959 to "read all of Samuel Beckett."[241] Having met Beckett on three or four occasions in Paris in 1974 and 1975, Johns later admitted to identifying with his "combination of elegance and austerity, of negativeness . . . [and] tragic aspect."[242] How appropriate then that Johns's grays have come to nominally embrace the character and disposition of Beckett. As curator Jeffrey Weiss has pointed out, *Malone Dies* (published in 1956, the very year Johns made his first gray monochromes) contains a characterization of the gray incandescence of the protagonist's room that lends itself to descriptions of Johns's own use of gray as both color and material.[243] In *L'Innommable* (the English version of which, *The Unnamable*, was published in 1957), Beckett wrote:

> Whether all grow black, or all grow bright, or all remain grey, it is grey we need, to begin with, because of what it is, and of what it can do, made of bright and black, able to shed the former, or the latter, and be the latter or the former alone. But perhaps I am the prey, on the subject of grey, in the grey, to the delusions.[244]

• • •

In 1970 Brice Marden made a painting *Three Deliberate Greys for Jasper Johns* (**FIG. 47**). Marden, who worked as a guard at the Jewish Museum during Johns's 1964 retrospective exhibition, came to Johns's work as a committed abstractionist who had studied the grays of Francisco Goya and Manet. Marden respected the restricted, rule-bound nature of Johns's practice—its intense feelings of reticence, denial, even repression—that simultaneously did not deny the pleasure of the painted surface:

> I have worked with many greys, not studying them, using them. Greys move around within themselves as they tend toward other colors. These greys don't, they had to stay grey. The problem was to get color using only these stone cold greys; values. It was a bitch because it kept being value and not going to color. It finally went to color. When it got up on a wall, it made me very happy to see it. Jasper Johns's paintings showed me paint dispersed on a surface being a surface, much about Cézanne, and has me always asking about realities. I find it difficult to paint. It is harder not to paint. But even harder to paint when you aren't painting. Painting says pain in it. Never dare think you're on top of grey.[245]

Fig. 47. Brice Marden. *Three Deliberate Greys for Jasper Johns*, 1970. Oil and beeswax on canvas; 182.9 × 381 cm (72 × 150 in.). National Gallery of Canada, Ottawa.

No other artist besides Johns has been linked to gray as closely as Gerhard Richter. The majority of his early works, including the first paintings he made in 1961 following his defection from East Germany, are gray (**FIG. 48**). Curator Robert Storr has written: "Not counting image paintings—townscapes and star pictures—that are almost but not quite abstractions, or the baked-enamel-on-glass mirror paintings, Richter has, to date, painted over one hundred gray monochromes. That is roughly one tenth of his entire production; and most recently he has gone back to making gray, or nearly gray, abstractions, in significant numbers."[246] Of his own commitment to gray, Richter has said:

> It makes no statement whatever; it evokes neither feelings nor associations; it is really neither visible nor invisible. . . . It has the capacity that no other color has to make "nothing" visible. To me, gray is the welcome

Fig. 48. Gerhard Richter. *Gray*, 1976. Oil on aluminum; 63 × 59 cm (24 ⅞ × 23 ¼ in.). Private collection, Cologne.

> and only possible equivalent for indifference, noncommitment, absence of opinion, absence of shape. But gray, like formlessness and the rest, can be real only as an idea. . . . The painting is then a mixture of gray as a fiction and gray as a visible, designated area of color.[247]

Unlike Johns, Richter has been drawn to gray in more expressly ideological contexts. Art historian Benjamin Buchloh observed: "For Richter, grey is the non-color par excellence, the sum of all colors in which various positions come to expression. Grey is the color of negation, of resistance, of an inability to unify, to reconcile."[248] Owing to certain shared attitudes, however, one might expect Richter to express admiration for Johns. Yet, when he named Roy Lichtenstein and Andy Warhol among the American artists he admired and not Johns, Richter—asked if the exclusion of Johns was purposeful—quite remarkably replied: "Yes, because Johns was holding on to a culture of painting that had to do with Cézanne, and I rejected that."[249]

Johns, Marden, and Richter are close contemporaries. It is more than curious that Richter's rejection of Johns is predicated, at least in part, on an aspect of his painting—the legacy of Cézanne—that Marden finds, in addition to their shared affinity for gray, affirming and elucidating. As seen through this prism of influence, and amplified by the specificities of Marden's and Richter's respective methodologies (in Richter's case, inclusive of both non-objective and representational painting), the difference of opinion must revolve around questions of touch and facture, and their larger implications. Even in his most reductive modes, Marden remains a painterly painter, massaging richly tactile objects that speak of human presence, while Richter always maintains an expertly cool, technically mediated distance from his surfaces. Beyond any questions of gray, however, Richter's unsurprising rejection of and Marden's near-filial allegiance to Johns may have to do with Johns's simultaneous insistence on both positions, unresolved. As ever, the middle ground between these two polarities might, ultimately, be the place to find Jasper Johns. Indeterminacy, in painting and otherwise, persists.

The author gratefully acknowledges Jesse Feiman, Research Assistant for *Jasper Johns: Gray,* for his assistance in the preparation of this essay.

1 Solomon 1964, p. 13.

2 For a useful summary of these various arguments, see Rosenthal and Fine 1990, pp. 18–19.

3 Kozloff 1968, p. 24.

4 Jean-Paul Sartre, "Introducing *Les temps modernes*," in *"What is Literature?" and Other Essays,* trans. Jeffrey Mehlman (Harvard University Press, 1998), p. 256. Originally published in *Les temps modernes* 1 (Oct. 1945), pp. 1–21.

5 Roberta Bernstein noted that the "c" of black and the "v" of violet are visible; Bernstein 1985, p. 40.

6 Kozloff diagnosed an "agitated" painting, "a consciously fabricated impasse" in which the "overall impression of combustion implies merely an imminent dissolution"; Kozloff 1968, p. 27.

7 Bernstein 1985, p. 41. The title was taken from a horse-racing print Johns saw at the Cedar Bar; see Hopps 1965, p. 36, in *Writings* 1996, pp. 110–12. The Cedar Street Tavern, located at 24 University Place, was a favored hangout spot for the Abstract Expressionists. For a discussion of that scene, see Irving Sandler, *The New York School: Painters and Sculptors of the Fifties* (Harper and Row, 1978), pp. 30–33.

8 Varnedoe 1996, p. 163.

9 "Johns sets perceptual and linguistic cues at odds by inducing discordance between the colors and the words that conventionally name them"; Varnedoe 1996, p. 163.

10 Ludwig Wittgenstein, *Philosophical Investigations* (1953), trans. G. E. M. Anscombe, 3rd. ed. (Blackwell, 2001), p. 192e.

11 Raynor 1973, p. 22, in *Writings* 1996, p. 145.

12 Kozloff 1968, p. 27.

13 The term grisaille has come to mean a "monochromatic rendering of tonal values ... between black and white." While the word is derived from the French *gris* (gray), many painters have chosen other colors as the basic hue from which to express a range of values, as in the green tones (*verdaccio*) of some early Italian Renaissance pictures, or umber tones (*bistre*) of Rubens; Frank Covino, "Review of 'Gray is the Color,'" *Leonardo* 9, 1 (Winter 1976), p. 80.

14 In conversation with the author on Aug. 18, 2006, Johns would neither confirm nor deny the presence of the flag, at one point suggesting the color underneath may be a collaged fragment from a woman's scarf. When pressed on the apparent "flagness" of the red, white, and blue underneath, Johns acknowledged that he was an artist who had previously painted the flag, and that he was playing. The *Jubilee* drawing (1960) and the *Jubilee* pastel over lithograph (1962 and 1994) are precise enough to replicate the painting's mysterious patch of partially concealed color patterning.

15 Rosenthal and Fine 1990, p. 158.

16 Sylvester 1965, in Sylvester 2001, p. 163.

17 Johns 1968, p. 6, in *Writings* 1996, p. 22.

18 Anonymous 1959, p. 58 (emphasis added), in *Writings* 1996, p. 82.

19 Of the eighteen paintings Johns presented in his first solo exhibition at Leo Castelli Gallery in 1958, twelve were monochrome: *White Flag* (1955; the Metropolitan Museum of Art, New York), *Figure 1* (1955; Peter and Irene Ludwig Foundation, on loan to Ludwig Museum, Cologne), *Figure 5* (1955; Collection of the artist), *Green Target* (1955; the Museum of Modern Art, New York), *Figure 7* (1955; Los Angeles County Museum of Art), *Canvas* (1956), *Gray Alphabets* (1956), *White Numbers* (1957; the Museum of Modern Art, New York), *Drawer* (1957), *Gray Target* (1957), *White Target* (1958; Whitney Museum of American Art, New York), *Green Target* (1958; Private collection).

20 Gray paintings have been shown together. For a group show at Castelli (Dec. 8, 1961–Jan. 10, 1962), Johns presented only four paintings, all of them gray from 1961: *In Memory of My Feelings—Frank O'Hara, No, Good Time Charley,* and *Liar.* Kirk Varnedoe installed John's 1996 retrospective exhibition at the Museum of Modern Art in New York in chronological order, with works grouped according to theme and color. One room contained multiple gray pictures. Installed together were *Canvas* (1956), *Gray Rectangles* (1957), *Drawer* (1957), and *The* (1957), and *Tennyson* (1958). In the next room, among other works, left to right, were *In Memory of My Feelings, No,* and *Fool's House* (1962) on a single wall, then, on a perpendicular wall, from left to right, *Good Time Charley, Disappearance II, Water Freezes,* and *Liar,* all from 1961. In the same room, *Painting Bitten by a Man* (1961) was in a vitrine with a selection of nine sculptures. *Periscope (Hart Crane)* (1963) was juxtaposed with *Device* (1962), the only two pictures on a small wall.

21 Lucy Lippard suggested the idea of an exhibition devoted to a single color, all black or all white; Lucy Lippard, "The Silent Art," *Art in America* 55, 1 (Jan./Feb. 1967), p. 62. Exhibitions that have focused on a single color, however, are relatively rare. Some examples include *White,* Alfred Schmela Gallery, Düsseldorf, 1965; *Weiss auf Weiss,* Kunsthalle Berne, Switzerland, 1966; *Itineraires Blanc,* Musée d'Art et d'Industrie, Saint-Etienne, France, 1970; *White on White,* Museum of Contemporary Art, Chicago, 1972; *Basically White,* Institute of Contemporary Art, London, 1974; *Marking Black,* Bronx Museum of Art, 1980; *Strictly Black,* Seibu Gallery, Tokyo, 1984; *Black,* Akira Ikeda Gallery, Tokyo, 1985; *Red,* Massimo Audiello Gallery, New York, 1986; *The Red Show,* Massimo Audiello Gallery, New York, 1987; *Les États du Noir,* Galerie Lambert-Rouland, Paris, 1992; *Un siecle d'Innocence: Le monochrome blanc,* Centre Rooseum pour l'Art Contemporain, Malmö, 2000; *Pure,* Sean Kelly Gallery, New York, 2007; *Simply Red,* The Fabric Workshop and Museum, Philadelphia, 2007. To date, only one exhibition that I am aware of has addressed gray as its principal theme: Institute for the Arts, Rice University, Houston, guided by the noted collector Dominique de Menil, organized *Gray is the Color: An Exhibition of Grisaille Painting, XIII-XXth Centuries* (Oct. 19, 1973–Jan. 19, 1974). The exhibition included over one hundred works by such artists as François Boucher, Thomas Eakins, Andrea Mantegna, Gustave Moreau, Odilon Redon, Frederic Remington, and Peter Paul Rubens. Twentieth-century practice was represented by Richard Artschwager, Alberto Giacometti, Robert Indiana, Fernand Léger, René Magritte, Man Ray, Pablo Picasso, James Rosenquist, Frank Stella, Mark Tobey, and Andy Warhol. Johns was represented by *Voice* (1964–67). Notably, the introduction authored by de Menil ends with a mention of Johns, and in his catalogue essay curator J. Patrice Marandel discussed Johns: "Gray in Jasper Johns's paintings seems to signify a withdrawal from the stance of personal involvement, of risk-taking, associated with his brushy Abstract-Expressionist handling. This deliberate neutralization, even pseudo-mechanization of that manner is not, finally, a put-down; rather, in retrospect, one can see it as feelingly conservative of Abstract-Expressionist handling in the context of his radically different problem formulation. Were it not so, his ironies would fail, because without really caring he could not arrive at those beauties of facture which lure us and then convince us that we have entered felt rather than fabricated ambiguities. Johns does not require his paintings to be abstract or not to be, which is to say that he means for us to know that he regards such an issue as passed. As to their sense, they have the sense fitting to a revery; but considering what he muses on, they may be called logical reveries"; J. Patrice Marandel, "Introduction," in *Gray Is the Color: An Exhibition of Grisaille Painting XIIIth–XXth Centuries,* exh. cat. (Rice University, 1974), pp. 22–23.

22 "He [Johns] came to California for a week and the weather was bad. A friend drove him to the airport and apologized for the gray weather and gloomy weather. 'That's all right,' he said. 'Gray is my favorite color'"; Crichton 1994, p. 16. Johns has also told Roberta Bernstein on more than one occasion that gray is his favorite color; Bernstein 1985, p. 221.

23 In the lithograph *Savarin* (1977–81), Johns combined a graphic representation of *Painted Bronze* with elements drawn from Edvard Munch's lithographic *Self-Portrait* (1895; see fig. 25 in the essay by Douglas Druick in this volume), replacing the face in Munch's composition with his own sculpture; see Goldman

1982; Francis 1984, pp. 9–10; Weinberg 1988, p. 47; and Orton 1994, p. 190; Bernstein 1996, pp. 50, 54.

24 Johns's art, Kozloff summarized, is an "essentially tonal pictorial vision, often literally inflected by grays and blacks"; Kozloff 1968, p. 46.

25 "I am not so much interested in dealing with images as working for form"; Johns, quoted in Nash and Holmstrand 1964, in *Writings* 1996, p. 105.

26 Taylor 1990, p. 100, in *Writings* 1996, p. 245.

27 Solomon 1964, p. 6.

28 Geelhaar 1980a, p. 48, in *Writings* 1996, p. 193.

29 Sketchbook A, p. 42, c. 1963–64, in *Writings* 1996, p. 54. See also a related statement, "More interesting to me is something equivalent to tone of voice that can change from picture to picture—that interests me—and the possibility of establishing an image that might not be susceptible to such manipulation"; Rosenthal and Fine 1990, p. 80.

30 Sketchbook A, p. 42, c. 1963–64, in *Writings* 1996, p. 54.

31 Geelhaar 1980a, p. 39, in *Writings* 1996, p. 191.

32 Johns was Artistic Director of the Merce Cunningham Dance Company from 1967 to 1980.

33 Mark Lancaster, who worked as Johns's assistant from 1973 to 1985, recalled: "In 1973, Merce Cunningham was commissioned to make a dance for the Paris Opera Ballet, for the Festival d'Automne.... Jasper agreed to design it and made some sketches for set and costumes, and asked me if I would go to Paris to supervise the work and then he would come for the performance.... After Jasper arrived and we re-dyed the costumes for the third time, all night in the bowels of the Opera, it happened and was generally well received." See www.warholstars.org/andywarhol/interview/mark/lancaster.html. Descriptions of the performance also appear in Rose 1993, p. 52 and David Vaughan, "Diaghelev/Cunningham," *Art Journal* 34, 2 (Winter 1974–75), p. 139.

34 Kozloff named *Three Flags* (1958; Whitney Museum of American Art) as the first instance in which actual shadows play a role in the composition of a Johns painting; Kozloff 1968, p. 18.

35 Conservator Carol Mancusi-Ungaro has recently cited a monochromatic gray field underneath the very colorful *Device Circle* (1959; Collection of Andrew and Denise Saul); Mancusi-Ungaro 2007, p. 253.

36 Klüver 1963, in *Writings* 1996, p. 85.

37 Crichton 1994, p. 36.

38 Ibid. In conversation with Henry Geldzahler (c. 1958), Johns did not reveal this: "There is a painting here called *Triple Flag* [*sic*], a flag, on top of a flag, on top of a flag. I asked Jasper, 'Did you bother to paint all the stripes all the way on the paintings, when we don't see them?' His answer to me was 'You'll never know'"; See "An Interview with Henry Geldzahler by Ingrid Sischy," in Henry Geldzahler, *Making It New: Essays, Interviews, and Talks* (Harcourt Brace & Co., 1994), p. 13.

39 Experimental psychologist Richard L. Gregory has stated, "As pictures, retinal images are very odd—unique—for although they are indeed perspective pictures of the world, they are never seen, for there is no eye looking at them and so they are not objects of perception. They are, rather, just one cross-section of the visual pathway from objects to perceptions of objects"; Rothfuss 2003a, p. 38. See also the essay by Douglas Druick in this volume, pp. 95–96.

40 Steinberg 1962/1972, p. 32, in *Writings* 1996, p. 83.

41 Kozloff 1968, p. 16.

42 "The rich texture and tonal variety of Johns' encaustic paintings of the middle and later 1950s is, in part, a function of the printed materials absorbed into their surfaces"; Carpenter 1977, p. 221.

43 Tomkins 1980, p. 72. Rauschenberg's transfer drawing technique extracted an essential "grayness" from the source material. Beginning in 1958, while he was working in the same building with Johns, his process involved soaking newspaper or magazine clippings in solvent, laying them facedown on paper, and then transferring the images and texts by rubbing.

44 Critic Michael Kimmelman of the *New York Times* took note of gray in a review of Johns's 1996 retrospective, observing: "You can see, for instance, the intense concentration of his early works, silent and passive, not just the flags and targets but also "Drawer" and "Canvas," which are gray on gray, closed off and melancholic.... "Tennyson" and "Disappearance II," with their overturned flaps of canvas, or in "Shade," with its makeshift window shade pulled down. One of the uses of a retrospective like this is to place these paintings along with what came later, and there turns out to be a kinship with Mr. Johns's hermetic pictures of the 1980's and 90's in the restraint, bordering on repression, of the art from the 1950's and early 60's"; Kimmelman 1996, p. C32. Other brief or isolated mentions of gray in the Johns literature include: Steinberg 1962/1972, pp. 17, 28; Kozloff 1964, pp. 537–38; Johnson 1974; Krauss 1976, p. 92; Bernstein 1985, p. 73; Clements 1990, p. 81; Rothfuss 1993, p. 270; Sylvester 1997b, p. 92; Wallach 1999, p. AR29; Field 1999, p. 29; Prather 2000, p. 147; Weiss 2007a, p. 52.

45 Ashbery 1962, p. 51.

46 Ashton 1963, repr. in Brundage 1993, n.pag. Ashton also wrote, "Particularly when he remains in the low-keyed grey to ochre to black range, Johns is able to achieve a vibrating, labyrinthine involvement; a kind of hide-and-seek verve which makes of his more recent works really engaging experiences"; Ashton 1964, p. 212.

47 Porter 1964, p. 62.

48 Greenberg 1962, p. 24.

49 Ibid., p. 26.

50 Ibid., p. 27 (emphasis added). Rosalind Krauss, praising this passage as one of "exemplary clarity and succinctness," later offered an apology of sorts for Greenberg's assessment of Johns's earliest colored works: "When in 1962 Clement Greenberg wrote that some of Johns' color paintings were weaker than his gray ones, he was probably not referring to the highly saturated hues of the flags and targets, in which Johns had been able to liberate the decorative impact of the colors themselves, but rather to the random type of color in the works after 1958"; Krauss 1965, p. 95. But Greenberg made his larger position on Johns's work clear on his own. Writing in 1960, he issued Johns (and others) a circuitous, somewhat contradictory, and ultimately cruel dismissal: "In a previous number of this magazine William Rubin dealt with some of the brighter as well as darker aspects of the present situation of New York art. While agreeing with much of what he said, I still found him a little too kind toward many of the artists he discussed.... There is a little too much of the received and the performed in even the best of the New York painters Mr. Rubin wrote about. I myself admire, or at least enjoy, the works of Raymond Parker, Ellsworth Kelly, Jack Youngerman, and Jasper Johns, but find them a little too easy to enjoy. They don't challenge or expand taste. This may not condemn their art, but it has made it, so far, less than major in its promise. And I do not see any reason why we, in America, should go back to celebrating what is less than major"; Clement Greenberg, "Louis and Noland," *Art International* 4, 5 (May 1960), p. 27.

51 *Oxford English Dictionary*, s.v. "gray."

52 Molly Teasdale Smith, "The Use of Grisaille as a Lenten Observance," in *Marsyas: Studies in the History of Art*, vol. 8 (Institute of Fine Arts, New York University, 1959), pp. 43–54.

53 Vasily Kandinsky, *Concerning the Spiritual in Art* (1910), trans. M. T. H. Sadler (Dover Publications, 1977), pp. 37, 39.

54 A recent article in the *Chicago Tribune*, for example, attests to the color's contemporary cultural currency. In an albeit frivolous vein, cultural critic Julia Keller invited a consideration of gray by proposing it as a tag for a then-unnamed rail line in the city's color-coded public transit network. Gray, the author opined is a "hymn to the middle distance. A nod to mists and murky in-betweens. A tip of the hat to indecision.... A bow to the marginal, the makeshift. Gray is the secret soul of the arts." Curiously apropos to the topic at hand here, the author not only valorizes gray, but views with suspicion the "showoff Crayola" qualities of those lines already named for the primary colors. "A Gray Line would celebrate the hushed and the unobtrusive. The beauty of ambiguity"; Julia Keller, "Think of Gray as a Salute to CTA Riders," *Chicago Tribune*, Feb. 26, 2006, Section 7, p. 9. A similarly wide-ranging discussion of the cultural and literary associations of gray can be found in Geoffrey

O'Brien, "Colors/Gray," *Cabinet* 17 (Spring 2005), pp. 7–8. See also David Colman, "For Neutral Grays, the Mood is Positive," *New York Times*, April 5, 2007, for a discussion of gray in men's fashion.

55 Charles Blanc warned, "Thus colorists can charm us.... But the taste for color, when it predominates absolutely, costs many sacrifices; often it turns the mind from its course, changes the sentiment, swallows up the thought"; Charles Blanc, *The Grammar of Painting and Engraving*, trans. Kate Newell Doggett (Hurd and Houghton, 1875), p. 168.

56 Bernstein 1985, p. 221 n. 7.

57 Young 1969, p. 51, in *Writings* 1996, p. 129 (emphasis added).

58 Preface in Georg Wilhelm Friedrich Hegel, *Hegel's Philosophy of Right* (1821), trans. T. M. Knox (Oxford University Press, 1967), p. 13.

59 David Katz, *The World of Colour*, trans. Robert Brodie MacLeod and Charles Warren Fox (K. Paul, Trench, Trubner, 1935), pp. 58–61. Alternately, Katz compared the experience of seeing in a dark room: "A considerable number report they see absolute blackness, yet their judgment is erroneous. A truly unprejudiced, descriptive attitude reveals that a dark room does not really produce the impression of absolute blackness. The unbiased observer sees a dark gray, which is termed subjective visual gray"; David Katz, *Gestalt Psychology: Its Nature and Significance*, trans. Robert Tyson (Ronald Press, 1950), p. 19.

60 Vija Celmins lecture at the Art Institute of Chicago, May 23, 2007. She further explained that the "gray room" is "like an interior room that's inside you... where everything's possible."

61 Steinberg 1962/1972, p. 54. Johns has also stated, "The prime motive of any work is the wish to give rise to discussion, if only between the mind and itself"; Kozloff 1968, p. 10.

62 Coosje Van Bruggen, *Bruce Nauman* (Rizzoli, 1988), p. 23.

63 Morris 2007, p. 224.

64 Glueck 1966, p. 26, in *Writings* 1996, p. 128.

65 Taylor 1990, p. 100, in *Writings* 1996, p. 245.

66 "With the destruction of their natural space, each of these species loses its distinctiveness"; Krauss 1976, p. 94.

67 Christian Geelhaar, "The Painters Who Had the Right Eyes: On the Reception of Cézanne's Bathers," in Mary Louise Krumrine, with Gottfried Boehm and Christian Geelhaar, *Paul Cézanne: The Bathers*, trans. John Mitchell and Dorothy Kosinski, exh. cat. (Harry N. Abrams, 1990), p. 298; quoted in Bernstein 1996, p. 42.

68 Robertson 1978, n.pag.

69 Sculp-metal was a commercial product marketed for amateurs and hobbyists and widely advertised in the art magazines of the 1950s. It could be extruded from a tube like paint, or perhaps more accurately like toothpaste, and modeled like clay with a knife, spatula, or by hand. It then hardened like metal. Mixed with thinners, it could be applied like oil paint. Sold in a ready-to-use compound made up of tints, fillers, vinyl, resin, aluminum powder, toluol, and methyl ethyl ketone, it proved to be highly toxic and is now no longer manufactured. See Orton 1996, p. 25.

70 Johns has stated, "I think most of my work is involved with a kind of ambiguous statement"; see *U.S.A. Artists 8: Jasper Johns* 1966, in *Writings* 1996, p. 127. Although in a different context, Johns admonished in one of his sketchbooks: "Beware of the body & mind. Avoid a polar situation"; Sketchbook A, p. 49, 1964, in *Writings* 1996, pp. 34, 56.

71 Tono 1964, in *Writings* 1996, p. 98.

72 Johns has stated, "Whatever idea one has, it's always susceptible to doubt"; Sylvester 1965, in *Writings* 1996, p. 117.

73 Sylvester 1965, in *Writings* 1996, p. 121 (emphasis added). For Wittgenstein, the meaning of something derives from the way it is used. In accounting for the discrepancies between intention and meaning, Johns relied upon Wittgenstein's logic: "Publicly a work becomes not just intention, but the way it is used. If an artist makes something—or if you make chewing gum and everybody ends up using it as glue, whoever made it is given the responsibility of making glue, even if what he really intended is chewing gum. You can't control that kind of thing"; Swenson 1964, p. 66, in *Writings* 1996, pp. 93–94.

74 Johns has used a lithograph by Henri Monnier (*Untitled*, c. 1835) as a source in recent works, echoing themes addressed in his Spy/Watchman note. Monnier's image of a young man spying a sexual act that is hidden from the viewer pertains to voyeurism, concealment, and what Scott Rothkopf called the "pleasure and alienation of looking"; Rothkopf 2005, p. 18.

75 Young 1969, p. 51, in *Writings* 1996, p. 130. See also Johns's remark, "An object that tells of the loss, destruction, disappearance of objects. Does not speak of itself"; Sketchbook A, p. 8, c. 1960, in *Writings* 1996, p. 50.

76 Sketchbook B, c. 1967, in *Writings* 1996, p. 64.

77 Sketchbook A, p. 31, c. 1963, in *Writings* 1996, p. 52. See also "He always regards neutrality as the expression of an intention, and therefore relative like all other conditions"; Solomon 1964, p. 15.

78 Johns 1966, p. 110, in *Writings* 1996, p. 22.

79 Sketchbook A, p. 9, c. 1960, in *Writings* 1996, p. 50.

80 Fuller 1978, p. 5, in *Writings* 1996, p. 182.

81 Kazimir Malevich, "Non-Objective Creation and Suprematism," in *Essays on Art*, ed. Troels Andersen, trans. Xenia Glowacki-Prus and Arnold McMillan (Borgen, 1968), p. 112.

82 Examples of gray include: *Composition with Gray Lines* (1918; Gemeentemuseum, Hague) and *Lozenge with Grey Lines* (1918; Van den Briel Collection, Gemeentemuseum, Hague). Other painters of the de Stijl movement, including Vilmos Huszar, produced gray monochromes around 1919; John Gage, *Color and Culture: Practice and Meaning from Antiquity to Abstraction* (Little, Brown, 1993), pp. 257–58.

83 Stevens and McGuigan 1977, p. 73, in *Writings* 1996, p. 165.

84 Tone 1996, p. 120.

85 Thomas McEvilley, "Seeking the Primal Through Paint: The Monochrome Icon," in *The Exile Returns: Towards a Redefinition of Painting for the Post-Modern Era* (Cambridge University Press, 1993), p. 26.

86 Critic Lawrence Alloway identified the years 1947–51 as the period of its greatest use; Lawrence Alloway, "Sign and Surface: Notes on Black and White Painting in New York," *Quadrum* 9 (1960), pp. 49–62. For a discussion of the use of black and white by the Abstract Expressionist artists, see also Clement Greenberg, "American-Type Painting," in *Clement Greenberg: The Collected Essays and Criticism*, ed. John O'Brian, vol. 3 (University of Chicago Press, 1993), pp. 226–27. In 1963 art dealer Ben Heller organized *Black and White* at the Jewish Museum (Dec. 12, 1963–Feb. 5, 1964), tracing the origins of black-and-white painting in the United States to the late 1940s. Evoking the precedents of Goya, Matisse, Mondrian, and Picasso, the exhibition included Josef Albers, Willem de Kooning, Jim Dine, Arshile Gorky, Hans Hofmann, Ellsworth Kelly, Franz Kline, Conrad Marca-Relli, Robert Motherwell, Barnett Newman, Jackson Pollock, Robert Rauschenberg, Frank Stella, Myron Stout, and others. Too wide-ranging to be polemical, Heller instead addressed his concerns in the most general terms. The catalogue essay does not mention Johns, who was represented by two works, *Reconstruction* (1959; Cleveland Museum of Art) and *Shade* (1959; State Museum, St. Petersburg).

87 Clement Greenberg, "The Present Prospects of American Painting and Sculpture," *Horizon* 93–94 (Oct. 1947), p. 29.

88 Quoted in Tracy Adler, "Seeing Red: The Project," in *Seeing Red: On Nonobjective Painting and Color Theory*, eds. Michael Fehr and Sanford Wurmfeld (Salon Verlag, 2004), p. 13. Although Hofmann's late work, for which he is best known, is characterized by radiant color, as a student and young artist struggling to master Cubism and its formal precedents, he worked for over twenty years—1915 to 1938—almost exclusively in black and white. Hofmann's influence as a teacher, particularly among Abstract Expressionist artists is legendary; following his own didactic trajectory, his classes worked frequently in black and white.

89 "In the Galleries: Shows One by One," *New York Times*, Jan. 11, 1948, p. x9. Pollock's 1950 exhibition at Parsons contained a number of predominantly black-and-white paintings, including *Number 32, 1950* (1950; Kunstsammlung Nordrhein-Westfalen, Düsseldorf) and *Number 28, 1950* (1950; Metropolitan Museum of Art, New York), together with unusually colorful works such

as *Number 19, 1950* (1950; Private collection).

90 Newman and Johns were neighbors. Newman's studio was at 100 Front Street between 1952 and 1968; Johns lived at 128 Front Street between 1959 and 1963.

91 Ann Temkin, "Barnett Newman on Exhibition," in *Barnett Newman*, ed. Ann Temkin, exh. cat. (Philadelphia Museum of Art, 2002), p. 40.

92 Newman also presented a small but powerful picture in black with a red stripe, *Joshua* (1951; Private collection). His abiding fascination with black and white was later expressed in the fifteen paintings of his magnum opus, *The Stations of the Cross* (1958–66; National Gallery of Art, Washington).

93 Stevens and McGuigan 1977, p. 77, in *Writings* 1996, p. 165.

94 Bernstein 1986.

95 See Temkin (note 91), p. 45 n. 95.

96 Tomkins 1980, p. 70.

97 John Cage, "On Robert Rauschenberg, Artist, and His Work," *Metro* 2 (1961), p. 43.

98 John Gruen, "Robert Rauschenberg: An Audience of One," *Artnews* 76, 2 (Feb. 1977), p. 47.

99 Richard Shiff, "Whiteout: The Not-Influence Newman Effect," in *Barnett Newman*, ed. Ann Temkin, exh. cat. (Philadelphia Museum of Art, 2002), p. 83.

100 Rosenberg 1977, p. 43.

101 Davvetas 1984, p. 12, in *Writings* 1996, p. 219; see also Bernstein 1996, pp. 40–41 n. 10.

102 Young 1969, p. 51, in *Writings* 1996, p. 129 (emphasis added).

103 Jespersen 1969. Consider also Johns's remark, "I decided to do only what I meant to do, and not what other people did. When I could observe what others did, I tried to remove that from my work. My work became a constant negation of impulses"; Crichton 1994, p. 29.

104 For a thorough discussion of the exhibition as a zeitgeist show, and its implications for the early framings of Minimal art in popular culture, critical writing, and art historical formulations, see James Meyer, "Introduction to the Minimal 1: 'Black, White, and Gray,'" in *Minimalism: Art and Polemics in the Sixties* (Yale University Press, 2001), pp. 76–81.

105 Samuel J. Wagstaff, Jr., "Paintings to Think About," *Artnews* 62, 9 (Jan. 1964), p. 62. Perhaps the editors of *Artnews*, not Wagstaff, were willing to characterize the affinity, in a sub-headline that read "A wide variety of new, far-out American painting and sculpture in Hartford *emphasizes the cool and intellectual stance*" (emphasis added).

106 Samuel J. Wagstaff, Jr., "Second Thoughts on Black, White, and Gray," The Black, White, and Gray Papers, Archive, Wadsworth Atheneum, Hartford, Connecticut, n.d., quoted in Meyer (note 104), p. 77.

107 In a letter to Mrs. Herbert Lee, who then owned *Newspaper*, Wagstaff, asking for the loan, wrote of Johns: "This show will attempt to give the most austere, regimented, severe side of the artist, and for that reason Jasper Johns thought that your painting would be perfect for this theme"; see letter dated Dec. 2, 1963, Wadsworth Atheneum archives. Other artists represented by all black or all white works included Dan Flavin, Robert Morris, Robert Rauschenberg, Ad Reinhardt, and Tony Smith. Also included were two of Johns's works on paper: *Coat Hanger I* (1960) and *Alphabets* (1957; Collection of Jane Rosenblum).

108 Meyer (note 104), p. 78.

109 "L'ennemi de toute peinture est le gris," in Eugène Delacroix, *Journal de Eugène Delacroix,* 3 vols. (Librairie Plon, 1932), vol. 3, p. 16.

110 Kirk Varnedoe, *Cy Twombly: A Retrospective*, exh. cat. (the Museum of Modern Art, New York, 1994), pp. 21–22.

111 Robert Rosenblum, *Cubism and Twentieth Century Art* (Thames and Hudson, 1960), p. 37.

112 For a brief discussion of Magritte's stone paintings in relation to Johns, see Kozloff 1968, p. 37.

113 Valerie Fletcher, *Alberto Giacometti: 1901–1966* (Smithsonian Institution Press, 1988), p. 49.

114 Sartre, quoted in ibid., p. 51.

115 Reinhold Hohl, *Alberto Giacometti* (Harry N. Abrams, 1971), p. 225.

116 Stevens and McGuigan 1977, pp. 73, 77, in *Writings* 1996, p. 165.

117 The two other colors Klein used were "madder red" (Monopink/MP) and gold (Monogold/MG).

118 Lippard (note 21), p. 62.

119 Young 1969, p. 52, in *Writings* 1996, p. 131.

120 Sylvester 1965, in Sylvester 2001, p. 167. See also Johns's remark, "If the painting is an object, then the object can be a painting....If on this area you can make something, then on *this* area you can make something"; Kozloff 1968, p. 21.

121 Johns's iconic, representational works of this period also explored "objectness." As Kozloff has pointed out: "Even the stretcher sides of the targets and flags are covered with heavy pigment, which lends each canvas an extraordinarily concrete, objectlike character"; Kozloff 1968, p. 12. Artist Robert Morris has also observed: "Johns took painting further toward a state of non-depiction than anyone else. The Flags were not so much depictions as copies.... Johns took the background out of painting and isolated the thing. The background became the wall. What was previously neutral became actual, while what was previously an image became a thing"; quoted in Varnedoe 1996, p. 99. Johns's trademark habit of occasionally leaving a strip along the bottom margin of the canvas unpainted reinforces his interest in painting as object, what he calls a "mannerism in the relationship between painting and canvas"; Pohlen 1978, in *Writings* 1996, p. 172.

122 Johns of this moment is not consciously quoting art historical precedent. He has said, for example, that he was not familiar before a 1957 trip to the Philadelphia Museum of Art with Duchamp's Readymades. He was, however, mindful of certain Cubist, Dada, and Surrealist precedents, notably Picasso, Kurt Schwitters, and Joseph Cornell; see Bernstein 1985, p. 31.

123 Varnedoe 1996, p. 27.

124 *Canvas* does apparently incorporate plain paper collage.

125 The idea of using paint to turn printed media *into* an object, as opposed to using printed media *in* painting, is confirmed by *Book* (1957; Collection of Martin Z. Margulies).

126 Prather 2000, p. 147. The English painter Howard Hodgkin singled out Johns as an artist who is able to "make autonomous and impersonal marks...with tremendous success....Marks which are emotive and cold all at once. Lucky man"; see Meyer 2006, pp. 58–59 n. 71. In terms of Hodgkin's overlapping areas of concern with Johns, see also Meyer 2006, pp. 47–48, 50–51.

127 Young 1969, p. 51, in *Writings* 1996, p. 129 (emphasis added).

128 Klüver 1963, in *Writings* 1996, pp. 87–88 (emphasis added). Consider also Johns's remark, "One of the extreme problems of painting as objects is the other side—the back. It can't be solved; it's in the nature of the work"; Crichton 1994, p. 34.

129 Willard 1966, p. 57, in *Writings* 1996, pp. 128–29. The actual image of paintings turned to the wall appears for the first time in *In the Studio* (1982; Collection of the artist).

130 It appears that this insert was painted separately, although the surface handling is worked in such a way as to create the illusion of continuous strokes over both surfaces. The size is curiously not standard; it is too large to be a common bedside table, too small to be an average dresser. It is, most likely, a handmade facsimile, or, more precisely, an abstraction, of household furniture.

131 Bernstein 1985, p. 34.

132 Strangely, the drawer suggests a contradictory depth; ultimately, of course, it is just the front of the drawer and thus reaffirms flatness. Unlike other paintings of this moment in which the sides of the canvas are painted to assert the object nature of the canvas, the sides of *Drawer* are not painted—seemingly to reaffirm the condition of surface with no depth.

133 Somewhat unusually, a drawing preceded the painting. In 1958 Johns made a Conté crayon drawing (Private collection) by tracing a real coat hanger from the dry cleaner and using this form to render an illusion of the object surrounded by a field of dense, dark strokes. In the drawing, the coat hanger rests parallel with the bottom edge of the sheet. When Johns made the painting the following year, he learned that the hanger naturally cants to one side or the other, refusing to remain aligned with the edge of the canvas, and by implication, the ground below. This discovery is incorporated into the subsequent prints *Coat Hanger I* and *II* (both 1960). Grayness also asserts itself here on the level of the incidental. Johns spray painted the coat hanger, which he suggested may have been kicking around the

studio for some time, gray (Johns to the author, June 23, 2006). The action amounts to a subtle, nearly undetectable alteration, and indicates the range and variety of signification within various thorough applications of gray media.

134 Kirk Varnedoe on *Tennyson*: "The canvas flap over the two panels suggests occlusion, while the bare strip at the bottom insists on the layered artifice of the surface; and the poet's name colors the gray monochrome with literary, elegiac associations"; Varnedoe 1996, p. 117. Robert Rosenblum wrote of "the chilly expanse of mottled gray geometries that becomes a tombstone for the Victorian poet whose name seems to be carved at its base"; Rosenblum 1960, p. 77.

135 Tennyson, quoted in Robert Bernard Martin, *Tennyson: The Unquiet Heart* (Oxford University Press, 1980), pp. 28–29. The anecdote is suggested, but not cited, by Shapiro 1984, p. 26.

136 Robert W. Hill, Jr., *Tennyson's Poetry: Authoritative Texts, Contexts, Criticisms* (W. W. Norton, 1999), pp. 203–04; Martin (note 135), pp. 174–88.

137 This reading was first developed in conversation with Kristin Lister.

138 Rauschenberg painted *Bed* in the spring of 1955 (Tomkins 1980, p. 136), a few months prior to moving into the loft above Johns's on Pearl Street (Tone 1996, p. 125). However, the work was not displayed until 1958 (Tomkins 1980, p. 137), so it is likely that Johns would have seen it frequently.

139 Crichton 1994, p. 33.

140 Klüver 1963, in *Writings* 1996, p. 89.

141 Rauschenberg moved out of the studio in winter 1961; Tone 1996, p. 192.

142 Bernstein 1985, p. 75, 226–27 n. 1.

143 Ibid., p. 73.

144 Varnedoe 1996, p. 191. This is an argument first suggested by Alan Solomon in 1964, who noted in his text for the Johns's survey at the Jewish Museum the connection between *Periscope (Hart Crane)* (1963) and the lines in Crane's "Cape Hatteras" section of *The Bridge* (1930): "These occasional overtones of feeling in the work have become more prevalent, in contrast with the complete personal detachment to which we were accustomed earlier"; Solomon 1964, p. 16.

145 Bernstein partially undoes her own argument—"the mood changes"—in a footnote, cautioning readers away from biography: "1961 is the year after his first retrospective exhibition at the Columbia Museum of Art in South Carolina; the year he got his studio on Edisto Island, South Carolina; and the year his close friendship with Rauschenberg drifts apart. *What is important about the works from this period, however, does not revolve around the specific details of Johns' life, but rather his shift to incorporating intense feelings as a subject in his art*"; Bernstein 1985, pp. 226–27 n. 1 (emphasis added). How, one might wonder, can intense feelings not be connected to one's own life? Bernstein, later Varnedoe, and, to a lesser extent, Fred Orton, who does offer a more complicated reading of the 1961 pictures viz. biography, all fail to accommodate a more open and differentiated approach to gray; see Orton 1994, pp. 56–76.

146 Leo Steinberg influentially saw in Johns "a solitude more intense than anything I had seen in pictures of mere desolation... a sense of desolate waiting.... of human absence from a man-made environment." Steinberg, quoted in Tomkins 1980, p. 137.

147 A show of Tapies's recent paintings was held at Galerie Stadler, 51, rue de Seine, June 15–July 14, 1961, while Johns was in Paris.

148 Kozloff 1968, p. 21.

149 Fred Orton wrote: "The grey brushstrokes that dominate the right and mark the white ground and turpentine-like brown-greyness of the left canvas are there not as the direct expression of feelings but as signifier of the expression of feelings appropriated from the pictorial language of Abstract Expressionism. In the context of Johns's surface they refer to the idea of the unmediated association of feelings and facture, but their very identity as appropriated signifiers inhibits our seeing and understanding them as marks directly expressive of Johns's feelings"; Orton 1994, p. 64.

150 Cage, quoted in Solomon 1964, p. 26. Cage's quotation from Johns's notes is an elision of two passages from Sketchbook A (c. 1960–65). The first, "A DEAD MAN/Take a skull/cover it with paint/rub it against canvas," appears on p. 18 and is dated c. 1960–61. The second, "Skull/against/canvas./Scull/against/canvas" appears on p. 57 and is dated 1964.

151 Donald Allen, ed., *The Collected Poems of Frank O'Hara* (University of California Press, 1995), p. 257.

152 *No* (1961) isolates a word of refusal against a much larger, nearly colorless gray encaustic field, a dark, even macabre, molten surface, almost completely colorless save for a streak of violent, blood red. The margin of exposed canvas at the base does little to lighten the mood. In this instance, the words are made of lead and are suspended from a wire running almost the full vertical length of the painting. At its terminus, the letters dangle in front of a Sculp-metal relief of the same word on the painting's surface in the bottom third of the canvas. There are coded references to sexuality and anatomy. Most notably, Johns identifies the abstruse trace in the upper left as an imprint of Marcel Duchamp's *Female Fig Leaf* (1961; Collection of the artist). The Duchamp multiple was ostensibly cast from a vagina. While several authors have stated it was molded from the nude figure in *Etant Donnés: 1° la chute d'eau, 2° le gaz d'eclairage* (1946–66; Philadelphia Museum of Art), Calvin Tomkins claimed that the original, from which all subsequent editions were made, was sculpted by hand; Calvin Tomkins, *Duchamp: A Biography* (Henry Holt, 1996), p. 377. Although, strangely, the argument has seemingly not yet been formally articulated, the sculptural rendering and surface indexing (in the case of NO as both imprint and shadow) of these two elements leads to one, perhaps excessively obvious, conclusion: Johns is refusing female sexuality. At the same time, depending, of course, on the height at which the painting is installed, the word NO does find its correspondence on the body of an average viewer roughly "below the belt," in the place of the genitals. (The word NO is also concealed behind Johns's self-portrait in *Souvenir* [1964].)

153 One can safely assume it was Johns's own decision to present *In Memory of My Feelings—Frank O'Hara*, as described, in both instances: "At Leo's, I always install my shows"; Hindry 1989, p. 16, in *Writings* 1996, p. 234.

154 Bernstein 1985, p. 84.

155 Ibid. According to the artist James Bishop, Viola Farber would cut Johns's hair. Bishop, in conversation with the author, Mar. 20, 2006.

156 Johns to author, July 11, 2007. This anecdote has also been recounted in a slightly different way in Eden Rafshoon, "In Memory of My Feelings Frank O'Hara: A Turning Point for Jasper Johns" (M.A. thesis, George Washington University, 1988), p. 31.

157 Taylor 1990, p. 100, in *Writings* 1996, p. 245.

158 Bernstein 1985, p. 8. For a further analysis of Johns's repetition of the flag, see Orton 1994, p. 97.

159 This list includes the gray flag at the bottom of *Flags* (1965; Collection of the artist).

160 It has often been written that William Jasper saved the American flag. He did not. He twice saved his regiment's colors. Johns recalled that, in the version of events told to him, William Jasper was portrayed saving the American flag; Stuckey 1976, p. 5; Taylor 1990, p. 100, in *Writings* 1996, p. 244.

161 Orton 1994, p. 107.

162 Diamonstein Spielvogel 1994, p. 118, in *Writings* 1996, p. 295.

163 Ibid., p. 114, in *Writings* 1996, p. 292.

164 It does have a correspondence to an unusual graphite pencil and collage drawing, *Two Flags* (1969; Menil Collection, Houston) which presents two inverted vertical flags, one in gray and one left white, with the lower-left corner of each flag folded in on itself.

165 Fisher 1990, p. 320.

166 Ibid.

167 Kozloff 1968, p. 16.

168 Tono 1964, in *Writings* 1996, p. 100. In regards to color as material, note that Johns spelled out the names of the primary colors in wooden letters, neon tubing, and cast aluminum in *Field Painting* (1963–64; Collection of the artist) and *According to What* (1964; Private collection).

169 This list is limited to the works that can be characterized as gray in the context of this exhibition. Other works with the flag motif, not under consideration here, were executed in bronze, resin, plaster, watercolor, colored

pencil, oil, charcoal, pastel, and tempera. See checklist in Sylvester 1996.

170 Swenson 1964, p. 67, in *Writings* 1996, p. 94.

171 Keenly observant of this aspect of Johns's process, Leo Steinberg commented: "We sense an unfamiliar deceleration of their [the flags] normal rate of existence. The flag stiffens, is slowly hand painted, and ... [finally] cast in bronze. The Stars and Stripes forever"; Steinberg 1962/1972, p. 29.

172 Robert Smithson, "A Sedimentation of the Mind: Earth Proposals," *Artforum* 7, 1 (Sept. 1968), p. 49.

173 Crichton 1994, p. 39.

174 "Johns is always involved in the play between tonal neutrality and chromatism"; Solomon 1964, p. 16.

175 Johns to author, July 30, 2004; see also John's comments in his interview with Nan Rosenthal in this volume, pp. 157, 160.

176 Cage 1964, p. 25.

177 Kozloff 1968, p. 38.

178 Johns observed in 1977: "I believe that I'm not a very accomplished colorist, although I do think that I've improved somewhat. I think that I can improve even more. I've always used schematic coloring and since there's always a tendency to move on to something, I want to do something different with color"; Olson 1977, p. 25, in *Writings* 1996, p. 169. See also Johns's comment of 1978: "My painting of the last few years has improved my color; I think I'm better at color than I used to be"; Fuller 1978b, p. 6, in *Writings* 1996, p. 185.

179 The best summary expression of Albers's ideas about the complex, adaptable relationships between colors is Josef Albers, *Interaction of Color* (1963), 2nd ed. (Yale University Press, 1971).

180 Quoted in Vincent Katz, "Black Mountain College: Experiment in Art," in *Black Mountain College: Experiment in Art,* ed. Vincent Katz, exh. cat. (Museo Nacional Centro de Arte Reina Sofia, Madrid/MIT Press, 2002), p. 34.

181 Thomas Hess, "Hommage to Albers," in *Albers*, exh. cat. (Galerie Beyeler, Basel, 1973), n.pag. For the artist's own account of this exchange, see the interview by Nan Rosenthal in this volume, p. 158. Of Albers, the artist Mel Bochner recalled hearing from Eva Hesse that she was the only student of Albers's to get all of the questions on the color test completely correct. Following this, however, Hesse, who was not inclined to Albers's theories, largely renounced color in her work. Bochner, in conversation with the author, Sept. 28, 2006. Hesse embraced gray. Indeed, the monochromism in her work after 1965 is largely traceable to an appreciation of Johns's work; see Robert Pincus-Witten, "Eva Hesse: More Light on the Transition from Post-Minimalism to the Sublime," in *Eva Hesse: A Memorial Exhibition*, exh. cat. (Solomon R. Guggenheim Museum, 1972), n.pag. One might also think of the artist Vija Celmins, who has worked exclusively in black, white, and gray since the early 1960s. Certainly Johns's solo exhibition at the Everett Ellin Gallery in late 1962, in which he showed, among other works, the all-gray *Drawer, Device, Fool's House,* and *In Memory of My Feelings—Frank O'Hara*, was hugely influential for Celmins; Lane Relyea, "Survey: Vija Celmins' Twilight Zone," in *Vija Celmins* (Phaidon, 2004), p. 61.

182 The work was damaged, broken into thirteen pieces, and was acquired by Johns in a trade with Rauschenberg, who had acquired it directly from Albers at Black Mountain College in 1948 or 1949. In 1964 Johns wrote to Albers and told him that Rauschenberg had passed the work on to him and to initiate a dialogue about its restoration, which was undertaken in 1972 (by Charles Tauss) and again in 1996 (by Lorna Barnes, an objects conservator at the Metropolitan Museum of Art, New York). This was confirmed in in a letter to the author from Lynn Kearcher, Sarah Taggert's assistant at the Johns studio, July 19, 2007, and in an e-mail to Jesse Feiman from Brenda Daniloquitz, Chief Curator, the Josef and Anni Albers Foundation, Aug. 3, 2006.

183 Charles Baudelaire, "On the Heroism of Modern Life," in *Art In Paris 1845–1862*, ed. and trans. Jonathan Mayne (Phaidon, 1965), p. 118.

184 Shapiro 1984, p. 35.

185 Johns, when asked about his work for another performance demurred. "You say that I made some costumes for a piece Merce did...in the early '60s, but I don't remember anything about it—I probably just dyed some tights and leotards. That was often my approach—to do nothing, basically"; Vaughan 1990, p. 140, in *Writings* 1996, p. 237. The description of *Exchange* was verified in an e-mail from Mark Lancaster to the author Dec. 14, 2006. A photograph of the performance appears in David Vaughan, *Merce Cunningham: Fifty Years*, ed. Melissa Harris (Aperture, 1997), p. 205. Vaughan writes: "*Exchange* seems irrefutably urban. The grisaille of *Inlets* was that of mist and soft rain; *Exchange* also featured grays, in Jasper Johns's backcloth and costumes, but they were gritty, like slag and anthracite, with touches of sooty color (Johns said he wanted 'polluted' colors)."

186 Li-Lin Tseng, "Jasper Johns *Untitled* 1980–84," in *Drawings of Choice from a New York Collection,* ed. Josef Helfstein and Jonathan Feinberg (Krannert Art Museum, 2002), p. 70, identifies the forms on the right margin as resembling elements of Duchamp's *Bride Machine*. Johns owned a reproduction of *Bride Machine* by Duchamp's brother, Jacques Villon, which he used for his own *Tracing* (1978). Tseng further identified the lines at the bottom margin as resembling the backhoe featured in an advertisement for Drainz which Johns traced into *Untitled* (1983–84; Collection of Mr. and Mrs. John Hilson).

187 Another example of the interrelationship between gray and the primaries can be found in *Voice 2* (1968–71; Kunstmuseum Basel). The sides of the three canvases that compose this predominantly gray triptych (each separated by a mandated six inches presumably to reveal all edges which would not happen if the panels were conventionally conjoined) are painted red, yellow, and blue, respectively.

188 See the essay by Kelly Keegan and Kristin Lister in this volume, p. 164.

189 Fisher 1990, p. 351.

190 Esterow 1993, p. 149, in *Writings* 1996, p. 284.

191 Shapiro 1971, p. 40.

192 Ibid.

193 Ibid., pp. 40–41.

194 Kent 1990, in *Writings* 1996, p. 259.

195 Much has been made about the title of the work. Michael Crichton, writing with the benefit of direct access to Johns, identified "Dutch wife" as a "board with a hole, used by sailors as a surrogate for a woman"; Crichton 1994, p. 60. He did not attribute the definition to the artist in his published text, and we cannot substantiate it in any other sources. In an e-mail correspondence of Sept. 26, 2006, to Jesse Feiman, Crichton wrote: "Johns himself explained the origin of the term to me in the interviews I did with him in 1976–77. His explanation was what I put in the text. But I never thought to question it, or pursue it further." The phrase is one of many in the English language that use Dutch as a shorthand for derogatory characterizations, such as "Dutch courage" (courage from alcohol) or "Dutch uncle" (a harsh or severe teacher). The phrase "Dutch wife" can also be used to refer to an open-frame bolster bed, made of bamboo or thick rattan, often used in tropical climates to allow air to circulate around resting limbs. It is possible that the title references the formal qualities of such a frame as related to the crosshatch pattern. It is more likely, however, given Johns's time in Japan, that the title's point of origin is the Japanese usage of "datch waifu" (Dutch wife) to refer to sex dolls.

196 In a few cases, along the bottom edge, the gestures appear flipped or mirrored.

197 The careful mimicry of left and right raises questions about the conscious intentionality of the artist's use of certain texts. Johns has consistently refused to invest meaning in his choices of texts, which he characterizes as random, accidental, and the result of happenstance more than choice. The careful repetition here, however, required at the very least the premeditation of obtaining a duplicate of the source or sources. Even if the artist was not particularly invested in the selection of texts, the doubling would certainly result in an acute awareness of fragments in use. Here, to take just two proximate examples from a vast field of possibilities, two texts are left visible and are verifiably repeated: "Organist's arrest shocks town" and "block window." In the context of an easily retrieved reference to masturbation, the suggestive puns

and hints of elicit behavior are not convincingly random. Such intentionality is bolstered by the singular rendering of the ejaculate-like splatter, a gesture borrowed from Duchamp, in this context. Incidents like this make it more difficult to insist on reading these text fragments as the result of chance. Indeed, there are statements to suggest Johns does at times use certain texts with a high degree of premeditation and intentionality. Carpenter 1977; Bernstein 1985, p. 12; Orton 1994, pp. 125–31; Orton 1996, p. 62.

198 Winkfield 1996, p. 24.

199 Johns also made three smaller versions in 1983. One could also take note of the colorful 1984 articulation of this motif in watercolor; Rosenthal and Fine 1990, pp. 266–67.

200 Bernard and Thompson 1984, in *Writings* 1996, p. 217. This self-reflexive phase of Johns's work has met with more critical skepticism than any other. Peter Schjeldahl in the *New Yorker* and Michael Kimmelman in the *New York Times* have led the charge, with harsh criticism verging on the retributive or mean-spirited: "His worst pieces are about the artist himself, and teem with gratuitous, bright ideas....The congested autobiographical and erudite impedimenta in his works of the eighties and nineties testified that he had fallen into the most common of traps for the creative and successful–he began to agree with his fans that whatever interests him has to be significant"; Schjeldahl 2005, p. 97. See also Kimmelman's coverage of Johns's solo exhibition at Matthew Marks Gallery in 2005: "A skeptical response to this show, Jasper Johns's first in New York since his retrospective at the Museum of Modern Art in 1996, is inevitable. Mr. Johns was last seen heading into the ether, toward ever more preening and self-mythologizing brands of obscurity, which made the later galleries of the MoMA retrospective feel suffocating and rather sad"; Kimmelman 2005, p. B32.

201 Tomkins 2006, p. 78. Referring to the Crosshatch and Flagstone motifs prevalent in the work of the 1970s, Johns remarked, "You consider that abstraction, those stupid marks....I don't know that I think of my other work as representational." For other discussions of these motifs as neither abstract nor representational, see Crichton 1994, pp. 52–53, 57; Rose 1977, p. 149.

202 *In the Studio* (1982; Collection of the artist) was, in fact, painted before the final Crosshatch paintings but belongs more cogently to the subsequent period of work.

203 Cork 1990, p. 21, in *Writings* 1996, p. 258.

204 Nan Rosenthal was the first to coin the term; Rosenthal and Fine 1990, p. 82.

205 The scenario is freighted. Artist Elizabeth Murray described *Racing Thoughts* as among "the saddest images that I have ever seen" because they evoke the image of the artist lying in a vulnerable position, naked and alone, "reviewing everything about fears and hopes and failures"; Varnedoe 1996, p. 107. In addition, after beginning the bathtub paintings, Johns read a book by Cocteau in which he recorded that Picasso said he was always amazed that when he took a bath, he didn't melt like a sugar cube; Wallach 1988, in *Writings* 1996, p. 226.

206 Marjorie Welish claims Mark Rosenthal calls it a "private museum," and she also suggests comparisons to both the curio cabinet, and the bulletin board. See Welish 1999, pp. 91–92. See also Yau 1996, p. 86.

207 Rosenthal 1993, p. 63, in *Writings* 1996, p. 282.

208 Goldman 1987, n.pag.

209 Solomon 1988, p. 64. For seasonal interpretations of color and winter, see also the following discussion by Philip Fisher: "The greatest of [Johns's] paintings have a somberness, even a solemnity. Having seized color as the essence of painting, Johns displays none of the sensuality of color that we find in Matisse or de Kooning. These are paintings from the winter of the history of color"; Fisher 1990, p. 351.

210 See Bernstein 1996, p. 57. Roberta Bernstein has also traced the influence of Paul Cézanne and the Japanese Zen master Sengai Gibon (1750–1838).

211 See Varnedoe 1996, p. 337, and Crichton 1994, p. 69. Also note the shadow migrates: it is, far left in *Summer* (1985; the Museum of Modern Art, New York), far right in *Winter*, split in *Fall* (1986; Collection of the artist), and centered in *Spring* (1986; Robert and Jane Meyerhoff Collection, Phoenix, Maryland).

212 Barbara Rose has observed, "Johns's quasi-transparent shadow is a poignant self-portrait of the artist who cannot be distinguished from his art, whose figure literally merges with his works"; Rose 1987, p. 199.

213 Goldman 1987.

214 This was first developed in conversation with Kristin Lister.

215 Roberta Bernstein points out that the arrows point counter-clockwise in *Spring*, *Summer*, and *Fall* but clockwise in *Winter*. See Bernstein 1991, p. 13 n. 6.

216 It may be that Johns initially intended to make more of the crack in the lower area. Through this section he painted a pale primary blue on the underlying canvas along the same fault line where the crack would be. He did this even before he adhered the canvas collages on top. This suggests that Johns initially intended the blue to be visible. I am indebted to Kristin Lister for this keen observation.

217 "In *Winter*, for example, Johns said he was trying to deal with kind of movement he associated with the phrase 'thin snow,' the title of a Japanese Noh drama that deals with the transience of beauty. 'I was trying to establish the idea of some kind of movement that couldn't be noticed but would still be there'"; Sozanski 1988, p. 31.

218 Richard Field makes such an argument, referring to *Catenary (Manet-Degas)* (2000; Private collection): "Johns's painting looks as if it had been ravaged over time, the decrepitude of its surface not unlike the scarred and pockmarked landscapes of the moon or the skin of the aged"; Field 1999, p. 22.

219 Rose 1987, p. 259.

220 In a series of etchings Johns transformed the concept into one of a continuous cycle, first by moving the position of the seasons to end with spring instead of winter, and then cross/wheel format. See Bernstein 1996, p. 65.

221 A. Walton Litz, *Introspective Voyager: The Poetic Development of Wallace Stevens* (Oxford University Press, 1972), pp. 99–100.

222 Ibid., p. 100. I am grateful to editor Robert Sharp, and to the artist Lisa Yuskavage, both of whom offered a similarly affirmative reading of Stevens's poem.

223 Johns thinks the string is very different from earlier collage elements. "I think it is quite different...It's the first time something had a dynamic of that kind. I have things in paintings that hang or that perhaps interfere, block, or change what you can see. But this curve takes a shape of its own–which becomes another element. I think that's the difference"; Field 1999, p. 17.

224 Johns began the series without knowing the term. In February 1997, a friend of the artist, Henry Cortesi, identified the form as a "catenary" while visiting the St. Martin studio. As we have seen, Johns prefers such unintentional appropriation of motif: "I'm not sure that the discovery of the word [catenary] didn't trigger all these other pictures. I know that it brought out some aspects that had not occurred to me. I had not thought, for instance, that as the points of suspension changed, the relationships were going to change, the curve was going to change"; Field 1999, p. 19.

225 For more on Johns and Hart Crane, see Solomon 1964, p. 16; Bernstein 1977, p. 144; Orton 1994, pp. 73–77; Pissarro 1999, pp. 42–45; Weiss 2007a, pp. 38–39. Richard Field, in a conversation in Johns, asked the artist about the parallel between Crane's poems and the Bridge paintings. Johns seemed delighted with Field's suggestion but quickly added: "I hadn't thought about that"; Field 1999, p. 54 n. 23.

226 See Pissarro 1999, pp. 38–39.

227 Rothkopf 2005, p. 5. One might also think of the wet-into-wet absorption of a sponge as a way to further modify the dry, chalky implications of a blackboard and eraser.

228 Ibid., pp. 8–9.

229 Admittedly, and typically, the trajectory from full to empty is not properly linear if one considers smaller works alongside the larger. Between *Bridge* and *Near the Lagoon,* intervening works show Johns in the business of accumulating still more, adding images associated with childhood memories of colored lanterns and a "Chinese" dragon-print Halloween costume. Conversely, the work just preceding *Catenary (I Call to the Grave)* was the first to be titled "Catenary" with no parenthetical references and the first to achieve a pure monochrome gray abstraction; six others followed

before the summary *Near the Lagoon*.

230 The proportions of the canvas fragments to the support in *Catenary (Manet-Degas)* do not precisely follow the proportions of *The Execution of Maximilian*. Johns claimed that the photograph of Manet's painting provided by the National Gallery, London, cropped a narrow area of blank canvas on the left edge of the original. After learning of the mistake, Johns used the corrected proportions of the Manet fragments as a motif in works such as, *Untitled* (2001) and *Near the Lagoon* (2002–03). Johns shared this with Douglas Druick at the time of the drawing's acquisition. This is also recounted in Rothkopf 2005, p. 21 n. 33.

231 Livingstone 2000, p. 180.

232 Quoted in John Elderfield, *Manet and the Execution of Maximilian*, exh. cat. (Museum of Modern Art, New York, 2006), p. 40.

233 See ibid., p. 146. The moment that the soldiers fired upon Maximilian is certainly the most dramatic to represent. However, Maximilian did not die from the firing squad's initial volley. Due to misfiring muskets and bad aim, he suffered several wounds before dying; see p. 139.

234 Looking through Zurbarán for precursors to the catenary pictures, one might also consider Johns's exposure to *Saint Francis in Meditation* (1635–40; National Gallery, London) in which a hanging, knotted cord is a preeminent feature. (Franciscans, sometimes called gray friars, originally wore a long, loose gray tunic girded with a cord. In the fifteenth century, the color was changed to brown.)

235 Smith (note 52).

236 Notions of weather in the Catenary paintings, although not specific to *Near the Lagoon*, have also been suggested by Catherine Craft: "Johns's earlier works in grey, such as *No* (1961) or *Souvenir* (1964), did not form 'grey pictures' but materialised surfaces whose implacable thereness constituted their identity as objects. In the new pieces, the grey areas transmute into something entirely different: metaphorical picture windows, suggesting among other things stormy seas and clouded heavens"; Craft 2000, p. 330.

237 Richard Field identified Johns's reference to Job (17:14). He believes that Johns encountered this passage in a letter from Larry Day in 1990. The version of the Book of Job from which Day copied this passage has yet to be identified; Field 1999, p. 21, 35 n. 11.

238 Cage 1964, p. 22.

239 Attributed to Beckett, recounted by Johns in "Jasper Johns: Take an Object. A Portrait: 1972–1990," 16mm film, directed by Hans Namuth and Judith Wechsler (1990).

240 *Zone* (1962; Kunsthaus Zürich) and other works dialogue the interaction between oil and encaustic on one surface. See *Study for "Wall Piece"* (1968–69; Collection of John and Kimiko Powers); Shapiro 1984, cat. no. 89.

241 Frank O'Hara wrote to Johns: "I think everyone should read all of Samuel Beckett"; Tone 1996, p. 165.

242 Pye 1990, p. 22, in *Writings* 1996, p. 256.

243 Weiss 2007a, p. 52.

244 Samuel Beckett, *The Unnamable* (Grove Press, 1958), p. 17.

245 Marden 1971, n.pag.

246 Robert Storr, *Gerhard Richter: Forty Years of Painting*, exh. cat. (Museum of Modern Art, New York, 2002), p. 56. "The earliest all-gray painting in Richter's oeuvre is a small-format townscape of 1968....That same year, Richter painted two more all-gray abstractions....In 1970 Richter embarked on a suite of four large-scale gray monochromes with fleshy, gestural surfaces, and also painted eleven other gray pictures in different, mostly, smaller formats....those completed in 1972 belonged to his Inpainting series, while the subsequent works were simply titled *Gray*. The next and largest group of gray paintings was made in 1974, and the final group—painted on aluminum and wood panels rather than on stretched canvases—was completed in 1976"; pp. 55–56.

247 See Richter's letter to Edy de Wilde, February 25, 1975, in Gerhard Richter, *The Daily Practice of Painting: Writings and Interviews, 1962–1993*, ed. Hans-Ulrich Obrist, trans. David Britt (MIT Press/Anthony d'Offay Gallery, 1995), pp. 82–83.

248 Buchloh in conversation with Harald Fricke, "A German Artist," *Deutsche Bank Art Magazine*, http://www.deutsche-bank-art.com/art/03/e/thema-achtgrau-buchloh.php.

249 Richter (note 246), p. 139. In the context of his own monochrome paintings, Richter has cited Robert Ryman, Brice Marden, Alan Charlton, and Yves Klein; ibid., p. 153.

Jasper Johns
Gray Matters

DOUGLAS DRUICK

JASPER JOHNS'S EARLIEST GRAY MONOCHROMES DATE TO 1956, the year after he completed *Flag* (1954–55; the Museum of Modern Art, New York), the first painting that he made after destroying his work to date, and that has been accorded the status of the first "Jasper Johns" canvas. Subsequently, the artist painted three monochromatic encaustics: in white (*White Flag*; 1955; the Metropolitan Museum of Art, New York), in green (*Green Target*; 1955; the Museum of Modern Art, New York), and in blue (*Tango*; 1955; Peter and Irene Ludwig Foundation, on loan to Ludwig Museum, Cologne). But once he began using gray tones in 1956, he largely abandoned all other colors but white for his monochromes. Gray became a Johns signature, its signatory properties imbricated in many of the issues and interests central to his practice.

Johns has spoken of colors as media, each possessing distinctive attributes. Just as he registers the variation in physical materials (oil, encaustic, lithography), so he does with colors: "When I used white and gray, there was a leap between them. When I used white and black, or green and red, I felt the difference between materials."[1] For Johns working in different media is working in "different situations," the material context in which the work is elaborated an essential constituent of meaning.[2] This approach recalls a tenet of Josef Albers's:

> . . . insight and skill depend on observation
> as well as on thought. And through manual work
> as through art, we realize that there is
> besides thinking in logical conclusions
> "thinking in situations,"
> which is just as necessary as thinking in numbers
> or figures or verbal terms.[3]

The intersection between observation and thought, seeing and knowing, is a central concern in Johns's art.[4]

Allying the medium of gray with that of encaustic, Johns created a particular situation in which to explore this intersection. In the late 1960s, looking back on his corpus of gray encaustics, the artist described the medium's particular utility:

> I used gray encaustic to avoid the color situation. The encaustic paintings were done in gray because to me this suggested a kind of literal quality that was unmoved or unmovable by coloration and thus avoided all the emotional and dramatic quality of color. Black and white is very leading. It tells you what to say or do. The gray encaustic paintings seemed to me to allow the literal qualities of the painting to predominate over any of the others.[5]

This positioning (and validation) of gray vis-à-vis spectral color on the one hand and black and white on the other stems from a historical discourse on color in Western culture, from Johns's particular moment and milieu, and from his abiding personal interest in issues of perception.

• • •

Medieval theologians were perhaps the first to identify color as problematic. At issue for church intellectuals was the nature of color, whether made of light or of matter.[6] Subscribers to the former view — chromophiles like the Abbot Suger in twelfth-century France — considered color to be the only element of the physical world that is both visible and immaterial and therefore believed it to be a manifestation of God. Hence, color could be deemed especially appropriate for use in church decoration, as Suger demonstrated when he commissioned the dazzling stained-glass windows for St.-Denis. However, chromophobes, among them Suger's contemporary Saint Bernard of Clairvaux, regarded color as material substance, a superficial covering over base matter — a vile, seductive mask that stimulates the senses and emotions. Because it thus distracted worshipers from thoughts of salvation, color was banned from Cistercian churches. This rejection of the worldly as incarnated by color — together with the Christian values of modesty and virtue and a spirit of abnegation — led to the black, white, and gray of religious habits.[7]

Such beliefs fueled the fashion for black clothing, in secular as well as religious society, that took hold following the Plague (1346–50). The proliferation of sumptuary laws and dress regulations throughout late medieval Europe signaled a moralizing trend that set the stage for the Protestant Reformation of the sixteenth century.[8] A parallel taste — for grisaille — had emerged in the visual arts of the late fourteenth and fifteenth centuries. The renunciation of polychromy and bright color, whether in painting or textile design, is an aspect of the general reaction against extravagant display that had already led to greater sobriety in the ecclesiastical realm.[9] An achromatic palette of black through gray to white seems to have had its first purposeful application in the hangings, liturgical objects, and paintings produced in observance of the penitential season of Lent; the colorless, gray representations evoked ashes and suggested a visual abstinence analogous to the customary fasting from foods and festivities.[10]

Chromoclasm paralleled iconoclasm in the sixteenth century. Protestant Reformers purged churches of both images and color, deeming offensive their appeal to the senses and their association with Catholic liturgy. For personal dress, an "honest," subdued palette dominated by white, gray, and black became standard. These signified humility and sobriety, echoing earlier codes that imposed drab colors on subordinates and the peasantry (hence "commoner's gray").[11] When Sir Isaac Newton's experiments with the prism led him to exclude black and white from the spectrum, science confirmed ideological distinctions in Western culture that would persist into the twentieth century.[12]

In aesthetics, as in theology, the question of color provoked disagreement. The relative virtues of *disegno* versus *colore*, debated since the Renaissance, became newly contentious in seventeenth-century France, when the "moderns" — the so-called "Rubenists" — began to challenge the dominant ideology of the Académie Royale de Peinture et de Sculpture (founded in 1648). In asserting the primacy of color as the "soul and ultimate achievement of painting," they countered the establishment, the "Poussinists," who maintained the supremacy of drawing. Governed by rules, transmittable through prescribed exercises, and judged according to set standards, drawing was the Académie's pedagogical foundation, considered to be the basis for abstract representation, spiritual in nature, and originating in thought.[13] Color, by contrast, "makes objects visible," in the words of Rubenist apologist Roger de Piles; it is the "part [of painting] full of charm and magic that knows so well how to deceive the eyes." Arguing the superiority of sight to touch, De Piles regarded the specifically visual component of painting, color, as superior to drawing, its tactile or "blind" aspect.[14] As Jacqueline Lichtenstein observed, drawing's partisans, in marshaling arguments against the Rubenists, rehearsed the moralizing distinction between the divine and the sensual established in medieval theology.[15] Thus painter and theorist Charles Le Brun, a founder of the Académie, argued that color "depends entirely on matter and is consequently less noble than drawing, which comes from the mind alone."[16] Unlike drawing, color could not be subjected to rules and therefore could not be taught; colorists were born and not made, with an arbitrariness that rendered color's seductive attractions and emotional appeal all the more dangerous from an academic point of view. Color, pronounced Le Brun, is "an ocean where many [painters] drown while trying to save themselves."[17]

The persistent question of the relative merits of color and *dessin*—the latter term including line and wash drawing as well as achromatic and monochrome painting—lies at the heart of a text critical to the development of early modern art: Charles Blanc's *Grammaire des arts du dessin*. Published in 1867 and translated into English within a decade, Blanc's book exerted a strong influence on Paul Gauguin, Vincent van Gogh, Georges Seurat, and other artists who came to maturity in the late nineteenth and early twentieth centuries. Blanc gendered the morally inflected debate, asserting that "drawing is the masculine sex of art, color the feminine sex. . . . Drawing must preserve its dominance over color. Otherwise, painting runs to its ruin; it will be lost by color like humanity was lost by Eve."[18] Color, feminized as nature, enchants the heart and senses, but requires reason—*dessin*—to express ideas.[19] (Johns, asked about the distinction between drawing and painting, responded, "I have always enjoyed drawings. In them, thought seems more concentrated, more suggestive.")[20]

Blanc's writing lent theoretical support to the fin-de-siècle deployment, by Symbolist artists like Odilon Redon, of monochrome as an antidote to Realism. Redon's early rejection of oil paint and color in favor of charcoal and chiaroscuro can be attributed to his desire to join the ranks of artists who were, as he put it, "thinkers as well as painters," such as Leonardo and Rembrandt. Jean-Baptiste Corot served as a more recent precedent, as his celebrated *Souvenir de Mortefontaine* (1864; Musée du Louvre, Paris) and other late landscapes, executed in a palette of silvery grays, thematize memory. A "fundamental *gray*," Redon wrote, distinguishes all masters.[21] His own drawn and lithographed images of a disembodied, free-floating eye focused heavenward (**FIG. 1**) signal a preoccupation with ocularity and, more specifically, with vision in terms of insight, imagination, and idea. Other contemporaries likewise sought to evoke interiority through a single-color palette: Eugène Carrière in his gray-brown landscapes and portraits; Pablo Picasso in his Blue Period works.[22]

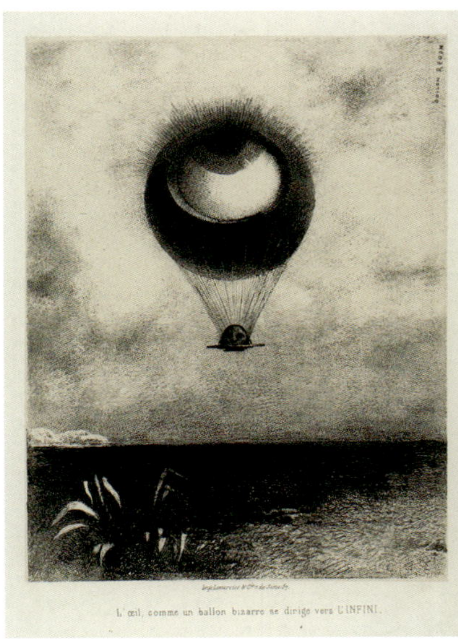

Fig. 1. Odilon Redon. *The Eye, Like a Strange Balloon Moves toward Infinity (L'oeil, comme un ballon bizarre se dirige vers l'infini)*, plate I from *To Edgar Allen Poe*, 1882. Lithograph in black on ivory chine affixed to white wove paper; image: 31.2 × 24.2 cm (12 ¼ × 9 9/16 in.), sheet: 45.3 × 34.9 cm (17 7/8 × 13 ¾ in.). The Art Institute of Chicago, Stickney Collection, 1920.1570.

For all its chromophobic bias, Blanc's book does include clear and extensive presentations of the latest findings in color theory. The very existence of scientific laws relating to color contradicted the belief that only drawing can be rationally understood and taught.[23] Thus, ironically, Blanc's book became a founding text for Neo-Impressionism. Key to the work of four Post-Impressionist masters—Paul Cézanne, Gauguin, Van Gogh, and Seurat—color became, by the turn of the twentieth century, a touchstone of vanguard art. The Analytical Cubism of Georges Braque and Picasso, with its dour palette of browns and grays, has been read as a repudiation of this tendency to place color at the center of formal and expressive innovation.[24] Similarly, Marcel Duchamp's early rejection of what he termed "retinal art" can be located within the context of longstanding debate and recent practice. In a television interview aired in early 1956, Duchamp maintained: "I consider that color is only a means of expression in painting and not an end. In other words, painting should not be exclusively retinal or visual; it should have to do with the gray matter, with our urge for understanding."[25] Johns, said to have first encountered Duchamp's writing and art in 1957, would observe: "[He] moved his work through the retinal boundaries which had been established with Impressionism into a field where language, thought and vision act upon one another"[26]—the field of "gray matter."

If, for Picasso and Duchamp in the early years of the century, the terms of the "color situation" had been set by Post-Impressionism, for Johns in the mid-1950s, the dominant practice was Abstract Expressionism. Robert Rauschenberg, whose close association with Johns began in 1954, recalled the two of them starting each day by having to "move out" from the movement's almost overpowering influence. Color was part of this. Rauschenberg would note that the Abstract Expressionists went so far as to assign "seriousness to certain colors."[27] Moreover, color featured in the new academicism resulting from Abstract Expressionist practice, with which both Rauschenberg and Johns consciously sought to break.[28] And although Rauschenberg described himself as a "pushover for color"—invoking the historical discourse of its seductions—he resisted it.[29]

Studying with Albers at Black Mountain College, Rauschenberg had learned that "if you thought one color was better than another you were just expressing a personal preference," which reflects the Abstract Expressionist ethos of self-revelation as art's final aim. In 1951, seeking to eliminate chromatic subjectivity, he made an initial monochrome series in white, followed by another using black enamel paint and newsprint. Of the latter, he would observe, "I was interested in getting complexity without their revealing much. In the fact that there was much to see but not much showing. I wanted to show that a painting could have the dignity of not calling attention to itself, that it could only be seen if you really looked at it." Rauschenberg subsequently explored a muted palette of what he termed "pedestrian color," associated with the experience of one's everyday environment, in which chromatically specific elements are perceived as a blurred average. He was developing what would be described as "the vernacular glance," a non-hierarchical mode of seeing the world. As the artist later put it, "It's possible that I discovered my originality through a series of self-imposed detours."[30]

Johns, who was Rauschenberg's junior in age and experience, held similar positions. Having tried and failed to operate like the Abstract Expressionists—collapsing personal identity and painting—Johns sought his own originality by means of "a constant negation of impulses."[31] He recalls that if he did something that reminded him of someone else's work, he would try to expunge it. Constantly on guard for influence, he has stated that his goal was to "[separate] myself from other artists, to clarify what I did as opposed to what I knew about what other people did." Johns has acknowledged "how hard it is to discard ideas or involvements that you already have, to come up with a different approach."[32] In the fall of 1954, he forced the issue by destroying his work to date.

On the tabula rasa of his new career, he created the now-mythic "first painting": *Flag* (1954–55; see fig. 5 in the essay by James Rondeau in this volume). He began the picture with enamel but completed it using a variant on the ancient technique of encaustic—painting with pigments in heated wax—which had been enjoying a modest revival among artists and art teachers since the 1930s.[33] Encaustic, which is applied warm and dries quickly as it cools, attracted Johns, like others before him who had been frustrated by the slow-drying properties of oil. The medium allowed him to work without pause and to preserve the character of each stroke and the "feeling for the time" between their consecutive applications, thus enhancing what he termed the picture's literal or object nature. Encaustic had another advantage in being largely unencumbered by associations with vanguard practice.[34] The medium (along with the image of the flag) quickly became a Johns signature. Rauschenberg would recognize Johns's proprietary claim: "I was very envious of his encaustic, I must admit, but too respectful ever to touch it."[35]

The motif of the American flag — "the old red, white, and blue" — allowed Johns to sidestep the "color situation" in *Flag*. His subsequent use, for the first Target paintings, of the three primary hues — red, yellow, and blue — was similarly an attempt at what Kirk Varnedoe termed a "found" palette, as "prelimited as the schema of a flag or target."[36] In a 1959 interview, Johns famously recounted that taking as subjects "things the mind already knows," like the American flag, freed him from the need to design and gave him room to "work on other levels," notably to convey that he "thought of a painting as a surface . . . [by] painting it in one color. . . ."[37] However, choosing the color — whether white for the first single-color Flag or green for the first monochrome Target — inevitably endangered the stance of chromatic impartiality, complicating what Leo Steinberg, apropos the artist's early images and palette, called his "refusal to advertise his subjective location."[38]

Fig. 2. *White Flag*, 1955. Encaustic and collage on canvas (three panels); 198.9 × 306.7 cm (78 5/16 × 120 in.). The Metropolitan Museum of Art, New York, Purchase, Lila Acheson Wallace, Reba and Dave Williams, Stephen and Nan Swid, Roy R. and Marie S. Neuberger, Louis and Bessie Adler Foundation Inc., Paula Cussi, Maria-Gaetana Matisse, The Barnett Newman Foundation, Jane and Robert Carroll, Eliot and Wilson Nolen, Mr. and Mrs. Derald H. Ruttenberg, Ruth and Seymour Klein Foundation Inc., Andrew N. Schiff, The Cowles Charitable Trust, The Merrill G. and Emita E. Hastings Foundation, John J. Roche, Molly and Walter Bareiss, Linda and Morton Janklow, Aaron I. Fleischman, and Linford L. Lougheed Gifts, and gifts from friends of the Museum; Kathryn E. Hurd, Denise and Andrew Saul, George A. Hearn, Arthur Hoppock Hearn, Joseph H. Hazen Foundation Purchase, and Cynthia Hazen Polsky and Leon B. Polsky Funds; Mayer Fund; Florene M. Schoenborn Bequest; Gifts of Professor and Mrs. Zevi Scharfstein and Himan Brown, and other gifts, bequests, and funds from various donors, by exchange, 1998.

In the same interview, Johns addressed the subjective location in which he envisioned his pictures: "Then I decided that looking at a painting should not require a special kind of focus like going to church. A picture ought to be looked at the same way you look at a radiator."[39] Suggestive here is the structure as well as the color of *Canvas* (1956; cat. no. 7), which consists of two stretched canvases, painted gray and affixed face to face so that they literally offer a "back side" to both the viewer and the wall.[40] The work reflects Johns's contention that at best "there is no difference" between the experience of looking at art and looking at everything else, that anything can sustain more or less "directed" visual attention — ideas consonant with Rauschenberg's but that Johns would develop differently.[41]

Canvas, one of Johns's first gray monochromes (see the interview by Nan Rosenthal in this volume), is among the early works which suggest (as the artist later put it) that they are "forms in space more readily than that they are 'windows.'"[42] In so saying, he invoked a metaphor dating back to the Renaissance, when linear perspective opened up a fictive, illusionistic world on the other side of the picture plane. But indeed walls, not windows, are more apt analogies for Johns's monochromes. He tells one anecdote about a visitor to his studio who leaned on *White Flag* (**FIG. 2**), failing to differentiate it from the white brick wall on which it hung; another of his own glimpse from a passing car of a wall painted to look like flagstones, which prompted a series of works incorporating this motif; and a third quoting Samuel Beckett's explanation of why he chose Johns's etching featuring flagstones as the endpaper for their collaboration, *Foirades/Fizzles*: "No matter which way you turn you always come up against a stone wall."[43] (The motif recurs in Johns's recent *Beckett*, cat. no. 138.) Johns has acknowledged that a viewer facing one of his works might have a sense of "nothingness, when in fact there is a great deal to be seen. One can look at a wall and have a similar experience of nothing of interest or one can find great interest in looking at an area of wall, or at anything."[44]

According to Leonardo, whose *Treatise on Painting* influenced Johns, an artist can "stimulate the mind to various discoveries [by looking] at walls splashed with a number of stains or stones of various mixed colors." This exercise prompts creative invention by engaging the eye in concert with the imagination to discern latent imagery—battles, faces, landscapes—in the textural irregularities and chromatic shifts of the wall's ostensibly neutral surface.[45] For Redon, Leonardo's exercise prompted a literal practice in making the charcoal drawings he called *noirs*; for Johns it contributed to a conviction that "at every point in nature there is something to see" and the correlate ambition to make work that "contains similar possibilities for the changing focus of the eye."[46]

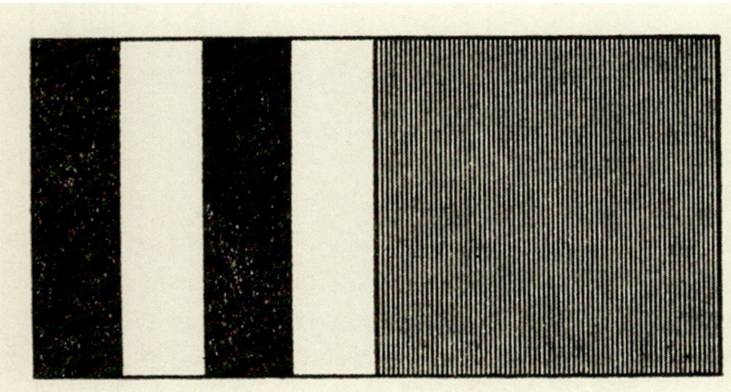

Fig. 3. Color diffusion, from Faber Birren, *Color Dimensions* (Crimson Press, 1934), p. 49, with the text: "At the left of the illustration the black and white strips have vivid contrast because they are well isolated in area and the eye can readily distinguish their total difference. At the right of the illustration when the white and black are split up into fine lines—forcing the eye to confuse them—all contrast is lost and the effect is a dull gray."

The complex surface variegations Johns created through the use of encaustic in conjunction with newspaper may be considered in this context. He liked the fact that the newspaper fragments afforded one "a different kind of information... that had nothing to do with the activity" of the painted surface, introducing an "intellectually different focus" into the viewing experience. By involving reading in addition to looking, these works engage the eye and the mind, vision and thought—and memory. Johns has suggested that the newspaper collage elements can engender what he called a "kinetic response" insofar as "what you're used to doing with a newspaper is turning [the pages]."[47] This response is elicited and thwarted in *Newspaper* (1957; cat. no. 8), in which facing pages are enveloped in a veil of warm-toned gray encaustic, the transient rendered permanent like an insect caught in amber. Combining encaustic with newspaper so that the wax medium obscures, partially reveals, and sometimes leaves headlines, passages of text, and bits of imagery tantalizingly evident, Johns realized his intention to create changing focal possibilities. Attention shifts as the viewer alternates between moving in for a close reading of the surface and its texts and pulling back to take in the painting as a whole. This is the restless, active attentiveness that the artist evoked when asked about the mood he sought in his pictures: "Mentally my preference would be the mood of keeping your eyes open and looking, ... without any constricted viewpoint."[48]

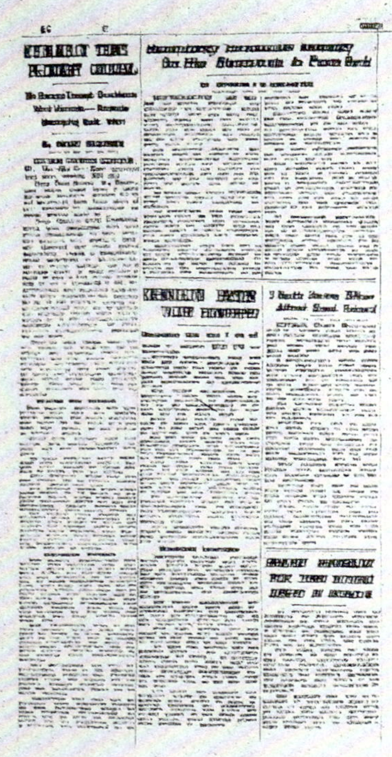

Fig. 4. Typofacture exercise, from Josef Albers, *Search Versus Re-Search* (Trinity College Press, 1969), p. 64, fig. 28, with the caption: "Relative to our *matière* studies, which aim at a special training of the hand, we show here only studies of so-called typofacture, that is, the overall appearance of printed text. Without making the individual letter forms or word groups, the hand movement makes marks which produce the impression of this special type of printed order."

Newspaper, as Johns incorporated it in encaustic paintings of 1955, may have factored into his privileging of gray monochrome beginning the following year. The farther from normal reading distance we see newspaper, the greater the tendency for the eye to confuse the distinction of letters and ground and to perceive the pattern of small units of black letters on white paper as an overall gray field. Covering newspaper with a thin skin of translucent white encaustic, notably in canvases such as *White Flag*, Johns facilitated this optical mixing or "color diffusion" (see **FIG. 3**).

Rauschenberg talked, vis-à-vis his 1951–52 black paintings, of newsprint providing a foundational "gray map of words," on which "even the first stroke in the painting had its own unique position."[49] This approach was possibly a legacy of the "typofacture" exercise that Albers assigned students in his "matière" class at Black Mountain College: to study the appearance of a commercially printed page of text and then simulate the letters by inventing an abstract mark and applying it row after row to produce drawings that had the character of (and appeared to the inattentive as) actual printed text (see **FIG. 4**). Like other drawing exercises in the class—which Rauschenberg took—the "typofacture" assignment reflected Albers's interests in commonplace materials, in perception and illusion, as well as in the idea that a drawing could develop incrementally, as it were, from the inside out.[50]

This inside-out approach is pertinent not only to Rauschenberg's gray-map metaphor but also to Johns's discussion of starting out by making marks responsive to the "elements which you use to begin the painting"; as the painting evolves, these elements "can be reinforced, can be made almost a subject matter, or can be obliterated. Usually they are both partly reinforced and partly obliterated."[51] *Gray Alphabets* (1956; cat. no. 55), which takes as its subject the building blocks of the written word as incorporated in its collaged newspaper substructure, plays with this idea as well as with the graying of the black-on-white printed elements when seen from the distance required to take in the full canvas. This was not only Johns's first alphabet painting but also the first in which gray has a titular presence.[52]

After *Canvas* and *Gray Alphabets*, Johns produced a series of gray pictures that foreground literalness while provocatively engaging the viewer in close looking and complex associational response. *Drawer* (1957; cat. no. 9) deploys a physical conceit similar to that found in *Canvas*, in this case arguably concretizing the motif of the table drawer from Cézanne's *Cardplayers* (1892; the Metropolitan Museum of Art, New York), which Johns saw in the artist's retrospective at the Metropolitan in 1952. Inserting a piece of wood with two attached knobs into a specially created aperture in a shaped canvas, Johns created a reasonable facsimile of a loose-fitting drawer. This construction makes reference to Cézanne's renowned ability to sustain compositional tension between the flatness of the picture plane and the illusion of space behind. While shutting down the trope of the canvas as window, *Drawer*—for all its presence as an object—is a trompe l'oeil nonetheless, visually proposing a functional use and a structural space behind the surface that do not exist.[53]

The, also of 1957 (cat. no. 11), explores painting's object status through language. Like most of his generation, Johns studied English grammar in school; he absorbed its rules and values precision (he would criticize Rauschenberg's grammatical errors).[54] In the English language, "the" functions primarily as a definite article, a word preceding and modifying a noun, a "thing" (or person or place). While the indefinite articles "a" and "an" are used before singular nouns to refer to any member of a group (*a* cat), the definite article "the" is used before singular and plural nouns to refer to a particular member of a group (*the* cat). In Johns's picture, "The" modifies an actual, immediately tangible thing, encaustic on a stretched canvas, not "*a* painting" or "painting" as an activity but rather "*the* painting" on which Johns painted the word. It recalls his concern with "the actual fact of a painting being an object, whatever you did to it, rather than making a statement on the front of it. I always wanted to be reminded that the canvas was there."[55]

Reminders are insistent in *Tennyson* (1958; cat. no. 12), which speaks eloquently to the complexity of Johns's anti-metaphoric strategies. The work comprises two narrow, vertically oriented canvases on separate stretchers, joined together and partially covered by another piece of canvas, pulled up from the bottom and folded back down (see the essays by James Rondeau and Kelly Keegan and Kristin Lister in this volume). Along the lower edge of the extra piece of canvas, in roman capital letters similar to those used to inscribe monuments, Johns painted the name of the Victorian era's most popular poet: TENNYSON literally extends across the stretcher bars. Just as he had literally constructed Cézanne's drawer, here Johns appears to have diagrammed the title and theme of one of Tennyson's most anthologized works, "Crossing the Bar" (1889), a sixteen-line meditation on mortality. Using the image of putting out to sea as a metaphor for his own death, the poet closed with the hope that he "will see my Pilot face to face / When I have crossed the bar."[56] But for all that Johns's *Tennyson* seems to take aim at the self-important grandiloquence commonly attributed to Victorian poetry and Abstract Expressionism, it remains a profoundly moving work. Steinberg, writing in 1962, imagined its construction in terms of the performance of a funeral rite, later comparing its form to an "upright stele."[57] The same year, the sculptor Dan Flavin, many of whose works are explicitly religious, invoked the emblematic nature of *Tennyson* in the context of one of his light icons.[58] With its combination of irony and elegy, *Tennyson* implies that, while the feelings articulated in "Crossing the Bar" are still with us, the rhetoric once used to express them is no longer viable.[59] It is hard to imagine that the painting would have had comparable affective impact in any other monochrome but gray.

This raises the issue of Abstract Expressionism's transcendental longings, addressed in Johns's stated interest in desacralizing the experience of looking at pictures.[60] His desire to shift from rose windows to radiators (or targets), as noted above, was fueled by a more personal, reformatory passion acknowledged in later comments on the destruction of his early works: "It wasn't a judgment on them. . . . It was more like reforming my identity"; it was "an attempt to destroy some idea about myself. . . . It gets to sound very religious, which I don't like, but it's true."[61] He followed this iconoclastic vehemence with the chromoclasm of gray.

Traditional associations of achromatic monochrome retained currency, as evidenced in the reception of two 1963–64 exhibitions devoted to black and white in which Johns participated.[62] Reviewing both shows, Barbara Rose wrote of the quality of asceticism implied by the "conscious rejection of what is ordinarily available" to a painter, namely color, with its inherent nuances of feeling. What struck Max Kozloff was an "ethos of deprivation" and a "Puritanical air."[63] Johns has been characterized in similar terms: Rauschenberg would recall that his own "sensual excessiveness" jarred the "intellectual" Johns; Rose saw Johns's work as a critique of hedonism and specifically of the hedonistic color of 1960s art.[64] Echoing and updating Redon's genealogy, she located Johns in the tradition of Leonardo, Poussin, Cézanne, and Duchamp: that of the "painter-philosopher" engaged with intellectual concerns.[65]

Interviewed by *Time* magazine in 1965 for a popular piece entitled "Pop's Dada," Duchamp reiterated that he had given up painting decades earlier because it was "too retinal. It didn't go beyond the eye." He went on to observe of recent art: "Abstract expressionism was not intellectual at all for me. It is under the yoke of the retinal; I see no grey matter there. Jasper Johns, one of our lights, and Rauschenberg are much more than that; they have intelligence . . . an original imagination."[66] Johns would in turn pay public tribute to "one of this century's pioneer artists" upon Duchamp's death three years later. Of Duchamp's *The Bride Stripped Bare by Her Bachelors, Even (The Large Glass)* (1915–23; Philadelphia Museum of Art), which Johns had traveled to Philadelphia to see in 1957, he would write: "Its cross-references of sight and thought, the changing focus of the eyes and mind, give fresh sense to the time and space we occupy, negate any concern with art as transportation. No end is in view in this fragment of a new perspective."[67]

The terms are precisely those of Johns's own stated ambitions in producing work "largely concerned with relations between seeing and knowing," but his solutions were different.[68] Even before encountering Duchamp, Johns had sought to engage "gray matter" by means that included avoiding color's appeal to the emotions. But he had also wanted to steer clear of dichotomous situations such as, literally, black and white. (A sketchbook note of around 1964 reads: "Avoid a polar situation," immediately following another cautionary: "Beware of the body / & the mind.")[69] Seeking to bridge the dualism of the retinal and the intellectual, Johns held that, in painting, "the way ideas are conveyed is through the way it looks and I see no way to avoid that, and I don't think

Duchamp can either."[70] Unlike Duchamp, Johns had no intention of quitting painting. Engaging with the older artist's work in 1957 affirmed his commitment to painting as a means of exploring the intersection between looking and thinking, an investigation already underway in his color and monochrome Flags.[71] Johns observed that at first people tended to regard the red, white, and blue version "as a flag, and not to take it for a picture," while they saw the painterly monochrome image in white "as a picture and not as a flag." He allowed that "It is the gray zone between these two extremes that I'm interested in — the area [where it] is neither a flag nor a painting. It can be both and still the neither."[72] With the metaphor of the gray zone, Johns posits a continuum in place of a dichotomy between knowing and seeing. As for the gray version (cat. no. 23), Johns allowed that it was perhaps "difficult to determine as a flag," but a viewer's prior knowledge of his involvement with the image would provide a clue to its recognition. "That interests me — the degree to which what we know affects what we see."[73]

Duchamp's example clearly had an impact on the development of Johns's thinking.[74] But he is impatient with attempts to trace influences, commenting that "what is of interest is in the 'air' from which all art comes."[75] When Johns first began working with Rauschenberg, in 1954, the ideas in circulation included those of John Cage, who spoke of art in terms of active discovery and "purposeless play," and who urged artists (and participants) to deemphasize personality and invite chance. Before this, Johns had evidently found stimulus for his interests through the reading he pursued in place of formal studies.[76] Salient to his autodidactic program was *Scientific American*, a long-established monthly reporting progress in industry that was reinvented in 1948 (the year Johns moved to New York) to occupy the middle ground between specialized scientific publications and popular illustrated magazines. The new *Scientific American* aimed to bring the latest findings in pure and applied science to a non-technical audience and, more specifically, to explain new advances and their implications with reference to the discipline's history, philosophy, and method.[77] In many contexts, *Scientific American* put forth the idea that progress depends not only on research, but also on the ability to extricate oneself from ingrained habits of thinking, including the "ancient verbal and metaphysical swamps" that perpetuated binary oppositions such as "mind versus matter."[78]

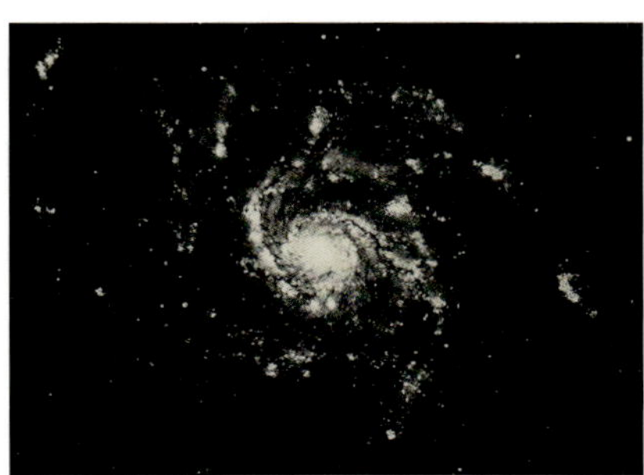

Fig. 5. Photograph of galaxy M 101, from Freeman J. Dyson, "Energy in the Universe," *Scientific American* 225, 3 (Sept. 1971), p. 54.

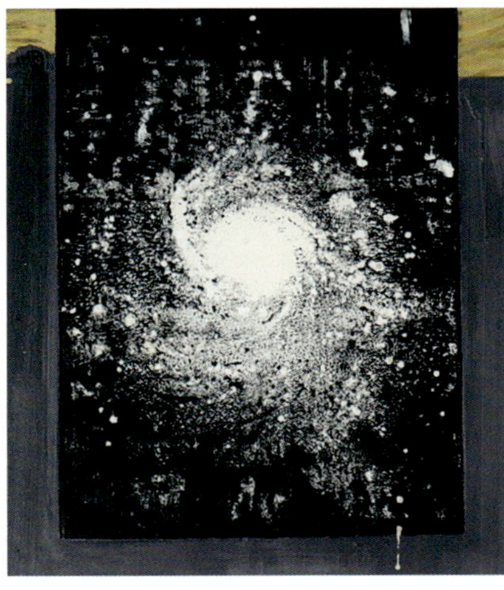

Fig. 6. Detail of *Bridge* (1997, cat. no. 128).

Johns was reading *Scientific American* by the time he was in the army (1951–52),[79] his interests seemingly as wide-ranging as the periodical's contents. He found certain illustrations compelling and subsequently useful. Barbara Rose connected the Crosshatch pattern that Johns began using in 1972 to diagrams in *Scientific American* explaining the theory of visual clustering.[80] Years later the artist would incorporate into his work (cat. no. 125) a drawing by a schizophrenic child from a 1952 article by Bruno Bettelheim and photographs of spiral galaxies that featured regularly in articles from 1948 onward (compare FIGS. 5 and 6 and see cat. nos. 126–28).[81] Most immediately relevant to the artist's early and abiding interests, however, were articles dealing with creativity, perception, and the certainty we attach to seeing — a leitmotif being our tendency to "mistake familiarity for understanding."[82]

Discussions of the late 1940s on Isaac Newton and Albert Einstein advanced several concepts pertinent to Johns's work and thinking: that great ideas emerge from the "common cauldron of intellectual activity" rather than from original recipes; that play is an aspect of creative discovery; that invention involves discernment, the choice of useful combinations, and the elimination of the useless; and that freedom of imagination depends on the realization that long-accepted ideas are not sacred, even in arenas

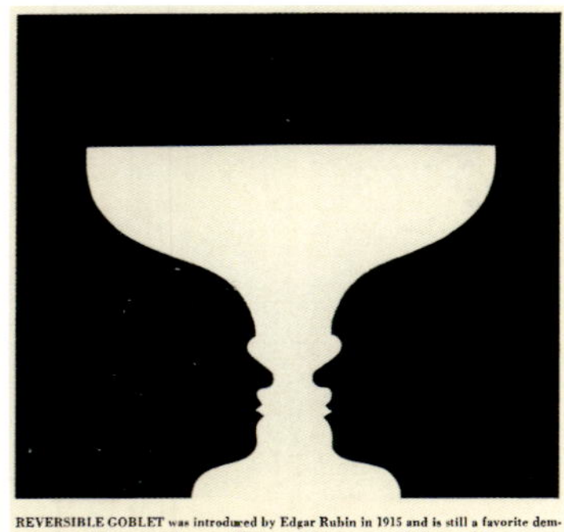

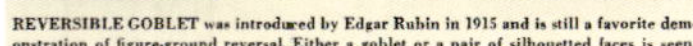

REVERSIBLE GOBLET was introduced by Edgar Rubin in 1915 and is still a favorite demonstration of figure-ground reversal. Either a goblet or a pair of silhouetted faces is seen.

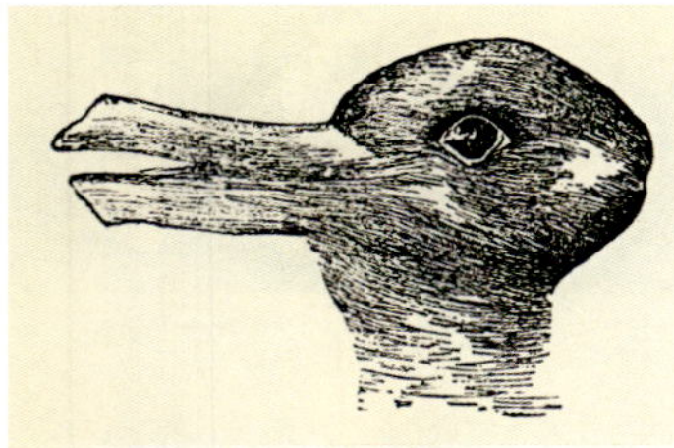

RABBIT-DUCK FIGURE was used in 1900 by psychologist Joseph Jastrow as an example of rival-schemata ambiguity. When it is a rabbit, the face looks to the right; when it is a duck, the face looks to the left. It is difficult to see both duck and rabbit at the same time.

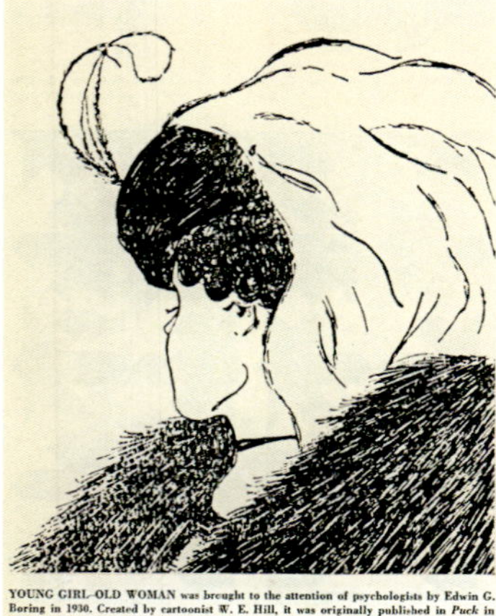

YOUNG GIRL–OLD WOMAN was brought to the attention of psychologists by Edwin G. Boring in 1930. Created by cartoonist W. E. Hill, it was originally published in *Puck* in 1915 as "My Wife and My Mother-in-law." The young woman's chin is the old woman's nose.

Figs. 7–9. Three ambiguous figures Johns employed beginning in the 1970s, from Fred Attneave, "Multistability in Perception," *Scientific American* 225, 6 (Dec. 1971), pp. 64, 66. Each image can be read one of two ways based on how the brain organizes the information in the picture. The possible readings for an image can only be recognized one at a time, never simultaneously.

such as atomic physics, where determinism and causality have ceded their authority to chance.[83] Articles on dreaming as a form of intelligence suggested an alternate framework in which to consider the connections between ideas and images.[84] An essay on the creative process of the intellect by mathematician Henri Poincaré (a source for Duchamp) similarly discussed the gift of intuition and the ways in which unconscious work is possible and fruitful only if preceded and followed by periods of conscious application. A creative individual, Poincaré posited, can be "present as his own unconscious work."[85] These and other articles of the period provide a context for understanding Johns's account of his first *Flag*. Initially, he attributed his use of the motif to an unconscious intuitive affinity; subsequently, he explained that he had acted on a dream of painting a flag, "the unconscious thought . . . accepted by my consciousness gracefully."[86]

Johns is deeply interested "in the idea of sight, in the use of the eye . . . in how we see and why we see the way we do."[87] Of singular relevance here are the many articles in *Scientific American* devoted to recent experiments in perception which, taken together, establish the idea that what we perceive does not directly correspond to reality, being instead a subtle blend of the external world and the lessons of our experience.[88] New scientific evidence supported the old Arabian adage that "the eye is blind to what the mind does not see": we see what we know; we don't look carefully; learning to see the world is a skill that begins in infancy and continues throughout our lives; seeing is as much a matter of experience as of physiology and as such is based on assumptions; we see what we believe we are looking at.[89]

Another thread running through the articles is that perception is subjective; our mental pictures are our own, neither shared by others nor by the objects themselves. If two people do not *look for* the same thing, they do not *see* the same thing. To put it another way, no two people live in exactly the same world, for no two are precisely identical in sense perception. Nonetheless, habit breeds inattentiveness. To see the world afresh involves close and conscious scrutiny, undertaken with the paradoxical aim of casting certainty into doubt. As one writer explained, "We enlarge our knowledge by making new comparisons, by looking about, as one might say, with an innocent eye. . . . In science and art . . . it is surprising how much progress results from merely cocking the head, changing the angle of view and uncovering unsuspected similarities."[90] In an ongoing cycle, new certainties yield to fresh doubts, requiring us to change our notions about the world as well as our verbal and visual means of representing it.

The lines of inquiry traced in *Scientific American* resonate with many of Johns's statements over the years. He has frequently distinguished between merely seeing and truly observing and expressed his interest in painting "things the mind already knows," things that are "seen and not looked at, not examined." He has asked how "life experience" affects what we see and has spoken of working in such a way as to create "doubt" and to make people "see something new." He has evoked the "novelty" of giving up what we know and of coming to know something we did not, advocating constant attentive looking.[91]

Within the general creative stimulus that his reading provided, specific instances can be identified. Richard Shiff, in a discussion of Johns's interest in questioning visual logic, traced the sources and implications of a notebook entry (c. 1960) in which the artist reminded himself to "find Scientific American" articles dealing with mirror imagery, parity, and anti-matter.[92] Johns himself described how his early "mannerism" of leaving a zone of largely untouched canvas at the bottom of his paintings accrued meaning when he subsequently read an article "in some popular science magazine" about the psychological interpretation of space.[93]

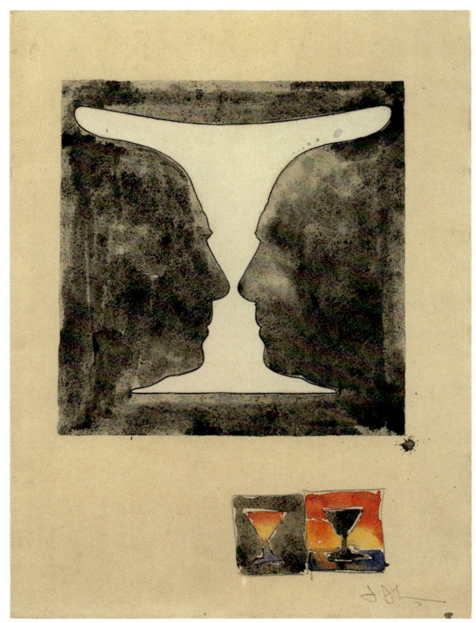

Fig. 10. *Sketch for Cup 2 Picasso*, 1971. Watercolor and graphite pencil on paper; 51.4 × 39.4 cm (20 ¼ × 15 ½ in.). Collection of the artist. Johns was invited by the Museum of Modern Art, New York, to make a print celebrating Picasso's ninetieth birthday. This drawing was the starting point for two lithographs of 1972 and 1973.

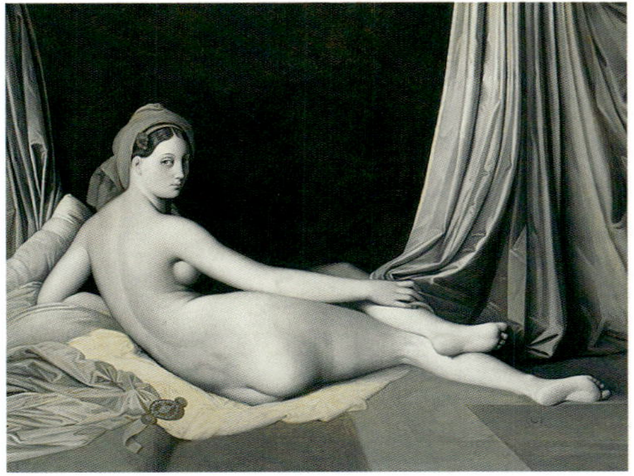

Fig. 11. Jean-Auguste-Dominique Ingres and workshop. *Odalisque in Grisaille*, 1824/34. Oil on canvas; 83.2 × 109.2 cm (32 ¾ × 43 in.). The Metropolitan Museum of Art, New York, Catharine Lorillard Wolfe Collection, Wolfe Fund, 1938.

As part of his interest in the psychological interpretation of visual data, Johns is especially fascinated with optical illusions, which set up the possibility "that something can be seen in two different ways" and raise the question "whether seeing it one way necessarily obliterates seeing it the other way."[94] A *Scientific American* article of 1971 entitled "Multistability in Perception" features the so-called ambiguous figures—the Rubin reversible goblet (FIG. 7), the duck/rabbit (FIG. 8), and the young girl/old woman (FIG. 9)—that "spontaneously shift in their principal aspect when . . . looked at steadily." Because these figures provide two possible representations that are quite different but about equally good, by whatever criteria employed by the perceptual system, the viewer will "lock in" or "stabilize" with one and then the other. More than an anomaly or a curiosity, this phenomenon points to issues of visual familiarity and learning, principles of ambiguity, and the physiology of perception (neural fatigue being one explanation for the spontaneous shift in one's reading of the representation).[95] Such imagery stimulated Johns's interest in "that aspect of seeing or knowing . . . [that] offers equal access to two possibilities" and desire "to create an image that when looked at becomes something else." Johns's late 1971 watercolor incorporating the Rubin goblet (FIG. 10) seems an immediate response to the article, published in December. While he adapted the motif at this moment to meet a specific need, it would appear (in different forms) in subsequent works, as would the duck/rabbit and the young girl/old woman (see FIG. 10 and cat. nos. 117 and 118).[96]

"Not knowing exactly" is a condition that Johns has said "moves one to see life in an ambiguous way."[97] This interest would seem to contribute to his interest in grisaille, which constitutes a literal gray zone. Originally associated with abstention from color, as noted above, grisaille early on assumed another role in facilitating the reproduction of unique works of art by professional printmakers for widespread dissemination. With the introduction in the nineteenth century of photography and photomechanical reproduction, artists took up grisaille to avoid the mistranslations of hue into value that were inevitable prior to the perfection of panchromatic film: a work executed in a palette of black through white permitted accurate photographic capture and translation into ink via photomechanical printing methods.[98] Just as earlier painters made grisaille translations of works in color to guide professionals working in the traditional black-and-white media of engraving, etching, and lithography, now they did so to serve the rotogravure, halftone, and offset processes. The burgeoning of the black-and-white press thus imparted a new valence to grisaille in the twentieth century, as reflected in its most celebrated exemplar, Picasso's *Guernica* (1937; Museo Reina Sofía, Madrid), once described as a "systematic metaphor of tabloid photography,"[99] which would later feature centrally in Pop Art.

Johns has said he likes seeing his own works in reproduction.[100] His delight in discovering in the Metropolitan Museum of Art's collection the grisaille translation of J.-A.-D. Ingres's *Grande Odalisque* (FIG. 11)[101] possibly factored into his idea, in the early 1960s, to paint a gray monochrome version of Cézanne's *The Bather* (c. 1885; see fig. 8 in the essay by Richard Shiff in this volume). The project, never realized, was tied up with his admiration for the picture's "synesthetic quality that gives it great sensuality—[and] makes looking equivalent to touching."[102] Johns thought a grisaille version would underscore this dimension, the absence of color reducing the optical in favor of the tactile.[103] His reasoning recalls De Piles in the seventeenth century dissociating *dessin* from sight—color and light—and relating it to touch. Also pertinent in this context is De Piles's illustration of the point with the story of a blind sculptor explaining his ability to execute wax portraits of remarkable verisimilitude: "I see nothing; my eyes are at my fingertips."[104]

Seeing and touching are thematized in the image of the target: hand and eye coordination are key in the act of taking aim and attempting to score a bull's

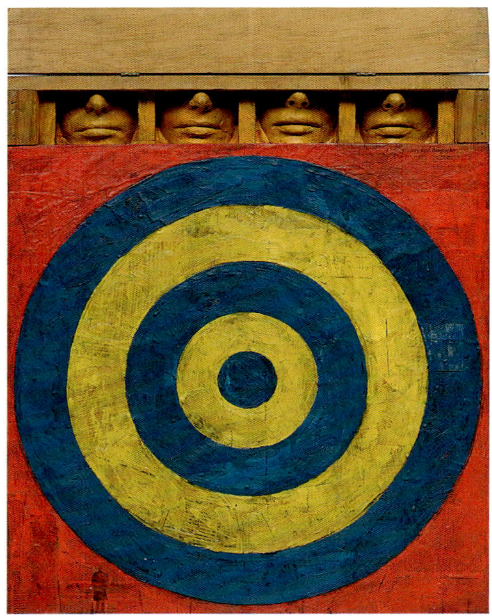

Fig. 12. *Target with Four Faces*, 1955. Encaustic on newspaper and cloth over canvas surmounted by four tinted-plaster faces in wood box with hinged front; overall, with box open, 85.3 × 66 × 7.6 cm (33 5/8 × 26 × 3 in.). The Museum of Modern Art, New York, gift of Mr. and Mrs. Robert C. Scull.

eye by penetrating, or blinding, the target's pupilar center. Johns's *Target with Plaster Casts* (1955; Collection of David Geffen) combines painting with plaster casts of various body parts that reference senses other than sight. In *Target with Four Faces* (FIG. 12), of the same year, Johns incorporated casts again; this time of four faces only, each cut off below the eyes.[105] Set into squat boxes, they appear as if blindfolded, recalling Redon's figurations of sightless insight and dream (FIG. 13). Allusion to Redon seems direct in a 1958 *Target* drawing (cat. no. 44) featuring an emphatic black center highly suggestive of the pupil of an eye.[106] Johns used this drawing as the model for one of his first lithographs (1960; see cat. no. 45), and the coupling of the motif and the medium for which Redon became famous seems a nod to the earlier artist, whom Duchamp also admired.[107] In the gray encaustic and Sculp-metal Targets (cat. nos. 41, 42, and 43), Johns combined pronounced surface textures and an achromatic palette to court an almost antiretinal tactility, thwarting ready visual apprehension and causing viewers to work harder to get the image in their sights.

• • •

Questioned in 1990 whether his early predilection for the achromatic was influenced by black-and-white mass media—whether newspaper, photography, or television—Johns replied that he did not remember but imagined "it was something more subjective than that."[108] Connected to his overall interest in questioning what Rose termed "the relativity of perception from a psychological, emotional, as well as optical point of view," this notion of the subjective finds echo in mid-century color theory.[109]

The subjective dimension of color perception is a recurring theme in the texts of the period on principles and practical application of color. First-year students at New York's Parsons School of Design, like Johns, took classes in the subject that drew on the holdings of the school's library, including books such as Faber Birren's *Color Dimensions*. In his popularizing volume, Birren stated that "the average color problem is a matter of psychological and visual judgment and is more concerned with the result of stimulation than with the nature of light itself."[110] Variations on the theme of color as subjectively and psychologically experienced, culturally and individually inflected are sounded in other instructional volumes.[111] But while the consensus was that "psychology knows more about the *sensation* of color" than physics or chemistry, authors also generally conceded that the human experience of color—a complex amalgam of seeing, feeling, and sensing, as well as associating and remembering—was imperfectly understood and still "a subject of active debate."[112]

At least one contemporary text gave painting students the assignment of "sizing up" different colors and one's subjective reaction to them in preparation for choosing a palette best fitted to "mood and purpose."[113] However, the literature assumed certain normative responses. Recent experiments with children considered too young to have absorbed cultural influences had yielded evidence supporting the notion that love of color is instinctive, as natural as the inclination to be more cheerful "on bright, colorful days than when the sky is gray."[114] Michael Crichton made a point of Johns's exceptional nature with an anecdote: "[Johns] came to California for a week and the weather was bad. A friend drove him to the airport and apologized for the gray and gloomy weather. 'That's all right,' he said, 'Gray is my favorite color.'"[115]

According to the psycho-diagnostic literature of the 1930s, '40s, and '50s frequently cited in color-theory texts, this inclination carries specific meaning. It was generally acknowledged that color has an effect on the emotions and that reaction to it is highly subjective, dependent on individual nature. While attempts to correlate color choice with personality might differ interpretively regarding specific color predilection (say red or blue), diagnosticians, including Max Lüscher and Hermann Rorschach, concurred that "normal persons" tend to favor the primaries and secondaries. A partiality for achromatism — for white, black, and gray over color — suggested psychological disturbance in children as well as adults.[116] Among the latter, predilections for black, white, and gray were regarded to be seldom "choices of the heart" but rather indications of the imposition of reason over passion, of individual will upon inborn traits. This was considered to be especially true of gray. In a particularly explicit formulation, Birren maintained that the "choice of gray may identify a person who has practically rebuilt his or her character. No matter what the primary color preference may be, the secondary selection of gray exposes the fact that the person has taken hold of life and attempted to regulate and adjust it."[117]

This characterization of gray can be traced to the traditional Western view of its representing an equivocal zone between the symbolic extremities of black and white, signifiers of darkness and light, of despair and hope. A blend of both and the midpoint on a sliding scale, gray indicated melancholy and tempered optimism, and as such was the color of *demi-deuil*, or "half-mourning" in the Victorian era.[118] Mid-twentieth-century color theorists continued to regard gray as a compromise between the negativity of black and the sublimity of white, but lacking the assertiveness of either.[119] Dutch psychologist Benjamin Kouwer reached some relevant conclusions based on an experiment in which subjects sorted cards printed with words into boxes labeled with color names. This matching exercise was designed to reveal the operation of conventional color symbolisms and associations, and their interaction with subjectivity. Gray turned out to be among the colors most frequently selected, particularly for such words as "boredom," "discouragement," "past," "sorrow," "theory," "business (things)," and "worry."[120] Kouwer traced gray's associations to familiar sayings and conceptions that share a subjective common denominator based on their difference from either black or white, both of which derive "specific force" from their antithetical relationship. Absent the "extreme significance" of black and white, Kouwer observed that, in "the case of gray... nothing remains but the aspects of neutrality, of indifference, of colorlessness."[121] Emotionally equidistant from the strong appeal of colors or black and white, gray is linked to "affective neutrality—the disciplined capacity to postpone immediate gratification," a quality deemed critical to scientific work and viewed as an attribute of "ascetic Protestantism.... [and] persons with a childhood experience of affectional frustration."[122] The color-theory books available during Johns's student days similarly refer to the "rationalism of gray," while diagnostically linking a preference for it with depression, introversion, and repression.[123]

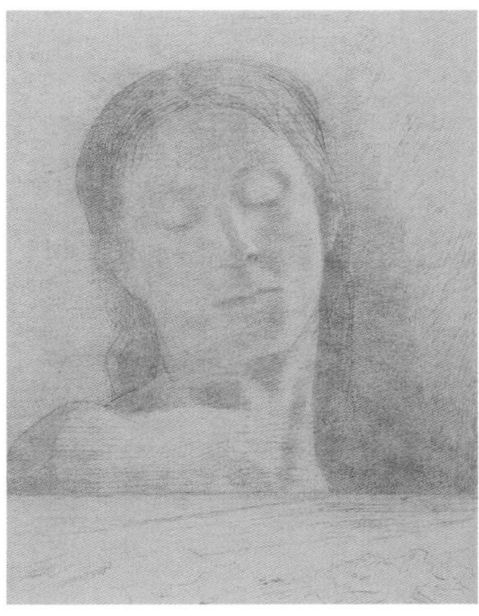

Fig. 13. Odilon Redon. *Closed Eyes (Yeux clos)*, 1890. Lithograph in green-gray on cream chine affixed to ivory wove paper; image: 26.3 × 19.8 cm (10 3/8 × 7 3/16 in.), sheet: 44.3 × 31.5 cm (17 1/2 × 12 7/16 in.). The Art Institute of Chicago, Stickney Collection, 1920.1672.

Johns's view of black and white as too "leading" and his related partiality for gray were informed by such current views, which are likewise echoed in critical responses to the "Black and White" exhibitions of 1963–64. Kozloff talked of black and white as achromatic "absolutes"; Rose saw dramatic intention and the allusion to "some Manichean opposition" in black-and-white paintings by Hans Hofmann and Jackson Pollock.[124] Such traditional symbolisms likewise informed Rauschenberg's inscription "the lily white" on an early white painting, as well the response of some contemporaries to his black series as negative.[125] The oppositional dynamic altered, as Rose observed, with the introduction of gray: more specifically, the perceived intention shifted to the ironic in the case of Johns's gray paintings, in which "the absence of color constantly evokes the presence of color."[126] The sense of an absent presence in the monochromes, intensified by the tantalizing traces of primary and secondary colors Johns often incorporates into or buries under the gray field (see the essays by James Rondeau and Kelly Keegan and Kristin Lister in this volume), contributes to a feeling of what Varnedoe termed "willed emotive shut-down."[127]

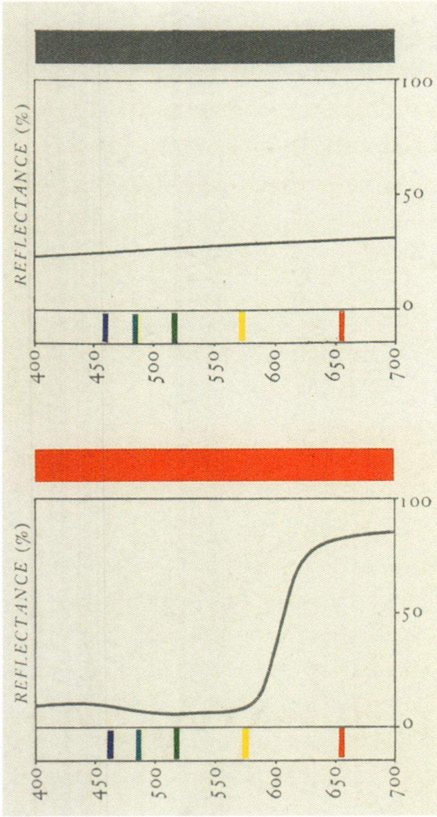

Fig. 14. Spectral reflectance of gray and red surfaces, from Interchemical Corporation, *A Series of Monographs on Color*, vol. 2, *Color as Light* (The Research Laboratories of the International Printing Ink Corporation, 1935), p. 13. "Gray materials generally have a uniform reflectance throughout the spectrum; the higher the reflectance, the lighter the gray. Brilliant colors are usually those which have a high reflectance in part of the spectrum and a low reflectance elsewhere."

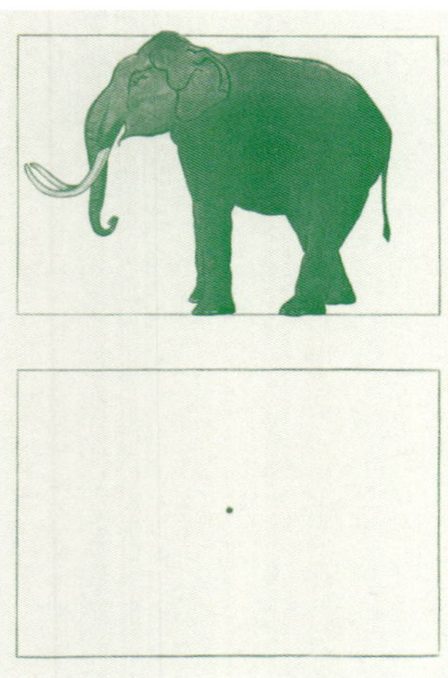

Fig. 15. Image and afterimage, from Jacques-Henri Bustanoby, *Principles of Color and Color Mixing* (McGraw-Hill, 1947), pl. 10. The motif here (a green elephant that generates a pink complement) alludes to the expression "seeing pink elephants," a euphemism for drunken hallucinations, thus introducing other aspects of subjectivity to the discussion.

Johns has acknowledged an awareness of "psychological tests showing that people who prefer gray are more emotionally repressed than people who prefer other colors."[128] And his comments about his early work have fed this perception; he has stated, "I tried to hide my personality, my psychological state, my emotions," an attempt that he has said had as much to do with "feelings about myself," the wish for "withdrawal into myself," and avoidance of "psychology or emotions," as it did with painting.[129] As part of an artistic identity that by 1961 could lead to his being described as "the great white, or the gray, hope of American painting," the color gray signified the limits the artist imposed upon himself, the "reserve" he would later "drop."[130] The neutrality perceived as central to gray's chromatic and affective identity served Johns's expressed desire to "feel removed from the work, neutral toward it."[131] Gray shared the "no particular quality" that Johns associated with his "kind of invisible images" like the Flags, Numbers, Alphabets, and Targets.[132] Moreover, gray signaled the intentionality of his position.

In a 1964 interview, Johns observed, "People say that my works are 'neutral.' But if you paint something, it is 'something,' and it cannot be neutral. Being neutral is a mere expression of a form of intention."[133] A notebook entry of about the same time pursues this idea: "Judd spoke of a 'neutral' / surface but what is meant? Neutrality / must involve some relationship (to other / ways of painting, thinking?) He would have to include these in his work / to establish the neutrality of that surface."[134] By including newspaper, objects, and other colors into his gray monochromes, Johns seems to underscore the neutrality of gray optically as well as affectively.

"In *gray* finally the maximum neutralization of antitheses is achieved. . . . Passively it yields to outside influence. . . . [It] is a neutral equation among the differentiations of the other colors (see also its use as background in psychological experiments)."[135] Kouwer's summary touches on particular optical properties of gray that supported commonly held ideas about its emotional valence. Gray can be produced in various ways, by mixing either chromatic or achromatic extremes. In other words, gray results from blending two complementary colors (or the three primaries) along with white, or blending black and white. Taken together, these grays are termed metameric: looking alike while being physically unlike.[136] The appearance of color traces on, in, and under Johns's monochrome surfaces suggests to the viewer that the grays are complex mixtures involving color, whereas in fact Johns makes gray primarily from black and white, and less frequently by combining complementaries (see the interview by Nan Rosenthal in this volume).

The phenomenology of metamers—in which vision, distinguishing results only, reads chromatic similarity where there is physical difference—is related to Johns's larger fascination with ambiguity. In the recent *Beckett* (2005; cat. no. 138), he experimented with the encaustic mixture employed for the left panel, adjusting its reflectivity to make the surface as similar as possible to that of the right panel, painted in oil.[137] Such ambiguities have also factored into Johns's printmaking (see the essay by Mark Pascale in this volume) and his practice of translating grays into different media, as in the two drawings after the encaustic *Tennyson*, which, though superficially similar in appearance, are constitutionally different: the earlier work elaborated in the friable media of pastel and charcoal (1959; cat. no. 13) and the other in the liquid medium of graphite wash (1967; cat. no. 14).[138] Only the former includes actual gray media, the latter, like the majority of the artist's drawings that appear gray are in fact made with various black drawing materials, the particulate matter extended across the white surface of the paper or plastics with the result that they read as gray. Metamers confuse assumed connections between means and ends.

Johns's stated attraction to gray as "unmoved or unmoveable by coloration" can be related to the properties that make it, optically, the quintessentially neutral color. Color physics had measurably demonstrated gray's unique spectral properties. As diagrammed in one of the books apparently used to teach color theory at Parsons in the late 1940s (**FIG. 14**), brilliant colors have a high reflectance in part of the spectrum and a low reflectance elsewhere: a red object absorbs all the rays but red, which are consequently perceived by the eye.[139] Gray by contrast has a uniform spectral reflectance; "a gray object absorbs some [light] rays and reflects others, doing so without disturbing the relative proportion of waves" in the light illuminating it.[140] This makes gray, as Kouwer noted, ideal for use in psychological experiments, particularly those having to do with the psycho-physiological phenomena known as afterimages.[141]

Afterimages are routinely explained and occasionally illustrated in color-theory textbooks: "When the eye is focused for a few moments on a small area of color and the attention then directed to a neutral background, the complement of that color becomes subjectively evident."[142] Physiologically, this phenomenon was commonly attributed to retinal fatigue: the eye, over-stimulated through excitation by a single color, compensates—restores its "balance"—by spontaneously generating that color's complement (**FIG. 15**).[143] This occurs as well in the experience of black and white, each being the complement of the other. The result, as contemporary textbooks alerted artists, is that compound color images affect the way we see paintings. The viewer "often fixes his gaze on one color after another or several colors at a time, though scarcely conscious that he does so. Then, as his gaze shifts, he transfers [chromatic] afterimages here and there.... When the eye wanders over a painting... the appearance of its colors (unless our glance is very hasty) depends somewhat on these afterimages which are being constantly produced by retinal fatigue." Nor are monochrome canvases exempt from the effects of complementarism; the longer we look at, say, a green canvas, the less vivid our experience of the color, which becomes duller right before our eyes as its afterimage—red—"forms and blends with it."[144]

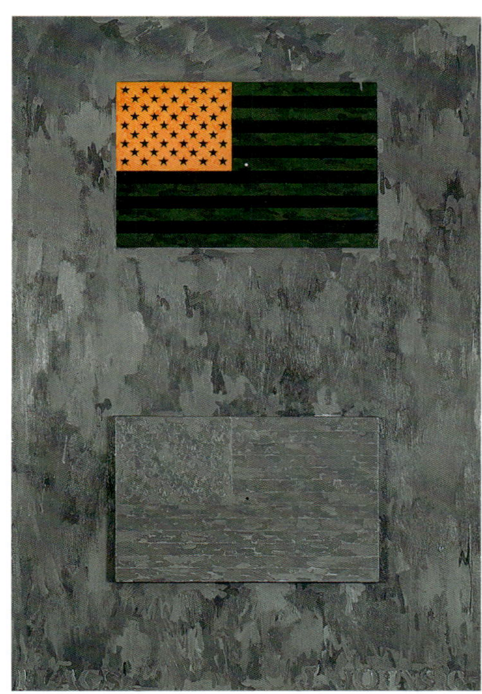

Fig. 16. *Flags*, 1965. Oil on canvas with raised canvas; 185.7 × 124.8 × 4.8 cm (73 ⅛ × 49 ⅛ × 1 ⅞ in.). Collection of the artist.

Gray is the sole exception to this rule, for medium gray generates what has been described as "a state of complete equilibrium in the eye," producing no afterimage.[145] If we view a neutral gray square on a blue background, the gray will seem to take on an orange cast while the blue remains undisturbed. However, if we look at a medium-gray square against a gray background, neither area will be affected by an afterimage. Johns's *Green Target* (1955) is susceptible to being "moved" by color in ways that are not operative for either *Gray Target* (both 1958; cat. nos. 41 and 42). Optically, gray was the most literal color—the least vulnerable to physiological subjectivity and hence the least expressive—available to Johns.[146] He refers to gray as "stable" (see the interview by Nan Rosenthal in this volume, p. 160).

Johns's most overt pictorial expression of interest in retinal afterimages is the 1965 oil *Flags* (**FIG. 16**), which he first thought to entitle *Optical Echo: Two Flags*:

> On the upper half of the canvas I will paint an American flag with the complementaries of red, white, and blue, with the stars and white lines in black, the background of the stars in orange, and the red li-nes in green. It will be a very ugly flag. Another flag of the same size will be painted all in gray, just under the first flag. I wonder if the background should be gray. If you gaze at the upper flag, and then suddenly look at the flag below, you will see the primary colors. Even if you don't, I don't care. But this idea is wonderful, isn't it? Is this multiplication or addition of a painting?[147]

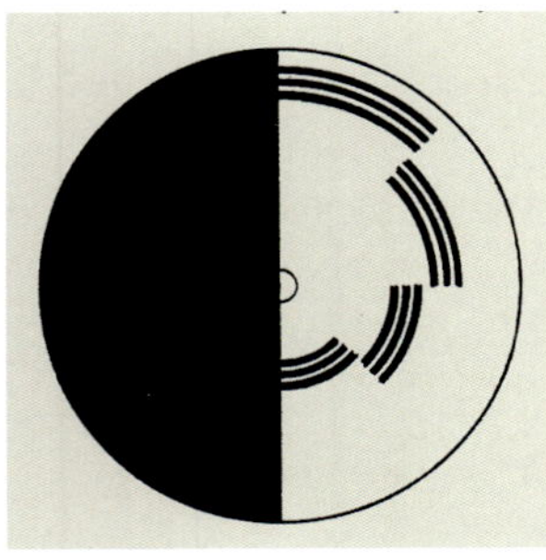

Fig. 17. Benham's disk, demonstrating subjective aspects of color, from Birren 1934 (see fig. 3), p. 47: "If a pin is inserted in the center and the disk spun . . . the series of black lines will instantly appear hued. When spun to the right under artificial light the outer ring will be blue, the second green, the third dull yellow, and the inner ring red. When spun to the left the order of hues reverses."

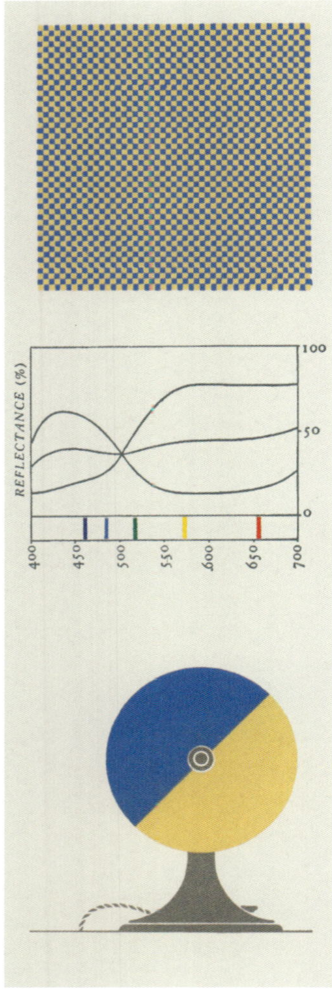

Fig. 18. The additive mixture of color pigments, from Interchemical Corporation 1935 (see fig. 12), p. 16. The upper diagram shows that alternate squares of yellow and blue are fused into gray when viewed from a distance; the chart at center shows equal areas of yellow and blue mix to the flat reflectance of gray; and the rotating device at the bottom mixes yellow and blue with the same result.

The painting's compositional organization—involving an initial focal site above and a neutral field below to receive the afterimage—recalls the designs used to demonstrate the phenomenon, down to the focal dot below the image. Here Johns calculated that color would move gray through a subjective process in which the viewer restores the "ugly" flag to its true colors. Gray is a field on which something happens but that does not itself necessarily cause something to happen. This is the situation of the gray monochromes.

Johns has long been attentive to his own subjective visual experience. When asked in a 1977 interview why he seemed more comfortable working in "grisaillelike tones," he ventured that he was "not a very accomplished colorist" (but added in the same breath that he had made improvements and had ambitions to do something different with color).[148] In an earlier conversation with Crichton, he connected what he perceived as his poor abilities as a colorist to a below-average capacity to discriminate between the colors he sees. In this context, he reported the following incident: "I was working on a colored numbers painting. When I worked on it for longer than a minute, the entire painting would turn gray to me. I couldn't see any of the colors, and I would have to stop." He mentioned this to Duchamp, who said, "Perhaps you have a physiological need."[149]

The anecdote, Crichton observed, "invites speculation for the entire body of Johns's work, so often characterized by muted grays."[150] While the psycho-physiological dynamics of the episode Johns described are unclear, the symptoms, as well as the discussion with Duchamp, are suggestive. It has been known since the early nineteenth century that sensations of color may be stimulated by the rapid alternation of light and dark, as demonstrated by rotating disks patterned with black-and-white forms (FIG. 17). Alternatively, sensations of gray can be produced through the optical mixture of complementary colors, a phenomenon demonstrated by two standard means: viewing alternate small patches at a distance from which their specificity is lost and the eye fuses them into a solid gray; or by a rotating disk designed with equal areas of two complementary colors (FIG. 18). However, it is anomalies in color vision that seem the point of the episode Johns related.

Duchamp, whose prohibition on retinal art exempted "looking defined as the physiological registering of an optical experiment," as Linda Henderson observed, had turned to optics himself in the 1920s. He collected optician's charts and, taking a lead from the spinning disks used to investigate perceptual phenomena, explored circular motifs in motion in his *Rotoreliefs* of 1935.[151] His fascination, and attendant familiarity, with virtual or subjective color experiments may explain Johns's confidence to him, which probably took place in the context of the Carnegie Institute's 1958 Pittsburgh Bicentennial International Exhibition of Contemporary Painting and Sculpture. Duchamp was part of the jury that awarded Johns a prize for *Gray Numbers* (FIG. 19).[152] In fact Johns was at work on the color version of this composition, *Numbers in Color* (FIG. 20) by the time he received news of the award in December 1958. His experience of the colored numbers turning gray—an eclipse of sorts—rehearses both the traditional sequence of going from color to grisaille, as well as the strong hold on Johns of the gray version, which in fact preceded the color translation.

The possibility of an inherent subjective preference for gray seems implicit in Duchamp's diagnosis of "physiological need," particularly when considered in light of the corresponding French phrase *besoin physiologique*, since *besoin* ("need") also conveys the sense of "want" or "lack." Possibly informed by Johns's freely avowed weakness in color discrimination—he would admit to taking Albers's test on color in 1964 and getting all the answers wrong[153]—Duchamp's conclusion raises the possibility of visual anomalies like those involved in the condition familiarly referred to as color blindness.

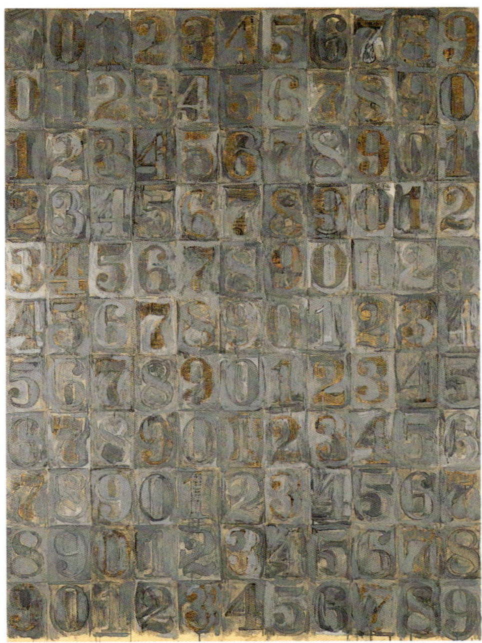

Fig. 19. *Gray Numbers*, 1958. Encaustic and collage on canvas; 170.2 × 125.7 cm (67 × 49 ½ in.). Collection of David Geffen, Los Angeles.

Twentieth-century research on the "mechanisms of colour-vision suggests the eye has two independent systems of polychromatic and monochromatic receptors." The retina's fovea is "sensitive to color . . . the periphery . . . only to white and gray."[154] In the literature current by the 1950s, colorless vision — an eye capable of black-white-gray perceptions only — was considered primitive, since characteristic of lower species, such as horses, dogs, and cats, which see the world in tones of gray and thus display the "equivalents of partial or total color-blindness" in humans.[155] Color vision had been a product of evolution, the normal human eye completely color-capable only at its center. Color blindness could thus be discussed as a kind of evolutionary throwback, an inherited sense defect that runs in families. At one extreme, the condition takes the relatively rare form of achromatism, in which the world has the appearance of a black-and-white photograph or a grisaille rendering. More moderate manifestations are found in the five to ten percent of the male population who exhibit degrees of dichromatism, or two-color vision, including the "color weak" whose impairment is so slight that only sensitive tests will reveal it.[156]

World War II had made the subject of color blindness topical. Normal color vision was considered essential for an efficient fighting force, and the accuracy and "fairness" of the screening tests that could lead to disqualification were much debated.[157] The armed forces favored the so-called pseudo-isochromatic plates — arrays of small, multicolored dots, each field containing one or more digits or letters, discernible or invisible according to the color sensitivity of the observer (see **FIG. 21**). These tests, as *Scientific American* noted, were designed to quickly reveal congenital color blindness on a sliding scale: from the rare instances of total color blindness, through the kind that involves deficiency in the red-green sense and weakness in the blue-yellow sense, to the more common red-green color blindness, wherein red, yellow, and green appear as degrees of yellow, while blue appears as it does to the normally sighted. Another expert wrote, "When [red and green] drop out — together, as they usually do — the differences between digit and ground, readily perceived by the color-capable, are obliterated. The entire field may turn to grey."[158]

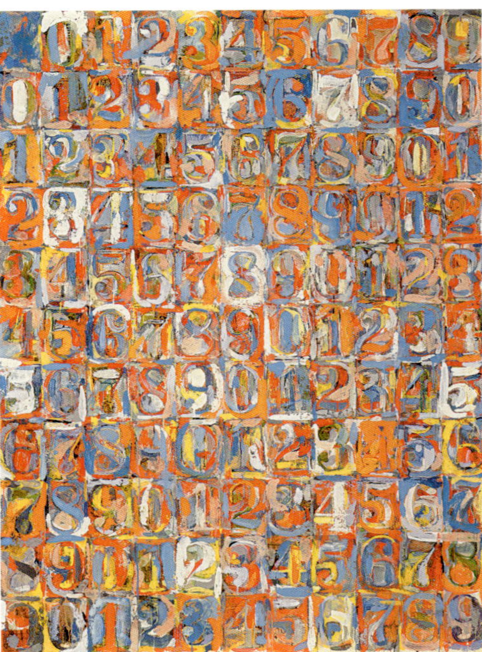

Fig. 20. *Numbers in Color*, 1958–59. Encaustic and collage on canvas; 168.9 × 125.7 cm (66 ½ × 49 ½ in.). Albright-Knox Art Gallery, Buffalo, Gift of Seymour H. Knox, Jr., 1959.

Those who protested military disqualification on the basis of test scores argued that the tests could not capture all gradations of color sensitivity; the average reject was not totally blind to color but merely color weak, with reduced systemic capacities. The most vocal protestors fell into the intermediate class of red-green blindness: "Their red is probably a reddish orange, their green bluish or grayish, their color fields restricted. At dusk, in rain or fog, their weakened red-green color pair is likely to fail them. They are subject to rapid color fatigue, and are likely to see vivid complementary color halos amounting to illusion on the neutral background of small color fields. . . . They can 'get by' in the majority of everyday situations . . . [but] are virtually color blind in slightly unfavorable or unusual circumstances."[159]

The cause of Johns's momentary loss of all color qualities — the achromatopsia that spontaneously translated the *Numbers in Color* before him into the grisaille of its precedent — remains unclear. However, his association of the event with his own color weakness suggests how personal experience of perceptual anomalies may have informed his interest in the subjectivity of vision. In one of the five identically sized versions of *0 through 9* painted in 1961 (**FIG. 23**), Johns seems to have alluded directly to the pseudo-isochromatic tests, which he had probably encountered when inducted into the army in 1951. (The series includes three versions in color, one in black and white, and another in gray [cat. no. 61]). In this oil on canvas, he introduced an overall pattern of differently colored and sized dots — the constituent elements of the digit-mosaic or "vanishing pattern" tests of figure/ground relationships — to the motif of superimposed numerals that emerge and disappear as our focus changes.[160]

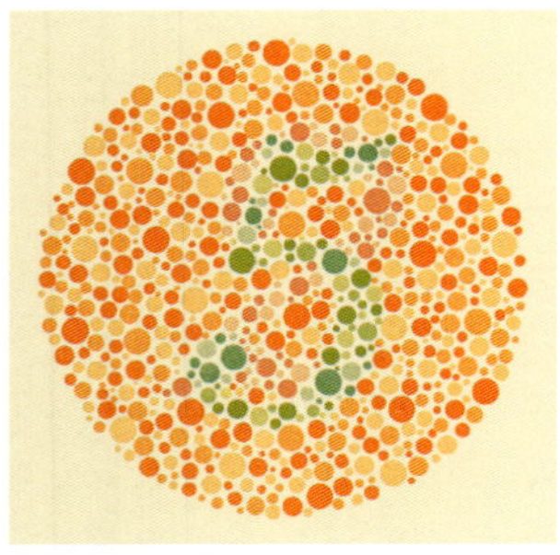

Fig. 21. Plate designed as a test for color blindness by Dr. Shinobu Ishihara, from *A Series of Plates Designed as Tests for Colour-Blindness*, 5th ed. (Kanehara, 1930), pp. 2–3: "The normal read the figure for 5. The red-green-blind read it for 2." "To one who is red-blind the red and bluish green parts of the spectrum are uncoloured, and moreover the red part appears to him dark. Consequently the spectrum is shortened at the red end.... To one who is green-blind, the green part of the spectrum is uncoloured.... The red and green blind... see only two colours, the yellow and blue of the spectrum, and do not see the rest of the colours. Consequently red and green are easily mistaken by them, but blue and yellow are never mistaken."

Johns's play with the shifting relationship between figures and ground is suggestively connected to this particular scientific interrogation of how the eye works differently in different people. As articles in *Scientific American* and elsewhere observed, this recognition made the study of the structure and function of the eye important for the philosopher as well as for the physiologist.[161]

Responses to the isochromatic tests underscored, as commentators of the 1940s observed, how each of us is "confined in his own sense world. The anomalous-visioned has no eyes but his own to see with... no more notion of the sense quality he lacks than the layman has of the fourth dimension." No one can appreciate what he or she has never sensed.[162] This called into question not only the commonality of visual experience but also the use of language as guide. Another *Scientific American* writer asked:

> What exactly do color-blind people see? This question is more difficult to answer than one might suppose. We cannot trust the color names used by color-blind individuals.... When a color-blind man describes a lemon as yellow, for all we know he may actually be seeing a color which we would call red.... In short, although two persons may use the same color names to describe their respective experiences, we cannot be certain that each man would recognize the other's sensations.[163]

Reliance on color names is misleading precisely because all of us learn correct color names for many common objects from infancy; experience habituates those with anomalous color vision to follow the names used by everyone else. With color, similarity of language usage can belie considerable difference in sense perception (see **FIG. 22**).

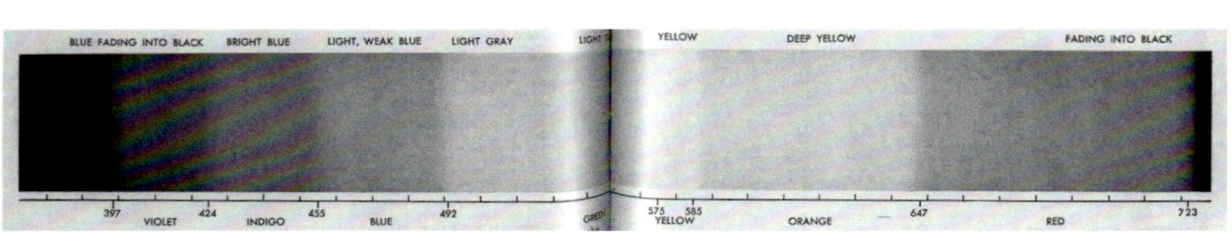

Fig. 22. Normal and abnormal color vision, from Alphonse Chapanis, "Color Blindness," *Scientific American* 184, 3 (Mar. 1951), pp. 48–49: "The colors indicated below the spectrum are those seen by a normal person. The numbers below the spectrum describe the limits of each color in millimicrons of wavelength. The colors indicated above the spectrum are those seen by a person suffering from protanopia, sometimes called red-blindness. In protanopia there is a neutral point in the area labeled 'light gray.' To the left of this point the protanope sees only blues; to the right, only yellows. The protanote also does not see as far into red as the normal person."

Such problematics regarding the relationship to color of sensation, experience, and language seem to inform another of the 1961 *0 through 9* series (see **FIG. 24**). Here Johns used oils to stencil color names against color backgrounds; in some instances, the relationship between either the color used to render the color name or the background that it labels is correct; in other cases, the relationships are at odds. The artist signaled his intention in such works as follows:

> In those paintings where colour names are used many times, the stencilled words were the only kind of objective thing in the painting for me.... I liked it that the words had a meaning.... I liked it that the meaning of the words either denied or coincided in the colored paintings, or reaffirmed the actual experience of the colour sensation. Those paintings to me were an accomplishment in ambiguity that previous paintings had not reached. I'm talking as the viewer.[164]

Painted two years earlier than the *0 through 9* series, *False Start* (1959; cat. no. 1)—literally a start in working in oil on a large scale—was the first major canvas in which Johns pursued this idea.[165] "A tissue of conflict between what is read and what is seen," is how Kozloff described it, the mind "bid to fuse that which the eye has no difficulty in distinguishing." But viewers have different abilities, and the "riot of illogical combinations" of colors and words might suggest not only "mischievous mislabeling" but also certain relatively commonplace visual abnormalities.[166] Indeed Crichton, invoking Johns's acknowledged challenges with color perception, suspected that *Jubilee* (1959; cat. no. 2), the grisaille version of *False Start* the artist painted soon thereafter, "may have

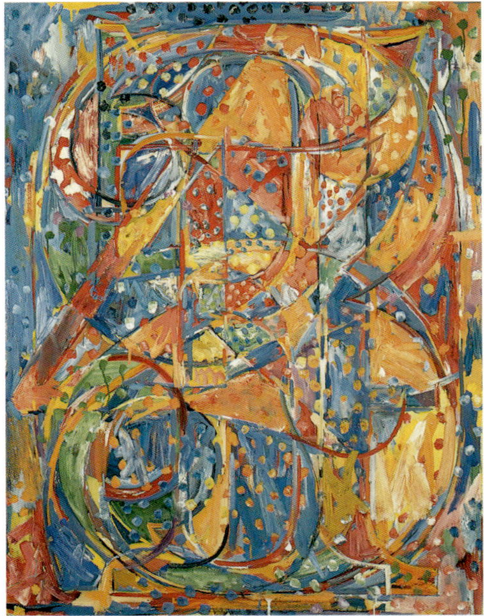

Fig. 23. *0 through 9*, 1961. Oil on canvas; 137.2 × 114 cm (54 × 45 in.). Hirshhorn Museum and Sculpture Garden, Smithsonian Institution, Washington, D.C., gift of Joseph H. Hirshhorn, 1966.

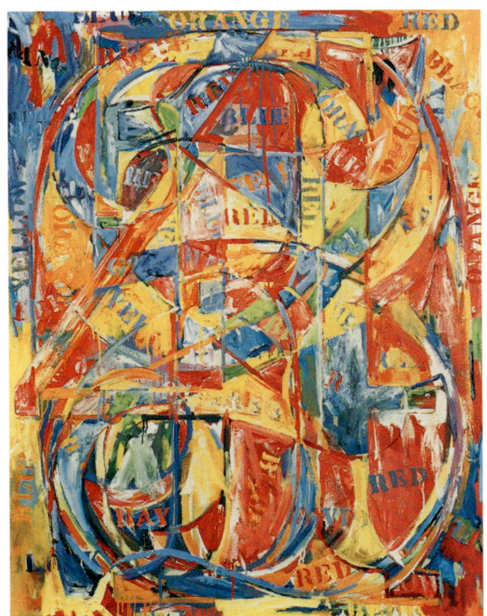

Fig. 24. *0 through 9*, 1961. Oil on canvas; 137.2 × 114 cm (54 × 45 in.). Collection of Ronald Perelman.

come from actual experience."[167] Sometimes the color words are inconsistent in brightness, as if mistranslated into value, as was common, before the invention of panchromatic film, in photographic reproductions of painting, and remains a common aspect of abnormal brightness sensitivity to hue of the color blind.[168] *Jubilee* and *False Start*—the experience of one informing the other—speak to Johns's larger aim to do something new with color: making its application less predetermined than in the Targets and Flags. He would make paintings inclusive of "all the colors—but all the colors by name, more than by visual sensation."[169] In the context of his first major venture into the Western tradition of oil painting, then, Johns would engage afresh with the question of gray and the "color situation."

Occupying mind and eye discordantly, these paintings featuring color names broach issues of language and naming, seeing and understanding resonant in Johns's contention that "painting has a nature which is not entirely translatable into verbal language."[170] In 1964 he spoke of his painterly activity in terms of an examination of the various conditions of the sign's ability to "adequately coincide with what's perceivable": "What is 'red' out of many shades of red, or which 'red' is the real red, this red or that red? When we gradually add yellow, exactly how much yellow will turn 'red' into 'orange'?"[171] Significant precedents here are René Magritte, Duchamp, and especially the philosopher Ludwig Wittgenstein, whose *Philosophical Investigations* (1953) had an impact on Johns's interest in the meanings of words and the use of labels. Johns is said to have started reading Wittgenstein only in 1961, but exposure to his ideas could have happened earlier.[172] A 1957 article in *Scientific American* introducing "an influential but little-known philosopher of science, Ludwig Wittgenstein," discussed the philosophical implications of key questions such as the relationships between sign and signification, and between naming, labeling or pointing, and meaning. In *Philosophical Investigations*, Wittgenstein posited that meaning resides in sentences rather than in words, in what is *said* rather than what is *named*; that "language games," governed by rules, determine the meaning of signs like "number-words" or "color-words"; and that meaning arises with the employment of such signs in normal and abnormal communication situations.[173]

Wittgenstein would also have been accessible to Johns through the review in a 1959 issue of *Scientific American* of a memoir by the philosopher's former student Norman Malcolm, published the previous year. This slim volume includes an anecdote about Wittgenstein's playful intelligence that, Johns would recall, immediately engaged his interest in the philosopher.[174] Moreover, Malcolm's recollections touch on topics belonging to the philosophy of psychology that spoke to Johns's interests. In his Cambridge University classes, Wittgenstein allowed that "there is philosophical question as to what one *really sees*," and acknowledged that "it's difficult to think *well* about 'certainty,' 'probability,' 'perception'"; he attempted to demonstrate that "to use 'I know' with sense-datum statements is silly. . . . The highest degree of certainty is nothing psychological but something logical"; and he employed the example of color—the supposition that the color red is specific and describable—to problematize the notion of explanation and its incompatibility with "private" language.[175] In *Philosophical Investigations*, which the memoir introduces and invokes, Wittgenstein frequently used numbers (including in one instance "the writing out of the series 0 to 9"), as well color words (especially red) to illustrate his ideas about the rule-governed, normative nature of language.[176]

The impact on Johns of *Philosophical Investigations*—said to be his bedtime reading during most of the 1960s—is echoed in interviews of 1963 and 1964, in which he made particular reference to red (as above) in explicating his conceptual interests. Johns stated that he is attracted to the philosopher's study of the "way we can abuse the structure of language to create new meaning."[177] It thus becomes interesting to consider *False Start* in light of Wittgenstein's rhetorical question about ambiguity and definition: "Could one define the word 'red' by pointing to something that was *not red?*" Direct influence need not be in play here, but rather amplification, Johns's existing involvement with perception's philosophical implications predisposing him to make use of Wittgenstein in the service of his own thinking.[178] It is similarly suggestive to consider Johns's magisterial drawing *Diver* (1962–63; cat. no. 102)—incorporating imprints of the artist's hands and feet and figuring a swan dive—in terms of the analogy that, as Malcolm noted, Wittgenstein liked to draw between philosophical thinking and swimming: "Just as one's body has a natural tendency towards the surface and one has to make an *exertion* to get to the *bottom*—so it is with thinking."[179] A fixed image implying kinesis that is ultimately modeled on Leonardo's iconic drawing *The Proportions of the Human Body According to Vitruvius* (c. 1492; Gallerie dell'Accademia, Venice), Johns's *Diver* can be read as a self-portrait of the painter-philosopher.[180]

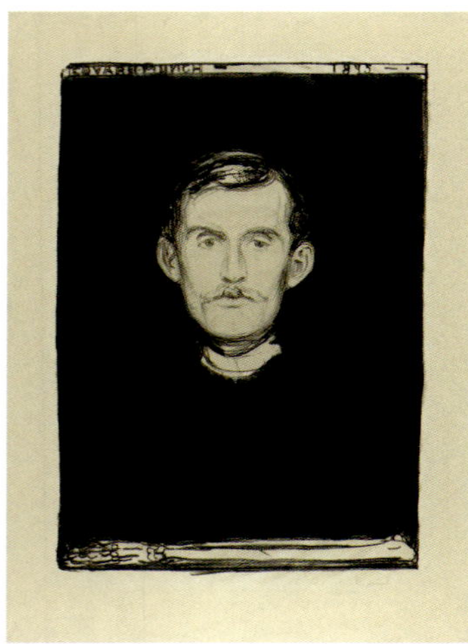

Fig. 25. Edvard Munch. *Self-Portrait*, 1895. Lithograph with tusche and scraping on stone, on paper; image: 46.2 × 32.4 cm (18 ⅛ × 12 ¾ in.), sheet: 59.5 × 44 cm (23 ⅜ × 17 ⅜ in.). The Art Institute of Chicago, Clarence Buckingham Collection, 1963.281.

• • •

As Johns has pursued his abiding interests over time, his work has changed. By 1969 he had come to re-evaluate ideas about painting he had articulated a decade earlier, in one of his first interviews (see p. 85 above):

> At that time, I was willing to take the radiator as a concrete object with definition and spatial characteristics.... I was even willing to take it as a reference—something steady and set. Art has so often involved ambiguities and the possibility of ambiguities. I originally thought the radiator was not ambiguous, that it was a basis on which we might agree. I am not sure any longer that I believe or am secure in that type of thinking. I would now question the reference as much as the work. Originally, I meant the radiator was a secure object one didn't have to bring any special psychological attitude to. Now, I not so sure.[181]

It was in the context of this same 1969 conversation that Johns made the often-quoted retrospective statement regarding his early use of gray encaustic to convey literalness.

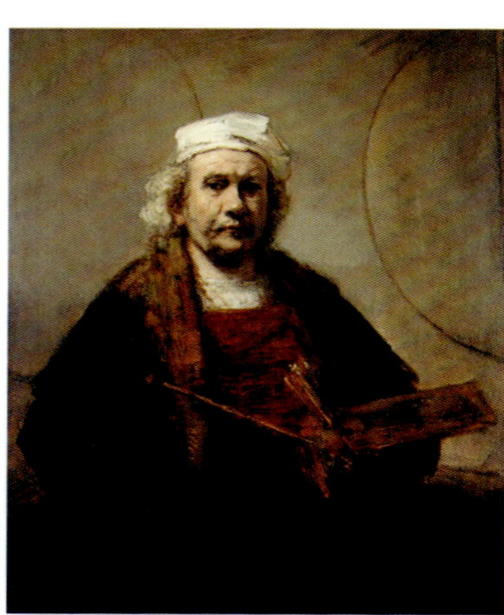

Fig. 26. Rembrandt Harmenszoon van Rijn. *Self-Portrait*, c. 1665–69. Oil on canvas; 114.3 × 94 cm (45 × 37 in.). Iveagh Bequest, Kenwood House, London.

As his situation changed—as he dropped his "reserve"—so did his use of the medium of gray. Johns pursued color, employing gray periodically in his painted work until the late 1990s, when he began to address the motif of the catenary curve (see cat. nos. 128 to 135; see also the essay by James Rondeau in this volume). Over the course of what became a series, he developed a field of gray that gradually subsumed elements alluding to his personal history and to the preoccupations sounded in the parenthetical phrase of the grand 1998 *Catenary (I Call to the Grave)* (cat. no. 129), taken from the Book of Job.[182] The expressiveness of the first-person here recalls Johns's answer, years earlier, to a question about titling: Noting that Duchamp considered a title as "an extra color," Johns added that, for him, it is "a sort of suggestive pleasure."[183]

The titular mournfulness of *Catenary (I Call to the Grave)* colors the experience of a work that, like others in the series, has the feeling of a deeply personal meditation. The assembly of near-weightless string—at once subject to gravity's laws, chance disturbances, and arbitrary rearrangement before backdrops of enveloping gray—takes on associations with human frailty.[184] The falling arcs recall the forms and pathos of draperies in representations of the Passion: the cloth with which the legendary Saint Veronica wiped Christ's face on the way to Calvary; the loin cloth Christ wore on the Cross, and the sheet used in the deposition of his body from the Cross.[185]

In its preoccupation with gray monochrome, the Catenary series can be seen as a return to the condition of Johns's early work—a retrospective attitude suggested in the title of the initial canvas, *Bridge* (1997; cat. no. 128).[186] The connection underscores the affective resonance of the early monochromes as well as the abiding signatory valence of gray for Johns. He once spoke of the need to "accept the responsibility for your personal coloring," the disposition that informs preference. The context of the remark—impatience with critics' propensity "to allocate precedents"—is cautionary.[187] But this is tempered by Johns's subsequent art historical borrowings for essays in self-portraiture: from Picasso, the shadow-presence incorporated as a gray silhouette into the Seasons (see cat. nos. 119–21); from Edvard Munch, the auratic title of a late meditation on mortality, *Between the Clock and the Bed* (1940–42; Munch Museum, Oslo; see also cat. no. 115).[188]

Johns looked to an earlier work by Munch on the theme of the artist's confrontation with time—*Self-Portrait* (FIG. 25)—for the lithograph *Savarin* (1977–81; see cat. no. 114). Here, in place of a literal self-representation, Johns substituted a drawing of his early sculpture of his paint brushes in a coffee can (see fig. 1 in the essay by James Rondeau in this volume), rendering this "surrogate self-portrait" in gray tones against a background of gray hatching; an imprint of his own arm printed in blood red replaces Munch's depiction of his skeletal limb.[189] To its right are printed initials of the Norwegian artist, E.M., which, the lithographic medium might initially suggest, he drew in reverse on the printing matrix—the "ME" beside Johns's arm print speaking to an intention to borrow another's self-portrait in order to create his own.[190]

The operation of identification and transformation openly acknowledged here lends credence to a possible new reading of the earlier *Device* (1962; cat. no. 93), one of a series of canvases from the late 1950s and early '60s in which Johns incorporated studio tools or devices—sticks, rulers, stretcher bars—used in their making to trace circles or parts of circles.[191] The resulting forms connote the faces of timepieces, their "hands" the implements that are extensions of the painter's arm, which in turn replaces them in subsequent pictures like *Periscope (Hart Crane)* (1963; cat. no. 103) and, more recently, the Seasons (see cat. nos. 119–21).[192] Devices of the artist's craft are a staple in the history of self-portraiture. But notably suggestive for Johns's *Device* is a famously enigmatic late Rembrandt in which the painter stands before a light wall marked with two semicircles, holding not only his palette and brushes but also a mahlstick, the wooden rod up to a yard long used by artists to steady the hand and keep it clear of the painting's surface (FIG. 26).[193] In Johns's *Device* (contrarily), two sections of a yardstick have been employed, compass-fashion, to smear the gray paint into partial circular forms, separated vertically by a board on which Johns painted the word "gray."[194] A self-portrait, perhaps, of the artist as his favorite color.

The author gratefully acknowledges assistance in the preparation of this essay from Susan Rossen, Britt Salvesen, Emma Bee Bernstein, Hilary Smith, and Tom Baron. Special thanks are due to Jesse Feiman, Research Assistant for *Jasper Johns: Gray*.

1 Tono 1964, in *Writings* 1996, p. 100.

2 Young 1969, p. 52, in *Writings* 1996, pp. 130–31. Here Johns was specifically referring to the "different situations" of painting and printmaking.

3 This is excerpted from a statement Albers drafted in the 1940s for the students of Black Mountain College. See Josef Albers, *Search Versus Re-Search* [three lectures by Josef Albers at Trinity College, April 1965] (Trinity College Press, 1969), p. 14.

4 Varnedoe 1996, p. 16; Steinberg 1962/1972, p. 54.

5 Young 1969, p. 51, in *Writings* 1996, p. 129.

6 On this subject, see John Gage, *Color and Culture: Practice and Meaning from Antiquity to Abstraction* (Little, Brown, 1993), and Michel Pastoureau, *Blue: The History of a Color*, trans. Markus I. Cruse (Princeton University Press, 2001).

7 Pastoureau (note 6), pp. 40–47. As Pastoureau noted, the debate began in the eighth century and continued to stir passionate arguments for hundreds of years. Enemies of color found one justification for its rejection in its etymology: "the Latin *color*, they believed, derived from the verb *celare*, to conceal." In Medieval Europe, the color of clothing could indicate the wearer's social status or religious affiliation. Black was popular among ecclesiastics and government officials because of its perceived moral connotations. Religious orders which took vows of poverty, such as the Benedictines and Franciscans, adopted austere costumes, black and gray (later, brown) respectively, as an aspect of their asceticism; Janet Mayo, *A History of Ecclesiastical Dress London* (B.T. Batsford, 1984), pp. 135–36.

8 Pastoureau (note 6), p. 87.

9 Ibid., pp. 90, 101.

10 See Molly Teasdale Smith, "The Use of Grisaille as a Lenten Observance," in *Marsyas: Studies in the History of Art*, vol. 8 (Institute of Fine Arts, New York University, 1959), pp. 43–54. See also J. Patrice Marandel, "Introduction," in *Gray Is the Color: An Exhibition of Grisaille Painting XIIIth–XXth Centuries*, exh. cat. (Rice University, 1974), pp. 22–23.

11 Alan Hunt, *Governance of the Consuming Passions: A History of Sumptuary Law* (St. Martin's Press, 1996), pp. 27, 129. See also Pastoureau (note 6), pp. 108–13.

12 One key twentieth-century instance is the Model T, which Henry Ford refused, on moral grounds, to manufacture in any color but black; see Pastoureau (note 6), pp. 113, 119.

13 On the early history of *disgeno* versus *colore*, see "*Disegno* versus *Colore*," ch. 7 in Gage (note 6), pp. 117–38. On the history of the debate in the seventeenth century, see Jacqueline Lichtenstein, "The Clash between Color and Drawing, or The Tactile Destiny of the Idea," ch. 6 in *The Eloquence of Color: Rhetoric and Painting in the French Classical Age*, trans. Emily McVarish (University of California Press, 1993), pp. 146–49.

14 Lichtenstein (note 13), pp. 153, 147, 158–59, respectively.

15 Ibid., pp. 152–55.

16 Charles Le Brun, "Sentiment sur le discours," in *Conference inédites de l'Académie Royale de Peinture et de Sculpture d'après les manuscripts des archives de l'École des Beaux-Arts*, ed. André Fontaine (A. Fontemoing, 1903), p. 37, quoted in Lichtenstein (note 13), p. 155.

17 Pastoureau (note 6), p. 200 n. 55.

18 Charles Blanc, *Grammaire des arts du dessin: Architecture, sculpture, peinture* (Jules Renouard, 1867), book 1, p. 23. Translated in Pastoureau (note 6), p. 200 n. 58.

19 Charles Blanc, "Peinture," in Blanc (note 18), book 3, p. 594. See also Charles Blanc, *The Grammar of Painting and Engraving*, trans. Kate Newell Doggett (Hurd and Houghton, 1875), p. 146.

20 Dannatt 2007, p. 35.

21 Douglas Druick et al., *Odilon Redon: Prince of Dreams 1840–1916*, exh. cat. (Art Institute of Chicago/Harry N. Abrams, 1996), pp. 48–50, 92. Redon used the phrase "thinker as well as painter" in reference to Jean-François Millet in "Millet" (Apr. 23, 1878), repr. in Odilon Redon, *À Soi-Même: Journal (1867–1915)* (José Corti, 1961), p. 144. The phrase "fundamental *gray*" [italics Redon] occurs in a discussion of Henri Fantin-Latour; see "Fantin-Latour" (Nov. 1882), repr. in Redon, *À Soi-Même*, p. 156.

22 Pertinent to Picasso is Blanc's discussion of "teintes mélancoliques" and the minor keys of blue that address the "tristesses de nôtre âme"; see Blanc (note 18), p. 26.

23 See Claire Barbillon, "L'esthetique pratique de Charles Blanc," in Charles Blanc, "Principes," in *Grammaire des arts du dessin: Architecture, sculpture, peinture* (École Nationale Supérieure des Beaux-Arts, 2000), p. 29.

24 See Linda Nochlin, "Picasso's Color: Schemes and Gambits," *Art in America* 68, 10 (Dec. 1980), pp. 105–23, esp. pp. 105–08.

25 "Regions which are not ruled by time and space...." edited version of "A Conversation with Marcel Duchamp," television interview filmed at the Philadelphia Museum of Art and conducted by James Johnson Sweeney, NBC, Jan. 1956, transcript published in Marcel Duchamp, *Salt Seller: The Writings of Marcel Duchamp*, ed. Michel Sanouillet and Elmer Peterson (Oxford University Press, 1973), pp. 135–36.

26 On Johns and Duchamp, see Tone 1996, p. 127. For Johns's comment on Duchamp, see Johns 1968, p. 6, in *Writings* 1996, p. 22.

27 Tomkins 1980, pp. 132, 89, respectively.

28 Tono 1964, in *Writings* 1996, p. 99: "...it was only Bob and I who were painting images (figurative art) during the age of action painting, when so-called images were not yet used. Today, what we used to do has become a matter of course. Yet I pride myself on the fact that our initial works broke with the latest academicism in those days." See also Rose 1965a, pp. 56, 61.

29 Quoted in Tomkins 1980, p. 200.

30 The following quotes are all from Tomkins 1980: "if you thought,"p. 70; "I was interested," p. 72; "pedestrian color" and "vernacular glance," p. 115; "It's possible," p. 63. The depersonalization of art making was an important aspect of Albers's teachings: "I feel unable to accept self-expression either as the beginning of art studies or as the final aim of any art"; Albers (note 3), p. 10.

31 Crichton 1994, p. 29.

32 "[separate] myself," Sozanski 1988, p. 30, in *Writings* 1996, p. 224; "how hard it is," Sozanski 1988, p. 30. See also Raynor 1973, p. 22, in *Writings* 1996, p. 145; Bernard and Thompson 1984, p. 65, in *Writings* 1996, p. 217; Cage 1964, p. 21.

33 For the most comprehensive history of encaustic and its practitioners during this period, see Gail Stavitsky, *Waxing Poetic: Encaustic Art in America during the Twentieth Century*, exh. cat. (Montclair Art Museum, 1999), pp. 17–19. In the course of her research, Stavitsky met and corresponded with Johns.

34 For Johns's comments on encaustic's quick-drying properties and appeal, see Crichton 1994, p. 30; Bernard and Thompson 1984, p. 65, in *Writings* 1996, p. 216; Davvetas 1984, p. 12, in *Writings* 1996, p. 218; De Antonio 1984, p. 97; and Francis 1984, pp. 113–14. For "feeling for the time," see Pohlen 1978, p. 22, in Varnedoe 1996, p. 36 n. 47 (not reprinted in *Writings* 1996). For "object character," see Pohlen 1978, p. 22, in *Writings* 1996, p. 172. James Fenton observed that Johns was attracted to encaustic "because it was *not oil paint*, and was therefore without intimidating associations"; Fenton 1996, p. 65.

35 Tomkins 1980, pp. 118–19.

36 Varnedoe 1996, p. 163. Crichton noted that, "if he needs color, he tries to find a way to make the selection happen according to some fixed rule he is not responsible for"; Crichton 1994, p. 35. Steinberg referred to the palette of primaries as a "schematic abstract of the whole spectrum"; Steinberg 1962/1972, p. 35.

37 Anonymous 1959, p. 58, in *Writings* 1996, p. 82.

38 Steinberg 1962/1972, p. 35.

39 Anonymous 1959, p. 58, in *Writings* 1996, p. 82.

40 Sylvester 1965, in Sylvester 2001, p. 166. In the loan agreement for *Canvas* (1956) for the 1964 exhibition "Black, White, and Grey" at the Wadsworth Atheneum, Hartford, the title of the work is given by the lender, Leo Castelli, as *Canvas (The Window)*; see Samuel J. Wagstaff, Jr., "Second Thoughts on Black, White, and Gray," The Black, White, and Gray Papers, Archive, Wadsworth Atheneum, Hartford, Connecticut, n.d.

41 Sylvester 1965, p. 168, in *Writings* 1996, p. 120.
42 Sylvester 1965, in Sylvester 2001, p. 166.
43 For *White Flag*, see Taylor 1990, p. 100, in *Writings* 1996, p. 245; for the Flagstones, see Crichton 1994, p. 52; for Beckett, see White 1977, p. 24, in *Writings* 1996, p. 153.
44 Sylvester 1965, p. 168, in *Writings* 1996, p. 120.
45 Leonardo da Vinci, *Treatise on Painting* (1651), trans. A. Philip MacMahon (Princeton University Press, 1956), no. 76, p. 50. On Johns and Leonardo, see Bernstein 1985, p. 60.
46 Johns 1959, p. 22, in *Writings* 1996, p. 20
47 Johns discussed the role of newspaper in an interview with David Bourdon; Bourdon 1977, p. 75, in *Writings* 1996, pp. 161–62.
48 Sylvester 1965, p. 157, in *Writings* 1996, p. 116.
49 Tomkins 1980, p. 72.
50 See Frederick A. Horowitz and Brenda Danilowitz, *Joseph Albers: To Open Eyes (The Bauhaus, Black Mountain College, and Yale)* (Phaidon, 2006), pp. 157, 188–89; the assistance of these authors is gratefully acknowledged. On Rauschenberg's participation in *matière* studies, see Tomkins 1980, pp. 30–32. See also Albers (note 3), p. 31.
51 Sylvester 1965, in Sylvester 2001, p. 149.
52 In interviews of 1965 and 1969, Johns referred to *Canvas* (1956) as *Gray Canvas*; see Sylvester 1965, in Sylvester 2001, p. 166; Hopps 1969, p. 35, in *Writings* 1996, p. 110.
53 Tuma 2007, pp. 171–72 and Bernstein 1985, pp. 34–35. There were five works with the motif of the table drawer in the 1952 Cézanne exhibition.
54 On Rauschenberg's grammar, see Tomkins 1980, p. 119. Johns also demonstrated skill at diagramming sentences, an exercise requiring students to analyze a sentence and portray its structure with a visual scheme; Tomkins 2006, p. 81.
55 Sylvester 1965, in Sylvester 2001, p. 167.
56 "Crossing the Bar" was first published in 1889. Later, Tennyson, who would die in 1892, expressed the wish that this poem be printed at the end of each edition of his works; see Robert Bernard Martin, *Tennyson: The Unquiet Heart* (Oxford University Press, 1980), p. 570. Standard interpretations identify the bar as a sand bar, a turbulent and potentially dangerous boundary between shore and open sea, between life and death.
57 Steinberg 1962/1972, p. 39.
58 See Rose 1965b, p. 68. Rose quoted Flavin's journal entry for August 9, 1962: "*Coran's Broadway Flesh* is my fifth electric light icon. It is an emblem much like Jasper Johns' *Tennyson*. It stands for a young English homosexual who loved New York City."
59 Holland Cotter recently characterized Johns's art as "unmystical, unromantic, unnostalgic but obsessed with transcendence and the reality of loss"; Cotter 2007, p. B35.
60 The painter Milton Resnick described this period as one in which in "the dream of art coming from heaven is nearly over"; Milton Resnick in "Is There a New Academy? Part II" *Artnews* 58, 5 (Sept. 1959), pp. 36, 60.
61 "Reforming my identity," see Pye 1990, p. 21, in *Writings* 1996, p. 254; "it gets to sound very religious," see Stevens and McGuigan 1977, p. 77, in *Writings* 1996, p. 165.
62 For further discussion of these exhibitions, see the essay by James Rondeau in this volume, pp. 39, 74 n. 86. "Black and White," at the Jewish Museum, New York, included Johns's *Reconstruction* (1959; Cleveland Museum of Art) and *Shade* (1959–60; The State Russian Museum, St. Petersburg). "Black, White, and Grey," at Hartford's Wadsworth Atheneum, included *Canvas* (1956), *Newspaper* (1957), *Alphabets* (1957; pencil, graphite wash, ink, and collage on paper; Collection of Robert and Jane Rosenblum, New York), and the lithograph *Coat Hanger I* (1960).
63 Rose 1964, p. 40; Kozloff 1964, p. 23.
64 Rauschenberg quoted in Tomkins 1980, p. 119. For similar commentary, see Rose 1977, p. 143; Rose 1993, p. 49.
65 Rose 1977, p. 149.
66 Anonymous 1965.
67 Johns 1968, p. 6, in *Writings* 1996, p. 22.
68 McKenzie 1965, p. 13B, in *Writings* 1996, p. 122.
69 Johns, Sketchbook A, p. 49, 1964, in *Writings* 1996, pp. 34, 56.
70 Hopps 1965, p. 35, in *Writings* 1996, p. 108.
71 Bernstein noted, "While his contact with Duchamp's ideas was expansive for him, it also crucially affirmed what was distinct about his own work, particularly his commitment to visual sensation, and to exploring the eye's relation to the mind"; Bernstein 1996, p. 43. See also Johns 1968, p. 6, in *Writings* 1996, p. 22.
72 Tono 1964, in *Writings* 1996, p. 98.
73 Taylor 1990, p. 100, in *Writings* 1996, p. 245.
74 See Bernstein 1985, pp. 59–68.
75 Young 1969, p. 54, in *Writings* 1996, p. 134.
76 See Tomkins 1980, pp. 68–70. Cage's now-famous formulation theorem of "Experimental Music" is found in *Silence: Lectures and Writings* (Wesleyan University Press, 1961), pp. 7–12 Rauschenberg described Johns as "always an intellectual" who wrote poetry and "read a lot"; Tomkins 1980, p. 119. What constituted Johns's early, formative reading—from high school until his artistic breakthrough in 1955—remains sketchy at best. Johns attended the College of Arts and Sciences, University of South Carolina–Columbia, for three semesters (Sept. 1947–Dec. 1948) and Parsons School of Design for one semester (Jan.–June 1949); Tone 1996, pp. 120–21. His disinclination for formal schooling is compatible with his belief that most artists are self-taught; Lewis 1990, p. F6, in *Writings* 1996, p. 241.
77 In the five months preceding the relaunch (Dec. 1947–Apr. 1948), the editors ran a column entitled, "An Announcement to Our Readers," outlining the rationale for and the nature of the changes; see *Scientific American* 177, 6 (Dec. 1947), p. 244; 178, 1 (Jan. 1948), p. 3; 178, 2 (Feb. 1948), p. 51; 178, 3 (Mar. 1948), p. 99; 178, 4 (Apr. 1948), p. 147. Before May 1948, *Scientific American* only published articles directly related to industry and manufacturing. In 1947 a publishing company bought the magazine and reinvented it as a vehicle to present the latest advances in science to a wider audience.Believing that "science has become a prime mover of modern history" (*Scientific American* [Apr. 1948]), the new editorial staff aimed to return it to the realm of common knowledge by bridging the gap between technical journals and the newspapers or magazines. They presented all branches of science, including physics, chemistry, biology, and psychology, along with applied sciences, like medicine and engineering, in a context which reflected the contributions of each to modern society. The editors saw "no inherent mystery in the nature of scientific knowledge which prevents its communication to the interested, though uninformed, layman"; *Scientific American* (Jan. 1948). They collaborated with scientists and specialists to present information using "language which is neither technical nor patronizing"; *Scientific American* (Mar. 1948). To aid in their endeavor, the editorial board placed a great emphasis on the graphic arts as a "resource...to extend the power of words in expressing the ideas of science"; *Scientific American* (Jan. 1948). They chose K. Chester, an artist and photographer for Life magazine, to oversee the presentation of ideas in the form of illustrations, photographs, diagrams, charts, and maps.
78 James R. Newman, "Review of J. Z. Young, *Doubt and Certainty in Science*," *Scientific American* 186, 3 (Mar. 1952), p. 78.
79 Bernstein 1996, p. 60. Other artists who found *Scientific American* of interest include Vija Celmins, who was attracted by the illustrations (conversation with Jesse Feiman, May 23, 2007), and Mel Bochner, who found it "a great source of ideas...[not] filled with all that purple prose of the '50s and early sixties art magazines" (e-mail to Jesse Feiman, May 18, 2007).
80 Rose 1977, p. 149.
81 Bruno Bettelheim, "Schizophrenic Art: A Case Study," *Scientific American* 186, 4 (Apr. 1952), pp. 30–34. Bernstein noted that Johns read the Bettelheim article in *Scientific American* while he was in the army in the early 1950s; see Bernstein 1996, p. 60. The artist would incorporate the drawing in several works beginning in 1991. *The Bath* (1988; Collection Joel and Anne Ehrenkranz), is the first instance in which Johns incorporated the galaxy motif. Field noted, "In the painting *Bridge*, 1997, and the print *Untitled*, 1999, the galaxy is printed from a photographic

screen or gravure, much as it was reproduced in the textbook Johns consulted"; Field 1999, p. 27. Whether or not *Scientific American* was Johns's immediate source, a reader of the periodical would have been familiar with the numerous photographs of spiral galaxies included in articles published between 1948 and 1984. See for example: George Gamow, "Galaxies in Flight" ("Spiral Nebula in Canes Venatici"), 171, 1 (July 1948), pp. 20–25; Cecilia H. Payne-Gaposchkin, "Why Do Galaxies Have a Spiral Forms?" ("Whirlpool Nebula in Canes Venatici"), 189, 3 (Sept. 1953), pp. 89–99; Robert P. Kraft, "Exploding Stars" (M 101), 206, 4 (Apr. 1962), pp. 54–63; Halton C. Arp, "The Evolution of Galaxies" (M 81 and M 74), 201,1 (Jan. 1963) pp. 70–78, 80, 82, 84; Freeman J. Dyson, "Energy in the Universe" (M 101), 225, 3 (Sept. 1971), pp. 50–59; Nick Scoville and Judith S. Young, "Molecular Clouds, Star Formation, and Galactic Structure" (M 101), 250, 4 (Apr. 1984), pp. 42–53. Johns incorporated images of galaxies and nebulae into the following works: nebulae similar to Spiral and Whirlpool nebulas appear in a group of touched intaglio prints, each called *Untitled*, executed in 2001; M 81 is featured in the drawing *Bridge* (1997; private collection, promised gift to the San Francisco Museum of Modern Art), and the painting *Untitled* (1997; private collection); a mirror image of a galaxy comparable to M 74 is present in the painting *Untitled (Halloween)* (1997; Collection of Marguerite and Robert Hoffman, Dallas); the galaxy M 101 appears in the intaglio print *Untitled* (1992), and in the painting *Mirror's Edge 2* (1993; Collection of the Robert and Jane Meyerhoff Modern Art Foundation, Inc., Phoenix, Maryland) (the source here is discussed in Mattison 1995, p. 46**).** All of the galaxy photos Johns would make use of predate those taken by the Hubble Space Telescope, launched in 1990. The Hubble telescope, the first put into orbit around earth, radically changed the imaging of outer space. The earth's atmosphere blurs and distorts photographs taken by ground-based telescopes. The Hubble's position outside of the atmosphere allowed (and continues to allow) it to capture stars, galaxies, and nebulas with greater clarity and detail than was previously possible.

82 Morris Kline, "The Straight Line," *Scientific American* 194, 3 (May 1956), pp. 105.

83 James R. Newman, "Books: A Fine Collection of Essays about Isaac Newton, Both the Man and His Accomplishments, on the Occasion of His Tercentenary," *Scientific American* 171, 1 (July 1948), pp. 57; Banesh Hoffman, "The Influence of Albert Einstein," *Scientific American* 180, 3 (Mar. 1949), pp. 54–55.

84 See for example Erich Fromm, "The Nature of Dreams," *Scientific American* 180, 5 (May 1949), pp. 44–47. Taking issue with Freud, Fromm argued that, while dreams may "express the fulfillment of irrational, asocial and immoral wishes which we repress successfully during the waking state," this is not the only way to interpret them. "We are often more intelligent, wiser...in our sleep....In sleep, no longer exposed to the noise of culture, we become awake to what we really feel and think. The genuine self can talk; it is often more intelligent...than the pseudo self which seems to be 'we' when we are awake"; p. 46. See also Calvin Hall, "What People Dream About," *Scientific American* 184, 5 (May 1951), p. 62: "Dreaming is thinking that occurs during sleep. It is a peculiar form of thinking in which the conceptions or ideas area expressed not in the form of words or drawings, as in waking life, but in the form of images, usually visual images. In other words, the abstract and invisible ideas are converted into concrete and visible images....The sleeping person can see his own thoughts embodied in the form of pictures."

85 James R. Newman, "Mathematical Creation: An Essay Written Early in this Century by the Great Mathematician Henri Poincaré Is Still a Remarkable Insight into the Creative Process of the Intellect," *Scientific American* 179, 2 (Aug. 1948), pp. 54–57. Poincaré was an important source of scientific knowledge for Duchamp, who was particularly interested in his writings on X-rays and non-Euclidian geometry; see Linda Dalrymple Henderson, *Duchamp in Context: Science and Technology in "The Large Glass" and Related Works* (Princeton University Press, 1998), p. 6.

86 Fuller 1978, in *Writings* 1996, p. 180. See also Orton 1994, pp. 97–104; Anonymous 1958b.

87 Jespersen 1969, p. 14, in *Writings* 1996, p. 136.

88 See for example W. H. Ittelson and F. P. Kilpatrick, "Experiments in Perception," *Scientific American* 185, 2 (Aug. 1951), pp. 50–55.

89 Ralph Evans, "Seeing Light and Color: One of Our Most Familiar Sensory Experiences Is Perhaps the Most Difficult to Define. The Study of It Requires the Application of Physics, Physiology, and Psychology," *Scientific American* 181, 2 (Mar. 1949), p. 55.

90 Newman (note 78), p. 75.

91 "Things the mind already knows," Anonymous 1959; "seen and not looked at," Hopps 1965, p. 34, in *Writings* 1996, p. 108; "life experience," Gratz 1970, p. 25, in *Writings* 1996, p. 137; "doubt," Sylvester 1965, in Sylvester 2001, p. 165–66, and McKenzie 1965, p. 13B, in *Writings* 1996, p. 122; "something new," Jespersen 1969, p. 14, in *Writings* 1996, p. 136; "novelty," Young 1969, p. 51, in *Writings* 1996, pp. 129–30.

92 Shiff 2003, p. 16, quoting Johns's Sketchbook A, p. 10, c. 1960, in *Writings* 1996, p. 50. Shiff identified the articles as Philip Morrison, "The Overthrow of Parity," *Scientific American* 196, 4 (Apr. 1957), pp. 45–53; Geoffrey Burbidge and Fred Hoyle, "Anti-Matter," *Scientific American* 198, 4 (Apr. 1958), pp. 34–39; and S. B. Treiman, "The Weak Interactions," *Scientific American* 200, 3 (Mar. 1959), pp. 72–80. Other articles of the 1950s that could have caught Johns's attention addressed topics that would feature in his work such as measurement and the concept of length; how water freezes and ice thaws at the identical temperature. See Nathaniel Kleitman, "Sleep," *Scientific American* 187, 5 (Nov. 1952), p. 37; Kline (note 82); George Miller, "Information and Memory," *Scientific American* 195, 2 (Aug. 1956), pp. 42–46; Bruce Chalmers, "How Water Freezes," *Scientific American* 200, 2 (Feb. 1959), pp. 114–22.

93 Pohlen 1978, p. 22, in *Writings* 1996, pp. 172–73.

94 Rosenthal 1993, p. 64, in *Writings* 1996, p. 283. Interviewed at the end of 1992, Johns made this remark in response to the question of whether the duck/rabbit—illustrated in Ludwig Wittgenstein, *Philosophical Investigations* (1953), 3rd. ed., trans. G. E. M. Anscombe (Blackwell, 2001), p. 166e—interested him in terms of the author's philosophical point. The Wittgenstein discussion is as follows: "I shall call the following figure, derived from Jastrow, the duck-rabbit. It can be seen as a rabbit's head or as a duck's. / And I must distinguish between the 'continuous seeing' of an aspect and the 'dawning' of an aspect. / The picture might have been shewn me, and I have never seen anything but a rabbit in it"; pp. 165e–66e. Johns denied this, stating his interest as quoted.

95 Fred Attneave, "Multistability in Perception," *Scientific American* 225, 6 (Dec. 1971), pp. 63, 66.

96 Weatherby 1990, p. 29, in *Writings* 1996, p. 257. On the Picasso print project, see Wallach 1988, in *Writings* 1996, p. 227; and Rosenthal and Fine 1990, p. 310. The duck/rabbit first appeared in *Untitled* (1984; watercolor and pencil on paper; Collection of the artist) and the young girl/old woman in *Untitled* (1983–84; ink on plastic; Collection of the artist). For discussion of motifs, see Rosenthal 1989, pp. 76, 84, 95; Rose 1987, p. 259; Crichton 1994, p. 66; Bernstein 1996, p. 55; Tone 1996, p. 322.

97 Weatherby 1990, p. 29, in *Writings* 1996, p. 257.

98 Beginning in the 1840s, publishers began printing photo-based illustrations in books and periodicals; Josef Maria Eder, *The History of Photography* (Columbia University Press, 1945), pp. 331–33. These were usually photo-mechanically generated images involving traditional print media (wood engraving, intaglio, or lithography). The various emulsions used in early photography were not sensitive to all wavelengths of the visible spectrum, and were therefore unable to accurately translate color images into grisaille. Artists who worked as illustrators, such as Frederic Remington and Winslow Homer, chose a grisaille palette for works intended for publication to minimize the degradation of their images as the result of the translation from

one medium to another; Estelle Jussim, *Visual Communication and the Graphic Arts* (R. R. Bowker Co., 1974), pp. 195–98.

99 Kozloff 1964, p. 22.

100 Taylor 1990, p. 100, in *Writings* 1996, p. 246.

101 Conversation with the author, July 30, 2004. The chromatic structure of *Odalisque in Grisaille*, with the cream color beneath the figure sounding the only chromatic note in a grisaille field, appears to have informed Johns's grisaille version of *Racing Thoughts* (1984), in which the hanging muted yellow pants function comparably in a largely gray surround.

102 Glueck 1977, p. 87, in *Writings* 1996, p. 166.

103 Conversation with the author, July 30, 2004. See also the interview by Nan Rosenthal in this volume, p. 160.

104 Lichtenstein (note 13), p. 158.

105 Steinberg 1962/1972, p. 32, in *Writings* 1996, p. 83. For discussion of this work in terms of the senses, see Bernstein 1980, p. 287, in *Writings* 1996, p. 202. Bernstein 1985, p. 19; Morris 2007, p. 227.

106 In other Target images, such as the graphite drawing of 1956 (see Weiss 2007, cat. no. 7), the artist's marks subtly emphasize the innermost spherical or pupilar form. Kozloff 1968, pp. 37, 47, observed that Johns admired Redon and the connection with the 1958 Conté crayon *Target* (cat. no. 44).

107 Walter Pach, *Queer Thing, Painting* (Harper and Brothers, 1938), p. 163, states that Duchamp once credited Redon as "my own point of departure."

108 Taylor 1990, p. 100, in *Writings* 1996, p. 248.

109 Rose 1987, p. 259.

110 Faber Birren, *Color Dimensions: Creating New Principles of Color Harmony and a Practical Equation in Color Definition* (Crimson Press, 1934), p. 10. Recalling his semester at the Parsons School of Design (Jan.–June 1949), Johns remembered being taught, "design and color theory...life drawing, anatomy"; Diamonstein Spielvogel 1994, p. 115, in *Writings* 1996, p. 291. Based on the Parsons School of Design 1948–49 curriculum, it appears that Johns participated in the first-year program for either the Costume Design or Advertising Design degree. Birren's *Color Dimensions* is among the books on color theory that were evidently in the school library (now the Gimbel Library at Parsons The New School of Design) by 1949. The library's practice was to lend books to faculty for use in class and to students at the faculty's discretion; Marjorie F. Jones, "A History of the Parsons School of Design, 1896–1966" (Ph.D. diss., New York University, 1968), p. 219.

111 "Color is highly personal. Many authorities maintain that it has no objective existence, but is a psychological experience"; William Longyear, *How to Use Color in Advertising Design, Illustration, and Painting* (Pitman, 1949), p. 39. "It matters little to the artist what color *is*....Our problem is not primarily a chemical or a physical one. It is and remains *psychological*"; Hilaire Hiler, *Color Harmony and Pigments* (Favor, Ruhl, and Co., 1942), p. 6.

112 "Psychology knows more," Birren (note 110), p. 11; "Seeing, feeling," Hiler (note 111), p. 7; "a subject of active debate," Birren (note 110), p. 11.

113 Arthur Guptill, *Color in Sketching and Rendering* (Reinhold, 1935), p. 62.

114 Ibid., p. 33. See also Maitland Graves, *The Art of Color and Design* (McGraw-Hill, 1941), p. 254.

115 Crichton 1994, p. 16.

116 See the overview of psychodiagnostic work relating personality to color preference, including, among others, Rose H. Alschuler, La Berta Weiss Hattwick, Max Lüscher, Max Pfister, and Hermann Rorschach. In Faber Birren, "Personal Color Preferences," ch. 9 in *Color and the Human Response: Aspects of Light and Color Bearing on the Reactions of Living Things and the Welfare of Human Beings* (Van Nostren Reinhold, 1978), pp. 114–18.

117 Faber Birren, *Your Color and Your Self* (Prang, 1952), p. 79. "In deciding upon the relative appeal of white, gray or black, an individual may clearly reveal what, if anything, he or she has imposed on inborn traits"; p. 77.

118 See Alice Planche, "Le gris de l'espoir," *Romania* 94 (1973), pp. 289–302. Planche noted that, in the fifteenth and early sixteenth centuries, gray was sometimes figured—given its contrast to black—as a symbol of hope, but that the signification of gray subsequently became negative (as if viewed from the perspective of white). See also John Morley, *Death, Heaven and the Victorians* (University of Pittsburgh Press, 1971), p. 68. Two years after bereavement, widows could go into half-mourning for six months, and the majority wore gray.

119 See Matthew Luckiesh, *Color and Colors* (D. Van Nostrand, 1938), pp. 78–79; Benjamin Kouwer, *Colors and Their Character: A Psychological Study* (M. Nijhoff, 1949), p. 131.

120 On the goals of the experiment, see Kouwer (note 119), p. 69. Kouwer further stated: "The character of the color is not completely given in the objective stimulus. The stimulus only means an appeal, an invitation to the observer to perceive something. *What* the observer actually will perceive not only depends on the stimulus, but on the total situation *including* the observer, his set and character. The stimulus provides only the *motive* for one perception or another. . . . The perception is essentially determined by the nature of the 'invitation.' In general it is impossible to perceive a 'red' stimulus as green"; p. 143. For the word associations with gray, see pp. 173–74. For the results, see Kouwer's ch. 2, "Discussion of the Results," pp. 131–32; and Appendix, tables A through C, pp. 173–78. The colors available for matching were black, white, red, yellow, orange, blue, green, purple, brown, and gray. Blue and red were most frequently used, closely followed by gray and white; p. 79. The most pronounced frequencies of color-specific word associations were found with red. Similar, though not so high, frequencies were found with gray, black, and white; p. 81.

121 Kouwer (note 119), p. 131.

122 Isidor Thorner, "Ascetic Protestantism and the Development of Science and Technology," *American Journal of Sociology* 58 (1952–53), pp. 25–26.

123 On gray's rationalism, see Birren (note 117), p. 80. On diagnostics, see Jacques-Henri Bustanoby, *Principles of Color and Color Mixing* (McGraw-Hill, 1947), p. 90; and Birren (note 117), p. 23 "Indifference to color which often goes with the sober introvert may rapidly change to an exciting attraction to hue when the same person is 'in his cups.' By actual clinical test, color response will be found to increase when a person is under the influence of alcohol."

124 Kozloff 1964, p. 23; Rose 1964, p. 40.

125 The painting *22 The Lily White* (c. 1950; Collection of Nancy Ganz Wright), a reference to a symbol of virginal purity, is said to reference a song the artist heard as a child. Tomkins 1980, pp. 52–53, noted the original title as *White Painting with Numbers*; see also pp. 71–73.

126 Rose 1964, p. 40.

127 Varnedoe 1996, p. 18.

128 Johns in conversation with Roberta Bernstein, November 15, 1974; Bernstein 1985, p. 221 n. 7.

129 Bernard and Thompson 1984, p. 65, in *Writings* 1996, p. 217. Johns's in interview with Demosthène Davvetas in 1984: "[This] had to do more or less with how I felt about myself, than towards painting. I had withdrawn into myself, I was avoiding psychology or emotions. But I lived through the work....When one is young, one imposes limits on oneself"; Davvetas 1984, p. 12, trans. Christel Hollevoet, in Varnedoe 1996, p. 18.

130 "The great white," Ashbery 1962, p. 51; "reserve...drop," Bernard and Thompson 1984, p. 65, in *Writings* 1996, p. 217: "Finally, one must simply drop the reserve. I think some of the changes in my work related to that."

131 *U.S.A. Artists 8: Jasper Johns* 1966, in *Writings* 1996, p. 123. Typical is the definition of gray in Bustanoby (note 123), p. 52: "neutral, dull; of the color of aluminum, nickel or silver"; see also p. 91.

132 *U.S.A. Artists 8: Jasper Johns* 1966, in *Writings* 1996, p. 125.

133 Tono 1964, in *Writings* 1996, p. 103.

134 Johns, Sketchbook A, p. 31, c. 1963, in *Writings* 1996, p. 52.

135 Kouwer (note 120), p. 135; the passage continues between ellipses: "Gray is nothing, neither good nor bad....It has no direction and it makes no claims."

136 Birren (note 110), p. 47: "In vision the eye distinguishes results only. For example, a gray formed with black and white will appear quite like a similar gray formed with red and green—although the physical conditions of the two

tones may differ. Metamic [*sic*] colors thus are those that look alike but which are physically unlike." Webster's defines metamer as "either of two colors that appear identical to the eye but have different spectral compositions"; Webster's New International Unabridged Dictionary, 3rd ed., s.v. "metamer," sense 2. The Oxford English Dictionary Online defines metamer as "*Optics*: a stimulus that is physically different from another stimulus but evokes the same perceptual response; especially each of two or more colours with different spectral properties that are perceived by an observer as being indistinguishable."

137 Conversation with James Meyer, Jasper Johns's studio assistant, on Aug. 18, 2006.

138 In *Tennyson* (1959), Johns used black, white, and gray pastel, with charcoal, over graphite to create a densely worked surface. In the later version (1967), the artist employed graphite wash with touches of white pastel to create a similarly dense field.

139 See Anonymous, *Color as Light* [number two of a series of monographs on color] (Research Laboratories of the International Printing Ink Corporation and Subsidiary Companies, 1935), p. 13.

140 Guptill (note 113), p. 36; anonymous (note 139).

141 Kouwer (note 119), p. 135; For Albers on after-images, see Albers (note 3), pp. 22ff.

142 Birren (note 110), p. 48.

143 See Guptill (note 113), pp. 57–59. He explained, "When portions of the retina are momentarily fatigued through the excitation set up by a distinct color, as in these recent experiments, [the eye's] balance is disturbed; the tired retinal areas are temporarily incapable of receiving the sensation of white. Being in a sense blinded to the rays of one particular color, they see only the sum total of the rays of the remaining colors of which white light is composed; these form the after-image, which obviously must be complementary to the color itself"; pp. 58–59.

144 Ibid., p. 59.

145 German physiologist Ewald Hering, as cited in Johannes Itten, *The Elements of Color*, trans. Ernst van Haagen (Van Nostrand Reinhold, 1970), p. 20.

146 Johannes Itten, *The Art of Color: The Subjective Experience and Objective Rationale of Color*, trans. Ernst van Haagen (Van Nostrand Reinhold, 1961), p. 20. Itten stated that "two or more colors are mutually harmonious if their mixture yields a neutral gray. Any other color combinations, the mixture of which does not yield gray, are expressive, or discordant, in character"; Itten (note 145), p. 20.

147 Tono 1964, in *Writings* 1996, p. 103.

148 Olson 1979, p. 25, in *Writings* 1996, p. 169.

149 Crichton 1994, p. 39.

150 Crichton 1977, p. 40.

151 See Henderson (note 85), p. 207, see also ch. 14, "Coda: Extensions and Echos of the *Large Glass*," pp. 207–23. She noted Duchamp's interest in optics for physics' rather than art's sake; p. 208, and stated that "Duchamp would have been familiar with the effects of virtual, subjective color produced in optical experiments by rotating black-and-white forms"; p. 212. See also Rosalind E. Krauss, *The Optical Unconscious* (MIT Press, 1993), pp. 120–24, 133–37.

152 The Carnegie Institute's Pittsburgh Bicentennial International Exhibition of Contemporary Painting and Sculpture ran from Dec. 1, 1958, to Feb. 8, 1959. The jury comprised Mary Callery, Marcel Duchamp, Vincent Price, James Johnson Sweeney, Raoul Ubac, and Lionello Venturi. *Gray Numbers* (1958) was the only painting by an American artist to receive an award. See Tone 1996, p. 129.

153 For this anecdote, see Thomas Hess, "Hommage to Albers," in *Albers*, exh. cat. (Galerie Beyeler, Basel, 1973), n.pag, as cited in the essay by James Rondeau in this volume, p. 55. For the artist's account, see the interview by Nan Rosenthal in this volume, p. 158.

154 Gage (note 6), p. 117. Birren (note 110), p. 12.

155 Elise Murray, "Anomalies in Color Vision," *Scientific Monthly* 57, 4 (Oct. 1943), p. 327; Birren (note 110), pp. 12; H. Kalmus, "Inherited Sense Defects (Concerning Color Blindness, Tone Deafness, and Certain Lesser-known Shortcomings of Men and Animals)," *Scientific American* 186, 5 (May 1952), pp. 64–65.

156 Murray (note 155), pp. 322–23; Alphonse Chapanis, "Color Blindness," *Scientific American* 184, 3 (Mar. 1951), pp. 49–50.

157 The medical examinations given to military recruits revealed many cases of deficient color vision. Diagnosis of color blindness prevented soldiers from serving in the Navy, Air Force, or Marines; Murray 1943, p. 329. Eager to serve and unaware of their condition, many men denied having any trouble seeing colors; Chapanis 1951, p. 51. Individuals protested and rumors circulated regarding the benefits of color blindness, such as an increased ability to detect camouflage. However, tests by the military disproved the latter and those who failed the color test were limited to serving in positions that would not be compromised by their condition.

158 Murray (note 155), p. 322.

159 Ibid., p. 323.

160 Bernstein 1985, pp. 26–27: "A new motif, polka dots, appears in this series for the first time."

161 See Kalmus (note 155), p. 64. In an interview of 1993, Johns observed, "There is always another way to see things, isn't there? It is interesting to me that the world is not the same to us"; Mattison 1995, p. 35.

162 See Murray (note 155), p. 324; Chapanis (note 156), p. 51.

163 Chapanis (note 156), pp. 50–51.

164 Sylvester 1965, in Sylvester 2001, p. 163.

165 See Bernstein 1985, p. 40; and Varnedoe 1996, p. 163.

166 Kozloff 1968, p. 27.

167 Crichton 1994, p. 39.

168 Chapanis (note 156), p. 50, noted that in the most common kind of color blindness—so-called two-color vision—color is essentially reduced to two types of hues, yellows and blues, which are clearly distinguishable. Particularly suggestive in Johns's painting is the placement of red near black and the incidence of correct labeling involving blue and yellow. Chapanis continued: "Among the red-yellow-green confusers visual scientists distinguish two principal varieties: those who see all colors in their normal brightness relations, though they may confuse one color with another, and those who have abnormal brightness sensitivity to certain colors. To the latter deep red, for example, appears so dark that it may be confused with black."

169 Crichton 1994, p. 39.

170 Tono 1975, in *Writings* 1996, p. 149.

171 Tono 1964, in *Writings* 1996, p. 97.

172 Bernstein 1996, p. 43. On Duchamp and Magritte, see Bernstein 1985, pp. 19, 43–44, 60–68, 92, 129, 131; Crichton 1994, pp. 50–51. On Johns and Wittgenstein, see Krauss 1965, pp. 91–92. Krauss noted (p. 97 n. 22) that Johns was prompted to read Wittgenstein late in 1961, when he heard a story about the philosopher that is recounted in Norman Malcolm, *Ludwig Wittgenstein: A Memoir* (1958; Oxford University Press, 1962), p. 51. According to Bernstein 1985, pp. 91–94, 228–29 n. 4, Johns informed her that he had heard about Wittgenstein through his friend David Hayes, from whom he borrowed *Philosophical Investigations*. She also referenced a November 1974 conversation and followed Krauss's dating of Johns's first interest to 1961. Rose 1965b, p. 66, noted that a number of artists of Johns's generation were interested in Wittgenstein. See also Higginson 1976.

173 Gilbert Ryle, "Books: The Work of an Influential but Little-known Philosopher of Science: Ludwig Wittgenstein," *Scientific American* 197, 3 (Sept. 1957), pp. 251–59. Wittgenstein discussed the speaking or "practice of the use of language" that he famously termed the "language-game" in Wittgenstein (note 94), p. 10e, sec. 23.

174 Norman Malcolm's *Ludwig Wittgenstein: A Memoir* (Oxford University Press, 1958) was reviewed in James R. Newman, "Books: The Tortured Life of an Influential Modern Philosopher: The Late Ludwig Wittgenstein," *Scientific American* 197, 3 (Aug. 1959), pp. 149–58. For the anecdote and Johns's response, see Krauss 1965, p. 97 n. 22.

175 Norman Malcolm, *Ludwig Wittgenstein: A Memoir* (1958; repr., Oxford University Press, 1977), pp. 49, 39, 91, 47.

176 William H. Brenner, *Wittgenstein's Philosophical Investigation* (State University of New York Press, 1999), esp. ch. 4, "Color and Number," pp. 117–38. For "0 to 9," see Wittgenstein (note 94), p. 48e, sec. 143.

177 Stevens and McGuigan 1977, p. 78, in *Writings* 1996, p. 165. Higginson 1976, p. 53. For more on the "abuse" of language, color names in particular, see

Klüver 1963, in *Writings* 1996, p. 89; and Tono 1974, in *Writings* 1996, p. 97.

178 Johns's study of the Dadaists and Duchamp, and of the philosopher Wittgenstein has been described as a kind of responsive reading, the artist finding in these sources ideas sympathetic to and enriching ones already espoused. See Krauss 1965, pp. 87–88, 91; Higginson 1976, p. 53; Bernstein 1985, p. 92; Tone 1996, p. 127.

179 Malcolm (note 175), p. 55.

180 On *Diver* as a self-portrait, see Bernstein 1977, pp. 142–43. Elderfield 2007, pp. 199–200, observed: "The possibility that we may use a fixed image to represent movement in our perception of it is called forth the more strongly by images placed in confining tracks. Johns discovered this when he made *Device Circle* in 1959, an anthropomorphic version of which composed a part of *Periscope (Hart Crane)*, made alongside *Diver*. And the more prescriptive these tracks the better. In this respect, the ultimate model for both *Device Circle* and *Diver* is, as often remarked, Leonardo da Vinci's *The Proportions of the Human Body According to Vitruvius*, done about 1492."

181 Young 1969, p. 54, in *Writings* 1996, p. 134.

182 Field 1999, p. 21.

183 Sylvester 1965, in Sylvester 2001, p. 148.

184 See Field 1999, p. 21.

185 For the religious symbolism in Johns's later work, see Bernstein 1996, pp. 61, 67, 89 fig. 71, who mentioned the impact on Johns of the depiction of the veil of Saint Veronica by Francisco de Zurbarán, which he saw in an exhibition at the Metropolitan Museum of Art, New York, in 1987; p. 74 n. 117.

186 On the Catenary series, see Garrels 1999, p. 10; Field 1999, pp. 17, 22–25, 29; and Pissarro 1999, p. 50. See also Rothkopf 2005, pp. 5, 9, 16.

187 Young 1969, p. 54, in *Writings* 1996, p. 134.

188 See Bernstein 1996, pp. 50, 54; for a reproduction *Between the Clock and the Bed* see p. 84, figs. 49–50. On Picasso, see Bernstein 1996, p. 59; *The Shadow* (1953; Musée Picasso, Paris) is reproduced as fig. 77 on p. 90.

189 Bernstein 1996, p. 50.

190 The possible significance of the inscription was pointed out by Jesse Feiman. Bill Goldston noted that the medium of this print is actually offset lithography; Johns would not have had to reverse the letters, as he would in traditional lithography, but, in Goldston's opinion, the artist was playing with the viewer's assumption of reversal in printmaking; conversation with Bill Goldston, ULAE, May 2, 2007.

191 See Bernstein 1985, pp. 45–47.

192 For a discussion of these motifs, see Weiss 2007, pp. 8–9, 11–13, 44–45.

193 Ernst Van de Wetering, *A Corpus of Rembrandt Paintings* (M. Nijhoff, 2005), pp. 564–68. Van de Wetering observed that the speculations to which the self-portrait gave rise "without exception...pertain to the meaning of the two semi-circles on the light wall before which Rembrandt has portrayed himself," and noted the hypothesis that the artist could have intended the two circles to signify a world map; p. 564. Christopher Wright speculated that the "famous half-circles could well have been introduced for decorative reasons in order to enliven an unusually large expanse of plain background...."; *Rembrandt: Self-Portraits* (Viking Press, 1982), p. 32.

194 Johns stenciled "gray" onto *Device* (1962) as a reference to his earlier *Painting with Ruler and "Gray"* (1960; Frederick R. Weisman Art Foundation, Los Angeles), in which he incorporated a found piece of wood stamped with the word GRAY; Mancusi-Ungaro 2007, p. 253; see the essay by James Rondeau, p. 31; see also the interview by Nan Rosenthal in this volume, p. 159.

Conditional States

The Appearance of Gray in Jasper Johns's Graphic Work

MARK PASCALE

JASPER JOHNS HAS ALWAYS HAD AN INTEREST IN WHAT THINGS are and how they appear. Over the course of his career, gray has been a constant stimulus, initially serving as a means of emphasizing the material or physical properties of an object by draining it of color or emotion. The artist's employment of gray throughout all his major serial motifs and in a wide range of media, however, has evolved into more than just an assessment of the specific forms that he depicts; rather, it can be considered an examination of gray itself. Indeed, for Johns, gray has become a condition — a separate idea or material of its own.[1] The artist often creates works on paper as further explorations of already extant paintings. How then, one might ask, has printmaking allowed Johns to investigate gray in a new way? The artist has his own literal definition of gray when he uses it: achromatic mixtures of only black and white yielding a range of value; monochromatic when a single color is added to shift the gray to the warm or cool side of the spectrum. Printmaking offered Johns a host of new variables to experiment with in the production of gray: different drawing materials and methods of application; the color, surface, and relative absorbency of paper; the pressure used to print the matrix; the order in which elements are printed; and the degree to which the matrices are inked. These factors proved difficult to master, and Johns was undoubtedly provoked by the ample challenges he encountered working with fairly traditional print methods. This essay offers detailed readings of the artist's printmaking processes that suggest the growth and trajectory of his graphic output, as well as how he subtly, at times even obsessively, mines the different properties of gray in his prints.

From his earliest printmaking experiences in 1960 working with Tatyana Grosman at the Long Island workshop Universal Limited Art Editions (ULAE), Johns understood that the medium afforded him the ability to retain each stage of his project and to rework or recontextualize it as he wished. Despite any initial frustrations with or inability to master printmaking, Johns nevertheless expressed a desire to continue working in it "because, knowing nothing about the process, he wanted to see how much he could complicate it."[2] With its subtle range of tonal values, gray provided a wealth of opportunity to fulfill this desire. Because one's appreciation of Johns's oeuvre is rewarded by careful and sustained looking, such prolonged consideration can lead to a perception of his work as something other than what he may have intended. In fact, many of the prints discussed in this essay are not necessarily called gray by Johns, and are not always the most obvious color gray; rather, they approximate its appearance. This is due to the artist's remarkable ability to coax subtleties from drawn marks that, when layered on papers of various colors and relative absorbency, often result in our *perception* of gray. As Johns became more adept at printmaking, he in turn became more skilled at concealing the discrete operations required of it. Indeed, his most mature prints display a seamlessness that masks any sense of process entirely.

Several authors have detailed Johns's earliest foray into lithography.[3] Much of what is known about the images and the order in which the artist drew

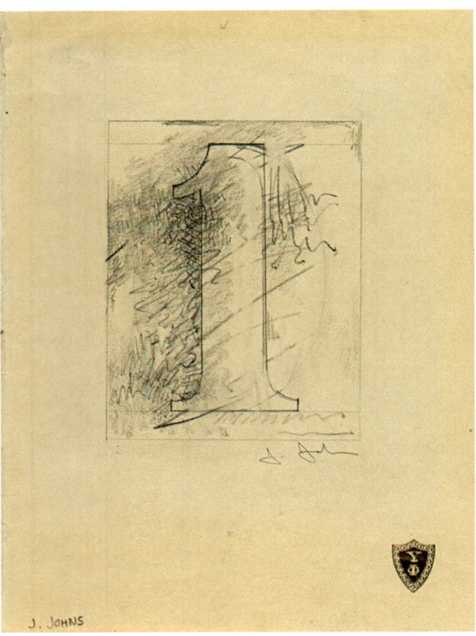

Fig. 1. *Figure 1*, 1957. Graphite on cream wove paper; 27 × 20 cm (10 5/8 × 7 7/8 in.). The Art Institute of Chicago, gift of Mr. and Mrs. B. C. Holland, 1969.6.

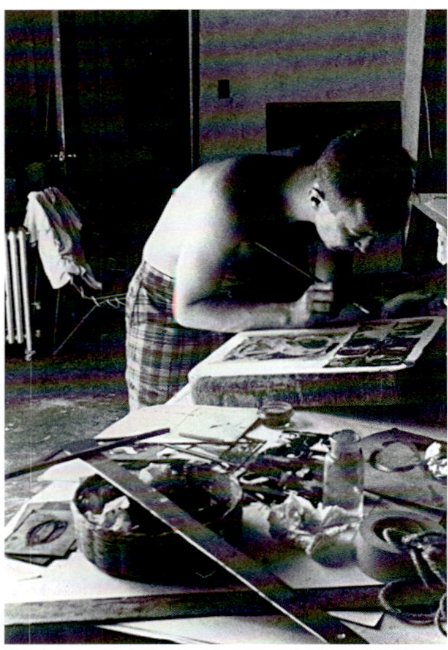

Fig. 2. Johns at ULAE working on the lithographic stone from the 0–9 portfolio.

them on the stones owes largely to his and Tatyana Grosman's recollections.[4] We know, for example, that Johns's first lithographic motif was the drawing of the large "0," which would become the basis for the *0–9* editions. To this image Johns later added the frieze of numbers that appears at the top of the editioned prints.[5] As with most of his prints, these first lithographs follow works in other media: the frieze is based on two paintings: a 1959–62 acrylic on canvas (cat. no. 65) and a 1958 encaustic and collage on canvas in a private collection.[6] What is unique to the print is Johns's inclusion of both the large single number and the frieze of smaller numbers in one composition. The artist's idea to change the large number as subsequent prints were made may have originated in a small drawing, *Figure 1* (**FIG. 1**). Although its proportion is slightly different from that of the "1" in the *0–9* portfolios, careful examination reveals the faint arc of a "0" along the right side of the paper.[7] In any event, early accounts of Johns's intent make clear that he planned to alter the stone after each number was printed.[8]

Johns's work on the "0" print saw him, like any unpracticed printmaker, learning to navigate the delicate process of printmaking. Indeed, the artist himself recalled that he began drawing the "0" stone as a test of the medium.[9] Using a stencil, Johns probably lightly sketched the frieze of numbers at the top with a lithographic crayon or pencil (see **FIG. 2**). He followed with tusche, applied with a brush full strength (and at times diluted with water) over the crayon, and sometimes later reinforced with the crayon again, because the tusche dissolved the crayon where it was wettest. This is especially apparent in the small "3" of the frieze (see **FIG. 3**). It is also possible that Johns used a water-laden brush to liquefy the crayon and create washes of tone. He also brushed tusche wet-into-wet, and especially in the lower "0," he drew back into the still damp wash with a soft crayon. Such accumulated layers of drawing might lead an artist inexperienced in lithography to believe that the final print would yield all of the textural qualities of the drawing.[10] Unfortunately, this is never the case, because to ready a lithographic drawing for printing, the actual drawing material is replaced with lithography ink, which flattens the image. The ink is necessary both to stabilize the image with one material that can be inked and transferred consistently and to bring the drawing to the surface of the stone, so that the worked and unworked areas alike are flush with the surface, held in place by the chemical balance between them. This is why lithography is called a "planographic" process. It is difficult to imagine what Johns's reaction was when he saw the inked-up stone and the first proofs. If he was disappointed at what he felt was lost to the process, the large number of proofs that were made of the "0" stone strongly suggests that the medium intrigued him and he was moved to master it.

Intermittently over the next three years, Johns produced three distinct editions of *0–9*, labeled "A/C," "B/C," and "C/C." These editions were printed in black, gray, and color, respectively. Taken together, the three suites of *0–9* constitute the locus of all of Johns's chromatic explorations up to that time, and, in fact, even now: color as value (edition A/C), achromatic gray (edition B/C), and the spectral colors plus black, white, gray, and brown (edition C/C). It is important to note, however, that Johns first conceived the project in gray, a fact underscored by his inscribing the "0" print from the gray edition B/C with the date "'60," while the rest of the prints are indicated as "'63."[11] Thus, the order of printing did not correspond to the sequence suggested by the letter-fractions. Two early trial proofs of the "0" print demonstrate how Johns experimented with different combinations of inks and papers in order to achieve his desired effect of gray. Both were made on sheets of handmade paper with a pronounced soft, fibrous surface, one in black ink on ivory paper (1960; cat. no. 77), the other in gray ink on unbleached gray paper (1960; cat. no. 78). In the former image,

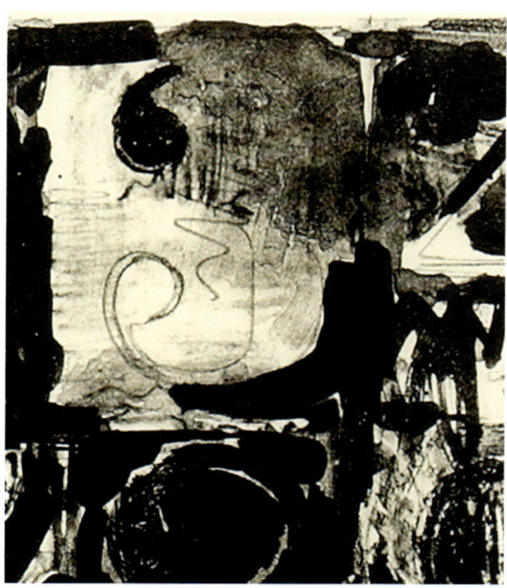

Fig. 3. Detail of the frieze of numbers from a "0" print (cat. no. 76), showing the dissolved tusche in the number "3."

the great absorbency and silkiness of the fibrous paper caused the black ink to flatten so that contrast is lower and the ink sits more prominently in a multitiered position, both in and on top of the paper fibers. This approximates the condition of the drawing on stone before it is processed. Depending on the way the print is lit, the ink appears black or a silvery dark gray with black undertones, which is in fact quite different from the final version of edition A/C. The second trial proof, mentioned above, is more closely aligned to the final version of edition B/C. In the B/C prints, the paper color approximates the warm gray of a lithographic stone, and the proportion of the paper border to image emulates that of the actual matrix.[12] Considering that Johns conceived the "0" print as a gray image, working on a warm gray lithographic stone would have provided the artist with the closest tonal approximation to envision how his drawing would have looked on the unbleached paper.

Target, the artist's second print (but the first published) was more an attempt at exploring how well lithography could mimic the properties of another medium. Although the composition is reversed, the lithograph closely follows that of Johns's 1958 drawing *Target* (cat. no. 44), but for various reasons it falls short of evoking the mysterious qualities of the earlier work.[13] The drawing was composed in layers; Johns first applied a painterly wash—presumably employing a combination of brush and perhaps a blending method—of gray and white pastels. These provide a subtle tone to the paper and also emphasize the concentric rings of the target, alternating the bands with warm and cool casts. Johns then used black Conté crayon and China marker (a greasy black crayon similar to a lithographic pencil) to delineate the target with hatches and his signature "W" stroke.[14] When Johns made the print, he first drew the key image in lithographic crayon using the same types of strokes that he had employed in the drawing. In addition, he added thin layers of tusche wash and scraped some of the edges of the rings, emphasizing the eyelike character of the image. At a very early point in the print's evolution, the artist took a proof of the key stone (the stone that bears the original drawing) on newsprint and laid a gray brush-and-ink wash into it (1960; cat. no. 46). Apparently happy with the way this wash extended the range of grays in the image—or perhaps urged on by Grosman or Johns's printer at ULAE, Robert Blackburn—Johns sought to re-create this effect by producing a second, or "tint," stone that would mimic the drawn wash, and a separate proof of this stone was pulled (1960; cat. no. 47).[15] Viewed by itself, the proof of the tint stone (printed in gray), appears similar to the subtlety of the pastel ground in the original drawing. When the tint stone was combined with the key image, however, the effect was ham-handed—the gray and black fail to coalesce (see cat. no. 48). Thus, still learning to feel his lithographic legs under him, Johns had yet to master the technical finesse needed to create a subtly layered print that fully simulated the property of the pastel and Conté crayon drawing. Nevertheless, the workshop prized these early proofs of *Target* perhaps as a harbinger of the success that was to come, and they were framed together in a grouping that hung prominently in the Grosmans' home for many years (see **FIG. 4**).

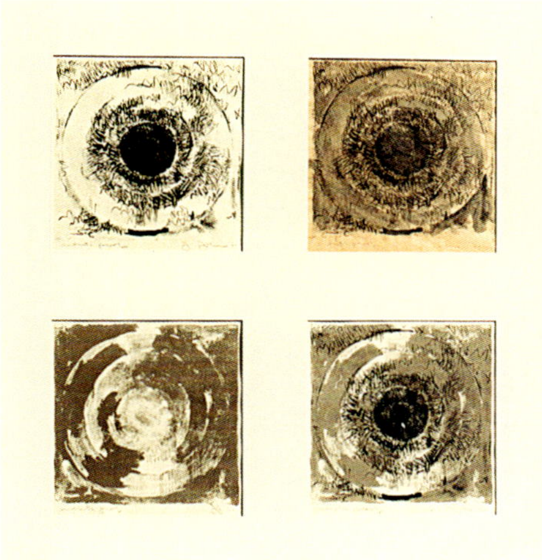

Fig. 4. The four early Target prints (all 1960), mounted together as they would have been displayed in the Grosmans' home.

In two other early groups of prints—Coat Hangers and Flags—Johns continued his broad experiments with papers and inks, much as he had done in the proofing stage of the *0–9* portfolios. Comparing his unpublished proofs with published editions on these themes, however, one can see the artist beginning to employ a more sophisticated use of materials to produce the effect of gray. At first inspection, *Coat Hanger I* (1960; cat. no. 17) appears to be a fairly conventional crayon lithograph—albeit a lushly drawn field of marks that seems to upholster the area behind the naked coat hanger, thus underscoring the absence of clothing from the device. In the painting on which this image is based (1959; cat. no. 16), Johns spray painted an actual coat hanger gray and

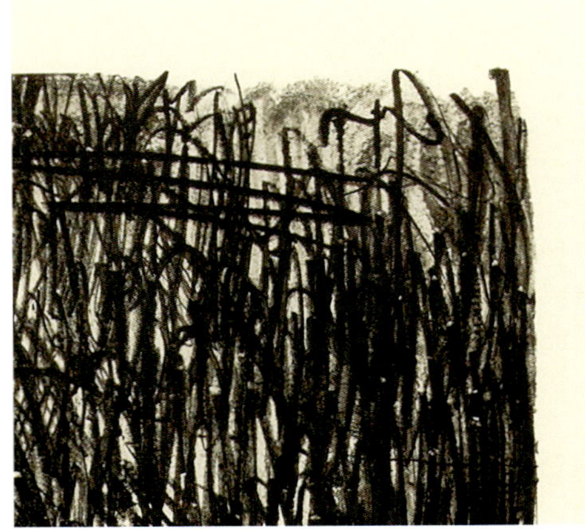

Fig. 5. Detail of the upper-right corner of *Coat Hanger I* (cat. no. 17).

hung it from a peg in front of the gray painted surface; here, in the first state of the lithograph, the hanger is rendered as a dark-colored object that similarly mimics the value of the field. Seemingly, this has nothing to do with gray, because the artist printed the image in black. Careful examination, however, reveals that he drew this field over a ground prepared for the stone. This is evident at the print's upper-right edge, where a lighter gray tone emerges from underneath the crayon marks (see FIG. 5). Johns may have achieved this effect by dipping a piece of cheesecloth into tusche and laying it onto the stone, leaving an impression of the textile on the matrix.[16] This operation calls to mind Johns's use of newspaper collage in his encaustic paintings, for which he dipped strips of newspaper into encaustic before applying them to a canvas.[17] The tusche creates a hazy gray backdrop for the crayon work in the foreground. The longer one examines the work, the more the coat hanger, heavy with dense black outlines, appears to float in front of a gray field of marks. The overall effect is quite similar to that of the pastel drawing *Tennyson* (1959; cat. no. 13). At first glance, the drawing displays a monotone field, but prolonged viewing reveals subtleties of warm and cool grays, as well as carefully plotted reserved whites, which the artist employed to depict the folded, painted canvas of the original encaustic (1958; cat. no. 12). Both *Coat Hanger I* and the *Tennyson* drawing undulate in a graphically controlled way, and while Johns maintained or insisted upon their shallow space—as if the compositions are hovering over the paper—his manipulations of the marks and gray fields add an objectlike quality to the drawn representations of the coat hanger and the folded canvas, respectively.

Johns continued to rework the Coat Hanger matrix, creating several interesting working proofs that demonstrate his manipulation of black media to appear gray. For one of these (1960; cat. no. 18), he drew with lithographic tusche and crayon over a dense field of printed black ink. The interplay of the very waxy black of the drawing material and the printed proof makes it appear as though the printed ink is in fact dark gray. This proof embodies gray created through the layering of black media. Yet another special proof (1960; cat. no. 19) further complicates the condition of gray. Here the field is nearly solid black, and the coat hanger is embossed and thus dimensional. The embossing casts a subtle shadow, or grayed area, around itself, underscoring the allusion of the hanger as three-dimensional.[18] Despite these varied experiments, Johns ultimately chose to print the second edition, *Coat Hanger II* (1960; cat. no. 20), in a mixed-gray ink.

Each of the three distinct versions of Johns's Flag prints from 1960 can be considered a representation of a specific color aspect of gray—hue, value, or chroma. Like *Coat Hanger I*, *Flag I* (cat. no. 26) was printed in black, the darkest value of the gray scale. Johns executed this image with several tools and methods—brush-applied tusche wash, smudging (the artist's fingerprints appear in several places), and stamping of a tusche-dipped cheesecloth or scrap of linen. It is possible that he was here experimenting with the density of a printed image, exploring how much drawing material he could add to the stone until the image filled in completely. In this aspect, the print is akin to another version of the Flag motif, a drawing that he executed in graphite washes (FIG. 6). In the print, the dark, glossy ink seems to shimmer in conjunction with the untouched reserves of the paper, and the image vacillates between negative and positive. Johns would later refine this effect in his Map prints. Having completed *Flag I* using conventional printmaking paper, the artist reworked the stone with tusche and crayon and printed it in white on tan wrapping paper, creating *Flag II* (1960; cat. no. 27). Although the image is printed in white ink, the interaction of the ink's density (it is nearly opaque) with the paper ground (a middle value) here makes it read as pale, silvery gray, representing chroma (the relative purity or impurity of hue). This would evolve

Fig. 6. *Flag*, 1959. Graphite on paper; 27.3 × 38.1 cm (10 ¾ × 15 in.). Private collection.

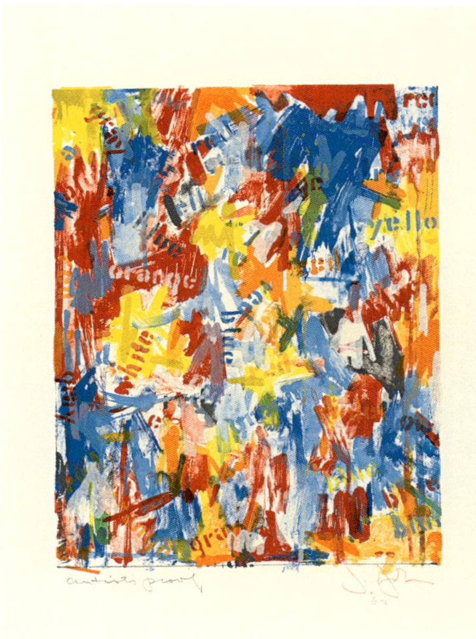

Fig. 7. *False Start I*, 1962. Lithograph from eleven stones on ivory wove paper (Rives BFK); sheet: 76.7 × 56.5 cm (30 3/16 × 22 1/4 in.). The Art Institute of Chicago, ULAE Collection acquired through a challenge grant of Mr. and Mrs. Thomas Dittmer; restricted gift of the supporters of the Department of Prints and Drawings; Centennial and Margaret Fisher endowments, 1982.941.

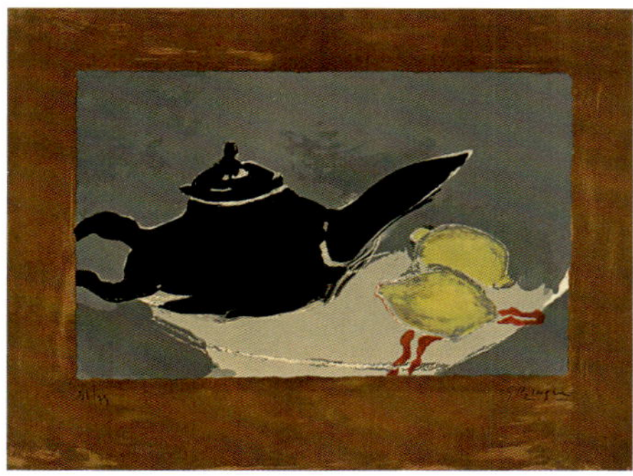

Fig. 8. Georges Braque. *Black Teapot and Lemons*, 1949. Lithograph on cream wove paper (Arches); sheet: 49.5 × 64.7 cm (19 1/2 × 25 1/2 in.). The Art Institute of Chicago, gift of Joseph R. Shapiro, 1954.977.

into Johns's interest in printing transparent white inks onto black papers to produce the effect of gray.[19] Finally, Johns reworked the stone yet again, covering it with a network of scratches that emphasize the flag's pattern of stars and stripes. And, as he had for the Coat Hanger series, Johns chose to print this final state—*Flag III* (1960; cat. no. 28)—in gray on ivory wove paper. Thus, it is as if the artist was playing with different ways of arriving at gray before ultimately deciding to print in the actual hue.

Within these few months of remarkable and intense work at ULAE, Johns established a life-long habit of printmaking as an integral part of his working scheme and established through the print medium an analogue to his interest in the use of gray in paint and drawing media. In 1962 the artist began producing lithographs for which he employed matrices printed first in color and later in grisaille. The color print *False Start I* (**FIG. 7**) and its gray counterpart, *False Start II* (cat. no. 4), were made after Johns's 1959 painting *False Start* (cat. no. 1). Using eleven matrices—representing all the primary and secondary colors or variations of them—Johns was able to capture in *False Start I* many of the optical blends of color that occur in the original painting. There are historical precedents in printmaking for the subtle overlaying of semiopaque, light colors over dark hues, and more transparent dark shades over light hues. Georges Braque employed these techniques extensively in his lithographs of the late 1940s and early 1950s (see **FIG. 8**).[20] While it is not clear whether Johns was familiar with these prints, Robert Blackburn certainly was and he used the technique in his own lithographs. This method helped Johns achieve the complex layering of warm and cool colors and, in particular, placing dark or cool hues on top of light or warm ones. This is especially apparent in the upper-left corner of *False Start I*, where Johns applied a muddy yellow-green over a lighter, more transparent yellow (see **FIG. 7**).

After printing the color version, Johns retained all eleven stones and had them reprinted in shades of gray, creating *False Start II*. Like the original painting's gray counterpart, *Jubilee* (1959; cat. no. 2), the gray print is in many ways more dimensional than the color version. Here Johns employed layering techniques similar to those in the color print, yet the subtlety of the gray tones yields a greater sense of depth, while maintaining lightness and avoiding the heavy quality in the upper-left corner of *False Start I*. The grisaille also speaks forcefully to the drawing *Jubilee* (1960; cat. no. 5). So physical is the surface of the graphite wash in *Jubilee* that one can discern actual dimension in many passages. Microscopic examination has revealed that Johns used letter stencils, sometimes building dimension around the form and sometimes within it. In addition, the artist applied fixative to the incomplete drawing and worked over it with additional wash. This allowed him to achieve passages that appear nearly black and opaque, but that also impart sheen. And while it is not clear exactly what Johns employed as the liquid vehicle to suspend the powdered graphite, heavy haloing on the sheet suggests turpentine or another petroleum solvent for some of the washes, which may have contributed to his ability to make the washes dimensional in several areas.[21] Johns use of powdered graphite suspended in a transparent base was a significant development; however, the artist would not fully refine this technique in his prints until he was working in Los Angeles at Gemini G.E.L. in 1968.[22] In *False Start II*, Johns achieved a dimensionality akin to that of the *Jubilee* drawing by using eleven matrices to build layer upon layer. Only after he became more adept at the manipulation of printing materials would he also become more economical, creating fewer matrices and using the properties of transparency and opacity more efficiently in conjunction with papers, ink conditioners, and printing pressure.

The condition of gray can also be understood photographically. As Arturo Herrera recognized, "The whole tone quality [of photography] is almost

Fig. 9. *Two Maps I* (detail), 1965–66. Lithograph from one aluminum plate on ivory wove paper, trial proof; 56.5 × 75.5 cm (22 ¼ × 29 ¾ in.). The Art Institute of Chicago, ULAE Collection acquired through a challenge grant of Mr. and Mrs. Thomas Dittmer; restricted gift of supporters of the Department of Prints and Drawings; Centennial and Margaret Fisher endowments, 1982.952a.

like graphite. It's almost like drawing. Usually photography is so much about perfect blacks and whites, and these are really about perfect grays."[23] Johns had used photographic reproductions in his work prior to undertaking the lithographic drawings for his Map prints,[24] but not as a way of creating continuous values of gray. The series began as a drawing in tusche wash on an aluminum plate, a surface that the artist was curious to try. On one of these plates, Johns drew a map of the United States without labeling the individual states, as he had in an earlier encaustic collage (1962; cat. no. 39). The plate was then processed and proofed in black, the result of which Johns found unappealing (see FIG. 9). Remembering something that John Cage once told him—"if something wasn't very pleasant once, then you should repeat it and perhaps it would become more interesting"—Johns decided to print two maps on one sheet of paper, a process that required careful realignment of the paper with the matrix.[25] At about the same time, the artist decided to explore the technique of printing white ink on black paper, and proofs of the single map were made in this way.[26] Over at least one of these proofs (1965–66; cat. no. 53), Johns drew extensively with black ink, probably lithographic tusche, the addition of which clarified the integrity of the individual shapes of the states. The graying effect that results calls to mind art historical precedents of layering black and white media that date back to the Renaissance.[27]

Johns then drew a second image of two maps on a stone and began another sequence of proofs. A seemingly unique proof of the two matrices, wherein the stone was printed in black over the original aluminum plate printed in white (1966; cat. no. 52), further extrapolates the optical effects created by layering black and white. The result gives the maps the appearance of the Sabattier effect in photography (see FIG. 10), whereby a partially developed negative is reexposed, reversing some of the values and emphasizing the dark gray tones.[28] The unfinished and jarring appearance of this version, however, prompted Johns to make further adjustments. For the first editioned state, *Two Maps I* (1965–66; cat. no. 51), Johns printed both the stone and the plate in white on black paper. The two densities of white ink on black paper read as silvery gray, and the delicate value range makes it at times difficult to distinguish the forms of the map. Moreover, in this version of the print, Johns achieved a fluidity in lithography that comes close to the manipulation of encaustic—literally, all the brushstrokes and pools of pigment are evident. And still, the effect of light ink on dark paper recalls a black-and-white photography negative.[29] The final printing, *Two Maps II* (1966; cat. no. 54), is in black on white Japanese paper mounted on a black support sheet. Unlike the first version of the motif, *Two Maps II* stresses the individual shapes of the states. Johns achieved this by printing the element in black (as a positive). Yet printing in black on a translucent white paper that is mounted on a black field creates the appearance of a negative. This undoubtedly is caused in part because one normally expects to see a map of the United States printed in color against a sea of blue—or light on dark—but Johns fundamentally reversed our expectation.[30]

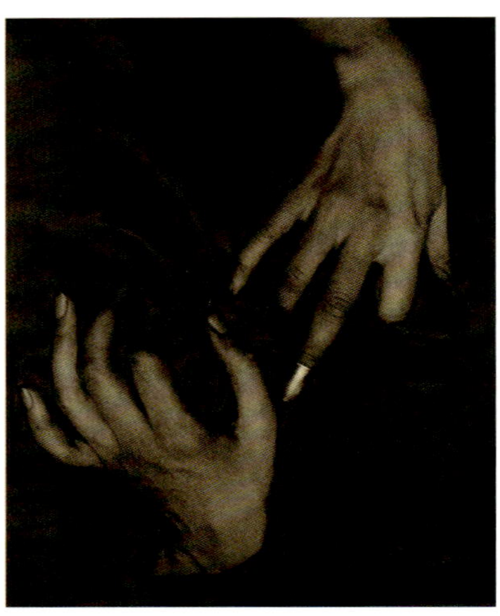

Fig. 10. Alfred Stieglitz. *Georgia O'Keeffe*, 1920. Solarized palladium print; 25.1 × 20.2 cm (9 ⅞ × 7 15/16 in.). The Art Institute of Chicago, Alfred Stieglitz Collection, 1949.745.

Johns's obsessive need to complicate the printmaking process grew exponentially as his confidence as a printmaker increased. In 1969 he said: ". . . the making of a print is actually accomplished by making discrete operations. . . . I like the idea of taking these discrete operations and using them in such a way that doubt is cast upon them, and one is not sure what to regard as a discrete thing."[31] This statement can certainly be applied toward understanding his rich but almost perverse accomplishments in the creation of *White Target* (1967–68; cat. no. 50) a year earlier. Johns made *White Target* by reusing six drawings on stones that he previously employed in the color prints *Target* and *Targets* (1967 and 1967–68, respectively). Of the six stones,

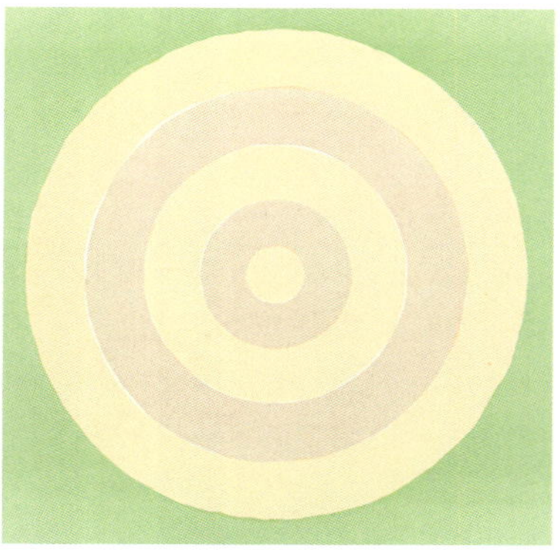

Fig. 11. Detail of a progressive print for *Targets*, 1967–68, printed in three colors from three stones. This print represents the three elements that formed the solid areas of color in the final print (see fig. 12).

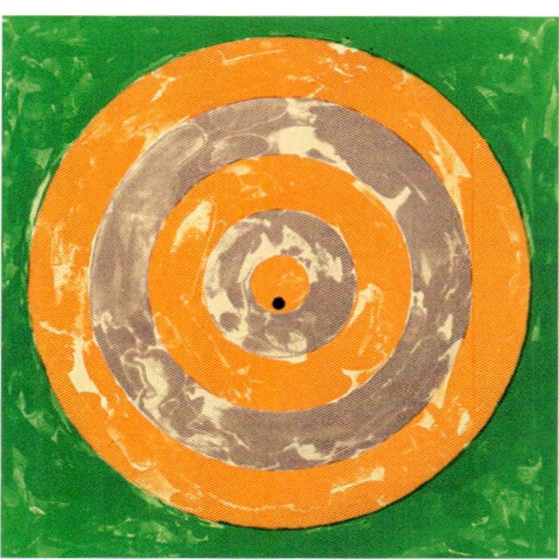

Fig. 12. Detail of the final editioned version of *Targets*, 1967–68, printed in six colors, from six stones.

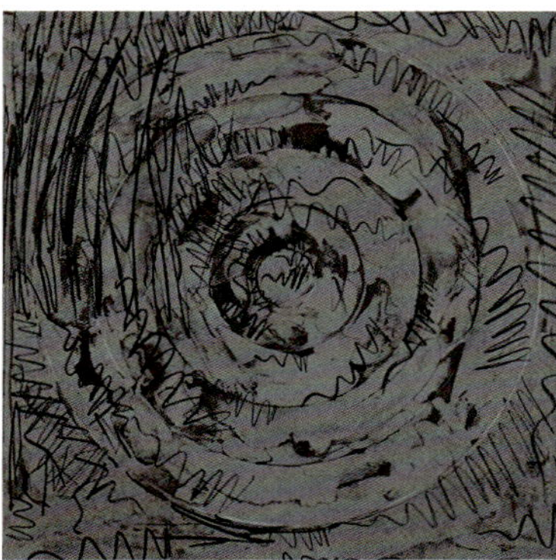

Fig. 13. Detail of a trial proof for *White Target*, 1967–68. This print represents the same three stones that were employed for the detail elements in *Targets* (see fig. 12), here printed in whites, along with an additional element printed in black.

three were used to define solid areas of color; the remaining three added detail elements to the finished print (see **FIGS. 11–12**).[32] For *White Target*, Johns had each of the matrices inked in various shades and transparencies of white; however, the inks were mixed and printed with such care that it is nearly impossible to distinguish the individual layers. This remarkable illusion was accomplished by printing the three solid elements in a similar value and density of white, over which were printed the detail elements in a variety of white values and degrees of transparency. The effects of printing were further diffused by Johns's choice of a soft black Japanese paper, which distributes the inks in a way that emphasizes their similarity of tone and allows an overall graying effect because the black paper mixes optically with the white inks to produce grays. Thus, an image that was once rendered in an obvious manner (the color targets) is now obscured; the many layers of process remain more-or-less mysterious to the viewer.

Further complicating things, Johns added a final, seventh printing element to *White Target*: a quickly drawn system of crayon strokes that, when printed in a nearly opaque white ink, hovers over the image. These strokes overshoot the boundary of the initial composition, and are thus cropped by the cut edges of the collé sheet. This device repeats, in reverse tones, a technique Johns employed in his 1964 lithograph *Ale Cans*, which also comprised seven printing elements. As Richard Field pointed out about this print, "The importance of this broken line should not be underestimated, for it at once separates and unites the image and the flatness of the paper."[33] This method is even more apparent in an uneditioned version of *White Target*, for which Johns printed four of the seven matrices, layering the three detail stones in white along with the seventh element in black on black Japanese paper (see **FIG. 13**). The addition of black creates the illusion of gray; thus, the appearance of gray is produced not only by the white ink on black paper, but also by the black ink on black paper (close observation, especially along the top edge of the image as well as in several areas of the concentric bands, reveals a subtle difference between the tone of the paper and the black ink). Typically, Johns created many such working proofs prior to finalizing the printing procedure for *White Target*. Of all of these, only one was printed by the artist as a small edition (1967–68; cat. no. 49). In this version, Johns further altered the transparency of some of the elements, which in turn emphasizes the target's concentric bands. The combination of white ink on black paper mounted on a mottled, blue-gray support sheet causes the image to thrust out at the viewer in a very different manner than the final editioned version of *White Target*, although both prints were essentially created from the same seven matrices.

Johns's ability to obfuscate such discrete operations in printmaking reflects his complete mastery of the lithographic process, which is epitomized by his refinement of working with graphite pigments. In 1960 the artist made a large graphite wash drawing (cat. no. 57) after his 1956 encaustic work *Gray Alphabets* (cat. no. 55). In 1968, when Johns turned to this motif in lithography, he was working at Gemini G.E.L. in Los Angeles. At three-quarters the size of the painting, the lithograph is larger than any he had previously created at ULAE. It is useful to compare the process and outcome of this print project with Johns's first published *Target* print. The reader will recall that, for this 1960 lithograph, the artist had experimented with a tint stone to support the key image, and that he based the tint upon a working proof of *Target* made by applying a bluish gray ink wash over a proof in black on newsprint. Johns made a similar working proof for *Gray Alphabets* (1968; cat. no. 58). It exhibits some of the same properties as the *Target* proof, but now, eight years after the artist's first lithographs, Johns and Gemini were able to finesse the optical and printing problems that occurred when creating the *Target* print. Realizing that he needed to separate his drawing into discrete layers or elements in order to achieve an effect comparable to the subtle warm and cool casts of the graphite wash drawing, Johns utilized four matrices in the final edition of the *Gray Alphabets* print (1968; cat. no. 59). Master printer Kenneth Tyler recalled that Johns mixed his own inks for the project and that metallic pigments were suspended in transparent base for at least one of the printed elements.[34] The image was printed on a smooth roll stock of Rives paper, the brightness of which, combined with the lustrous grays of the printing elements, produced a masterwork of nacreous brilliance. Insistently flat, and relying entirely on optical rather than dimensional properties for its illusion, *Gray Alphabets* is utterly different from either the painting or graphite wash drawing of the same motif, contrary to what some surmise as a reproductive quality due to the print's refinement. Here, for the first time, Johns mastered the sophisticated use of multiple gray pigments in a print.

Another group of prints of Target and Flag motifs executed contemporaneously at ULAE profited from this experience, as well as from the introduction of a new piece of equipment at the Long Island workshop—an offset proofing press. An earlier drawing, *Flag* (1958; cat. no. 22), displays visual properties on which Johns's Flag prints of the late 1960s and early 1970s may have been modeled. The drawing was made with several types of graphite wash, which the artist applied with brush and fingers, as well as graphite pencils of various types and hardness, and carbon pencils.[35] The overall effect is that one sees all the marks simultaneously; they seem to be suspended in a narrow transparent space, weaving in and over one another. This spatial ambiguity is similar to what the artist captured in his 1970–72 lithograph *Two Flags* (cat. no. 30), which was printed in part using graphite inks.[36] The print was constructed using five matrices that were previously employed in the printing of *Flags II* (FIG. 14). In the earlier print, Johns positioned the flags in their proper orientation, but separated them so that the lower flag is cropped by the bottom edge of the paper. The visual effect suggests that one is looking at an interrupted filmstrip. In the later print, the flags are set vertically—or turned 90 degrees counterclockwise—directly next to one another, though the artist playfully left a horizontal "drip" at the lower-right corner of the image. Further complicating one's understanding of the flags is that they are reversed. Johns accomplished this by printing the plates and stones on an offset press, which prints the matrices as they are drawn.[37] To an untrained eye, the five layers of drawing might appear to be one, because the values and relative transparencies of the marks are so close—calling to mind *White Target*. Here the offset press provided the lightest possible touch in printing, compared to direct lithographic printing, wherein the paper and matrix are subjected to tremendous friction and pressure (which causes the paper fibers to flatten). In offset the image is practically kissed onto the sheet, which in turn leaves its fibers uncompromised. *Two Flags* was printed on a soft Japanese paper, an extremely absorbent, fibrous sheet that intensifies the sensitivity of the printing. The paper shows every nuance possible in each of the elements and projects an extra degree of dimensionality due to light reflected back through the transparent inks. Given the close value range of the inks and the soft sheen inherent to the graphite component, the image practically pulsates on the paper surface. Of all the artist's lithographs, this print comes closest to approximating the texture and visual properties of graphite wash.

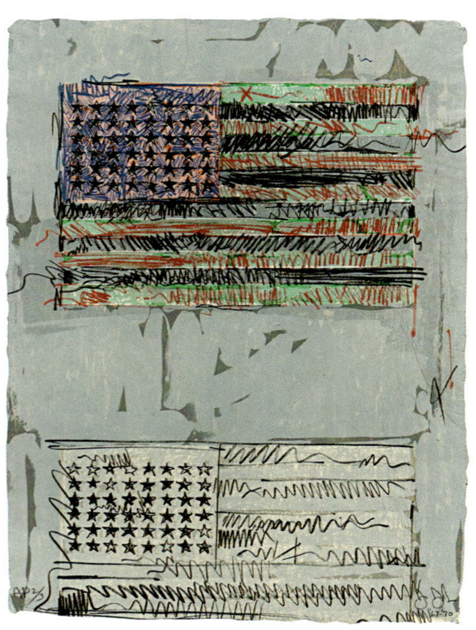

Fig. 14. *Flags II*, 1970. Lithograph from five stones, five aluminum plates, and one rubber stamp on white wove paper (East India); sheet: 86.4 × 63.5 cm (34 × 25 in.). The Art Institute of Chicago, gift of Mr. and Mrs. Edwin A. Bergman, 1983.1769.

The optical breakthrough that Johns achieved in *Two Flags* would be extended a year later when the artist began a decade-long relationship with Simca Print Artists. Unlike the airy quality of *Two Flags*, a density of surface characterizes the screenprint *Flags II* (1973; cat. no. 31), such that the print takes on an entirely new quality. It is neither painting, drawing, nor relief sculpture, but a bit of all three. By adding varnish to some of the printing inks—notably on the right side—and using cut stencils in concert with more painterly resist stencils, Johns was able to make a surface that emulates encaustic on one side, oil paint on the other.[38] In spite of this technical success, the artist has been quite dismissive about the process of screenprinting, in essence referring to it as "simpleminded."[39] Johns has also vacillated about the attractiveness of etching. In 1969 he said, "I don't like the medium, although I'm going to do some more etchings.... Within a short unit of an etching line there are fantastic things happening in the black ink, and none of those things are what one had in mind."[40] And while Johns made numerous etchings that might be considered "gray" prior to the 1992 *Untitled* (cat. no. 126), this multiplate print best represents a combination of blacks and grays that yields an effect similar to the conditions previously described. Here those effects color the work and underscore simultaneous readings of darkened interior and firmament, qualities that coexist in many of Johns's works of the 1980s.[41] What sets the etching apart, as often is the case in intaglio, is the inherent transparency of aquatint, the predominant medium in this work. With a layer or two of aquatint, Johns accomplished what would take many more matrices in lithography or screenprinting. The very processes that first inhibited him were used to great effect in his later work.

It is fitting, therefore, to conclude with the artist's most recent print, *Within* (2007; cat. no. 137), which was completed just prior to the time of publication. If *Untitled* exemplifies the light, transparent possibilities of intaglio processes, as well as those same qualities of gray, *Within* makes use of a more literal aspect of the color. The print is the result of several plates, the key image of which is a conflation of Johns's Flagstone and Crosshatch motifs. In an earlier painting of the same title (1983 and 2005; cat. no. 136), Johns reworked an abandoned 1983 crosshatched canvas, covering it with the flagstone image. One motif is thus encased or frozen within the other. Similarly, in the new intaglio, Johns created etched plates of crosshatched strokes and printed them, especially on the margins of the composition, paired in complementary colors—yellow/violet, red/green, and blue/orange. Over these passages, he added a plate of flagstone imagery printed in nearly opaque, but extremely luminous, gray. Around the periphery of the composition, the artist placed strips of molding as in his Catenary series with a frayed string hanging freely from the right-hand strip. This framing device, in concert with the compressed or encased center, lends the composition the air of a reliquary. And so, with these later etchings, Johns has employed gray in contradictory ways—in the former as an open and airy condition, and in the latter as closed and private. They reflect the general trajectory of Johns's output of the past twenty-five years—from introducing personal iconography in the early 1980s, to his more recent work, which in part, looks back to the mystery and ambiguity of *Tennyson*, among other examples from the first decade of his career.

Over the course of nearly fifty years, Jasper Johns has produced a profoundly diverse corpus of printed and drawn art, subjecting a fairly limited number of motifs to a rich variety of graphic examination and experiments. As I have attempted to show, throughout his printmaking campaigns, Johns consistently employed the color and/or relative appearance of gray. For an artist obsessed with the idea of complicating things, gray has served as the ideal form of concealing and revealing objects and how they appear. Viewed together, these gray works on paper prompt reflection upon their conditional states, illuminating a myriad of subtle differences and similarities that stretch across media, subject, and indeed the color gray itself.

The author would like to gratefully acknowledge several colleagues for their assistance and generosity in accessing many of the works discussed in this essay: Bruce Day at the Hirshhorn Museum and Sculpture Garden, Washington; Martin Bansbach, Rachel Mustalish, and Samantha Rippner at the Metropolitan Museum of Art, New York; Karl Buchberg, Raimond Livasgani, and David Moreno at the Museum of Modern Art, New York; Ian Alteveer, Carlotta J. Owens, Charles Ritchie, and Nan Rosenthal at the National Gallery of Art, Washington; Joseph King and Joan Rothfuss at the Walker Art Center, Minneapolis; and Claire Gerhard at the Whitney Museum of American Art, New York.

1 For an extended discussion of the condition of gray, see the essay by James Rondeau in this volume, pp. 26–31.

2 Calvin Tomkins, "Profiles: The Moods of a Stone," *The New Yorker* (June 7, 1976), p. 64.

3 Richard Field has published extensively and famously on Johns's prints, including two catalogues raisonné and numerous essays and articles; Field 1970 and Field 1978. Other excellent interpretive texts on Johns's prints are Castleman 1986, Geelhaar 1980b, Goldman 1981, Goldman 1993, Rose 1970, and Young 1969, in *Writings* 1996, pp. 129–34. In addition, see Ruth Fine, *Gemini G.E.L.: Art and Collaboration*, exh. cat. (National Gallery of Art, Washington/ Abbeville Press, 1984).

4 It is not certain that any written record exists at the workshop, but see Douglas Davis's notes from an interview with Tatyana Grosman in Aug. 1973, copied in Esther Spark's research notebook, pp. 1–3, The Art Institute of Chicago, Department of Prints and Drawings, with thanks to Esther Sparks Sprague for making this notebook available.

5 This disputes what Michael Crichton wrote in 1977: "[Johns first drew] all the numbers zero through nine at the top in two rows, and then, because there was more space below, he drew a large zero"; Crichton 1977, p. 44.

6 For a reproduction of the latter, see Rosenthal and Fine 1990, no. 20a, p. 124.

7 Thanks to Jesse Feiman for this observation.

8 Grosman interview (note 4).

9 Crichton 1977, p. 44.

10 The quality I am describing can be seen clearly in the ink-on-plastic drawings *Disappearance II* (1962) and *Two Flags* (1985), in which the accretive media is physically dimensional. The same phenomena occur when drawing a lithograph with many materials, as Johns did for the "0." Tusche and crayon are different shades of black, and the more one layers them, the more media accumulates on the surface. A similar rich, dimensional surface occurs in certain graphite wash drawings, such as *Jubilee* (1960). Here the build-up of media is also pronounced—so much so that it brings to mind Johns's Sculp-metal reliefs.

11 Bill Goldston, master-printer and director of ULAE, alerted me to this when I asked about the proofs.

12 See figure 2, which shows that, as Johns was working on the image, the relationship to the untouched border gave it an objectlike appearance. Borders are left blank on stones and plates because it is necessary to engage the pressure of the press (a scraper bar), on top of the matrix, but away from the image. Failure to follow this method results in incomplete transfer of the ink—literally a light horizontal streak where the image should be. Johns pushed his composition to the top edge of the stone; as a result, the upper-left corners of the prints reveal the embossed corner of the stone's irregular upper-right edge.

13 For an earlier comment about the relationship between the drawing and the print, see Geelhaar 1980b, pp. 59–63.

14 Harriet Stratis and I examined the unframed drawing in the Paper Conservation Laboratory at the Metropolitan Museum of Art, New York, where various drawing materials were compared under a microscope with those Johns used for *Target*. We determined that the waxy, black marks were in fact not only Conté crayon, as previously described, but a combination of Conté overlaid with China marker, which is used to label laundry and is often mistaken for a lithographic crayon. We thank the lenders, Mr. and Mrs. Andrew Saul, as well as paper conservator Rachel A. Mustalish and senior consultant Nan Rosenthal and her assistant Ian Alteveer at the Metropolitan Museum, for allowing us to examine this work unframed, and to Martin Bansbach for unframing the work for our examination.

15 Aloys Senefelder, the inventor of lithography, made early and frequent use of tint stones. This technique mimicked the properties of chiaroscuro woodcuts and was employed when a key stone alone could not depict the full range of values, or the overall mood or intent of the composition. Johns sometimes refers to the monochromatic states of his prints as the "Black" state or version, as in the number or "Figure" sequences he created at Gemini G.E.L.

16 Conversation with Bill Goldston, Dec. 2006.

17 Johns has used this "collage" technique in his lithographs with success as both passage within a larger field of marks (*Flag I*) and as a subject within a composition. For his 1970 lithograph *Souvenir*, he replicated a collage element from the 1964 encaustic of the same title using a tusche-laden piece of cheesecloth stamped onto the stone; Field 1970, n.pag.

18 This result pleased Tatyana Grosman so much that she ordered an edition of ten impressions with embossing, but the entire edition was never completed.

19 The first use of white ink on black paper that I have found in the artist's oeuvre appears in a unique trial proof of *Painting with Two Balls II* (1962; Castelli Collection). For an illustration of this proof, see Slavin 1991, p. 64. As a device within Johns's work, it reached full potential with the prints *Two Maps I* (1965–66) and *White Target* (1967–68).

20 Dora Vallier, "Théière et citrons," in *Braque: L'ouevre gravé catalogue raisonné* (Flammarion, 1982), pp. 94–95. This print was made using only five colors, although it achieves some of the same optical effects seen in Johns's *False Start II*.

21 It is also possible that Johns used a commercially available form of liquid graphite, which has as its vehicle some form of petroleum solvent. This drawing was carefully examined in the Paper Conservation Laboratory at the Museum of Modern Art, New York. Harriet Stratis and I are grateful to Karl Buchberg for allowing us to use the lab, and to David Moreno for unframing these works for our examination.

22 Johns's first use of graphite pigment in printmaking is a test print of *Figure 1* (1963). The result was not satisfying enough to produce a large edition, but its use of graphite looks forward to the more technically sophisticated prints that Johns made at Gemini.

23 Arturo Herrera, *Art:21: Art in the Twenty-First Century*, third season of "Play," premiered on October 7, 2005, on Public Broadcasting Service.

24 In painting, his most obvious use was to screenprint the newspaper passage that bisects the right two-thirds of the painting *According to What* (1964; Private collection). Johns was aware of Robert Rauschenberg's and Andy Warhol's use of photo-screenprinting in their paintings and works on paper, which may have led him to use this largely commercial technique to duplicate the newspaper image.

25 *U.S.A. Artists 8: Jasper Johns* 1966, in *Writings* 1996, p. 125. Perhaps at the risk of confusing the reader even more, but to clarify how this print was made, I should point out that in examining our proofs of *Two Maps I*, I observed a matrix of pinholes through the paper that explains how the printer was able to align the single map image on the plate so that it would be positioned one over another. Additionally, one can see how the paper passed under the pressure of the scraper bar, because it imparts a pattern, visible on the verso of the sheet, which shows that the pressure started and stopped along the periphery of a single image—twice. The paper fibers were subjected to so much pressure, and so many times, that this pattern of pressure compressed the fibers of the sheet in the margin, leaving a "grayed area" or halo around the image, and the unpressed sheet very black. I believe this haloing may have played a role in suggesting the extreme manipulation of similar values of white printing ink that Johns employed in the printing of *White Target* (1967–68), as well as Johns's choice to print *White Target* on black paper, laid down on black paper, which creates the illusion that the paper is dark gray against the black secondary support sheet.

26 Johns had played with this technique much earlier in his 1962 encaustic *Map* but a 1965 *Map* drawing (Collection of John and

Kimiko Powers) displays an entire section in which Johns remembers painting with a transparent medium over an area densely covered with charcoal. For a color illustration of this work, see Rosenthal and Fine 1990, no. 14, pp. 112–13.

27 For an explanation of the effects among Renaissance painters—notably Leonardo, of whom Johns is fond—of painting transparent white over black and vice versa, see John Gage, *Color and Culture: Practice and Meaning from Antiquity to Abstraction* (Little, Brown, 1993), pp. 133–34. On page 133, a passage from Leonardo's *Codex Hammer* (1506/09) describes the artist's observations about the atmospheric conditions of smoke, haze, and deep space, and how specifically to create these effects by painting "a board with...an intense black; and over all let him lay a very thin and transparent white. He will then see that this transparent white will nowhere show a more beautiful blue than over the black....The creation of a beautiful blue-grey by overlaying a white ground with transparent black had long been known in the studio—it was to be used by Titian...but one modern scholar who has repeated the painter's 'experiment' has found it to result only in 'unpleasant greys with a greenish cast'." While it may have been an unpleasant result for the historian, we can imagine Johns's delight at discovering these ways of creating various grays. My sincere thanks to Jesse Feiman for finding this passage.

28 Gordon Baldwin described the Sabattier effect: "...named for Armand Sabattier (1834–1910), who discovered the technique in 1862, is an intentional darkroom technique, employed to produce tone reversals." It became a major tool of art photography in the 1930s; Gordon Baldwin, *Looking at Photographs: A Guide to Technical Terms* (J. Paul Getty Museum/British Museum Press, 1991), p. 77. I thank Newell Smith for clarifying this definition for me.

29 This idea about photography has been discussed in writing about Johns's *Two Maps* prints; Sparks 1990, p. 364. It was also reinforced for me in conversation with Riva Castleman.

30 John's reuse and isolation of the second element here recalls the same choice made by Pablo Picasso when he created his masterful reduction linocut *Still Life with Bottle* (1962). Picasso printed the final state of the linoleum block in black—as Johns did for *Two Maps II*—after the completed state was finished in three colors. And just as Johns has denied any knowledge of Picasso's great lithographic sequences of the late-1940s (*Bulls*, for example) prior to undertaking his 0–9 portfolios in 1960–63, Johns probably was not aware of this linocut by Picasso when he created *Two Maps* a few years later. Rather, this is ample evidence of both artists' profound discernment of the possibilities inherent in the printmaking media.

31 Young 1969, p. 52, in *Writings* 1996, pp. 131–32.

32 The complete information for the details in figs. 11–13 is as follows: Fig. 11: lithograph from three stones on ivory wove paper; 86.7 × 64.6 cm (34 ¼ × 25 ⅜ in.). Fig. 12: lithograph from six stones on handmade paper (India); 86.5 × 65.3 cm (34 × 25 ¾ in.). Fig. 13: lithograph from four stones on black Japanese paper; 63.5 × 47.4 cm (25 × 18 ⅝ in.). All are The Art Institute of Chicago, ULAE Collection acquired through a challenge grant of Mr. and Mrs. Thomas Dittmer; restricted gift of the supporters of the Department of Prints and Drawings; Centennial and Margaret Fisher endowments, 1982.966d, 1982.966, and 1982.967c, respectively.

33 Field 1970, cat. 47.

34 The Print Documentation sheet for *Gray Alphabets* lists the following order for printing: "1. Warm Grey Transparent; 2. Warm Green Grey Transparent; 3. Cold Grey Transparent; 4. Transparent Cool Grey (Flake pigments added to ink)." I am grateful to Kenneth Tyler for suggesting in a phone conversation in Oct. 2006, that I refer to the documentation, and to Sidney Felsen and My Linh Miles at Gemini G.E.L. for providing me with same. Tyler also thought that the "flake" pigments are probably mica chips or dust, which is typically added to paints with a pearlized finish.

35 Harriet Stratis and I carefully examined the drawing. We thank Barbara Bertozzi Castelli for allowing us to see this work.

36 As a printmaking student in the 1970s, I was inspired by this print, wrongly [now] believing that it was the first successful use of graphite printing inks. Still, I recall many of my peers were also excited by Johns's achievement with this print because of its subtlety and use of graphite.

37 Because the paper comes in direct contact with the printing element on a hand press, the drawing is reversed. However, an offset press produces the image right-reading because it is transferred to the paper indirectly—by means of a rubber blanket which makes contact with the printing element and then "offsets" it to the paper.

38 The screenprint is based on the painting *Two Flags* (1973; encaustic and oil on canvas; Collection of Michael Crichton). For an illustration, see Field 1978, p. 88. Johns also revisited this technique for the 1977 screenprint *The Dutch Wives*.

39 Martin 1990, p. 51, in *Writings* 1996, p. 204.

40 Young 1969, p. 52, in *Writings* 1996, p. 131.

41 See especially *Untitled* drawings of 1983 and 1984, and *Racing Thoughts*.

Johns Metanoid, Metanoid Johns

RICHARD SHIFF

Change Your Life

PEOPLE SURPASS THEMSELVES. THE AIM OF AN ARTIST AS A creative individual, Jasper Johns suggested recently, is to do "something a little more worthwhile than oneself."[1] If your established worth is the culture and learning that your customary actions reflect, then to be worth a bit more than yourself—more than the self shaped by and confined within its socialization—would entail undoing cultural protocols, probing new modes of thought and behavior. To be worth more, you would need to change in a fundamental way—change your life—or, at the least, experience change and become a channel for its communication.

Johns acts as a human medium of change, not expression. Conventionally understood, the concept of expression implies a certain stability: the preexistence of the thing expressed, whether an object represented or a person creating a representation. You express yourself by showing how you see, or desire to see, an object available to the competing visions of others. "A portrait is a model complicated by an artist," Charles Baudelaire wrote in 1846, providing a pithy account of what his Romantic contemporaries understood—to every artist, a consistently individual vision reflected in each rendering.[2] With varying degrees of emphasis, modern artists who followed Baudelaire accepted still another complication: the independent play of the material medium. When the artist complicates the model, we have Romanticism. When the medium complicates the artist, we have what many call modernism.

Just as the material medium yields to forces of self-expression, it resists them. Intentions, desires, established habits, even a person's physical tics: all are subject to modification in accord with the exigencies of the medium. Every medium becomes a distorting agent of anamorphosis. To accept this, however, is to reject the more orthodox transference of an artist's mentality, straight through skills of the hand to an aesthetic product. According to traditional theories of art, a practiced hand masters the difficulties presented by the medium, facilitating the mind's desires. Charles Blanc's *Grammaire des arts du dessin* (1867), a comprehensive account of aesthetic practice that set standards for several generations after Baudelaire, relegated the material medium to the far side of the design process, an impediment to be overcome, subordinate to an artist's conceiving mind and executing hand. Blanc explained: "We can no longer deny that there is a secret accord between the hand that guides the pen and the mind that guides the hand.... Touch is the handwriting of the painter, the stroke [*frappe*] of his mind."[3] Blanc's second sentence can be paraphrased: The painter's touch or brushstroke corresponds to the draftsman's or writer's stroke of the pen, which corresponds in turn to a stroke of forceful thought. The mind conceives, the hand renders, and the medium falls into line: end of theory, origin of art.

This orderly system collapses when an artist recognizes that a portrait in oil on canvas and a portrait of the same model in graphite on paper must differ in emotional valence, and that the difference holds even if the psychological dynamic between artist and model remains constant during the time of the two representations. Johns is explicit about this independent, agonistic aspect of a medium: "I like to repeat an image in another medium to observe the play between the two: the image and the medium... the stress the image takes in different media."[4] His imagery and marks are usually ordinary enough not to cause stress in themselves. Yet they may be responsible for whatever emotional tenor the viewer perceives. Commonplace marks, such as Johns's slanted, parallel hatchings and sinuous waves—see *Flag* (1958; cat. no. 22)—fall within the normal range of movement of the human hand and readily adjust to the physical demands of a medium. They hardly require parallel effort on the part of an inventive mind. "But anyone else could do this" is the thought that often occurs to Johns when an interviewer imputes an aura of uniqueness to one of his graphic techniques.[5] No doubt, he has a distinctively practiced touch; but this does not imply that he himself regards his marks as distinctive. His personal way of making an ordinary mark looks ordinary to him. Why would it not?

It may be that our culture will always insist on applying a hierarchy of value to works in relation to their origin in a named hand. Inherently neither beneficial nor detrimental, this is merely the way things have been. What if it were otherwise? Johns offers a lesson for aesthetics: nothing but cultural inertia compels us to follow the likes of Baudelaire and Blanc in assuming that the mentality and emotional state of an artist is paramount, that mind and mood prescribe the mark and render its value. Perhaps instead, the artist's mark, or any mark, transfers value to the mind. It changes the attentive viewer's mind and even the artist's. Johns observed this in himself and in others. "Seeing [his art] becomes thinking," Leo Steinberg concluded in the first evaluative account of the scope of Johns's practice.[6] The judgment still holds, not only for viewers of the imagery, but for its creator: Johns thinks according to what he sees, and he learns by doing. The following essay considers why he allows such an open exchange of eye and mind to occur.[7]

This Happens

Technology affects both the routine and the idiosyncracies of life in a society. The play of a medium and its associated techniques affects an artist analogously, especially one who remains open and sensitive to what a medium does. ("One who remains open" may be the operative modern definition of "artist.") Barnett Newman stated the situation succinctly in 1966: "It is as I work that the work itself begins to have an effect on me."[8] His attitude discouraged speculation on the existence of a specific program that might have determined the abstract series he titled *Stations of the Cross* (**FIG. 1**). He discovered his program in the course of executing it with his chosen materials. Like Newman, Johns settles on the name of a work only after its completion. Titling in advance would limit possibilities.[9]

Often, retrospective interpretation proceeds with such specificity and conviction that the category of the possible closes down. Critics regard acts of artistic expression as if they revealed singular relationships and correspondences, preserved in fully decipherable form (if not for the artist, then decipherable for the critic). When disagreements occur, it is a matter of which singularity is the true one. Troubled by prevailing standards of interpretation, Steinberg asked a rhetorical question: "Who would need pictures if they were [readily] translatable?"[10] Pictures offer feelings that other forms of human expression cannot match without risk of significant distortion or reduction. Despite Steinberg's admonition, interpreters continue to seek consistency in thematic expression just as connoisseurs, often at their peril, seek it in stylistic expression. Given the

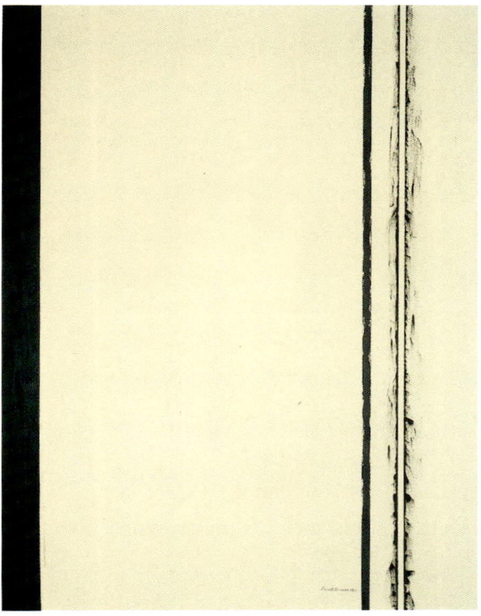

Fig. 1. Barnett Newman. *Third Station*, 1958, from *The Stations of the Cross*, 1958–66. Oil on canvas; 197.8 × 153.7 cm (77 7/8 × 60 1/2 in.). National Gallery of Art, Washington, Robert and Jane Meyerhoff Collection.

nature of criticism, artists seem fated from birth to express their character by one means or another—the same character regardless of variation in the material means.

Resisting the certainty of character, Johns knows better than to offer interpretations of his art. Instead, he provides substantial biographical and technical information concerning the conditions under which a particular work was made. To an unusual extent, he attributes his results to the material circumstances in which he chooses to operate. At work, it is as if he were attending to his process more than directing it. Refusing to set limits even after the fact, he remains aware that any particular feature of his practice could have been otherwise. His personal intervention seems less than fully active as he describes what he does, for he tends to substitute the impersonal pronouns *one* and *you* for the intimacy of *I*. "If you do this, this happens," he states, indicating that between a material cause and its material effect, a change is to be observed.[11] The common failing is that people try "to figure out what's going to happen, rather than seeing what happens."[12]

Johns's explanation might be applied to every process equally. As a cause converts into an effect, human agency merely provides the energy and cannot guarantee the consequences. Turn a figure upside down. Will it look like the same figure, only inverted? Or will it seem to be something else? When an interviewer imagines Johns conceiving of a situation and thinking to himself, "It would be interesting to see that," the artist extends the notion: "Or 'it would be interesting to do that,' which is not the same."[13] Seeing can be restrictive because it often follows a fixed conception of the thing seen: to ordinary habits of vision, an object upside down appears inverted. Doing is open-ended, its results far less certain. Having moved the object into an inverted position, you may have a different sense of it.

Johns avoids speculation. (Why speculate when your guess excludes equally valid possibilities?) He has no aversion, however, to personalizing the principle of "this happens" when the situation he addresses is sufficiently specific, objective, and factual: "I will sometimes apply ink on a sheet of plastic and let it dry. I put it there and it does something. . . . Some people would see that as chance, but I would see it simply as a way of working."[14] The medium is his choice, "a way of working." And it works: the ink puddles on the nonabsorbent plastic and then dries as the artist watches. At a certain point in what remains an integrated process, the central mover becomes the observer, emotionally affected by whatever appears. Whereas Baudelaire featured the artist as a force of change in rendering the model, Johns features the medium. His *Two Flags* (1985; cat. no. 33) has the irregular fluidity and deep gray profundity of ink on plastic. It responds to gravity as much as to a self, despite the presence of the handprint at the lower right. This too has no stable self-identity because it assumes whatever form the medium allows. Johns's handprints are his, but their actual appearance is always changing.[15]

Any medium sets at least some limit to an artist's own worst instinct, a monomaniacal desire to shape the world to his or her desire; in this respect, ink on plastic presents a particularly strong challenge to an assertive ego. An image as blotchy and runny as *Two Flags* or *Tracing* (1989; cat. no. 122) might suggest that the draftsman either was cultivating spontaneity or had overworked the surface. Both conclusions place an exclusive emphasis on the artist as cause. The medium is also the cause, conceivably self-motivated:

> I like the way [ink on plastic] removes itself from my touch. . . . It isn't difficult to control, if that's what one wants, but . . . one can apply the wet ink in a way that allows it to change its form as it dries—and I like that part of it. . . . Not the surprise. I like its independence, that it is difficult to tell from the finished drawing what gestures were used to produce it.[16]

Johns implies that ink on plastic is an unreliable index of the character of the artist. No style can be applied to it; it receives no autograph. Johns must be present in his ink drawing, but his presence will not be visible there.

Ink is changeable, versatile, polyvalent. In this respect, it resembles Johns's waxy encaustic—a paint that can be brushed as a warm liquid that solidifies as it cools, and can be reheated and manipulated repeatedly. Johns represented the physicality of this process by creating *Iron* (**FIG. 2**); its layer of encaustic has been melted away *by* an iron to produce the image *of* an iron. This imprinted shape, like all imprints, is at once indexical and iconic. It translates an object into a tactile happening (the indexical factor), resulting in a visual form (the iconic factor). Johns's attraction to printmaking has a similar foundation. The various print processes offer an extraordinary capacity for manipulation, which Johns extends in unusual ways by reworking print images in different media (see *Jubilee*, 1962 and 1994 [cat. no. 6], a pastel over a lithograph, and *Flag*, 1972 and 1994 [cat. no. 32], a carborundum wash over a lithograph).[17]

Fig. 2. *Iron*, 1962. Encaustic on wood; 24.8 × 18.1 cm (9 ¾ × 7 ⅛ in.). Collection of the artist.

At work with whatever medium, Johns uses materials in recognition of how their properties relate to a specific physical environment. Ink, for example, can be applied as a runny liquid or relatively dry, and on absorbent paper or impervious plastic: you choose certain conditions, *these* conditions, and as a result, *this* happens. Everything has its condition. Long ago, Heinrich von Kleist applied this notion to thought: "Ideas come as we are speaking. . . . For it is not *we* who 'know'; it is rather a certain condition, in which we happen to be, that 'knows.'"[18] The self, its identity, and its self-knowledge must be conditional, dependent on the circumstances of what happens.[19] Johns's friend John Cage may have alluded to this realization when he wrote: "Looking around his thoughts, [Johns] sees them in the room where he is"—in his material circumstances. Cage added: "There are evidently more persons in him than one."[20] The diversity of Johns's interests and productivity caused Cage to observe more than one creative agent at work. "My experience of life is that it's very fragmented," Johns himself has stated; "I would like my work to . . . [indicate] those differences."[21] In his case, the work itself generates the differences he feels and thinks.

Johns is wise to doubt the stability of his character, the impossibility of isolating it within a room of unchanging conditions. He can hardly be content with the familiar language of self-expression, which treats the self and its mentality as an integrated entity. In his estimation, individual words are as conditional as thoughts; and, as an artist, he wants to *do something* in recognition of the situation. So he puns on the ambiguities of language and manipulates the graphic signs for words as if they were material objects to be pictured in ever-changing ways: "I thought that one thing to do with the written word was to pretend that it was an object that could be bent, turned upside-down, and I began more or less folding words, or painting the illusion of a folded word" (*Jubilee* [1959; cat. no. 2]; *Periscope (Hart Crane)* [1963; cat. no. 103]).[22] Subjected to a medium and a context, word-objects are no more fixed than the mental concepts they form and the self they identify: "The idea of 'thing' or 'it' can be subjected to great alterations"; "Thingness itself can become ambiguous."[23] "Things" of every kind would be more true to life were they to remain fluid like runny ink. In this respect, Johns is Nietzschean: "Nothing is really equal. . . . In order that the concept of substance [Johns's 'thingness'] could originate, [it was] necessary that for a long time one [neither] see nor perceive the changes in things."[24] To unfix the thing, counteracting its integrity and reintroducing its multiple ambiguities, is to enter, or return to, an expanding world of change. This would affect not only object-things but also words, self-images, and even the individual "self."

Not I

The subject of a work of art ordinarily acts as both source and limit of meaning. A Johnsian subject does otherwise. His pictures tend to have curiously restricted, nominal subjects—a mere name or characterizing quality, which may seem to refer to itself rather than open itself to interpretive elaboration. The Johnsian subject or theme can be a specific word (*The*, 1957; cat. no. 11), a familiar sign (*Map*, 1962; cat. no. 39), a type of mark (the hatchings of *Between the Clock and the Bed*, 1982–83; cat. no. 115), or an array of disparate yet identifiable images (*Racing Thoughts* [1984; cat. no. 116]; *Untitled* [1992–95; cat. no. 127]). Johns is eclectic. His formal appropriations stand in passive opposition to Newman's drive to reach a fundament of personal expression. Newman absorbed himself in aesthetic relationships that he understood as solely of his making.[25] At work with his direct sense of color and scale, surrounded by his paintings in his studio, he could become sufficiently impassioned to "create himself" (a phrase he used in advocating an openly opinionated art criticism, another form of self-expression).[26]

Because Johns believes that the self is neither the origin nor the end of art, self-creation is not at issue. This is not an unusual attitude for a late-twentieth-century American. In 1967, Newman complained that the word *self* was being "repudiated by young artists."[27] Many of Johns's contemporaries, especially those a few years his junior—artists associated with minimalism and conceptualism, as well as those deriving imagery from photography, film, advertising, and all forms of popular culture—dismissed the expressionism with which others (misguidedly) were extending the art of Jackson Pollock.[28] Yet we would unfairly represent the import of Johns's attitude were we to reduce it to a mere supercession of generations. Johns does not actively reject the self, its self-expression, or its self-creation; nor is he concerned to negate the work of others. Rather, he evades the self and the objects it defines as it exercises its wants. The less reliance on the self and its expression the better, as he intimated in 1964: "If we come closer and closer to [a thing] to identify it . . . we will begin to wonder whether that 'something' is really 'something' or not. . . . I have begun to want an object to be free from the way I see it. . . . I want images to free themselves from me."[29] Images are not limited; artists are, and they limit images to mirror themselves.

"Free from the way I see it": Johns may be someone with cause to hide his more extreme emotions. He identifies himself as a "highly flawed person," one who avoids "expressing my flawed nature, or my *self*."[30] Statements on the order of "I want images to free themselves from me" plausibly acknowledge either a troubled psyche or its active repression. Repeatedly admitting to the situation, Johns hides nothing. In 1973: "I have attempted to develop my thinking in such a way that the work I've done is not me . . . I didn't want my work to be an exposure of my feelings."[31] In 1978: "I wanted to have an idea, or an image . . . that was not *I*."[32] In 1984: "In my early work I tried to hide my personality, my psychological state, my emotions."[33] Repentence for the sin of concealment comes in a frequently cited statement, also of 1984: "Finally, one must simply drop the reserve."[34] Ironically, here the voice remains depersonalized ("one"); and Johns's pursuit of an image "that was not *I*" surely continues to this day. Identifying his personal flaws may not be the most fruitful way to approach his art, which neither indulges his flaws nor remedies them. Of more relevance is the realization that everyone is flawed.

"I didn't want my work to be an exposure of my feelings." Why? Perhaps it was not so much that Johns was driven to hide his feelings, but rather that his feelings merited no exposure, at least not in art. Exposure might be therapeutic and might satisfy an exhibitionist ego (if Johns had one), but in his case—he is not a politician—personal expiation would serve no social purpose. To put his retrospective remark of 1973 in context is to displace the personal psychology ("my feelings") with issues that are more public, stemming from perceptual and behavioral psychology: the question of how people see, how people think, or better, how a mind thinks. This is a worthy issue for Johns, one that goes beyond the self and self-expression.

Referring to the problem of "exposure," Johns was comparing himself to the Abstract Expressionists and noting an early failing of his that was as much technical as emotional: "Abstract Expressionism was so lively—personal identity and painting were more or less the same, and I tried to operate the same way. But I found I couldn't do anything that would be identical with my feelings. So I worked in such a way that I could say that it's not me."[35] Whether because of inadequacy or prescience, Johns realized that he wanted something more than self-expression from his art, "something a little more worthwhile than oneself." He wanted to think thoughts not himself.

Imagine a mind for which all relations between "things" continually change. Johns seeks this mind in himself. We normally suppress change to create a discourse of manageable entities, giving each its sign or identity. This is the foundation of our logic of symbols. Images of a conventional kind, including self-images, express symbolic identities. But if such identities mask the reality of change, if they disguise the unstable, inapprehensible nature of things (Johns's ambiguity of "thingness"), then change should come equally to one's *self*, also a "thing," an artificial construct deceptively fixed in place for social and political expediency. The aim of knowing yourself and expressing yourself is the trap of Western culture. Self-expression is no liberation for an artist determined to know something other than the tautology of his or her personality and its cultural formation. Self-expression is self-censored: knowing yourself, you will refuse to do anything out of character.

Resurrection, Metamorphosis, Conversion

Religious miracles and conversions represent extremes of a character change we call spiritual. When Johns first saw Matthias Grünewald's *Isenheim Altarpiece* in 1976 (and again in 1979), he may have been moved by its aesthetic properties far more than by its religious mythology: "I found the details so interesting and handsome . . . I wanted to trace this [compositional factor], and get rid of the subject matter . . . . I only got a few [traced details] to work, from my point of view . . . free of the original imagery." Johns's "point of view" guided his pursuit of an intuition—that "there was something in the way these things are structured that [is] free of the information that the images convey."[36] Why certain of his tracings "worked," while others proved ineffective, must remain mysterious. Apparently, some failed to separate the image from its function as a sign; that is, they failed to expose feelings independent of what the thematics of the picture already indicated. In at least two instances, however, Johns observed that his tracing released the potential of the given form beyond all conventional meaning and beyond the preconditions of his own "point of view" as well. In each of his tracings, his hand is recognizable, just as in his other renderings; but this is hardly relevant to the express purpose of tracing. His effort had nothing to do with distinguishing himself or, to the contrary, identifying himself with another. The process was open: "When you do this"—when Johns was tracing—"this happens."

Ironically, the two Grünewald configuations that "worked," which Johns eventually transferred to numerous compositions of his own, have strong thematic identities. One is a fallen soldier—actually two soldiers, but one is dominant—overcome by being witness to an astonishing physical transformation, the Resurrection of Christ (see **FIG. 3**, bottom left, and compare the left side of *Untitled* [1992–95; cat. no. 127]). The soldier suffers a spiritual or moral conversion, a transformation pressed upon him, a change-your-life experience leaving him in physical disarray.[37] His condition resembles the physical incapacity of the other figure of Johns's choice, the victim of a skin disease, a likeness to those who once sought aid from the hospital for which Grünewald created the altarpiece. A diseased person's corporal healing is a conversion, too (see **FIG. 4**, bottom left, and compare the background elements in *Untitled* [1984; cat. no. 118], and at the left side of *Racing Thoughts* [1984; cat. no. 116]).

Beginning in 1978 and continuing into the early 1980s—a few years in advance of his actual use of the Grünewald figures, but subsequent to his viewing them—Johns developed the visual theme he titled *Cicada*. From pupa to adult, the cicada undergoes a dramatic physical change marked by its emergence from its shell as a winged creature. In the symbolism of the East, the cicada is analogous to the butterfly in the West, which represents the ascension of the soul.[38] The cicada/butterfly sheds its skin, "yet the vital principle, the Psyche [soul] survives."[39] In several instances, Johns evoked this change of life by establishing a central area of hatching marks of vibrant primary colors (red, yellow, blue), surrounding it with somewhat deeper tones of secondary colors (green, violet, orange); the secondaries present a darker effect, primarily because of the absence of yellow (see **FIG. 5**). Optically, the central area bursts forth from its environment, as if an organic force were emerging, the physical conversion being powered by spiritual energy.[40] Johns enhanced the quality of outward projection by aligning the hatchings left to right and top to bottom as the pattern reached the four edges of the painting. The effect is to imbue *Cicada* with a sense of ovoid convexity and the potential to rotate either vertically or horizontally on an axis.

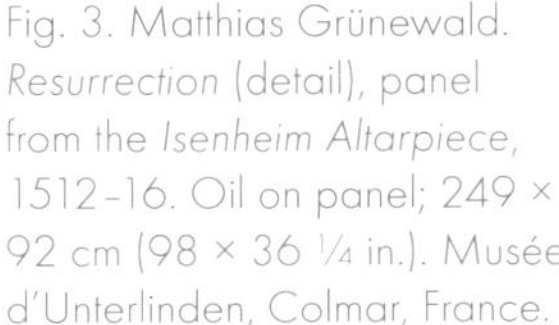

Fig. 3. Matthias Grünewald. *Resurrection* (detail), panel from the *Isenheim Altarpiece*, 1512–16. Oil on panel; 249 × 92 cm (98 × 36 ¼ in.). Musée d'Unterlinden, Colmar, France.

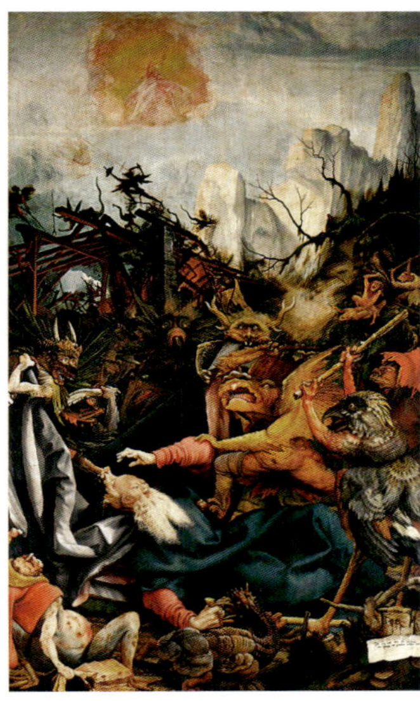

Fig. 4. Matthias Grünewald. *The Temptation of Saint Anthony* (detail), panel from the *Isenheim Altarpiece*, 1512–16. Oil on panel; 249 × 92 cm (98 × 36 ¼ in.). Musée d'Unterlinden, Colmar, France.

The metamorphosis of the cicada recalls one of Johns's sketchbook notes from around 1960: "Make something, a kind of object, which as it changes or falls apart (dies as it were) or increases in its parts (grows as it were) offers no clue as to what its state or form or nature was at any previous time."[41] Considered as a theme, the cicada holds an attraction similar to that of ink on plastic in its application as a medium: "It is difficult to tell from the finished drawing what gestures were used to produce it."[42] This was not the case when Johns shed his own skin-surface by pressing his head against a sheet of (skinlike) paper to leave a flat imprint of his visage in the round. I refer to *Study for "Skin II"* (1962; cat. no. 98), which readily reveals its generative technique of rotation (if *Cicada* evokes convexity or rotation out from a core, *Study for "Skin II"* evokes concavity or rotation into a core). The true revelation, the conversion factor of the *Skin* series, must lie beyond the rotational movement, which is easy enough to grasp kinesthetically while performing it. As Johns turned his head, he could not have known the precise form his imprint would take; nor could he have drawn it by eye, viewing himself in the round from a distance. Physical contact was his only possible means—intimate touch. Making these works necessitated change in his mental-sensory orientation.

Johns has evoked physical conversion in disparate ways: by rotating his body into the flat images of the *Skin* drawings; by representing Grünewald's astonished soldier and diseased man; by alluding to the metamorphosis of the cicada. Each physical conversion implies a spiritual or emotional one—a transformative change of mind. In pictorial terms, this association might be

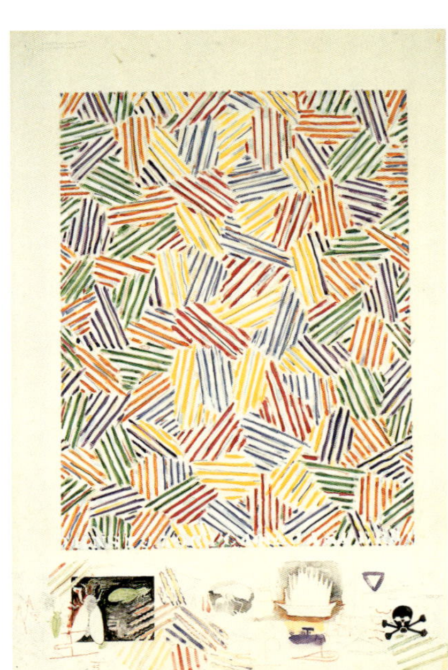

Fig. 5. *Cicada*, 1979. Watercolor, crayon, and graphite pencil on paper; 109.2 × 73 cm (43 × 28 ¾ in.). Collection of the artist.

clearest with respect to Grünewald's *Resurrection* panel, not only because the dominant soldier falls backward, a figure of organic disharmony, but also because the risen Christ bursts forth from a sepulchral shell in the splendor of a spectrum of primaries and secondaries. The soldier must be affected violently by what he sees, because he has neither foreknowledge nor insight; he experiences a change with "no clue." Spiritual conversion is a radical change of mind and heart, a turning of the soul, often, but not necessarily, from a lesser to a greater moral capacity. As a consequence of spiritual conversion, there is a change in what people want and how they think—a selfish person may become altruistic. Perhaps the rainbow of light surrounding the Christ would move the soldier toward repentance: if so, he is changed. As so often, the power of religious faith and faith in the power of art converge, for morality can be a matter of cultural indoctrination by imagery, and aesthetics develops the spirit. Religious leaders often rely on the sensory experience of art to change a person's thinking. Artists who take spiritual matters into their own hands, expanding their thinking by sensory exploration, reach a quasi-religious goal in a suitably demystified form: they achieve "something a little more worthwhile than oneself." This may be the insight that motivates Johns's art.

Metanoia

> The repentance required in Scripture, *the Passing into a new mind*, into a new and contrary Principle of Action, this *Metanoia*, is [it] in the Sinner's own power? at his own liking?...[It] borders...on a contradiction in terms [to propose] this volunteer *Transmentation*, this Self-change, as the easy means of Self-salvation!
>
> —Samuel Taylor Coleridge, 1825[43]

> Most of us have an underlying sense of helplessness, a necessity to make what we call our work. Many have the odd sensation of being called upon to do it.
>
> —Jasper Johns, 2005[44]

> To make choices [to gain] an effect is to eliminate the life which is at work.... The conception of the self-portrait...[cuts] oneself off from one's life.... What finally gives the [painting] its life is "life."
>
> —Jasper Johns, 1965[45]

By one means or another, philosophers have argued that positive experience, life as we feel we live it, ever changing, derives from negative effects: every memorable sight, every significant sound, disturbs the individual's psychic equilibrium and easy inertia.[46] All experience worthy of the designation comes as a shock, at least a mild one—experience with "no clue." Because we shape our perceptions as they come along, arrogantly we may think we control them. But the shaping can be no more than an accommodation, the best—given a degree of luck—to be made of an imposed condition. In the ordinary course of events, a person lives through extraordinary shifts in mentality, forced reorientations, each analogous to the singular experience of Grünewald's soldier, converted by trauma, or Coleridge's penitent, graced by the fate of "passing into a new mind." With a similar range of metaphors, Johns sometimes alludes to a transcendent faith in art: "One hopes for something resembling truth, some sense of life, even of grace, to flicker, at least, in the work."[47] In the *work*, not necessarily in the artist: grace itself is something to be experienced through materials and the sensations they induce. It is not the individual ego that has grace and is redeemed, but a collective condition. Johns does not create for the sake of self-expression or to impose belief on others. He creates to have something to look at, to edify him, which he will share with others.[48]

All but the most timid souls desire to be edified and enlightened in life. People want events to occur, things to happen: for them, to them. For those dissatisfied with the given cultural environment and, above all, dubious of the merit of the culturally generated desires and character that they share with others in their society, novel experience may offer a way out of the dilemma of distrusting the self and its acculturated instincts. An individual's creative practice opens routes of escape to a different order of experience and a different self. Like Coleridge, Matthew Arnold referred to repentance and conversion as metanoia—literally, change of mind—and he equated metanoia to "a change of the inner man."[49] Johns intends his material practice of art to change "the inner man" by changing his mind: "The mind can adjust itself in different ways to anything. I try, when I recognize something is a kind of repetition or is a habit, I try to disregard it and to get rid of it and to find something else to work with."[50] Yet Johns throughout his career has repeated certain clusters of images and techniques, including not only early motifs such as flags and targets, but also later ones, such as the two Grünewald configurations. So either he deceives himself on the question of repetition and habit, or the interpreter needs to explain how slight differences might bring about a significant spiritual conversion. What strikes the casual observer as a set of minor variations seems to shape the world of the artist as a series of unforeseen wonders.

Even when faith in art assumes no more than a weak form, art retains the potential to save aesthetic life from tedium and degeneration. When the faith assumes a strong form, art accomplishes much more: it mimics religion in offering spiritual guidance beyond what many would regard as the limits of aesthetic pleasure. By aesthetic means, art develops "the inner man"; it alters a person's mentality through sensory stimulation. To effect such change, art circumvents the conservative forces of social organization: every social construction, doctrine, and norm. Is all this actually possible? Reasoned, academic study—at least our current form of it—says no. Yet there are degrees of effort and corresponding degrees of success. Relative successes are points of failure worth reaching. Johns moves within whatever space remains available to an artist between the absolutes of divine salvation and social determination. Each of these polarities threatens to render individual initiative "helpless"—a characterization Johns often uses but with an oddly contrary implication. He refers to the helplessness, the irresistible force, of a person's creative calling, as when feeling "called upon to do it." The "helpless" aspect of thought is the thinking you do without having consciously willed it—the thinking that constitutes an involuntary change or turn of mind.[51] Negative thinking. New thinking. Thinking otherwise.

When Johns negotiates the narrows between divine intervention and social construction, we might expect his operation to require a plan or at least a clear intention, a voluntary program to bring about a desired degree of what Coleridge called, dismissively, "Self-change." Johns, however, associates self-change with a "helpless" situation: "Your thought takes a certain form and you have to follow it."[52] Artists take matters into their own hands, displacing forces ordinarily attributed to either the will of a god or the demands of a social institution. But at some point, in some situation, the artist's will paradoxically becomes involuntary—it does so for Johns, in any case. This may be where art begins, with its strange acceptance of helplessness that yields neither to a god nor to a social institution. It is also where art and religion and society, so often allied, divide. Johns instructs the nonreligious soul in survival tactics for a modern world: allow your thinking, your very life, to change.

Hand-Eye Alienation

> This has given me the greatest trouble and still does: to realize that what things *are called* is incomparably more important than what they are.
>
> —Friedrich Nietzsche, 1882[53]

> The picture of a busy street, say, as Monet painted it, in which nothing whatsoever coincides with the form which we think we know in life, [presents a] bewildering alienation of the sign from the thing.
>
> —Heinrich Wölfflin, 1915[54]

Like the art historian Heinrich Wölfflin, Johns is quick to detect alienated signs, in which visual appearance takes leave of referential meaning. Alienated signs are representations that stray from what they represent, usually because of material interference. In the case of the early Claude Monet, invoked by Wölfflin, reflections in water become coarse, heavy strokes, and mere dabs of black or blue indicate individual figures, whether on a Parisian boulevard or in one of its railway stations (FIG. 6). Wölfflin regarded Monet's impressionism as the extreme of a "painterly" vision, a tendency to perceive the environment in terms of atmospheric illumination, continuous space, and the massing of forms—all superceding discrete objects contained by linear contours. The fact that Monet's paint looked like paint and neither water nor people, that it remained pasty, viscous, and hardly more formed on the canvas than on the palette—all this was disturbing. Comparing Monet to Rembrandt and Velázquez, Wölfflin hinted that alienation of this material kind had become excessive without developing a distinct cultural benefit in the process. The change in perception seemed gratuitous and without conceivable limit: "It would be difficult to fix the point at which the merely 'painterly' [Rembrandt] ceases and 'impressionist' [Monet] begins. Everything is transition."[55]

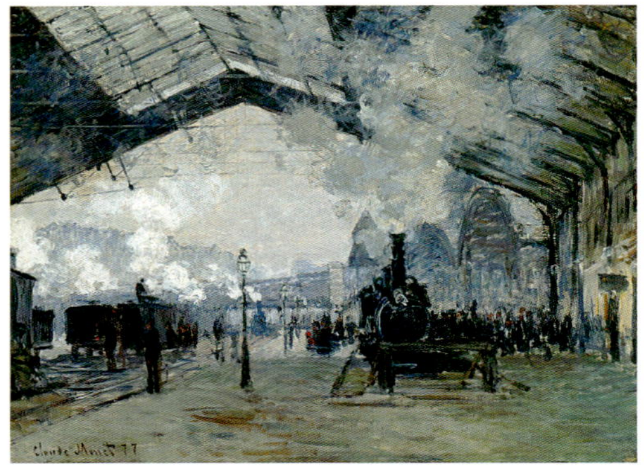

Fig. 6. Claude Monet. *Arrival of the Normandy Train, Saint-Lazare Station*, 1877. Oil on canvas; 59.6 × 80.2 cm (23 ½ × 31 ⅝ in.). The Art Institute of Chicago; Mr. and Mrs. Martin A. Ryerson Collection, 1933.1158.

Johns might agree that "everything is transition," but—more of a Nietzschean—he would assign a positive value to the modern alienation of the representational image, recognizing that it had been offering an exit from the tedious dialectic of society and self, collective and individual. Unlike painters of the Romantic-Expressionist tradition, unlike critics eager to find a repressed psyche under every mark, Johns broke the cultural habit of viewing every rendering as a surreptitious portrait of its creator—a "model complicated by an artist." His early flags, targets, alphabets, and numbers gave him the "opportunity to feel removed from the work, neutral toward it, involved in the making but not involved in the judging of it."[56] Judging would reflect Johns's values, and through them, his social and cultural identity. Were he to follow the pattern of his judgment, his imagery would agree with the prevailing social use of signs, and agree as well with his own conscious desires as an "I." His practice would implicitly acknowledge the dialectical play of social convention and personal expression. It would hardly touch the "not I" he was actually seeking.

Neutrality expresses no preference and is neither proper nor improper. Johns used neutrality in his imagery to alienate his desire; and he used neutrality in his rendering to alienate the sign itself.[57] His imagery was no longer beholden to its assigned truth value; it was responsible only to its actual appearance. The same image that Johns traced from Grünewald, orienting it to the right in one work and to the left in the next, held a constant thematic "truth" in relation to the Resurrection. The figure as a visual truth, however, became radically different from one position to the other. In 1886, Nietzsche had asked: "Why should we be forced to assume that there is an essential difference between 'true' and 'false' in the first place? Isn't it enough to assume that there are various grades of apparentness [*Stufen der Scheinbarkeit*]?"[58] Either no orientation of the Grünewald figure was the correct one, or all were correct. Every possibility was equally a variation, developed without a "clue as to what its state or form or nature was at any previous time." Johns's imagery is untouched by the self, untouched by origins.

A sketchbook note from about 1963–64 indicates the nature of the value-neutral but relentless change: "Take an object, do something to it. Do something else to it. Do something else to it."[59] Johns indicated the second "Do something else" by ditto marks, implying that there should be numerous distinct actions in succession. His instruction to himself represents an attitude more than a prescription to do this or that. His sequential actions need be no more than slight variations or adjustments, so long as he concentrates on each "this happens" for what it is in itself—treating each as if it were a figure removed from thematic demands. If he renders Grünewald's diseased man facing up, he can focus all the more by plotting the same figure facing down or rotated to the side in a subsequent composition. Reversals, inversions, rotations, and mirrorings generate new emotional sensations and force new thoughts upon him—mental curiosities, frissons of the brain.

Just as the positioning of a figure results in a significant but ineffable change, so does a shift in the direction or density of marking, or in the character of hue or value. Concentric, symmetrical circles define the image of a target as a "target" (a conventional sign). To turn the target on its side should make no communicative difference. Yet the directional movement and material substance of the clusters of marks within the rings of a hand-rendered target have the potential to alienate the artist's process from the sign; the rendering introduces irregularities that affect an open mind and perhaps open a closed one. When Johns shifted from the narrow range of tone in the encaustic *Gray Target* (1958; cat. no. 41) to the loose crayon strokes of *Target* (1958; cat. no. 44), he made the changes as a positive action. He also experienced them in the philosophical, negative sense, as an imposition on his given mental state. Rather than extending or completing a dominant gesture, each mark amounted to a redirection, an adjustment of the implications of the previous mark. The familiarity and simplicity of Johns's early imagery provided a dispassionate structure within which change freely occurred. He was caught up in the movement of the marks. "How my mind must move," was his broader realization, as he questioned the concept of free choice.[60]

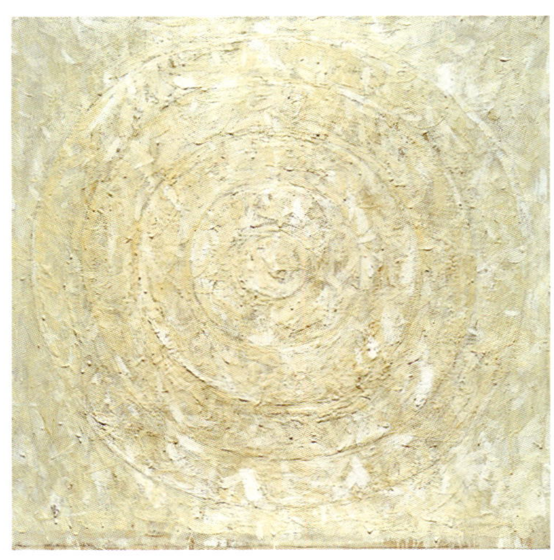

Fig. 7. *White Target*, 1957. Encaustic on canvas; 76.2 × 76.2 cm (30 × 30 in.). Whitney Museum of American Art, New York, Purchase.

A play on his thought—"how my hand must move"—justifies the variety of marking that Johns's signs have had to accommodate. *White Target* (1957; **FIG. 7**) and *Gray Flag* (1957; cat. no. 23) are examples of a range of "choices" exercised within a limited format of neutralized chromatics. Works of this type seem to neutralize the self. Successive deposits of encaustic interfere with the legibility of the underlying schemata of target and flag, but never so much that the template disappears. It is neither projected nor suppressed. The nearly monochromatic surfaces cause the subtle play of separate strokes to become all the more evident in a material, tactile sense. Here, too, gray suited Johns's interest: "It puts perception on a more tactile level perhaps.... Through the use of gray, the object nature of the materials would come forward."[61] The preservation of the visual pattern of Johns's early sign-subjects depends to a great extent on strokes that retrace the straight or curved contours, providing a texture of ridges that catch the light—a tactile feature deployed to an optical end.

In works on paper, such as the graphite wash *Two Flags* (1960; cat. no. 25), elements of the fundamental design vie with a range of marks inserted as surface covering or infilling. In some instances, the marking seems to reinforce the standardized design, saving it from oblivion; in other instances, the graphite actively confuses the underlying structure by transgressing contours or establishing arbitrary points of emphasis. Johns's application of gray graphite wash eliminates the distinction that blue in opposition to red might have established, leaving a difference in density between stars and stripes to maintain an analogous effect. Because the flag configuration barely survives the graphite marking process, a material impulse to change seems to have overcome the stabile motif.[62] The subject itself is transformed—but into what? The mark becomes as much the motif as does the emblematic flag, and perhaps more so. It represents the thinking, the signifying. Better, it *does* the thinking. Every mark is itself a thought, rather than the representation of a thought.

Johns's renderings of the American flag in its normal position privilege the upper left, the location of the concentrated array of stars. Analogously, a map of the United States has an area of relative density at its upper right because of the number of state lines to be traced for the Northeast. Asked why the upper-right quadrant of *Map* (1965; cat. no. 40) has a quality different from the remainder of this drawing (as if manipulated for contrast or some other compositional effect), Johns replied that a map of the United States *is* different in this area—a proper, yet ambiguous, response.[63] If something novel has developed from the pictorial composition of Johns's flags and maps—a new sense of asymmetrical order, perhaps—then he perceived this innovation in the signs themselves, rather than imposing it. His imagery presents nothing that was not always present to be seen.

Johns's signs happen to mirror each other: an upper-left quadrant in one, the flag, becomes an upper-right quadrant in the other, the map. This relationship supports his sense that "there are no literal qualities to anything—everything is unstable."[64] To represent an American map, set an American flag in reverse (or view it from the back). Similarly, a round target in a square format can be alienated from its symmetry, growing asymmetrically maplike and flaglike. Johns scribbled a set of anomalously long lines over the upper-left quadrant of *White Target* (1967–68; cat. no. 49), a lithograph in white ink on black paper (optically, a "gray" image). As a result, the target acquires the appearance of a flag compressed to a square. It has its own upper-left concentration. If this description seems farfetched, recall Johns's general concern "to extract the abstract quality of the work . . . from the figurative meaning . . . trying to uncover *something else* in the work, some other kind of meaning."[65] "Do something else" was Johns's credo, certainly so during the 1960s. *White Target* does "something else."

Johns has many ways of changing his mind about an image—or rather, having it changed for him. Applying a process to a medium will do it; it will change the concept of the image as the image is produced. He has often shifted from chromatic marks to gray or black-and-white, whether in a single work or in a series: *False Start* (1959; cat. no. 1) uses the primary (and some secondary) colors; the closely related *Jubilee* (1959; cat. no. 2) opposes this effect with tones ranging from deep black to bright white, including a few inconspicuous touches of chromatic color, a reminder of the difference. A variant work in black and white pastel, *From False Start* (1960; cat. no. 3), represents the conversion from one type of color, the chromatics of *False Start*, to the other, the neutrals of *Jubilee*. Just as chromatic change can be the crux, so can a change in scale: the marking pattern of *Between the Clock and the Bed* (1982–83; cat. no. 115) shifts internally at the bottom right, rendering the relation of the pattern to its associated gesture indeterminate.

An account from 1977, similar to Johns's "do something" statement, lacks the memorable, epigraphic quality of the earlier note but explains more. There is a difference, however. Rather than beginning with a physical object,

Johns now refers specifically to "doing something else" to an image, that is, altering an image or sign as if to unfix the conceptual meaning of it. This type of change all the more obviously affects the mind—a metanoia or transmentation, as Coleridge would say, but devoid of its religious dimension. Change comes in various sizes. If the finality of repentence and conversion constitutes a *grand metanoia*, then the kind of change of mind (and heart) embodied within a material art like Johns's is a *petit metanoia*. Such a turn in thought and sensation will be repeated many times over in the course of an artist's inventing a work, perhaps with every mark made. Petit metanoia is the form of conversion experienced by secular believers in art:

> I usually begin with some sort of an idea of what I want to do. Sometimes it is an image. I always want to see what it will make. Then, I actually start working. During the process I don't have any morality about changing my mind. In fact, I often find that having an idea in my head prevents me from doing something else. It can blind me. Working is therefore a way of getting rid of an idea.[66]

Image to Object (Metanoiac Touch)

Johns releases himself, his self-image, to the work process, as if he were volunteering for "Transmentation, this Self-change." His inventions "get rid of an idea"—the initial image—by converting it into an object, an emergent construction, cognizant of its medium. With *Canvas* (1956; cat. no. 7) he attached one stretched canvas to another, face to face, so that neither of the two surfaces for painting functions in the usual way; if they were to contain images, we would not see them. Their evident physical contact causes a viewer's sensory focus to turn to touch as a way of comprehending the situation, just as, for Johns himself, touch provided the way to comprehend *Study for "Skin II"* (1962; cat. no. 98). A canvas surface is the visual face of a painting; skin is the visual face of a body. *Canvas* changes the "mentality" or self-image of painting, converting its visual features into tactile ones. The *Skin* drawings do the same with respect to the artist's body. *Painting Bitten by a Man* (1961; cat. no. 90) has a related effect. Johns articulated its surface by biting through two relatively thick layers of wax encaustic to the level of the coarse canvas support. He followed his own instruction to "do something to it"—anything. In this instance, he applied an action to a surface he could not see during the act. Investigative touching (with the mouth) displaced investigative looking. In both *Study for "Skin II"* and *Painting Bitten by a Man*, works of the same years, Johns achieved a change in the life of the mind by diverting its sensory orientation.

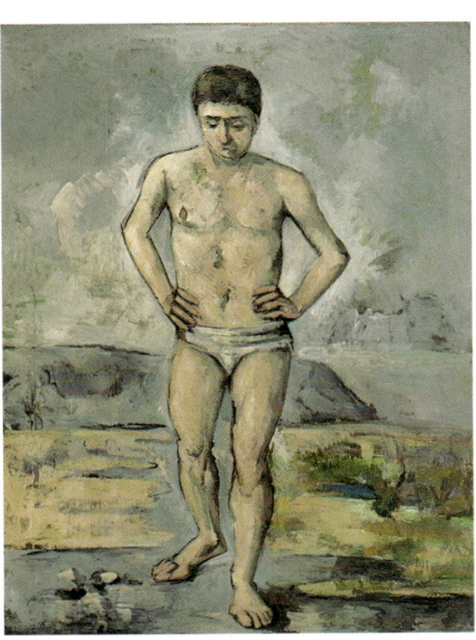

Fig. 8. Paul Cézanne. *The Bather*, c. 1885. Oil on canvas; 127 × 96.8 cm (50 × 38 ⅛ in.). The Museum of Modern Art, New York, Lillie P. Bliss Collection.

Canvas, *Study for "Skin II,"* and *Painting Bitten by a Man* are among a significant number of Johns's works that accomplish with objects and imprints what he claimed Paul Cézanne achieved as he marked out an image, *The Bather* (**FIG. 8**). This work, Johns stated, "has a synesthetic quality that gives it great sensuality—it makes looking equivalent to touching."[67] Johns may have noticed how arbitrarily Cézanne applied his mark, his touch, with respect to representational consistency. The fingers of his bather project outward as an independent pattern, much like Johns's hatchings of the 1970s, including those in *Cicada* (1979). The nipple of the body's right side is grossly exaggerated. The fingers and the nipple seem to have become alienated points of physical concentration for the painter, his metanoiac distraction.

During the 1960s, Johns had an interest in copying Cézanne's *Bather* entirely in gray.[68] Why gray? The temptation is to argue that gray would allow

Johns to appropriate Cézanne since it was his color, virtually a Johns trademark. It may even have been a way to compete with Cézanne. Imagining this kind of egoistic motivation, we become critic-sleuths, exposing aspects of the artist's inner desire to which he would never admit. But in Johns's case, a more suitable interpretation would be more neutral in tone, like gray itself: Johns considered suppressing the chromatic values in order to perceive the tactile energy, enhancing the degree to which looking *is* equivalent to touching. He would take the Impressionist air out of Cézanne to leave only the substance, just as he would take the Resurrection out of Grünewald's fallen soldier by tracing the configuration in isolation.

Gray does for color what metamorphosis does for the cicada: it removes the traces of previous states. Every optical gray disguises a myriad of potential components, as Johns suggests: "The clues that the color gives [to the nature of whatever is represented] are lost"; as the optical order becomes unrevealing, so perception rests "on a more tactile level."[69] Gray is the unrevealing neutral among neutrals: beyond neutralizing the spectrum, it becomes the neutral value between extremes of black and white. Accordingly, Johns coated many of his early canvas-objects with a textured gray encaustic (in addition to *Canvas*, see *Drawer* [1957; cat. no. 9] and *Coat Hanger* [1959; cat. no. 16]). With the visual color subdued, the tactile "object nature" shone as if *it* were now the color—grayness ambiguates the visual and the tactile. Interviewer: "Do you think of gray as a positive color?" Johns: "Yes, I think so. I don't know, I don't really often think about gray." Interviewer: "Does the color gray carry for you a suggestion of ambiguity?" Johns: "*Everything* carries for me a suggestion of ambiguity."[70]

Johns is strong on ambiguity, which is change incarnate. In some respects, Cézanne was the opposite but perhaps only superficially the opposite. Early in his career he stated that he had unusually "strong sensations."[71] He offered this remark as a provocative way of justifying what others regarded as his exaggerated, aggressively personal style. Many of his contemporaries preceived nothing but alienation in his technique, as they did in Monet's. Yet the mature Cézanne's coarse network of individual strokes was rather anonymous in character and offered impressionist advantages. The broken, fragmented surface of marks connoted direct, spontaneous observation, as if any given image of a landscape, or any other subject, were still in a stage of formation. With this technique, painting would represent no more extensive and protracted a vision than could possibly be the case if the time of painting was to be coordinated with the time of seeing. Cézanne's manner of painting brought about a radical sense of hand-eye coordination, such close coordination that (as Johns perceived) the emphasis could shift over to the hand: a conversion. Rather than painting what he was seeing, Cézanne may have been seeing whatever he was touching: the paint, the canvas. This reversal in sensory orientation would apply regardless of the theme—a landscape in the local environs, a model or still life in the studio, an imaginary invention—and the emotional force of the work would derive from the ineffable features of the configuration, just as Johns believed must be the case with Grünewald. Had he painted Cézanne's imagery in gray—he never did—its textured, neutral surface would have projected the substance of the form and whatever emotional content was basic to it. Johns and Cézanne did eventually make contact, touching at a different point, as tracers. Not only has Johns made a number of ink-on-plastic tracings of Cézanne's later compositions of bathers, but he is also the owner of Cézanne's traced drawing after an engraving of Caravaggio's *Entombment* (**FIG. 9**). Johns associates the physicality of this drawing with Cézanne and not Caravaggio, for the actual lines are Cézanne's. But Cézanne, like Johns, may have been using tracing to alienate himself from the line that could only remain his: whether intending it or not, he substituted self-alienation for self-expression.[72]

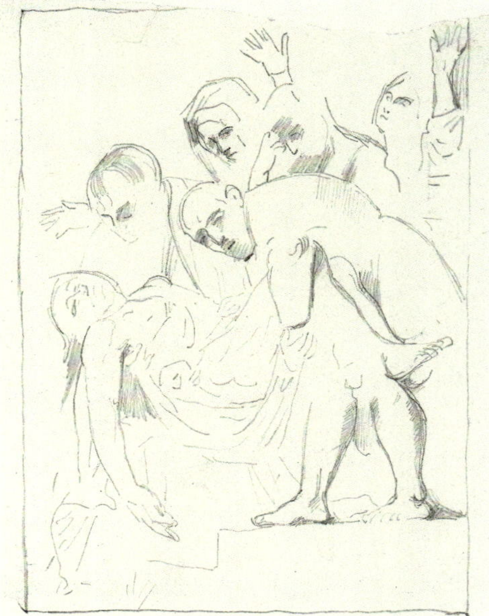

Fig. 9. Paul Cézanne. *Tracing of an Engraving after Caravaggio*, c. 1877–80. Pencil on paper; 14.5 × 10.5 cm (5 ¹¹⁄₁₆ × 4 ⅛ in.). Collection of Jasper Johns.

Images are visual; they are not held in the hand. But to trace an image is a tactile, corporeal experience that must change the visual sense of the source: you explore the image by touch, rendering it physical not only as a drawing-object of a specific size but also as a drawing-action that occupies your bodily space. In Johns's art, images become objectlike (recall his "bent" letters); and when he adds physical attachments to an image on canvas, it becomes all the more objectlike. *Near the Lagoon* (2002–03; cat. no. 135) has an attached cord and strips of wooden lattice, intended to appear as themselves. Because the lattice is also painted, by a kind of sympathetic transference it renders the entire painted construction objectlike. The predominantly gray field of *Near the Lagoon* becomes so physical that it may seem more like very low relief than a flat plane for a painter's illusion.

How much of an object will this painting appear to be? It might be countered that it remains an image. Johns derived the form of the gray field in *Near the Lagoon* from the composition of a reconstruction of Édouard Manet's *Execution of Maximilian* (c. 1867–68). Manet's painting had been dismembered after the artist's death and subsequently reassembled from four fragments by Edgar Degas (see fig. 6 in the essay by Kelly Keegan and Kristin Lister in this volume).[73] The "picture," as a collage, is something of an "object." Each fragment retains a strong material presence, for its external shape is unrelated to (alienated from) the pictorial composition within it. Johns treated the shapes themselves as together comprising an abstract image, a composition. He mimicked their placement and proportions with his own collaged pieces, then rotated the entire configuration clockwise 90 degrees so that it assumed a vertical orientation. Images tolerate such intensive manipulation because gravity has no effect on weightless pictorial elements. Yet, to think of gravity is to realize that Johns's image is a physical construction, a collage with attachments; and turning it sideways (in relation to an imagined initial position) must be as much a physical operation as it is a geometrical variation.[74] Responding to gravity, the suspended cord of *Near the Lagoon* forms a catenary taller than it is wide, the reverse of the situation in most of the earlier paintings having this type of attachment, such as *Bridge* (1997; cat. no. 128) and *Catenary (I Call to the Grave)* (1998; cat. no. 129). It is as if Johns regarded the image as a set of objects that could be rotated as one rotates any physical thing—"do something to it"—with gravitational consequences that bear an aesthetic effect. If you turn a hanging cord, "this happens": the catenary changes.

Signs are generalized cultural tokens, visual configurations to be formed of any material. An American "flag" fabricated by Johns from collage and gray Sculp-metal (*Flag*, 1960; cat. no. 34) or cast in relief in achromatic silver (*Flag*, 1960 and 1987; cat. no. 36) remains identifiable as an image of a flag but not necessarily as an American-flag object. As an object, a gray or achromatic "flag" has become something else, because "something" and "something else" have been done to it. It has changed. Johns's tinkering with the pragmatics of signs converts them into specific material things that acquire new potential. The hand-rendered lettering of *The* (1957; cat. no. 11) is so precise that the visual sign, a decontextualized lexical fragment, makes a synesthetic appeal to a viewer's touch. The sharp, incised edges of the letters appear as if Johns had chiseled them into stone. The content of *The* has little to do with the word and its potential meaning, much to do with the sensory aspects of its material. Becoming an object, the sign changes its orientation, the mentality it projects, its "mind." Or rather: the sign changes Johns's mind as he gradually shapes it into what it is and how it appears.

Working "gets rid of an idea"; it eliminates the mental construct by converting it to a physical construct subjected to material change. "Take up the space 'with what you do,'" Johns noted in 1964, seemingly puzzled, perhaps merely amused, by this ambiguous way of defining *occupation*. He gave the term a double definition, active and passive: occupation is the thing you do, your work; occupation is also the activity that fills your consciousness, your mental "space" as much as your physical sphere of action, causing you to think whatever thoughts you think as a response to the (negative) experience that comes with acting.[75] Perhaps we more commonly feel that we use thinking to *direct* actions. After all, *we* are the conscious agents of action. Yet actions are occupying. Doing one thing implies that you are not doing some other thing at that moment. Just as "having an idea . . . prevents [Johns] from doing something else," to be occupied with handwork is his "way of getting rid of an idea." If preliminary thought generates the idea, then the hand that renders the concept as an image and a certain object, changes it. The hand, its touch, is metanoiac; it changes the mind.

"I usually begin with some sort of an idea," Johns says. Gray, grayness, and graying are ideas. Think of gray as a verb, and graying as a process. Johns sometimes grays values of black and white, as in *Gray Target* (1958; cat. no. 41), by imposing lighter tones on darker ones and darker tones on lighter ones, reducing the overall contrast, and perhaps also the conceptual opposition of the polar terms. A more targetlike target would preserve the contrast from circle to circle; to some extent, this is the case in *Target* (1960; cat. no. 46), a lithographic working proof with additions of gray wash. The two types of marks are of two minds: washes freely brushed yet reaffirming the essential circularity of the target form; lithographic crayon strokes that sometimes violate the circles, attending to their own rhythmic placement. By comparison, the latter element seems black-and-white with the tones of the washes graying its effect. On a number of occasions, Johns has also mixed pigments to gray the chromatic intensity of an entire surface, as in *Untitled (Red, Yellow, Blue)* (1984; see fig. 33 in the essay by James Rondeau in this volume). Here, he neutralized the primaries to the point that they appear gray within a colorful environment but colorful within a gray environment. Chromatic grayness is especially unstable and changeable, but all grays tend to change. As a neutral, gray hovers between its extremes of black and white. Johns nevertheless recognizes gray as distinct from other types of color, not a mere variant. It establishes a "leap from one material to another. . . . When I used white and gray" — *White Target, Gray Target* — "there was a leap between them."[76] Many would regard the nature of the distinction between white and gray as conceptually clear, no experience necessary; but the difference Johns perceived was experiential. When "there was a leap," it moved his mind.

"How my mind must move," expresses Johns's feeling about his condition. "Existing units become details in other works; something connects the images, but I don't know what it is."[77] He speaks of his mind as if it were an object of his observation. His thoughts come to him helter-skelter; and when pathological, we call this condition "racing thoughts."[78] His thoughts also come from someplace other than his willful choice, his self-volition; and when pathological, we call this other condition "thought insertion."[79] The psychoanalytic terminology can only be applied metaphorically, because Johns's condition is supremely human and hardly pathological. Artists *ought* to have racing thoughts. Stimulated by his materials as much as by the images he engages, Johns is in a position to be converted — now, later, and again.

Clueless

> Ambiguous figures put our perceptual system at a curious disadvantage; because they give no clue of which bet to make, [perception] never settles for one bet.
>
> —Richard L. Gregory, 1979[80]

> What interests me . . . is that something can be seen in two different ways, and the question whether seeing it one way necessarily obliterates seeing it the other way. Or whether it's possible to see both at once. . . . Sometimes I think that I'm able to see two things at once, but I'm not sure, because I play with that kind of material so much that there are probably very rapid shifts of perception. . . . In seeing one thing we probably see many.
>
> —Jasper Johns, 1992[81]

Being occupied by two or more visual images simultaneously, like thinking two or more thoughts at once, ought to be impossible. Yet there are borderline cases, "as if there were two things represented in the same place."[82] To demonstrate this, psychologists often present images of figure-ground reversal called "Rubin's figures."[83] One appears prominently in Johns's pastel and charcoal drawing *Untitled* (1983; cat. no. 117)—a vase whose irregular contours define the profile faces of Queen Elizabeth II and Prince Philip. Psychologists would argue that "each perception is entertained alone."[84] Johns counters: "I am not certain that one can't see both at once."[85] Obviously, if shifts in perception are rapid enough, seeing two things in succession will feel like seeing them simultaneously—like seeing the still frames of a projected film strip as continuous movement rather than separate images. But the comparison strays by mixing our sensory, observational capacity with our perceptual, interpretive capacity, two different worlds of experience, seeing and thinking. Does Johns's art allow seeing to morph into thinking (as Steinberg once suggested and I concurred)? Clueless ambiguity: what we feel we see is one reality; what we know about what we see is another reality. We need to see something that will confirm the reality of what we think we know about seeing. Or not.

Psychologists have designated as "ambiguous figures" a particularly puzzling class of separate-but-unified double images. What else could they be called? An "ambiguous figure" has no figure-ground relationship to keep its two active configurations apart, each in its own space and category: "The two alternating figures interpenetrate each other spatially and there is no definite division of the field by a contour. . . . Neither figure is favored over the other."[86] If neither is favored, then neither can be assigned a relative value. Each remains fluid and neutral in relation to the other, like an indefinite gray in relation to its two extremes of black and white. Alternating figures, like grayness, are strangely devoid of psychological tension. We have no impetus to bet that one of the two is more real than the other. Their situation, whatever it is, has already changed before a psychological investment can be made.

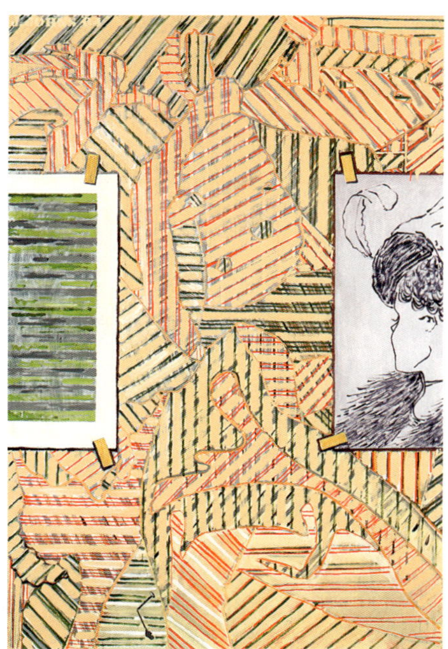

Fig. 10. *Untitled*, 1984. Oil on canvas; 190.5 × 127 cm (75 × 50 in.). Milwaukee Art Museum, Purchase, with funds from Friends of Art, Contemporary Art Society, and the Virginia Booth Vogel Acquisition Fund.

A famous example is the wife/mother-in-law figure, first devised in 1915 for humor, then converted to a somewhat more schematic form in 1930 for psychological study (for a version of it, see fig. 9 in the essay by Douglas Druick in this volume).[87] Johns has used the 1930 variant many times (see **FIG. 10**). It appears as if mirrored in a watercolor and pencil drawing, *Untitled* (1984; cat. no. 118), along with another ambiguous figure, the duck/rabbit, as well as an Elizabeth-and-Philip vase, a "Rubin's figure." It may be that the *naming* of the alternatives for certain ambiguous figures introduces cultural value—the "wife" positive, the "mother-in-law" negative. But the visual switch occurs despite a moral or emotional preference for one figure over the other. This phenomenon forces the mind out of its cultural and psychological predispositions, disrupting

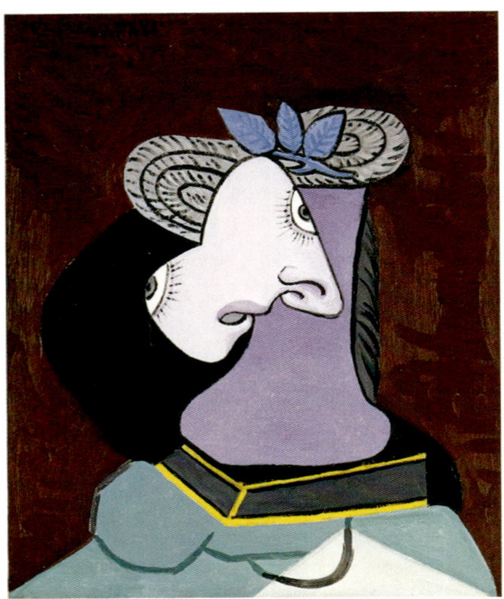

Fig. 11. Pablo Picasso. *Woman in a Straw Hat*, 1936. Oil on canvas; 61 × 50 cm (24 × 19 ¾ in.). Musée Picasso, Paris.

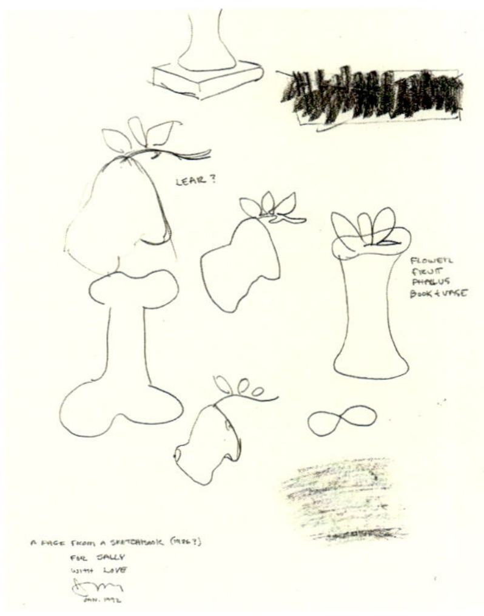

Fig. 12. Page from Sketchbook E, c. 1986. Pencil on paper; 34.6 × 27.3 cm (13 ⅝ × 10 ¾ in.). Collection of Sally Ganz.

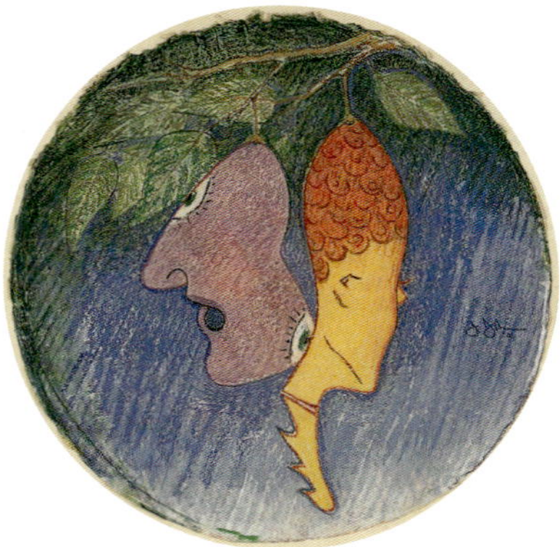

Fig. 13. *Untitled*, 2001. Pastel; d.: 66 cm (26 in.). Collection of the artist.

the rule of the culturally formed self. Ambiguous figures must be Nietzsche's natural allies; they demonstrate that "what things are called" and how we value them need not determine our experience. The wife/mother-in-law is an inherently metanoiac figure.

At some point during the early 1980s, Johns noticed another metanoiac figure illustrated in a book, Pablo Picasso's *Woman in a Straw Hat* (**FIG. 11**). "It became extremely poetic," he explained, "something that conveys many meanings at once. . . . Picasso had constructed a face with features on the outer edge. I started thinking in that direction, and it led me to use the rectangle of the paper as a face and attaching features to it."[88] For Johns, the Picasso face became both an image and—when stretched taut through the medium of drawing—a surface for drawing other figures and faces, just as drawing is sometimes done on the skin of a living body, including one's own.[89] His line of thought may have recalled his early studies for the *Skin* drawings, some of which stretch the imprinted facial features out to the periphery of the sheet. His interest in the Picasso face also led him back to an illustration he had seen many years before—a somewhat similar image drawn by a schizophrenic child. He combined the two "faces," Picasso's and the child's, in *Untitled* (1991; cat. no. 125).[90] (The "wife" in the wife/mother-in-law has its features at the periphery of the rendered face as well; we perceive this figure in extreme lost-profile perspective.)

Picasso recognized that seen from certain angles, a person's eyes migrate to the edges of the self-contained body and seem to project from the contoured head or face, just as a nose, lips, or ears may project beyond the generally established periphery. Yet the eyes in *Woman in a Straw Hat* do not actually project; instead their location is just at the edge, contained by it. The picture of a face conceived in this manner is already objectlike in being entirely self-contained—the antithesis of Wölfflin's impressionist alienation. If there is a "bewildering alienation of the sign from the thing" in this case, it must involve the image as a whole, considered as if it could be displaced. Beyond the migrating features, Johns recognized the potential for such displacement: "It's a still life with a book and a vase. The head can be seen as a [fruit hanging from] a branch. It's rich in a kind of sexual suggestion, and extremely complicated on that level."[91] Around 1986 he sketched these interpretations on a single sheet: the flower in a vase, the vase resting on a book, the anthropomorphic fruit hanging from a branch, the phallus (**FIG. 12**).[92] Then his mind moved: at some point, he saw that what applied to the Picasso face might apply to the wife/mother-in-law as it passed through a drawing medium. A tondo in pastel, *Untitled* (2001; **FIG. 13**), tests the validity of the notion by hanging as fruit on the same branch the Picasso face and the wife/mother-in-law. Johns stripped both (the Picasso and the wife/mother-in-law) of their original clothing, leaving just the skin of the face. In an earlier pastel, *Untitled* (1990; **FIG. 14**), the same two "objects"—not as "fruit," but merely as object-entities—appear to have fallen to the floor of an interior room or a box. Perhaps I surmise that the two ambiguous heads have fallen only because I previously thought that I saw them suspended from a branch. My mind remains open to be changed. Nothing I learn from Johns's art seems definitive. This in itself is a lesson.

A flexible length of cord suspended from two points will hang in the form of a catenary. Johns attached cords to works such as *Near the Lagoon* and let them hang. He also drew the motif in various media, without "real" attachments. *Untitled* (2002; cat. no. 133) is one example, a study in ink on plastic with characteristic vertical runs of the fluid medium, the effect of gravity. Here, gravity both acts and is represented acting—represented by the catenary motif that mimics a cord affected by gravity when hung at different lengths from the

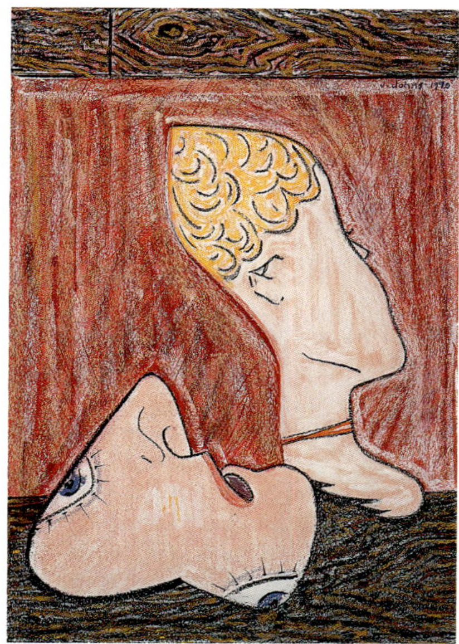

Fig. 14. *Untitled*, 1990. Pastel; 78.7 × 57.2 cm (31 × 22 ½ in.). Collection of the artist.

same two points. The pictorial effect of the hanging motif converts the image of the cord into a swag of drapery with several pleats.[93] The transformation depends on the same type of visual metaphor that converts heads to fruit when shown suspended from a branch. At the top of *Untitled*, Johns drew a broad squiggle-mark: a horizontal stroke to the right, a diagonal drop to the left, a diagonal recovery upward, another diagonal drop. Under the conditions, the mark reads ambiguously, signifying at least two possibilities: alienated from any representational sign, it is a natural gesture of the arm and hand, similar to the squiggles seen in Johns's early motifs of targets and flags; motivated by the motif of the cord-catenary-swag, it assumes the sense of something hanging (suspended, it also drops). The squiggle is viciously metanoiac.

Metanoia: reorientation, repentance, conversion, change of heart, change of mind. The prefix *meta-* signifies change, but also refers to operations taken to a higher level. Obscure but etymologically fluid, the word *metanoia* ought to mean thinking beyond thought, having your mind go elsewhere, beyond the cultural store of knowledge. Did Johns "know" what he was doing when he made the very ordinary squiggle at the top of *Untitled*? Perhaps he would say that it seemed like the thing to do as he was doing it: "It's what I did; it's what I've done. . . . I don't know if it's out of choice or out of necessity—how my mind must move."[94]

"How my mind must move" is not something to be known but something to keep finding out.

1 Jasper Johns, interview by Richard Field, Apr. 23, 1999, audiotape transcript, unpublished (courtesy Jasper Johns and Richard Field); see also Shiff 2006, pp. 294, 297. I am especially grateful to Caitlin Haskell for aid in research.

2 Charles Baudelaire, "Salon de 1846" (1846), in *Oeuvres complètes*, ed. Claude Pichois, 2 vols. (Gallimard, 1975–76), vol. 2, p. 456 (my translation). See also Richard Shiff, "Expression: Natural, Personal, Pictorial," in *A Companion to Art Theory*, ed. Paul Smith and Carolyn Wilde (Blackwell, 2002), pp. 159–72.

3 Charles Blanc, *Grammaire des arts du dessin: Architecture, sculpture, peinture* (1867; Henri Laurens, 1880), p. 574 (my translation).

4 Geelhaar 1980a, p. 39, in *Writings* 1996, p. 191. One of the most explicit of Johns's works in this respect is the lithograph *Hand* (1963), which consists of two impressions of a right hand, one using soap as a medium for leaving an imprint on the lithographic plate, the other using oil.

5 "I've only drawn something that everyone knows how to draw"; Shiff 2006, p. 294.

6 Steinberg 1962/1972, p. 54. This sentence appears only in the revised (1972) edition of the essay.

7 My concern is for those aspects of Johns's practice that seem the most public, the least hermetic—those features that any other person might adopt to benefit his or her understanding and experience. Johns's art has pragmatic social value to the extent that others learn something from it, extending their sensory, intellectual, and emotional capacities in the process. See below, "Not I."

8 Barnett Newman, "The 14 Stations of the Cross, 1958–1966," *Artnews* 65 (Sept. 1966), p. 26.

9 "Sometimes I change the [projected] title because it seems to me the painting has changed"; Sylvester 1965, in Sylvester 2001, p. 147.

10 Steinberg 1962/1972, p. 54. This sentence appears in the original (1962) version of the essay (compare note 6).

11 Johns was explaining that although people would be inclined to associate an interest in accidental effects with the use of ink and its drips, "what is accidental about it? If you do this, this happens." See Rosenthal and Fine 1990, p. 74.

12 Raynor 1973, p. 20, in *Writings* 1996, p. 142.

13 Sylvester 1997, p. 466.

14 Robertson and Marlow 1993, p. 46, in *Writings* 1996, p. 287.

15 See above, note 4.

16 Rosenthal and Fine 1990, p. 73.

17 Johns has even used drawing to convert published reproductions of his art into new works; see Fine 1990, pp. 51–53.

18 Heinrich von Kleist, "On the Gradual Fabrication of Thoughts While Speaking" (1805–06), in *An Abyss Deep Enough: Letters of Heinrich von Kleist with a Selection of Essays and Anecdotes*, ed. and trans. Philip B. Miller (Dutton, 1982), pp. 218, 222 (original emphasis).

19 "The only unity we truly possess is perhaps that of the name"; Michel Leiris, "Keaton (Buster)" (1930), in Georges Bataille, ed., *Encyclopaedia Acephalica: Comprising the Critical Dictionary and Related Texts*, trans. Iain White (Atlas Press, 1995), p. 56 (reference courtesy Cord Bynum).

20 Cage 1964, p. 22.

21 Fuller 1978a, p. 6, in *Writings* 1996, pp. 173–74.

22 *U.S.A. Artists 8: Jasper Johns* 1966, in *Writings* 1996, p. 127.

23 Sylvester 1965, p. 155, in *Writings* 1996, p. 114; statement to the author, Jan. 22, 2007.

24 Friedrich Nietzsche, *The Gay Science* (1882), trans. Walter Kaufmann (Vintage, 1974), p. 171.

25 See Richard Shiff, "To Create Onself," in Richard Shiff, Carol C. Mancusi-Ungaro, and Heidi Colsman-Freyberger, *Barnett Newman: A Catalogue Raisonné* (The Barnett Newman Foundation, 2004), pp. 3–115.

26 Barnett Newman, "For Impassioned Criticism" (1968), in *Barnett Newman: Selected Writings and Interviews*, ed. John P. O'Neill (Knopf, 1990), p. 135: "What I am asking from the art critic is...that each time he writes, he create himself."

27 Newman, "Response to the Reverend Thomas F. Mathews," (1967), in *Barnett Newman* (note 26), p. 288.

28 Accordingly, they preferred Newman to Pollock as a representative of the New York School, giving him a phenomenological as opposed to a metaphysical spin; see Richard Shiff, "Whiteout: The Not-Influence Newman Effect," in *Barnett Newman*, ed. Ann Temkin, exh. cat. (Philadelphia Museum of Art, 2002), pp. 77–111.

29 Tono 1964, in *Writings* 1996, pp. 97, 100.

30 Fuller 1978b, p. 7, in *Writings* 1996, p. 187 (original emphasis).

31 Raynor 1973, p. 22, in *Writings* 1996, p. 145.

32 Fuller 1978b, p. 7, in *Writings* 1996, p. 187 (original emphasis).

33 Bernard and Thompson 1984, p. 65, in *Writings* 1996, p. 217.

34 Ibid.

35 Raynor 1973, p. 22, in *Writings* 1996, p. 145.

36 Johns's statements were made in late 1991–early 1992; see Crichton 1994, p. 64. Johns explained his motivation in the same way when interviewed by Bryan Robertson and Tim Marlow; see Robertson and Marlow 1993, p. 46, in *Writings* 1996, pp. 287–88. He began making the tracings in 1981. For an extended account of his involvement with Grünewald's art, see Rosenthal 1990, pp. 34–41.

37 Johns speaks of the soldiers (there are several) as "in a state of awe": see Rosenthal 1993, p. 63, in *Writings* 1996, p. 282. Grünewald's image differs somewhat from the account in Matthew 28:2–4, New Revised Standard Version: "Suddenly there was a great earthquake; for an angel of the Lord, descending from heaven, came and rolled back the stone [of the tomb] and sat on it....For fear of him the guards shook and became like dead men."

38 "As the metamorphosis of the butterfly supplied to old Greek thought an emblem of the soul's ascension, so the natural history of the cicada has furnished Buddhism with [the notion that] man sheds his body only as the [cicada] sheds its skin"; Lafcadio Hearn, "Sémi (Cicadae)" (1900), in *The Writings of Lafcadio Hearn*, 16 vols. (Houghton Mifflin, 1922), vol. 10, p. 67. Furthermore, "in Buddhist conception, not only a person may change into a cicada, but a cicada may also change into a human being"; Gaines Kan-Chih Liu, "Cicadas in Chinese Culture," *Osiris* 9 (1950), p. 331. On the cicada as an emblem of resurrection among American Indians and the ancient Chinese, see also Lucy W. Clausen, *Insect Fact and Folklore* (Macmillan, 1954), pp. 128–29.

39 Samuel Taylor Coleridge, *The Notebooks of Samuel Taylor Coleridge, Volume 4: 1819–1826*, ed. Kathleen Coburn and Merton Christensen (Princeton University Press, 1990), entry 4824 (1821). Coleridge relates this metamorphosis to repentance and metanoia (see below).

40 A black-and-white etching of 1975–76 titled *Hatching* produces the same effect with relatively light, gray tones at its center in opposition to relatively dark blacks toward its edges (see fig. 75a in Rosenthal and Fine 1990, p. 244). This may be a prototype for the *Cicada* images, and its title perhaps puns on "hatching" as both a graphic mark and the bursting forth from an egg or shell. Metaphorically, one can hatch a plot or, simply, an idea—that is, experience hatching as metanoia (change of mind).

41 Sketchbook A, p. 9, c. 1960, in *Writings* 1996, p. 50. See my previous discussions of Johns's evasion of cause and effect: Shiff 1987 and Shiff 2003.

42 Rosenthal and Fine 1990, p. 73.

43 Samuel Taylor Coleridge, *Moral and Religious Aphorisms* (1825), in *The Collected Works of Samuel Taylor Coleridge, Volume 9: Aids to Reflection*, ed. John Beer (Princeton University Press, 1993), p. 132 (original emphasis). Compare *The Notebooks of Samuel Taylor Coleridge, Volume 4: 1819–1826*, entry 5270 (Nov. 1825): "O! would the Jew and the Unitarian say—We have only to *repent* and God has promised to *pardon* us!—As if a metanoia, a transmentation, were but the holding up a finger, or a nodding of the Head—the immediate consequent of a self-produced Volition" (original emphasis; Greek words omitted).

44 Shiff 2006, p. 277.

45 Sylvester 1965, in Sylvester 2001, p. 161.

46 "It is the compulsion, the absolute constraint upon us to think otherwise than we have been thinking that constitutes experience"; Charles Sanders Peirce, "The Categories in Detail, Secondness: Shock and the Sense of Change" (c. 1905), in *Collected Papers*, ed. Charles Hartshorne, Paul Weiss, and Arthur W. Burks, 8 vols. (Harvard University Press, 1958–60), vol. 1, p. 170.

47 Shiff 2006, p. 297.

48 The phrasing is Newman's: "An artist paints so that he will have something to look at"; see "From 'The Ides of Art: The Attitudes of Ten Artists on Their Art and Contemporaneousness'" (1947), in *Barnett Newman* (note 26), p. 160. Johns readily shares his work, placing many of his major paintings on extended loan to public institutions.

49 Matthew Arnold, *Literature and Dogma* (1873), in *Dissent and Dogma*, ed. R. H. Super (University of Michigan Press, 1968), pp. 288–89: "We translate [*metanoia* as] *repentence*, a groaning and lamenting over one's sins; and we translate it wrong. Of 'metanoia,' according to the meaning of Jesus, the bewailing one's sins was a small part. The main part was something far more active and fruitful—the setting up an immense *new inward movement* for obtaining one's rule of life. And 'metanoia,' accordingly, is: *A change of the inner man*" (original emphasis).

50 *U.S.A. Artists 8: Jasper Johns* 1966, in *Writings* 1996, p. 124.

51 When asked to expand on his thoughts about helplessness, Johns replied: "I felt or wanted my work to have a sense of the inevitable, the unavoidable"; Yau 2007, p. 22. See also Johns's remark, in Sylvester 1965, in *Writings* 1996, p. 118: "The final statement, has to be not a deliberate statement but a helpless statement. It has to be what you can't avoid saying, not what you set out to say." And see Sylvester's subsequent reflection on this aspect of Johns's thinking; Sylvester 1997, pp. 464–65. Johns also put the matter this way: "If you avoid everything you can avoid, then you do what you can't avoid doing, and you do what is helpless, and unavoidable"; Klüver 1963, in *Writings* 1996, p. 87. Kirk Varnedoe commented relevantly (but perhaps too strongly) on Johns's "self-denials and throttlings of will"; Varnedoe 1996, pp. 30–31.

52 Wallach 1991, in *Writings* 1996, p. 261.

53 Nietzsche (note 24), p. 121 (original emphasis).

54 Heinrich Wölfflin, *Principles of Art History* (1915), trans. M. D. Hottinger (Dover, 1950), p. 21.

55 Wölfflin (note 54), p. 22.

56 Johns, statement in *U.S.A. Artists 8: Jasper Johns* 1966, in *Writings* 1996, p. 123.

57 Johns's attitude has affinities not only with Nietzsche but with the Nietzschean Georges Bataille: "It is vain to see in the appearance of things only those intelligible signs that allow various elements to be differentiated one from another. What strikes human eyes determines not only knowledge of the relations between various objects, but just as much a specific, inexplicable state of mind"; Georges Bataille, "Le langage des fleurs" (1929), in *Oeuvres complètes*, ed. Michel Foucault, 12 vols. (Gallimard, 1970–88), vol. 1, p. 173 (my translation).

58 Friedrich Nietzsche, *Beyond Good and Evil* (1886), trans. Marion Faber (Oxford University Press, 1998), p. 35 (translation slightly altered).

59 Sketchbook A, p. 42, c. 1963–64, in *Writings* 1996, pp. 31, 54.

60 Bernstein 1980, p. 286, in *Writings* 1996, p. 201 (emphasis eliminated).

61 See the interview by Nan Rosenthal in this volume, pp. 160–61.

62 See the similar effect in Johns's lithographs of 1960: *Flag I, Flag II, Flag III*.

63 Conversation with the author, Sharon, Connecticut, Oct. 1, 2005.

64 Kent 1990, in *Writings* 1996, p. 258.

65 Cork 1990, p. 21, in *Writings* 1996, p. 258 (emphasis added). Here Johns refers to his work with the Grünewald figures, but the statement applies more generally.

66 Olson 1977, p. 25, in *Writings* 1996, p. 168.

67 Glueck 1977, p. 87, in *Writings* 1996, p. 166. Johns also linked Cézanne to his own interest in rotation: see Shiff 2003, including relevant studies by others listed on p. 22 n. 50 of that essay.

68 See Christian Geelhaar, "The Painters Who Had the Right Eyes," in *Paul Cézanne: The Bathers*, trans. John Mitchell and Dorothy Kosinski, exh. cat. (Kunstsammlung Basel, 1990), p. 298.

69 See the interview by Nan Rosenthal in this volume, p. 160.

70 Ibid., p. 160 (original emphasis).

71 "J'ai les sensations très fortes"; Cézanne's words as quoted by the journalist "Stock," *Le Salon*, Mar. 20, 1870; see John Rewald, *Histoire de l'impression-nisme* (Albin Michel, 1986), p. 163.

72 See Johns's remarks on the Cézanne tracing in Shiff 2006, p. 288.

73 See Livingstone 2000, pp. 178–89; John Elderfield, *Manet and the Execution of Maximilian*, exh. cat. (Museum of Modern Art, 2006), p. 99.

74 Johns prevents the possibility of many of his signlike images from being turned sideways or upside-down by leaving the very bottom edge free of paint and, in a significant number of early works (such as *White Target*, 1957 [fig. 7]), taking care to stretch the canvas with a blue selvage thread visible just above the bottom edge as well. Both practices definitively mark the chosen edge as "bottom." For an extended discussion, see Richard Shiff, "Breath of Modernism (Metonymic Drift)," in *In Visible Touch: Modernism and Masculinity*, ed. Terry Smith (University of Chicago Press, 1997), pp. 184–213.

75 Sketchbook A, p. 47, 1964, in *Writings* 1996, p. 55.

76 Tono 1964, in *Writings* 1996, p. 100.

77 Rosenthal 1993, p. 63, in *Writings* 1996, p. 282.

78 See Robert Berkow, ed., *The Merck Manual of Diagnosis and Therapy* (Merck Research Laboratories, 1992), p. 1599; Irving I. Gottesman, *Schizophrenia Genesis: The Origins of Madness* (Freeman, 1991), pp. 14–15. See also Shiff 2003, pp. 13–16.

79 See Christopher D. Frith, *The Cognitive Neuropsychology of Schizophrenia* (Lawrence Erlbaum Associates, 1992), p. 5 and passim.

80 Richard L. Gregory, *Eye and Brain: The Psychology of Seeing*, 4th ed. (1979; Princeton University Press, 1990), p. 230.

81 Rosenthal 1993, p. 64, in *Writings* 1996, pp. 283–84. Compare Johns, in Weatherby 1990, p. 29, in *Writings* 1996, p. 257: "You see the one or the other with no in between....Not knowing exactly is something that I find fascinating. Whatever the basis, it probably moves one to see life in an ambiguous way."

82 James J. Gibson, *The Senses Considered as Perceptual Systems* (Houghton Mifflin, 1966), p. 246.

83 See Richard L. Gregory, *The Intelligent Eye* (McGraw-Hill, 1970), pp. 15–18.

84 Gregory (note 80), p. 229.

85 Yau 2007, p. 22.

86 Edwin G. Boring, "A New Ambiguous Figure," *American Journal of Psychology* 42 (July 1930), pp. 444–45.

87 For the first publication of the more graphic version of the figure, see Boring (note 86), p. 444, and *Puck*, Nov. 6, 1915, p. 11, for the original version as drawn by W. E. Hill.

88 Johns's statement was made in late 1991 or early 1992; see Crichton 1994, p. 71. The book in question was David Douglas Duncan, *Picasso's Picassos* (Harper and Row, 1961). See Bernstein 1996, p. 73 n. 108.

89 Picasso drew on skin around 1961; see Shiff (note 74), pp. 189–91.

90 On Johns's use of the two flattened images of faces, see Shiff 2003. See also Bernstein 1996, p. 60.

91 Wallach 1988, p. 154, in *Writings* 1996, p. 226. See also Bernstein 1996, pp. 60–61, 73 n. 109.

92 Johns wrote "Lear?" next to his drawings of fruit, a reference to the nineteenth-century English artist Edward Lear who had made similar renderings (for an illustration, see Edward Lear, *The Complete Verse and Other Nonsense*, ed. Vivien Noakes [Penguin, 2001], p. 252). The Royal Academy of Art, London organized a Lear retrospective in 1985, but Johns did not see it (statement to the author, Jan. 22, 2007).

93 Of relevance to Johns's development of this image is his interest in Francisco de Zurbarán's paintings of Veronica's veil; see Bernstein 1996, p. 61. *Untitled* (2001; cat. no. 132) is another example of Johns's veil-catenary motif.

94 Bernstein 1980, p. 286, in *Writings* 1996, p. 201 (emphasis eliminated).

Mapping the Mind

BARBARA ROSE

My mind was a mirror:
It saw what it saw, it knew what it knew.
In youth my mind was just a mirror
In a rapidly flying car,
Which catches and loses bits of the landscape.
Then in time
Great scratches were made on the mirror,
Letting the outside world come in,
And letting my inner self look out.
For this is the birth of the soul in sorrow,
A birth with gains and losses.
The mind sees the world as a thing apart,
And the soul makes the world at one with itself.
A mirror scratched reflects no image—
And this is the silence of wisdom.

Epitaph for Ernest Hyde
Edgar Lee Masters, *Spoon River Anthology*

DURING THE FALL OF 1962, JASPER JOHNS BEGAN PAINTING A large gray map of the United States, in encaustic. The work was made to be sold to help fund the newly formed Foundation for Contemporary Performance Arts, which was to have its first benefit exhibition in early 1963, at the Allan Stone Gallery in New York. The original purpose of the Foundation, formed by John Cage and Johns, was to finance a Broadway season for the Merce Cunningham Dance Company.[1] Collector Marcia Weisman saw the gray *Map* (1962; cat. no. 39) in Johns's studio on Front Street and wished to buy the painting immediately. Johns agreed to the purchase on the condition that the funds would go to the Foundation and the work would be included in the benefit exhibition, where it was first seen publicly. Following that event, *Map* hung in Weisman's California dining room until it was bequeathed to the Museum of Contemporary Art, Los Angeles.

According to Johns, this gray *Map* was inspired by the brightly colored 1961 *Map* now in the collection of the Museum of Modern Art, New York (FIG. 1).[2] Thus, the 1962 gray encaustic may be thought of as a pendant to the 1961 oil.[3] The two related paintings are among a number of doubled or paired works, one executed in the bright hues of the spectrum, the other in subdued gray. Perhaps the most obvious "twins" are the 1959 colored *False Start* (cat. no. 1) and its slightly smaller grisaille complement, *Jubilee* (1959; cat. no. 2). These paintings are among the first in which Johns loosened his previously tight and restricted brushwork. This is not to say, however, that either one is spontaneously expressive. The artist's brushstrokes are organized into patterned bursts that carefully maintain their disciplined decorum.[4] Yet within this context of a style evolving into a freer way of painting, the brush was still controlled by the hand and wrist, and not by the arm and body as in "action painting."

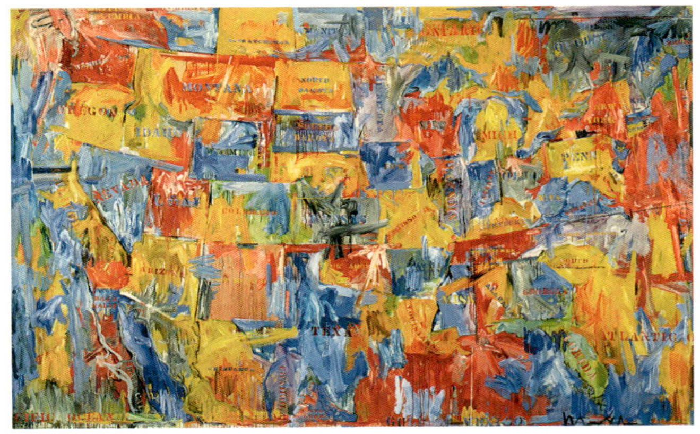

Fig. 1. *Map*, 1961. Oil on canvas; 198.1 × 312.7 cm (78 × 123 1/8 in.). The Museum of Modern Art, New York, gift of Mr. and Mrs. Robert C. Scull.

Johns owed his use of the map motif to Robert Rauschenberg, who, sometime in 1960, had given Johns a small printed map of the United States, typical of the kind used to teach geography in public schools.[5] Maps appear collaged into a number of Rauschenberg's early works such as *Monk* (1955; Gundlach Collection, Los Angeles), one of his first Combines, probably named for the great, improvisatory jazz musician Thelonious Monk. *Charlene* (Stedelijk Museum, Amsterdam), a 1954 Combine, contains, along with pieces of fabric and a letter from the artist's mother, a map of Rauschenberg's home state of Texas.[6] Previously, he had collaged a map into the monochrome white *Mother of God* (FIG. 2).

So much has been conjectured about the relationship between Rauschenberg and Johns that it seems idle to add to this bourgeoning literature. But there is still a lot to be said about the complex artistic dialogue between the two, an exchange that began in collaboration and ended in competition.

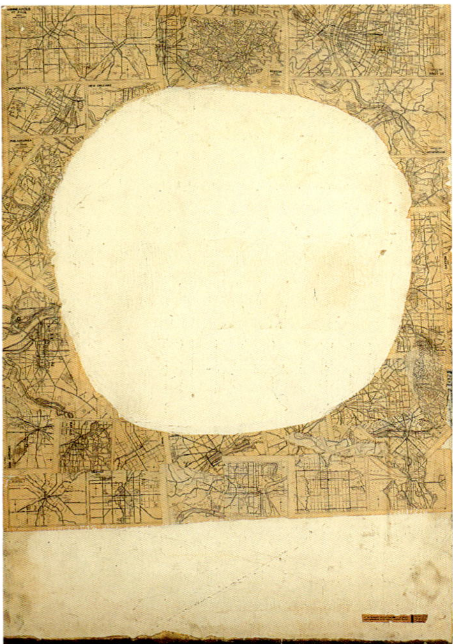

Fig. 2. Robert Rauschenberg. *Mother of God*, c. 1950. Oil, enamel, printed maps, newspaper, and copper and metallic paints on Masonite; 121.9 × 81.6 cm (48 × 32 ⅛ in.). San Francisco Museum of Modern Art, fractional purchase through a gift of Phyllis Wattis and promised gift of an anonymous donor.

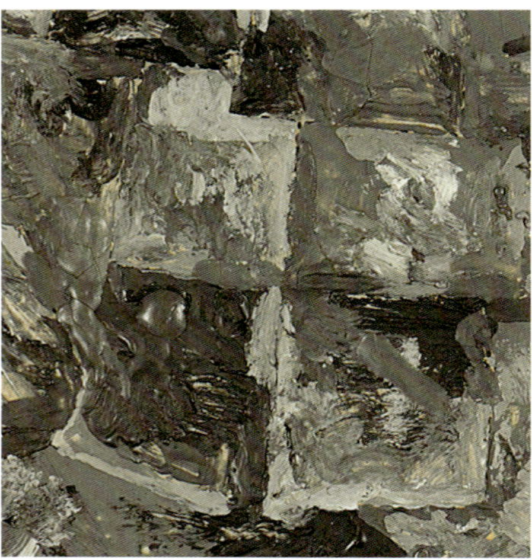

Fig. 3. Detail of *Map*, 1960 (cat. no. 38).

Coincidentally, this historic interchange, from 1954 to 1961, lasted exactly as long as that of Pablo Picasso and Georges Braque, who, working together during a period of intense interaction from 1907 to 1914, invented Analytic Cubism, the basis for advanced art in the first half of the twentieth century. During the seven years of their dialogue, Rauschenberg and Johns similarly created a new visual language that radically altered the history of art in the second half of the twentieth century.

The extroverted Rauschenberg was famous for giving away objects, ideas, and personal fetishes. Presenting Johns a map could well have been a suggestion for a motif that was a logical succession to the flags, numbers, and alphabets that had become his signature images. The point was not lost on Johns, who turned the ordinary 8 × 11 inch paper diagram into a precious artwork, covering its surface with delicate impressionist strokes — painted in encaustic in the shades of the gray scale — that stop at the edge of the sheet, later mounted on canvas (1960; cat. no. 38). The states are not named as they are in the artist's later versions. Their outlines, more similar than in reality, approximate gridded rectangles to the point that this work appears to be a missing transition between the alphabet and number series and Johns's later works (FIG. 3). The broad constructive strokes and standard notebook-page size suggest that this first gray map could itself be a pendant to the colorful *Alley Oop* (FIG. 4), the comic strip that Johns covered with similarly measured, flat brushstrokes, this time in the primary and secondary colors.

Alley Oop, as painted by Johns, resembles Paul Sérusier's *Talisman* (1888; Musée d'Orsay, Paris) — his protoabstract landscape on the lid of a cigar box — more than it does a crude comic strip with its blunt outline drawing. As an image, it is unique in Johns's production. Newspapers are part of John's life: he reads the headlines and does the crossword puzzles (scraps of which have found their way into his paintings), but he largely leaves the funny pages to others.[7] Because he painted the American flag, a familiar image from the common culture, Johns has been considered the father of Pop Art. His work, however, is not a comment on mechanical reproduction, mass culture, or consumerism — all of which are thought to lie at the heart of that movement.[8]

The gray *Map* stands out among Johns's masterpieces, but he used the motif in other works, including a miniature oil sketch on board (FIG. 5) that he gave to Toiny Castelli, the wife of his dealer, Leo Castelli, on the birth of their son Jean-Christophe in 1962 — possibly a maquette for the large painting we are discussing. Far more than its 1961 colored doppelgänger, the gray *Map* pictures a terrain that is slippery and sharply discontinuous, with spatial elisions and extreme light-dark juxtapositions suggesting precipices or craters. The 1962 gray *Map* also has a crusty uneven surface, which peels away in places to reveal suggestive fragments sutured into the layers of wax that cover the canvas. The volume-describing function of tonal modulation ironically creates no sense of space, while the knowledge that a map is flat is sabotaged by an inevitable reading of chiaroscuro as indicating depth. This territory of uncertainty becomes familiar in Johns's subsequent works, just as the multiple contours of Paul Cézanne's blurry objects are an indication of a permanent condition of doubt.[9]

In addition to the three large maps of 1961–63, Johns painted a sizeable *Double White Map*, in encaustic, in 1965 (Whitney Museum of American Art, New York). There are also a number of maps on paper, including a 1965 work in graphite and metallic powder (cat. no. 40), lithographs from 1965 and 1966 (cat. nos. 51–54), and the 1965 black *Map*, executed for collectors John and Kimiko Powers: a large charcoal drawing in which the Southeastern states are covered in black oil, making their names difficult to read, as if they were "condemned to anonymity."[10]

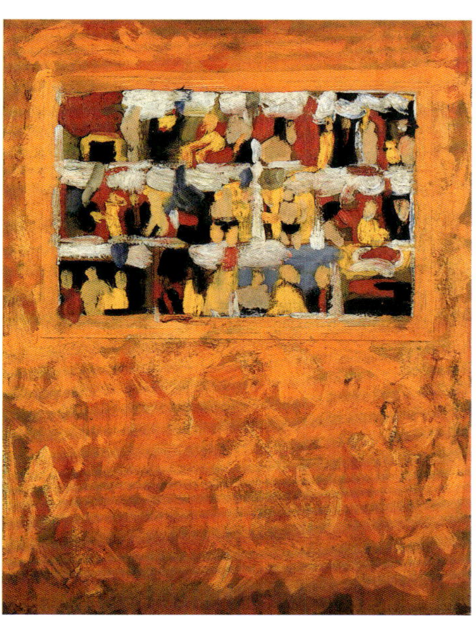

Fig. 4. *Alley Oop*, 1958. Oil and collage on cardboard; 58.4 × 45.7 cm (23 × 18 in.). Private collection.

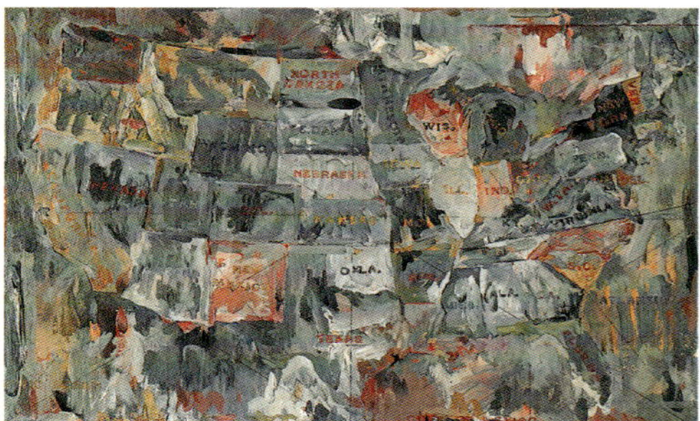

Fig. 5. *Small Map*, 1962. Oil on board; 16 × 26.4 cm (6 5/16 × 10 3/8 in.). Collection of Jean-Christophe Castelli.

On one level, maps tell about location—where you are—and about boundaries—the limits of where you may go without trespassing. In 1962 Johns, along with the other, most ambitious artists of his generation, was involved in testing both. After the success of the Flags, Targets, Numbers, and Alphabets, all paintings based on simple, recognizable images, he was obviously seeking other directions, a fresh place to take a stand. Maps are indispensable in times of war, when familiar landscapes suddenly become dangerous battlefields. Beyond any personal meaning the image of the map may have had for him, the public context for Johns's early maps was a country reevaluating its divided past, in the opening stages of a faraway foreign war that would divide it once again. Maps mark combat zones. The raised and fractured surface of Johns's gray *Map* gives it a topographical feeling, suggesting the kind of map that generals inspect when strategizing moves. The battleground implicitly referenced in this 1962 painting, however, was not Saigon. Given its historical context and personal references, it was more likely Antietam, the crucial engagement fought one hundred years earlier which decided the future of the United States.

The Battle of Antietam was the turning point of the Civil War because it ended General Robert E. Lee's strategic first invasion of the North, permitting President Abraham Lincoln to issue the Emancipation Proclamation only five days afterward, on September 22, 1862, at Gettysburg, Pennsylvania. One hundred years later, President John F. Kennedy proclaimed the end to segregation, the remaining legacy of slavery, in all public schools and facilities, as well as in the armed forces of the United States. Since we know that Johns was painting the gray *Map* in his Front Street studio in New York in the fall and early winter of 1962 and that he was sensitive to historical events, it is not unlikely that he would make reference to these events, which were much in the news at the time.[11]

The Civil War centennial began on December 6, 1960, when President Dwight D. Eisenhower issued a national proclamation recalling the bloody strife that had torn the country apart and urging Americans "to plan and carry out their own appropriate Centennial observances during the years 1961 to 1965."[12] Frank Stella was the first artist to respond, using the primary and secondary colors to make monochrome "stripe" paintings known as the *Benjamin Moore* series, the name of a popular commercial brand of house paint. These works—each titled after a different Civil War battle—were exhibited at the Galerie Lawrence, in Paris, in the fall of 1961.[13] Like Stella's series, or Larry Rivers's slightly earlier *Last Civil War Veteran* (1959; the Museum of Modern Art, New York), Johns's Maps may be seen as a response to the Civil War centennial.

For each series of stripe paintings, Stella planned a culminating horizontal work. The finale of the *Benjamin Moore* group was a double concentric-square painting titled *Jasper's Dilemma*, done in 1962–63 (**FIG. 6**). The precedent for such an abstract portrait can be found in a number of examples executed in the mid-to-late 1920s by Charles Demuth in honor of friends and colleagues. Originally, Stella made diagrammatic drawings for a series of works as well, but the only one actually executed was his tribute to Johns. A psychological portrait symbolizing the issues facing Johns at the time, *Jasper's Dilemma* may be read as both homage and character analysis.[14] A mirrored image of two halves that do not match, it pictures irreconcilable oppositions. The mitered concentric squares on the left are painted in bright spectrum hues, while the receding squares on the right are painted in the gray shades that were Johns's alternate palette. Thus, one might conjecture that "Jasper's dilemma" is Johns's refusal or inability to choose—between representation and abstraction, object and image, chroma and chiaroscuro, hard edge or blurred contour.

While Johns was painting the gray *Map*, the cutting issue in art was the nature of pictorial illusionism. Stella had articulated the stance of the younger generation in his frequently quoted, "What you see is what you see."[15] Johns's response is that what you see is not what you see.

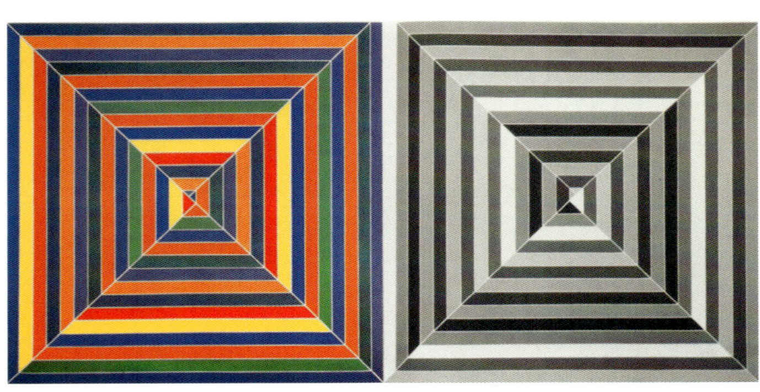

Fig. 6. Frank Stella. *Jasper's Dilemma*, 1962–63. Alkyd on canvas; 195.6 × 391.2 cm (77 × 154 in.). Collection of Mr. and Mrs. Paul Anka, Carmel, California.

The most powerful critic of the moment, Clement Greenberg, devoted much of his writing then to defining illusionism, along with tactility, as the enemies of advanced painting. For his argument for the superiority of a purely optical style, addressed to eyesight alone and rejecting tactile surface concerns as superfluous to visual experience, to be consistent, Greenberg had to find a reason to exclude Johns from the roster of the masters. But Johns clearly continued to bother him. When he published his "post painterly" painting manifesto in the form of the essay "After Abstract Expressionism," Greenberg devoted considerably more space to arguing that Johns was no more and could be no more than a "minor master" than he did to explaining what was great about Jules Olitski, whom he often compared to Titian.[16]

Greenberg had to expunge Johns from the canon for a number of reasons, most pointedly because it was obvious that Kenneth Noland—whom Greenberg celebrated—had pilfered the format of his concentric-circle paintings directly from Johns's targets.[17] Even more troubling was the fact that if Johns were allowed into the ranks of the chosen, the keystone of Greenberg's argument that painterliness was dead would crumble. Greenberg had to admit that Johns had a nice hand. But he dismissed this talent with a brush as minor—in an inversion of the old criticism that Claude Monet was just an eye—implying that Johns was nothing more than a hand, ignoring the multitude of new issues that Johns's paintings placed at the center of contemporary aesthetic practice.[18]

For the champion of color field painting, Johns's flaw was that he practiced "homeless representation," a hybrid style mixing elements of illusionistic representational art with those of anti-illusionistic "flat" abstraction. Earlier, Greenberg had pinpointed Willem de Kooning as the source of this heresy that tied the New York School to figurative art, in his eyes now an academic relic. Greenberg's antagonism to de Kooning had a long history: he trashed de Kooning's series of Women of 1952–55 as "outspokenly representational." De Kooning, according to Greenberg, was now guilty of practicing "homeless representation," because his descriptive painterliness suggesting a spatial cavity behind the picture plane indicated illusionistic space, the enemy of flatness fundamental to "post painterly painting." Worse still were the disdained European *Art informel* artists like Jean Dubuffet, Jean Fautrier, Nicolas de Staël, and Antoni Tàpies, who piled matter on the surface and so were practitioners of "furtive bas relief."[19]

It was easy for Greenberg to dismiss the *informel* painters: for one thing, they were far away in Paris. Johns, on the other hand, was too prominent on the New York scene to avoid attacking directly. Greenberg had to make the case that Johns was just another of de Kooning's "Tenth Street" followers for the freight train of progress to move forward. For Greenberg, Johns "brings de Kooning's influence to a head by suspending it clearly, as it were, between abstraction and representation."[20] This was, of course, Johns's intention, but for Greenberg it spelled his damnation. In Greenberg's black-and-white categories, gray had no place. Comparing Greenberg's pronouncements with Johns's paintings, however, reveals how prejudice blinded the critic. Johns's attitude toward figuration is quite different from that of de Kooning, whose collapsing space and agitated expressionist style has much in common with Chaïm

Soutine's intense colors, loaded brush, and passionate execution. The hot palette and splashy style of de Kooning's grotesque and distorted Women are the antithesis of the elegant hauteur of Johns's cold sexless "figures." The pallid encaustic of *Figure 1* (1955; Collection of Peter and Irene Ludwig Foundation, on loan to the Museum Ludwig, Cologne), Johns's surrogate for figure painting, is a repressed chalky geisha compared to the plush, Rubensesque flesh of de Kooning's painted versions of the "Venus of Willendorf" figurine.

For Greenberg, Johns's gray paintings are his best because the shading tones are those that become "the most exhibitedly and poignantly superfluous when applied to ineluctably flat images."[21] In other words, the mind knows they are flat, whereas the eye is trained to interpret shaded forms as three-dimensional volumes. Tonal modeling is superfluous if it cannot communicate three dimensionality when experience tells us the image is flat. Johns's insistence on light/dark contrasts juxtaposing shades of the gray scale led Greenberg to conclude that "Johns sings the swan-song of 'homeless representation' and like most swan-songs, it carries only a limited distance."[22] In Greenberg's judgment, Johns was wrong because he remained a painterly painter of sensuous surfaces at a time when abstraction presumably should have been addressed to eyesight alone. Greenberg put forth this argument in his influential and widely read 1961 essay "Modernist Painting."[23] Given the date, it is likely that Johns's gray sculpture of that year, in which mouths displace eyes, *The Critic Sees* (cat. no. 84), was addressed to Greenberg, whose eyes, Johns implies, were in his mouth.

Greenberg's understanding of what Johns was doing at the time he was painting the 1962 gray *Map* was perceptive and to some degree correct. His misreading was the result not of what Greenberg saw, but what he did not see. Provoking such misreadings was intentional on Johns's part. Greenberg wrote that he did not mean that Johns's painting depended on a "device," although John's titles explicitly proclaim the opposite. That Johns's paintings may be seen as a series of maneuvers to expose its processes, as Jeffrey Weiss explained in his recent essay on the meaning of Johns's early works, was not visible to Greenberg.[24]

The Maps stress the varying qualities of surface, of boundaries of permeable and unfixed contour, and the nature of illusion and allusion in terms of their constant interaction. They are among Johns's most redundant images, mirroring only themselves and their antecedents, speaking only of their own plangent, echoing history. This pressure on surface indicates a shift from conventional spatial construction based on the recession of parallel planes. The separation of surface from what is depicted ruptures space and risks incoherence. Pictorial continuity is preserved, however, by the cognition of a familiar image that the mind already knows to be a singular unity.

Like the numbers that are surrogates for "figures," the maps are surrogates for landscapes; but they represent horizontal space spread out on a flat surface as opposed to landscapes that define distance as depth receding behind the frontal picture plane. In the Maps, Johns, the stickler for accuracy, suddenly plays havoc with known definitions. In the gray *Map* under consideration, the two oceans and the Gulf of Mexico flood the coastline, blurring its boundaries. Virginia swamps Washington and California slides into the Pacific Ocean. It is precisely this blurring and transgression of limits that interests Johns. The boundaries and borders of the individual states divide the whole into parts. These fragments of the whole may be reconstituted in other formations. The relationship of parts to the whole and their shifting possibilities, an idea of growing importance for Johns, was first articulated in the Maps.

In Johns's interpretation of the map of the United States, the states are separated from one another by a change of color rather than by sharp outlines.

The clearest and most emphasized division in the gray *Map*, however, is not the boundary of an individual state: it is the horizontal demarcation known as the Mason-Dixon Line that divides North from South, the boundary that divided the free states of the Union from those of the slave-holding Confederacy. In the 1961 colored *Map*, North Carolina is spelled out in small letters in yellow. On the 1962 gray *Map*, N.C. is written on the area that in the colored work is identified as South Carolina. Cape Hatteras is divided from the mainland by a long black line drawn across the top of North Carolina. Among the other liberties Johns has taken is moving the Mason-Dixon Line south, from the northern border of Maryland to southern limit of Virginia (FIG. 7).[25]

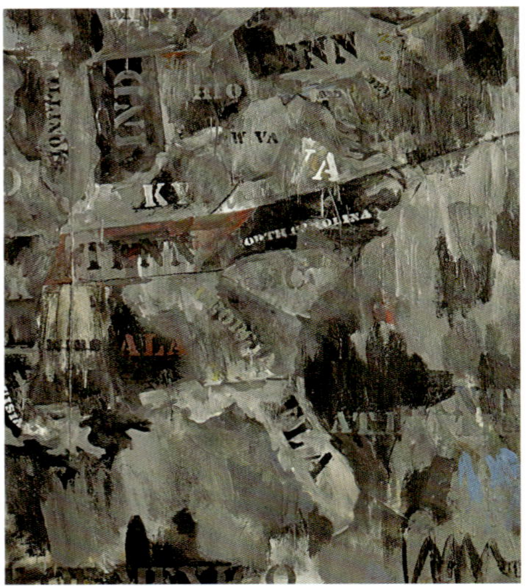

Fig. 7. Detail of *Map*, 1962 (cat. no. 39), showing the Southeast.

Given that he was born in Georgia and brought up in South Carolina, the Civil War was bound to have special personal meaning for Johns.[26] The first state to secede from the Union (on December 20, 1860), South Carolina initiated the War between the States, leading Mississippi, Florida, Alabama, Georgia, Louisiana, and Texas to follow suit within little more than a month. Virginia, Arkansas, North Carolina, and Tennessee withdrew in the spring of 1861. Perhaps the most remarkable of the alterations Johns made in the gray *Map* is that the only state not identified, except with vaguely discernable initials, is South Carolina. We do not know why he annulled the place where he grew up and the state whose secession started the Civil War, although surely the omission was no accident.

Is anything in the life of a highly conscious artist an accident? Is the fact that Francisco Goya lived at no. 1 Calle del Desengaño — Disillusionment Street — a coincidence? The concept of *engañar* (to dissimulate, to create false illusions) and its opposite *desengañar* (to reveal the truth, to rip away the veil of unreality) runs through Goya's mature work as a recurrent leitmotif. One might say the same is true of Johns, whose engagement with illusion and its unmasking is more than simply a formal issue.

The difficult realities of Johns's personal life coincide with the idea that this map pictures a battlefield; beyond that, as I have proposed above, its historical context suggests not only the Civil War but also a particular conflict, fought on September 17, 1862, at Antietam, outside Sharpsburg, Maryland, when the gray-uniformed Confederate army lost a decisive struggle against the blue-clad Union forces. So bloody was the fighting that the date is remembered as "the day Antietam Creek ran red." A hundred years later, in Johns's painting gray is the predominant color, but the purples and reds beneath the surface are sometimes exposed to a greater or lesser degree, giving the painting a richness and variety that it would not have if it were a uniform gray. On the right is a red horizontal streak that could well refer to the encounter that would, in a single day, claim more than 23,000 lives. Moreover, the patching of the surface with paper and fabric calls to mind images of wounds and bandaging.

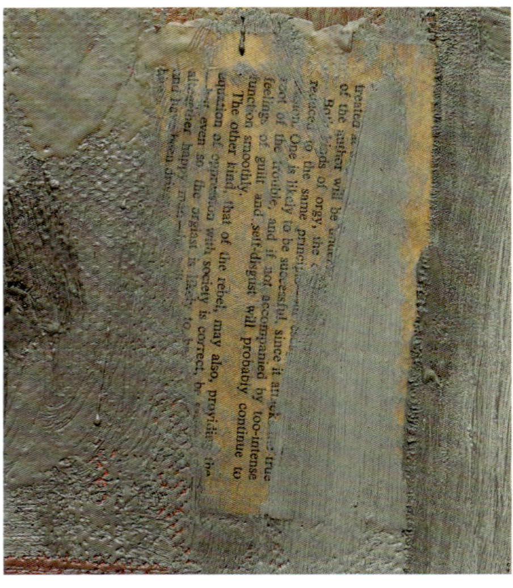

Fig. 8. Detail of *Map*, 1962 (cat. no. 39), showing collaged fragment of printed matter.

Topographically, the hills, ridges, and ravines of Johns's gray *Map* suggest geological strata bursting. Paint washes over the surface like sea spume or waves eroding coastlines. Known borders are changed or blurred. This transgression of boundaries is a physical fact of art historical as well as personal significance. The surface is scarred and scraped in areas so that the printed matter sealed into it with adhesive encaustic is visible. The most tantalizing fragment is not newsprint but part of a page probably ripped from a paperback book Johns had in the studio. One can make out the words "intense feelings of guilt and self-disgust," as well as "rebel" and "orgiast" (FIG. 8). These chosen and deliberately revealed phrases participate in Johns's game of peekaboo, which he plays with his audience, much as a stripper suggests that more will be revealed with each succeeding fan flutter.[27]

In the early 1960s, the marginal misfit, the rebel with a cause, was much discussed when Colin Wilson's *The Outsider* was a best-seller and neo-Freudians such as Herbert Marcuse and Norman O. Brown were publishing critiques of social conformity. The transgression of the boundaries of the states, borders, and coastlines of Johns's *Map* may be interpreted as metaphoric trespassing as his work moved farther and farther from accepted norms into uncharted territory. (His game of hide-and-seek, of concealing and revealing, was announced in the shuttered compartments of *Target with Plaster Casts* [1955; Collection of David Geffen, Los Angeles]).

In 1957 Johns left the brilliant light of the spectrum for the shadowy gray encaustic of *Gray Rectangles* (cat. no. 10) and *The* (cat. no. 11), whose surfaces are covered by a regular blending of gray markings saved from formlessness by geometric cutouts into the surface or by inscriptions painted in lapidary capital letters of the type found on tombstones. His growing focus on process and craft received an impetus from his initiation into printmaking in 1960, in that working in black and white may have prompted a greater consideration of executing works in gray shades rather than in brilliant hues. Certainly, about the time he began making prints, there appeared a darker and bleaker tone in his paintings, which were increasingly focused on themes of loss and morbidity. By comparison, his earliest gray paintings—including *Canvas* (1956; cat. no. 7), *Drawer* (1957; cat. no. 9), and *Gray Rectangles*—are dulled, virtual monochromes that lack the activity and variation of the gray *Map*. They are secretive hiding places, whereas the Maps lay out their contents and ask to be read. The connection between these two types of gray paintings is Johns's poignant 1961 masterpiece *In Memory of My Feelings—Frank O'Hara* (cat. no. 85). In addition to the vague outline of a skull in the upper right, at the bottom of the painting beside the stenciled title, barely visible in the tangle of bluish gray brushstrokes, is the inscription DEAD MAN, the opening words of a dirge that was to occupy Johns for the next several years (see also the essay by James Rondeau in this volume, pp. 50–51).[28]

In Memory of My Feelings—Frank O'Hara is one of Johns's first mirrored images that juxtaposes similar but unidentical halves. The idea that we are now dealing not with the present tense but with the memory of things past, their imprints and associations, complicates the meaning of what is pictured. To interpret the suggestive title of the painting simply as nostalgia is to miss the reason the painting retains its compelling mystery. Johns deliberately provokes iconographical interpretations of his work with his carefully chosen titles and his unexpected contexts for the displacement of familiar objects. The works are so obviously charged with innuendo that one begins to suspect a ruse by the master of the game to throw the viewer off the track of a more difficult reading of what is and is not pictured. Just as in the opening chapters of a detective novel where suspicion is cast on the wrong subjects, iconography becomes a red herring, with clues strewn about to make amateur sleuths of nosey critics. Beneath this superficial reading, there is another story that is far more complex and serious.

It is increasingly obvious that Johns's works are connected to one another and that these connections constitute a narrative or more likely a series of intertwined and braided narratives. Within this context, the gray *Map* plays an important role, in the entire concatenation of Johns's grisaille works, as well as in his treatment of the themes of morbidity, voyeurism, and auto-analysis. In his recent essay in *Jasper Johns: An Allegory of Painting, 1955–1965*, Jeffrey Weiss contends that the first ten years of Johns's work may be defined as a record of the artist's inquiry into the divergent meanings of painting as art, craft, and process. The probing self-reflexiveness and self-consciousness of modernism is linked to another type of analysis, that of the author's own investigation of what his subconscious is bringing to the surface.

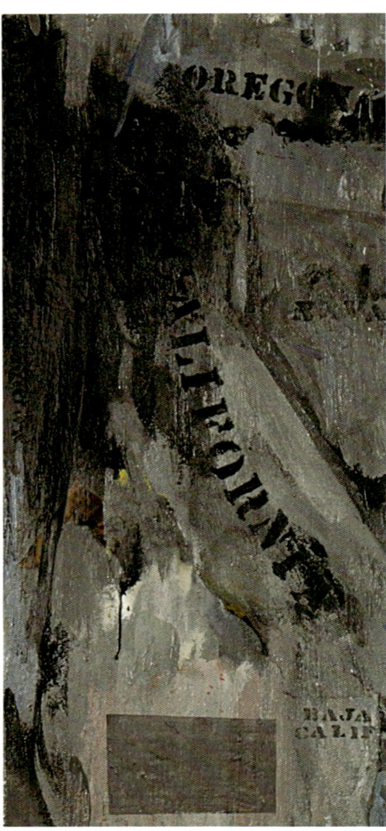

Fig. 9. Detail of *Map*, 1962 (cat. no. 39), showing the West Coast.

The idea that art should elicit participation was articulated in 1957 by Marcel Duchamp in "The Creative Act."[29] But Duchamp's chess strategy is not Johns's model. The objective of chess is either victory (checkmate) or else a stalemate that ends the game. Johns is not interested in closure: he clearly wants his engagement with the spectator to continue, and so he connects work to work in an open-ended chain by repeating, inverting, and recycling images that reemerge from consciousness and refuse to be forgotten. In effect, Johns coaxes the riveted viewer into filling the role of absent siblings or playmates. If this strategy of luring the spectator to fall into the "trap" of interpretation succeeds, then the artist is no longer alone, as Johns was for most of his childhood. He has a willing partner to tease into games of peekaboo and hide-and-seek.

The antinomy of absence and presence became a major theme in the works revolving around memories, such as the Maps. Originally, Johns asked Carolyn Brown, a lithe and elegant dancer with the Merce Cunningham Company, to have a strip of images taken in a photo booth of the type Andy Warhol used in making the screenprints for his portraits. Johns intended to incorporate the strip in the 1962 *Map*, yet when he saw the results, he thought the dancer looked too much like a fashion model even in an unposed mechanical photograph. She offered to have more pictures taken, but Johns opted instead to acknowledge her presence only by her absence, which is recorded in the hand-printed block letters that occupy a vertical passage at the left of the painting, MACHINE PHOTO: CAROLYN BROWN (**FIG. 9**). The beautiful woman has become a memory.

In his writings and interviews, Johns has stressed the importance of transfer in his work. In 1959, for example, he wrote that he was impressed by Duchamp's ambition "to reach the Impossibility of sufficient visual memory to transfer from one like object to another the memory imprint."[30] For Johns, the transference of the imprint of an object to another image meant using one thing to stand for another, not as metaphor or surrogate but in a way that short-circuits recognition, leading to multiple associations. Fred Orton has described the relationship between the objects Johns represents or incorporates in his paintings and their referents as metonymy rather than metaphor.[31] In other words, it is not the object itself but rather its associations or references that are the key to its meaning in the context of the work. The object, like Marcel Proust's madeleine, is the link to a chain of experiences. Its function is like that of a switching station that transfers trains from one track to another, loading the departing train with the significance of the arriving freight.

Johns's attachment to the painterliness of early modernism reveals an antipathy to the slickness of quickly communicated and easily absorbed imagery, the hallmark of the art of the 1960s. The split between the instant impact of his familiar Flag and Target images, which are immediately recognizable, and the durations required to read the elaborate surfaces that Johns built up while painting them creates a tension between optic mental cognition and haptic sensuous, tactile response.

Splitting divergent types of cognitive systems deliberately induces perceptual schizophrenia. This incongruity is not to be confused with Surrealist synesthesia, which mixes rather than separates the senses. It is the key to the enduring enigma of Johns's art. Beginning in 1959, Johns freed the strokes of the brush from their original function as building blocks of images, permitting them to be autonomous of the single unified image, which now tends to be a literal object affixed to the canvas such as a thermometer or a stick—both coincidentally instruments of literal measure—in an ambiguous, fluid space that suggests the immeasurable. Johns's experiments with multiple ways of altering surface include adding objects or their impressions, leaving visible pentimenti, and bending stretchers.

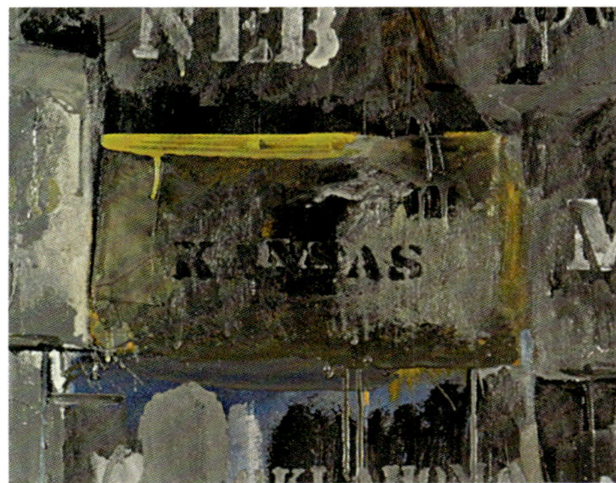

Fig. 10. Detail of *Map*, 1962 (cat. no. 39), showing collaged elements underneath encaustic.

Individual brushstrokes stand out in relief in Johns's early works, especially those painted in encaustic. The raised and isolated strokes engage the eye longer than the untextured uniform surface and minimal detail characteristic of the dominant styles of the 1960s such as Pop, minimal, and color field painting. Infrared photographs permit us to penetrate the surface layer to see how Johns constructed his images of the early encaustic Targets and Flags. The strips of newsprint were applied as rectangular ribbons that follow the structure of the image to literally build their forms, stroke by constructive stroke. The brushstrokes themselves follow the design of the images they create. Those in the *Target with Four Faces* (1955; the Museum of Modern Art, New York; see fig. 12 in the essay by Douglas Druick in this volume) proceed in a circular pattern, while ones in *Flag* (1954–55; the Museum of Modern Art, New York; see figs. 5–6 in the essay by James Rondeau in this volume) echo the horizontal stripes of the object itself. Comparing these with infrared photographs of the 1962 gray *Map* reveals the difference in facture and the freer movements of the brush. The latter also isolate rectangles patched into the surface whose images are not legible, but whose shape and placement suggest the irregular spread of tombstones in a field (**FIG. 10**).

The separation of the object from what it references is characteristic of Johns's oblique treatment of imagery. Displacement and reconfiguration are the essence of his need to transfer feelings, experiences, and memories from one thing or person or place to another. Among the most self-conscious artists in history, Johns certainly must have been aware that what he described in his sketchbook notes as his process of making was a description of perversion: "one thing used as another."[32]

Psychological transference, first articulated by Sigmund Freud, was elaborated on by later psychoanalysts, especially Jacques Lacan in his theory of the "mirror stage" of development and Donald W. Winnicott in his discussion of "transitional objects."[33] Lacan's "mirror stage," which he considered as the critical moment of psychic development, corresponds in suggestive ways to Johns's idea of transferring aspects of one thing to another through processes of grafting or mirroring. This transference of properties is not the same as Freud's concept of the patient transferring emotions to the analyst, who is a specific person not a generic thing. Winnicott, an English follower of Karen Horney, also spoke of transference as the crucial moment of personality formation in his theory of "transitional objects," which permit the formation of the autonomous self. According to Winnicott, the actual characteristics of "transitional objects" that the infant substitutes for the mother are not as important as the fact that they allow the infant to transfer the emotions tied to the mother to familiar objects, like toys. This process of transferal leads to the formation of the concept "not-I," that is, of the Other, which establishes the boundaries of the self.

We have observed that Johns makes a point of linking his paintings to those that precede and follow them. Frequently, images from one painting spill over into the next group of related works. Johns's imagery is sequential rather than serial; it suggests the type of evolution over a period of time we normally associate with narrative. The overlapping narratives in his sequences, however, are interwoven, like the skeins in a Pollock painting and just as difficult to unravel. The result is a kind of gumminess that resists, indeed discourages, disentanglement. Many of the links are not obvious. Even his chosen medium may suggest other associations. Our knowledge of the history of encaustic painting, for example, leads back through archaeology to its practice by the ancient Egyptians, who covered their wooden sarcophagi with wax depictions of the individual whose mummified corpse lay inside. Thus, the very material with which Johns constructs his images is tied to the grave.[34]

Painting with molten wax mixed with pigment and fused through heat appealed to Johns for several reasons. Wax is useful in the transfer process because, in its molten state, it accepts impressions of objects that leave their trace or memory without remaining present. Because wax dries quickly, layers may be added without losing the lustrous finish of fresh paint. Encaustic paint does not need to dry but to cool, which it does in minutes, allowing additional coats to be added almost immediately. Reheating permits alterations—corrections, additions, and subtractions—to be made. Rather than merely painting on top of a surface, or allowing paint to sink into the canvas support in the manner of stained color field painting, Johns could physically construct a surface of many layers. By dipping strips of newsprint or other printed matter into the wax and applying them to canvas, he sealed their words and images permanently, as if suspending flies in amber.

The contents of the encaustic strokes can be seen but not touched, no matter how much their smooth and articulated surfaces beg to be fingered. The frustration aroused by this results in a form of exquisite torture for the viewer, and thus raises the issue of sadomasochism, which is so blatant and so consistent in Johns's work that it is surprising that so little has been written about it. Not, of course, that the artist exempts himself: the process of oiling his skin and then covering his face and body in graphite to leave their impressions on paper must have been extremely unpleasant.

In this connection, Johns's sketchbook notes are curious in that they are written as commands to be carried out, splitting the authority (the conscious, inhibiting superego) from the subordinate (the subconscious agent) who is to dispatch the orders. If one takes the imperative literally, there are two people involved in making a Johns work: the disembodied voice, who gives directions, and the subordinate worker, who is supposed to follow them. Within a few years Johns would direct himself to make a work incorporating the "watchman" and the "spy," two secretive Peeping Toms, one a legitimate guardian keeping intruders out, the other a detective searching for secrets. The implication is of two separate viewers, both employed by a third party to look and report back. But suppose both the watchman and the spy are the artist himself? And that his questioning whether they will meet is an expression of a desire for the wholeness and unity achieved only by the discovery and confrontation of the Other.

In an analysis of Johns's relationship to poetry and language, James Cuno observed that Johns was concerned with preserving memory and evoking lost experiences.[35] He discussed in particular the suite of works related to Hart Crane's suicide at sea, returning to New York from Mexico. In 1962, the year he painted the gray *Map*, Johns also painted *Passage* (Museum Ludwig, Cologne), presumably inspired by the title of Crane's 1926 poem. As usual, there is more than one meaning to Johns's words and images. The French word *passage* also denotes the shading and tonal modeling that creates the illusion of volume or depth. Used in relationship to Cubism, it means the fading from dark to light, characteristic of the planes of Analytic Cubism. In John's painting, the poet as well as the process of making the work is simultaneously referenced in the title of the piece. The last line of Crane's poem—"Memory, committed to the page, had broke"—suggested to Cuno the poignancy of the works Johns painted in 1962–63 with titles connected to Crane's tragic life and death. As Cuno pointed out, Johns frequently read poetry aloud to his friends in these years.[36] Undoubtedly, the poems he chose had specific significance for him.

In a 1965 interview with Richard Francis, Johns explained: "Seeing a thing can sometimes trigger the mind to make another thing. In some instances, the new work may include, as a sort of subject matter, references to the thing that was seen. And, because works of painting tend to share many aspects, working itself may initiate memories of other works; naming or painting these ghosts seems a way to stop their nagging."[37] In order to be laid to rest, the nagging ghosts must be entombed, mummified in the cemetery of memory. The gravestones that mark the fallen soldiers of the Civil War or the cemeteries of Spoon River—or even Edwin Arlington Robinson's epitaph for the unfortunate Minniver Cheevy, which Johns could recite from memory—link a train of thought saddened by loss and heavy with morbid associations. The role of memory, which became paramount in Johns's work beginning in 1961, has remained so for the rest of his career. His sense of overlapping narratives is related to Proust's continuous consciousness established in the technique of the *roman fleuve*, which consists of a series of simultaneous narratives recording memory from multiple, often contradictory viewpoints. The "story" that unfolds in this manner can only be that of the author's own consciousness of the internal perceptions of experience as it is remembered, correctly or incorrectly. *Map*, 1962, represents the geography of the United States, but its gray and cloudy brooding passages reference not an objective fact but rather an emotional climate. It pictures no place on earth but rather "the sky above," the stormy weather immortalized by Billie Holiday in her melancholic torch song.[38]

As we closely examine the 1962 gray *Map*, which along with the large, incomparable charcoal drawing *Diver* (1962–63; cat. no. 102), begun the same year, represents the pinnacle of Johns's grisaille works, we begin to understand it as a stylistically crucial work in the artist's oeuvre and one that also represents the cenotaph of an emotionally charged relationship. This map may be seen as a point of departure for a journey that once had a "false start."[39] The journey is the search for the Other, the lost and hidden, unconscious self reflected in the distorted and unmatched mirror image of an inner world that does not correspond to the outer world. Johns's mirroring is not that of Narcissus in love with the image he sees reflected in the water. Rather, it is an attempt to encounter the "not-I." The search for the Other (that is, the authentic self that resides in the uncensored unconscious) requires excavating graveyards piled high with corpses. The hope is that the discovery of the buried Other will ultimately lead to unity and completeness, the integration of the self that eludes the divided personality.

The annihilation of the pain of memory—dimmed, blurred, distorted, and out of necessity transferred to transitional objects—is possible only through the transcendence of artistic transfiguration. The solution to the cycle of sadomasochistic relationships, as described by Maria Condor, in her study of the structural role of jealousy in Proust's *Remembrance of Things Past*, is to be found only in the transcendence of art. Fusion, coherence, or wholeness is not achieved in personal relationships. The injured psyche—indeed, often injured by the self—finds wholeness and completion only in the construction of a work of art.[40]

As pictured by Stella, "Jasper's dilemma" represents not only a divided, unmatched mirror image but also, given its inverse receding linear perspective, a labyrinth. That there is a beast caged inside the labyrinth is implicit, given the labyrinth's history. Whoever cares to join the artist in his search for the buried self that will unify the fragments and their mirrors of memory risks confronting the beast, as well. Because it is so full of promise and seduction, the artist's invitation to accompany him on this treacherous journey, despite its obvious hazards, is irresistible.

1 Artworks by Willem and Elaine de Kooning, Marcel Duchamp, Ellsworth Kelly, Wifredo Lam, Marisol, Frank Stella, Saul Steinberg, Jean Tinguely, and Andy Warhol, among others, were donated, exhibited, and sold to benefit performing artists.

2 Personal communication to the author.

3 Johns painted another gray encaustic map, now in a New York private collection, the same size as the original as a commission for a collector.

4 There is a relationship between the five pronged strokes, the handprint that Johns begins to impress on his works as a physical signature and the carefully grouped "hatch" marks of his later works.

5 The rudiments of reading and writing, alphabets and numbers, as well as the saluting of the American flag every morning with the Pledge of Allegiance, were mandatory in all United States public schools when Johns was a student in the one-room school house in Climax, South Carolina, where his aunt Gladys was the teacher. Similarly, Cy Twombly's white abstract cursive script on a gray ground resembles the chalk writing on blackboards that taught American children to write in cursive script when they were forced to give up "childish" block printing.

The rigid conformity imposed on American children until the progressive education of the 1960s took hold (even to a degree in public schools) rewarded following orders and thinking in terms of preexisting multiple choices. Those who did not conform were singled out for criticism as examples of "bad" conduct. The drill-like instruction aimed at creating so-called democratic uniformity caused some children to rebel. A study of the signatures of American artists would be psychologically revealing. These same children were further ostracized when they insisted on coloring outside the lines in the printed books that accompanied their lessons. Johns's Flags, stenciled Numbers, and Alphabets usually respect their given boundaries. His Maps do not. The color extends outside the boundaries, constituting an act of rebellion and proclaiming a psychic independence.

6 *Charlene* also contains a clipped newspaper headline; a scarf from the Metropolitan Museum of Art, New York; various art reproductions; and a postcard of the Statue of Liberty; see Paul Schimmel, "Autobiography and Self-Portraiture in Rauschenberg's Combines," in *Robert Rauschenberg: Combines*, exh. cat. (Museum of Contemporary Art, Los Angeles, 2005), pp. 215–16.

7 See Katz 1998.

8 On the other hand, he was very much a part of the younger New York art world in the early 1960s that liked movies, pop music, and dancing. But the Peppermint Lounge, a small midtown nightclub favored by black clients where Johns did a mean "twist," was not the mobbed and depersonalized Studio 54 drug den frequented by the Warhol Factory group. Among the first discotheques in Manhattan was the Dom, a Polish restaurant on the Lower East Side, which had a dance floor with strobe lights. Clement Greenberg was a particularly good dancer and insisted on dancing through the night with the younger crowd. I recall an evening of frugging with the esteemed critic to Peter and Gordon's 1964 hit *A World without Love* ("I don't care what they say I won't stay in a world without love").

9 See Maurice Merleau-Ponty, "Cézanne's Doubt" (1945), in *Sense and Non-sense,* trans. Hubert L. Dreyfus and Patricia Allen Dreyfus (1964; rpt. Northwestern University Press, 1991), pp. 9–25.

10 See the remarks by John Powers that appeared in *Aspen*, no. 3 (Dec. 1966), item no. 8. Powers and his wife, who were collectors of Japanese as well as contemporary art, observed that Johns's calligraphic effects gave the piece an Asian feeling reminiscent of the Sumi ink painters of China and Japan, who recognize eight distinct shades of black. The observation was prescient, since Johns had just returned from a trip to Japan. He had earlier been stationed in Sendai, Japan, while in the Army during the Korean War.

11 Rauschenberg, too, was thinking of the Civil War. A screenprint made from the reproduction of Louis M. D. Guillaume's painting of Robert E. Lee's surrender to Ulysses S. Grant at Appomattox—which ended the bloody conflict that tore America apart—appears in *Cove*, the 1963 screenprint painting that Johns purchased from Rauschenberg's exhibition at the Castelli Gallery that year.

12 See "Proclamation 3382: Civil War Centennial," on the Web site of the American Presidency Project, http://www.presidency.ucsb.edu/ws/index.php?pid=12029.

13 Johns also showed in Paris that year at the Galerie Rive Droite. The intense exchange between Paris and New York in 1961–62 is documented in *Paris–New York*, one of the first catalogues published by the Centre Pompidou. The Coupole on the Boulevard Montparnasse was a favorite meeting place of American artists like Claes Oldenburg and Larry Rivers. Niki de Saint Phalle and Jean Tinguely staged "happenings" together with American artists in Paris and New York. Yves Klein and Arman came to New York, and gallery owners Sidney Janis and Leo Castelli especially encouraged this interchange, comparing the French *nouveaux réalistes* to the American Pop artists.

14 Jasper's Dilemma is also the name of an Australian rock trio that plays moody, atmospheric, and dirty "indie" guitar mixes with electronic elements and interludes. Their first CD was appropriately a concept album, flowing from track to track, suggesting dark personal experiences and frustrations.

15 The statement was made during a radio interview with Bruce Glaser, entitled "New Nihilism or New Art?" broadcast on WBAI-FM, New York, in Feb. 1964. The conversation was later edited by Lucy R. Lippard and published as "Questions to Stella and Judd," *Artnews* 65, 5 (Sept. 1966), pp. 55–61. Stella's epigrammatic remark appears on p. 59.

16 Greenberg 1962.

17 Thomas B. Hess was so stunned by Johns's first show at Castelli that he borrowed *Target with Plaster Casts* and took it in a taxi to be photographed for the January 1958 cover of *Artnews*, where the image immediately created an art-world sensation.

18 Greenberg distinguished between linear and painterly, but not between haptic and optic, Alois Riegl's more complex categories. Greenberg's elevation of the optic—what appealed exclusively to eyesight alone—above the haptic, which appealed to the sense of touch and sensuality rather than intellect, is explicable in the context of his prudish inhibitions, a caricature of his aspiration to high WASP elegance.

19 Greenberg 1962, p. 25.

20 Ibid., p. 25–26.

21 Ibid., p. 27.

22 Ibid.

23 Clement Greenberg, "Modernist Painting," *Arts Yearbook* 4 (1961), pp. 101–08.

24 Weiss 2007a.

25 The Missouri Compromise of 1820 established a boundary between the slave states of the South and the free states of the North, which became known as the Mason-Dixon Line, after the two English surveyors who mapped it. Understandably, the Mason-Dixon Line has long been symbolic of the nation's contentious struggle over slavery. Johns moved the Mason-Dixon Line south and had it pass straight along the northern border of North Carolina, rather than between Pennsylvania and Maryland, where the actual division exists.

26 In addition to the scraps of newspaper, a laundry ticket, a bank receipt, and other items with personal significance for Johns, Joan Carpenter discovered that South Carolina is referenced in the photograph of native son Billy Graham sealed in the wax layers of *Target with Four Faces;* Carpenter 1977, p. 223.

27 Johns was fascinated with Joanne Woodward's performance in the 1963 film *The Stripper*. He was also aware that the house he later purchased on East 63rd Street had belonged to Gypsy Rose Lee.

28 Orton 1994, pp. 64–65.

29 Marcel Duchamp, "The Creative Act," in *Salt Seller: The Writings of Marcel Duchamp*, ed. Michel Sanouillet and Elmer Peterson (Oxford University Press, 1973), pp. 138–40.

30 Johns 1959, p. 22, in *Writings* 1996, p. 20. That same year, Rauschenberg referenced Duchamp's remarks on the surface of his painting *Wager* (1957–59; Kunstsammlung Nordrhein-Westfalen, Düsseldorf).

31 "Metonymy is based on a proposed contiguous or sequential link between the literal object and its replacement by association or reference....It is the record of a lacuna, of a move or displacement from cause to effect, container to contained, goal to auxiliary tool, whole to part....With metonymy the move is escape. It represents not the object or thing or event or feeling that is its reference but that

which is tied to it by contingent or associative transfers of meaning"; Orton 1994, pp. 27, 31.

32 Johns, Sketchbook A, 1964, p. 49, in *Writings* 1996, p. 56.

33 On Jacques Lacan's theories, see his 1949 essay "Mirror Stage as Formative of the Function of the I as Revealed in Psychoanalytic Experience," in *Écrits: A Selection*, translated by Alan Sheridan (W. W. Norton, 1977), pp. 1–7; on Donald Woods Winnicott, see, among his numerous scholarly contributions, his essay "Transitional Objects and Transitional Phenomena," *International Journal of Psychoanalysis*, 34 (1953), pp. 89–97, and his *Collected Papers: Through Paediatrics to Psycho-Analysis* (Tavistock Publications, 1958).

34 Johns may also have known Karl Zerbe's encaustic painting of an interpretation of Pablo Picasso's seated *Harlequin* (1943; Whitney Museum of American Art, New York).

35 Cuno 1987*a*.

36 Ibid., p. 225.

37 Francis 1984, p. 98.

38 Like many Americans of his generation, especially those from the South, Johns often listened to Blues singers and Billie Holiday was one of his favorites.

39 The title of Johns's 1959 painting is coincidentally a Proustian concept; see Maria Condor, *En Busca de Sodoma y Gomorra: Un Estudio Sobre Proust* (Huerga & Fierro, Madrid, 2006).

40 Ibid., p. 29.

A Conversation with Jasper Johns

NAN ROSENTHAL

The conversation took place at Johns's homes in northwestern Connecticut on August 28, 2006, and in St. Martin, French West Indies, on February 22, 2007.

NAN ROSENTHAL: Would you say that the place you work affects what you're doing?

JASPER JOHNS: I don't think so. Earlier, it may have. My first loft in New York had a very low ceiling and no windows—some windows at either end of the long space, but very dirty windows. Later I had a studio at Edisto Beach, South Carolina, which had one long wall of screen wire to keep out the insects. There I would usually begin to paint very early in the morning by electric light and, as the sun came up, the room would gradually fill with daylight, and, at some point, the electric lights would no longer be needed and I would turn them off. So I think that was different, and I adjusted to it. But the works made earlier in New York were made by electric light, only by electric light, whether it was day or night when I was working. And I remember once when I was moving some paintings and saw them outside on the street, I found it very odd, the way they looked in sunlight. But, later, works were made under varying lighting conditions and didn't seem drastically different in one kind of lighting or another.

And then, as you got in the position where you could adjust what your studio situation was, there would be even less difference.

Yes, I think so.

So, back then, what happened in the studio was really a situation involving you and the canvas, or you and the paper.

Yes.

What do you think of as the first gray painting?

I don't remember what it was. Do you know what it was, in terms of dates?

There are *Gray Alphabets* (1956; cat. no. 55) and *Canvas* (1956; cat. no. 7).

Well, I think *Gray Alphabets* would have been first. It was certainly my first large painting in gray.

Jasper, Roberta Bernstein has written that you told her several times that gray is your favorite color.

Was it several times? Or was it once?

According to Roberta, it was several times. But does that mean for you gray is a color?

Yes, I think so, but, I suppose, one also might think of it as an absence of color.

There are various ways to make gray. What are the colors that you usually use to make gray? Are they black and white?

Yes, but I sometimes mix complementary colors with white. Most often I use a combination of three blacks and one or more whites, sometimes adding a bit of color to alter its warmth or coolness.

What kind of qualities are you seeking?

I don't know. It may depend on the particular work and, I suppose, is highly subjective. I think one dislikes describing what one "does." It may be what one has done, but one may hope that one will do something different in the future.

I had the opportunity the other day to see two of your early gray paintings, *The* (1957; cat. no. 11) and *Gray Target* (1958; cat. no. 41), hanging near each other. It was wonderful to see how very different they are from each other. *The* seemed to have three layers of gray, getting progressively darker, but it didn't seem to be tinted different colors.

Well, at that time, probably not.

Adding color and slightly changing the grays—that has evolved over the years, you were saying?

Yes, in the earlier paintings the colors were modulated enough in intensity to keep the eyes busy but I aimed for an overall effect of pure, simple color. If it was red, it was red. If it was blue, it was blue. And I treated gray in the same way. Later, as the canvases were often less sharply divided and areas of color less clearly demarcated, colors—gray included—were more obviously nuanced.

When did that change?

I imagine it was a gradual change, just part accident and part boredom—but I don't know. One does such things to amuse oneself.

Some discovery, too, of the way that the color worked?

Probably that, and things seem to happen of their own accord—the materials that you're using, you notice, begin to behave in certain new ways.

Working with encaustic, how did you add hue to the beeswax in order to create a color?

Originally, I used oil paints, tube paints, but mostly I use dry pigment now. I visited a wonderful shop on Fulton Street—I forget the name of it—that sold supplies. They had things like powdered pigments which were sold for various purposes, and, at some point, I became interested in the possibility of using them. And I had read about it.[1]

And then you had to add a few other things, too, that would have made them mix?

There is not too much that you add—gum damar and some linseed oil to make it more flexible. I'm still uncertain about the proportions. No one seems to know really. Artists develop their own ways of doing it.

But you don't ever buy those bricks?

I have bought a few of the colored bricks, but I've rarely used them. I prefer adding the pigment myself, so that I can obtain different degrees of opacity and translucence.

When did you learn about color in the first place?

I don't think I ever learned much about color, but I studied it in school. When you study it as a child, you learn red-yellow-blue, green-orange-violet.... That's about all I learned.

Really? I mean, did they teach you things like, I don't know, the Munsell color sphere, or the color wheel, for example?

Well, I suppose that at various times we must have had to construct such things, but in a casual way. I doubt that I took it very seriously.

But that would have been in college?

I don't really remember. Of course, I played with color in elementary school, learning what color mixed with what to make another color. At the University of South Carolina I took a design course or two that must have included something of that sort. At Parsons, briefly, there must have been a good deal of it

You never studied with Albers?

No, but I did meet him. What were the names of those two men who had a screenprint place in New Haven, Connecticut? Ives-Sillman?

Yes, Norman Ives and Sewell Sillman. They did the fancy version of Albers's *Interaction of Color*.[2]

Exactly. I think they printed many of Albers's graphic works. In 1964, Lois Long and I accompanied John Cage to Hawaii, where John was lecturing or performing. The Albers book had just been published and Norman Ives, who was also in Honolulu, brought it over for us to look at. Included with the book was a kind of test of color perception. I studied each of the sheets very carefully and said what I saw. I got every one wrong. John Cage barely glanced at the things before saying what he saw, and was correct each time. Later, I met Albers, when Irving Penn photographed us together for some magazine, and I said, "Mr. Albers, I took this test of yours and got everything wrong." I had often heard from Bob Rauschenberg, who had studied with him, how precise Albers required everything to be, so I was surprised when he replied, "But that's the point. It doesn't make any difference!"

I wonder if you've ever used a gray scale. I don't mean including one as you did in paintings such as *Diver* (1962; Collection of Irma and Norman Braman), but if you ever used it as a working tool in the studio.

Not really. I've used one in printmaking, occasionally. That is the only place where I have thought about it deliberately. A printer may show you a scale and say, "If you leave the acid on for so many minutes, you get this value." So, on an aquatint, if you etch a short while, you'll get a gray, and if you etch longer, you'll get a black, and variations in between.

You use so many different metallic materials—aluminum, Sculp-metal, silver, and lead, and a great deal of graphite wash. Do you consider these to be versions of gray?

They are. But I think more importantly, they're versions of materials. It was probably the material aspect of those things that interested me more than their grayness. But once you are working with them, you are dealing with all their attributes. I suppose it is all connected.

You could've used metallic materials that produced other colors.

Perhaps. What, for example?

Well, gold.

I once tried to use gold for a sculpture, but I couldn't get anyone to settle on a price. Gold is very costly.

With a medium like Sculp-metal, then, it is its material aspect that interested you, more than its grayness?

Probably they were the same for me—or closely related—the grayness and the material. The material *suggests* metal: it has metallic powder in it, and it's intended to look like solid metal. So the color, the metallic look, and its imitative role all interested me—the fact that it mimics but is not metal.

That's very interesting, the imitative aspect, that it's not metal. Because even though there are so few sculptures, really, and so few Sculp-metal pieces, it seems to me that they are particularly influential works, because of the nature of the material and the dullness, in a way, that peculiar dullness that Sculp-metal has. I mean, it's very different from seeing, say, a child's shoes cast in bronze. It's just a very unusual use of material. Is that something you were conscious of?

Well, I don't know whether I was conscious of it, but once you use something, you know, you tend to be more conscious of it than you were before you used it. So you pay attention to what you're doing. The material was—I don't know how I knew that the material existed.

Was it a crafts store find?

I think an art store called Rosenthal's is where I got it, but how I knew about it, I don't remember.[3]

Two works of yours include the word "gray" on their vertical wood centerpieces—*Painting with Ruler and "Gray"* (1960; Frederick R. Weisman Art Foundation, Los Angeles) and *Device* (1962, cat. no. 93). What prompted you to inscribe them this way?

If I remember correctly, in *Painting with Ruler and "Gray,"* the inscription was already printed on the board, which was something I found in the studio or wherever I was at the time.

How fascinating.

And then, when I made *Device*, I painted the word on the board because I wanted to mimic what had happened by chance, or whatever you want to call it, in the earlier painting.

Do you think of gray as a positive color?

Yes, I think so. I don't know, I don't really often think about gray. I mean, I work with it, and I guess that's a form of thought, but I don't have particular ideas about it that can be separated from the work.

Well, I'm intrigued by your use of gray to cover colorful areas of painting. Take your recent painting *Near the Lagoon* (2002–03; cat. no. 135). It's underpainted with areas of red, yellow, and blue, am I right?

Very subdued red—not very bright. Not in very brilliant colors, but nevertheless in clearly distinct areas.

What was the point of that underpainting?

Thinking of my work and its references to Degas's attempt to reassemble Manet's painting, I divided the surface into three categories—my canvas, the ground provided by Degas to contain the Manet fragments, and the Manet fragments themselves.[4] I indicated each of the three categories with a subdued primary color, a sort of underpainting as you say. I thought to distinguish these three things, one from the other, as a beginning.

And how did you make the embedded line?

I had the canvas hanging on the studio wall and I hung the cord against the canvas, painted over it, and then pulled the cord away. And so on. I think I did the same thing three times, didn't I?

Yes. So you weren't tracing the shadow of the string on the painting?

Well, I may be describing it incorrectly, because I'm not sure that I remember precisely what I did. In some paintings, I put a string, painted over the string; pulled the string away, and it left an impression. Is there an impression there? I don't remember.

There is.

The painting is largely made of things put down on other things.

There's also red, yellow, and blue in the much earlier *Gray Rectangles* (1957; cat. no. 10), right? Under the three boxes, so to speak?

There was and there still may be. I think I began that picture by painting those rectangles bright primaries but, during the process, decided that eliminating the color would enhance the perception that they were embedded objects.

Jasper, what's the ball made of in *Gray Painting with Ball* (1958; cat. no. 15)?

Wood.

Did you order a sphere of the dimensions you wanted?

Of course not, but I don't remember where it came from.

And what are the sides made of?

One-by-two-inch lumber, I think. Originally, I planned simply to use commercial stretchers. But when I did, I discovered that the short outer edges were pulled inward when the longer sides bowed to accommodate the ball. So I had to construct it to justify the distortion. This was true of *Painting with Two Balls* (1960; Collection of the artist), also. I had not thought through my preconception.

With the works that come around 1961, such as *Liar*, *No*, or *Water Freezes* (cat. nos. 87, 91, and 86), gray seems to be used symbolically to suggest a mood. Do you think that's true?

Well, I think it doesn't matter if it's true or not, because the subjects and the titles of the paintings are suggestive of moods. They go together very nicely.

Jasper, are there other artists, historically, who've used grays in ways that you find attractive?

I haven't paid that much attention.

Picasso and Braque? I guess that's more gray-*ish*, but... the Analytic Cubists?

I think of those as brown.

Brown? But there's a lot of gray. Any seventeenth-century Spanish painters?

Not really.

Whistler?

Well, I don't usually think of my work in such art historical contexts. It is something that others may want to do. Originally, the gray may have seemed an absence of color.

An attempt to get away from the expressiveness of color?

That could be a thought, I suppose. To get away from a *kind* of color that leads one and to get to something that I thought of as *real* or *stable*.

What you've called "literal"? What does that mean, exactly?

I'm not sure it means anything, exactly. It was a way of proceeding at that time. I'm not sure how to say it. One may look for facts and hope to be able to contemplate facts. Such thought was useful to me very early on in my work. But then the problem perhaps disappears as you continue, or becomes something else.

What was the attraction of getting down to the literal, or the fact? I can understand getting away from Abstract Expressionism's purported expressionism.

Well, for me, there was no art historical problem—I was not that sophisticated.

Was encaustic particularly suitable for the literal?

It seemed useful to me.

It wasn't just because it dried quickly? And it often has a certain materiality.

I enjoyed those qualities. But it may have helped that when I began to work with it, no other artists that I knew were using it. The events that happened with it seemed discoveries.

And *Painting Bitten by a Man* (1961; cat. no. 90)?

Well, it's heavily built up, so that I could get a good bite out of it.

When you did your Catenary series, you seemed to return again to a predominance of grays. Was there any specific reason for linking the Catenary series to the color gray? I mean, was there a mood that you had in mind, particularly, initially?

I don't think one sets out to establish a mood. That's not the way one goes about it. One work may trigger another, and you may end up with a kind of chain or series of works. I don't know what causes it; but obviously, there is a relationship from one to the next. Among the group there are relationships, and they tend to be tied together by certain constants, certain repetitions, which allow the differences to be examined or to be put forward. The gray seemed to help to give unity to the group, a sort of school uniform.

Does the color gray carry for you a suggestion of ambiguity?

Everything carries for me a suggestion of ambiguity.

Fair enough. I was thinking that it could be argued that gray casts attention away from figuration or imagery. I'm talking especially about the early work, such as a flag or a number and so on. I don't know if you agree, but do you think gray pulls attention away from figuration because it isn't the natural or conventional color?

The clues that the color gives are lost, of course. It puts perception on a more tactile level, perhaps.

But then I'd ask: how does gray differ in your work from other kinds of monochromes, like the *Green Target* (1955; the Museum of Modern Art, New York) or the *White Flag* (1955; the Metropolitan Museum of Art, New York) and so on?

I don't know that it does. I think if you think it does, that's for you to say.

Do you have any idea why you've used gray so much?

Well, I don't know how much I've used it. I mean, I guess I'm going to learn, from this exhibition. I really don't have a thought about it. You know, I don't do it *because*.

And your use of gray continues in your newest works—*Beckett* (2005; cat. no. 138), for example. I remember your story of Samuel Beckett's reaction, when he saw the etchings with flagstones for *Foirades/Fizzles* in Paris.[5] He looked through your etchings and said, "No matter where you go, you come up against a wall," which I think is classic Beckett.

Well, it's like he's telling a short story of his, isn't it?

Yes. And I wonder, does the composition of the flagstones in *Beckett* have a specific precedent in earlier flagstone works?

No.

I'm relieved to hear that, because I looked and looked and looked, and I couldn't find one!

You mean the precise imagery, I assume.

The imagery, and the pattern of the imagery . . . the way the flagstones go with one another.

Well, it's a similar motif but there is no repetition of the exact pattern.

And was the idea partly in relation to the Beckett centennial? He was born in 1906.

No, I didn't think of that.

Well, gray seems a perfectly Beckettian color.

Well, yes.

Is there more I should know about gray?

I don't know much about gray. I think we will find out something about it, I hope, from this show.

In the context of your statement to Richard Field, "I think that what one wants from a painting is a sense of life,"[6] and talking to Christian Geelhaar frequently, the word lively comes up in that wonderful catalogue.[7] I'm wondering how gray works in that context of a sense of life and liveliness, since we sometimes think of gray as something inert.

I, too, may have felt that it was inert, but I think in these early works, a feeling of a reality was being stressed; through the use of gray, the object nature of the materials would come forward, their physical existence isolated or intensified. I don't know what it is that color does to a work, but, in a sense, gray drained the work of the excitement that color afforded. One was left with what I must have thought of as reality. It's hard to recover the sense that one had then, such a long time ago.

This is what you mean when you say you want to stress the work's "materiality?" Inertness transferred over to reality?

I don't know if inertness and reality are useful terms, but obviously, I was concerned with physicality in all of these early works, whether they used colors or not. Using gray made that very clear... or at least for me, it made it clearer.

1 The shop was Fezandie and Sperrle, at 205 Fulton Street. See Gail Stavitsky, *Waxing Poetic: Encaustic Art in America during the Twentieth Century*, exh. cat. (Montclair Art Museum, 1999), p. 23.

2 *Interaction of Color* was originally published in 1963 by Yale University Press in collaboration with Ives-Sillman as a limited screenprint edition with color plates.

3 Rosenthal's Art and Hobby Supply Company, in Greenwich Village, was a favorite store of the downtown New York art community. Owned by Louis H. Rosenthal (d. 2007), it later became New York Central Art Supply Co.

4 For more on Degas's reconstruction of Manet's *The Execution of Maximilian* in relation to *Near the Lagoon*, see the essay by James Rondeau in this volume, pp. 67–68.

5 *Foirades/Fizzles*, a book with thirty-three intaglio prints by Johns printed at the Atelier Crommelynck in Paris and accompanied by five texts by Samuel Beckett was issued in 1976 in an edition of 250. See Field 1993, cat. no. 173.

6 Field 1999, p. 15.

7 Geelhaar 1980a, pp. 37–56.

A Shifting Focus

Process and Detail in *Tennyson* and *Near the Lagoon*

KELLY KEEGAN
& KRISTIN LISTER

I think the processes involved in the painting in themselves mean as much or more than any reference value that the painting has.[1]

TWO PAINTINGS BY JASPER JOHNS, *TENNYSON* (1958; cat. no. 12) and *Near the Lagoon* (2002–03; cat. no. 135), painted forty-four years apart, invite comparison by their striking similarity in format, their construction using added pieces of canvas, and their overall covering with strokes of gray encaustic. Close examination by conservators has also revealed that before the gray was applied, both pictures were initially painted with the triad of primary colors—red, yellow, and blue—almost an axiom in Johns's work that in these two served as a point of departure for painting in gray.[2]

> I prefer work that appears to come out of a changing focus—not just one relationship or even a number of them but constantly changing and shifting relationships to things in terms of focus. . . . I am concerned with a thing's not being what it was, with its becoming something other than what it is, with any moment in which one identifies a thing precisely and with the slipping away of that moment.[3]

It is worth identifying the steps in Johns's painting process to consider how his focus may have changed as he worked, how the relationships within a piece may have shifted, and how a painting may have grown in complexity. At the same time there may be opportunities to compare how this working process might be expressed differently in an early and a later work.

Construction and Color: *Tennyson*

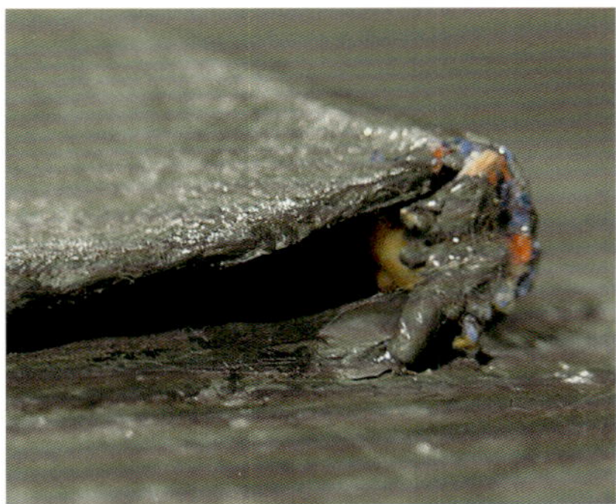

Fig. 1. *Tennyson*, upper right, showing canvas folded over the horizontal dowel.

Johns acknowledged in the mid-1960s that he "was very much concerned with the actual fact of a painting being an object," and although he attributed his manner of working in discrete "unartful" operations to the influence of printmaking, which he did not take up until 1960, this practice is already evident in *Tennyson*.[4] For this painting Johns took two vertical, unprimed, cotton duck canvases, stretched on separate strainers—each 186.7 cm tall (6′ 1 ½," about his own height)—and joined them with wing-nuts.[5] He then stapled an additional piece of canvas along their bottom edges and stretched it across the front of both the panels, pulling it up to about shoulder height, and then folding it back down, much like the top sheet on a bed.[6] It is interesting to note that the two panels underneath maintain their separate identities by being wing-nut joined rather than nailed or bracketed, as if with a flick of a finger the two could be separated, though the later trappings of the piece—the covering sheet that Johns adhered with unpigmented wax—would make this difficult and ultimately destructive. Johns's respect for the separate identity of the individual elements in the piece might be likened to his preference for discrete steps in the painting process, both the result of literal thinking.

With his canvas construction Johns created a variation on the theme of what a stretched canvas is, and by extension, what a painting is: taking the

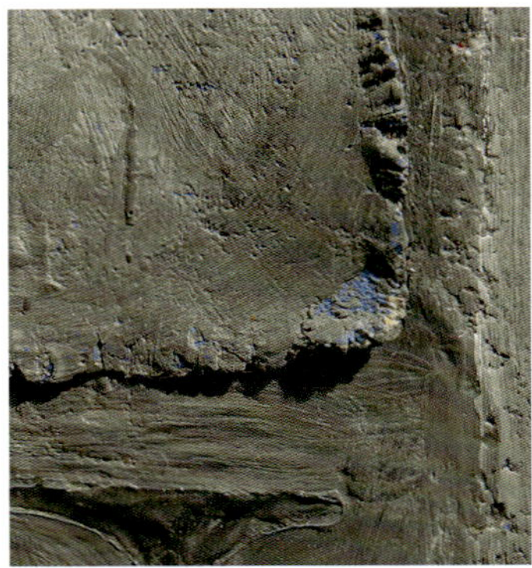

Fig. 2. *Tennyson*, lower right, showing two layers of canvas on top of the stretched canvas, above the letter N.

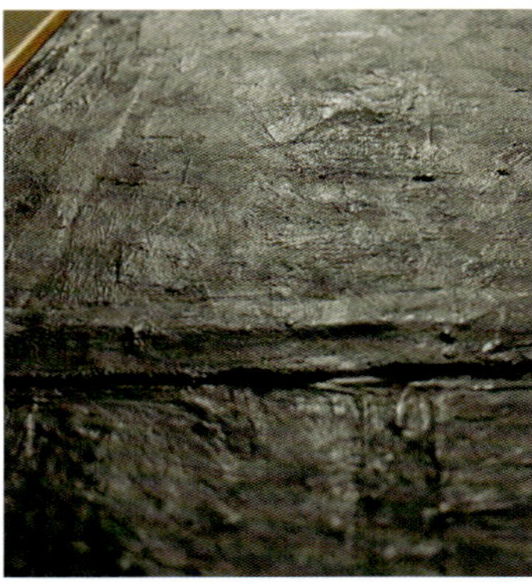

Fig. 3. *Tennyson*, lower left, showing raised border around edge of top canvas, above letters TE.

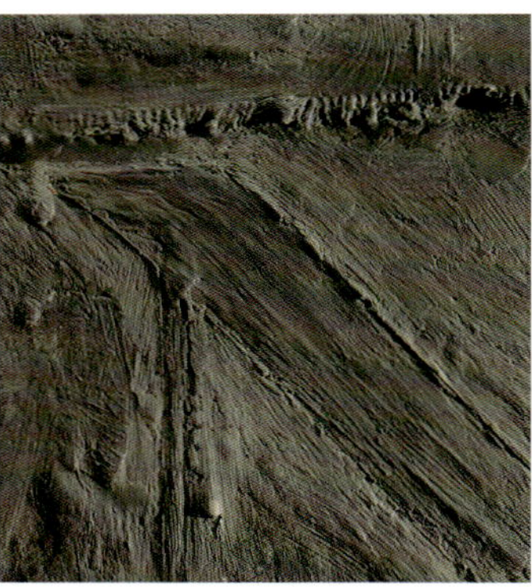

Fig. 4. *Tennyson*, in raking light, showing the first letter N.

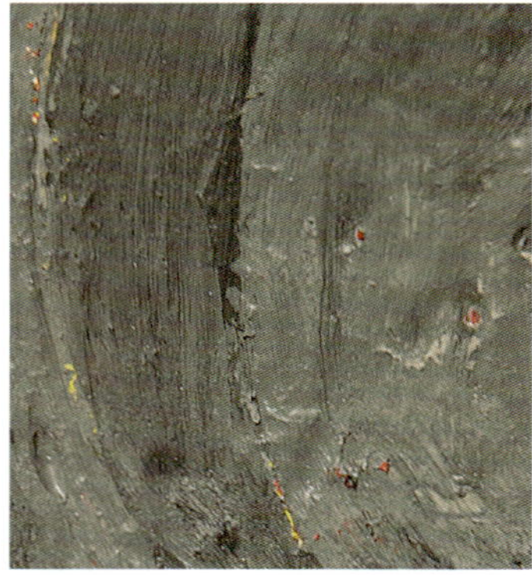

Fig. 5. *Tennyson*, left edge of the letter O, showing vivid underpainting in yellow and red.

simple act of stretching a canvas and subverting it to make something different.[7] After stapling one edge in the normal manner, the canvas was pulled up across the face without restraining and stapling it on the other sides. The portrayal of stretching is relayed visually by the way the fabric narrows as it nears the fold. Johns then wrapped it around a length of dowel at the top and pulled it back (FIG. 1); here again stretching is demonstrated, for Johns pulled the sides out toward the corners. At the word TENNYSON, the tension dissipates: the extra canvas ends at the top of the letters.[8] All three layers, offset by the coarsely frayed edges that naturally tend to splay out and curl away from the layer below, are revealed sequentially at the sides, and attest to the process (FIG. 2). The topmost layer has been folded twice and released, creating a raised border around the side and bottom edges, reminiscent of creases left after stretching, and described by the artist Robert Morris as "part of a canvas ripped from its stretcher bars" (FIG. 3).[9] This artistic artifact may have been added as an embellishment on the theme of the stretched canvas, but it also adds a sculptural accent to the largest flat area of the composition.

Of the triad of primary colors composing the initial paint layers, the overriding one was blue, both for the top sheet and for the twin panels that show above it and along the outer edges.[10] The lower layer of the added canvas was painted bright red, which would have been visible under the area of the inscription and as a sliver up the sides, between the top and bottom blues.[11] In this state the layers along the sides would have alternated in color, blue-red-blue, which one might think would make the construction more pronounced. But by adding color, it is the flat colored shapes themselves, rather than the structural build-up of layers, that would be emphasized. *Gray Rectangles* (1957; cat. no. 10), painted the previous year, had also first been red, yellow, and blue, but Johns thought that painting it gray would reveal the structure more clearly.[12] When Johns did paint over the surface of *Tennyson* with grays, he underscored the dimensionality of the added canvas further by painting the semblance of a darker gray shadow along the edges.

Johns had first used bright yellow for the roman capital letters he painted over the red area. Below the overall blue, the yellow-on-red TENNYSON would have seemed highly charged. The red on the sides, clearly painted to extend some distance under the blue top sheet, might have seemed to hint of some action behind the sheet, which, like a stage curtain, was raised just high enough to reveal the title. When he repainted the entire picture with gray, he reworked the yellow TENNYSON in a purposeful manner, covering the letters in dark gray strokes. Leaving the dark gray letters in reserve, he imitated stenciled letters by carefully outlining freehand a lighter gray raised edge around them. Whereas true stenciled letters would stand in relief, these appear to be chiseled out rather than built up (FIG. 4).[13] This portrayal of cutting into the surface brings to mind an inscription chiseled into a gray tombstone—a stark contrast to the colorful earlier state. Though heavily covered in gray now, little bits of the original colors are left visible (FIGS. 1, 2, and 5), particularly along the edges of the canvas layers, adding a prismatic glint to the gray, highlighting the structural dimension, and lending a hidden complexity to the work, as do the drips of red, yellow, and blue along the bottom edge.

Construction and Color: *Near the Lagoon*

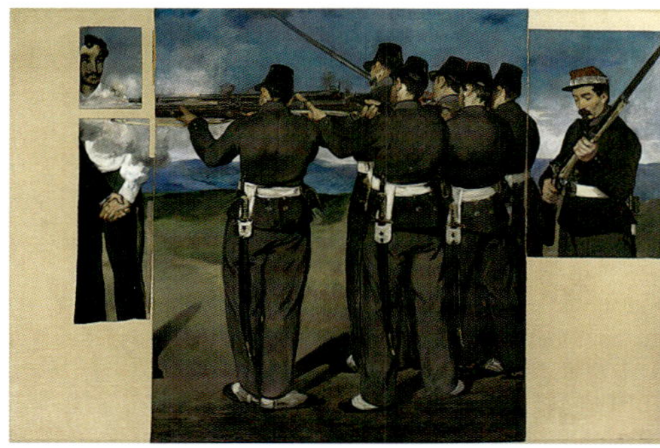

Fig. 6. Édouard Manet, reconstructed by Edgar Degas. *The Execution of Maximilian*, c. 1867–68. Oil on canvas; 193 × 284 cm (76 × 111 ⅞ in.). The National Gallery, London.

The format of *Near the Lagoon* is based on Edgar Degas's reconstruction of the salvaged fragments from Édouard Manet's *The Execution of Maximilian* (FIG. 6), which Degas had collected from various sources after Manet's death and had mounted onto a new canvas, leaving blank areas to represent missing sections of the original. For *Near the Lagoon,* Johns mounted four blank pieces of canvas corresponding to Manet's fragments onto a 3 × 2.1 m canvas, only slightly larger than Degas's reconstruction (1.9 × 2.8 m), basically preserving the proportions of his efforts, but turning the composition vertically.[14]

The steps in constructing *Near the Lagoon* were thoughtfully determined. The canvas was first coated with a layer of unpigmented wax, which like size, would stabilize the canvas and prevent it from soaking up the hot encaustic paint when it was applied and later reheated. A muted, earthy red (iron oxide red mixed with titanium white) was then painted over the entire canvas, functioning as a colored ground (FIG. 7).[15] The four patches corresponding to Manet's fragments are of the same linen and are painted the same muted red. Johns roughly outlined the fragments' positions on the reverse in black and ruled off the area with an extensive 5-inch (12.7 cm) grid in blue crayon. The red fragments were then systematically tacked to the stretched canvas with a knotted stitch of waxed thread at each interval where the grid lines intersected, adding extra knots at some edges (FIG. 8).[16] The careful measuring, grid-work, and sewing are the engineering behind this last and largest project in the Catenary series, which had begun with *Bridge* (1997; cat. no. 128).[17]

The compositions for *The Execution of Maximilian* and *Near the Lagoon* are interesting in terms of what can be considered a part, a whole, and space.

> Such things run through my work, relationships of parts and wholes. . . . the shifting nature of anything . . . how it varies when it's taken to be whole and when it's taken to be a part. Aside from such problems of identity, the way that we use space and decide that something in the space is a thing and the rest of it isn't a thing is odd and is always changing.[18]

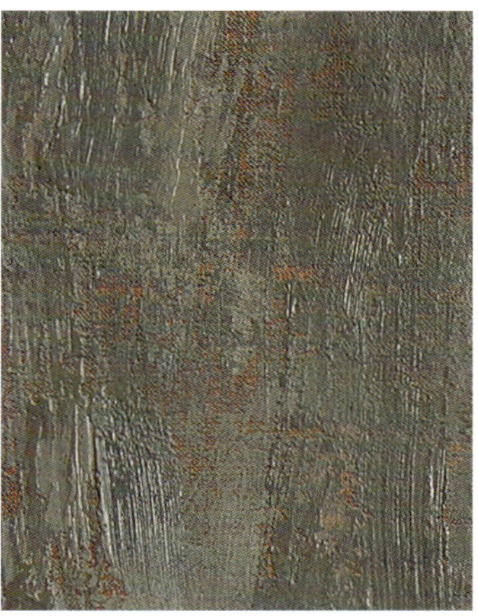

Fig. 7. *Near the Lagoon*, lower right, showing varied grays, thinly applied, revealing red underpainting.

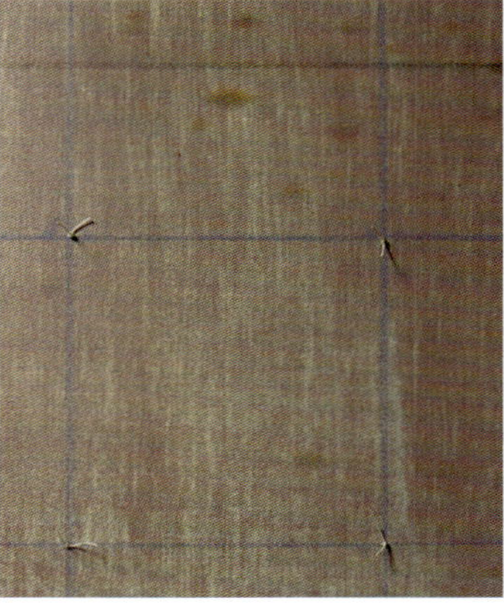

Fig. 8. *Near the Lagoon*, reverse, showing grid (blue) and horizontal center line (black) with knotted stitches that attach canvas pieces on the front.

In signifying the relationship between the fragments and their background, or the parts and the whole to which they were joined, Johns had already departed from Degas's scheme, cutting them both from the same red encaustic-covered cloth, as if the smaller pieces were closely bound to or born from the larger. Red is the only primary color of the red-yellow-blue triad that does not play a significant part in Degas's reconstruction.[19] Once the fragments were in place, Johns began by painting the thing that isn't—the blank spaces that in Degas's reconstruction appear as yellow canvas, standing in for the missing parts of Manet's painting. Using a yellow similar to the color of the blank canvas (yellow ocher mixed with titanium white), Johns painted in the area not covered by his fragments. But he painted this as a positive "thing," not as negative space. Painting along the cut edges of the fragments, his yellow strokes extend over them, functioning like scar tissue, sometimes breaking open to reveal the reddish underlayer below, like a cut that has not healed—the soft yellow translucent encaustic suggestive of skin (FIG. 9).[20] He painted passages within the "blank" areas, not simply as solid yellow, but developing them in response to lines, shapes, previous strokes, etc., so that the lighter yellow strokes began to stand out against the flat outlined shapes of the fragments. He also used yellow to demarcate the outside edge of the entire Degas reconstruction, and later reinforced this line with dark paint and charcoal to imitate a shadow, creating a faux canvas edge. In this way he marked more strongly the edge between Degas's canvas, which he made the same size as the original source, and the beginning of the remaining outer border. His border,

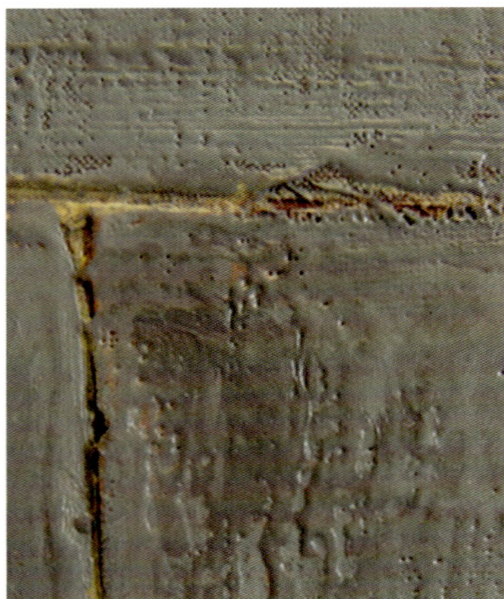

Fig. 9. *Near the Lagoon*, bottom edge of largest fragment and upper-left corner of lower fragment.

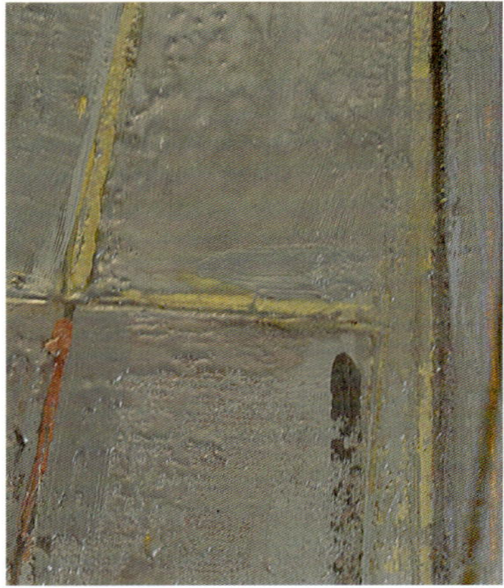

Fig. 10. *Near the Lagoon*, right edge, showing triad underpainting: blue border and edge between red fragment and yellow area.

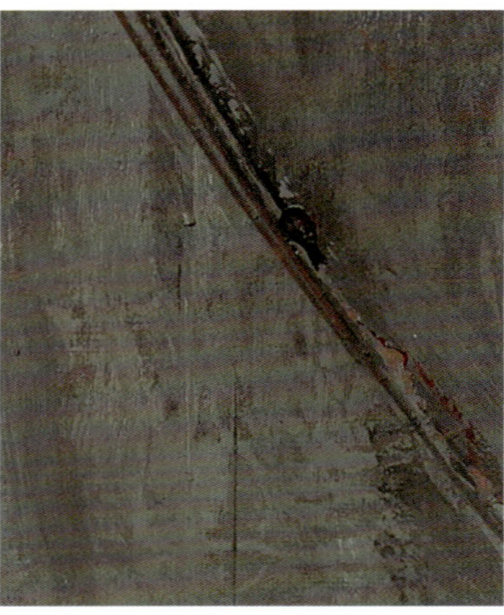

Fig. 11. *Near the Lagoon*, lower left of middle catenary curve, showing multiple impressions and reworking.

which he painted blue, served to surround the red fragments and yellow areas as one united whole (FIG. 10), and completed the triad of red, yellow, and blue in muted tones.[21]

The remaining parts of the construction are the hinged wooden side wings (one on the left and two on the right), and the white cord that hangs down in a curve in front of the painting (the catenary), looping up through a hole in the top of each outer wing, with the ends dangling down to the bottom behind the wings. These create the three-dimensional aspects of the piece. The wings project obliquely outward and hold the cord slightly away from the painting's surface. The outer wing on the right side is hinged so it folds back outward, accordion style. It also reveals the warm reddish tone of the wood slats' unpainted inner edges, the color enriched by a thin coating of wax. Since the string is attached to the extra wing, the catenary curve is pulled off-center to the right, offsetting it slightly from its own impression in the paint, as if projecting a shadow, which lends it a heightened illusion of depth.

With his catenary curve, Johns discovered a new "device"—a tool that creates a particular shape. He had once been struck by Robert Rauschenberg's impromptu use of a jar rim dipped in paint to make circles on a canvas, and he continued to make use of that particular device as part of his repertoire: two such rings appear in *Near the Lagoon*. Johns's classic device is a piece of wood fixed at one end that marks out a circle of smeared paint when turned, but even his stencils can be considered devices, in that they form set shapes, contradicting traditional notions of artistic process. The catenary device creates a perfectly curved line, and as with other devices, Johns can imprint it into the soft encaustic paint. In *Near the Lagoon,* he suspended a cord from tacks in the top two corners of the canvas, allowing it to drape down to the measured center. To set the curve, he impressed the cord into the paint and also layered strokes of gray encaustic over its edges. Once he had captured the cord's position, he pulled it out of its groove, sometimes leaving broken edges, or pulling up the paint beneath (FIG. 11). The cord that now hangs in front of the painting is too pristine to have been the one used in the actual process. Johns has given it a token splash of gray paint, making it the artist's representation of the real thing. He repeated the embedding procedure for the two other recessed curves, measuring their drop to be evenly spaced from the top one.[22] Sometimes the string would move slightly, so that there are two or three impressions made alongside one another. There is a sense of movement inherent in the Catenary paintings from the free-hanging string itself, which will swing if touched. Movement is further underscored here by the string's length, which is not fixed and changes if pulled; by the hinged side wings through which the string is threaded; and even by the multiple impressions of the string, which relay the gentle movement made by the string during the painting process.

> It's important that one sees the instability of what one is looking at—that it could be changed. I like that you're aware of other possibilities, whether you wish to set them in motion or not.[23]

Like the edges of the canvas fragments, the catenary lines later became a focus for Johns's brushwork, as he painted up and down their length once again, varying the colors to reflect what was underlying. Johns went back into the grooves with varied strokes, accenting them with more intense color, shading with darker tones, and highlighting with lighter strokes, sometimes cutting back into the groove with a heated tool or brush, sometimes apparently restriking the cord's impression—thus accentuating the dimensionality of the curve and centering a complex and varied history within this narrow space.

Painting in Gray: *Tennyson* and *Near the Lagoon*

One of the effects of graying over a colored painting is attenuation: as the range of colors shrinks, gradations that remain assume finer nuances; as colored shapes are muted, prominence is given to lines, leaving the possibility of space more open. In *Near the Lagoon* one is aware of the edges of the fragments as lines, more than of the whole fragments as shapes. To this end, Johns would sometimes enhance a fragment's outline with a soft undulating indentation drawn with a heated tool (FIG. 12). As he shifted the focus in this direction, toward edges and lines, he also added the additional lines of the catenary curves, cutting flat canvas forms into open spaces. It is formally expedient that most of the catenary lines span the largest unbroken space of the central fragment. The shift in focus, from color toward gray, from flat shapes toward lines and space, would impose a visual reorientation, engaging Johns as a painter.

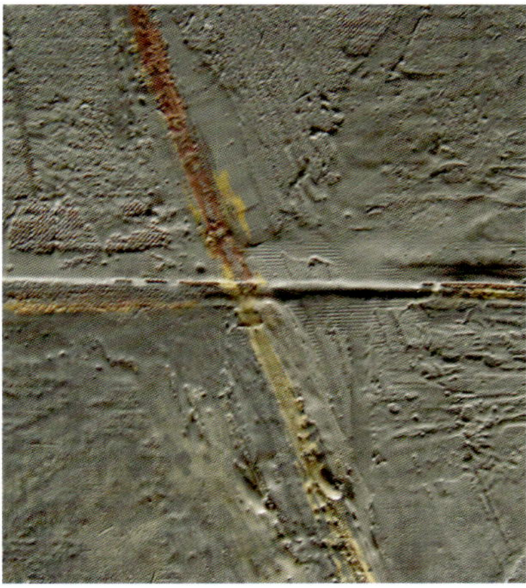

Fig. 12. *Near the Lagoon*, lower edge of central fragment, left of center, showing the indentation made with a heated tool.

Johns applied many more layers of grays in *Tennyson* than he did in *Near the Lagoon,* to the point that the underlying colors have been mostly obliterated. On this level, *Tennyson* seems very much about covering up: layer upon layer of paint over layer upon layer of canvas. The strokes themselves were freely applied as short, animated marks in varied directions. This provides a natural quality to the facture, as does the way the strokes become more awkward near the bottom where they are outside the artist's natural range. While the individual marks appear freely made, the mixtures of gray tones in *Tennyson* were carefully modulated and built up. Lighter tones were applied underneath, working generally toward darker strokes on top, but where the latter appeared too strong, or a configuration of marks too dominant, Johns lightened them with a thin scumble, and then went back to add dark strokes more modestly. He worked over the entire surface, adding and correcting, to achieve strokes that mingle in a lively mass dispersed across the entire surface. With no dominant points of focus, the viewer experiences an unanchored way of seeing.

> The early paintings of mine . . . tended to be a sum of corrections in terms of painting, in terms of strokes. So that there are many, many strokes and everything is built up on a very simple frame but there is a great deal of work in it. . . . Whereas the more recent works don't have that involvement. There isn't the constant attempt to do something over and over and over in the more recent works.[24]

Near the Lagoon has a much thinner covering of gray strokes through which the reddish underlayer glows in many spots. There is both the sense of surface and of space. The central area of the painting presents a surface that can be penetrated through to a greater depth, as if one were looking straight down at a pool of water and seeing beneath. By contrast, looking at the top and bottom sections is like peering across the surface of water, and being unable to penetrate it. The penetration is in part actual: throughout this large central fragment there are scattered reveals of the red-toned canvas in between the gray brushstrokes that are most easily glimpsed straight on. One perceives a greater spatial separation in this area, which Johns has carefully orchestrated through an extended range of steps in tonal contrast. He has used the very darkest and lightest tones of grays here, which are mostly missing from the other areas. In the area between the top and middle catenary curves, he set the darkest strokes against very light areas, and the very lightest spot in the painting, which he placed just off center, is surrounded by dark strokes. The careful ordering in this section can be contrasted to the area above the top catenary curve, where the marks are crowded together in a high-energy mixture. The catenary curves seem to act as a series of sieves, distilling the marks. After passing through the top curve, all the salient strokes are ordered in a vertical direction, while very few verticals pass through the second catenary curve, below which calm waters seem to prevail.

When asked if he was conscious of the different ways in which he made marks, Johns replied:

> At times, yes. At times I am conscious of making a mark with some directional idea which I've got from the painting. Sometimes I am conscious of making a mark to alter what seems to me the primary concern of the painting, to force it to be different.[25]

This statement is a rather remarkable attempt to break down the innately subjective and complex act of painting into discrete, "unartful" steps. It appears that Johns often begins painting very logically, as he does with the grays in *Near the Lagoon*, taking cues from the lines in the painting, which are the reference points—the facts—rather than just breaking out in the middle somewhere and making up some fiction. Many strokes follow a line or fill in a shape between lines; then these painted areas become further reference points leading to a follow-up action, development, or reaction. In *Near the Lagoon*, the identity of the individual parts was respected in the mark-making process—the lines made by the fragment or border edges and the catenary cords were not crossed by the gray strokes even when the same tone of gray appears on both sides. It was only later when the painting in gray was complete, and Johns added the long, colored streak marks, indentations, and drips that he purposefully bridged the divisions. Furthermore, each fragment and each surrounding space was painted in a slightly different manner. Though the effects are subtle and do not disrupt the unity of the work as a whole, the different processes seem to signal different choices, accompanied by various possible modes of thinking, adding crosscurrents of complexity to the work.

While one might view the catenary curves as a series of sieves, they might also suggest ripples moving out across the surface of water. To extend this association further, the strokes at the top of the painting seem to flow around the top two fragments and cascade fluidly over the left side, like water running over rocks and down into a pool. In the lowest section of the picture, the paint strokes seem to collect on the bottom line, like sediment resting on the floor of a lagoon. The strokes in *Near the Lagoon* are not as gestural as those of *Tennyson* and also less literal. There is a different kind of physicality—less connected with human mark making and more with a substantive materiality. Initially one of the reasons Johns took up encaustic was that it "preserves the character of every stroke of the brush."[26] By zooming in on the encaustic surface itself, one encounters a new spatial dimension. In many areas of *Near the Lagoon,* Johns has transformed the surface by melting and masterfully manipulating the encaustic with a heat gun. The paint looks like a planetary surface seen from a thousand miles away, with miniaturized mountain ranges, smooth glacier fields, craters, rivers, drifting sands, and melting ice flows (**FIG. 13**).[27]

With *Near the Lagoon* there is the constant temptation to change one's focus: to look *into* the painting from close at hand, or *at* the painting from a broader perspective. Its various textures, gestures, and surface effects recall the process used in *Tennyson*, at least initially. There is a sense of arduousness to both works, as if in looking at each, one can picture Johns jutting around, moving away from the painting, considering it, reacting to multiple impulses at a time. There is an unsettling quality to the brushstrokes in *Tennyson*, an almost antsy uneasiness of a man taking great pains to make his point.

Near the Lagoon seems to convey a kind of ease, a comfort within one's own skin and a confidence in the mark making. Smoother, more carefully blended with more subtle effects and textures, the later painting shows Johns continually pushing the boundaries of a medium with which he is quite familiar. The brushstrokes often appear to be applied in threes, perhaps the current

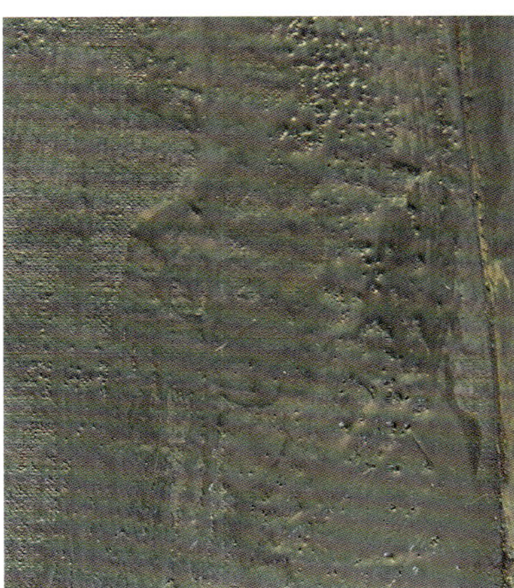

Fig. 13. *Near the Lagoon*, lower-right corner of top-center fragment, showing melting formations.

incarnation of the characteristic curving M-shaped strokes the artist developed in his paintings of the 1960s and 1970s, appearing more discreet toward the center of the painting and slowly shifting out of focus. There is a vertical quality throughout the central section of the painting, a kind of waterfall of encaustic strokes placed side by side. The physicality of the process is evident, strokes painted from top to bottom; toward the top, where Johns likely employed a ladder or flipped the painting, the brushstrokes clearly change direction, moving around the collage elements. Unlike *Tennyson*, where there is a clear intention of one stroke on top of another, a kind of competitive energy between strokes, the softer movements of the brush in *Near the Lagoon* function more collectively, and are more nuanced in texture and color. The perceived visual softness of the painting is further reinforced by an increased physical softness of the medium itself, evidence of the development of Johns's encaustic technique.

The concentration has clearly shifted between *Tennyson* and *Near the Lagoon* as Johns's increased comfort with the medium and perhaps with his artistic ability in general has led to not only a variety in mark making but also a subtlety of color and surface. *Near the Lagoon* is most clearly linked to and simultaneously separated from its predecessor by the application and function of gray in the conception and execution of each as a gray painting. *Tennyson* went through extreme compositional stages before ending in gray, which functions in some ways to shift the focus of the work to the inherent structure, allowing "the literal qualities of the painting to predominate."[28] In *Near the Lagoon* there are fewer layers of gray paint, and the manipulation and coloration of these grays give the sometimes false impression of visual penetration to the lower toned layers.

Both paintings have, in different ways, a number of secrets, hidden surfaces and meanings. Despite this, in *Tennyson* there is an immediateness to the application of paint, a straightforward quality to the use of color, of gray being simply black and white. In *Near the Lagoon*, Johns utilized what decades of manipulating encaustic and color had taught him, and seemingly nothing is as simple as it appears. The grays are no longer exclusive mixtures of black and white, but may be complex mixtures that appear tinged slightly red, yellow, or blue, and the subtle grays within the picture change markedly when viewed under different qualities of light. Some of the gray mixtures in *Near the Lagoon* were found to incorporate not only titanium white with bone black and lamp black, but also iron oxide red, iron oxide yellow, ultramarine blue, and possibly cadmium red and cobalt blue in various proportions.[29] Underpainting in muted shades of iron oxide red, iron oxide yellow, and ultramarine blue, Johns departed from the intense underpainting seen in *Tennyson* for a more subdued, earthy palette. In contrast, the artist also incorporated the underpainted colors as well as others into the upper layers of paint, not only to give the illusion of translucency, but also to contrast the gray tones. Despite these colored grays in *Near the Lagoon*, the strokes appear much more blended and closely related than in *Tennyson*. There is an overall coolness to the earlier painting, perhaps heightened by the predominantly blue underpainting, that occurs when black and white paints are mixed without additional colors, although there are also strokes of less heavily pigmented beeswax that provide a slightly yellow tonality; here the medium itself is called upon as a coloristic influence.

Since his 1954–55 *Flag* (the Museum of Modern Art, New York; see figs. 5–6 in the essay by James Rondeau in this volume), encaustic has been a medium favored by Johns, as it preserves the painted gesture and dries quickly, allowing for multiple paint layers in a single session without smearing. Johns has often been elusive about the origins of his medium and his recipe, but has stated that it generally involved bleached beeswax and a small bit of damar resin and linseed oil.[30] Originally, Johns mixed tube oil paints with the beeswax,

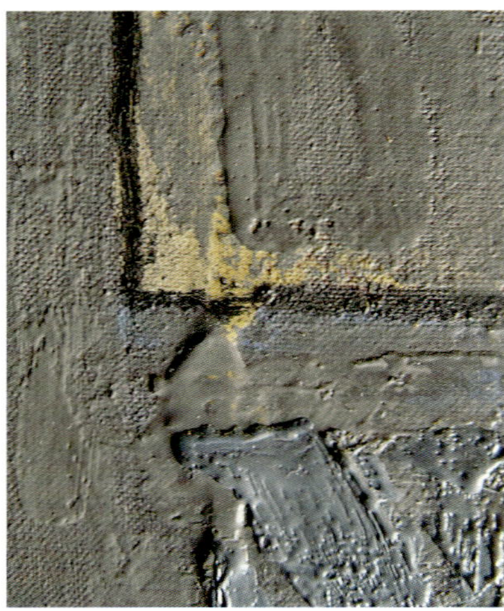

Fig. 14. *Near the Lagoon*, lower-left corner of charcoal edge between blue border and yellow area.

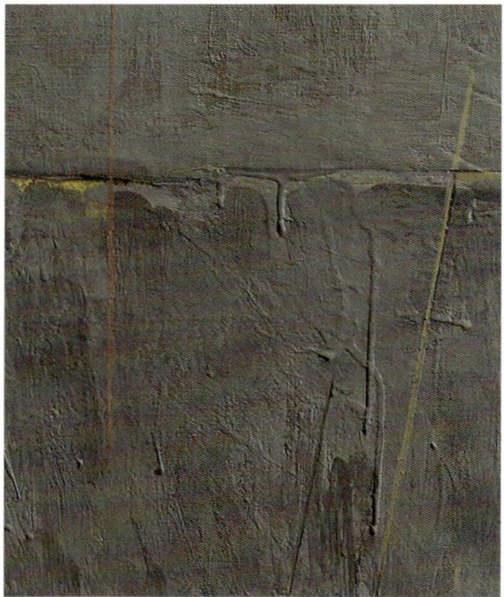

Fig. 15. *Near the Lagoon*, lower left, showing colored drips.

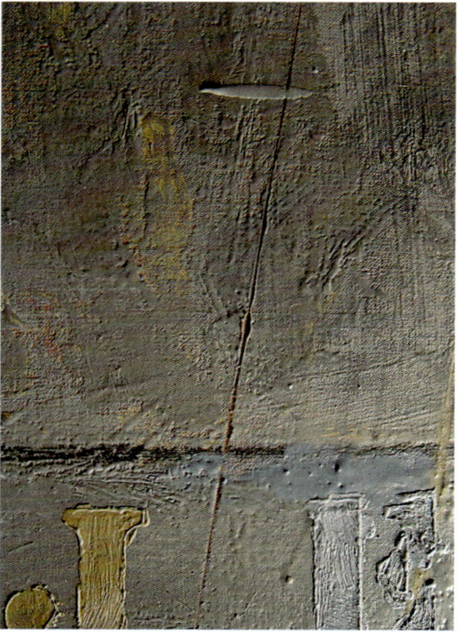

Fig. 16. *Near the Lagoon*, lower left, showing the artist's indentation at center.

purchased from Fezandie and Sperrle near his Pearl Street loft in New York, and later moved to mixing raw materials with dry pigments.[31] Media analysis of *Near the Lagoon* revealed the predominant binding medium to be bleached beeswax, with little or no additives other than pigment.[32] This represents a departure from published recipes, previous interviews with Johns, and his earlier methods. The result is a physically softer and more pliable paint surface that is more easy to manipulate. Johns's way seems to have been simplified over the years, as the artist stripped the medium of its additives, discarding ready-made tube oil paints and additives for powdered pigment and beeswax. The pigment mixtures themselves tend to range in complexity, as many are relatively simple, with two or three main components and a number of minor pigments reflecting either intention or chance. Other hues seem much more tailored with four or more major components; one imagines the artist like a cook sprinkling various colored ingredients into a single mixture, altering tonality and translucency slightly with each addition.

Studio images of Johns often show the artist with a small rolling cart, easily maneuverable before a large painting, packed with materials including, a small hot plate, a heat gun, a can of brushes, and a crowded array of metal pots of paint, each color individually mixed to be heated and reheated as needed. The individual nature of each color mixture is evident in the layer structure and analysis of the paint. While the palette is predominantly muted primary colors, black, and white, a rich green, the only secondary color present, used solely in the carefully manipulated "drips" across the surface, is perhaps the most complicated mixture, mainly of a cobalt-titanate green and carbon black, with additions of viridian and ultramarine, as well as small amounts of pale yellow (perhaps cadmium), iron oxide yellow, titanium white, and iron oxide red.[33] It is unclear whether these various added colors in small amounts are intentional or part of the process, resulting perhaps from his dipping a brush into various pots of color, but Johns's mindset seems to point toward the latter.

In addition to multiple layers of encaustic paint, Johns made use of charcoal both as a planning and aesthetic element in *Near the Lagoon,* incorporating it into the lower and upper paint layers (FIG. 14). Like the uneven application of yellow around the collage elements, the charcoal line marking off the blue perimeter undulates as the artist periodically darkened sections of the line that, on either side when abutting the largest collage element, run in tandem with thickened areas of yellow, functioning to set the collage elements off against the background for a kind of trompe l'oeil effect.[34] The traditional drawing medium was also utilized along the bottom margin in a preparatory manner, where Johns made small tick marks to mark the lower-left edge of the stenciled letters that alternate to form the title, signature, and date of the work and on the surface in a number of faux "drip" marks, drawn freehand across borders like detached shadows of drips found elsewhere throughout the work. The stenciled letters themselves, all capitals, alternate in gray tonality mostly between bluish and yellow-tinted shades of gray.

Johns varied the application of his paint widely throughout the work using splatters, possibly a spray, and various "devices," as well as the brush and stencil methods. In addition to a number of small dabs of paint in various colors and naturally occurring drips, the artist also created straight indentations in the work by impressing a hot tool into the surface, probably along a straight edge. Later in the process, Johns executed long, straight "drips," likely created by running a thin, warm bead of encaustic down a straight edge (FIG. 15). Often Johns would combine these methods, alternating them along the same line to create colored indentations similar to the reworked impressions of the catenary cord.[35] Like the catenary curves, these straight lines and well-placed drips tend to cross borders throughout the work, fracturing the careful outlines Johns

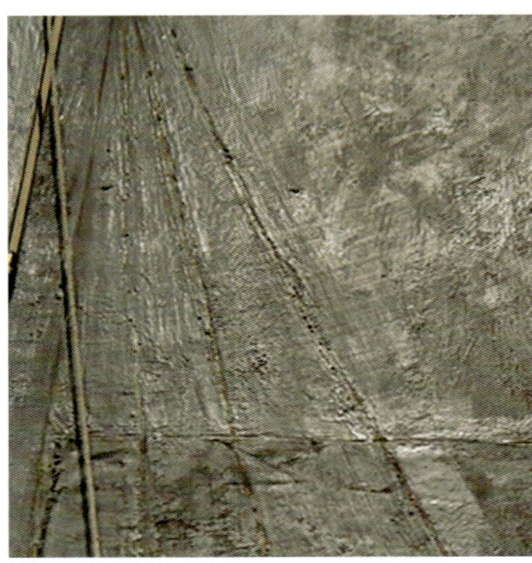

Fig. 17. *Near the Lagoon*, upper left, in raking light, showing semicircular sweep.

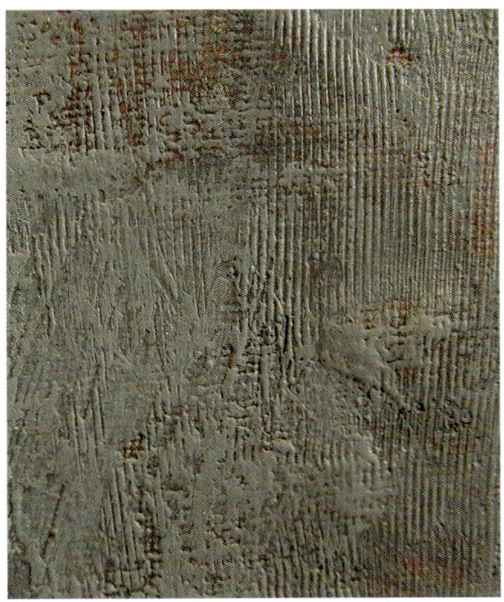

Fig. 18. *Near the Lagoon*, lower center, macro-detail showing the crosshatching pattern made by a tool (possibly a mezzotint rocker).

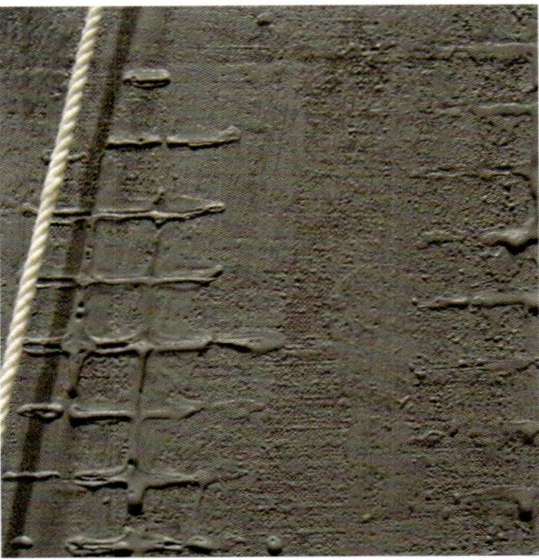

Fig. 19. *Near the Lagoon*, right side, showing the imprint of a hardware screen.

had previously taken such pains to define (FIG. 16). The drips themselves have long been one of Johns's devices, occurring naturally during the painting process and helped along by the artist.

Perhaps the most intriguing and initially puzzling manipulation of materials is Johns's treatment of the surface in *Near the Lagoon*, for it is indeed the surface of his paintings that has become increasingly more complex and subtle throughout his career. Rather than concentrating simply on the brushstroke, making it the subject of the painting as he has said in the past,[36] Johns engages the surface as a whole, a separate entity from the individual strokes as the skin of the lagoon is separate from the depth below, employing a variety of methods to shape the overall texture and sheen of the work. Over the entire surface, especially noticeable in the upper half, a fine textile imprint is most likely the effect of soft encaustic pushed into the canvas support. Perhaps in an attempt to counteract this or the gloss from reheating, Johns imparted an additional surface texture on the upper half. Close inspection of the surface reveals a series of concentric semicircles radiating from the upper left like ripples in a pond (FIG. 17), and a mirrored, less intense echo of them at the upper right. It appears Johns swept an instrument such as a squeegee across the surface, lightly grazing and alternately glossing the soft encaustic paint in a pattern of streaky rotation around a stationary point (the corner) and in a very subtle way echoing the semicircular form first seen in *Good Time Charley* (1961; cat. no. 92).

In another attempt to break up various sections of homogenous, melted, glossy former brushstrokes, Johns employed a small instrument—possibly a mezzotint rocker—to create a series of parallel striations, resembling the marks left by a brush. In some cases, the artist used single passes within a melted brushstroke and in other areas he varied the direction creating a kind of crosshatched patch that revealed the underpaint along the intersecting lines (FIG. 18).

As the painting neared completion, Johns added a number of personal marks to the surface that can be read as carrying a certain humorous intent. These are signature marks, for he had used them on many other paintings, and thus, like the drip-covered strip of bare canvas he left along the bottom of numerous works, they had become part of his personal style, his mannerisms. Most of these marks are displayed down the right side of *Near the Lagoon*, as though, with the painting completed, Johns was making his exit stage right. Whereas he may have used the mezzotint rocker from printmaking to imprint the very subtle sets of parallel lines into the painting's surface, Johns now created a pattern that is a parody of the screenprinting process. In screenprinting, paint is squeegeed through a fine fabric mesh, but here he used coarse hardware screen instead, placing it against the painting's surface and perhaps even using a squeegee to press the paint through and deposit the grid pattern in light gray impasto on the surface (FIG. 19). Instead of portraying a fine brushstroke as the mezzotint rocker would have, this treatment left a deposit more like a tire tread.[37] Another humorous notation in *Near the Lagoon* is several groups of perfectly formed, light gray drips that clearly run horizontally (FIG. 20). Sideways drips are often found in Johns's paintings, but because the surfaces are such an orgy of drips they do not immediately catch one's attention as completely unnatural. Johns had to turn the painting on its side to form them—an ordeal with a painting the size of *Near the Lagoon*—but they force the realization that a painting is an object, not just a surface.[38]

Johns's use of a jar rim to leave a ring of paint implies more strongly still a sense of completion, as if he were so comfortable with the painting he might set a cup or can down on it.[39] Two such rings are found on *Near the Lagoon*: the first (a full circle with a partial circle offset by 2 cm) bridges the seam between the bottom fragment and the "blank" canvas at the right edge (FIG. 21); and the

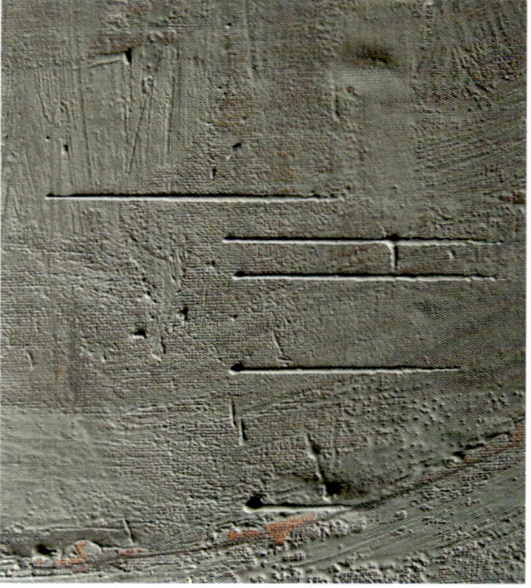

Fig. 20. *Near the Lagoon*, lower center, in raking light, showing horizontal drips.

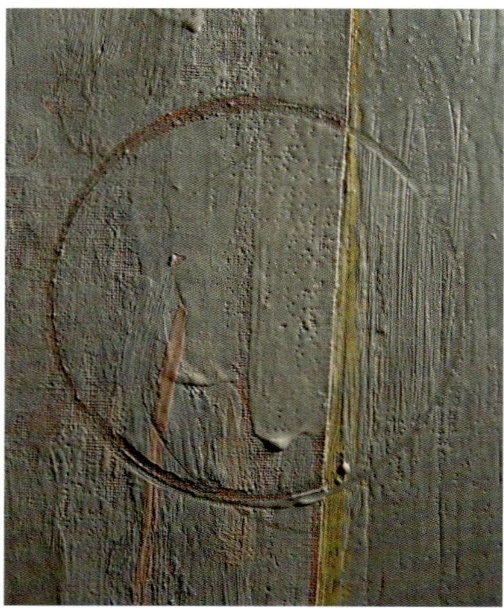

Fig. 21. *Near the Lagoon*, lower right, showing ring impression across outer edge of largest fragment.

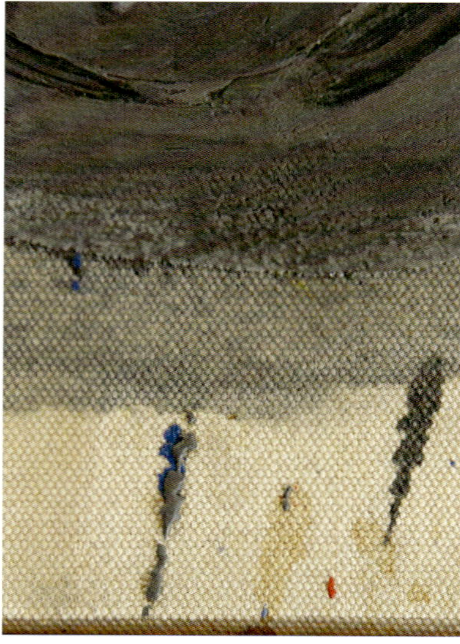

Fig. 22. *Tennyson*, unpainted lower margin, showing drips and flicks below the letter S.

second (a partial circle, slightly smaller) a little farther down, bridges both right side wings and extends into the space beyond the painting, annexing the room into the field of focus.[40] To make the ring on the fragment, Johns first pressed the rim into the encaustic, leaving a light impression that reveals the muted red underlayer. He then filled in the half circle adjacent to the fragment with a pattern of vertical lines, as if the circle had subsumed the area into a new whole. Next he dipped the can rim into darker gray paint and tried to place it on top of the first impression in order to make the circle a stronger color, but, as if by mistake, he placed it off the mark, so quickly lifted it again, leaving only a partial circle. Then he dipped the rim in the gray paint again, very purposefully this time—the rim is thickly covered—and set it down dead-on, leaving a heavy gray circle superimposed on the first one. All of this was done like a knife thrower in a circus act who clowns around with his first throw, but then amazes with his hair-raising accuracy. When Johns pressed a ring onto the outer wooden wing on the right, he also superimposed the ring twice. The encaustic on the wood is not thick enough to take a complete impression, but a dark brown substance from the rim was lightly deposited on the outside wing, reinforcing the form. Where the ring continues onto the adjacent inner wing, Johns has fooled the eye, for the mark was not made by the can as it appears. Instead he took a heated tool or a brush dipped in solvent, and drew a freehand continuation of the curve, melting or dissolving the existing encaustic with his tool, stopping just when it had collected as a bead about to drip from the bottom of the stroke, once again demonstrating his delicate precision. All these signature details lie on the very top layer of the painting like reflections of the artist on the lagoon's surface.

Tennyson also has a humorous aside hidden in the details. At the bottom Johns left a strip of unpainted canvas, what he has called "a mannerism in the relationship between painting and canvas."[41] Often this strip contains only the random drips from paint strokes that were applied higher up. Together with the canvas, these are the raw materials; revealed thus, it is as though the magician were showing his hand. But in the case of *Tennyson* the drips of red, yellow, and blue did not occur when Johns was applying the colored underlayers, as they seem to portray. This is a sleight of hand, for they are faux drips that appear to have been flicked on afterward, not even downward like real drips, as most of these flicks of paint travel from the bottom up and go over the edge of gray paint (FIG. 22).[42] Nevertheless, they still attest to the presence of colors that are hidden under the gray, and to the painting process. Whether they are residues of the actual process or the artist's simulated portrayal of drips, they are both valid forms in Johns's vocabulary, and that may be the point here.

> Details offer a kind of thought. Details offer a way of thinking.
> I'm picky that way.[43]

The actual steps in a work's construction can be seen as distinct decisions, accompanied by a variety of possible thoughts, separate pathways leading to the same result. And while the actual process of applying the paint remains intrinsically instinctive, Johns has attempted to deconstruct the process into discrete steps that can be understood as a language of choices. In examining individual steps in the process, as the details become smaller, the language seems clearer, yet stepping back, looking at a larger view, the rich and complex mosaic of the artwork and Johns's vision materializes.

The authors gratefully acknowledge Gwenäelle Gautier, Anikó Bezúr, Inge Fiedler, and Francesca Casadio of the Conservation Science Department at the Art Institute of Chicago for undertaking the paint analysis and for their helpful assistance in interpretation and discussion.

1 Sylvester 1965, in *Writings* 1996, p. 117.

2 Since *Near the Lagoon* is in the collection of the Art Institute of Chicago, as conservators we have had an opportunity to examine it very closely. We were only able to examine *Tennyson* for about three hours with a brief look at the reverse, and without a microscope, on a visit to the Des Moines Art Center. We are very grateful to the staff in Des Moines for facilitating our visit.

3 Swenson 1964, p. 23, in *Writings* 1996, pp. 92–93.

4 Sylvester 1965, in Sylvester 2001, p. 167.

5 A strainer is a more primitive form of stretcher that cannot be expanded. The canvas is relatively coarse, 18 vertical threads/cm × 13 horizontal threads/cm.

6 See the article by James Rondeau in this volume, pp. 46–47. To adhere the layers of canvas to the stretched panel, Johns used unpigmented wax and heat. The wax saturated the canvas and is visible on the reverse.

7 Similarly he had used the stretched canvas, in a more literal way, to explore this idea, by presenting the back of a stretched canvas, painted gray, in *Canvas* (1956).

8 There are possibly several shorter sections of dowel. The dowel(s) may have been nailed to the strainers before the canvas was folded back over them.

9 Morris 2007, p. 218. The creases were not from an actual stretching.

10 Seen between the covering layers of gray, some of the blue on the stretched panels was unmixed blue, some mixed with white, and some a thinner blue wash. The blue also penetrated through to the reverse on the top portion of the stretched panels.

11 It is not possible to determine how far under the top canvas this red might extend.

12 See Johns's remark in his interview with Nan Rosenthal in this volume: "I think I began that picture by painting those rectangles bright primaries but, during the process, decided that eliminating the color would enhance the perception that they were embedded objects" (p. 203).

13 In an exchange with Douglas Druick (July 11, 2007), Johns stated that he had not used stencils on *Tennyson*, a claim borne out by the fact that each N in the title is a slightly different size.

14 The relatively fine canvas is 20 vertical threads/cm × 23–24 horizontal threads/cm.

15 Iron oxide was identified by polarized light microscopy and confirmed with Fourier Transform Infrared Spectroscopy (FTIR); Gwenäelle Gautier, Anikó Bezúr, and Inge Fiedler, analytical report, Jan. 11, 2007.

16 The horizontal centerline was also measured and marked on the reverse. Heat was also used to lightly adhere the wax-infused patches to the underlying canvas.

17 The appearance of the reverse of *Near the Lagoon* with the myriad starlike knots suggests constellations in space—a topic visited in the early Catenary paintings.

18 Geelhaar 1980a, p. 55, in *Writings* 1996, p. 196.

19 Manet's fragments are painted primarily in grays, against a blue sky and a yellow and gray foreground, and the bare canvas on which they are mounted, standing in for the missing sections, appears as yellow. Where one would expect to find red in Manet's painting is the one major fragment that is still missing: the section on the left where Maximilian stood with his general, the target who, with his head and arms thrown back, has just been shot. Johns's red underlayer could stand in for this more visceral part of the scene that had been excised.

20 A similar link was made early on by Johns when he noted: "encaustic (flesh?)"; Sketchbook A, p. 48, 1964, in *Writings* 1996, pp. 33, 56.

21 It appears he may also have painted one small "blank" space of Degas's reconstruction blue before changing it to yellow: the bottom right corner, seen to bleed through to the reverse. This small fragment, missing from the top of Manet's painting, is only a thin section of blue sky.

22 The measured marks below the center of the curves appear to have been reinforced after the curves were made, but were probably measured and marked with a vertical and horizontal line previously. He also marked the cords' positions with pencil lines visible at the top.

23 Rothkopf 2005, pp. 9–10.

24 Klüver 1963, in *Writings* 1996, p. 85.

25 Sylvester 1965, in *Writings* 1996, p. 115.

26 Davvetas 1984, p. 12, in *Writings* 1996, p. 218.

27 Such a detailed spatial landscape created by melting and manipulating the surface is particularly evident at the top of the painting where the paint is particularly thick.

28 Young 1969, p. 51, in *Writings* 1996, p. 129.

29 Many of the gray mixtures containing iron oxide pigments also contained small amounts of calcium carbonate and silicates. Silicates likely indicate the iron oxide red and yellow were natural rather than synthetic inorganic pigments. The presence of calcium carbonate may be a contaminant or filler; the small amount present in most gray samples does not indicate it was an intentional additive. Pigments were identified by polarized light microscopy and FTIR. Analytical report prepared by Gwenäelle Gautier, Anikó Bezúr, and Inge Fiedler, Mar. 8, 2007.

30 Francis 1984, pp. 113–14.

31 Gail Stavitsky, *Waxing Poetic: Encaustic Art in America during the Twentieth Century*, exh. cat. (Montclair Art Museum, 1999), p. 23.

32 A total of five samples were analyzed with FTIR including samples from the blue border, yellow and red underpaint, various gray layers and the green surface drips. In all samples, the main component most closely matched a bleached beeswax from Kremer Pigmente in the reference library spectra. With FTIR, the concentration of additives such as damar or linseed oil would be approximately 5% or greater to be above the detection limit; it is therefore assumed if Johns added oil or resin as he had in the past it was in very small quantities. The green sample was the only sample where traces of a possible oil component were found, however further analysis would be needed to confirm its presence, and it is unclear whether it was an intentional additive or a contaminant. FTIR analysis by Gwenäelle Gautier, analytical report, Mar. 8, 2007.

33 Pigments identified by polarized light microscopy and FTIR. X-ray fluorescence was used to confirm the presence of cobalt in the green, which also detected nickel, titanium, zinc, iron, chrome (from viridian), and calcium. FTIR spectra for the cobalt-titanate green most closely resembled a cobalt-titanate green spinel. Samples of this pigment, called kelly green, and others used for comparative testing, were generously provided by Ferro Corporation; analysis and report by Gwenäelle Gautier, Anikó Bezúr, and Inge Fiedler, Mar. 8, 2007.

34 In addition, it seems that Johns may have imbedded string or slightly impressed the paint around the edges of the collage elements in order to enhance this effect, making them appear more like the frayed, upturned edges of the collage canvas in *Tennyson*.

35 He had used these long diagonal slash lines throughout the Catenary series. They may have had their genesis in *Spring* (1986; Robert and Jane Meyerhoff Collection, Phoenix, Maryland). A number of these indentations also occur in the lower layers of the painting. Mostly horizontal in nature, they closely resemble those on the collage canvas of *Tennyson* and can best be seen here in raking light throughout the center of the painting.

36 "Eventually I pushed the brushstrokes forward and made them the subject of the painting"; Sozanski 1988, p. 30, in *Writings* 1996, p. 225.

37 This appears to have been used as early as 1968 in *Screen Piece 3* (Private collection) and *Wall Piece* (Collection of the artist).

38 Johns has stated that he first used horizontal drips in *According to What* (1964; Private collection); Coplans 1972, p. 31, in *Writings* 1996, p. 140.

39 Johns's use of the ring began to make a regular appearance in the Crosshatch paintings such as *Corpse and Mirror II* (1974–75; Collection of the artist). It appears in several paintings in the Catenary series, always bridging edges.

40 The larger ring is the size of a Melitta coffee can and the smaller ring, an Illy coffee can.

41 Pohlen 1978, p. 22, in *Writings* 1996, pp. 172–73.

42 While the placement of many drips and flicks is somewhat random, Johns does appear at times to go back and reinforce them, widening or changing their color and strengthening their aesthetic presence.

43 Wallach 1977, p. 5, in *Writings* 1996, p. 155.

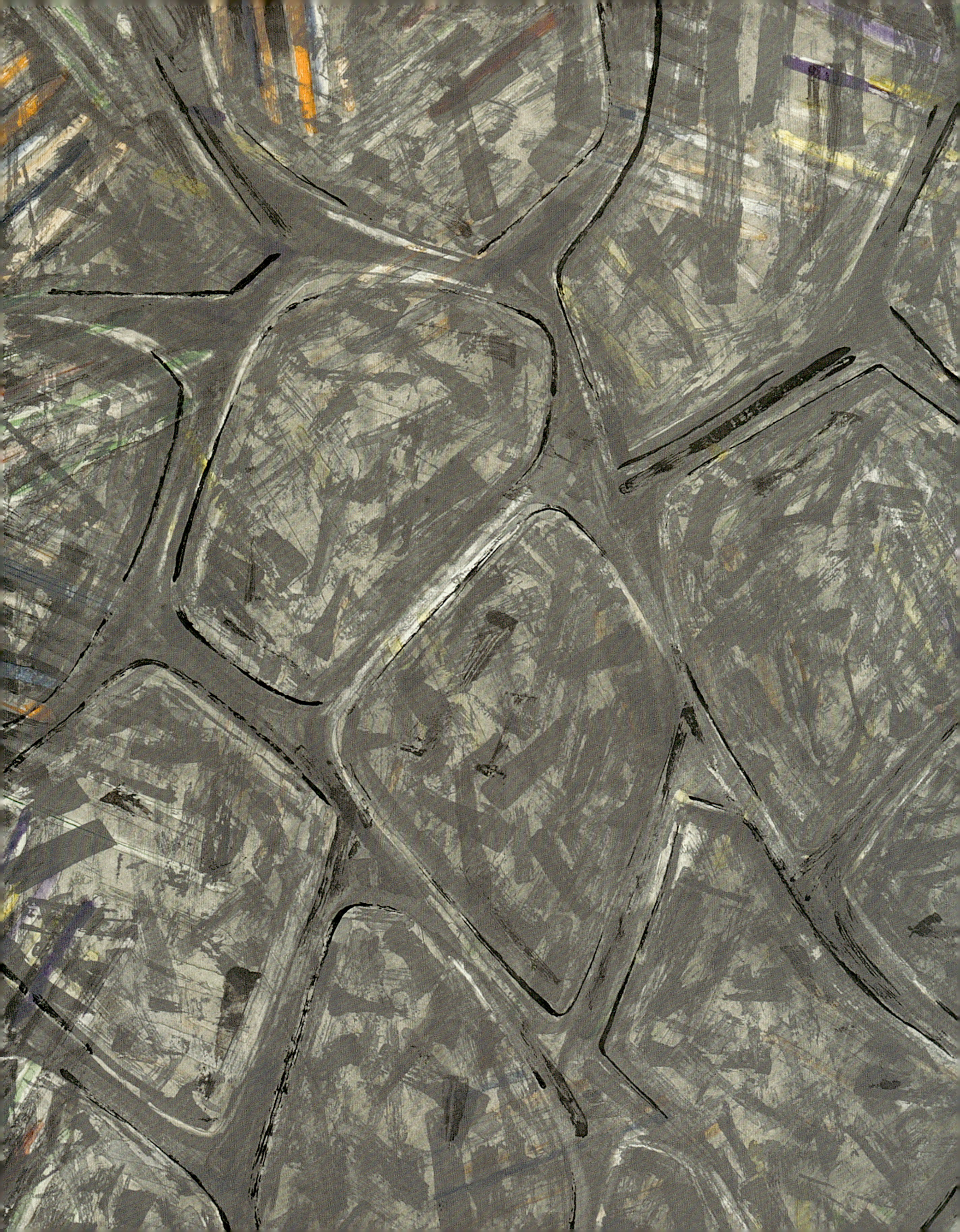

Plates

1. *False Start*, 1959
Oil on canvas
170.8 × 137.2 cm (67 ¼ × 54 in.)
Kenneth and Anne Griffin

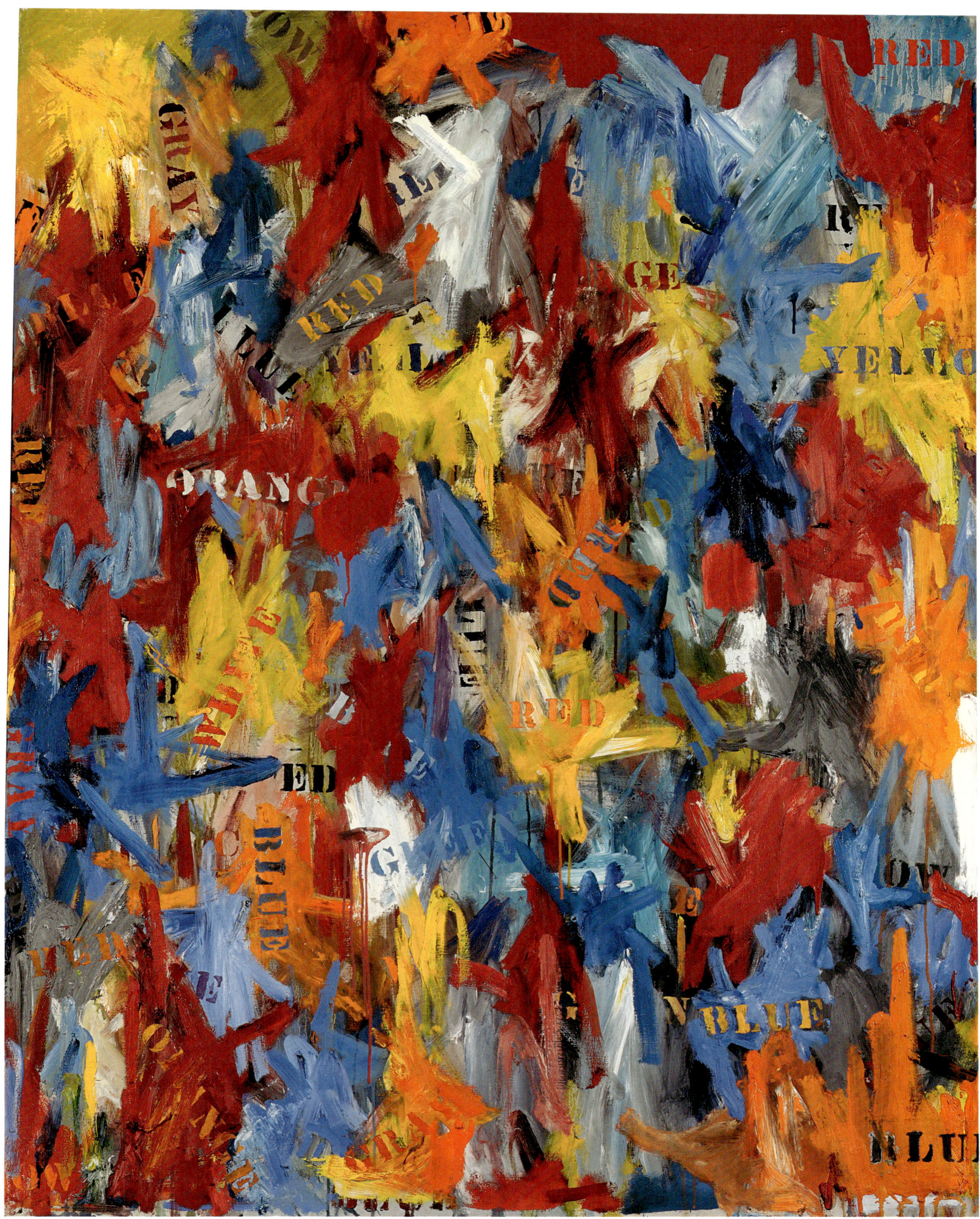
RED
GRAY
RED
YELLO
ORANG
RED
ED
BLUE
BLUE
BLU

2. *Jubilee*, 1959
Oil and fabric collage on canvas
152.4 × 111.8 cm (60 × 44 in.)
Private collection

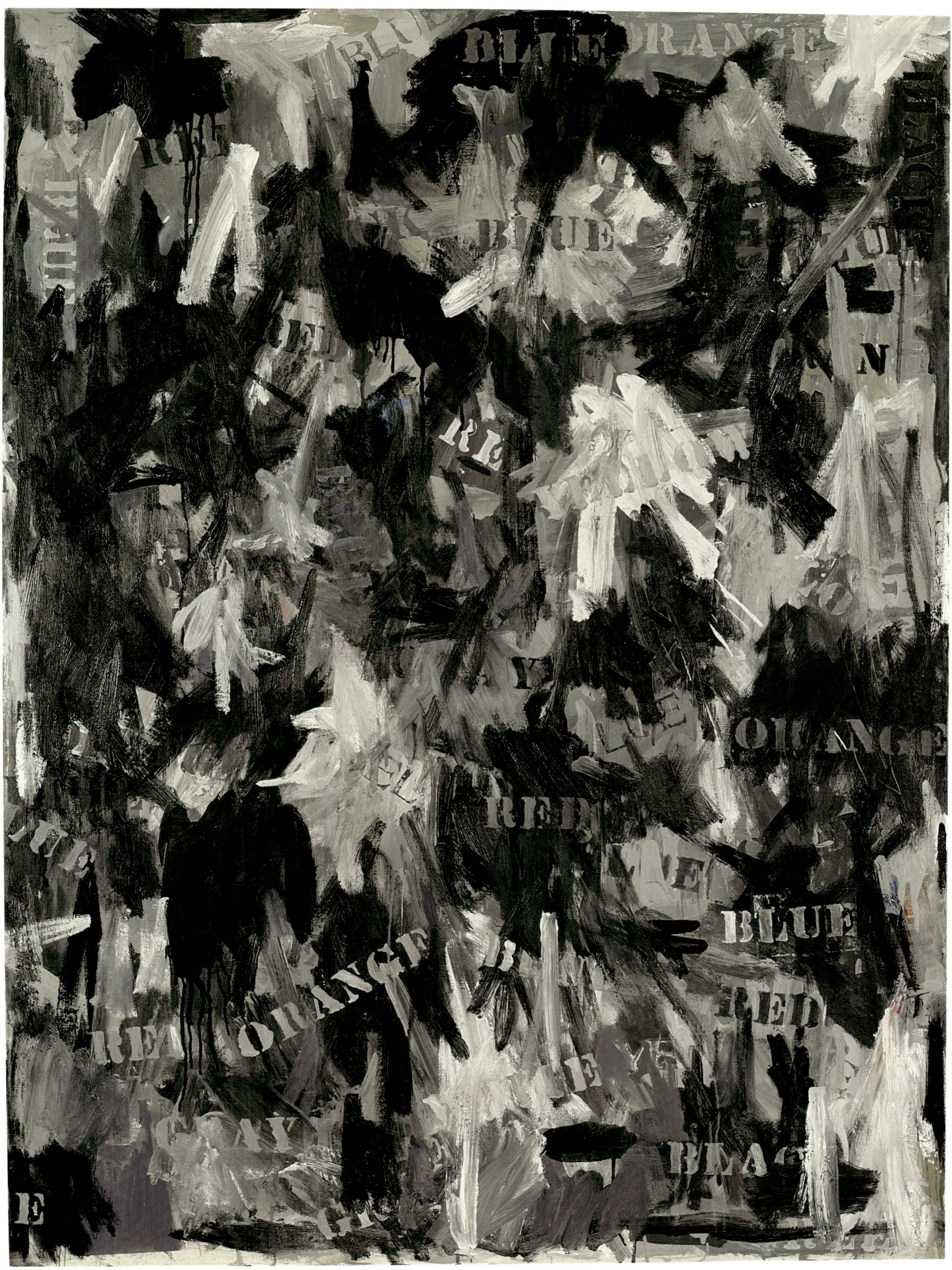
BLUE
ORANGE
BLUE
ORANGE
RED
BLUE
ORANGE
RED

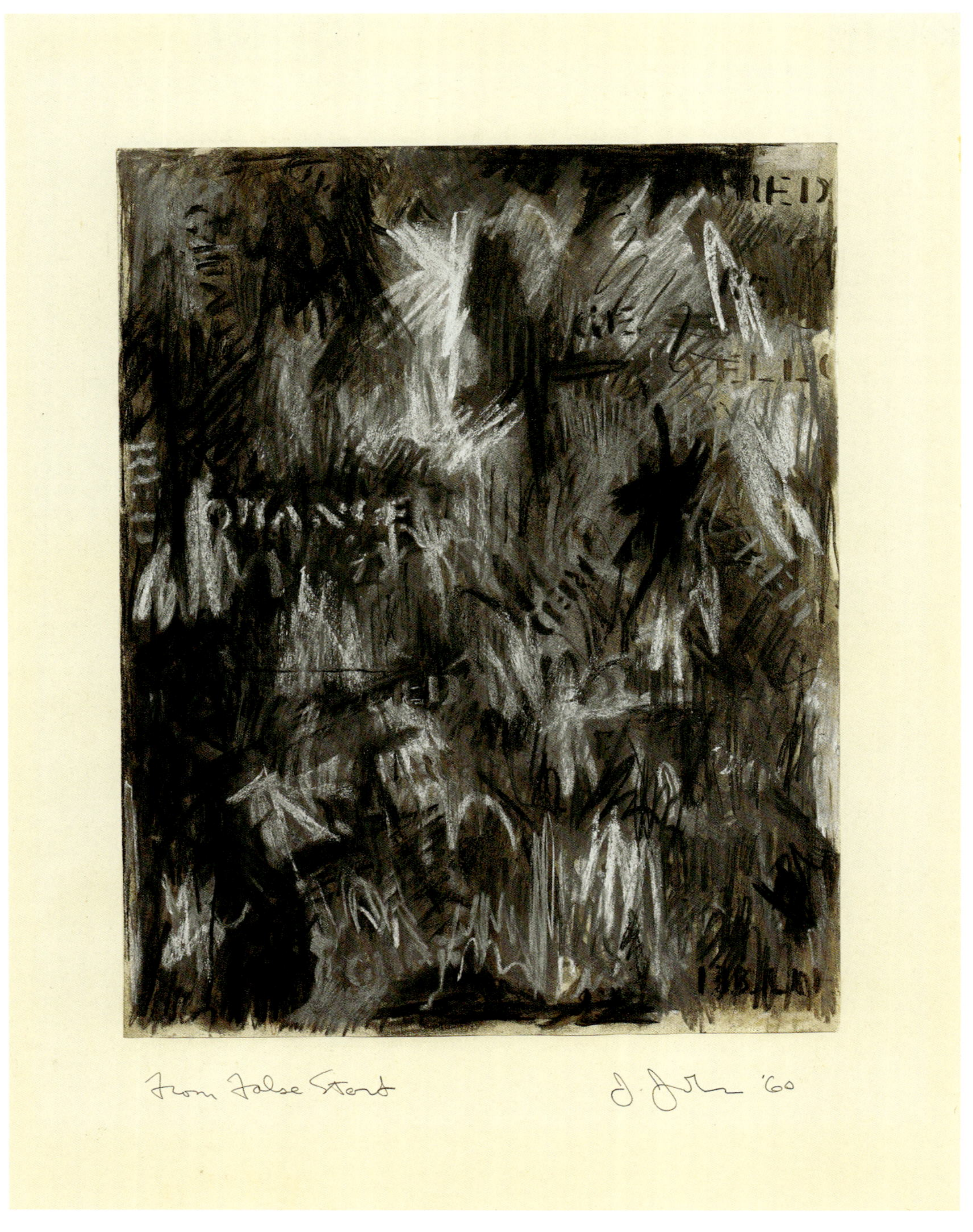

3. *From False Start*, 1960
Pastel with charcoal and powdered graphite on cream wove paper, tipped onto cream wove paper
image: 34.9 × 27.3 cm (13 ¾ × 10 ¾ in.)
secondary support: 41.3 × 33.5 cm (16 ¼ × 13 3⁄16 in.)
Collection of Barbara Bluhm-Kaul, Chicago

4. *False Start II*, 1962
ULAE, 1962
Lithograph from eleven stones on ivory wove paper (A. Milbourn & Co.)
image: 44.5 × 34.9 cm (17 ½ × 13 ¾ in.)
sheet: 77.5 × 55.9 cm (30 ½ × 22 in.)
ULAE/Johns cat. raisonné 10
The Art Institute of Chicago, ULAE Collection acquired through a challenge grant of Mr. and Mrs. Thomas Dittmer; restricted gift of supporters of the Department of Prints and Drawings; Centennial Endowment; Margaret Fisher Endowment Fund, 1983.533

violet
red
blue
30/30 II

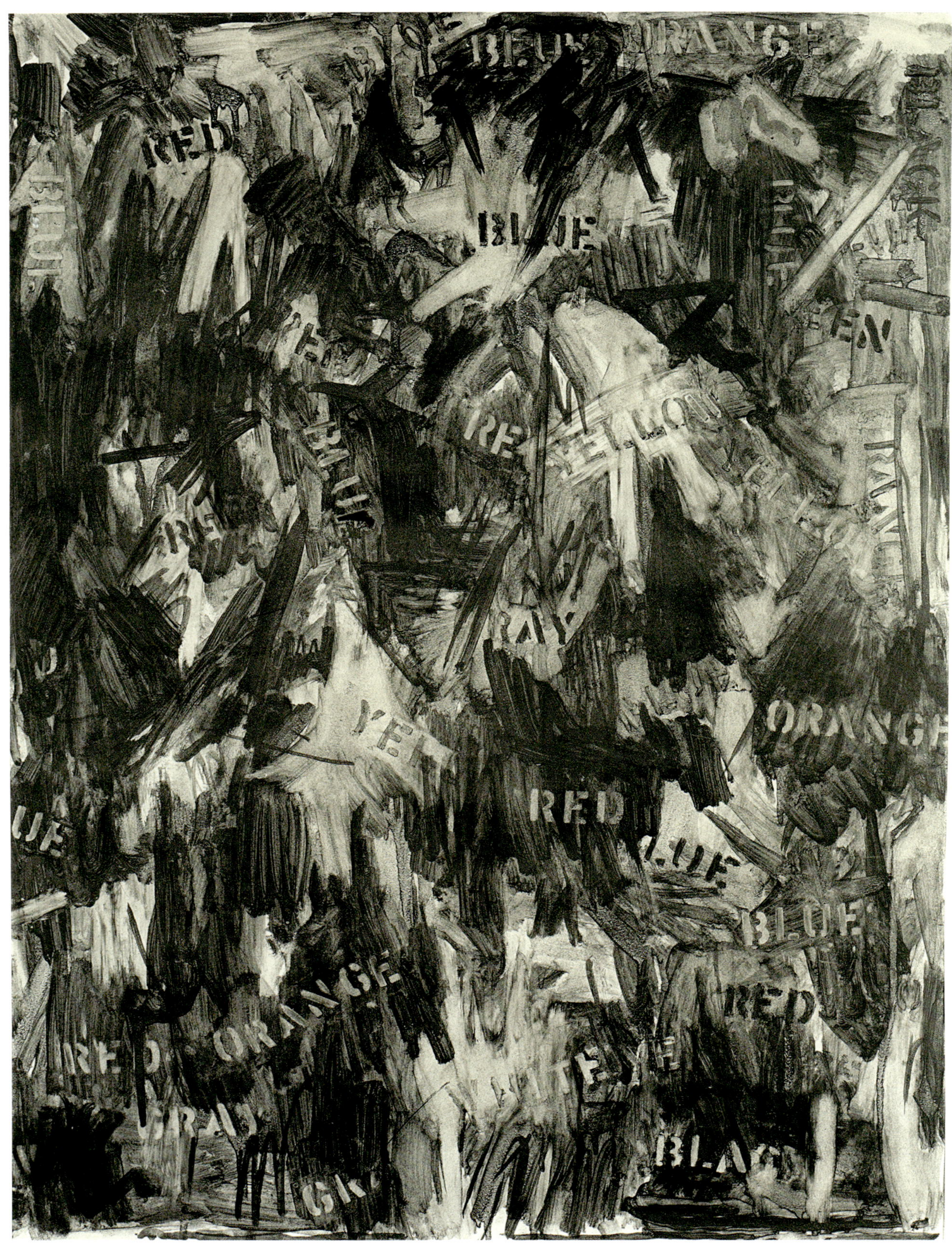

5. *Jubilee*, 1960
Graphite wash on ivory wove paper
79 × 63.5 cm (31 ⅛ × 25 in.)
The Museum of Modern Art, New York,
The Joan and Lester Avnet Collection, 1978

6. *Jubilee*, 1962 and 1994
Pastel over lithograph on ivory wove paper
61.9 × 50.5 cm (24 ⅜ × 19 ⅞ in.)
Collection of the artist

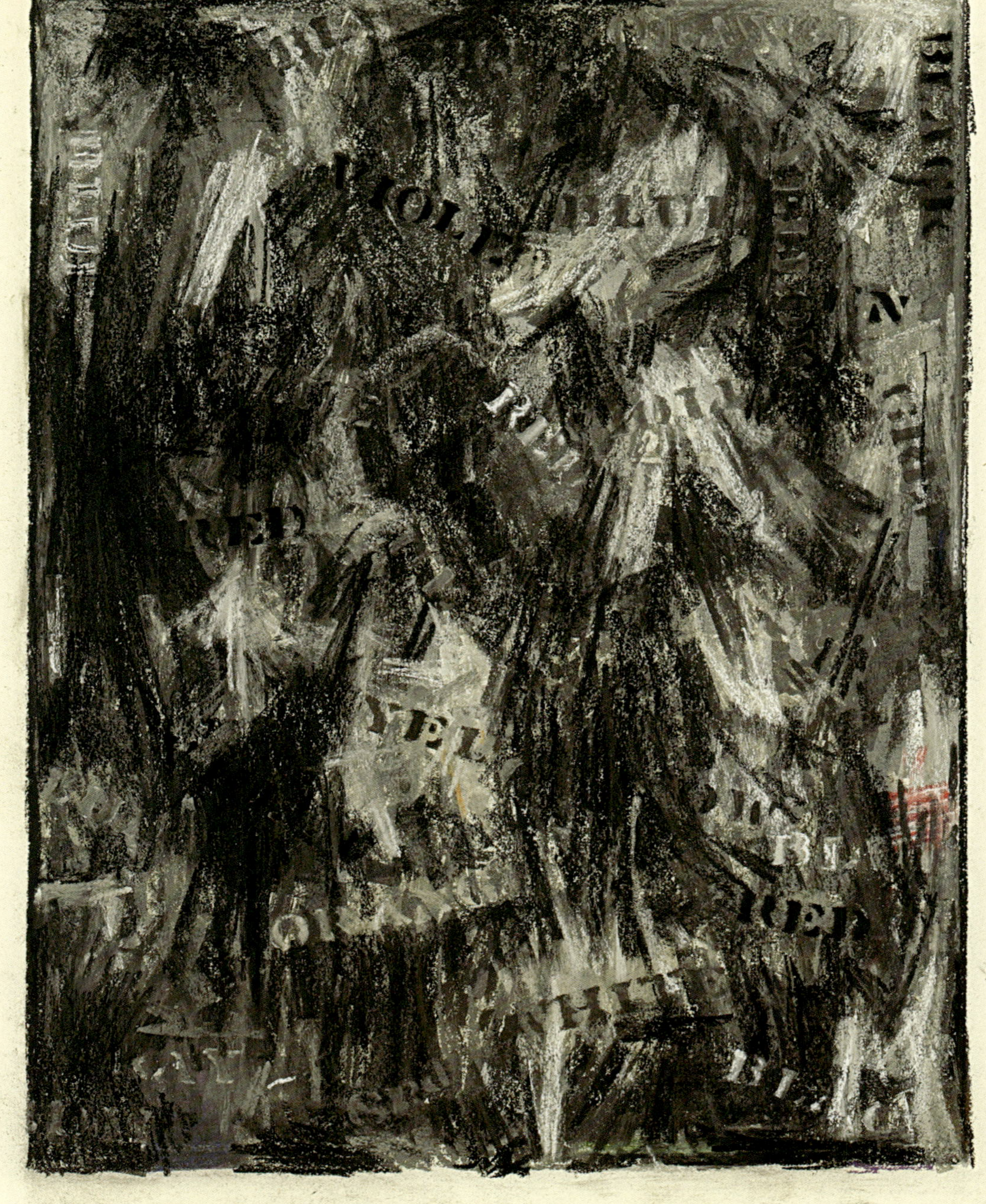
JUBILEE 1994 OVER FALSE START II 1962
1994

7. *Canvas*, 1956
Encaustic and collage on wood and canvas
76.2 × 63.5 cm (30 × 25 in.)
Collection of the artist

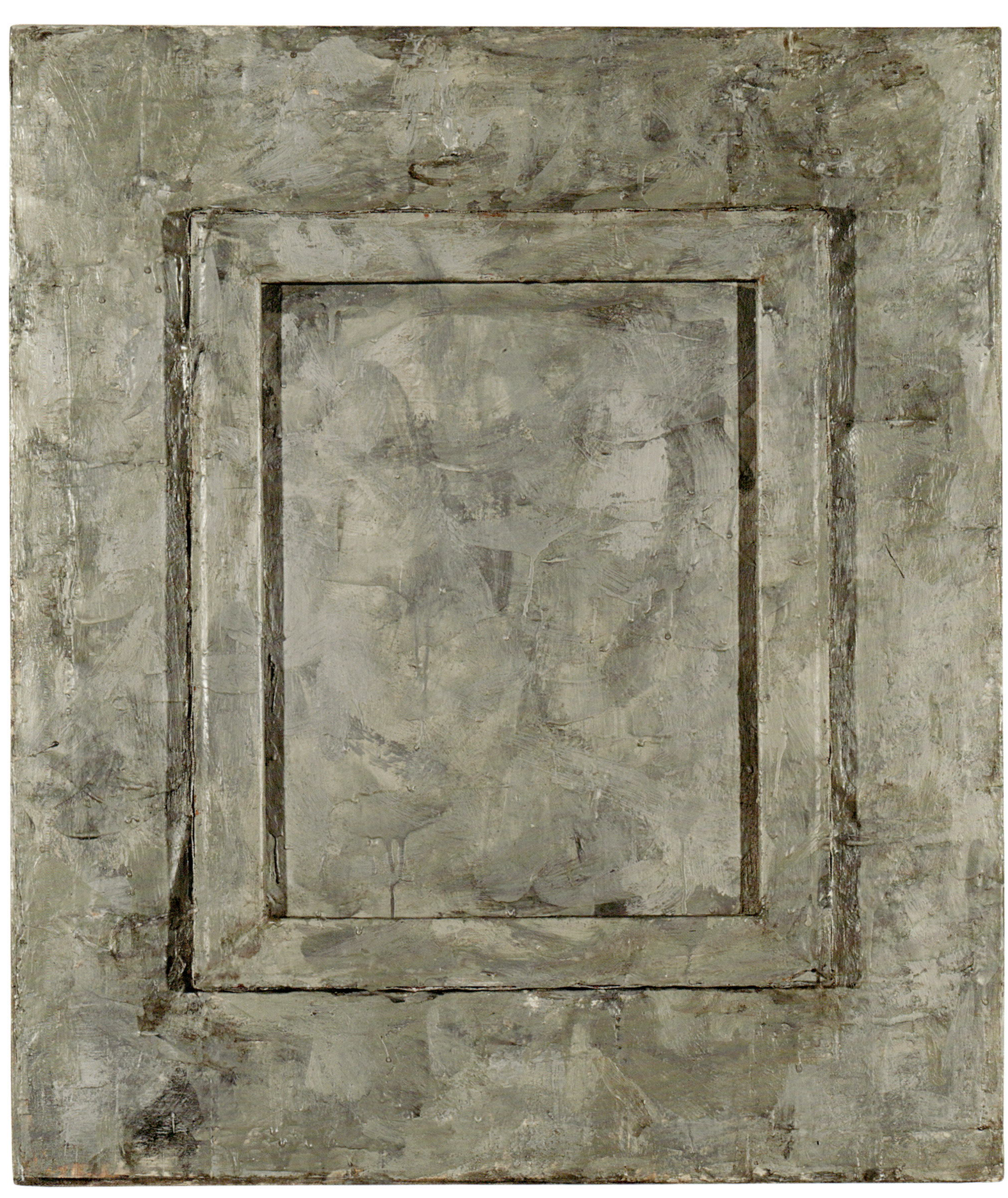

8. *Newspaper*, 1957
Encaustic and collage on canvas
68.6 × 91.4 cm (27 × 36 in.)
Private collection, New York

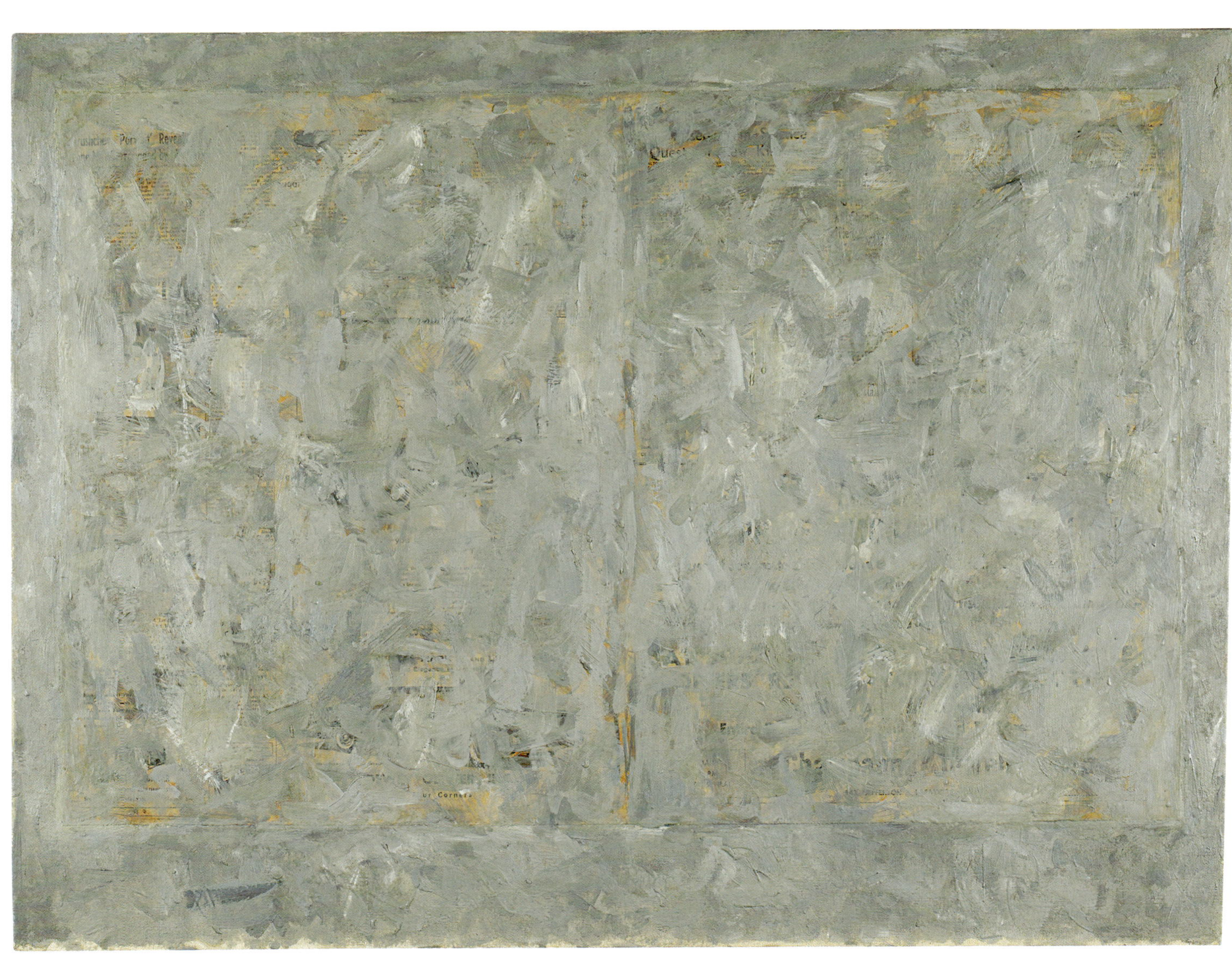

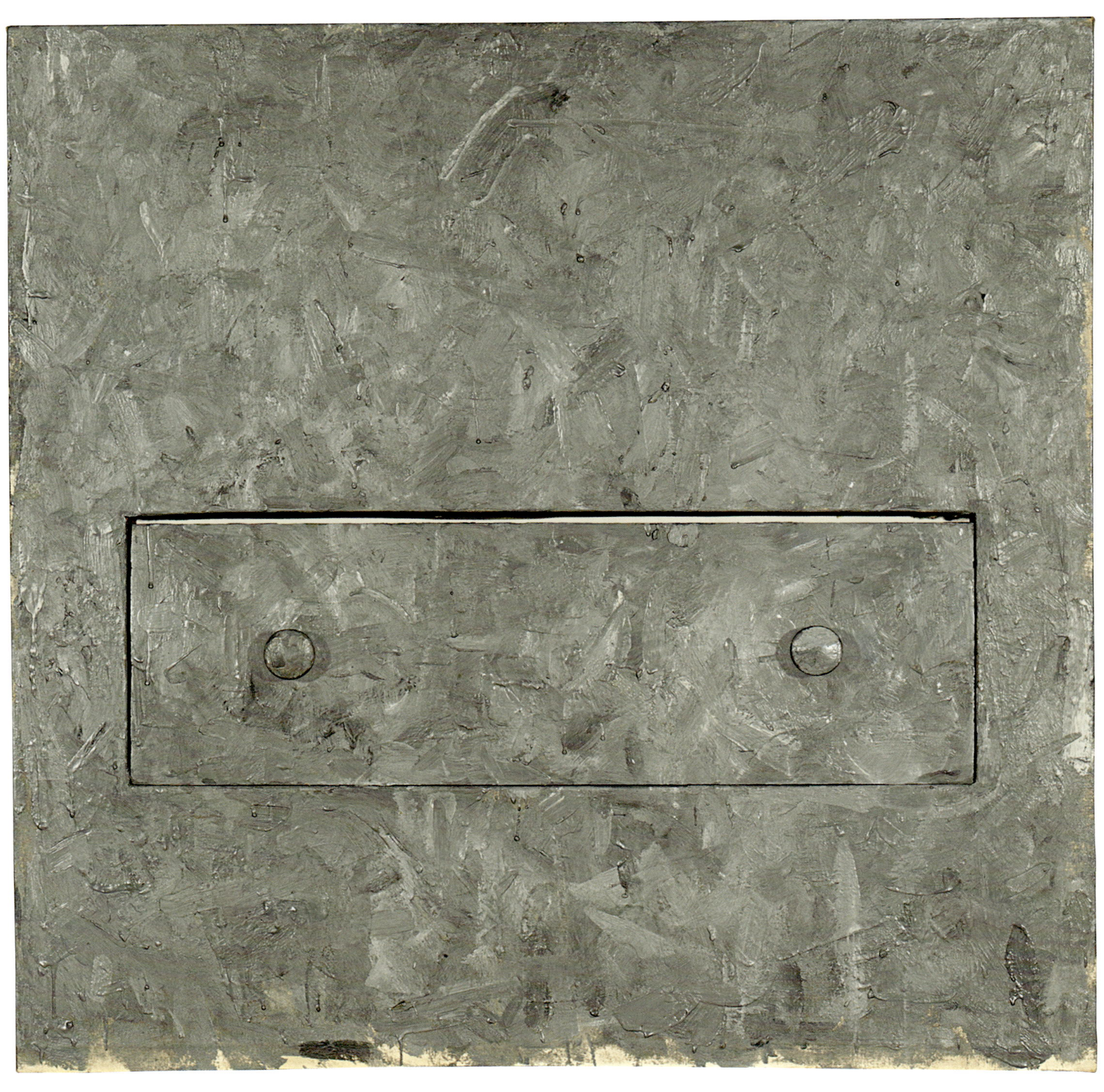

9. *Drawer*, 1957
Encaustic on canvas and wood with objects
78.1 × 78.1 cm (30 ¾ × 30 ¾ in.)
The Rose Art Museum, Brandeis University, Waltham, Massachusetts, Gevirtz-Mnuchin Purchase Fund, 1962.133

10. *Gray Rectangles*, 1957
Encaustic on canvas
152.4 × 152.4 cm (60 × 60 in.)
Collection of Barney A. Ebsworth

11. *The*, 1957
Encaustic on canvas
61 × 50.8 cm (24 × 20 in.)
Private collection

THE

12. *Tennyson*, 1958
Encaustic and collage on canvas
186.7 × 122.6 cm (73 ½ × 48 ¼ in.)
Des Moines Art Center, purchased with funds from the Coffin Fine Arts Trust; Nathan Emory Coffin Collection, 1971.4

TENNYSON

13. *Tennyson*, 1959
Pastel, charcoal, and graphite on ivory wove paper
image: 66 × 45.7 cm (26 × 18 in.)
sheet: 76.7 × 55.3 cm (30 3/16 × 21 3/4 in.)
Hirshhorn Museum and Sculpture Garden, Smithsonian Institution, Washington, D.C., gift of Joseph H. Hirshhorn, 1966

14. *Tennyson*, 1967
Graphite wash and pastel on cream Japanese paper
image: 74.9 × 52.1 cm (29 1/2 × 20 1/2 in.)
sheet: 92.7 × 62.2 cm (36 1/2 × 24 1/2 in.)
Collection of Kate Ganz

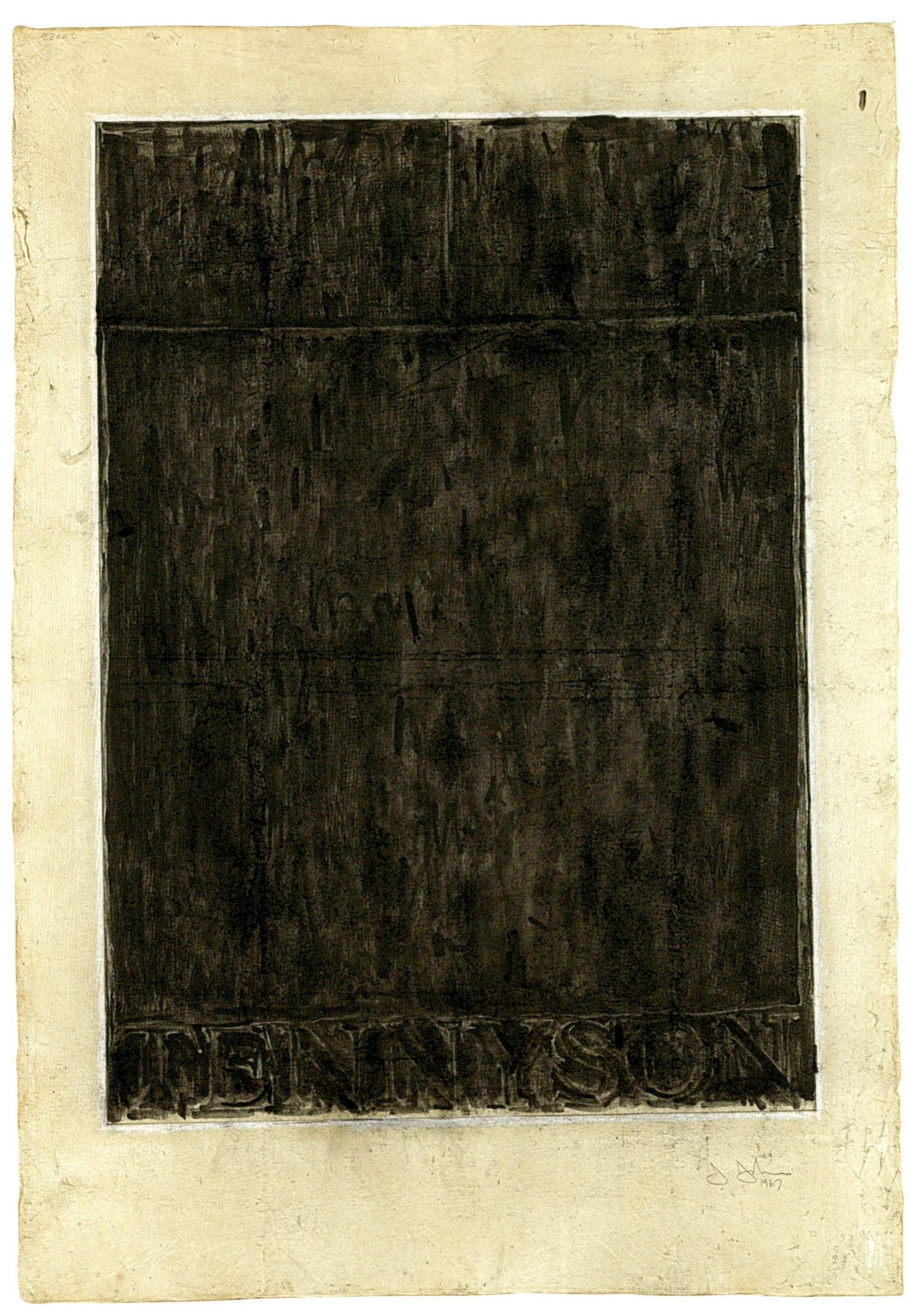
TENNYSON

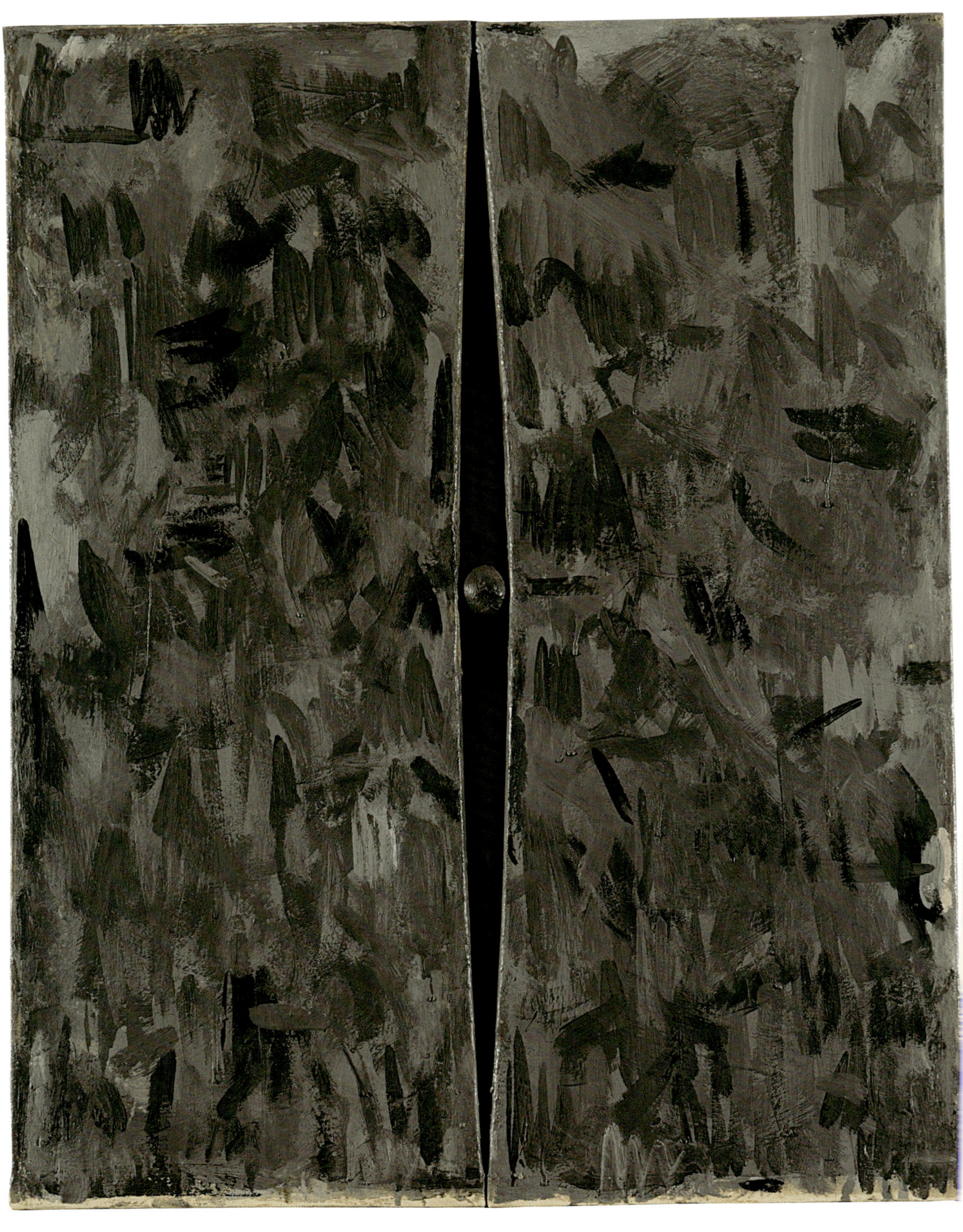

15. *Gray Painting with Ball*, 1958
Encaustic on canvas with objects
80 × 61.6 cm (31 ½ × 24 ¼ in.)
Collection of Michael Crichton

16. *Coat Hanger*, 1959
Encaustic on canvas with objects
70.5 × 54 cm (27 ¾ × 21 ¼ in.)
Private collection, Switzerland

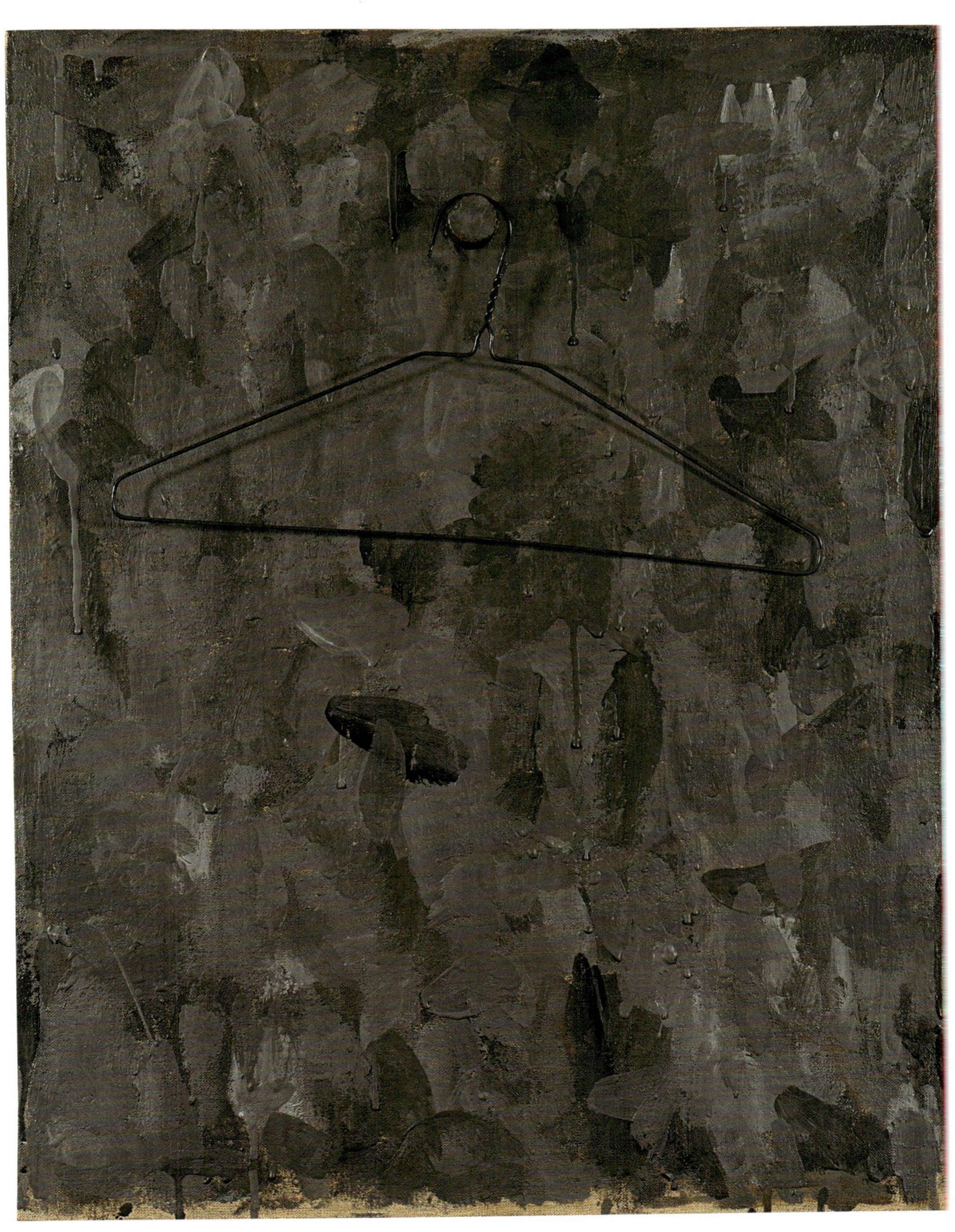

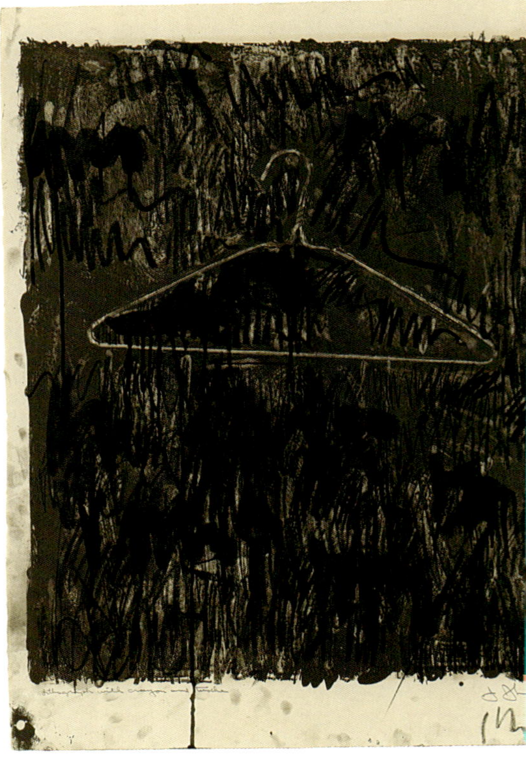

17. Coat Hanger I, 1960
ULAE, 1960
Lithograph from one stone on ivory wove paper (Copperplate Deluxe)
image: 65 × 53.2 cm (25 ⅝ × 21 in.)
sheet: 91.4 × 68.6 cm (36 × 27 in.)
ULAE/Johns cat. raisonné 2
The Art Institute of Chicago, ULAE Collection acquired through a challenge grant of Mr. and Mrs. Thomas Dittmer; restricted gift of supporters of the Department of Prints and Drawings; Centennial Endowment; Margaret Fisher Endowment Fund, 1982.933

18. *Coat Hanger II*, 1960
ULAE, 1960
Lithographic crayon and tusche over lithograph from one stone on buff wove paper; working proof
image: 66.6 × 55 cm (26 ¼ × 21 ⅝ in.)
sheet: 93 × 68.6 cm (36 ⅝ × 27 in.)
ULAE/Johns cat. raisonné 6
The Art Institute of Chicago, ULAE Collection acquired through a challenge grant of Mr. and Mrs. Thomas Dittmer; restricted gift of supporters of the Department of Prints and Drawings; Centennial Endowment; Margaret Fisher Endowment Fund, 1982.933b

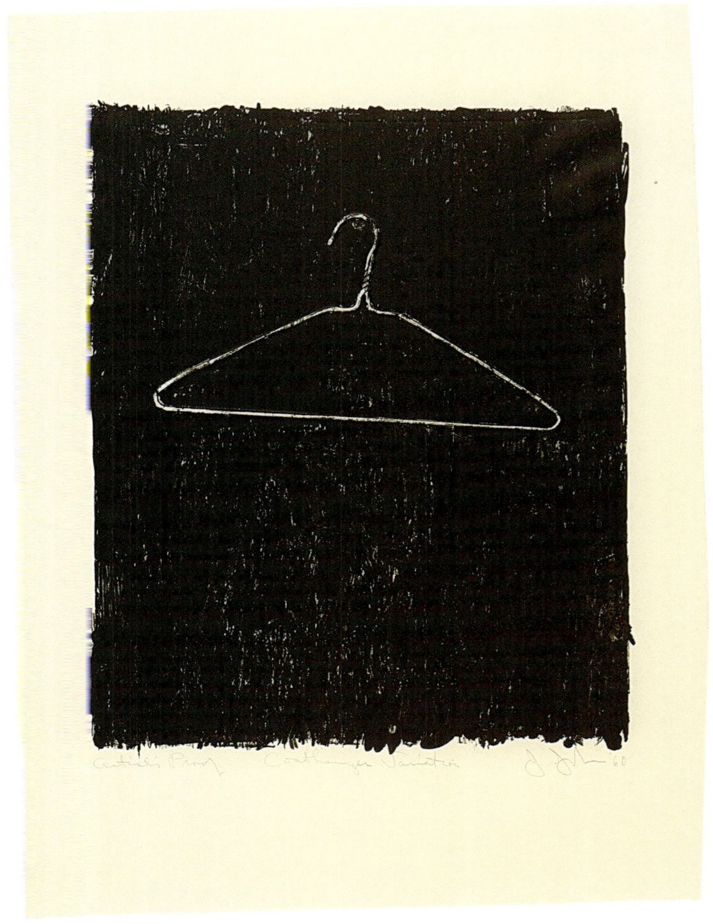

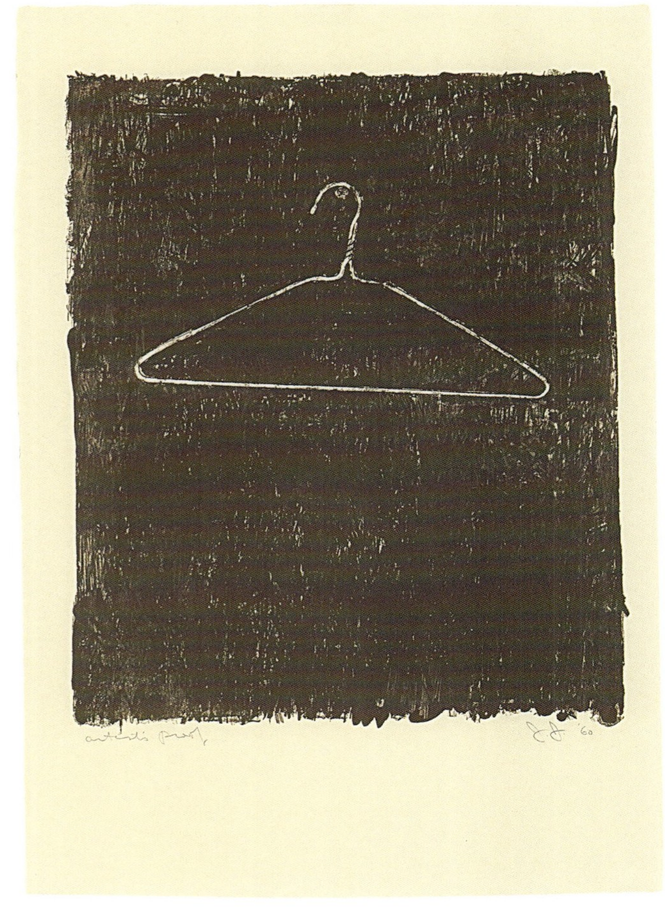

19. *Coat Hanger Variation,* 1960
ULAE, 1960
Lithograph from one stone with embossing on ivory wove paper; trial proof
image: 67 × 54.2 cm (26 3/8 × 21 3/8 in.)
sheet: 93 × 68.8 cm (37 × 27 in.)
ULAE/Johns cat. raisonné 6
The Art Institute of Chicago, ULAE Collection acquired through a challenge grant of Mr. and Mrs. Thomas Dittmer; restricted gift of supporters of the Department of Prints and Drawings; Centennial Endowment; Margaret Fisher Endowment Fund, 1982.933a

20. *Coat Hanger II,* 1960
ULAE, 1960
Lithograph from one stone on cream wove paper (wmk.: Japan)
image: 67 × 55 cm (26 3/8 × 21 5/8 in.)
sheet: 88.9 × 63.5 cm (35 × 25 in.)
ULAE/Johns cat. raisonné 6
The Art Institute of Chicago, ULAE Collection acquired through a challenge grant of Mr. and Mrs. Thomas Dittmer; restricted gift of supporters of the Department of Prints and Drawings; Centennial Endowment; Margaret Fisher Endowment Fund, 1982.934

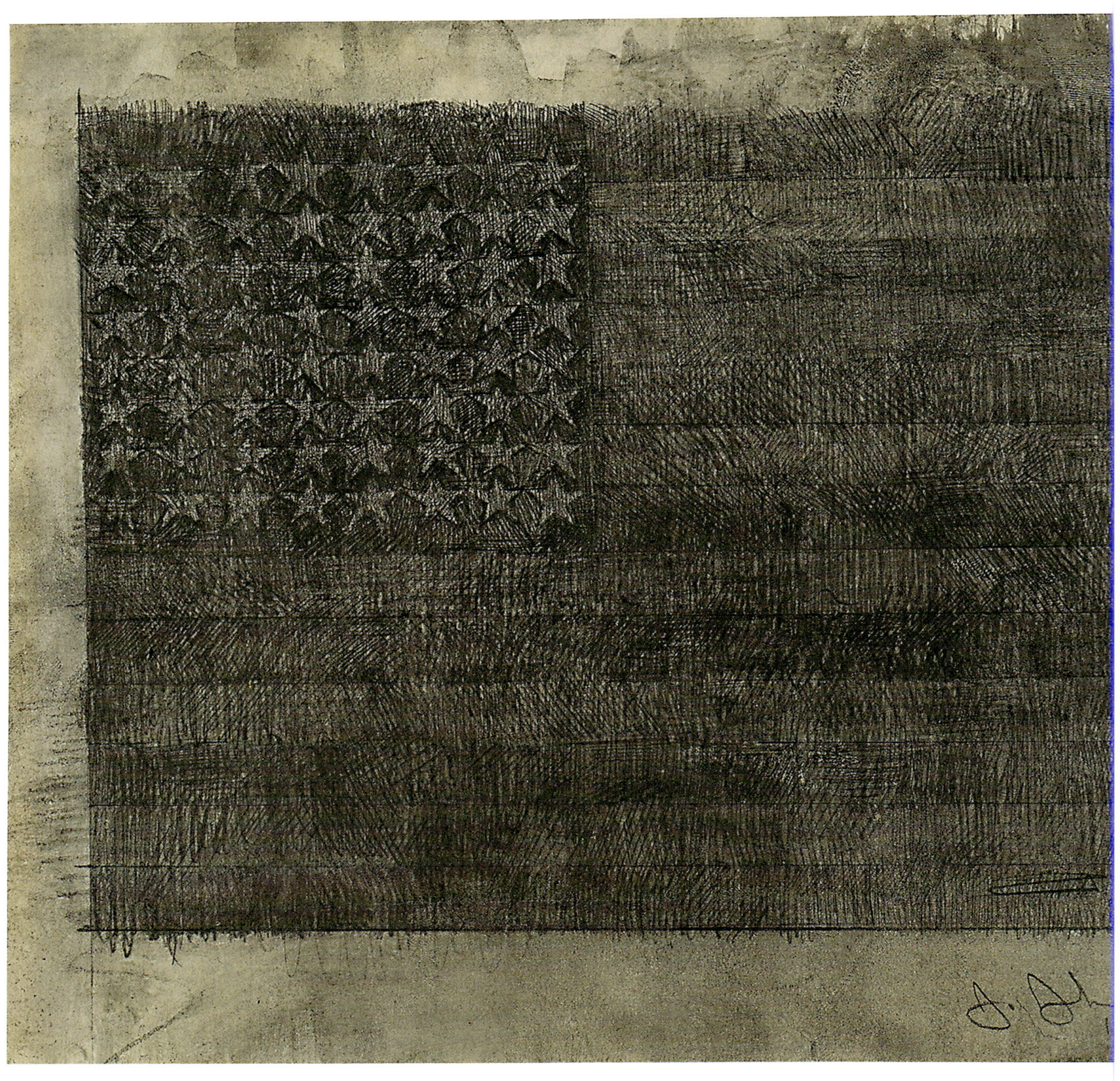

21. *Flag*, 1955
Graphite and graphite wash on cream wove tracing paper, prepared with a white ground
image: 21.9 × 25.7 cm (8 5⁄8 × 10 1⁄8 in.)
sheet: 21.6 × 25.7 cm (8 1⁄2 × 10 1⁄8 in.)
The Museum of Modern Art, New York, gift of Edgar Kaufmann, Jr. (by exchange) and purchase, 2004

22. *Flag*, 1958
Graphite, carbon pencil, and graphite wash on cream wove tracing paper
image: 18.4 × 26.4 cm (7 1⁄4 × 10 3⁄8 in.)
sheet: 22.5 × 30.5 cm (8 7⁄8 × 12 in.)
Collection of Barbara Bertozzi Castelli

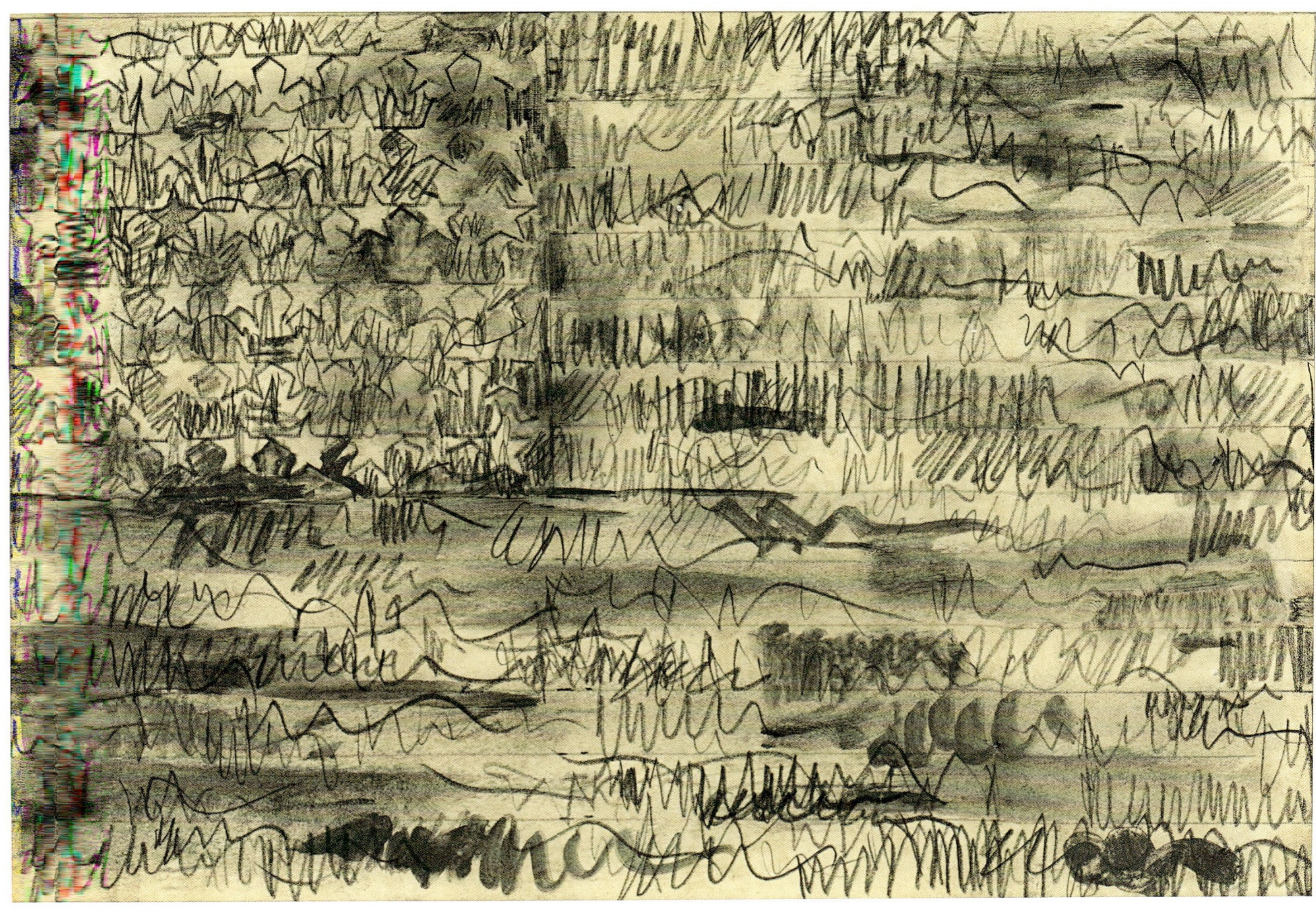

23. *Gray Flag*, 1957
Encaustic on canvas
66 × 96.5 cm (26 × 38 in.)
Ohara Museum of Art

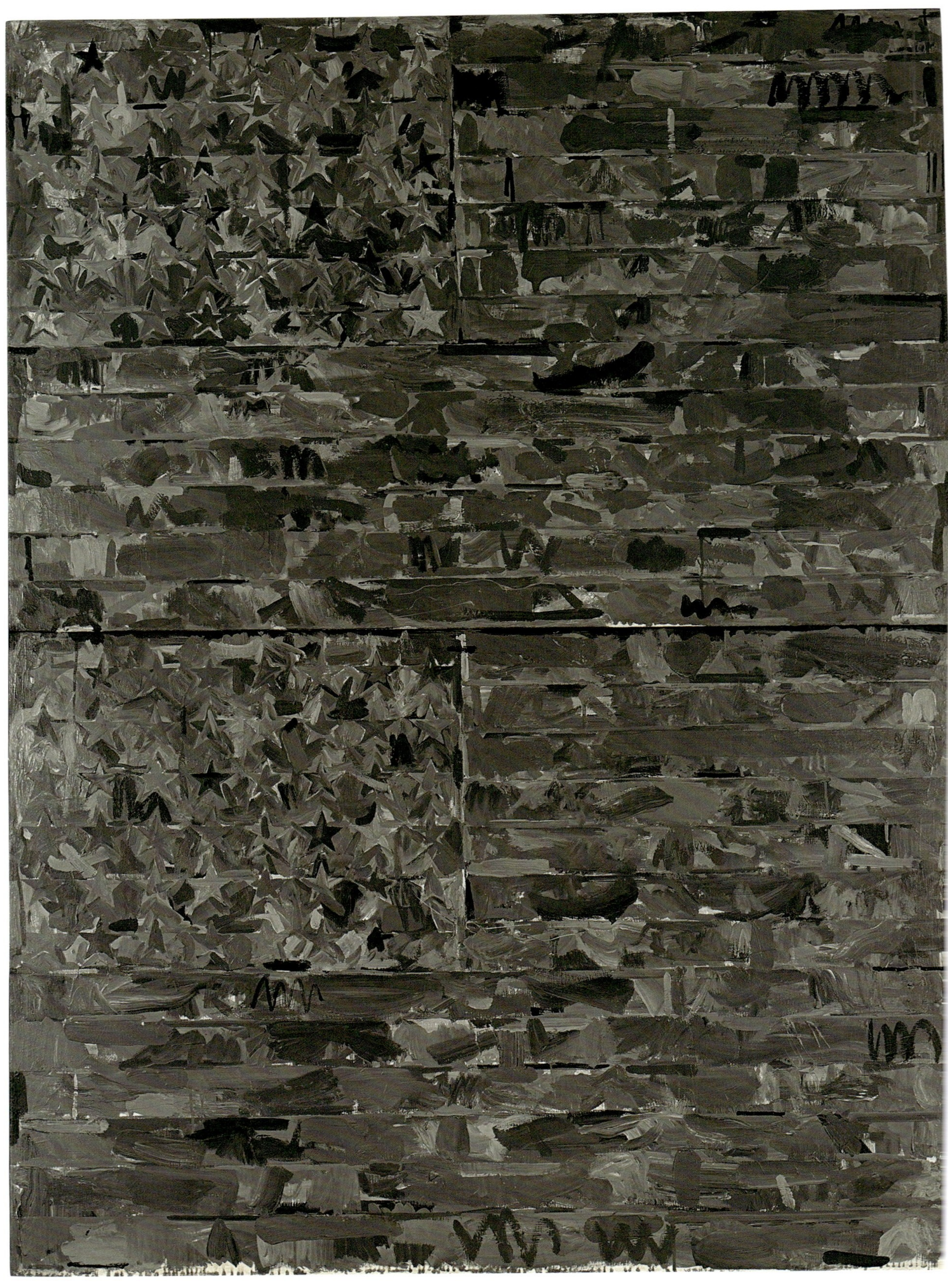

24. *Two Flags*, 1959
Acrylic on canvas
200 × 145 cm (79 ¼ × 58 ¼ in.)
Museum Moderner Kunst Stiftung Ludwig, Vienna, on loan from the Ludwig Collection, Aachen

25. *Two Flags*, 1960
Graphite wash on ivory wove paper
sheet: 74.9 × 55.3 cm (29 ½ × 21 ¾ in.)
Collection of the artist

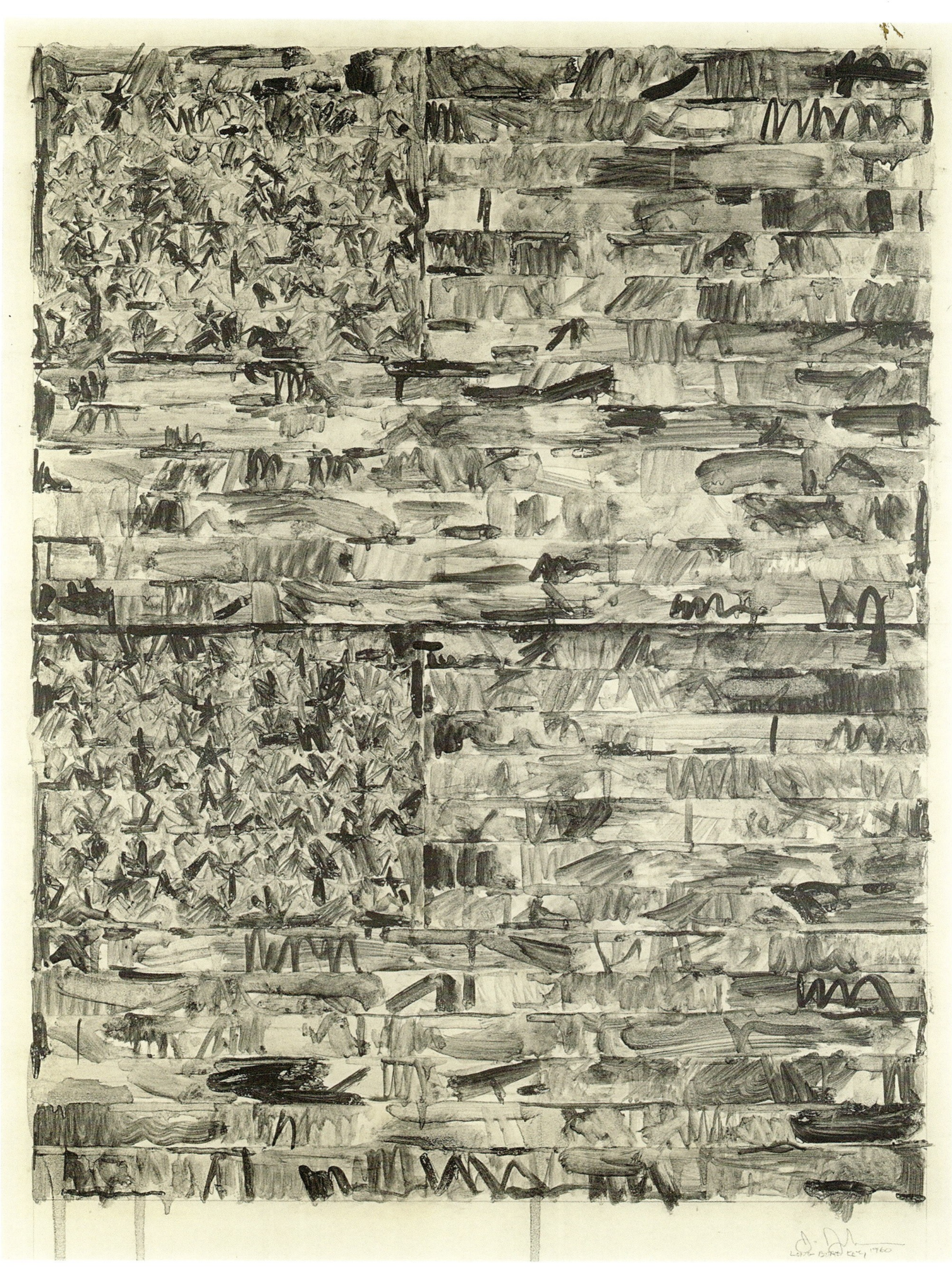

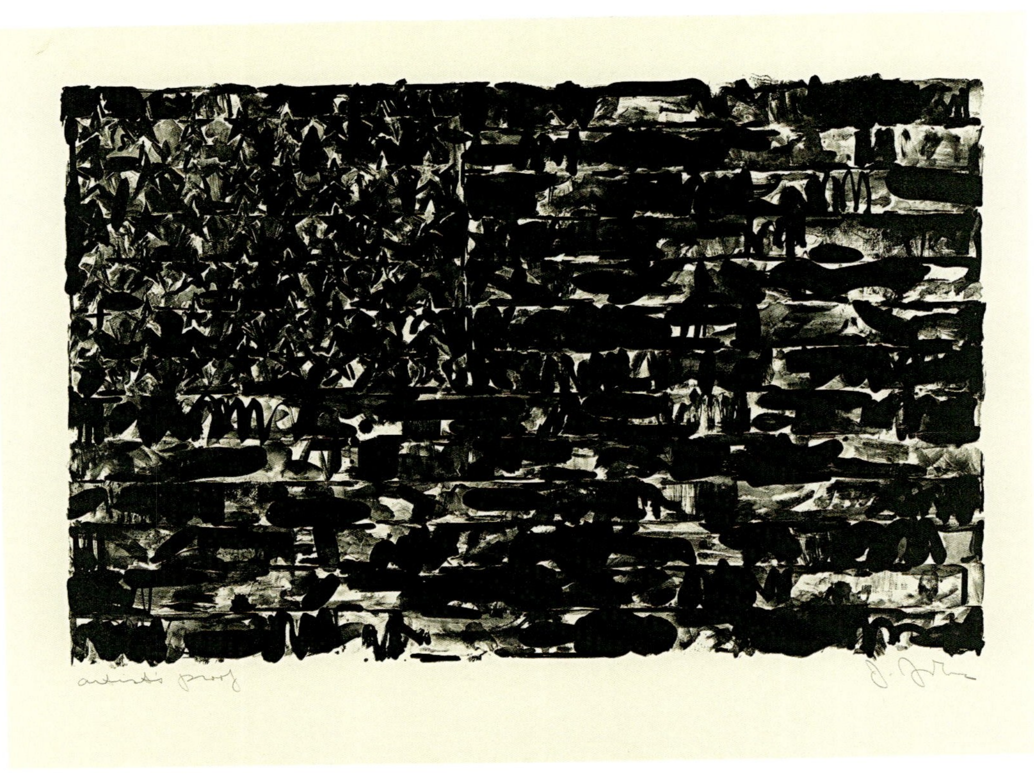

27. *Flag II*, 1960
ULAE, 1960
Lithograph from one stone on tan wove paper (Kraft)
image: 44.5 × 68.5 cm (17 × 27 in.)
sheet: 60 × 81.6 cm (24 × 32 in.)
ULAE/Johns cat. raisonné 5
The Art Institute of Chicago, ULAE Collection acquired through a challenge grant of Mr. and Mrs. Thomas Dittmer; restricted gift of supporters of the Department of Prints and Drawings; Centennial Endowment; Margaret Fisher Endowment Fund, 1982.936

26. *Flag I*, 1960
ULAE, 1960
Lithograph from one stone on ivory wove paper (Arches)
image: 44.5 × 67.5 cm (17 × 27 in.)
sheet: 56.7 × 76 cm (22 × 30 in.)
ULAE/Johns cat. raisonné 4
The Art Institute of Chicago, ULAE Collection acquired through a challenge grant of Mr. and Mrs. Thomas Dittmer; restricted gift of supporters of the Department of Prints and Drawings; Centennial Endowment; Margaret Fisher Endowment Fund, 1982.935

28. *Flag III*, 1960
ULAE, 1960
Lithograph from one stone on ivory wove paper (Arches)
image: 44.5 × 68.5 cm (17 × 27 in.)
sheet: 57.2 × 76.5 cm (23 × 30 in.)
ULAE/Johns cat. raisonné 7
The Art Institute of Chicago, ULAE Collection acquired through a challenge grant of Mr. and Mrs. Thomas Dittmer; restricted gift of supporters of the Department of Prints and Drawings; Centennial Endowment; Margaret Fisher Endowment Fund, 1982.937

29. *Flag*, 1971
Encaustic and collage on canvas
66 × 43.8 cm (26 × 17 ¼ in.)
Private collection

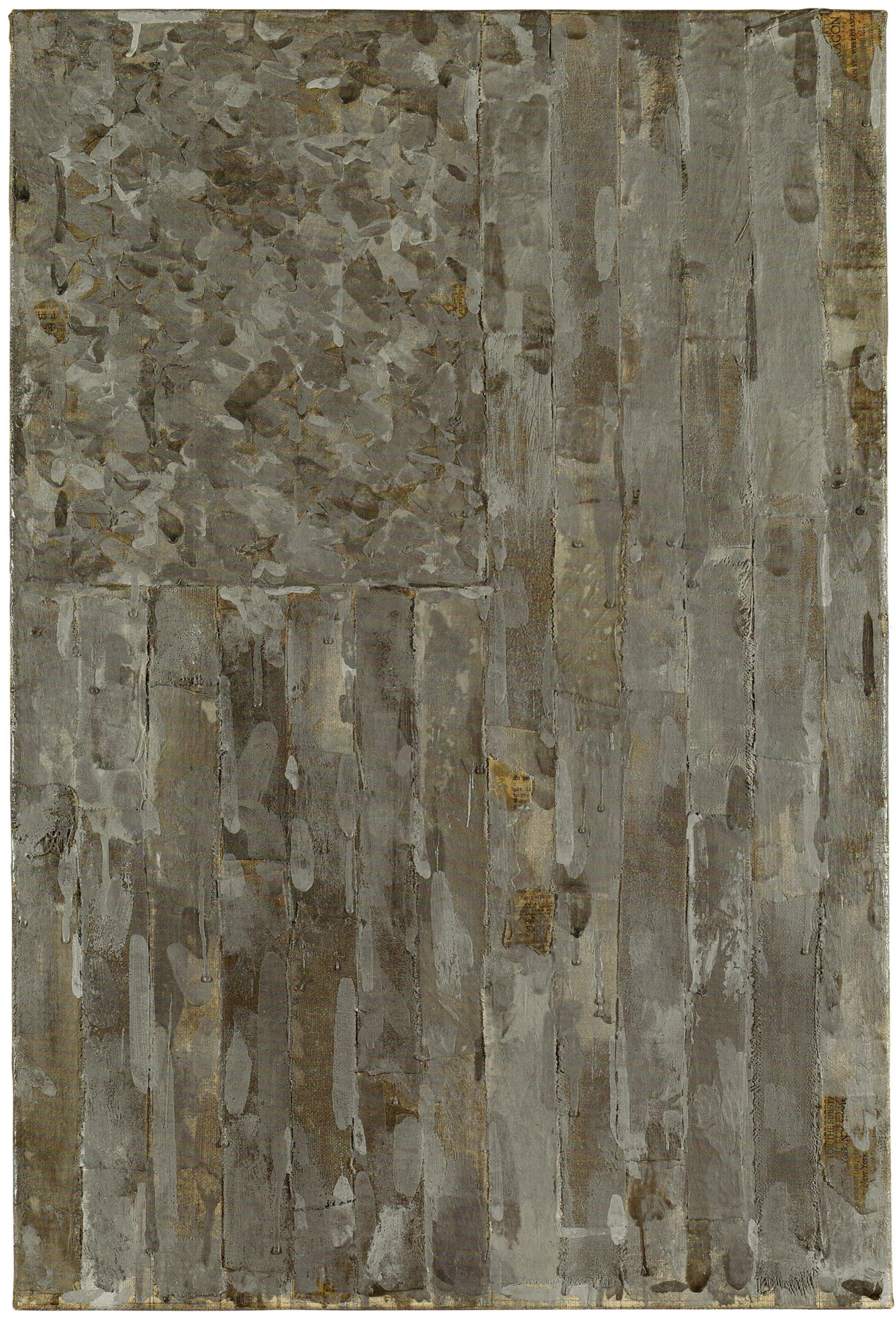

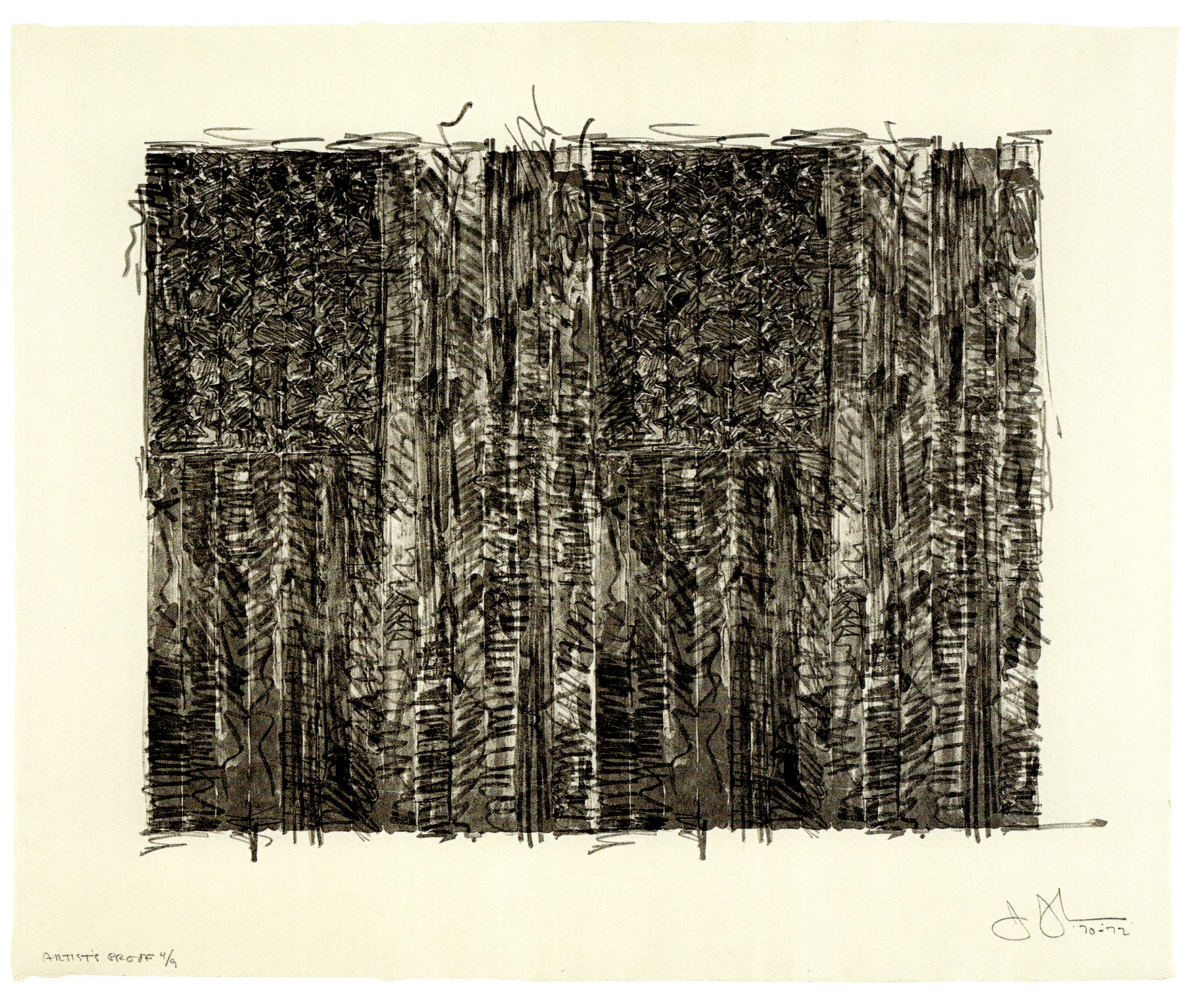

30. *Two Flags*, 1970–72
ULAE, 1972
Lithograph from two stones and three aluminum plates on cream Japanese paper (Hanga)
image: 55 × 68.3 cm (21 5/8 × 26 7/8 in.)
sheet: 69.5 × 82 cm (27 3/8 × 32 1/4 in.)
ULAE/Johns cat. raisonné 120
The Art Institute of Chicago, ULAE Collection acquired through a challenge grant of Mr. and Mrs. Thomas Dittmer; restricted gift of supporters of the Department of Prints and Drawings; Centennial Endowment; Margaret Fisher Endowment Fund, 1982.978

31. *Flags II*, 1973
Simca Print Artists, Inc., 1973
Screenprint from thirty screens on white wove paper (J. B. Green)
image: 64.8 × 83.8 cm (25 1/2 × 33 in.)
sheet: 69.2 × 89.5 cm (27 1/4 × 35 1/4 in.)
ULAE/Johns cat. raisonné 129
Walker Art Center, Minneapolis, gift of Judy and Kenneth Dayton, 1988

32. *Flag*, 1972 and 1994
Carborundum wash over lithograph on ivory wove paper
sheet: 43.5 × 59.7 cm (17 ⅛ × 23 ½ in.)
Collection of the artist

33. *Two Flags*, 1985
Ink on plastic
image: 53.3 × 41.9 cm (21 × 16 ½ in.)
sheet: 58.4 × 45.7 cm (23 × 18 in.)
Whitney Museum of American Art, New York, gift of the American Contemporary Art Foundation, Inc., Leonard A. Lauder, President, 2002.240

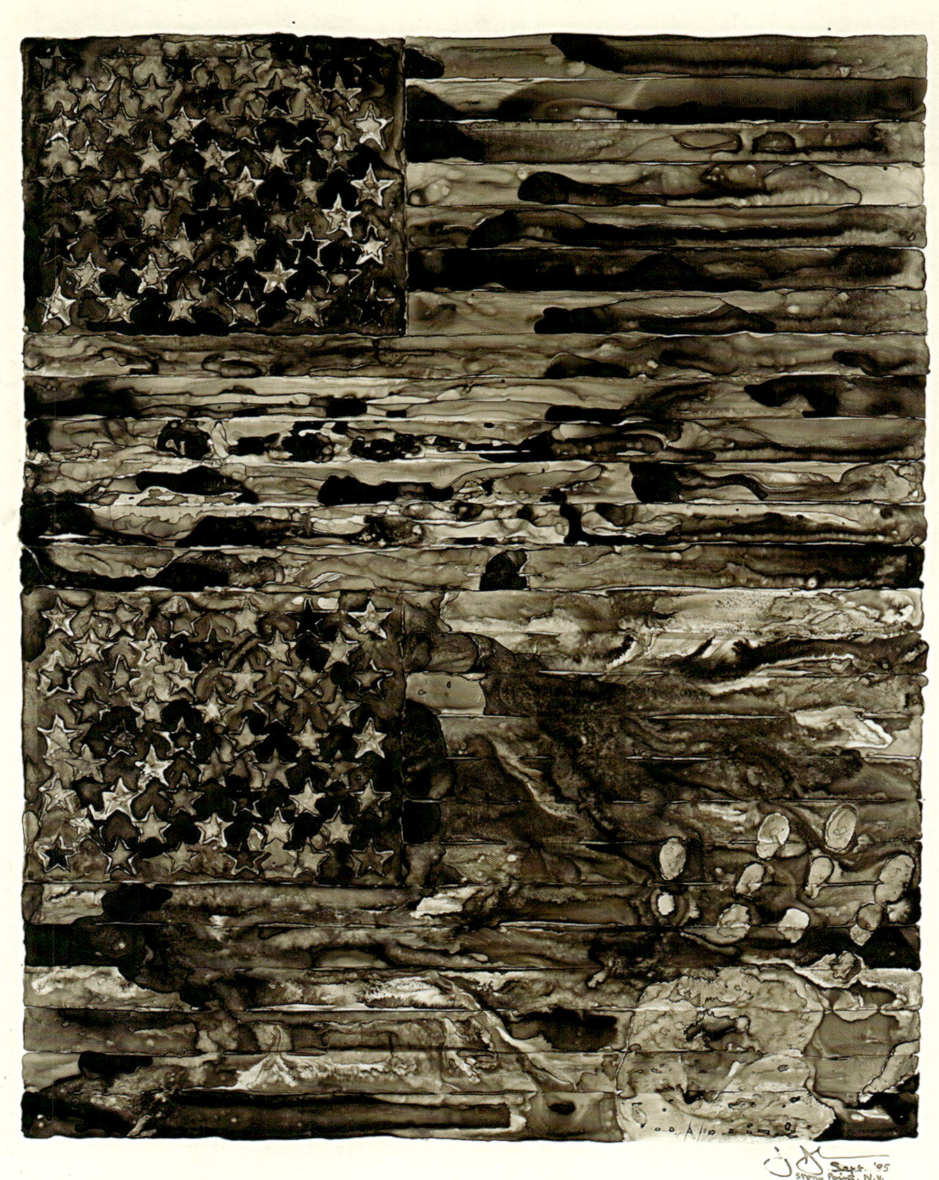

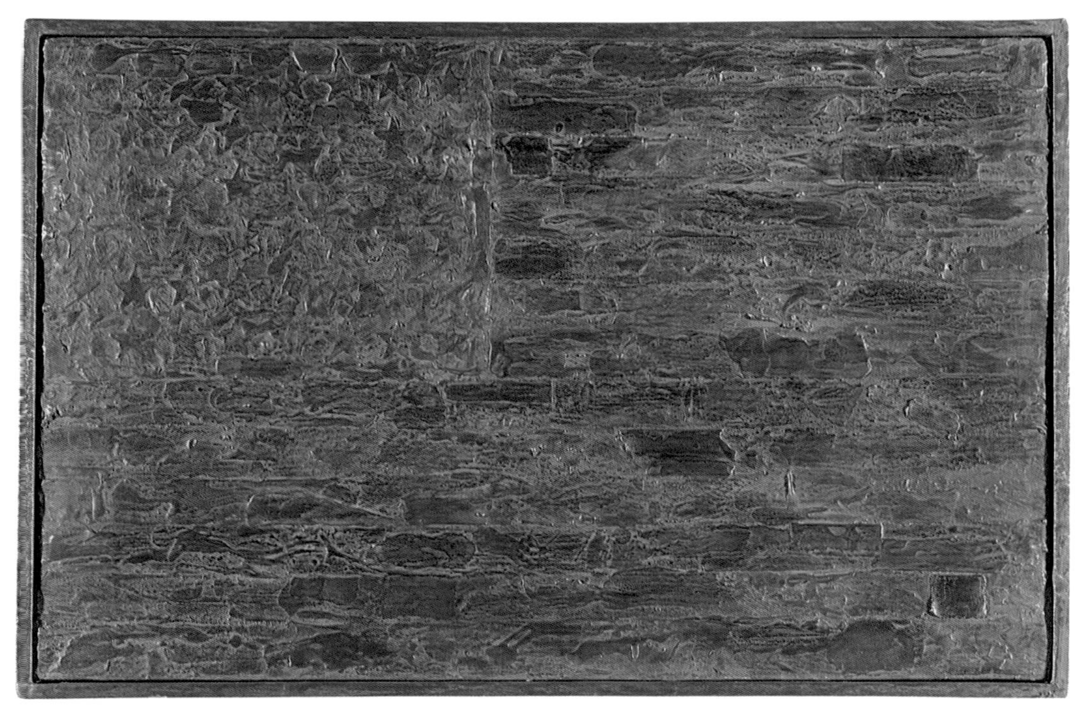

35. *Flag*, 1969
Gemini G.E.L., 1969
Embossing on lead sheet
43.2 × 58.4 cm (17 × 23 in.)
Stenn Family Collection, Chicago

34. *Flag*, 1960
Sculp-metal and collage on canvas
33 × 50.2 × 3.8 cm (13 × 19 ¾ × 1 ½ in.)
Robert Rauschenberg Collection

36. *Flag*, 1960 and 1987
Silver cast from a moulage of *Flag*
32.4 × 48.9 × 3.8 cm (12 ¾ × 19 ¼ × 1 ½ in.)
Collection of the artist

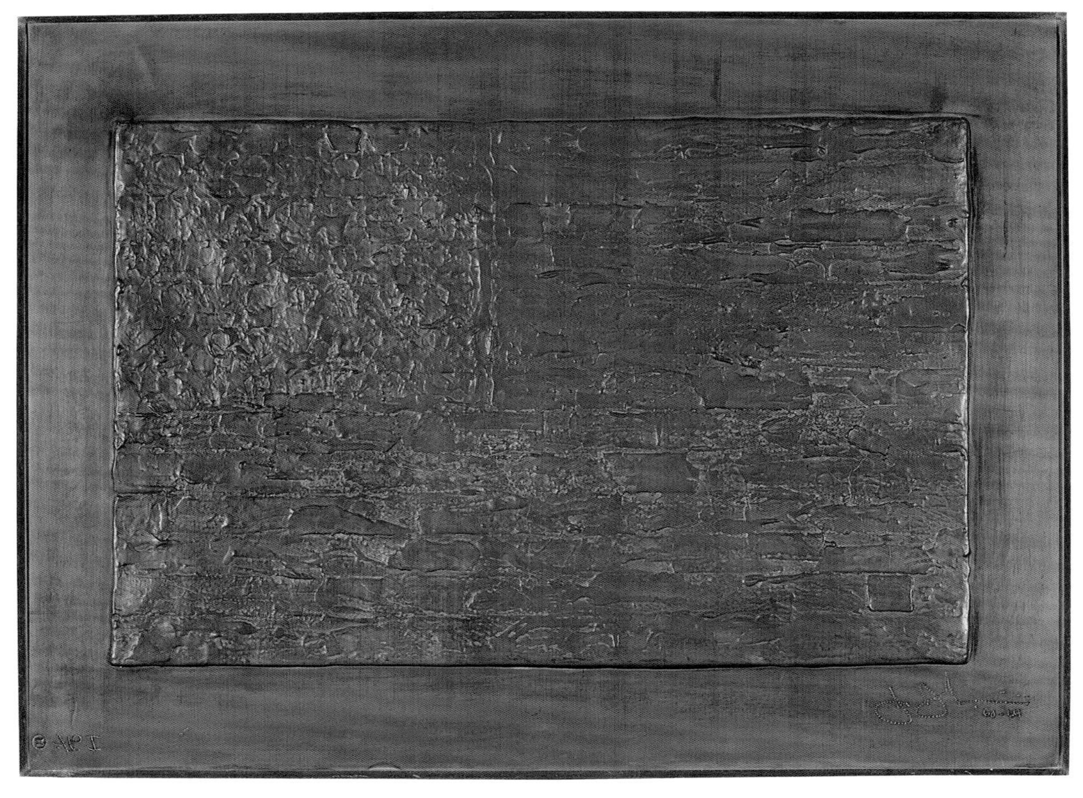

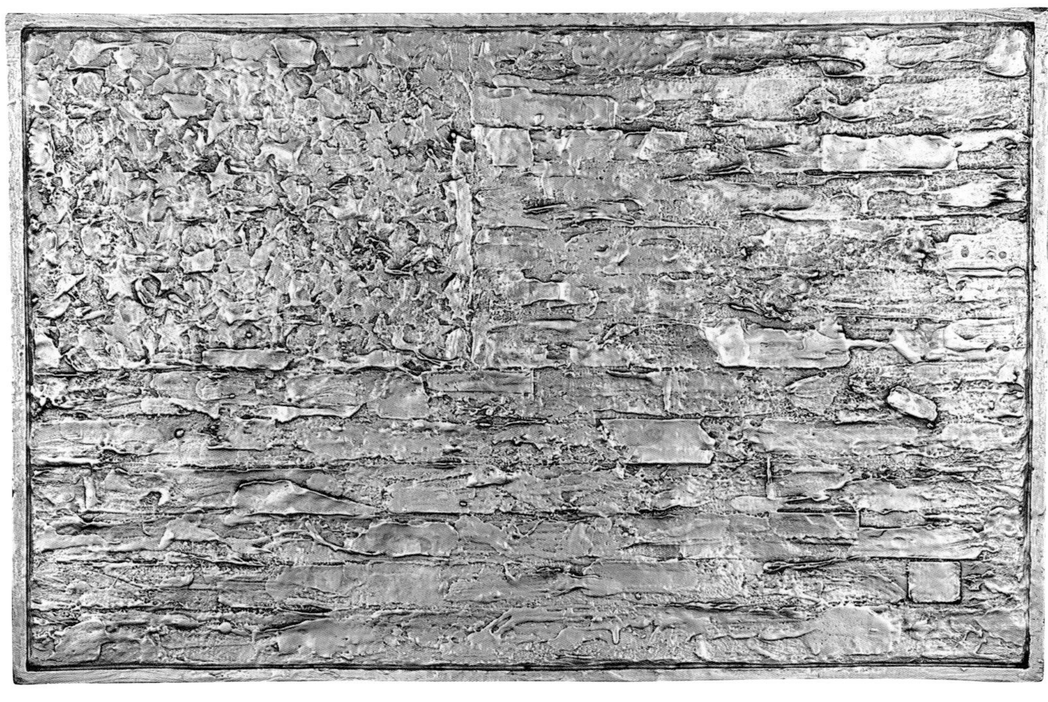

37. *Flag*, 1994
Acrylic on canvas
32.2 × 48.7 cm (12 11/16 × 19 3/16 in.)
The Eli and Edythe L. Broad Collection, Los Angeles

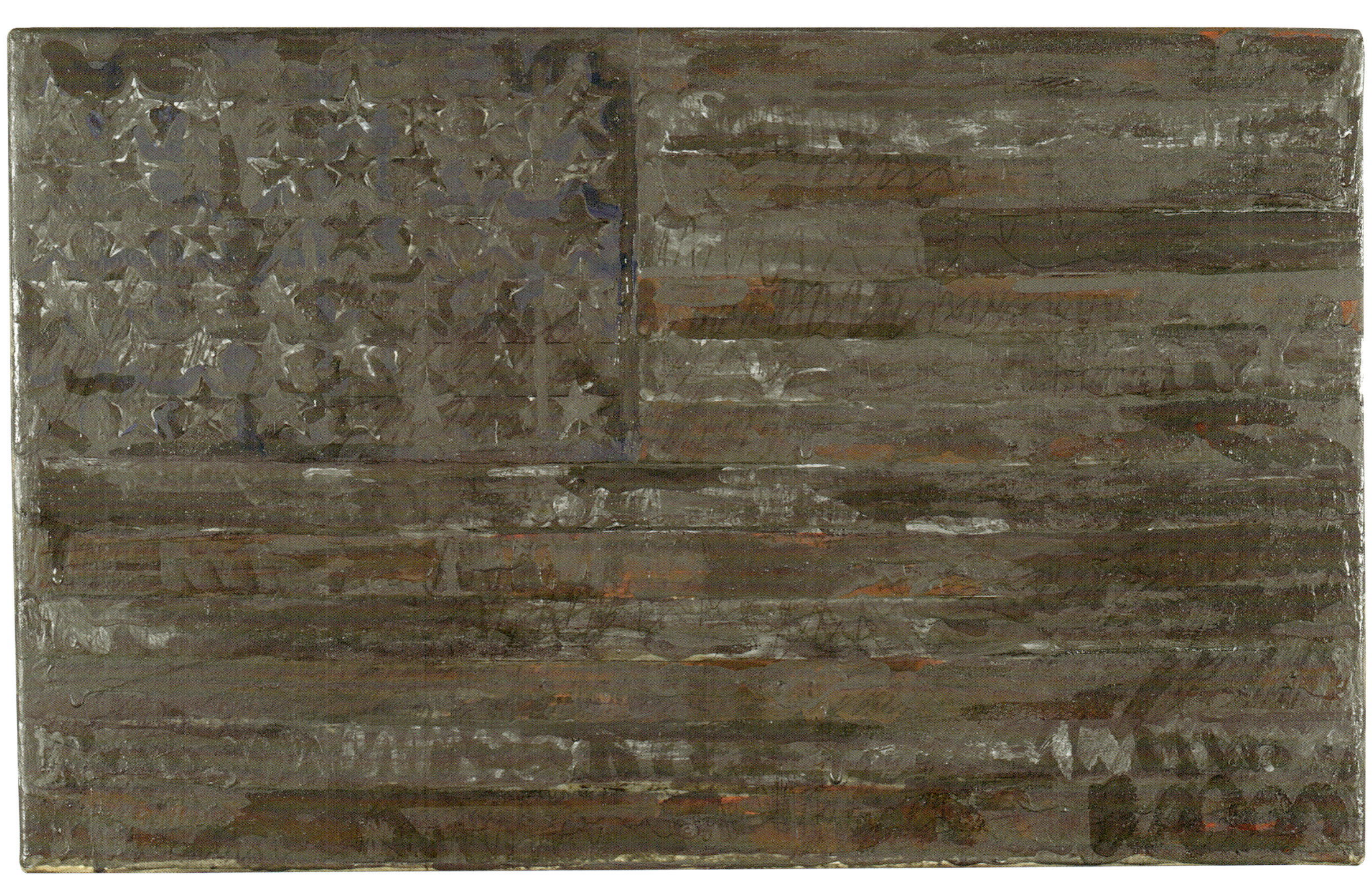

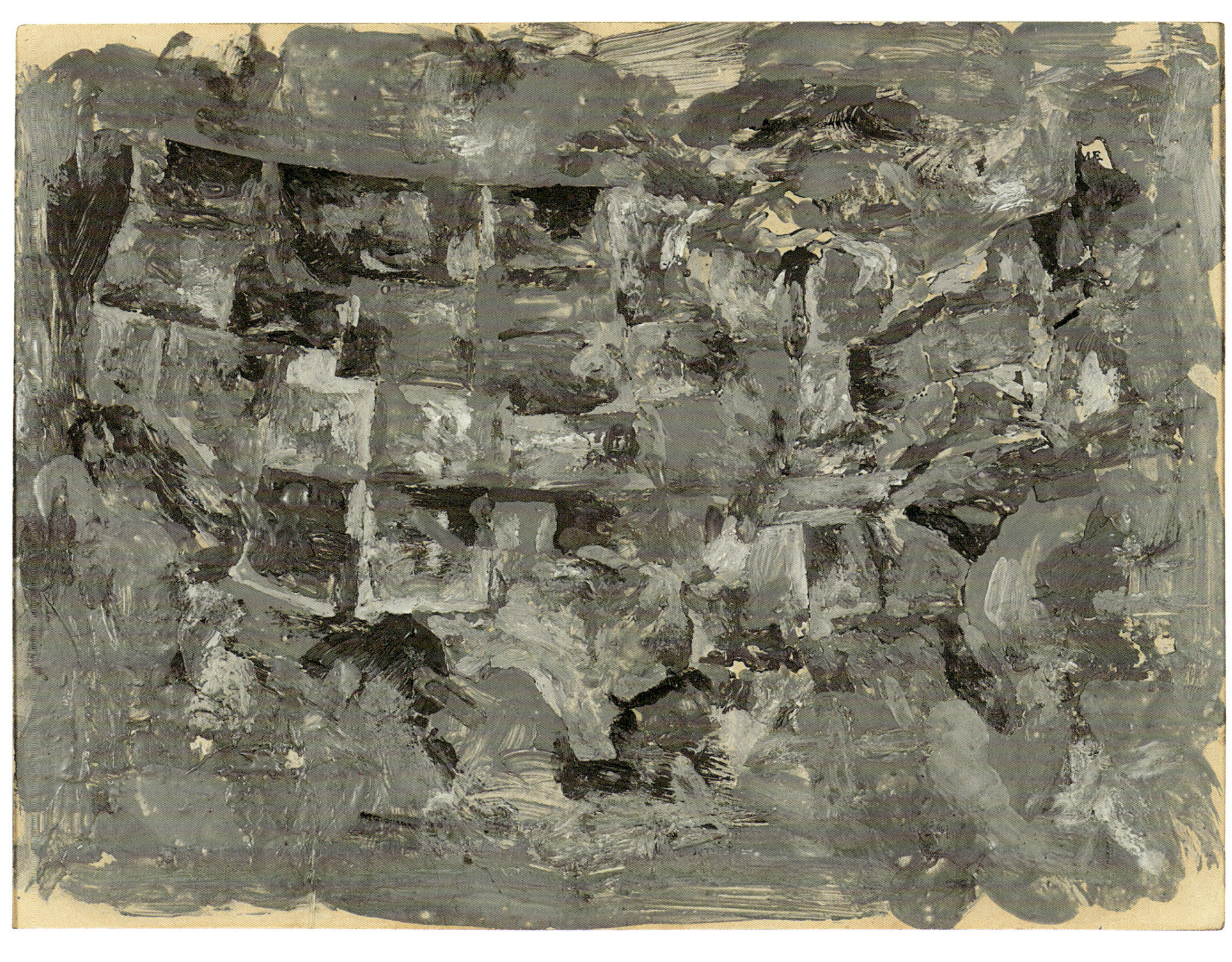

38. *Map*, 1960
Encaustic on printed paper, mounted on board
20.3 × 27.9 cm (8 × 11 in.)
Robert Rauschenberg Foundation Collection

39. *Map*, 1962
Encaustic and collage on canvas
152.4 × 236.2 cm (60 × 93 in.)
The Museum of Contemporary Art, Los Angeles,
gift of Marcia Simon Weisman

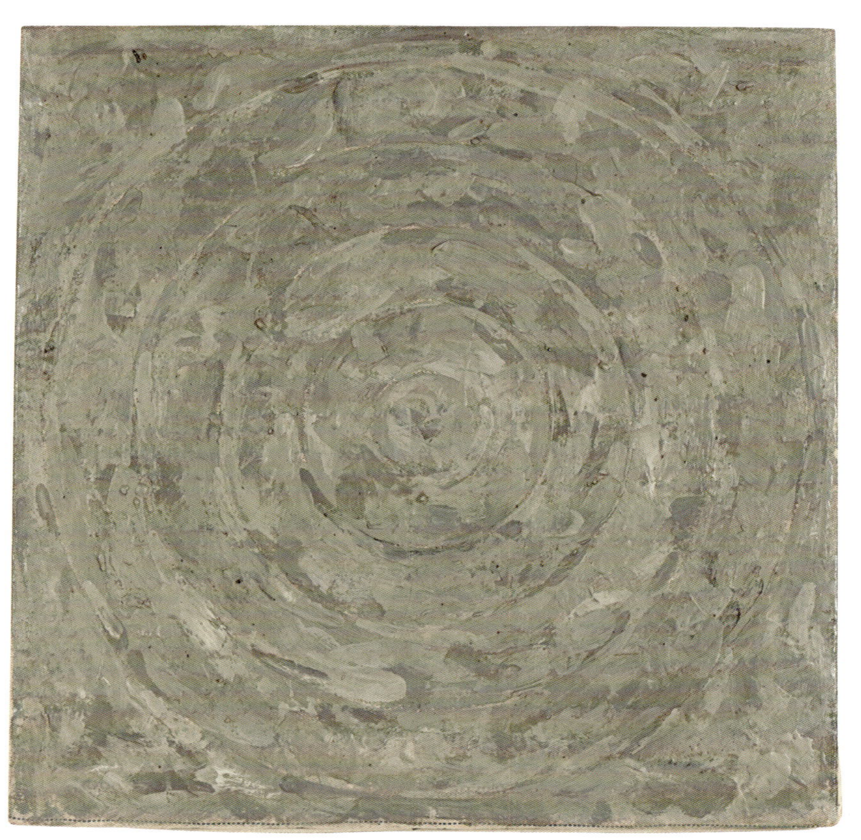

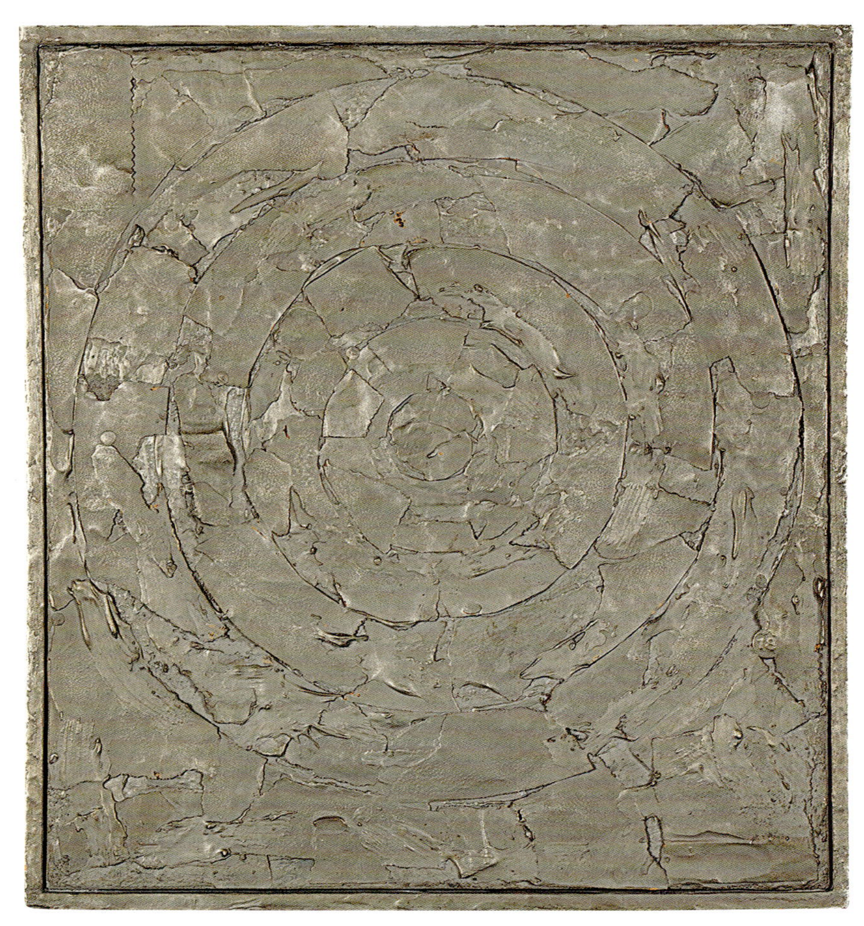

44. *Target*, 1958
Conté crayon, wax pencil, and pastel on ivory wove paper
image: 38.7 × 37.2 cm (15 ¼ × 14 ⅝ in.)
sheet: 39.4 × 38.1 cm (15 ½ × 15 in.)
Mr. and Mrs. Andrew Saul

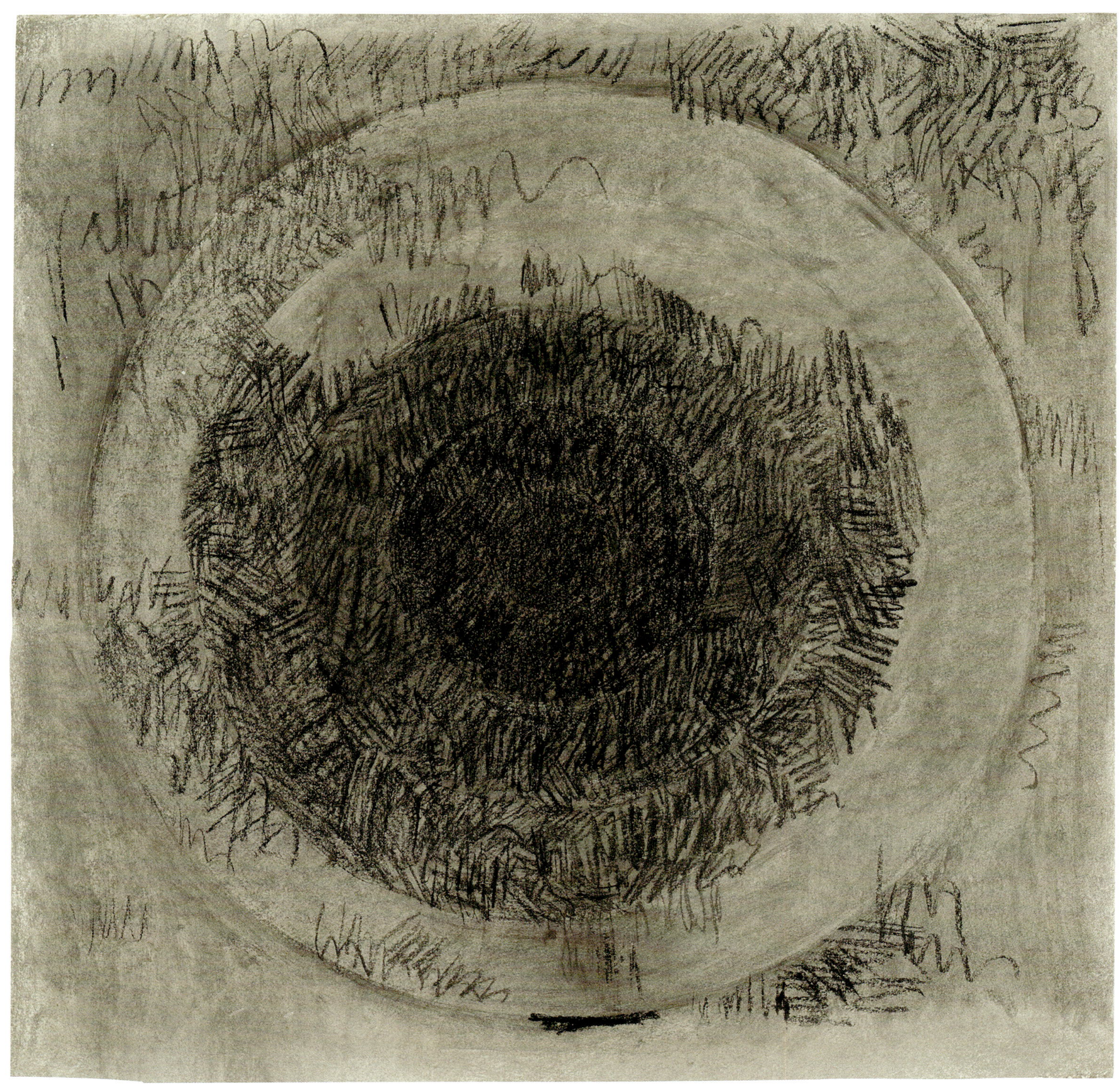

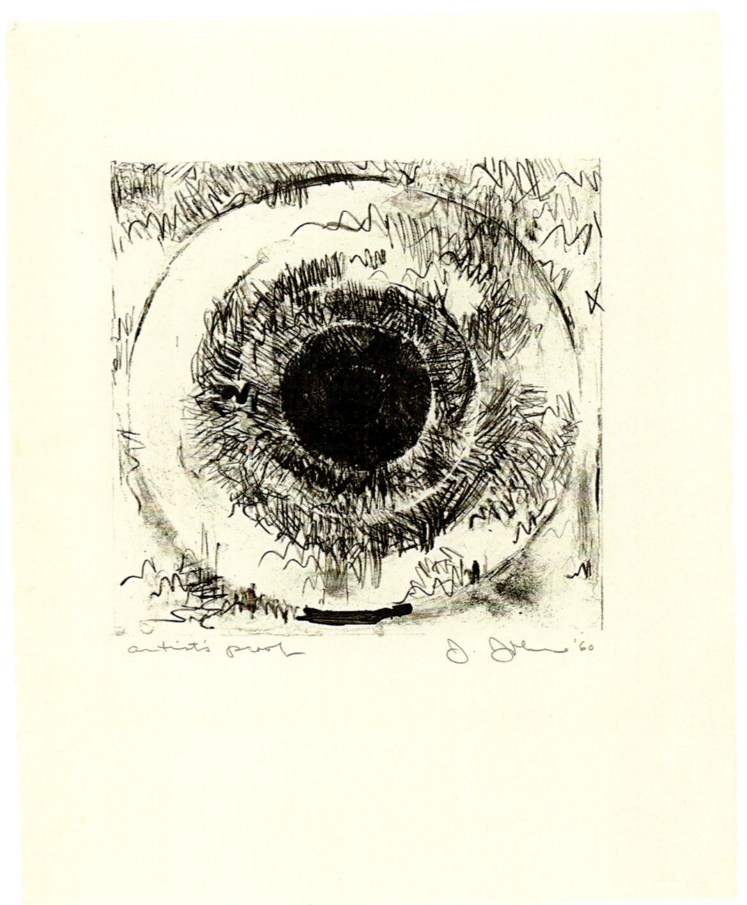

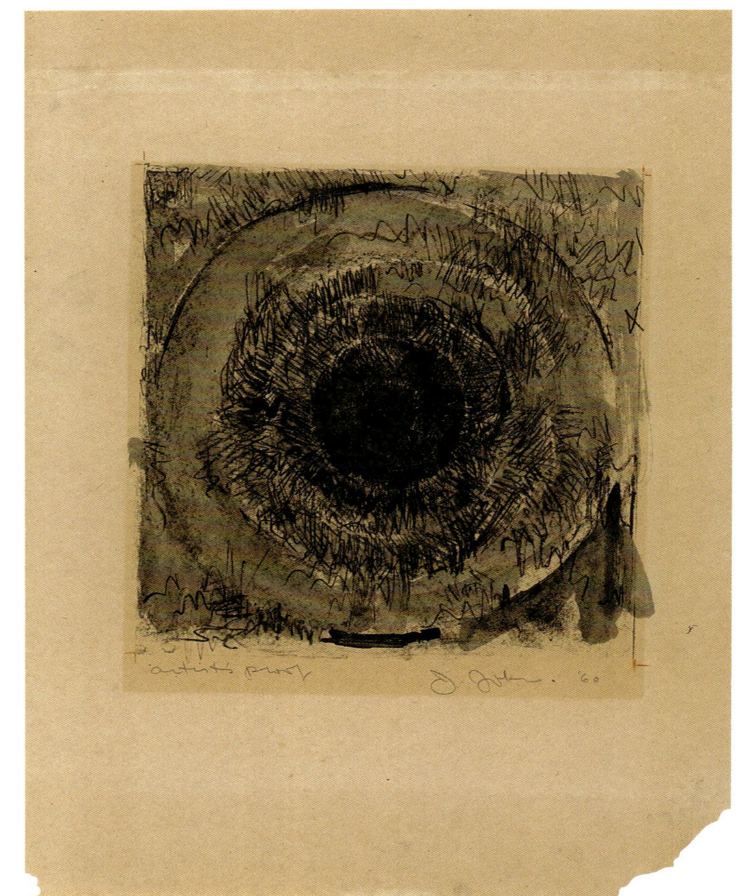

45. *Target*, 1960
ULAE, 1960
Lithograph from one stone on ivory wove paper (wmk.: Japan)
image: 30.5 × 30.5 cm (12 × 12 in.)
sheet: 57.4 × 44.8 cm (22 5/8 × 17 5/8 in.)
ULAE/Johns cat. raisonné 1
The Art Institute of Chicago, ULAE Collection acquired through a challenge grant of Mr. and Mrs. Thomas Dittmer; restricted gift of supporters of the Department of Prints and Drawings; Centennial Endowment; Margaret Fisher Endowment Fund, 1982.938

46. *Target*, 1960
ULAE, 1960
Wash over lithograph from one stone on newsprint; working proof
image: 31.5 × 32 cm (12 3/8 × 12 5/8 in.)
sheet: 56 × 43.4 cm (22 1/8 × 17 1/8 in.)
ULAE/Johns cat. raisonné 1
The Art Institute of Chicago, ULAE Collection acquired through a challenge grant of Mr. and Mrs. Thomas Dittmer; restricted gift of supporters of the Department of Prints and Drawings; Centennial Endowment; Margaret Fisher Endowment Fund, 1982.938a

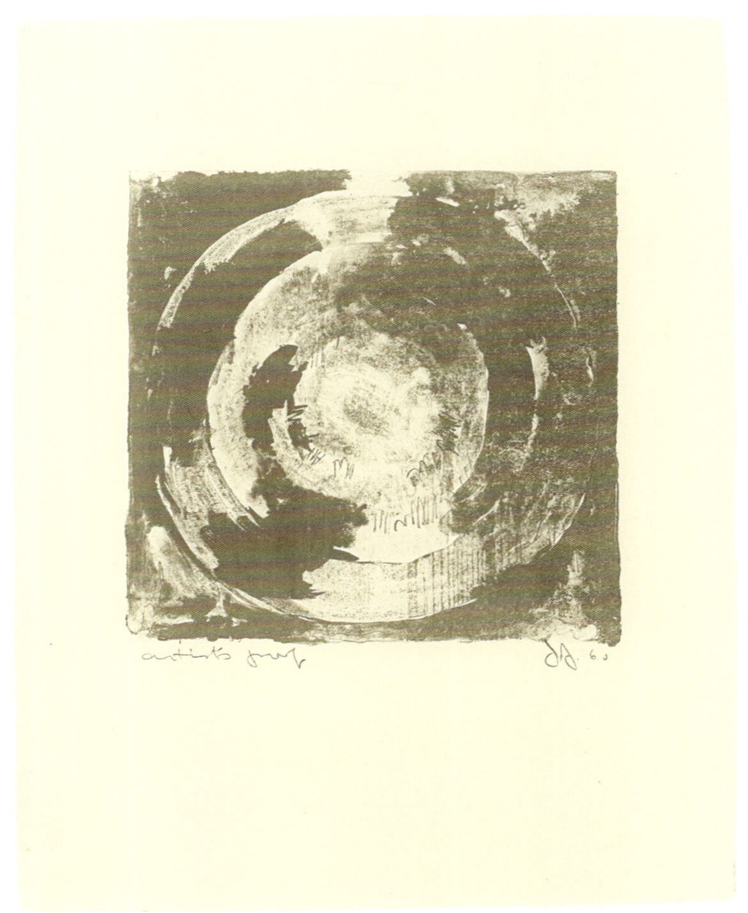

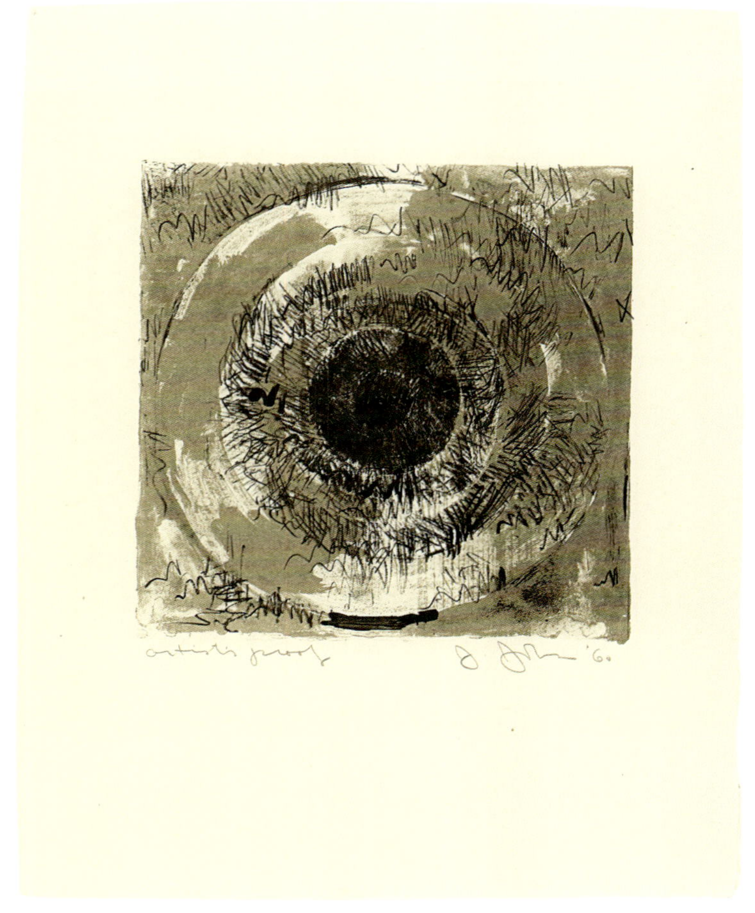

47. *Target,* 1960
ULAE, 1960
Lithograph from one stone on ivory wove paper (wmk.: Japan); trial proof
image: 30.5 × 30.5 cm (12 × 12 in.)
sheet: 57.9 × 46 cm (22 ¾ × 18 in.)
ULAE/Johns cat. raisonné 1
The Art Institute of Chicago, ULAE Collection acquired through a challenge grant of Mr. and Mrs. Thomas Dittmer; restricted gift of supporters of the Department of Prints and Drawings; Centennial Endowment; Margaret Fisher Endowment Fund, 1982.938b

48. *Target,* 1960
ULAE, 1960
Lithograph from two stones on ivory wove paper (wmk.: Japan); trial proof
image: 30.8 × 30.8 cm (12 ⅛ × 12 ⅛ in.)
sheet: 58 × 45.3 cm (22 ⅞ × 17 ⅞ in.)
ULAE/Johns cat. raisonné 1
The Art Institute of Chicago, ULAE Collection acquired through a challenge grant of Mr. and Mrs. Thomas Dittmer; restricted gift of supporters of the Department of Prints and Drawings; Centennial Endowment; Margaret Fisher Endowment Fund, 1982.938c

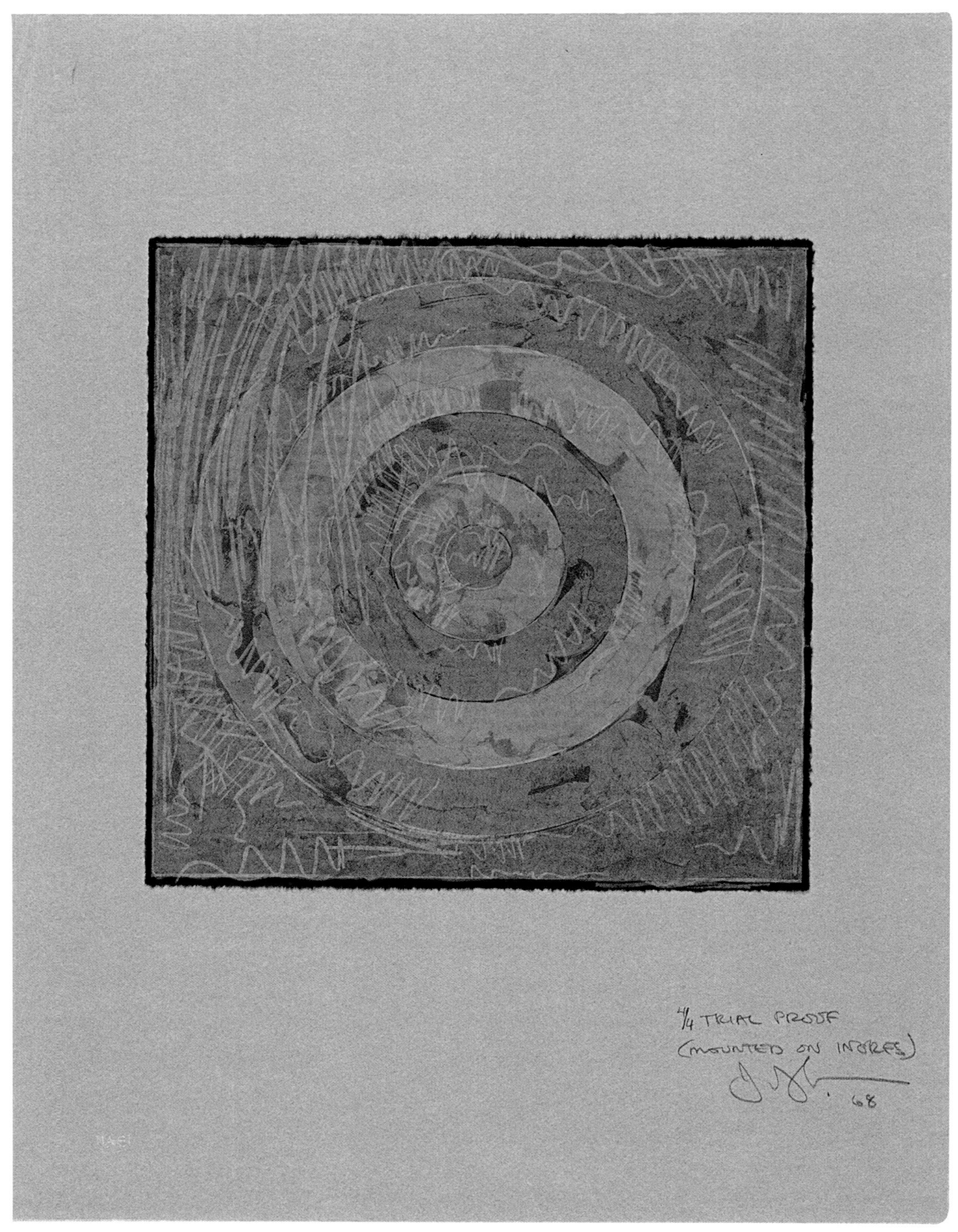

49. *White Target*, 1967–68
ULAE, 1968
Lithograph from seven stones on black Japanese paper laid down on mottled blue-gray wove paper (wmk.: Ingres); trial proof
image: 34.2 × 34 cm (13 ½ × 13 ⅜ in.)
secondary support: 63.8 × 48 cm (25 ⅛ × 18 ⅞ in.)
ULAE/Johns cat. raisonné 54
The Art Institute of Chicago, purchased from ULAE, 1982.967a

50. *White Target*, 1967–68
ULAE, 1968
Lithograph from seven stones on black Japanese paper laid down on black wove paper (bls.: Canson)
image: 33.8 × 33.8 cm (13 ¼ × 13 ¼ in.)
secondary support: 75 × 55 cm (29 ½ × 21 ⅝ in.)
ULAE/Johns cat. raisonné 54
The Art Institute of Chicago, ULAE Collection acquired through a challenge grant of Mr. and Mrs. Thomas Dittmer; restricted gift of supporters of the Department of Prints and Drawings; Centennial Endowment; Margaret Fisher Endowment Fund, 1982.967

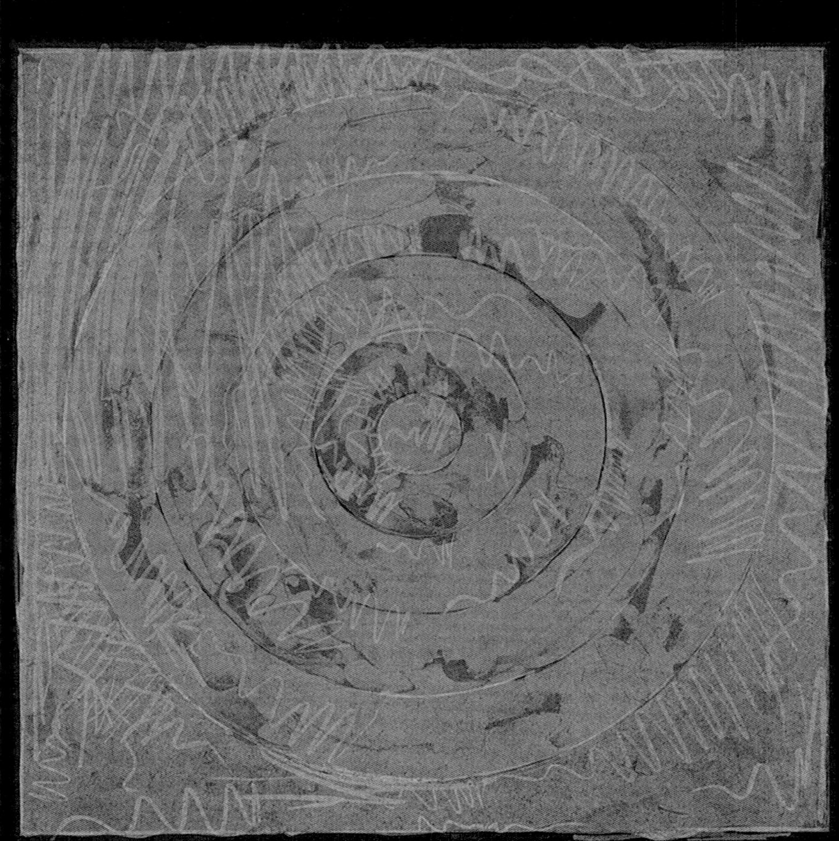

3/5 ARTIST'S PROOF

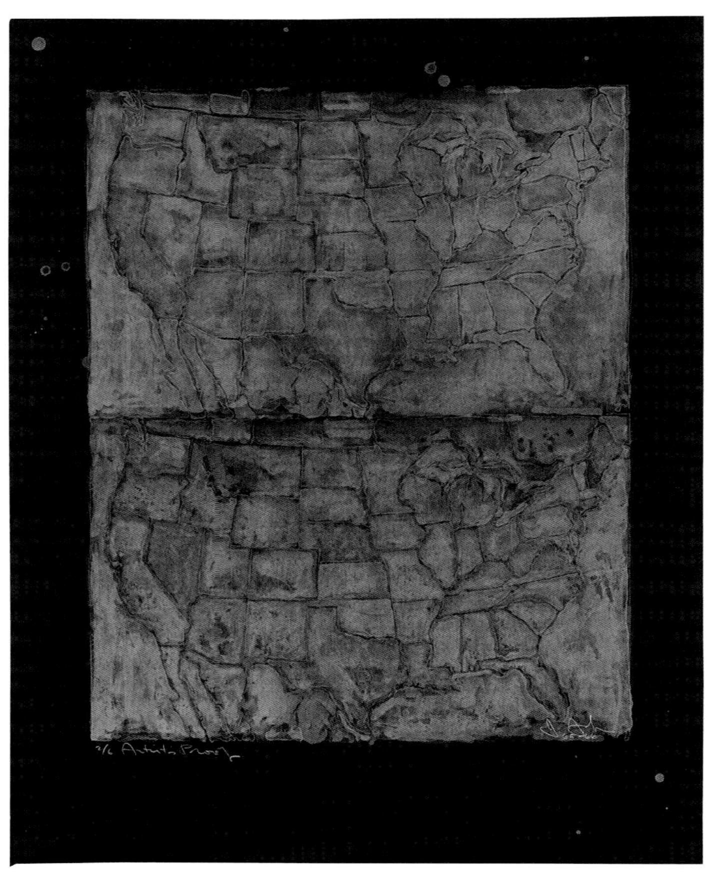

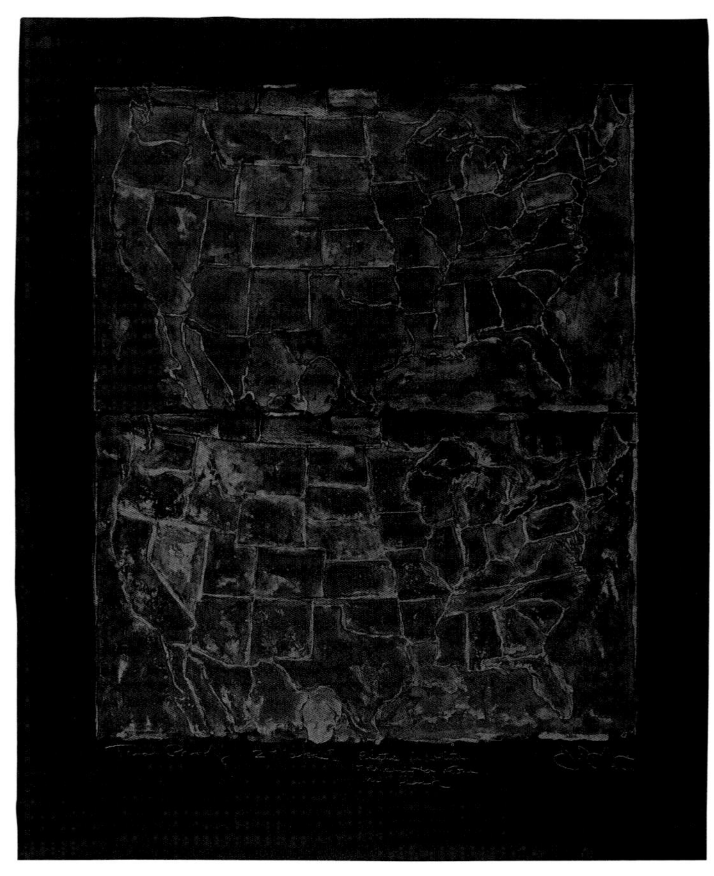

51. *Two Maps I*, 1965–66
ULAE, 1966
Lithograph from one stone and one aluminum plate on black wove paper (Fabriano)
image: 66 × 53.5 cm (26 × 21 1/8 in.)
sheet: 84.5 × 67.5 cm (33 1/4 × 26 5/8 in.)
ULAE/Johns cat. raisonné 23
The Art Institute of Chicago, restricted gift of the Albert Kundstadter Family Foundation, 1982.952

52. *Two Maps I*, 1966
ULAE, 1966
Lithograph from one stone and one aluminum plate on black wove paper (Fabriano); trial proof
sheet: 84.5 × 67.3 cm (33 1/4 × 26 1/2 in.)
ULAE/Johns cat. raisonné 23
National Gallery of Art, Washington, Patrons' Permanent Fund, 2004

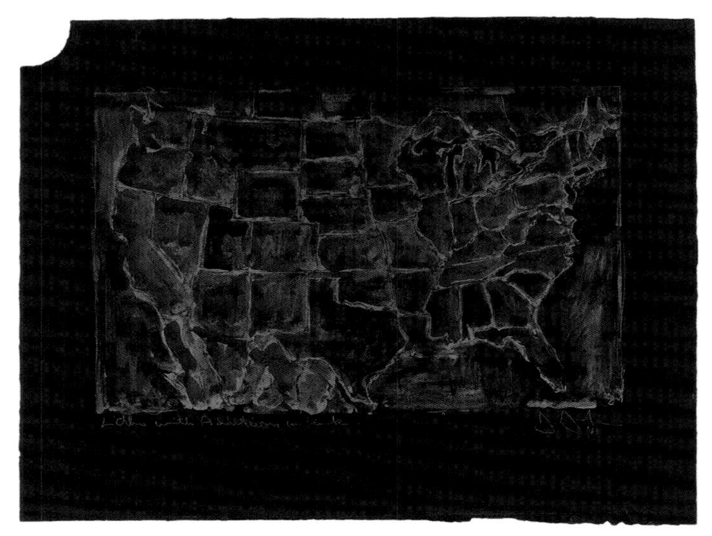

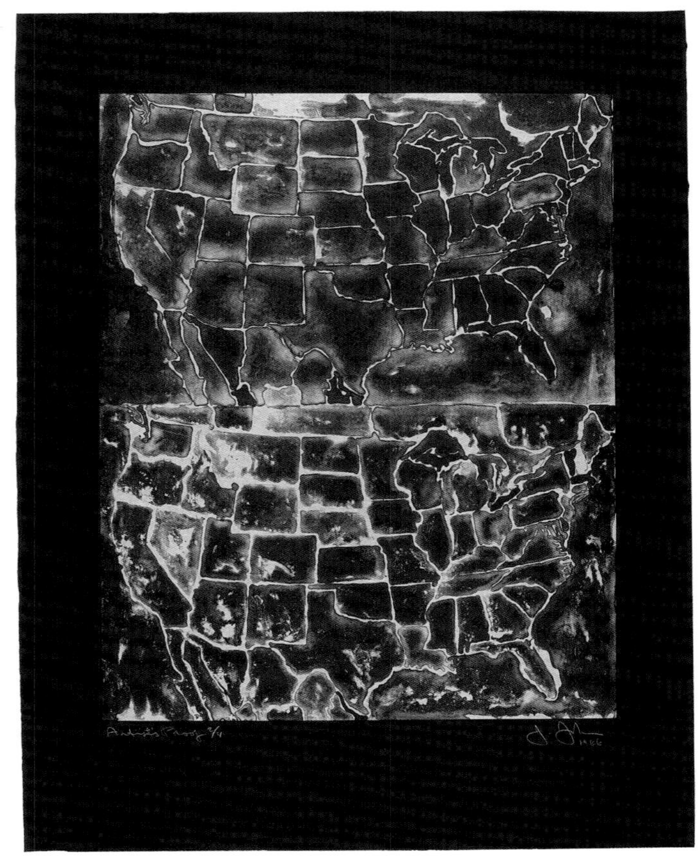

53. *Two Maps I-II*, 1965–66
ULAE, 1966
Ink over lithograph from one aluminum plate on black wove paper (Fabriano); working proof
image: 33.3 × 53 cm (13 1/8 × 20 7/8 in.)
sheet: 51.8 × 67.5 cm (20 3/8 × 26 5/8 in.)
ULAE/Johns cat. raisonné 23
The Art Institute of Chicago, ULAE Collection acquired through a challenge grant of Mr. and Mrs. Thomas Dittmer; restricted gift of supporters of the Department of Prints and Drawings; Centennial Endowment; Margaret Fisher Endowment Fund, 1982.952f

54. *Two Maps II*, 1966
ULAE, 1966
Lithograph from one stone on white Japanese paper, laid down on black wove paper (Fabriano)
image: 64.5 × 51.5 cm (25 3/8 × 20 1/4 in.)
secondary support: 86 × 67.5 cm (33 7/8 × 26 5/8 in.)
ULAE/Johns cat. raisonné 26
The Art Institute of Chicago, Prints and Drawings Purchase Account, 1982.953

55. *Gray Alphabets*, 1956
Encaustic and collage on canvas
168 × 123.8 cm (66 1/8 × 48 3/4 in.)
The Menil Collection, Houston

56. *Gray Numbers*, 1957
Encaustic on canvas
71.1 × 55.9 cm (28 × 22 in.)
Private collection, Seattle

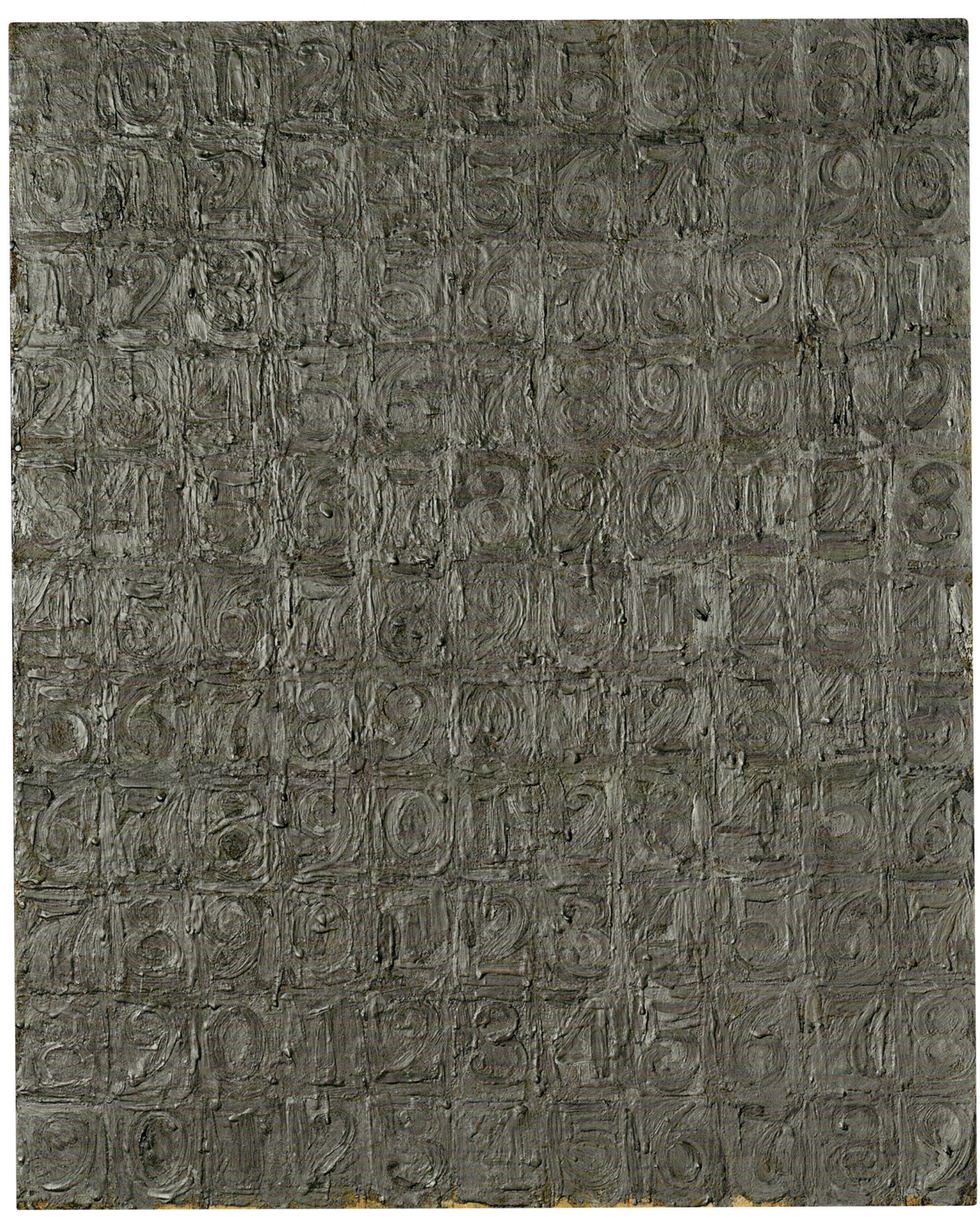

57. Gray Alphabets, 1960
Graphite and graphite wash on cream wove paper
image: 89.5 × 62.9 cm (35 ¼ × 24 ¾ in.)
sheet: 97.5 × 70.8 cm (38 ⅜ × 27 ⅞ in.)
Fogg Art Museum, Harvard University Art Museums, Cambridge, Massachusetts, on loan from the collection of Jean-Christophe Castelli, class of 1985

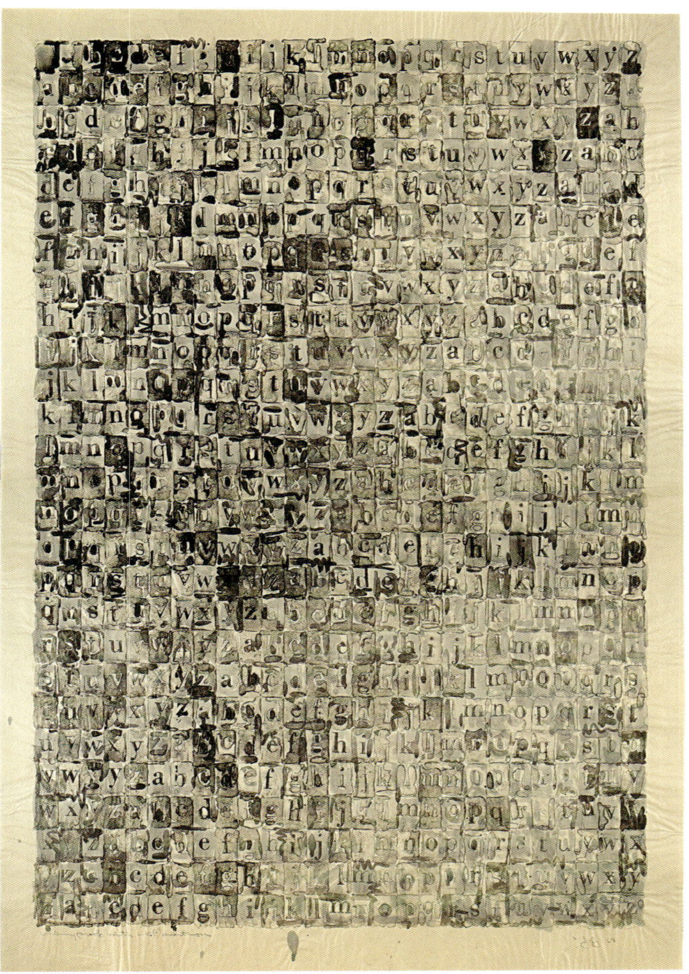

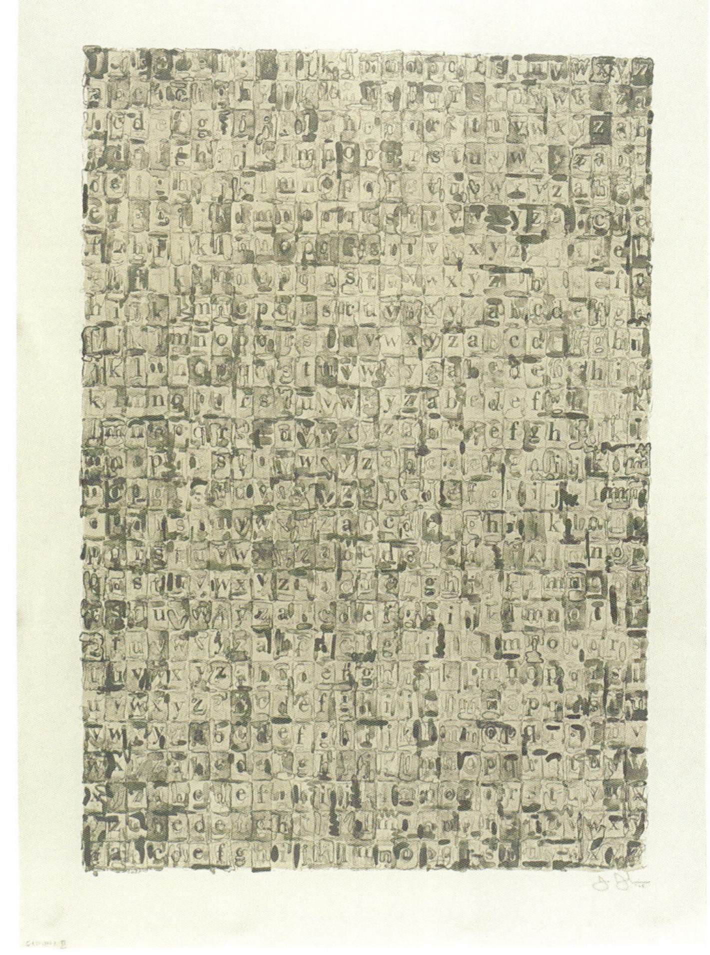

58. *Gray Alphabets,* 1968
Gemini, G.E.L., 1968
Wash over lithograph from one aluminum plate on newsprint; working proof
sheet: 140.3 × 95.9 cm (55 1/4 × 37 3/4 in.)
ULAE/Johns cat. raisonné *57*
National Gallery of Art, Washington, Patrons' Permanent Fund, 2005

59. *Gray Alphabets,* 1968
Gemini G.E.L., 1968
Lithograph from four aluminum plates on ivory wove paper (Rives BFK)
image: 129.5 × 86.4 cm (51 × 34 in.)
sheet: 150.8 × 105.4 cm (59 3/8 × 41 1/2 in.)
ULAE/Johns cat. raisonné *57*
Walker Art Center, Minneapolis, gift of Kenneth E. Tyler, 1985

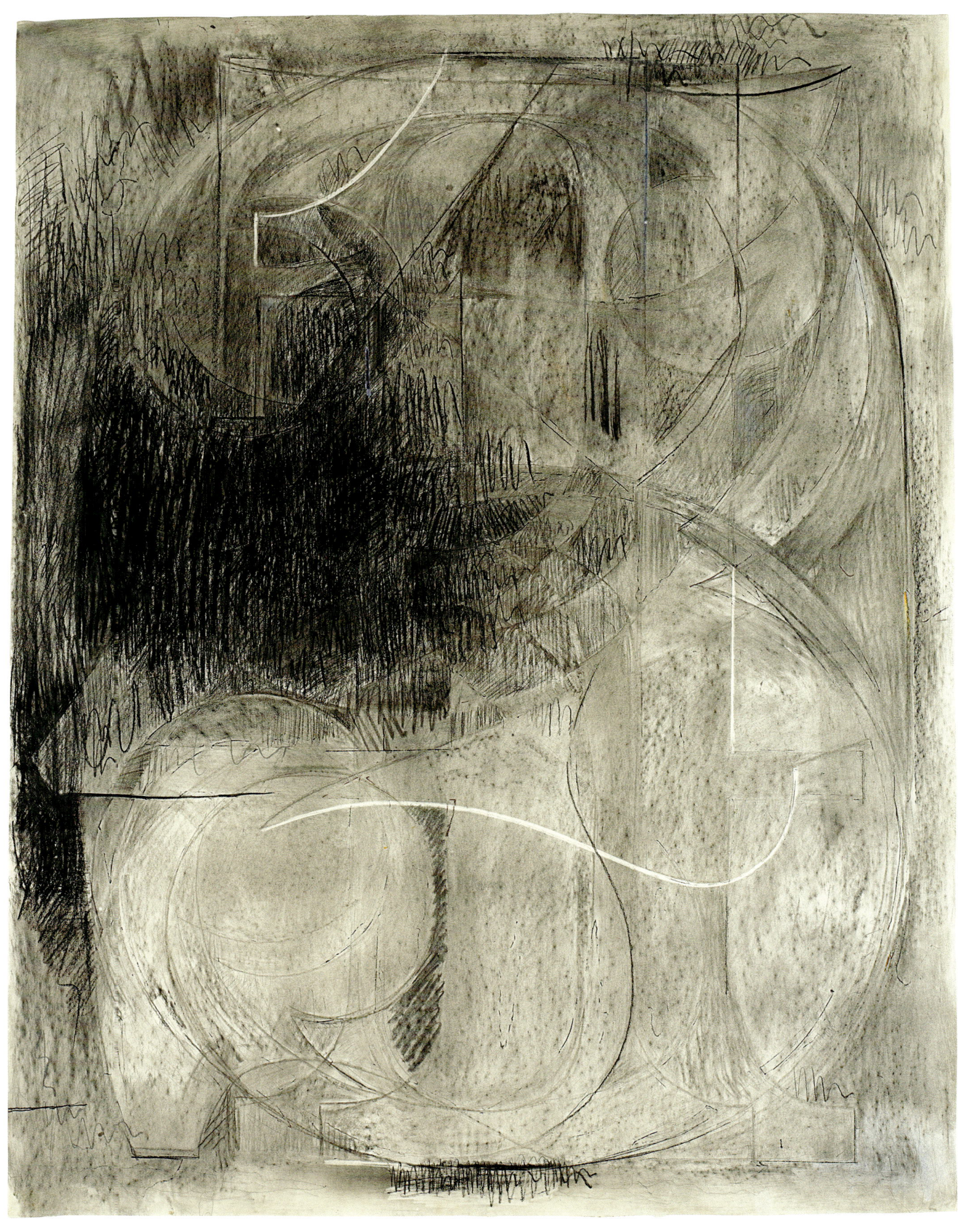

60. 0 *through* 9, 1961
Charcoal and pastel on ivory wove paper
137.8 × 105.7 cm (54 ⅛ × 41 ⅝ in.)
Private collection

61. 0 *through* 9, 1961
Oil on canvas
137.2 × 114.3 cm (54 × 45 in.)
Collection of Michael Crichton

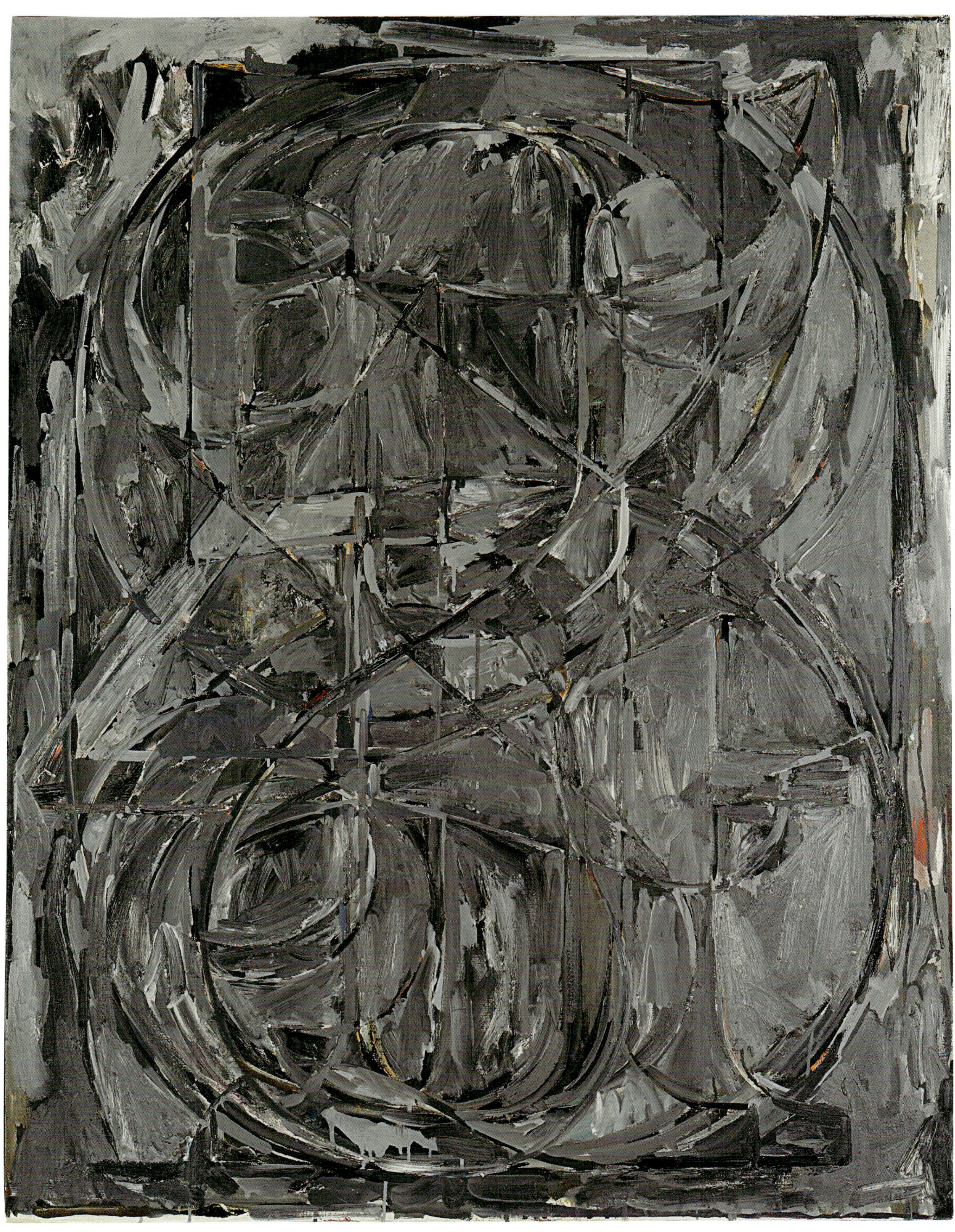

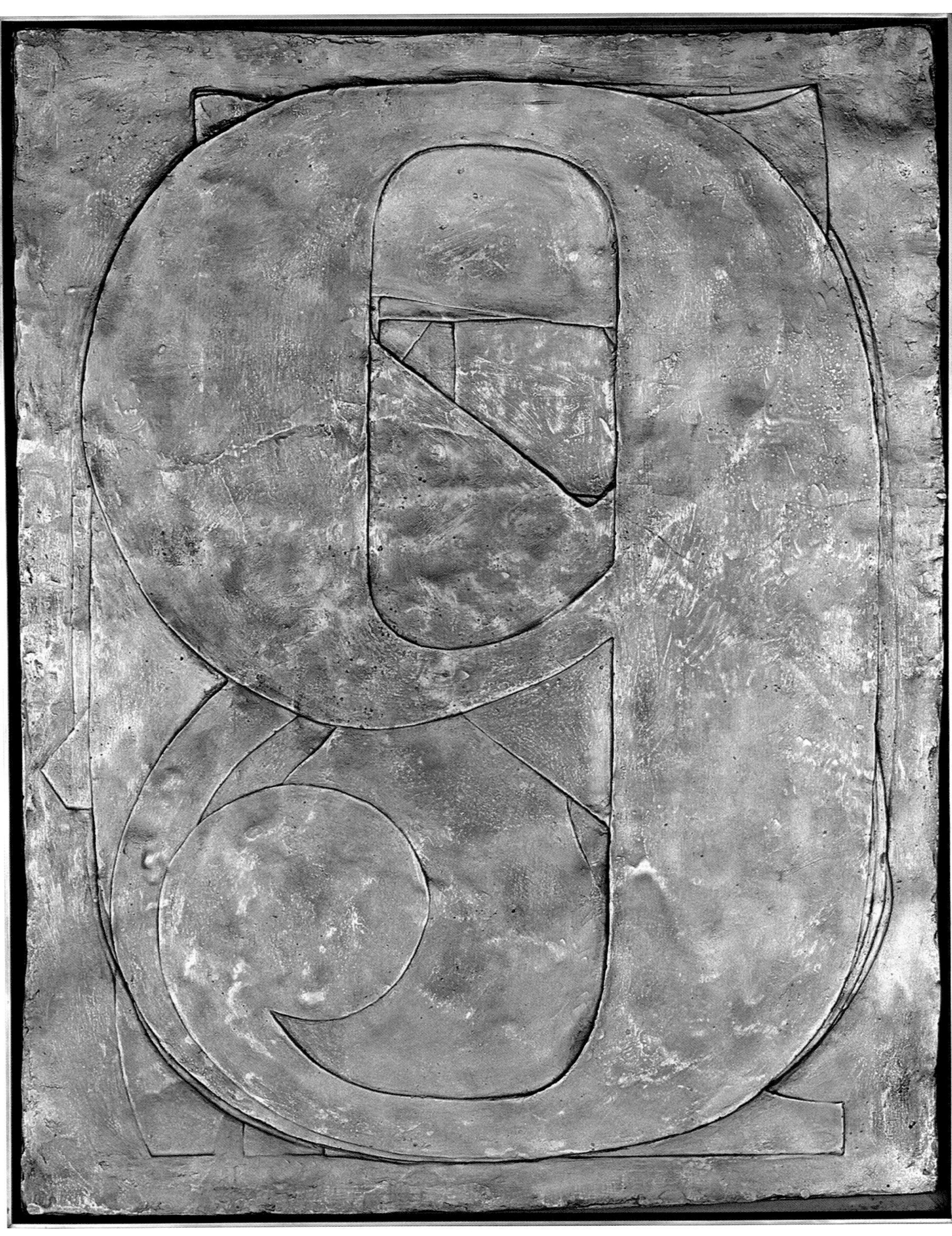

62. *0 through 9*, 1961
Aluminum
67.3 × 50.8 × 2.9 cm (26 ½ × 20 × 1 ⅛ in.)
Collection of the artist

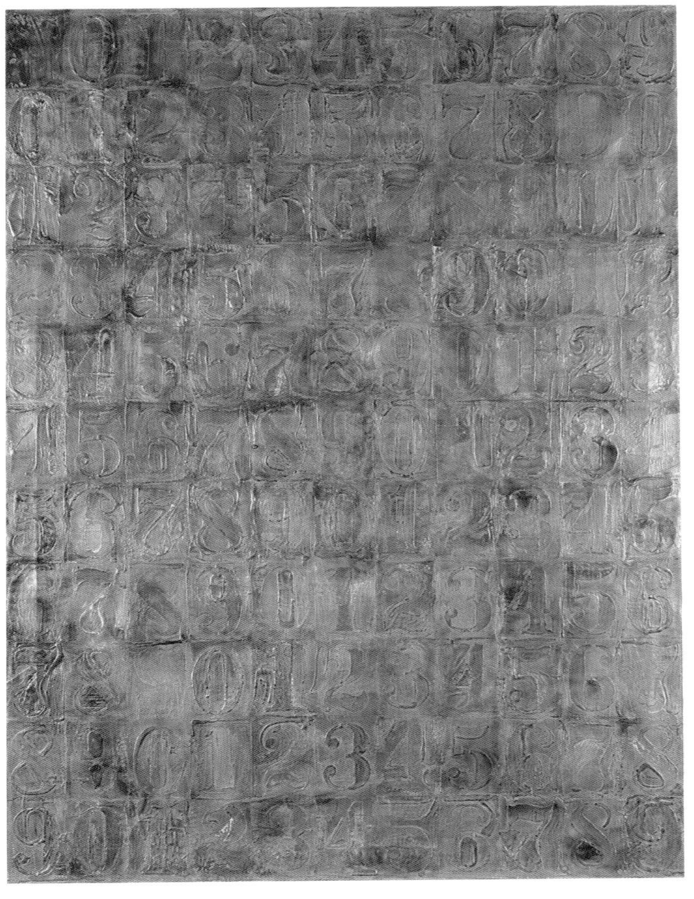

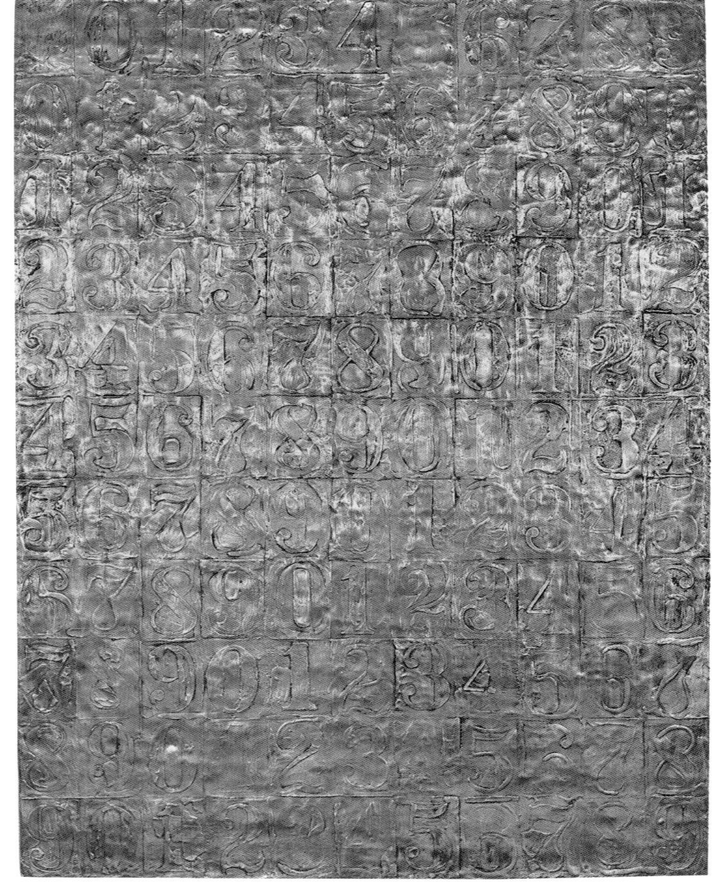

63. *Sculpmetal Numbers*, 1963
Sculp-metal on canvas
147 × 111.4 cm (57 7/8 × 43 7/8 in.)
Philadelphia Museum of Art, centennial gift of the Woodward Foundation, 1975

64. *Numbers*, 1963–78
Aluminum with oil paint
145.1 × 110.2 cm (57 1/8 × 43 3/8 in.)
Collection of Lady Belle Partnership,
Courtesy of Margo Leavin Gallery, Los Angeles

65. *0-9*, 1959–62
Acrylic on canvas
52.1 × 90.2 cm (20 ½ × 35 ½ in.)
Collection of Martin Z. Margulies

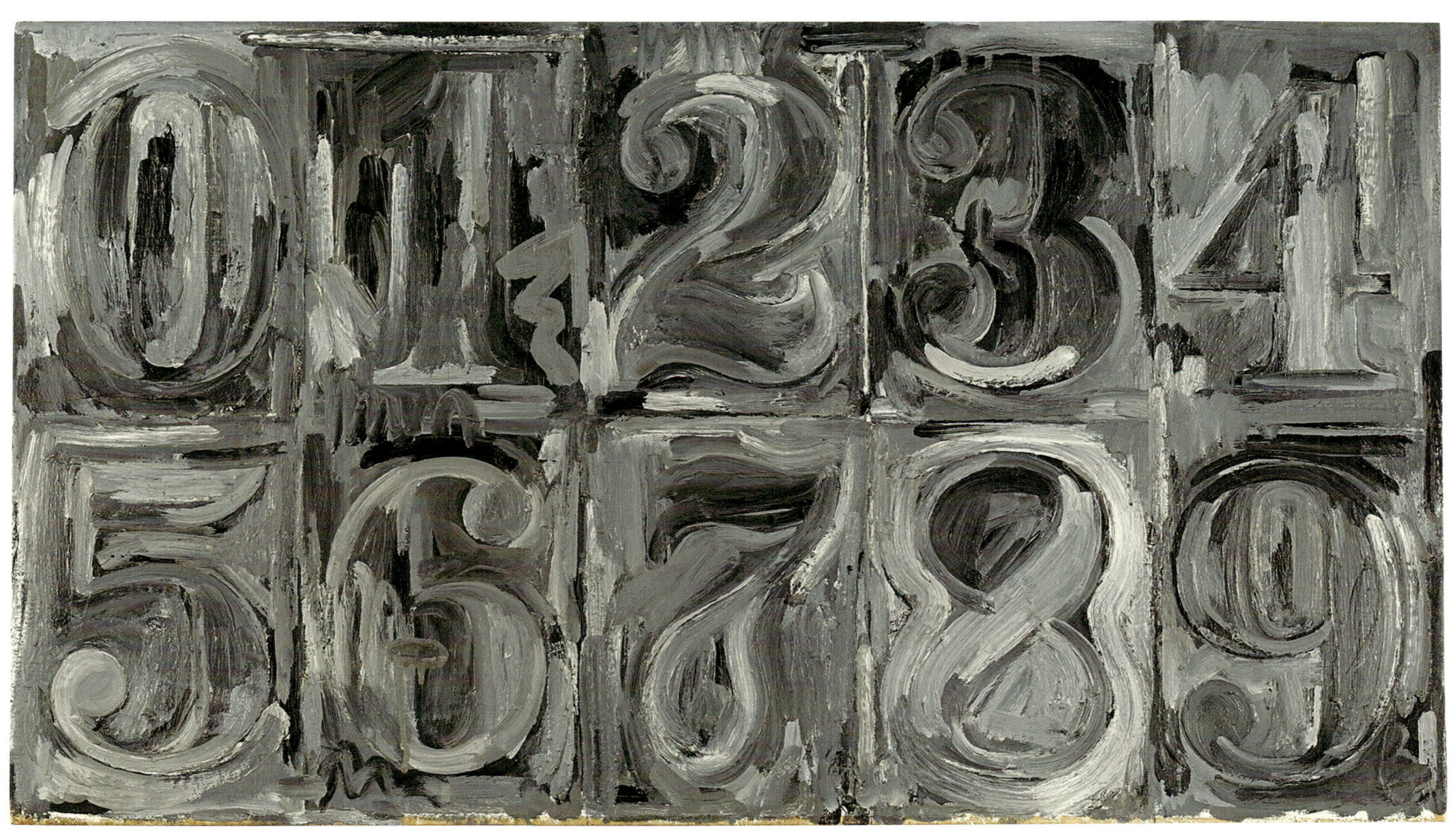

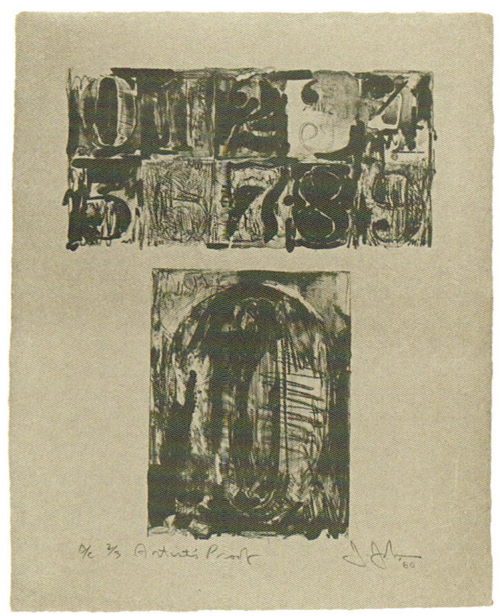
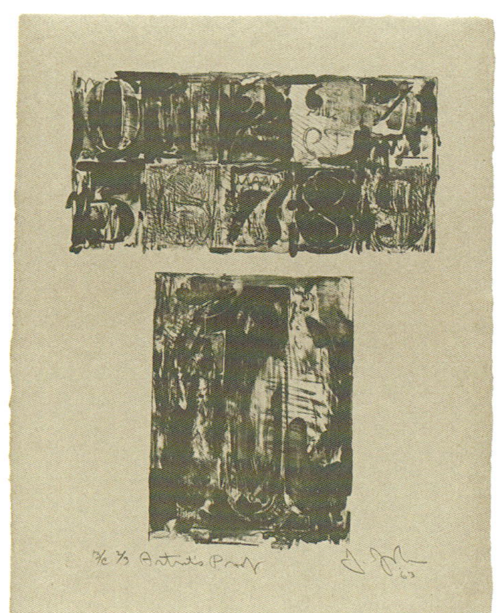
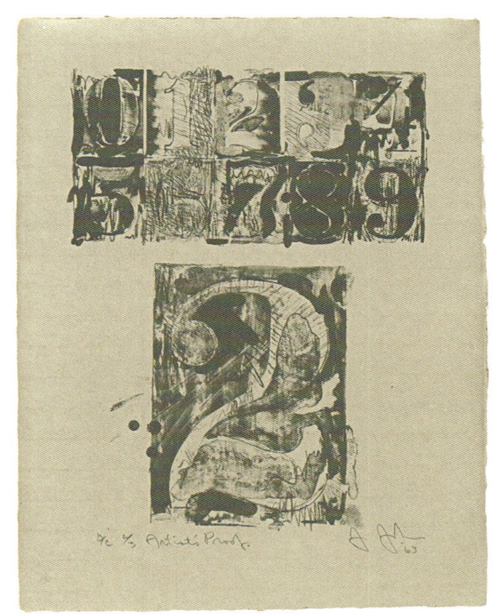
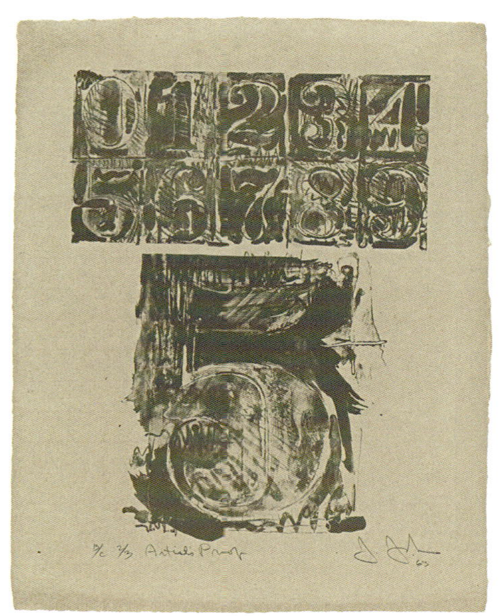

66–75. 0–9, 1960–63
ULAE, 1963
Lithographs from one stone on unbleached gray wove paper (wmk.: Angoumois J Johns); edition B/C
image: 40 × 30.7 cm (15 ¾ × 12 ⅛ in.)
sheet: 51.5 × 40 cm (20 ¼ × 15 ¾ in.)
ULAE/Johns cat. raisonné 18
The Art Institute of Chicago, ULAE Collection acquired through a challenge grant of Mr. and Mrs. Thomas Dittmer; restricted gift of supporters of the Department of Prints and Drawings; Centennial Endowment; Margaret Fisher Endowment Fund, 1982.945.b4–1982.945.b13

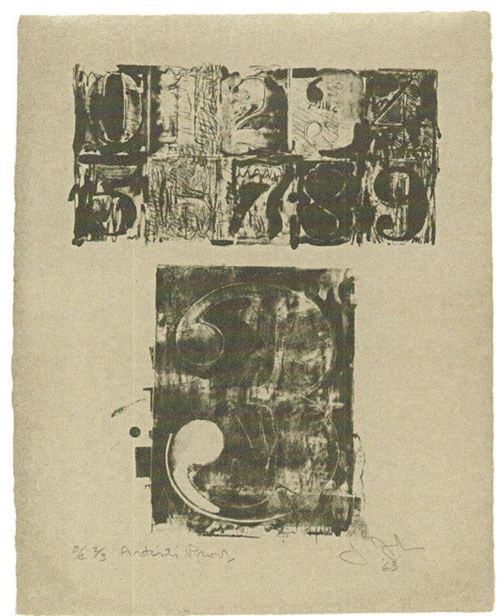

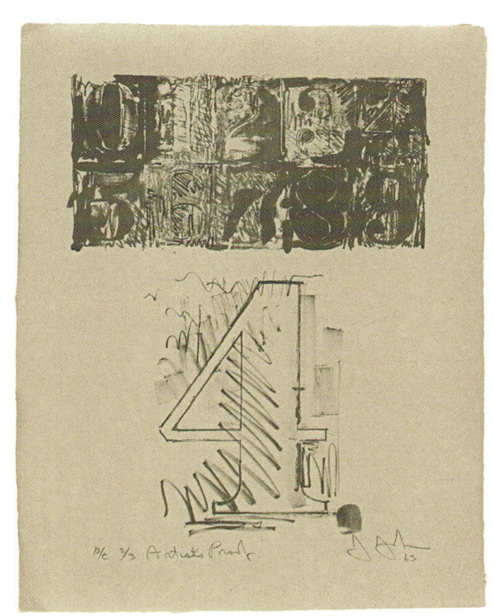

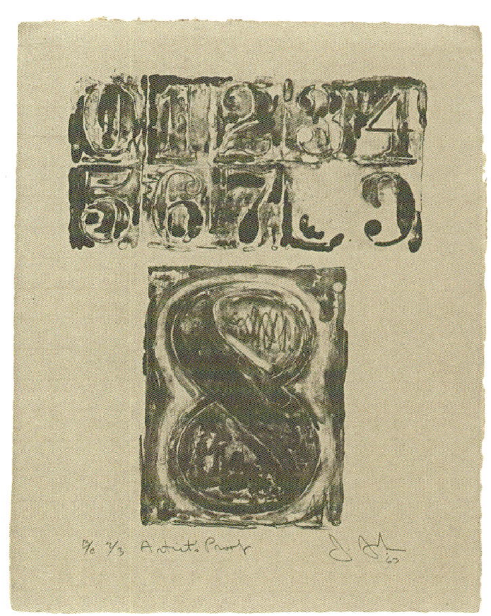

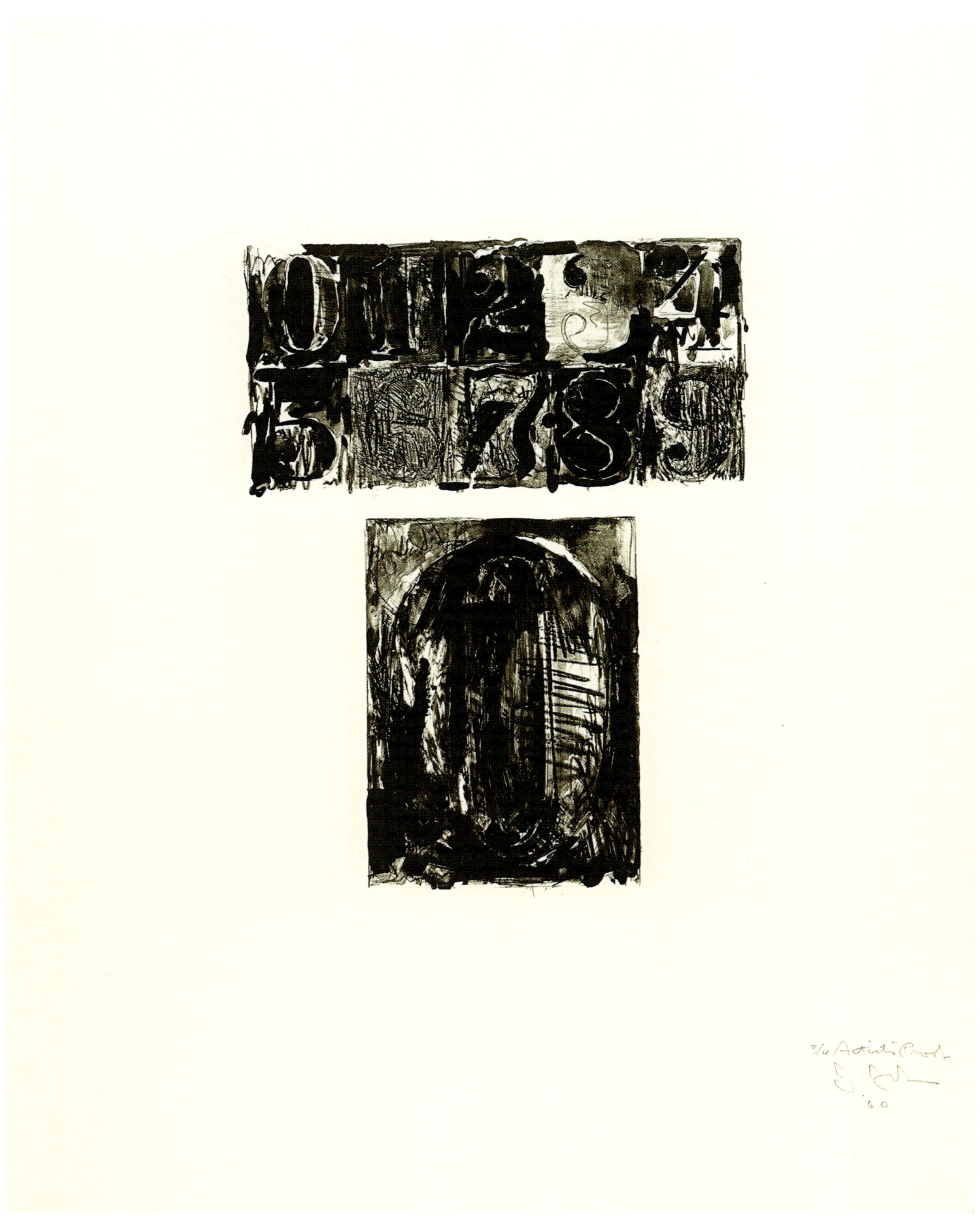

76. 0–9, 1960–63
ULAE, 1960
Lithograph from one stone on ivory wove paper
(bls.: Strathmore)
image: 39.8 × 30.1 cm (15 5/8 × 11 7/8 in.)
sheet: 73.8 × 58.3 cm (29 × 23 in.)
ULAE/Johns cat. raisonné 18
The Art Institute of Chicago, ULAE Collection
acquired through a challenge grant of
Mr. and Mrs. Thomas Dittmer; restricted gift
of supporters of the Department of Prints
and Drawings; Centennial Endowment;
Margaret Fisher Endowment Fund, 1982.945a

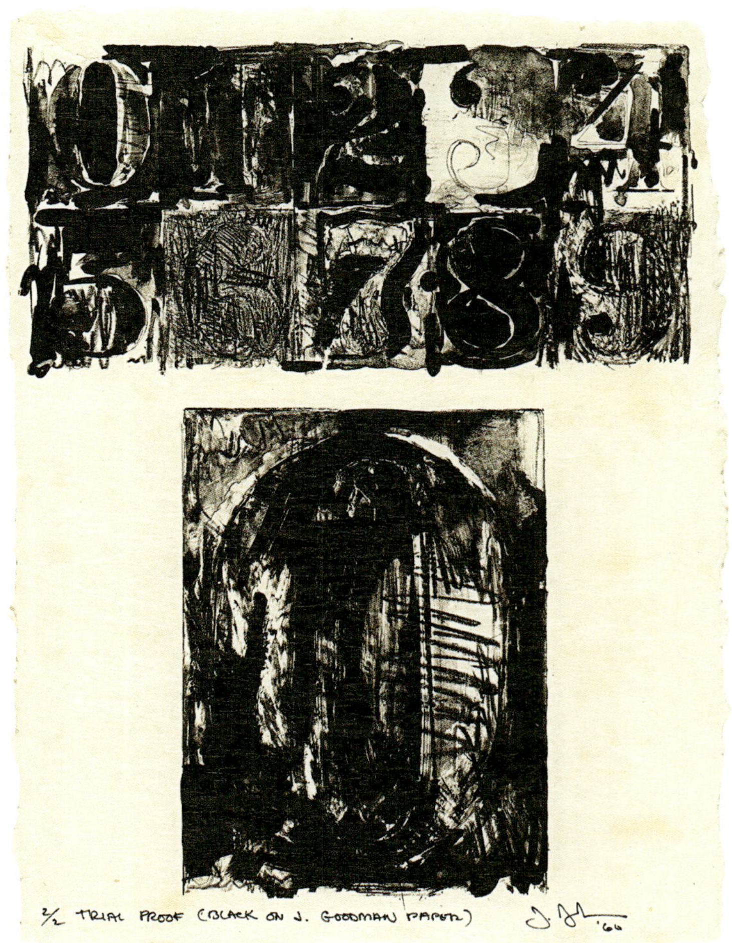

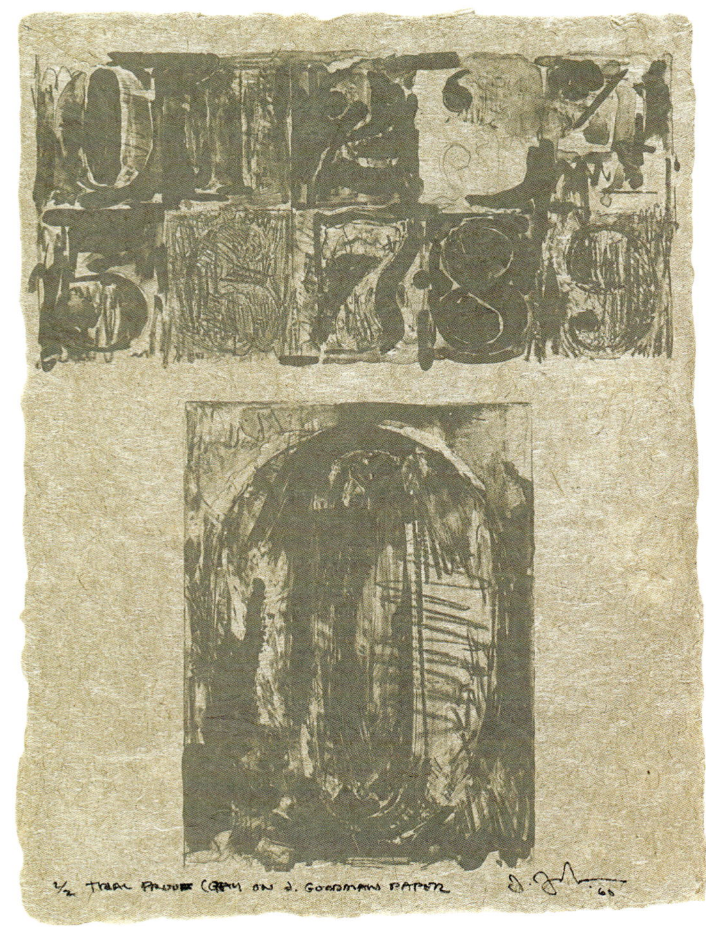

77. 0–9, 1960–63
ULAE, 1960
Lithograph from one stone on cream wove paper (Jeff Goodman); trial proof
image: 40.3 × 30.7 cm (15 7/8 × 12 1/8 in.)
sheet: 44.5 × 32.7 cm (17 1/2 × 12 7/8 in.)
ULAE/Johns cat. raisonné 18
The Art Institute of Chicago, ULAE Collection acquired through a challenge grant of Mr. and Mrs. Thomas Dittmer; restricted gift of supporters of the Department of Prints and Drawings; Centennial Endowment; Margaret Fisher Endowment Fund, 1982.945c

78. 0–9, 1960–63
ULAE, 1960
Lithograph from one stone on unbleached gray wove paper (wmk.: JG); trial proof
image: 40.3 × 30.7 cm (15 7/8 × 12 1/8 in.)
sheet: 44.8 × 32.8 cm (17 5/8 × 12 7/8 in.)
ULAE/Johns cat. raisonné 18
The Art Institute of Chicago, ULAE Collection acquired through a challenge grant of Mr. and Mrs. Thomas Dittmer; restricted gift of supporters of the Department of Prints and Drawings; Centennial Endowment; Margaret Fisher Endowment Fund, 1982.945b

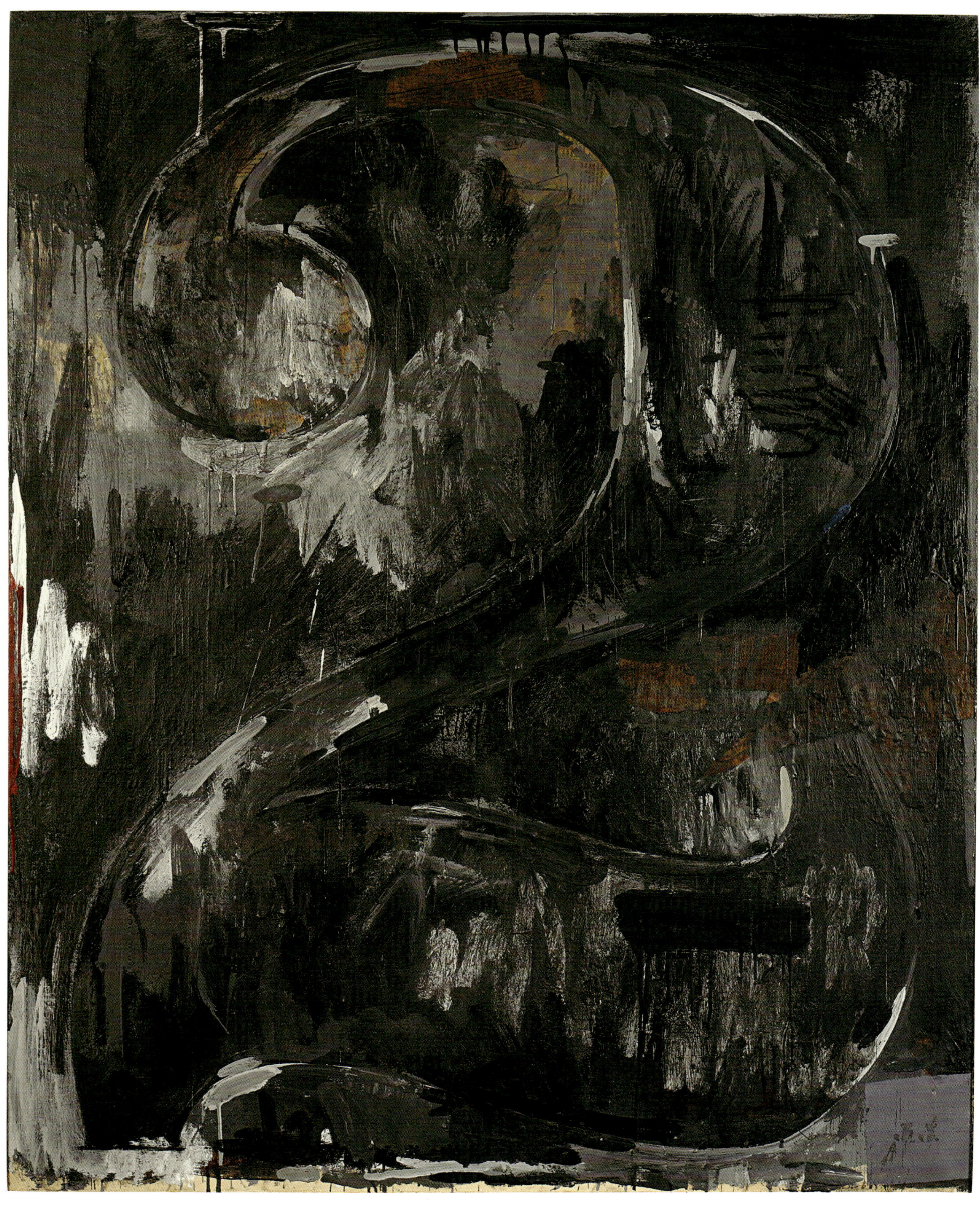

79. *Figure 2*, 1962
Encaustic and collage on canvas
127.5 × 102 cm (51 ½ × 41 ½ in.)
Kunstmuseum Basel, purchase 1970

80. *4 Leo*, 1970
Encaustic and collage on canvas
128.9 × 90.8 cm (50 ¾ × 35 ¾ in.)
Collection of Barbara Bertozzi Castelli

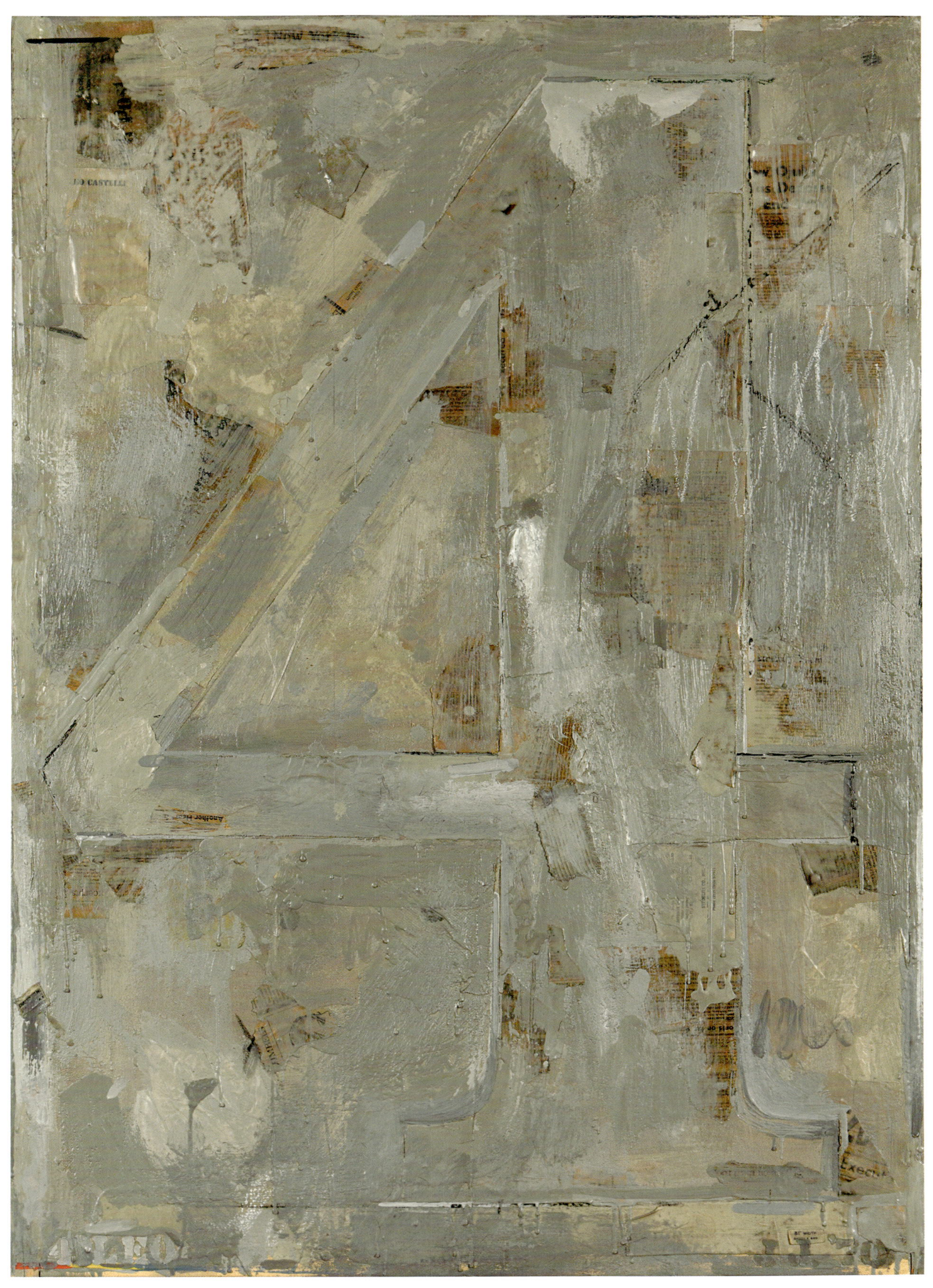

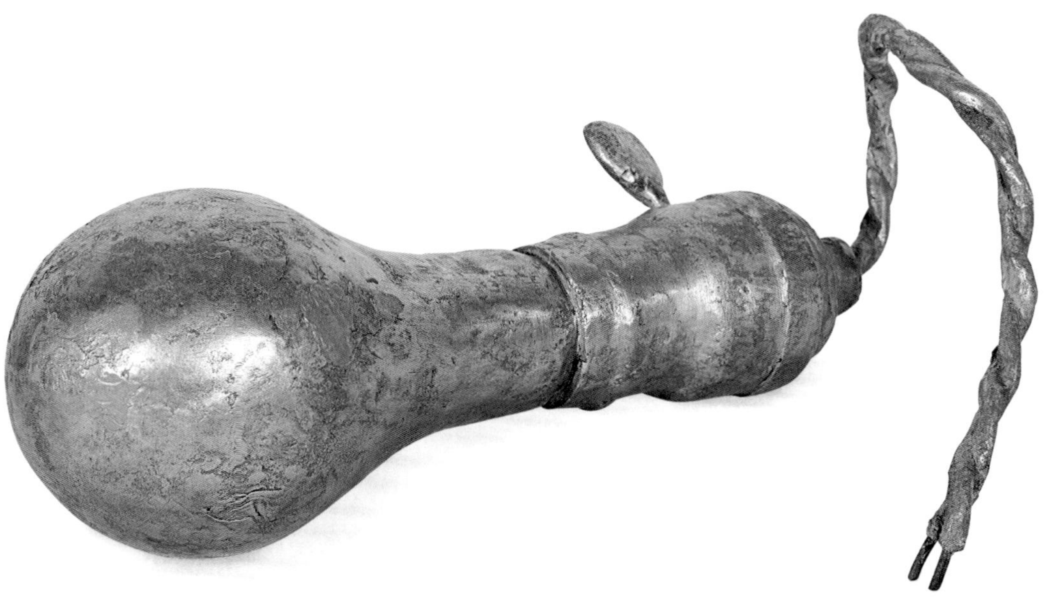

81. *Light Bulb II*, 1958
Sculp-metal
7.9 × 20.3 × 12.7 cm (3 ⅛ × 8 × 5 in.)
Collection of the artist

82. *Flashlight I*, 1958
Sculp-metal over flashlight and wood
13.3 × 23.2 × 9.8 cm (5 ¼ × 9 ⅛ × 3 ⅞ in.)
Sonnabend Collection

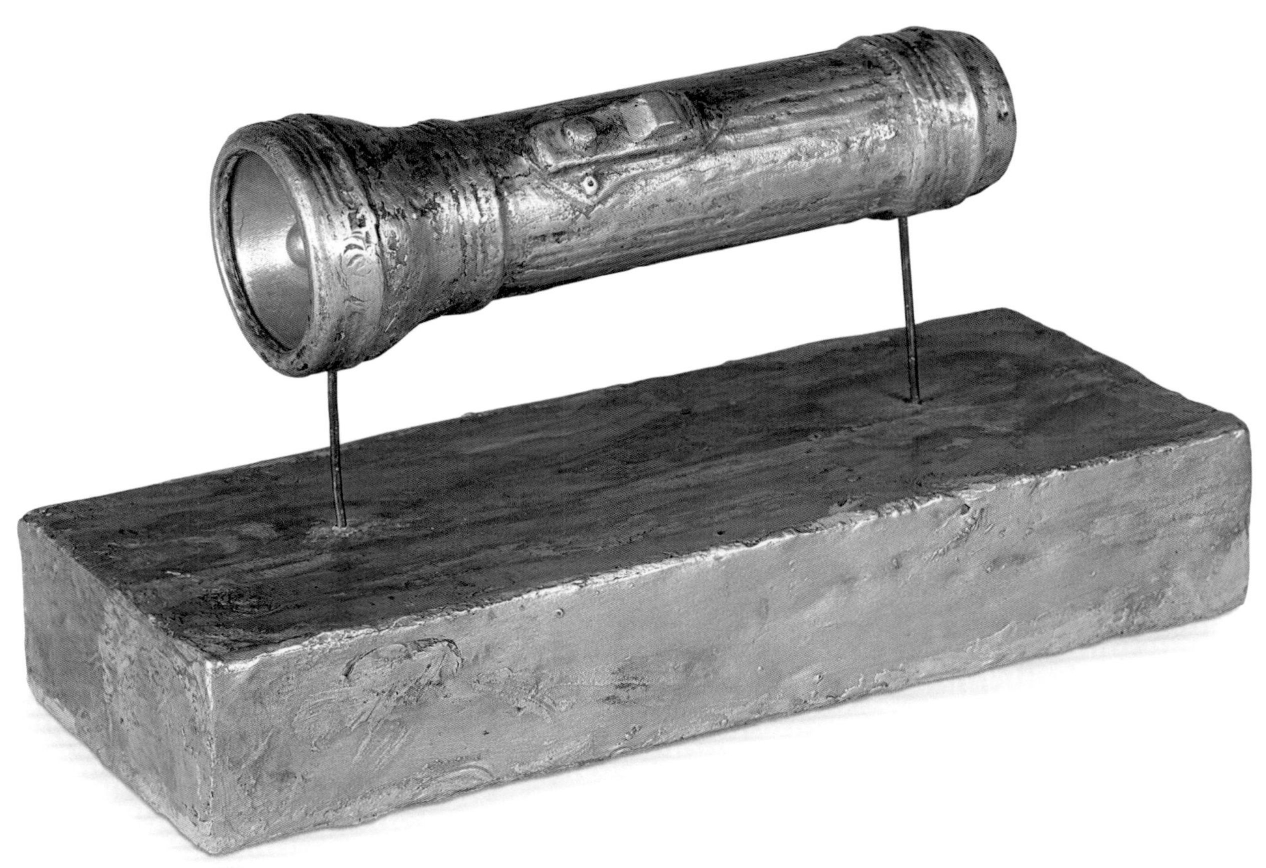

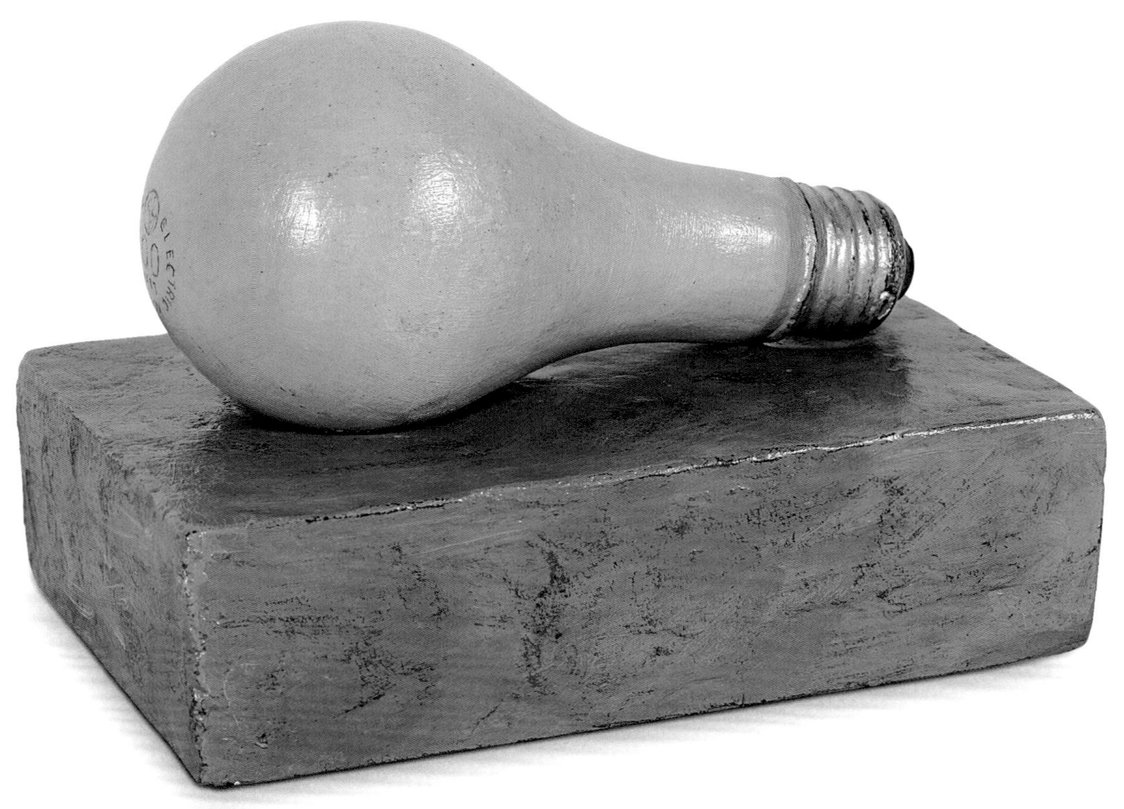

83. *Light Bulb*, 1960
Oil on bronze
10.8 × 15.2 × 10.2 cm (4 ¼ × 6 × 4 in.)
Collection of the artist

84. *The Critic Sees*, 1961
Sculp-metal over plaster with glass
7.9 × 16.5 × 5.7 cm (3 ⅛ × 6 ½ × 2 ¼ in.)
Collection of Steven A. Cohen

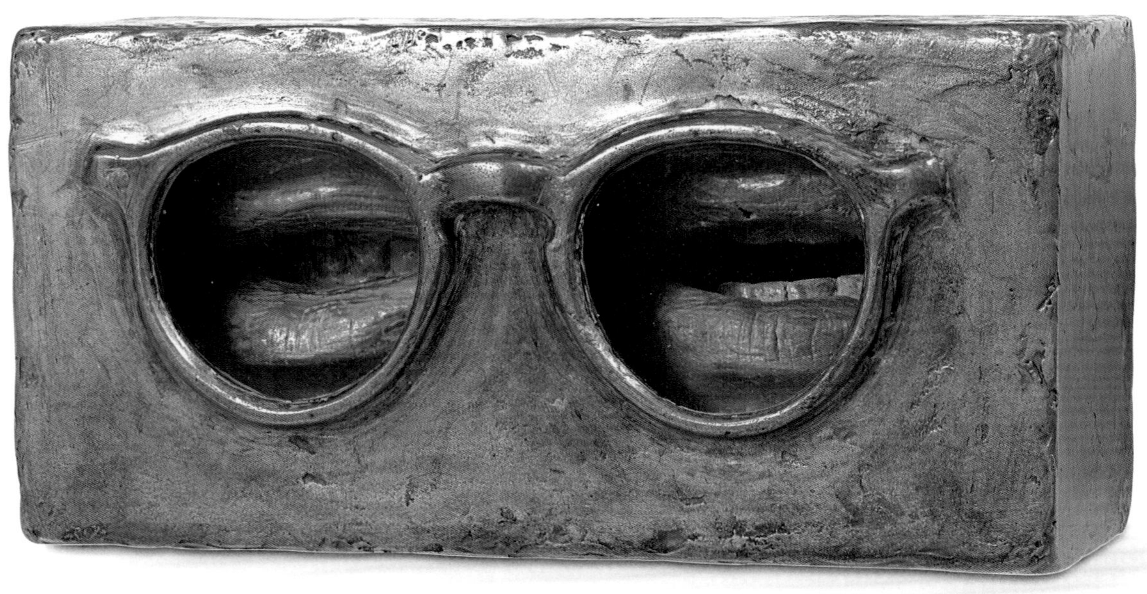

85. *In Memory of My Feelings—Frank O'Hara*, 1961
Oil on canvas with objects (two panels)
102.2 × 152.4 × 7.3 cm (40 ¼ × 60 × 2 ⅞ in.)
Museum of Contemporary Art, Chicago, partial gift of Apollo Plastics Corporation, courtesy of Stefan Edlis and H. Gael Neeson

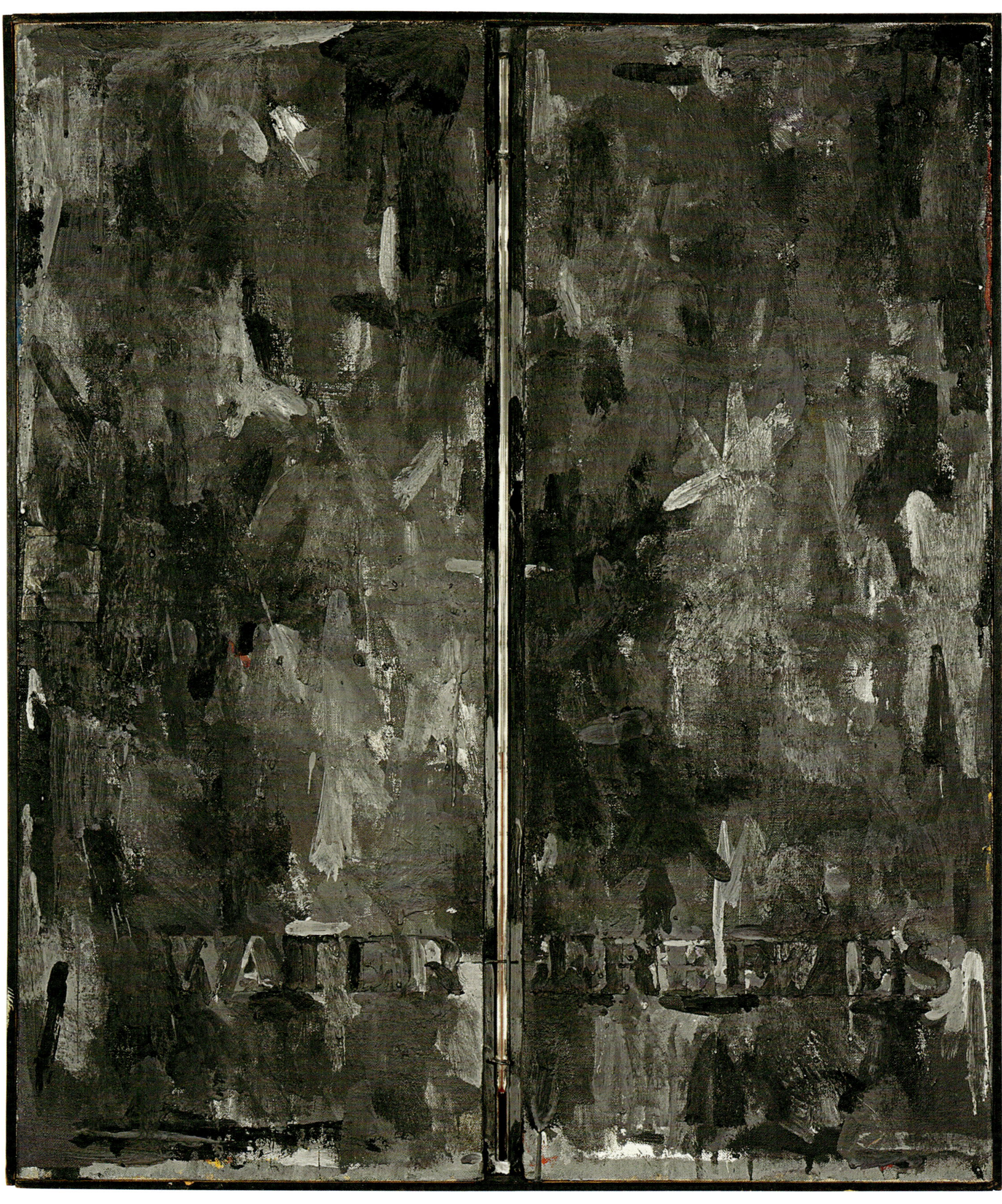

86. *Water Freezes*, 1961
Encaustic on canvas with objects
78.7 × 64.1 cm (31 × 25 ¼ in.)
The Marguerite and Robert Hoffman Collection

87. *Liar*, 1961
Encaustic, Sculp-metal, and graphite on cream wove paper
54 × 43.2 cm (21 ¼ × 17 in.)
Collection of Gail and Tony Ganz, Los Angeles

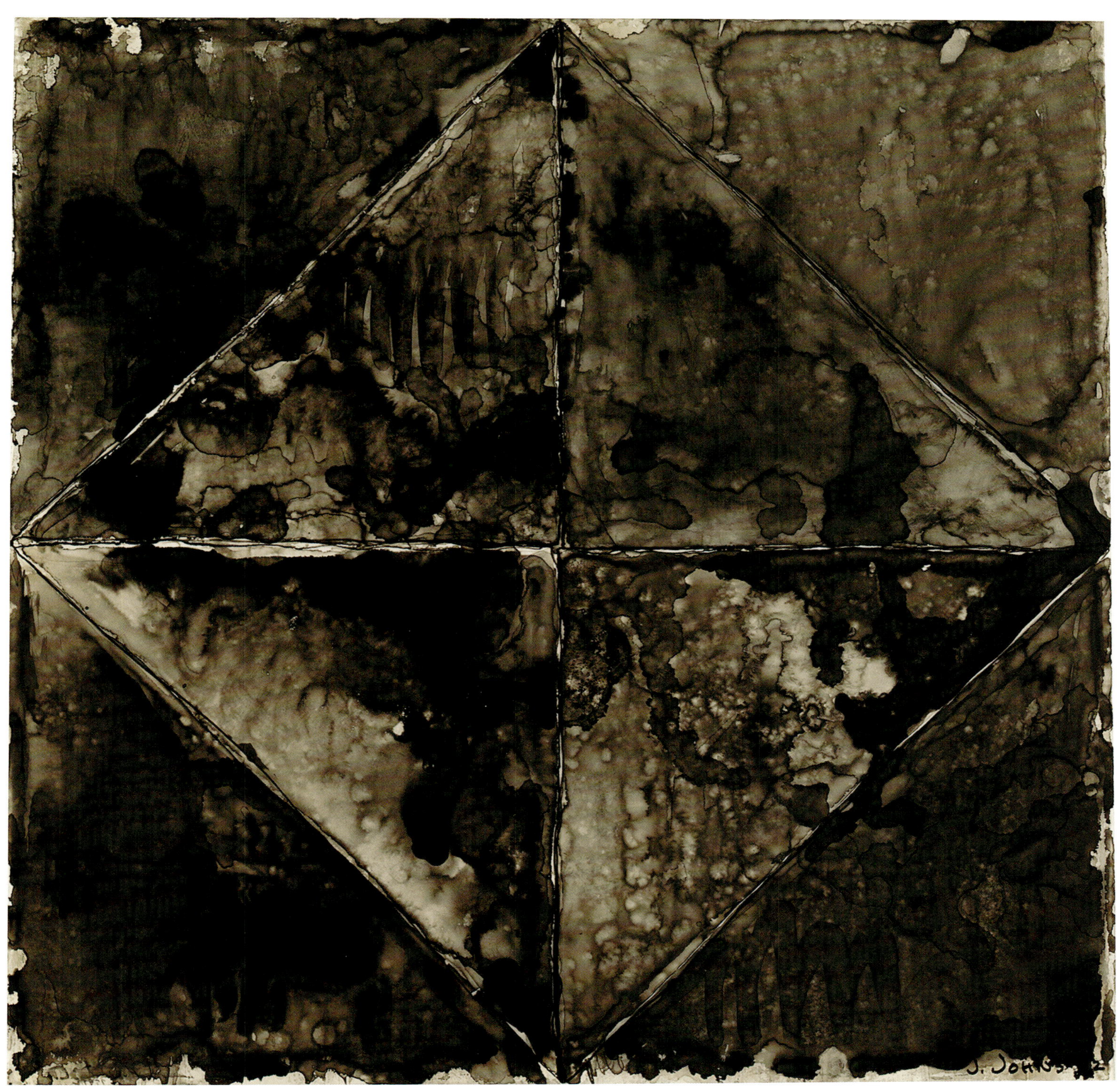
J. JOHNS

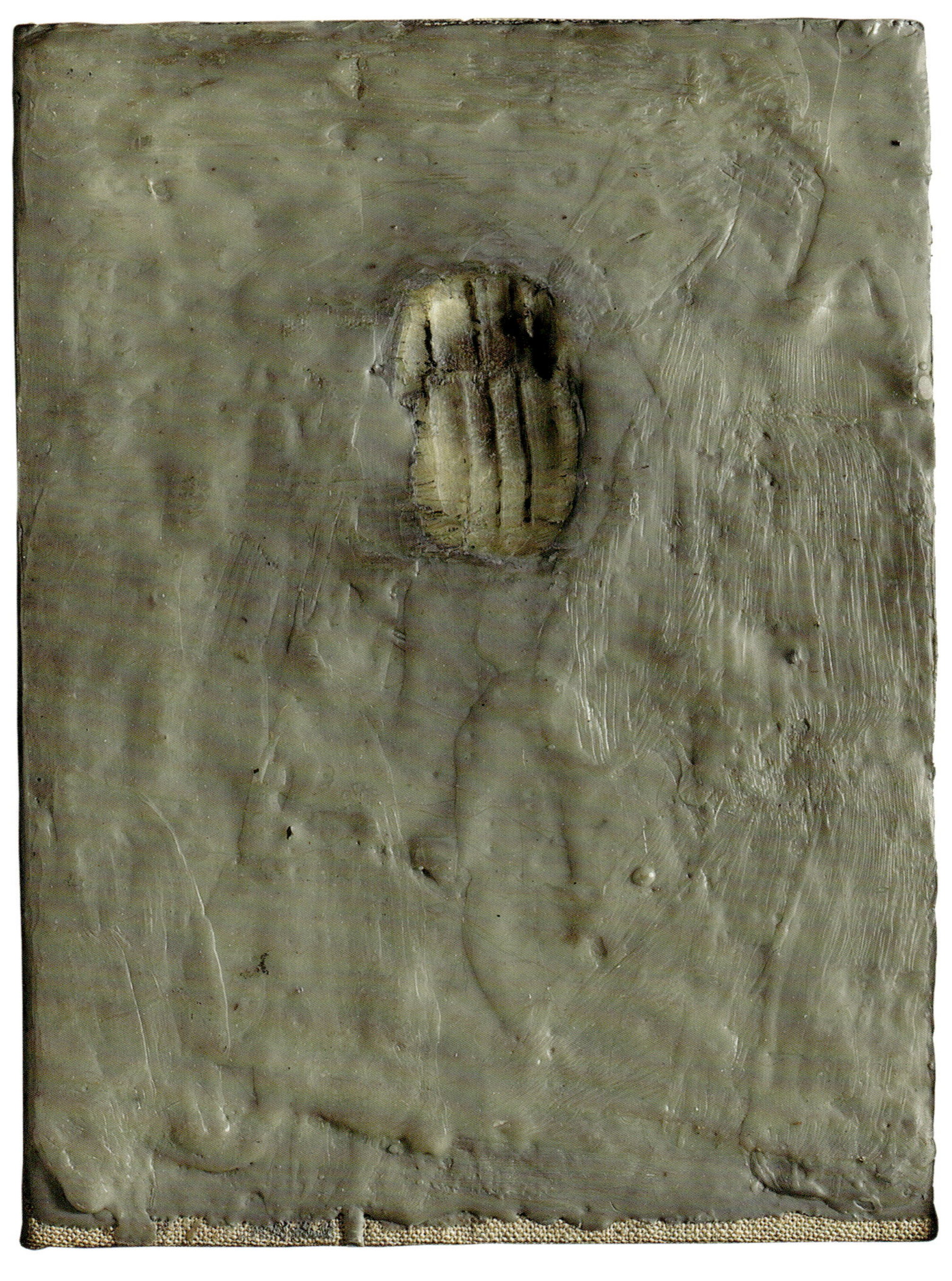

90. *Painting Bitten by a Man*, 1961
Encaustic on canvas, mounted on wood
24.1 × 17.5 cm (9 ½ × 6 ⅞ in.)
The Museum of Modern Art, New York,
gift of Jasper Johns in memory of Kirk Varnedoe,
Chief Curator of the Department of Painting
and Sculpture, 1989–2001

91. *No*, 1961
Encaustic, collage, and Sculp-metal
on canvas with objects
172.7 × 101.6 cm (68 × 40 in.)
Collection of the artist

NO

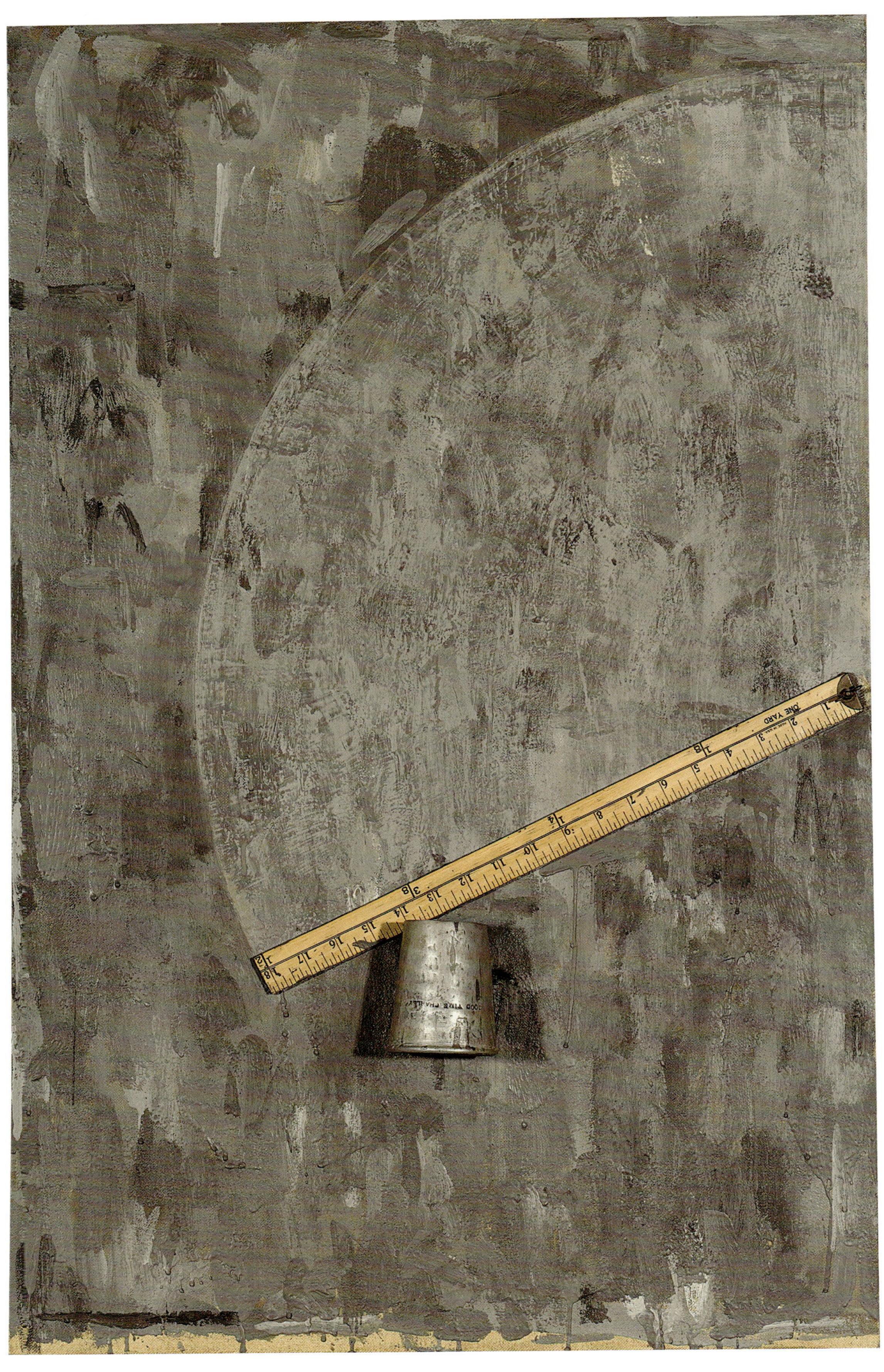

92. *Good Time Charley*, 1961
Encaustic on canvas with objects
96.5 × 61 × 11.4 cm (38 × 24 × 4 ½ in.)
Collection of Mark Lancaster, courtesy of the Philadelphia Museum of Art

93. *Device*, 1962
Oil on canvas with objects
101.6 × 76.2 cm (40 × 30 in.)
The Baltimore Museum of Art, Purchased with funds provided by the Dexter M. Ferry, Jr., Trustee Corporation Fund, and by Edith Ferry

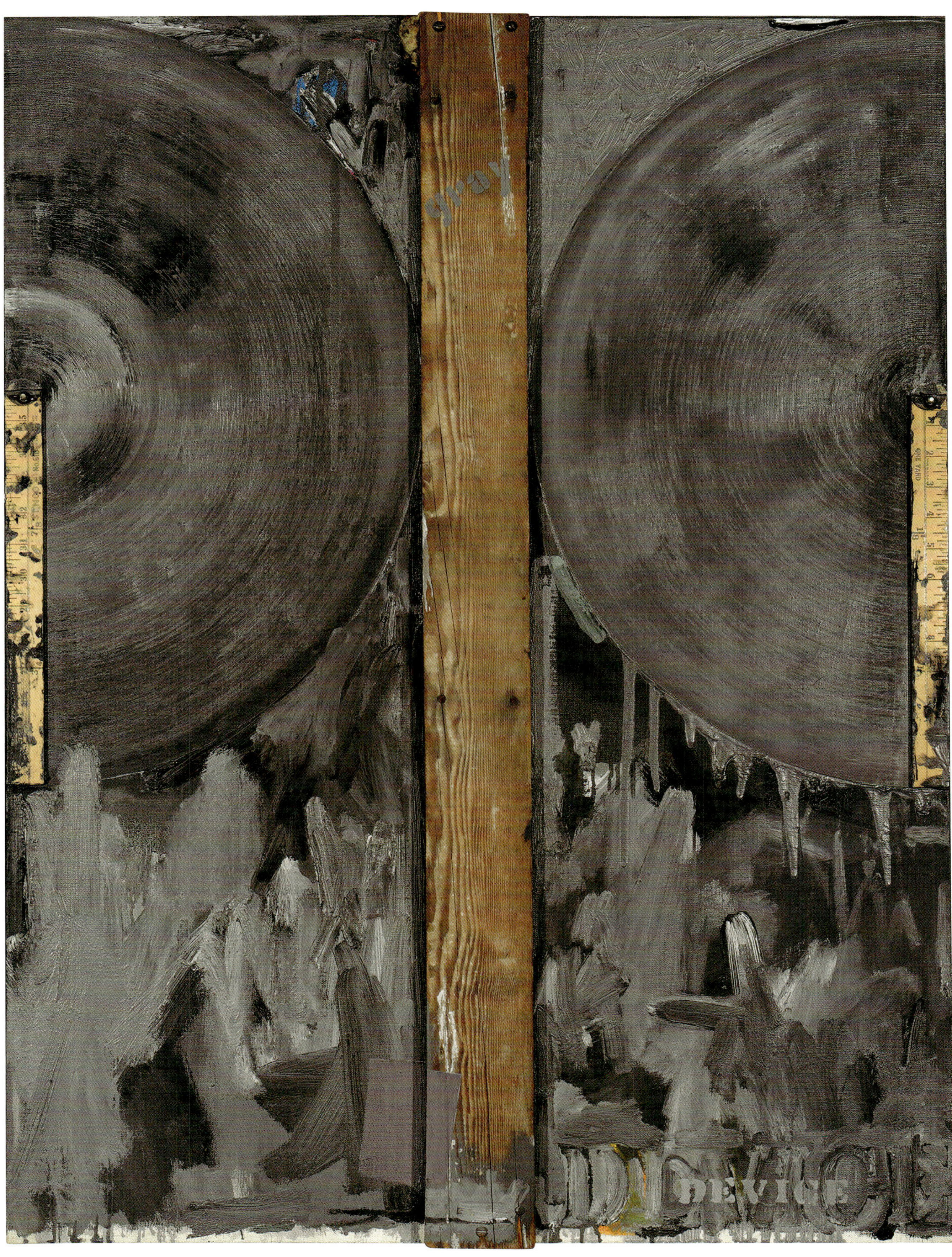
gray
DEVICE

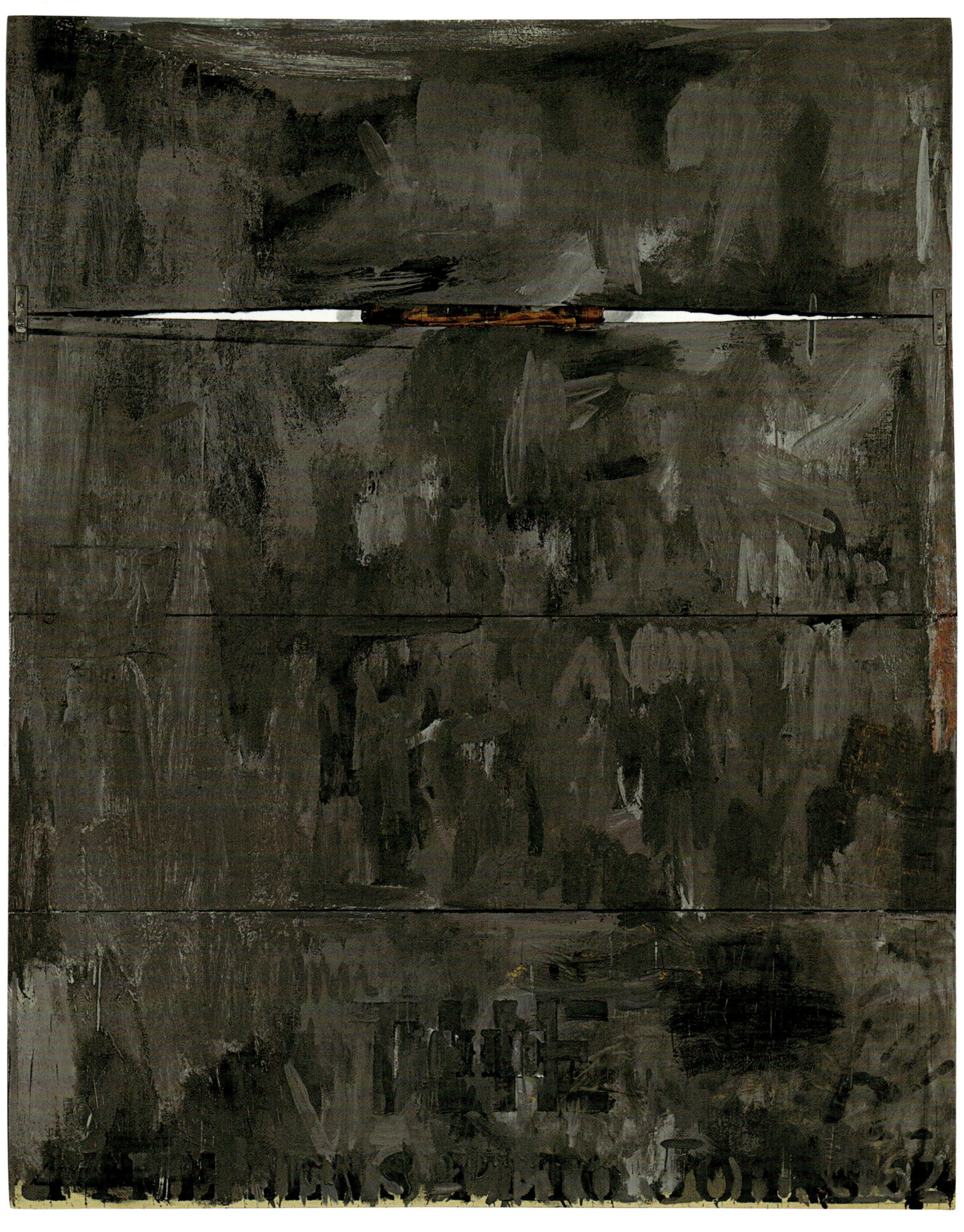

94. *4 the News*, 1962
Encaustic and collage on canvas with objects
165.1 × 127.6 cm (65 × 50 ¼ in.)
Kunstsammlung Nordrhein-Westfalen, Düsseldorf

95. *Fool's House*, 1962
Oil on canvas with objects
182.9 × 91.4 cm (72 × 36 in.)
Collection of Jean-Christophe Castelli, New York

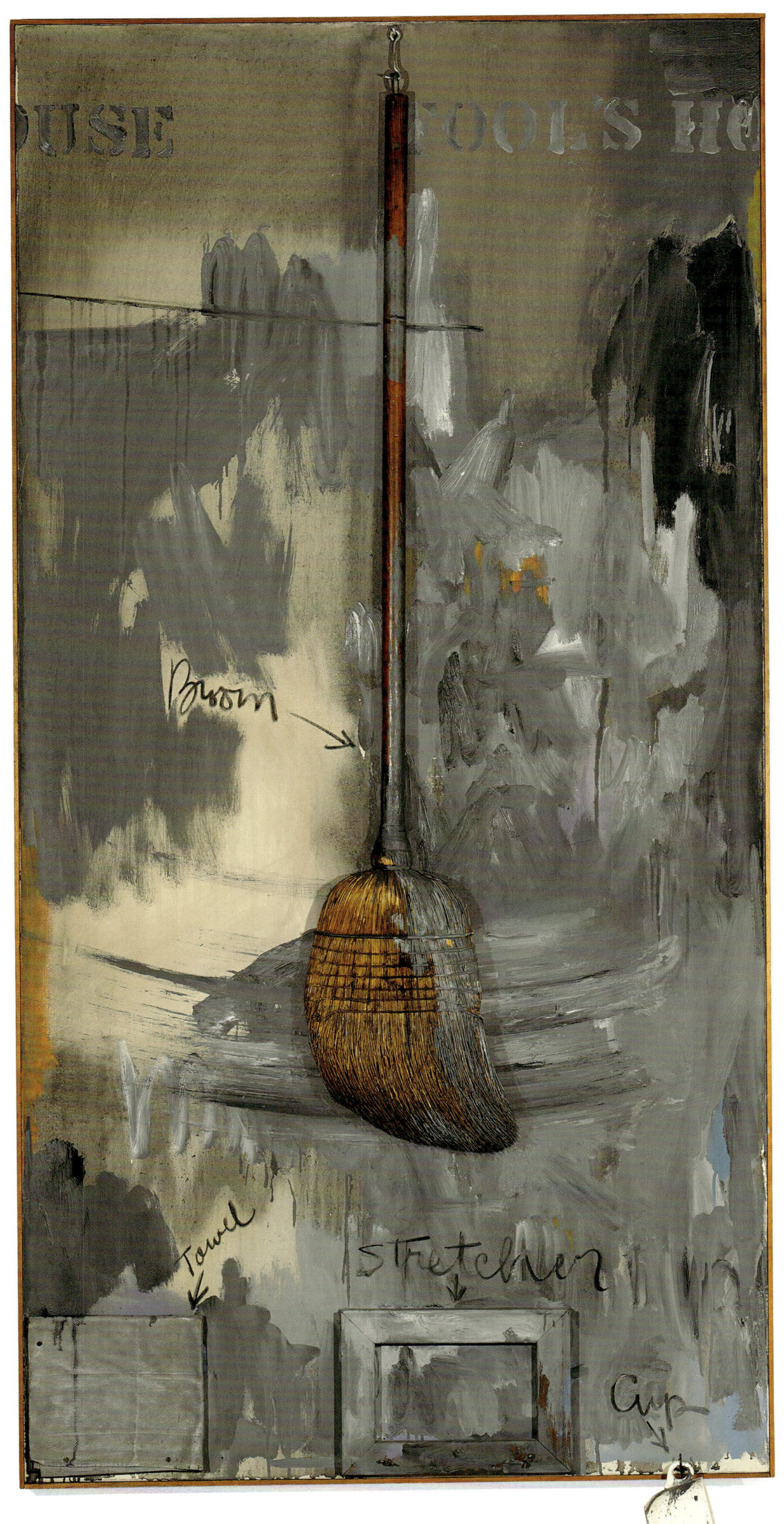
FOOL'S
Broom
Towel
Stretcher
Cup

96. *Portrait–Viola Farber*, 1961–62
Encaustic on canvas with objects
122 × 158 cm (48 × 62 in.)
Private collection, courtesy of MaxmArt, Mendrisio

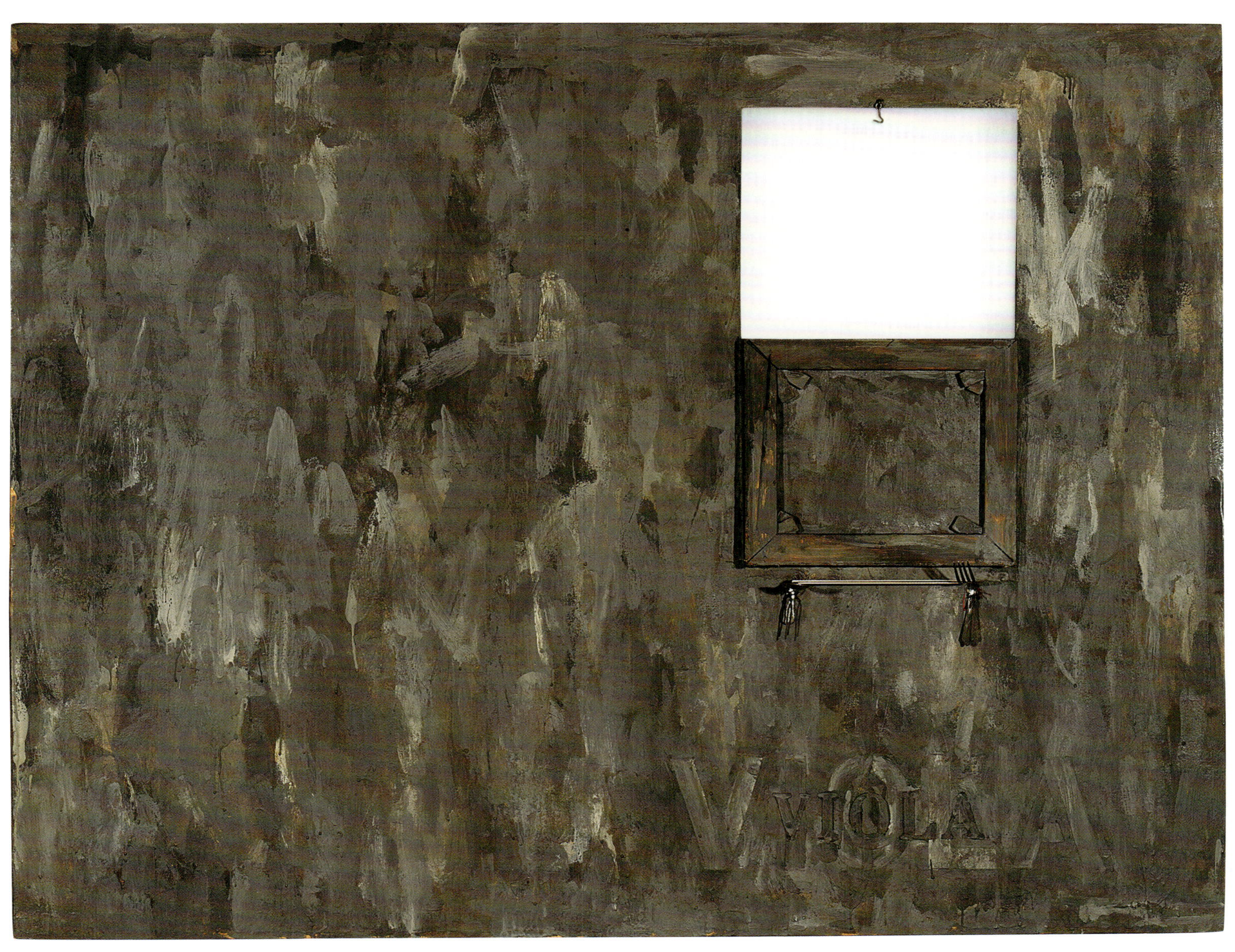
VIOLA

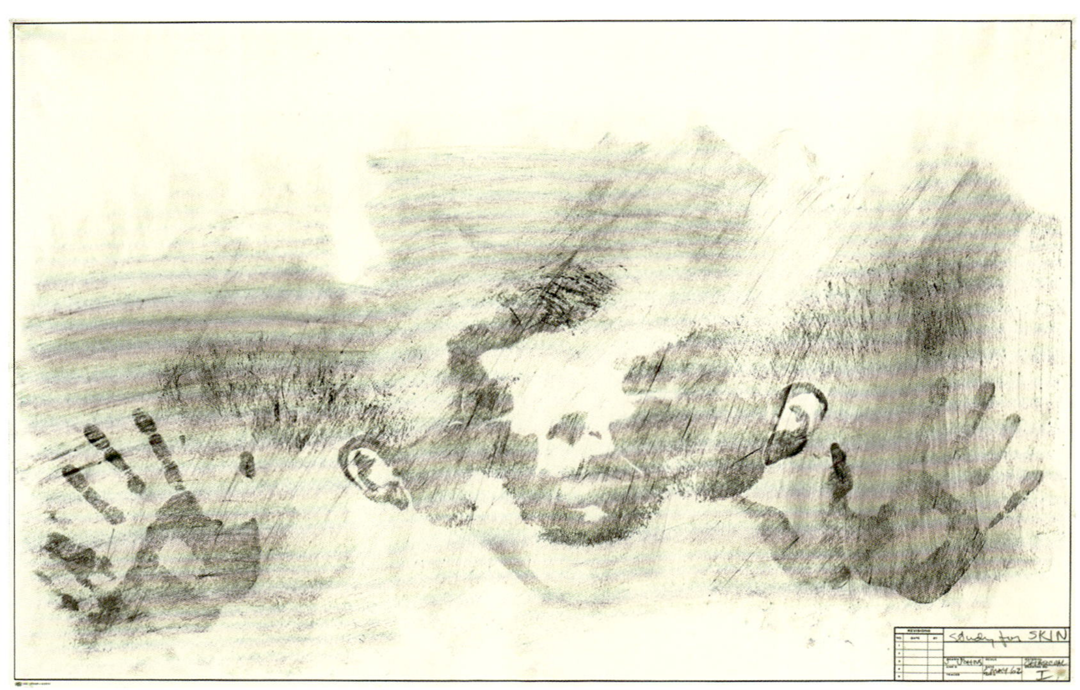

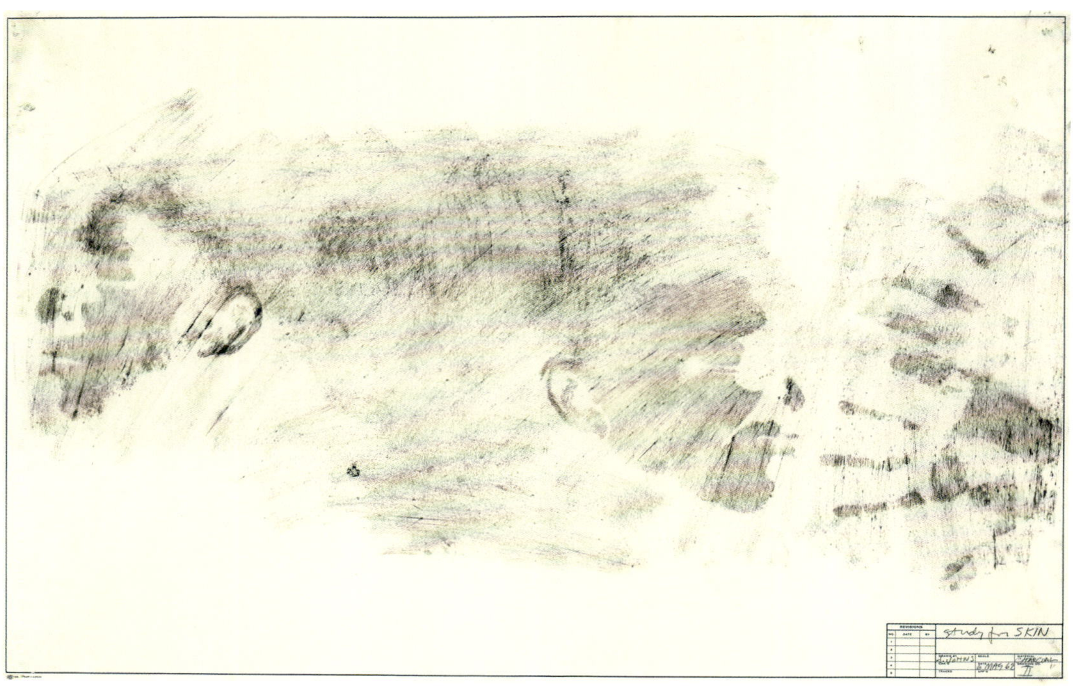

97. *Study for "Skin I,"* 1962
Charcoal and oil on ivory wove drafting paper
55.9 × 86.4 cm (22 × 34 in.)
Collection of the artist

98. *Study for "Skin II,"* 1962
Charcoal and oil on ivory wove drafting paper
55.9 × 86.4 cm (22 × 34 in.)
Collection of the artist

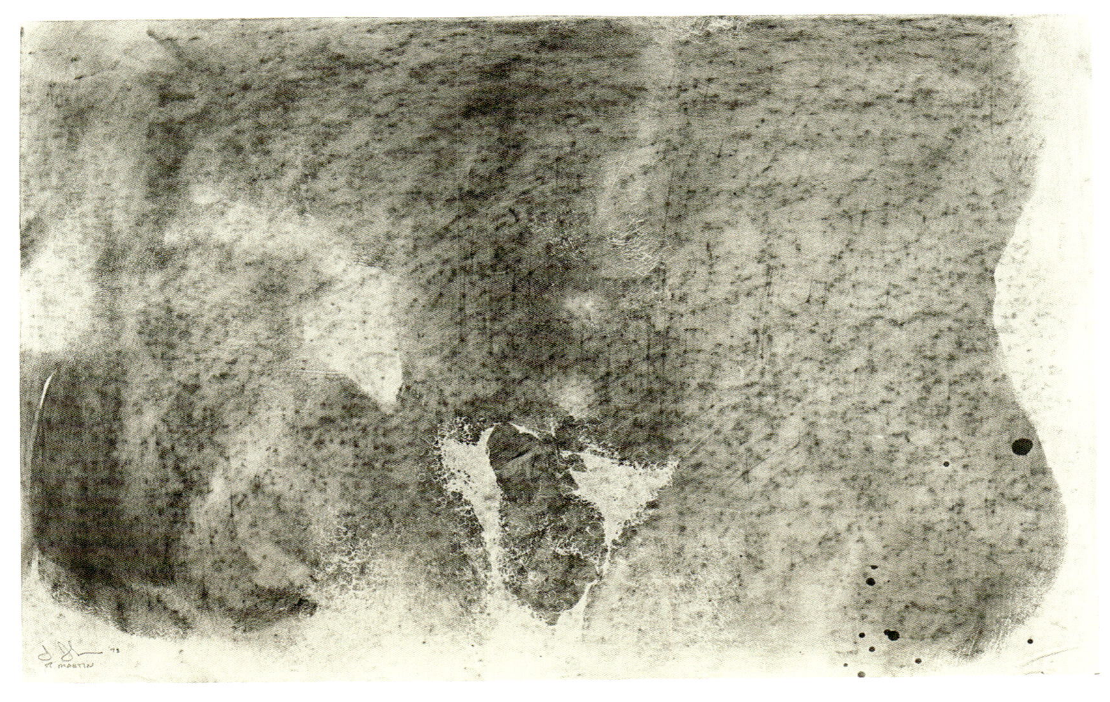

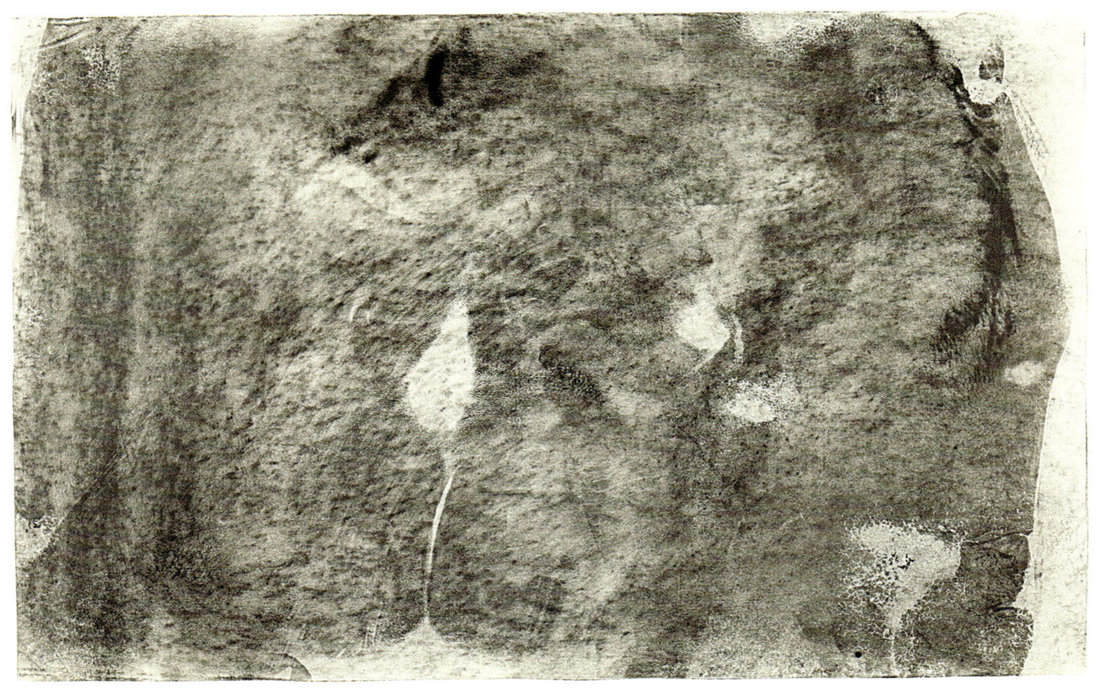

99. *Skin I*, 1973
Charcoal and oil on ivory wove paper
64.8 × 102.2 cm (25 ½ × 40 ¼ in.)
Collection of the artist

100. *Skin II*, 1973
Charcoal and oil on ivory wove paper
64.8 × 102.2 cm (25 ½ × 40 ¼ in.)
Collection of the artist

101. *Skin*, 1975
Charcoal and oil on ivory wove paper
103.5 × 78.1 cm (41 ¾ × 30 ¾ in.)
Collection of Richard Serra and
Clara Weyergraf-Serra, New York

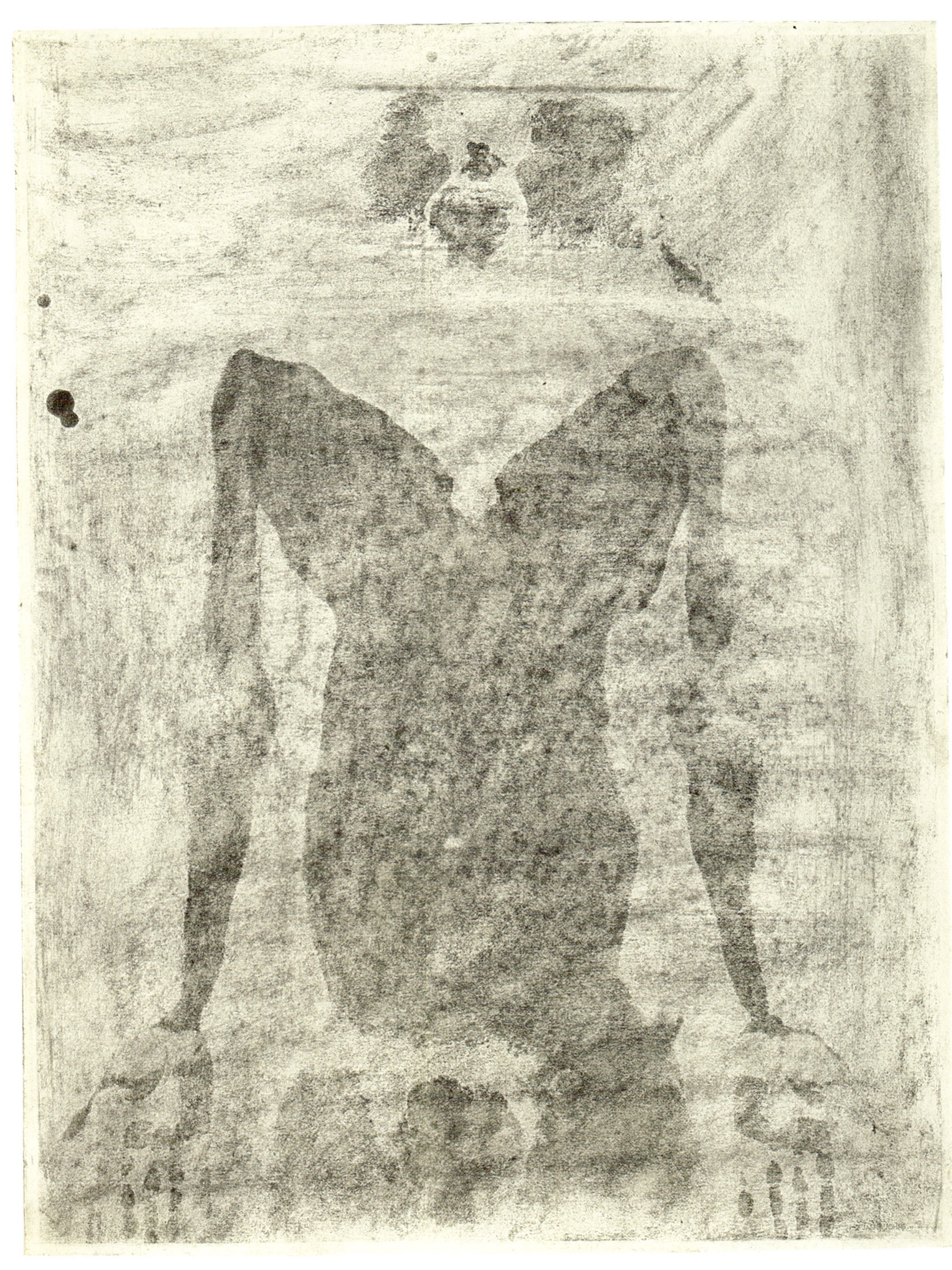

102. *Diver*, 1962–63
Charcoal, pastel, and watercolor on tan wove paper, mounted on canvas (two panels)
219.7 × 182.2 cm (86 ½ × 71 ¾ in.)
The Museum of Modern Art, New York, partial gift of Kate Ganz and Tony Ganz in memory of their parents, Victor and Sally Ganz, and in memory of Kirk Varnedoe; Mrs. John Hay Whitney Bequest Fund; gift of Edgar Kaufmann, Jr. (by exchange) and purchase; acquired by the Trustees of the Museum of Modern Art in memory of Kirk Varnedoe, 2003

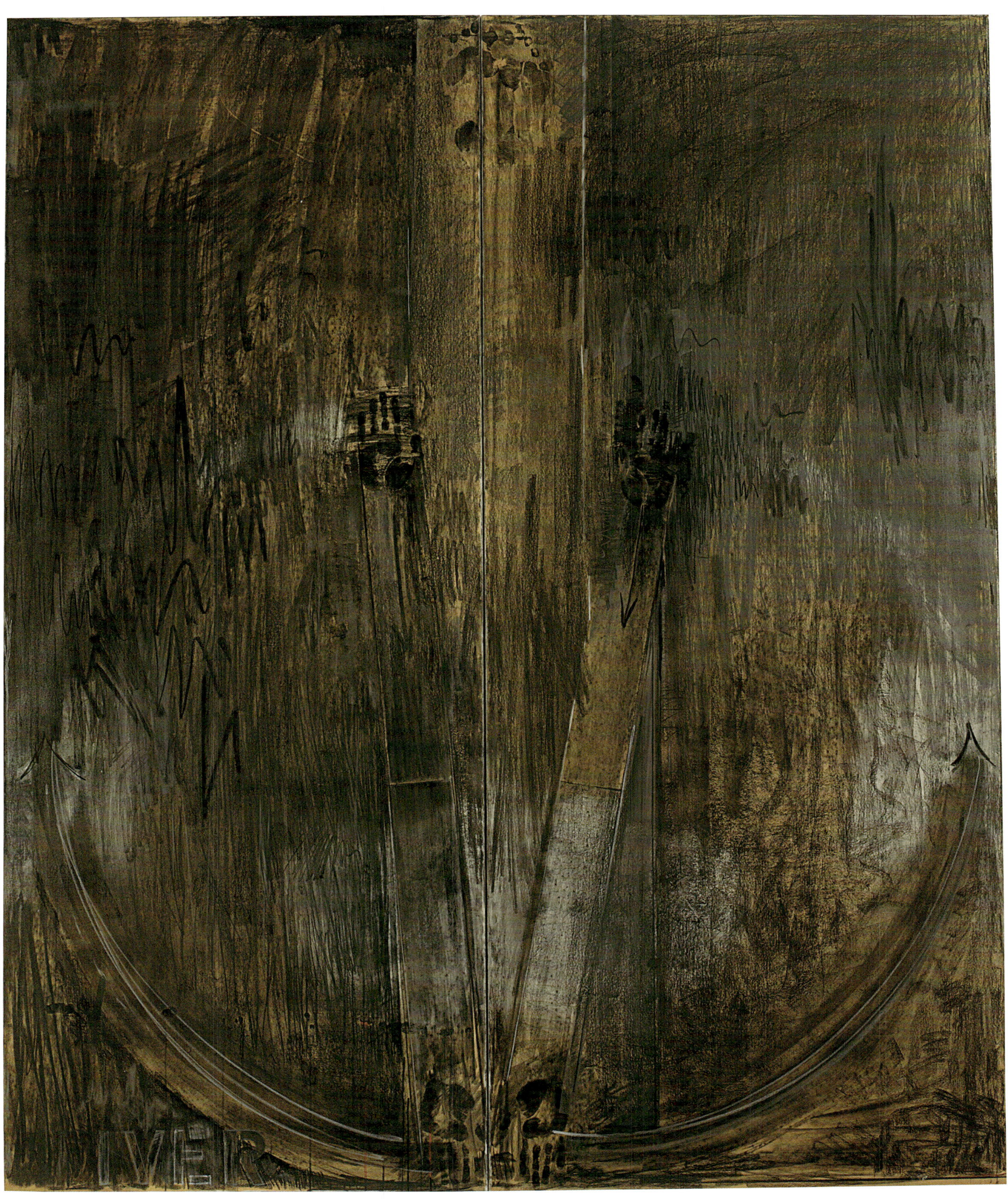
IVER

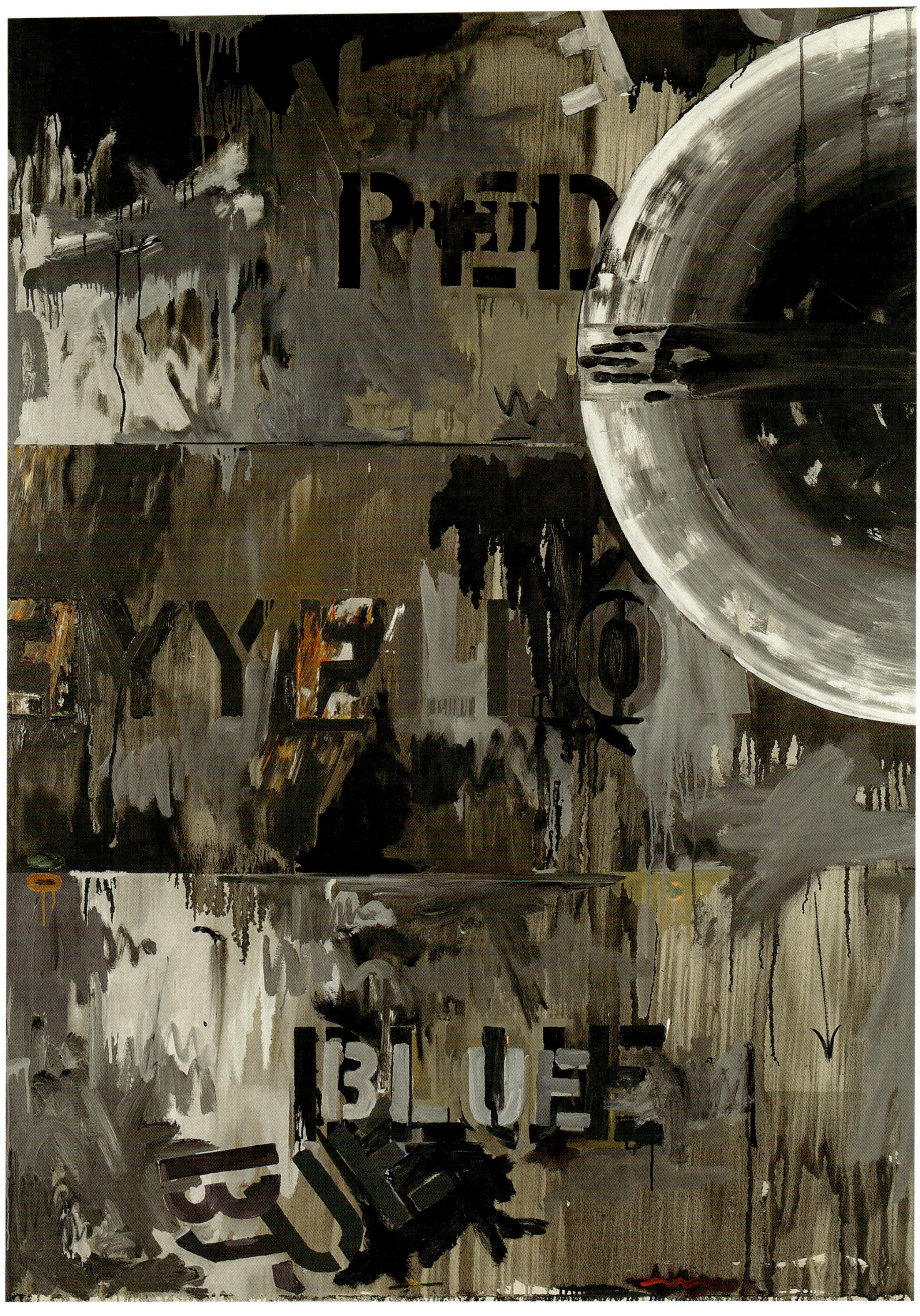

103. *Periscope (Hart Crane)*, 1963
Oil on canvas
170.2 × 121.9 cm (67 × 48 in.)
Collection of the artist

104. *Periscope (Hart Crane)*, 1977
Ink on plastic
88.9 × 62.2 cm (35 × 24 ½ in.)
Nerman Collection, Kansas City

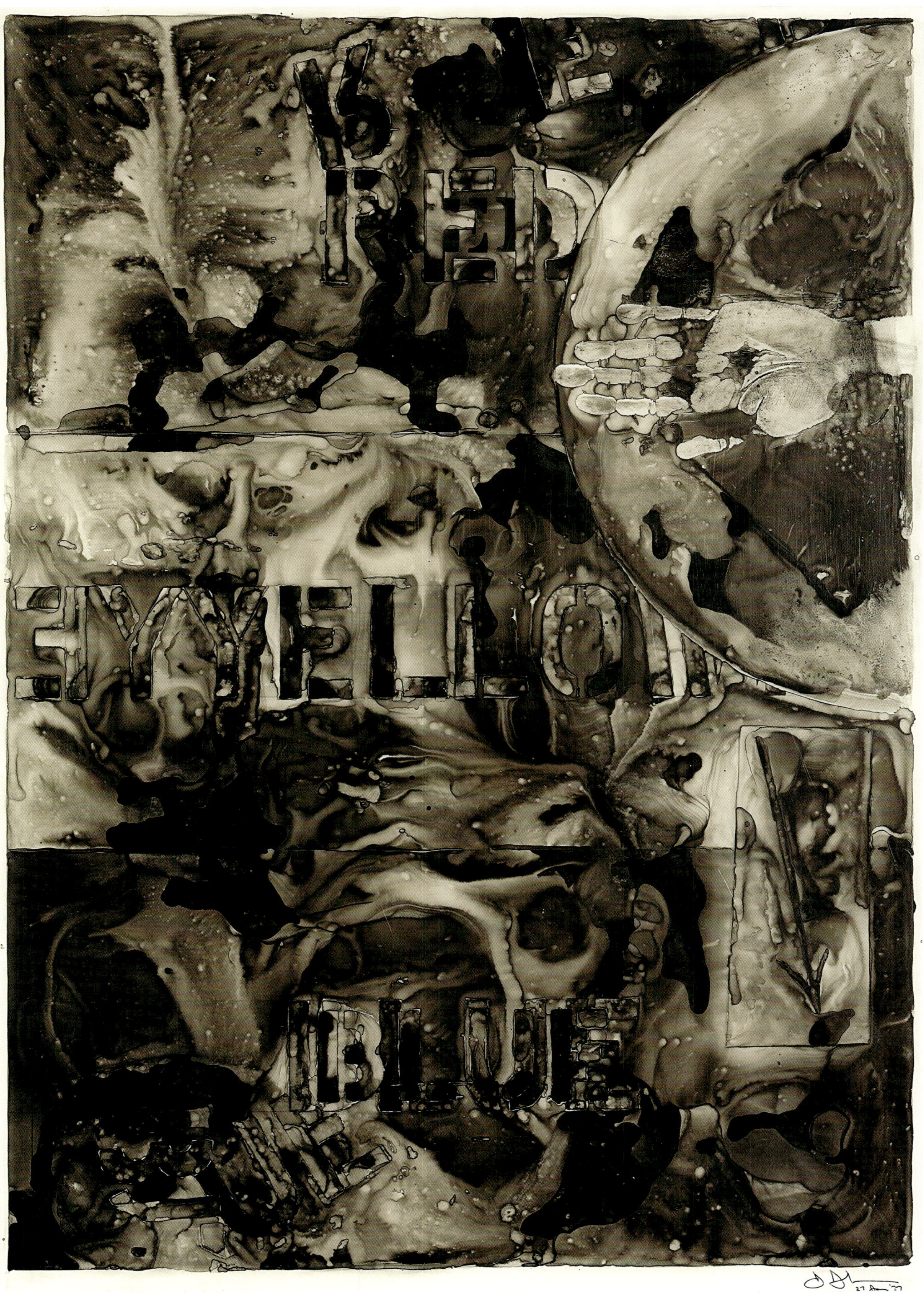
RED
BLUE

105. *Souvenir*, 1964
Encaustic on canvas with objects
73 × 53.3 cm (28 ¾ × 21 in.)
Collection of the artist

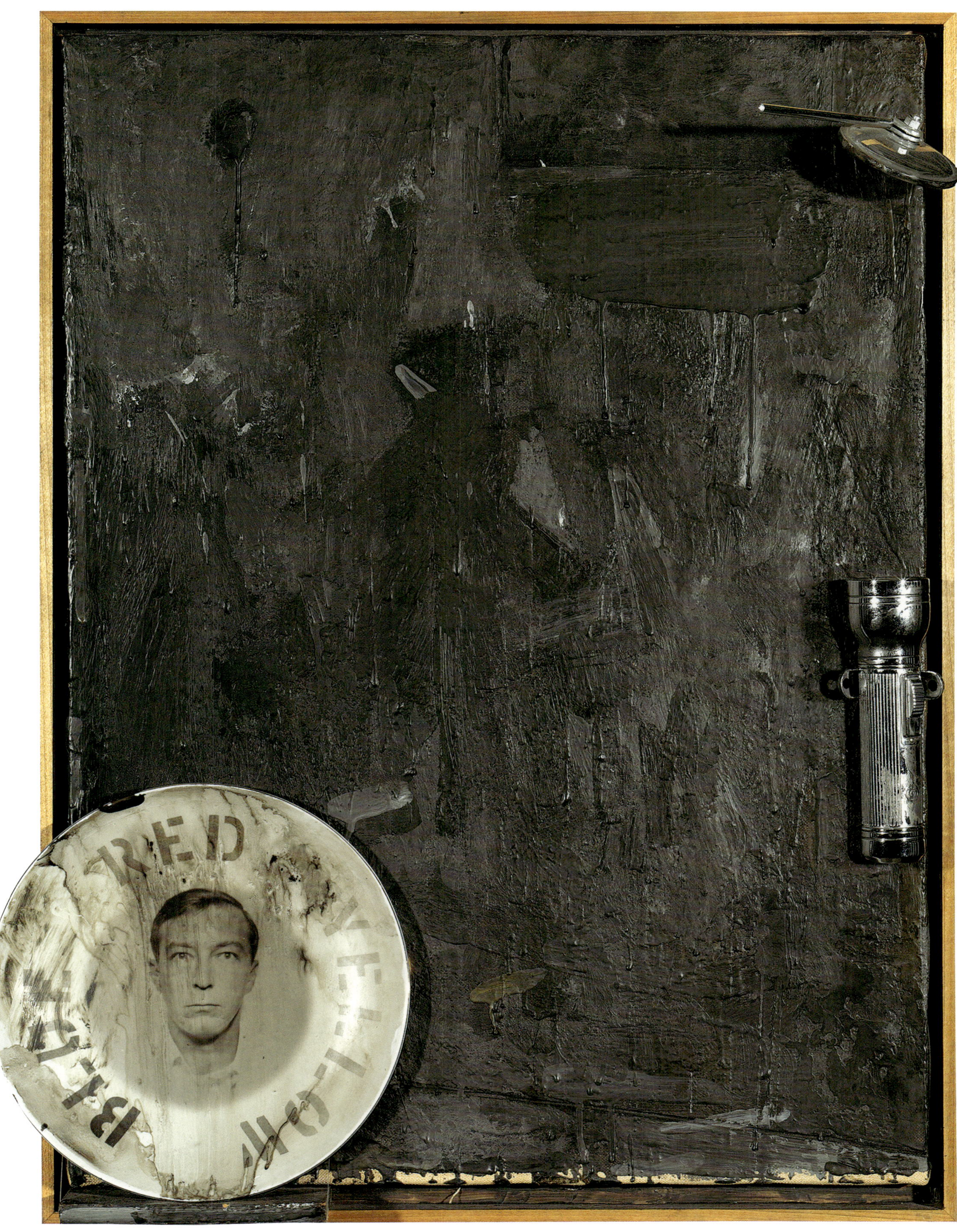
RED

106. *Voice*, 1964–67
Oil on canvas with objects (two panels)
243.8 × 176.5 × 6 cm (96 × 69 ½ × 2 ⅜ in.)
The Menil Collection, Houston

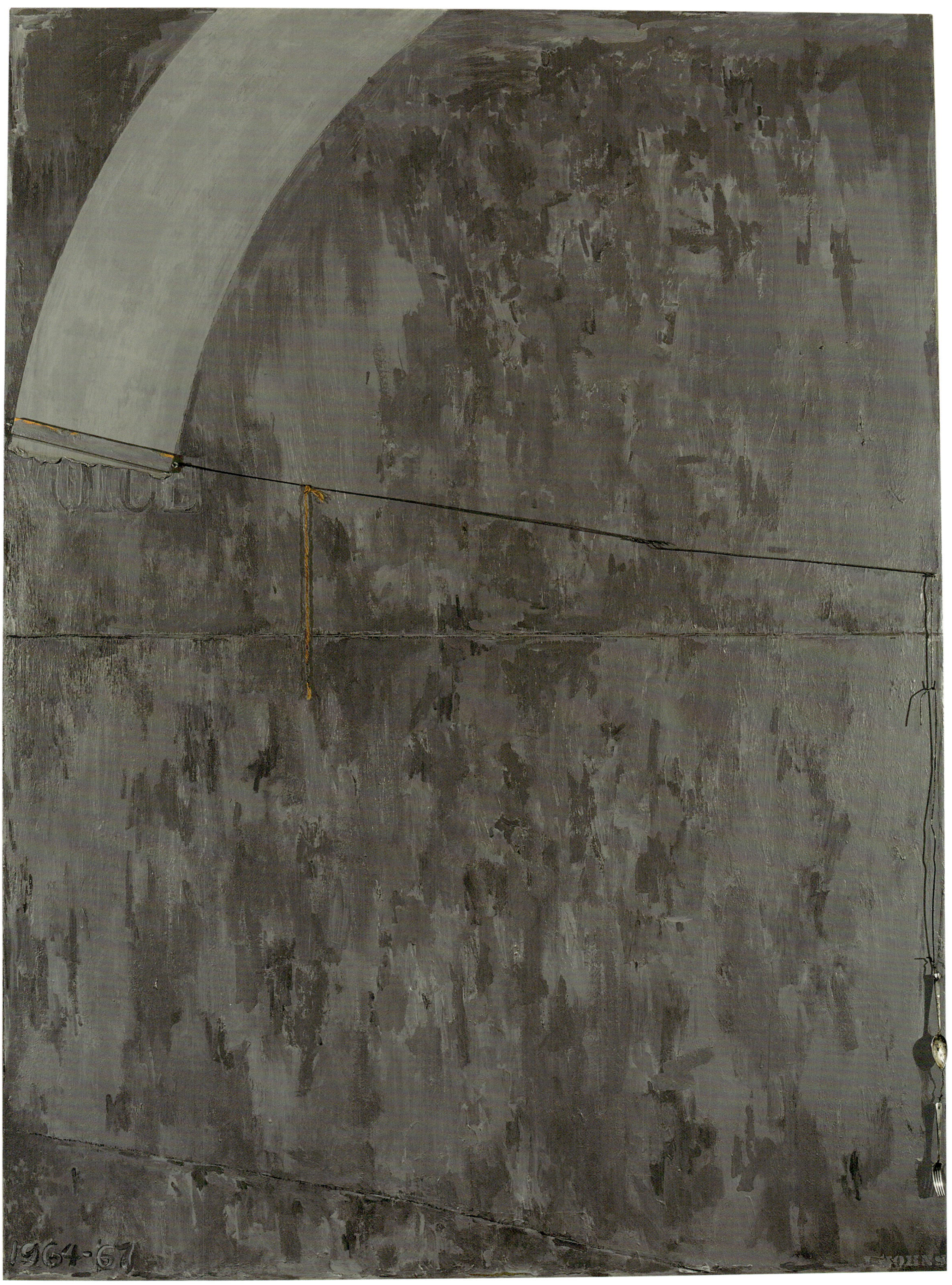
1964-67

107. *Screen Piece 3*, 1968
Oil on canvas
182.9 × 127 cm (72 × 50 in.)
Nerman Collection, Kansas City

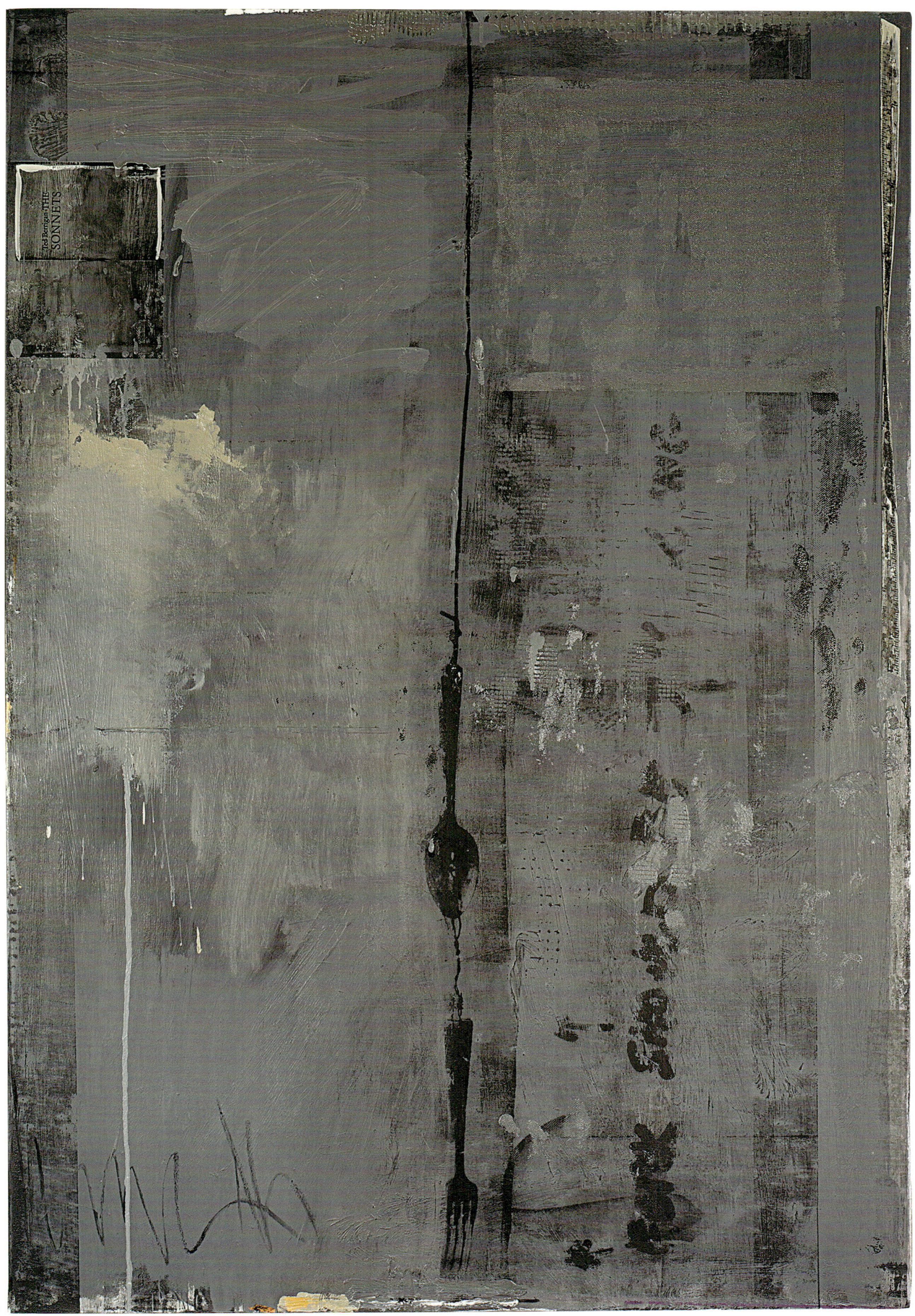
Ted Berrigan · THE
SONNETS

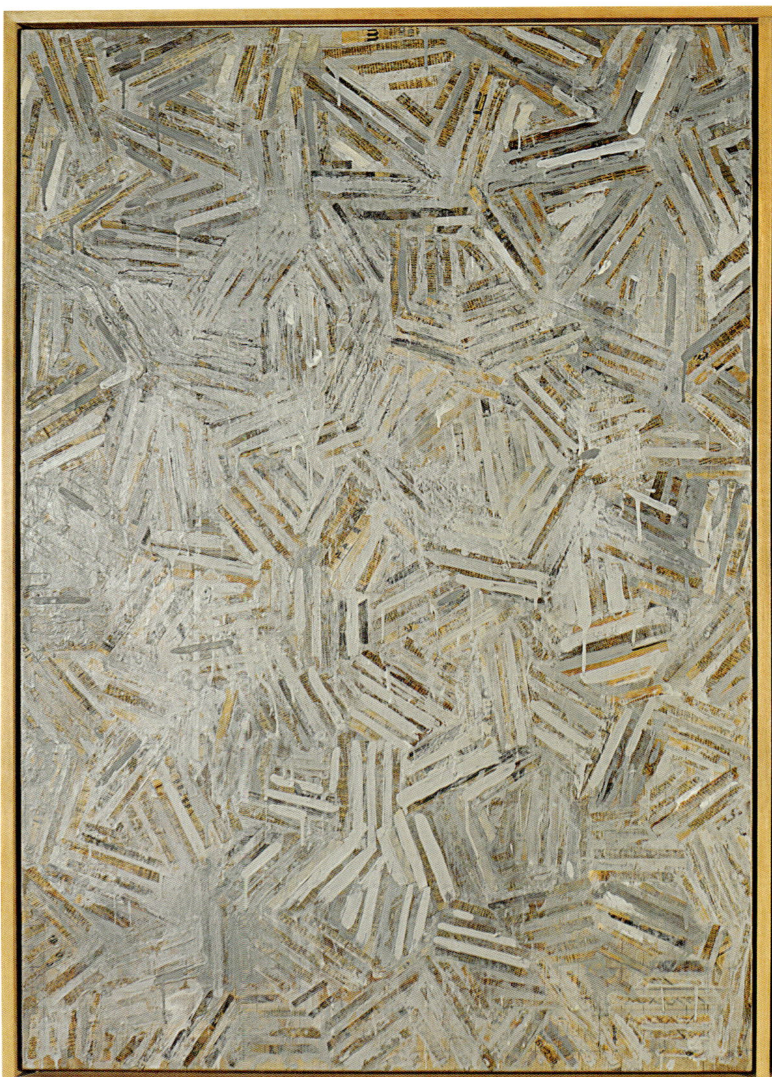
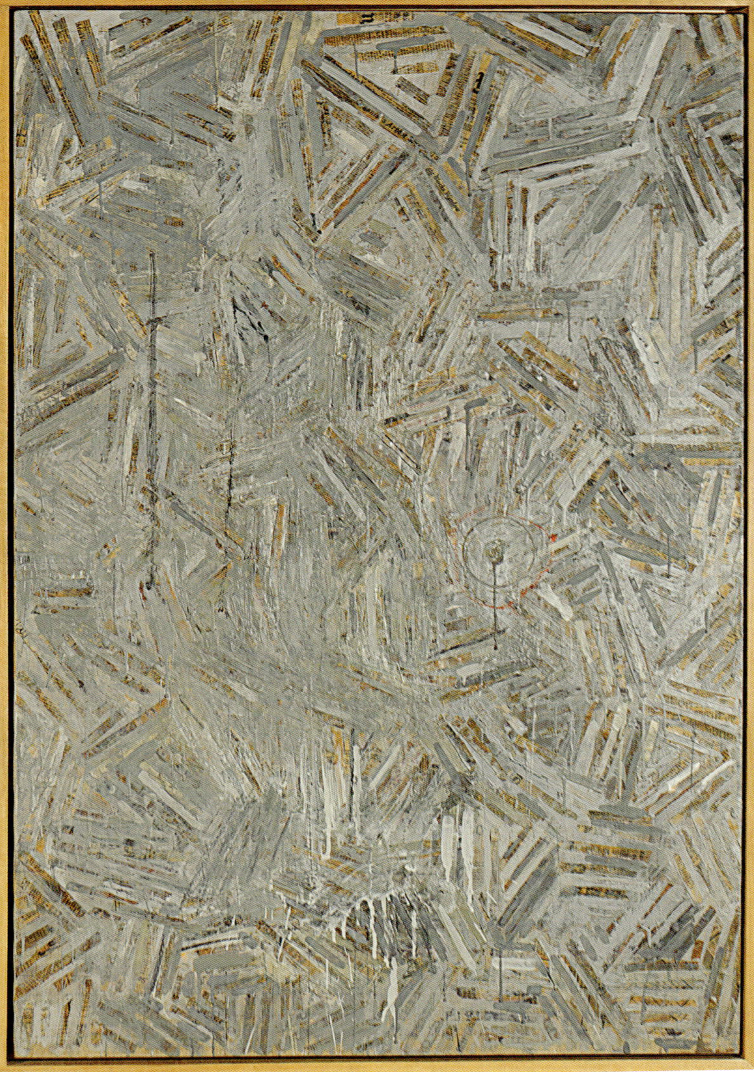

108. *The Dutch Wives*, 1975
Encaustic and collage on canvas (two panels)
131.5 × 180.3 cm (51 ¾ × 71 in.)
Collection of the artist

109. *The Dutch Wives*, 1977
Simca Print Artists, Inc., 1977
Screenprint from twenty-nine screens on
cream Japanese paper (Kurotani Kozo; wmk.:
The Dutch Wives J Johns 1977)
image: 95.3 × 124.5 cm (37 ½ × 49 in.)
sheet: 109.2 × 141 cm (43 × 56 in.)
ULAE/Johns cat. raisonné 187
Walker Art Center, Minneapolis, gift of Judy and
Kenneth Dayton, 1988

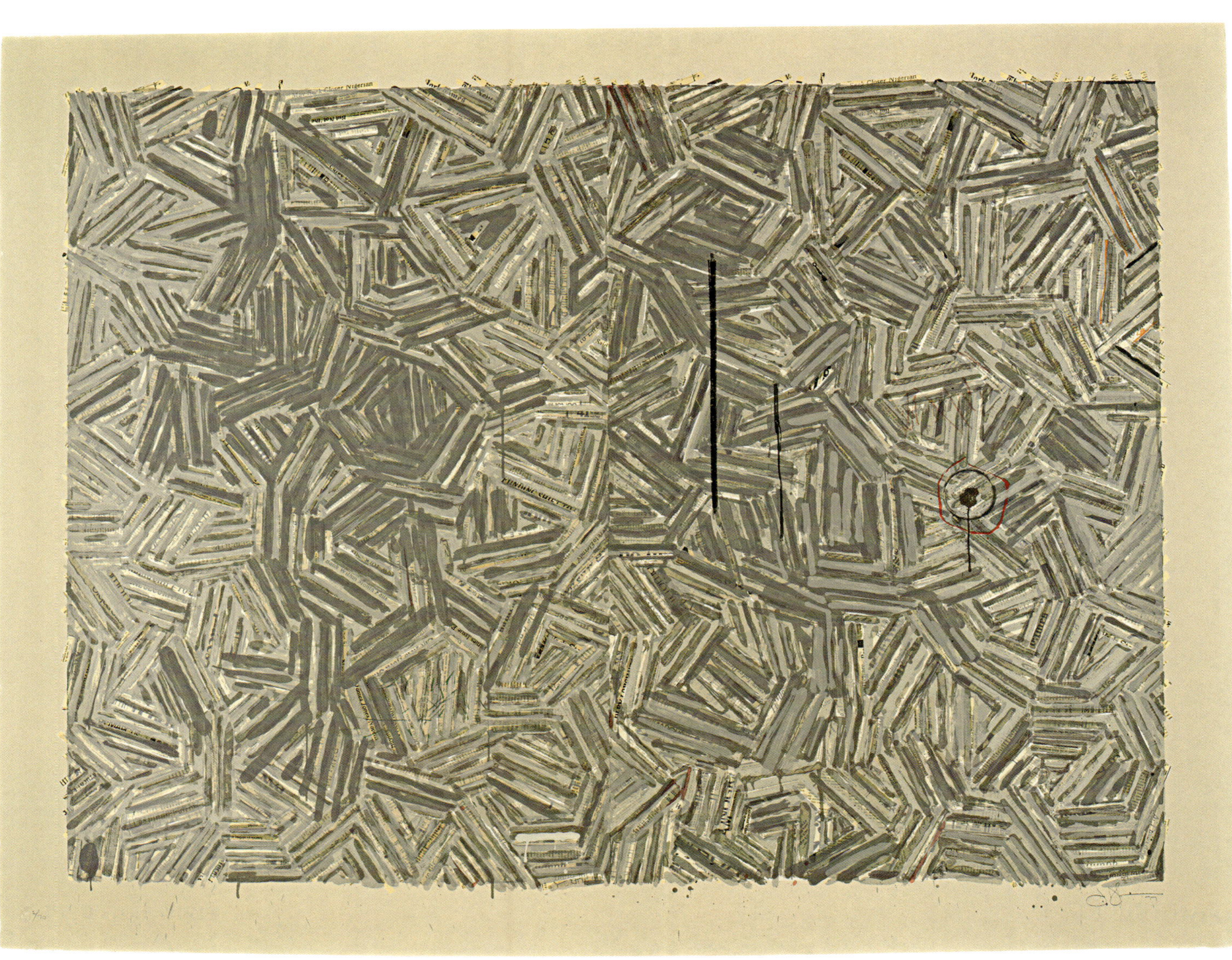

110. *Céline*, 1978
Oil on canvas (two panels)
215.5 × 122.5 cm (84 7/8 × 48 1/4 in.)
Kunstmuseum Basel, acquired with a contribution from the Max Geldner Foundation, 1979

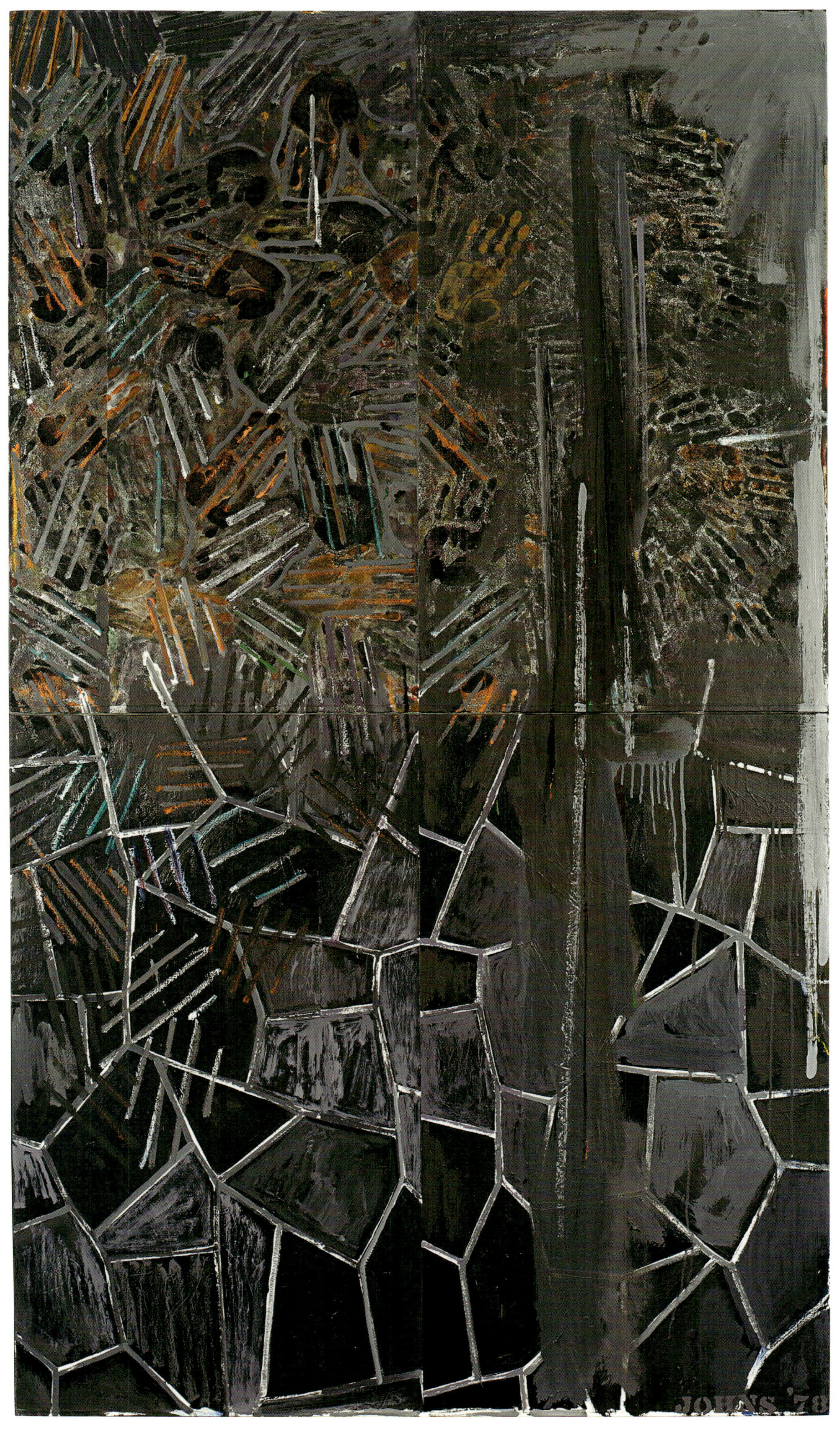
JOHNS '78

111. *Tantric Detail I*, 1980
Oil on canvas
127.3 × 86.7 cm (50 1/8 × 34 1/8 in.)
Collection of the artist

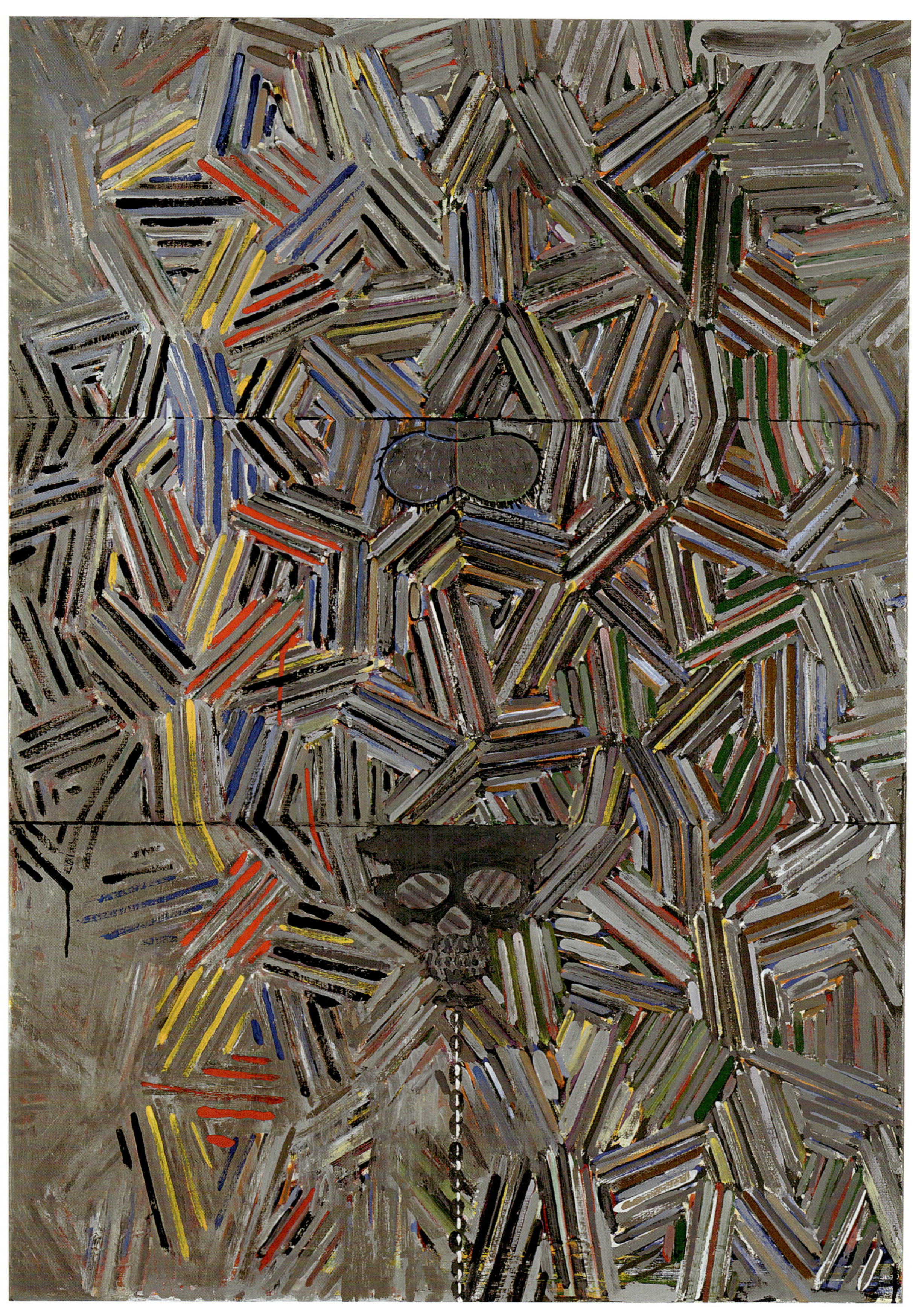

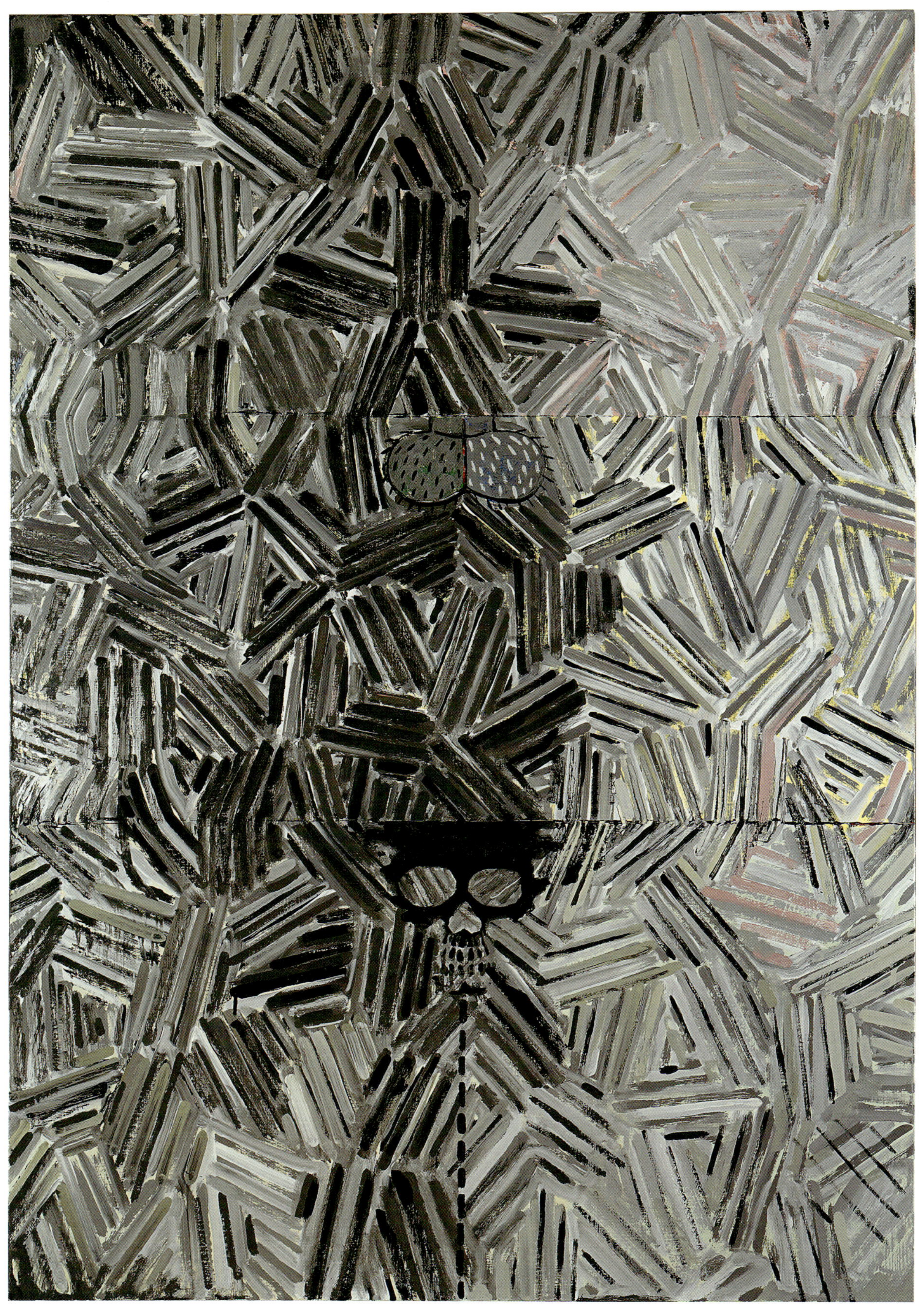

112. *Tantric Detail II*, 1981
Oil on canvas
127 × 86.4 cm (50 × 34 in.)
Collection of the artist

113. *Tantric Detail III*, 1981
Oil on canvas
127 × 86.4 cm (50 × 34 in.)
Collection of the artist

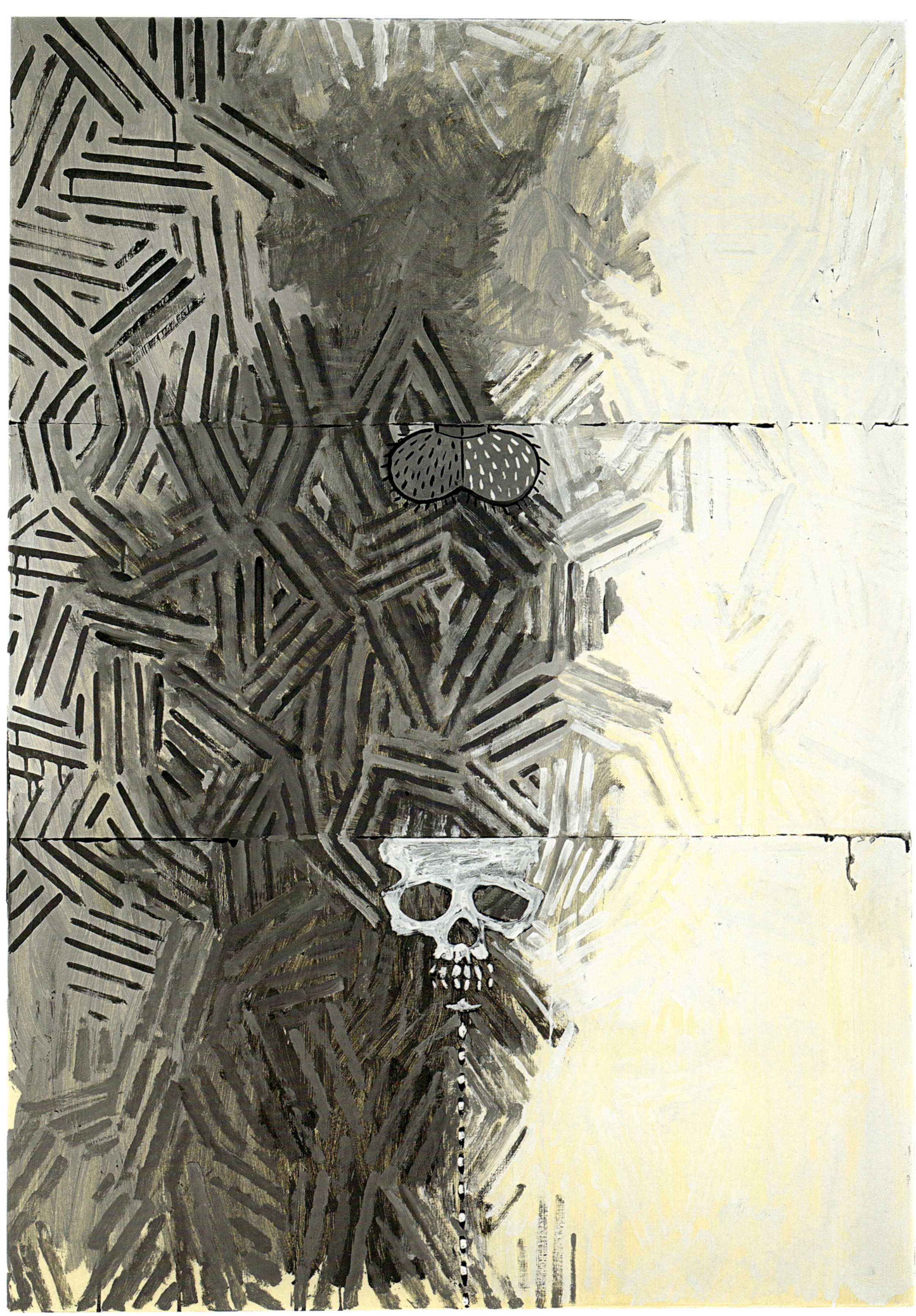

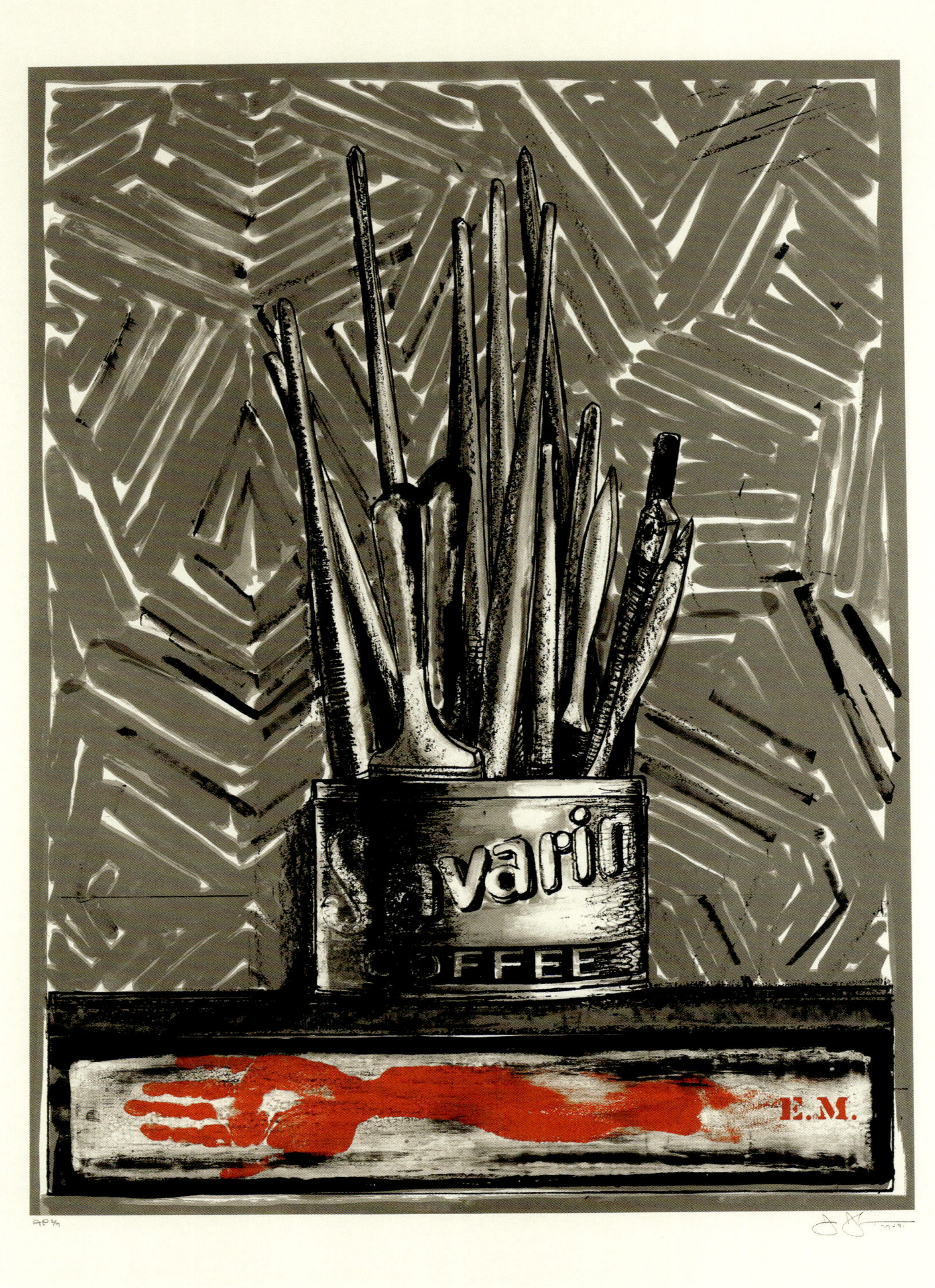

114. *Savarin*, 1977–81
ULAE, 1981
Lithograph from seven aluminum plates on white wove paper (Rives BFK)
image: 101.2 × 75 cm (39 7/8 × 29 1/2 in.)
sheet: 127.5 × 97 cm (50 1/4 × 38 1/4 in.)
ULAE/Johns cat. raisonné 220
The Art Institute of Chicago, ULAE Collection acquired through a challenge grant of Mr. and Mrs. Thomas Dittmer; restricted gift of supporters of the Department of Prints and Drawings; Centennial Endowment; Margaret Fisher Endowment Fund, 1982.411

115. *Between the Clock and the Bed*, 1982–83
Encaustic on canvas (three panels)
182.9 × 320.6 cm (72 × 126 1/4 in.)
Virginia Museum of Fine Arts, Richmond, gift of Sydney and Frances Lewis, 85.411

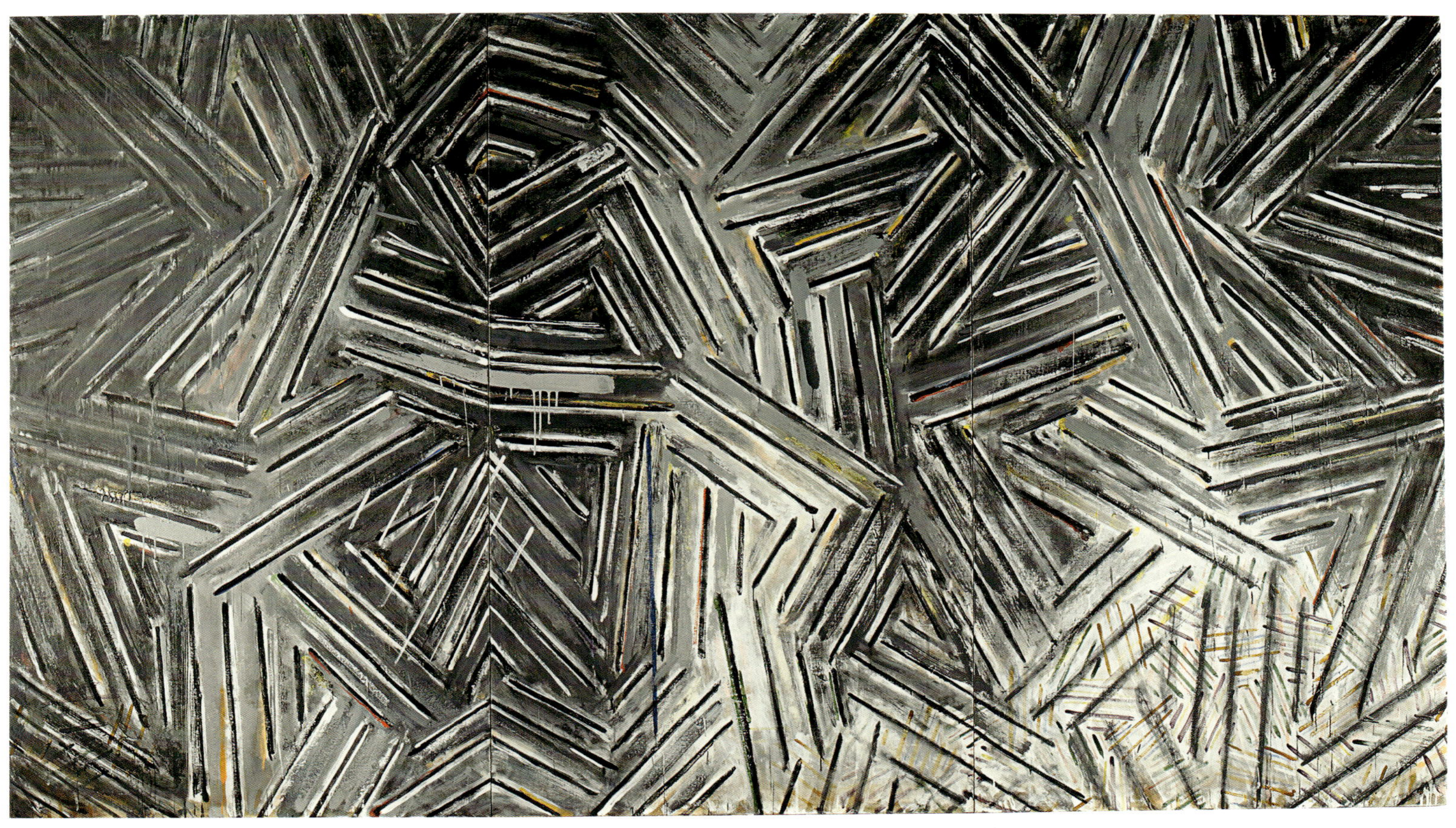

116. *Racing Thoughts*, 1984
Oil on canvas
127 × 190.5 cm (50 × 75 in.)
Robert and Jane Meyerhoff Collection,
Phoenix, Maryland

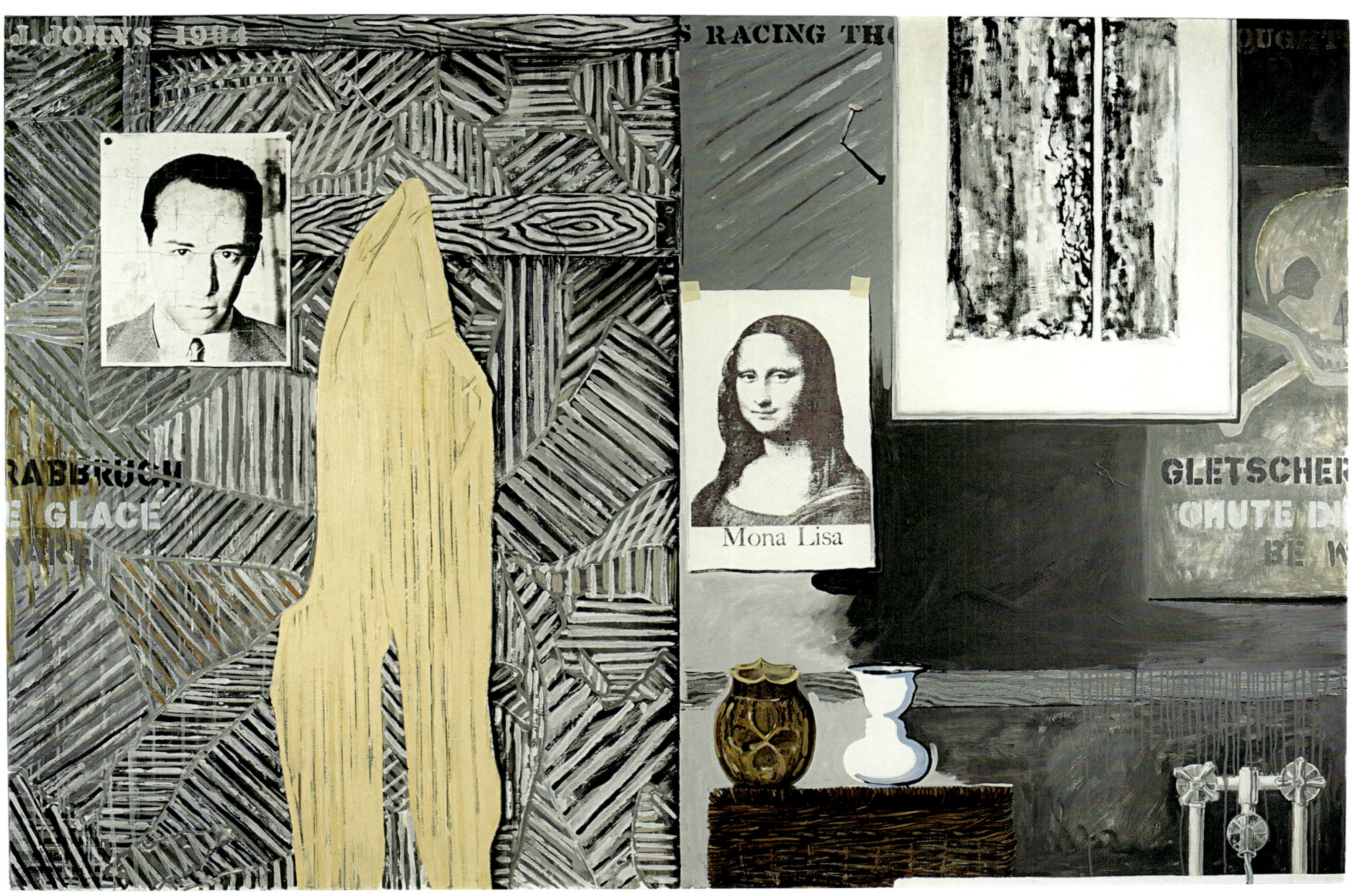
J. JOHNS 1984
S RACING TH
RABBRUCH
E GLACE
Mona Lisa
GLETSCHER
CHUTE D
BE W

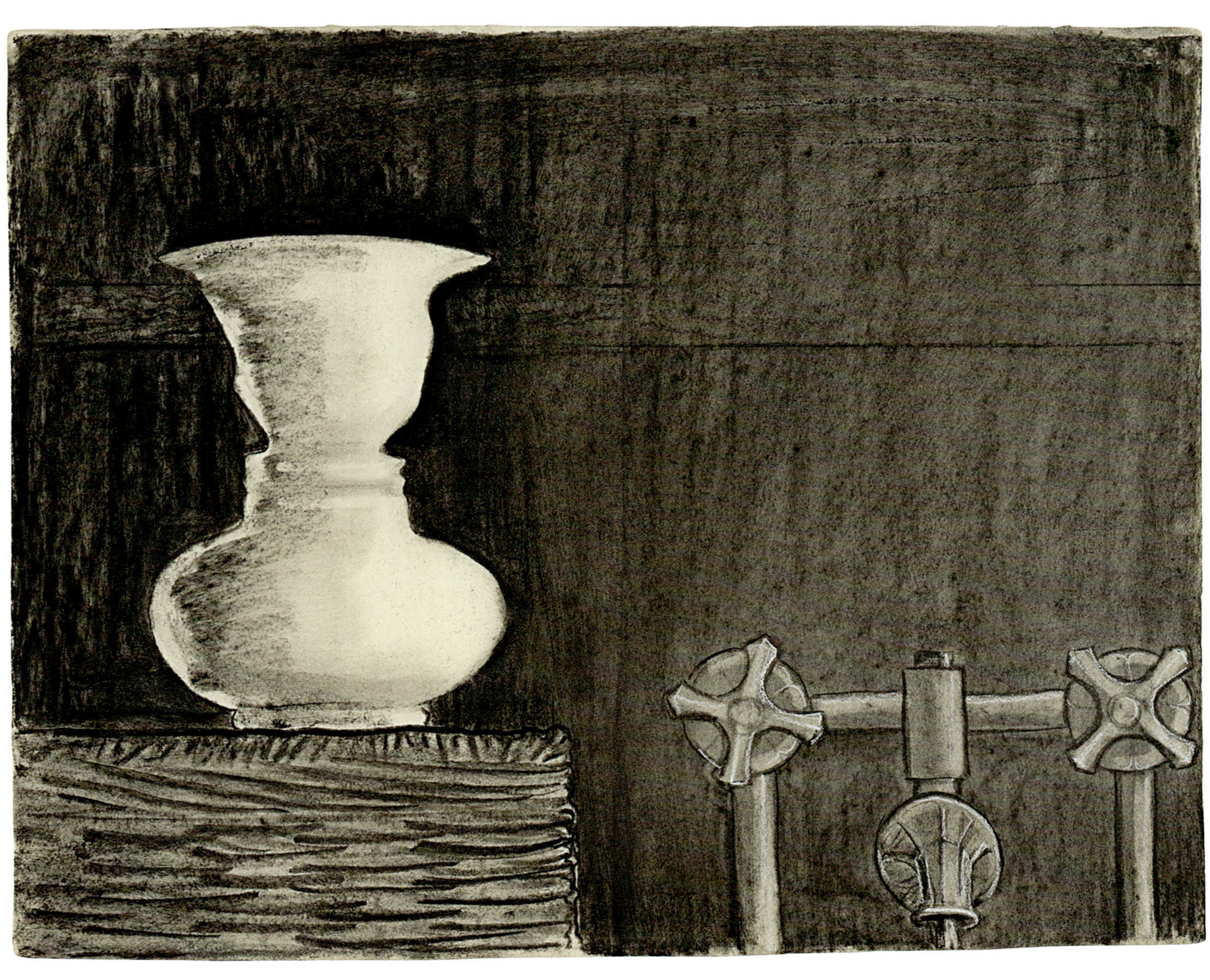

117. *Untitled*, 1983
Charcoal and pastel on ivory wove paper
48.9 × 61.6 cm (19 ¼ × 24 ¼ in.)
Collection of Lenore and Bernard Greenberg

118. *Untitled*, 1984
Watercolor and graphite on cream wove paper
image: 68.6 × 89.2 cm (27 × 35 ⅛ in.)
sheet: 74.6 × 100 cm (29 ⅜ × 39 ⅜ in.)
Collection of the artist

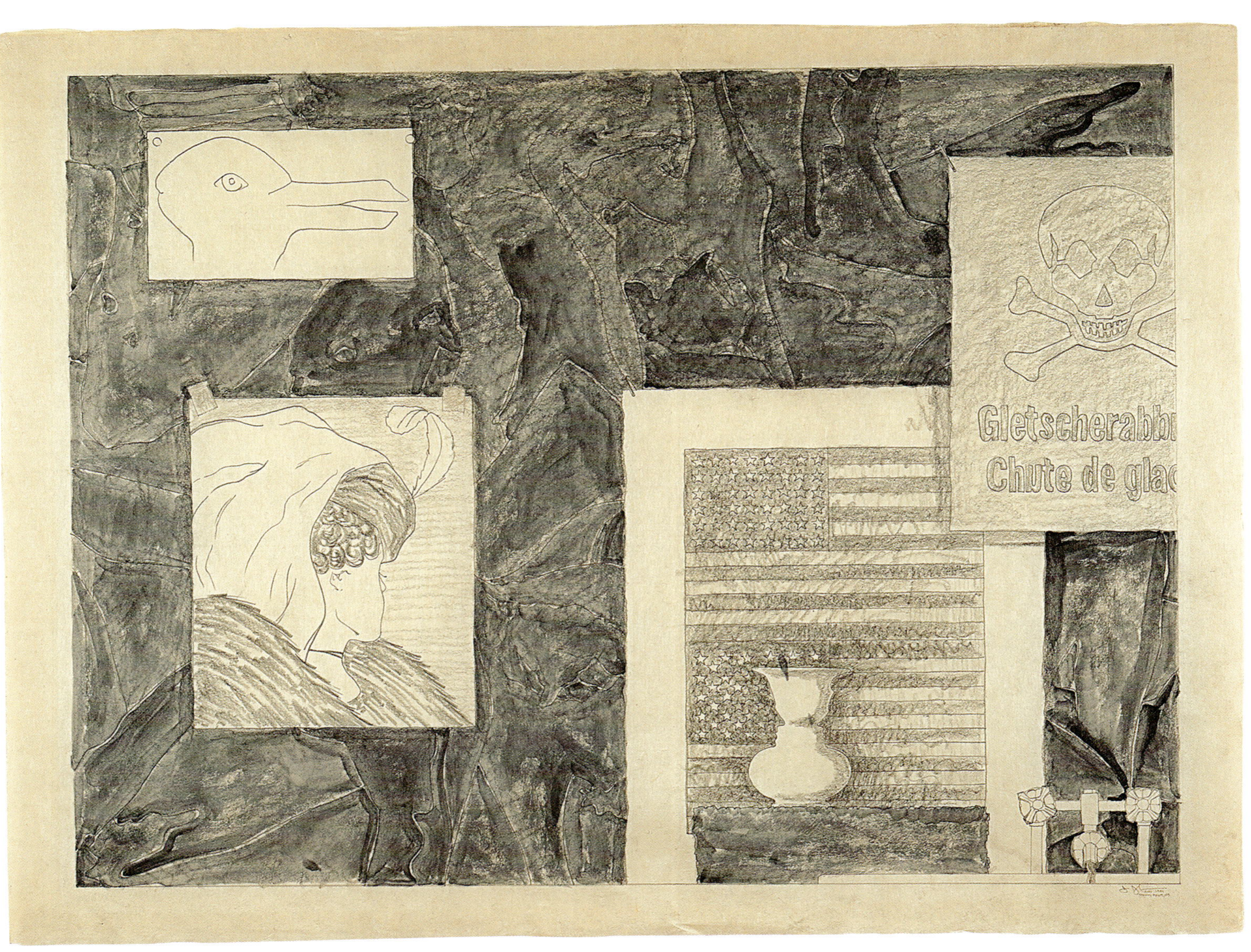
Gletscherabbr
Chute de glac

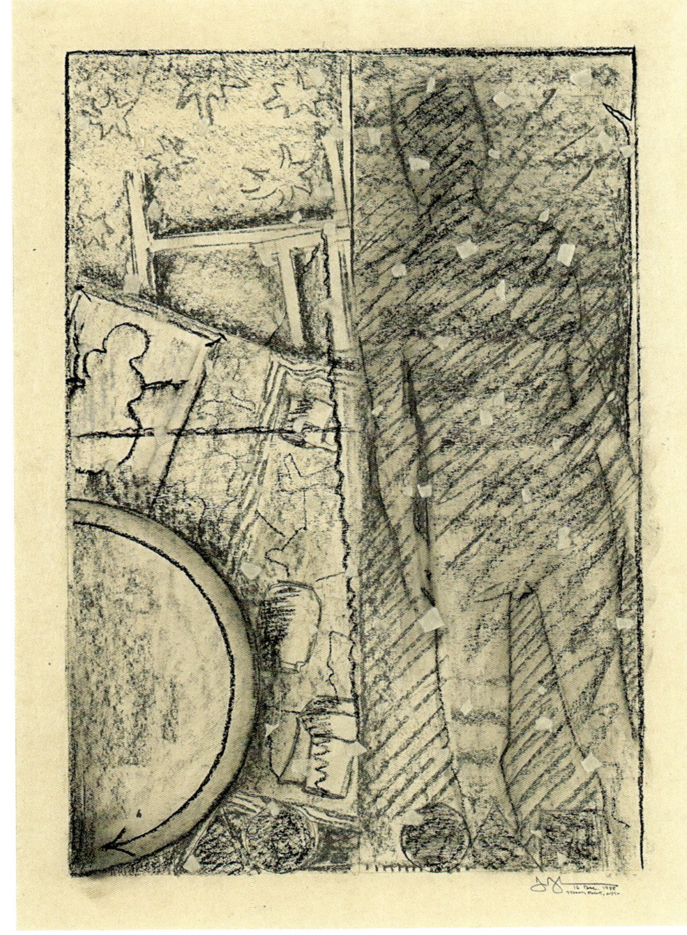

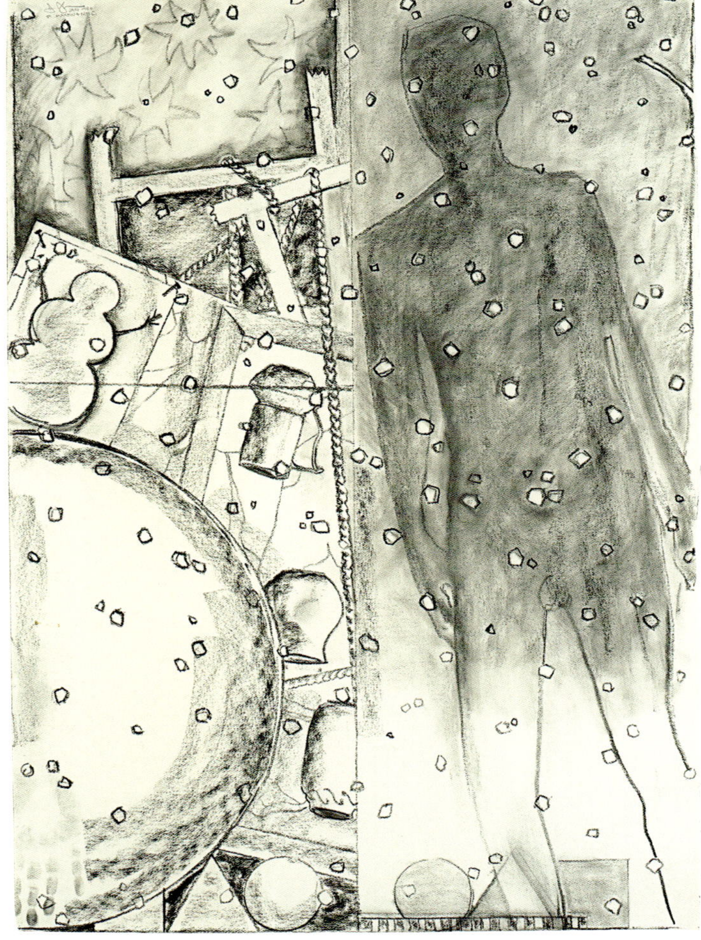

119. *Winter*, 1985
Chalk and collage on cream wove paper
image: 55.9 × 39.4 cm (22 × 15 ½ in.)
sheet: 61.9 × 48.9 cm (24 ⅜ × 19 ¼ in.)
Collection of the artist

120. *Winter*, 1986
Charcoal on ivory wove paper
106.7 × 75.6 cm (42 × 29 ¾ in.)
Robert and Jane Meyerhoff Collection,
Phoenix, Maryland

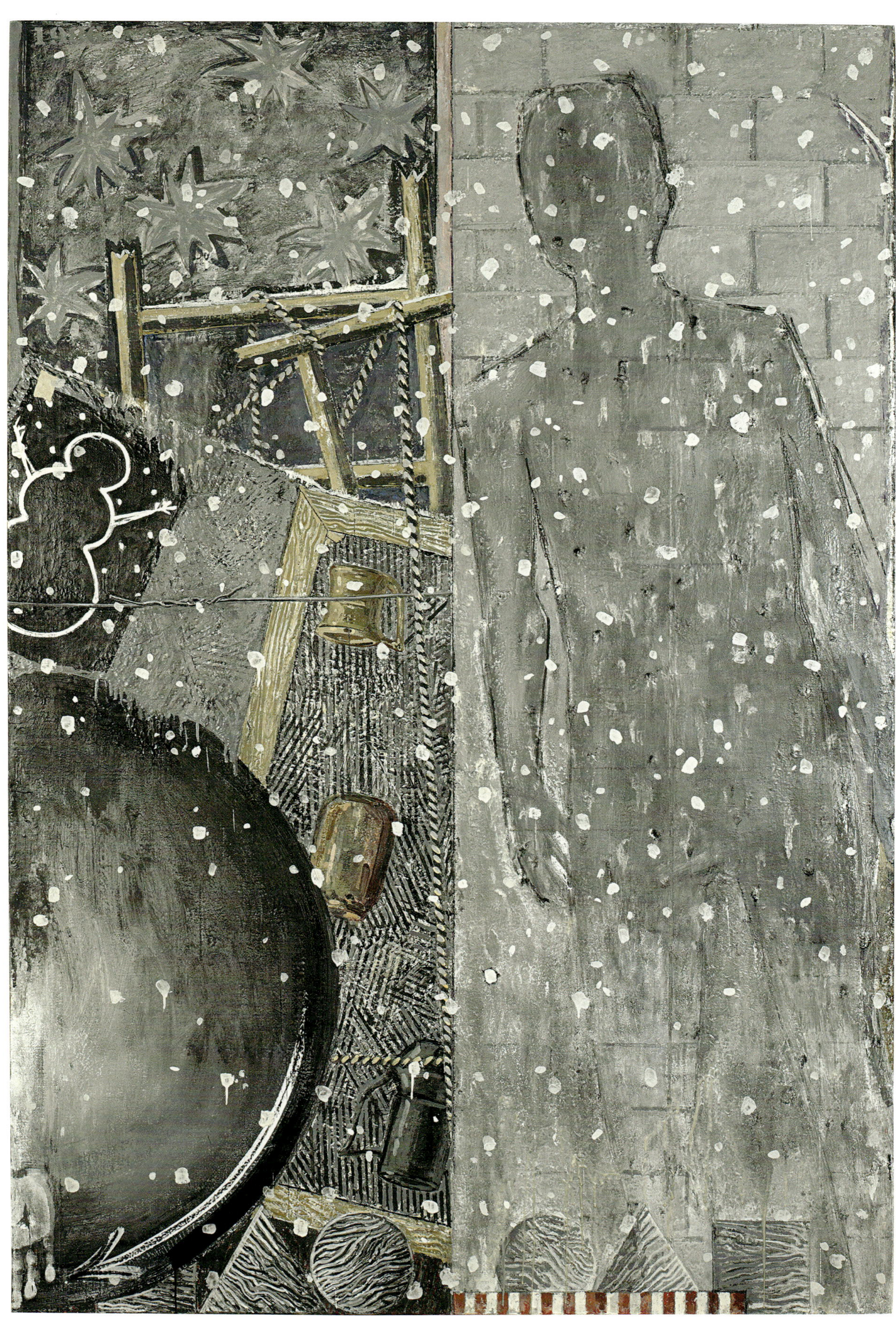

121. *Winter*, 1986
Encaustic and collage on canvas
190.5 × 127 cm (75 × 50 in.)
Private collection

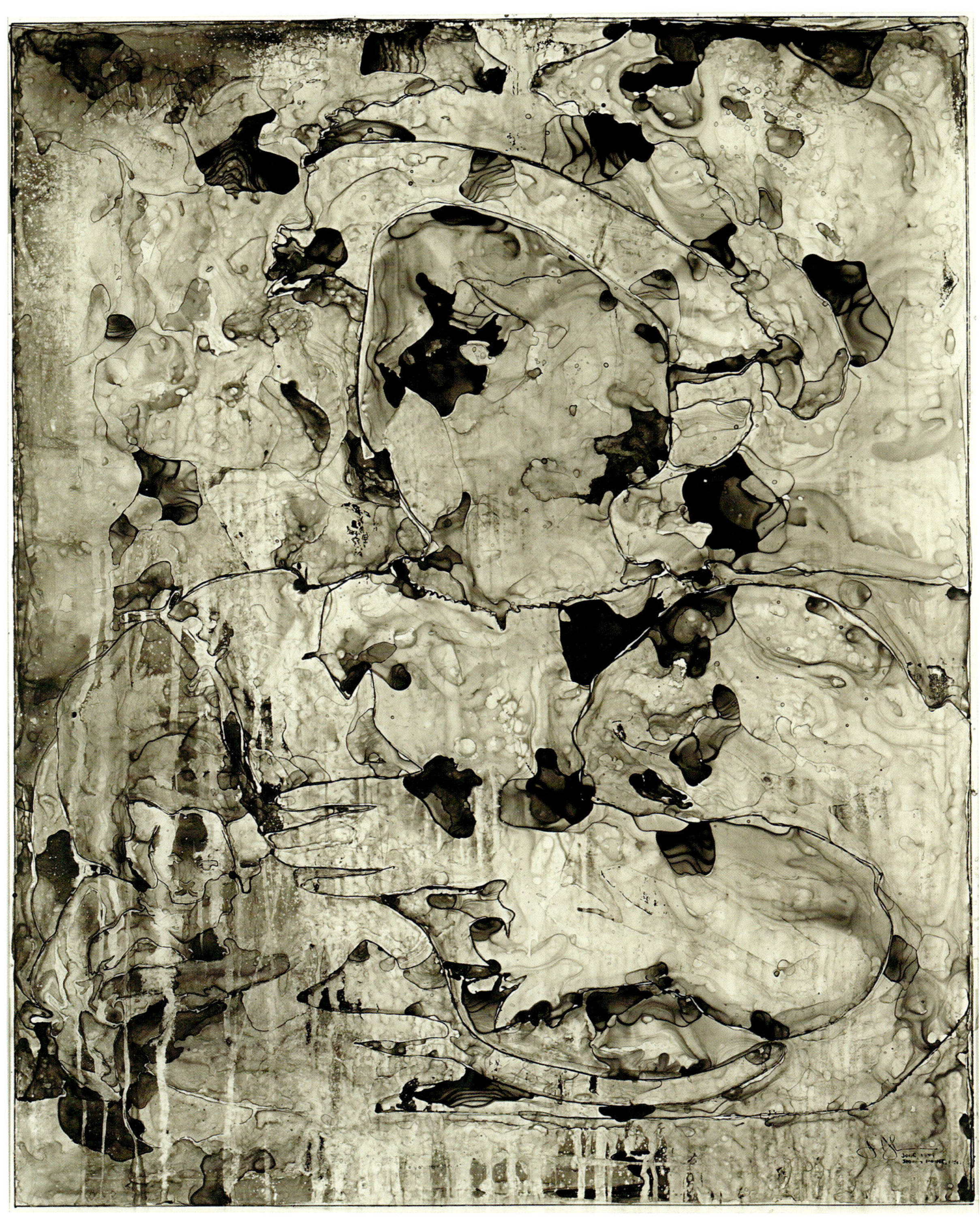

122. *Tracing*, 1989
Ink on plastic
92 × 78 cm (36 ¼ × 31 in.)
Private collection, London

123. *Untitled (After Holbein)*, 1993
Encaustic on canvas
85.2 × 65.1 cm (32 $\frac{9}{16}$ × 25 ⅝ in.)
Private collection

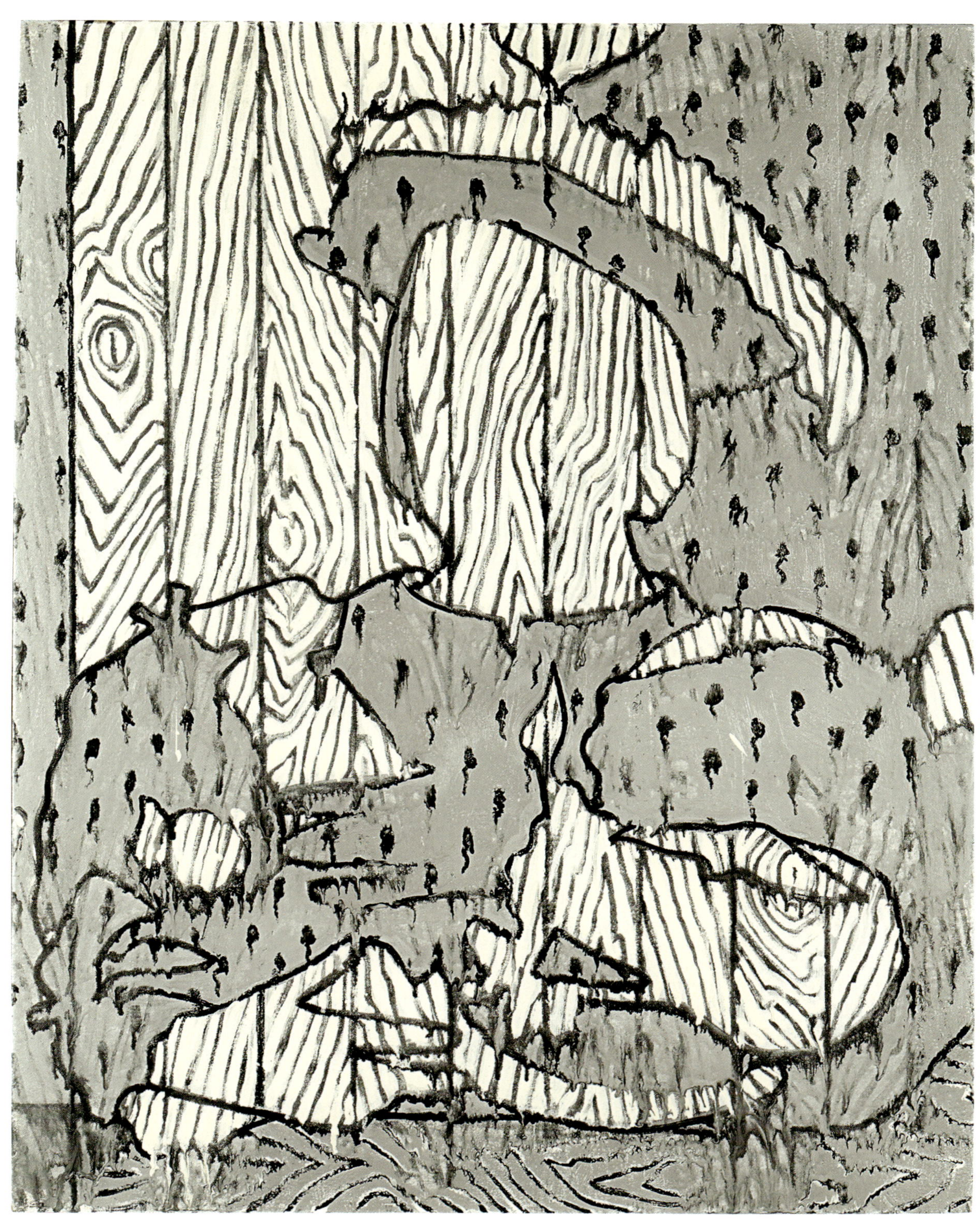

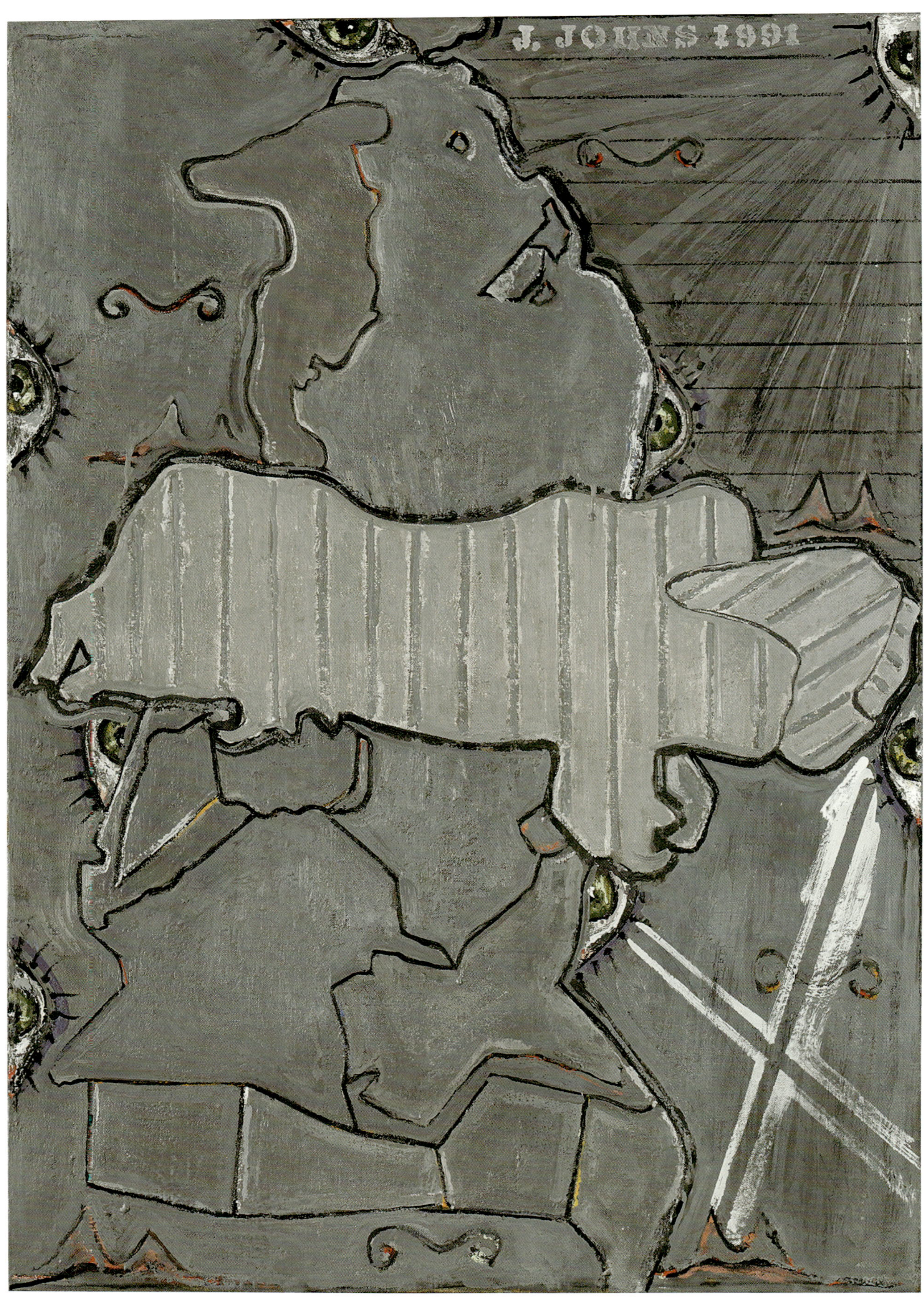

124. *Untitled*, 1991
Encaustic on canvas
81.3 × 56.8 cm (32 × 22 3/8 in.)
Collection of Tom Levine

125. *Untitled*, 1991
Oil on canvas
156.2 × 104.8 × 4.8 cm (61 1/2 × 41 1/4 × 1 7/8 in.)
Collection of the artist

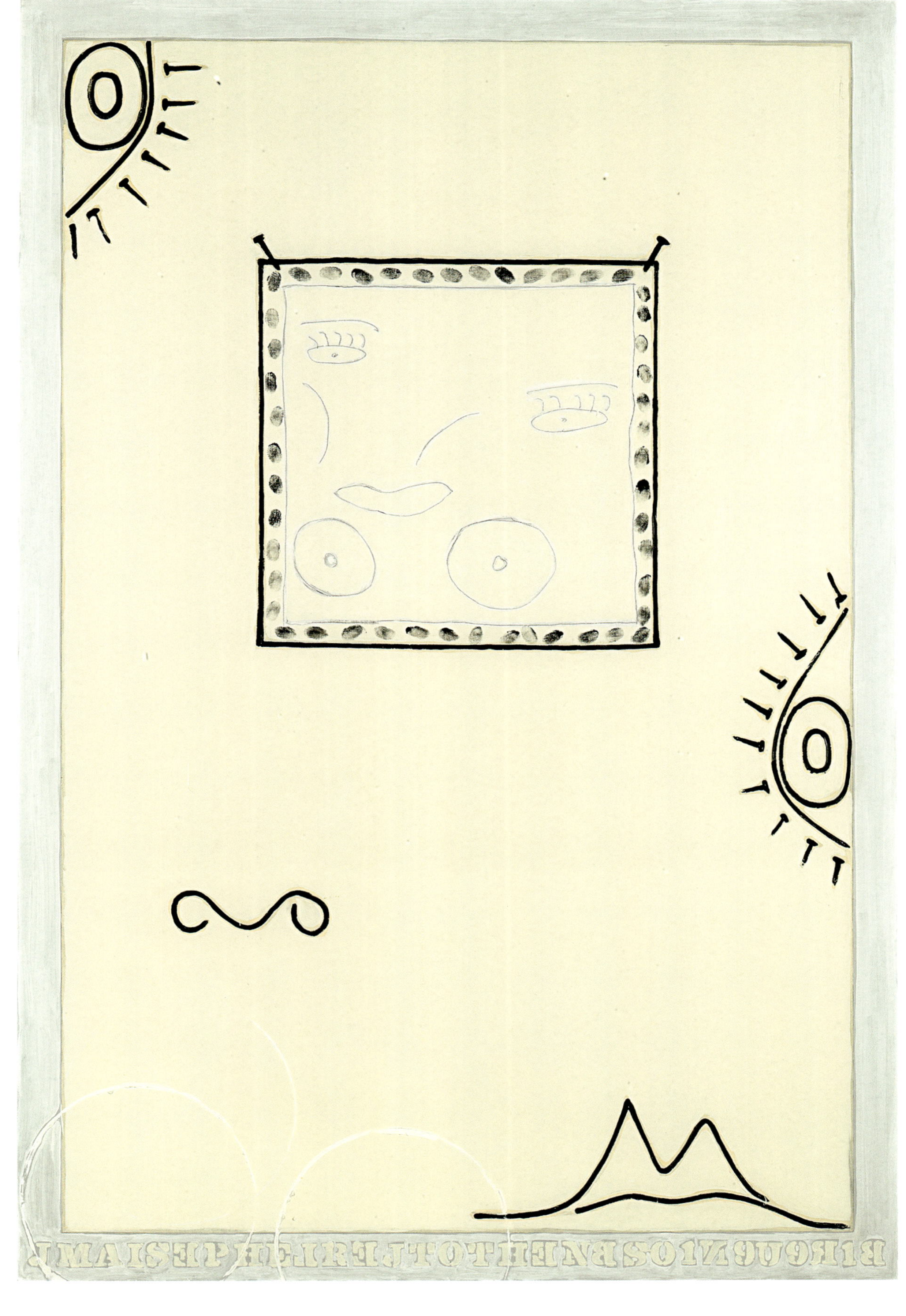

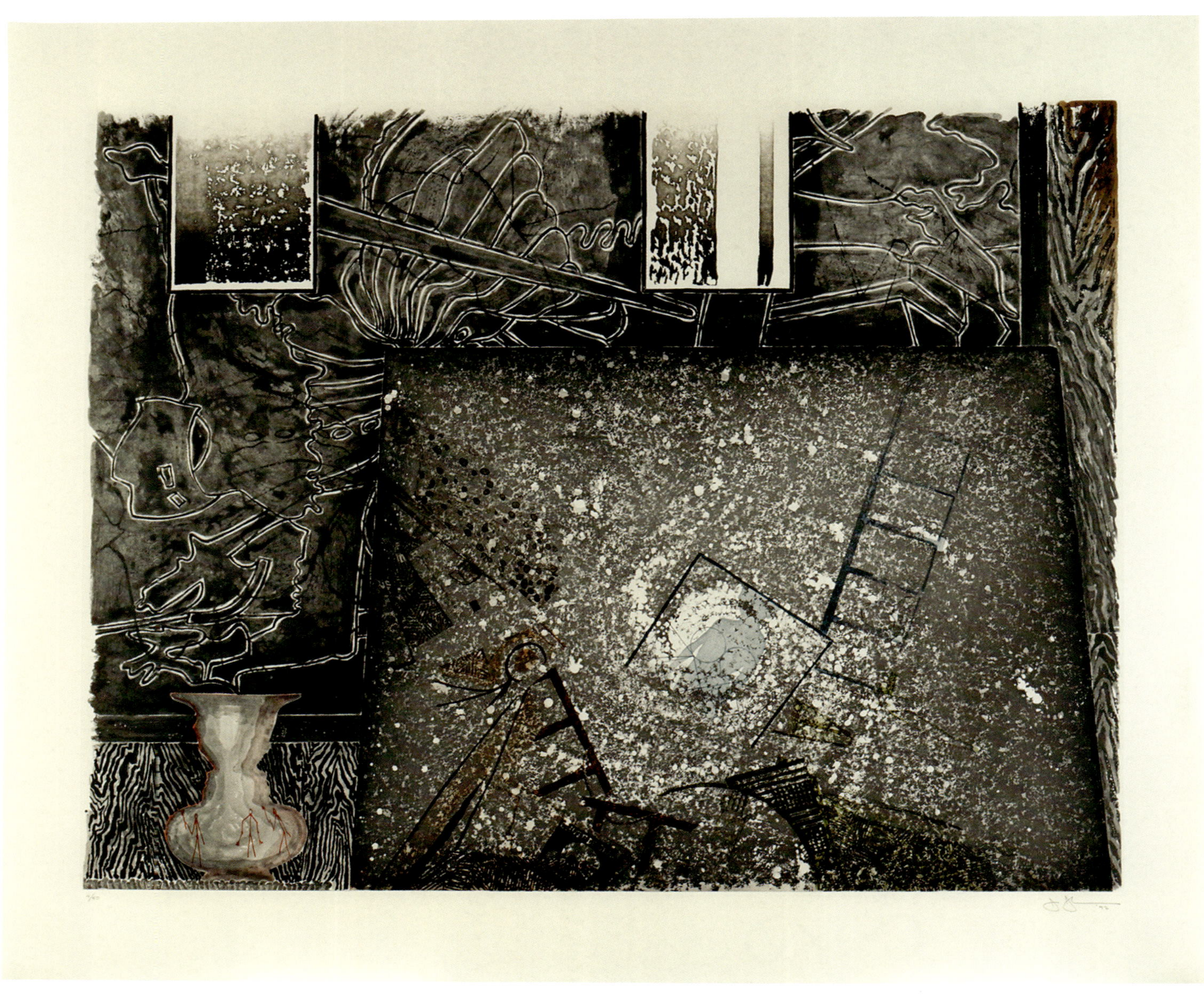

126. *Untitled*, 1992
ULAE, 1992
Intaglio from seven copper plates on off-white Japanese paper (To-inoko)
image: 91 × 115.5 cm (35 7/8 × 45 1/2 in.)
sheet: 110.5 × 133.5 cm (44 × 53 in.)
ULAE/Johns cat. raisonné 256
The Art Institute of Chicago, Mr. and Mrs. Robert O. Delaney Fund and Endowment, 1994.263

127. *Untitled*, 1992–95
Oil on canvas
198.1 × 299.7 cm (78 × 118 in.)
Private collection

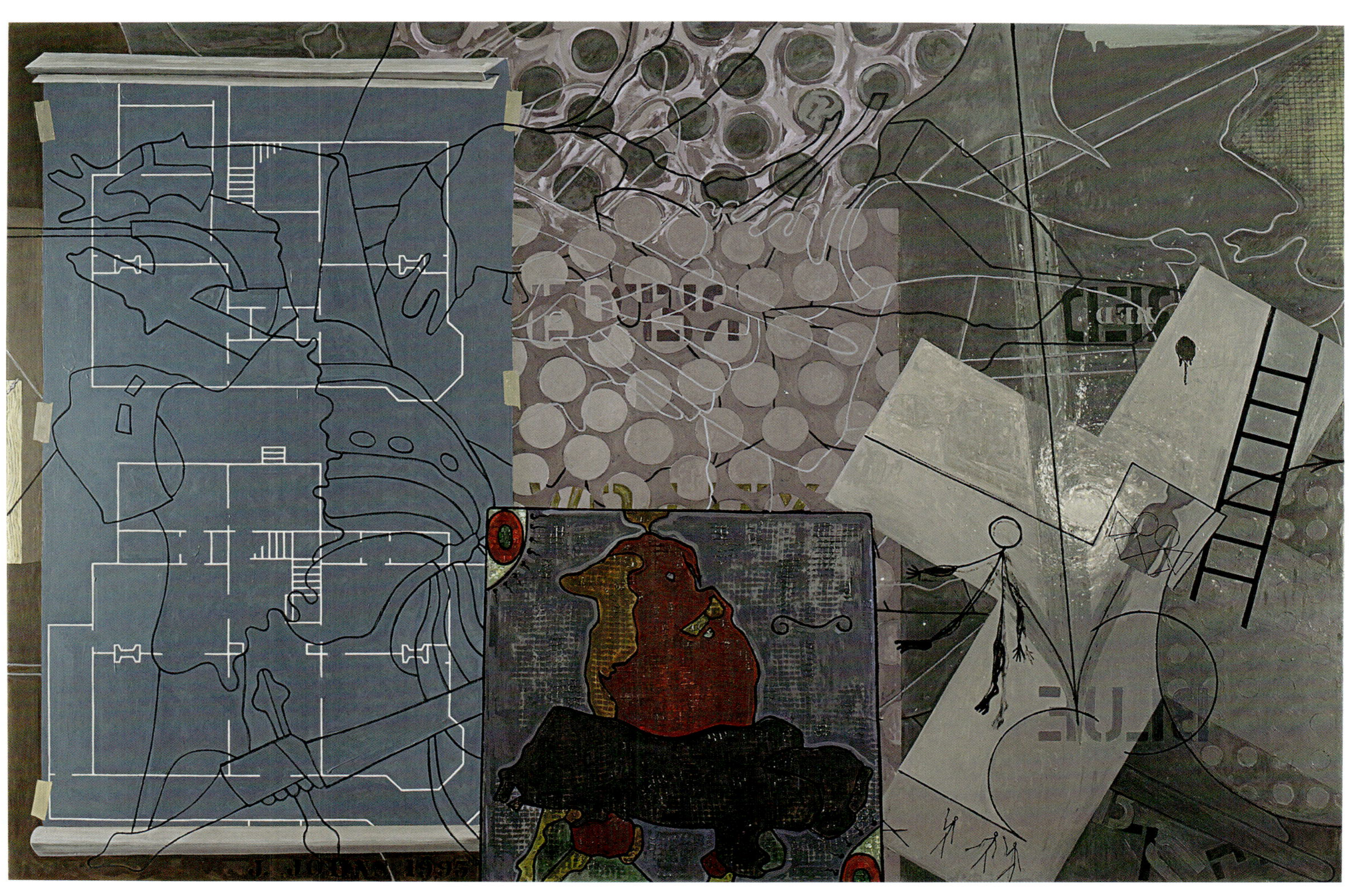

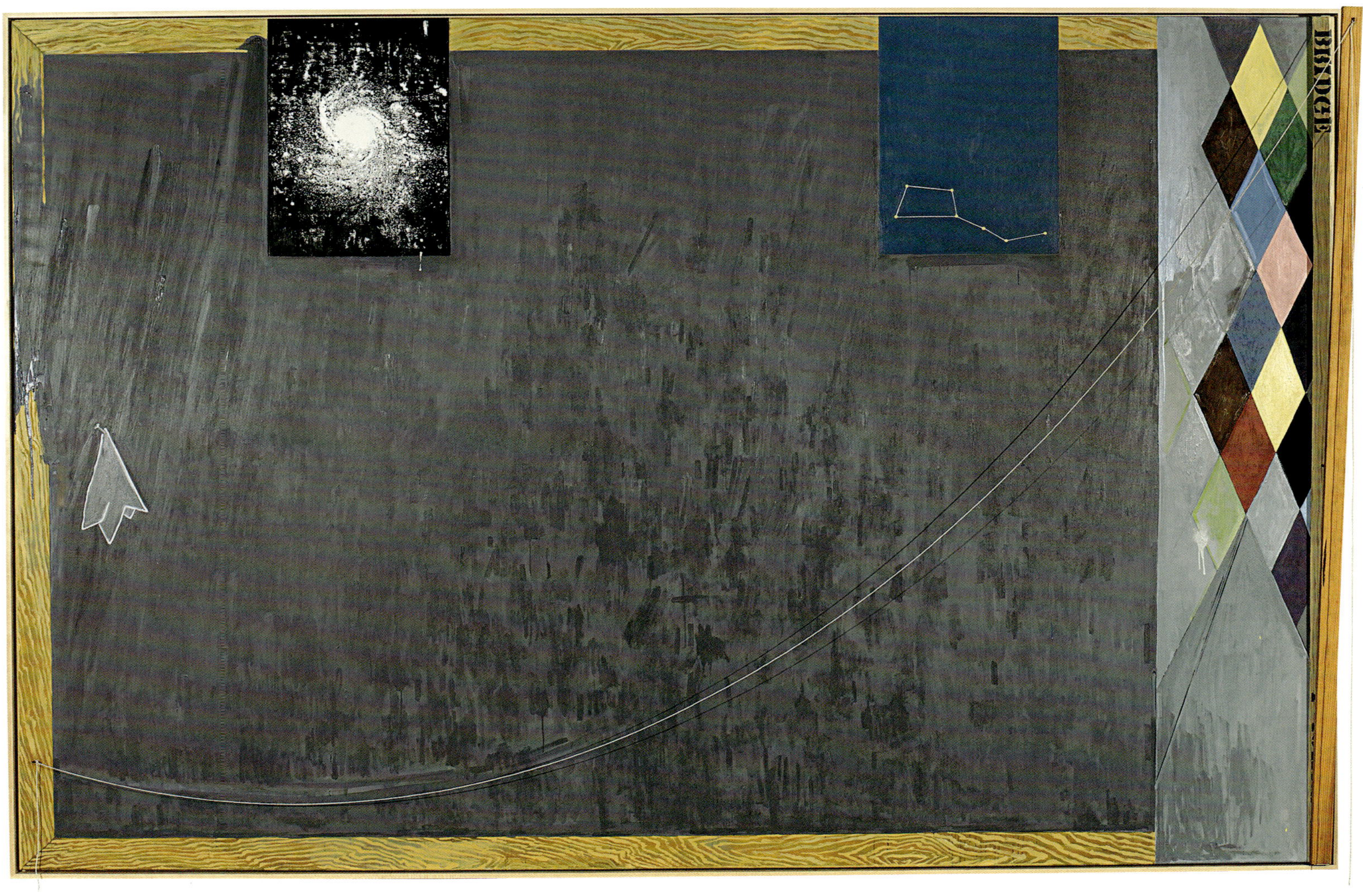

128. *Bridge*, 1997
Oil on canvas with objects
198.1 × 299.7 × 20.3 cm (78 × 118 × 8 in.)
Promised gift to the San Francisco Museum of Modern Art

129. *Catenary (I Call to the Grave)*, 1998
Encaustic on canvas with objects
198.1 × 299.7 × 20.3 cm (78 × 118 × 8 in.)
Philadelphia Museum of Art, purchased with funds contributed by Gisela and Dennis Alter, Keith L. and Katherine Sachs, Frances and Bayard Storey, The Dietrich Foundation, Marguerite and Gerry Lenfest, Mr. and Mrs. Brook Lenfest, Marsha and Jeffrey Perelman, Jane and Leonard Korman, Mr. and Mrs. Berton E. Korman, Mr. and Mrs. William T. Vogt, Dr. and Mrs. Paul Richardson, Mr. and Mrs. George M. Ross, Ella B. Schaap, Eileen and Stephen Matchett, and other donors in honor of the 125th Anniversary of the Museum, 2001

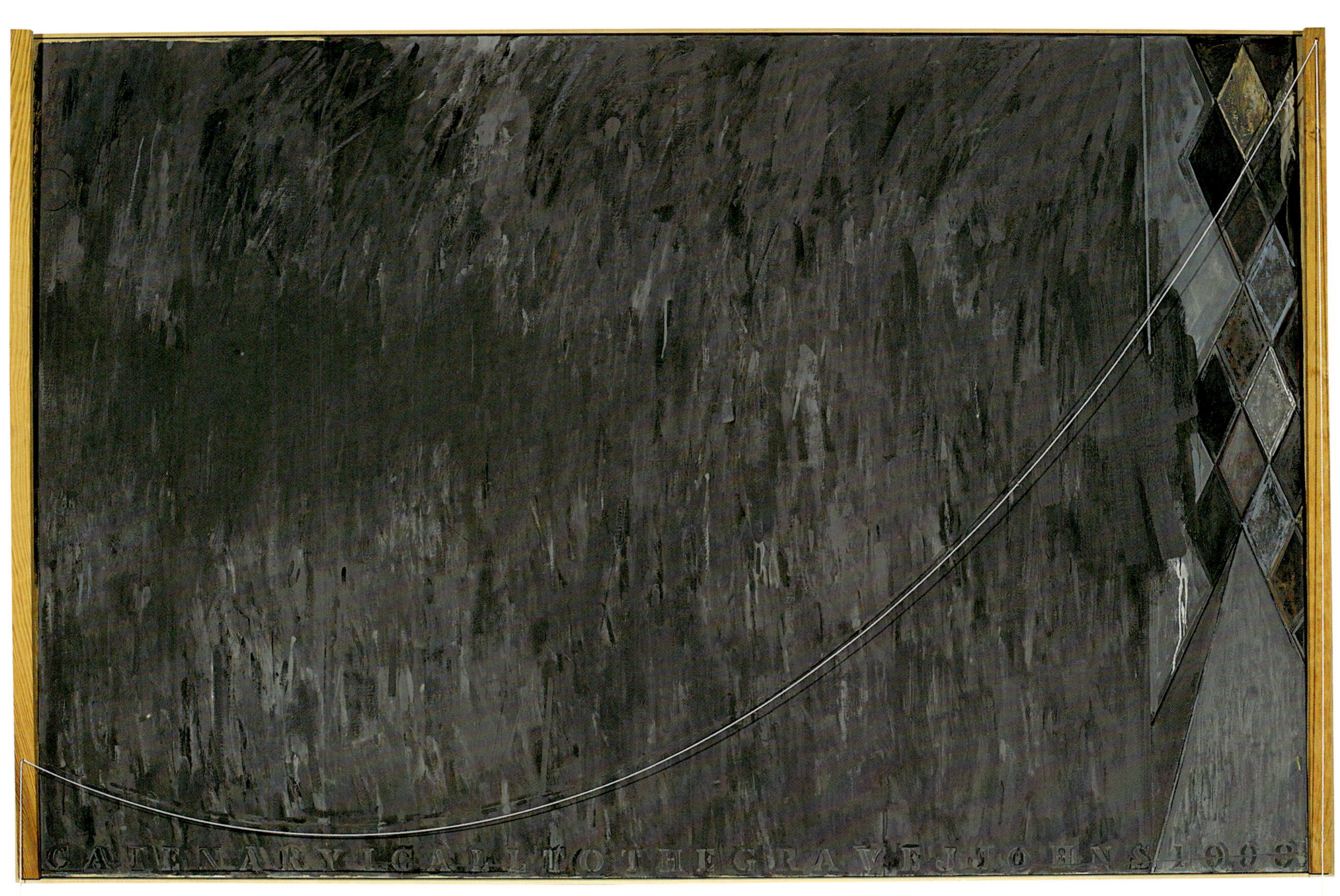
CATENARY I CALL TO THE GRAVE J JOHNS

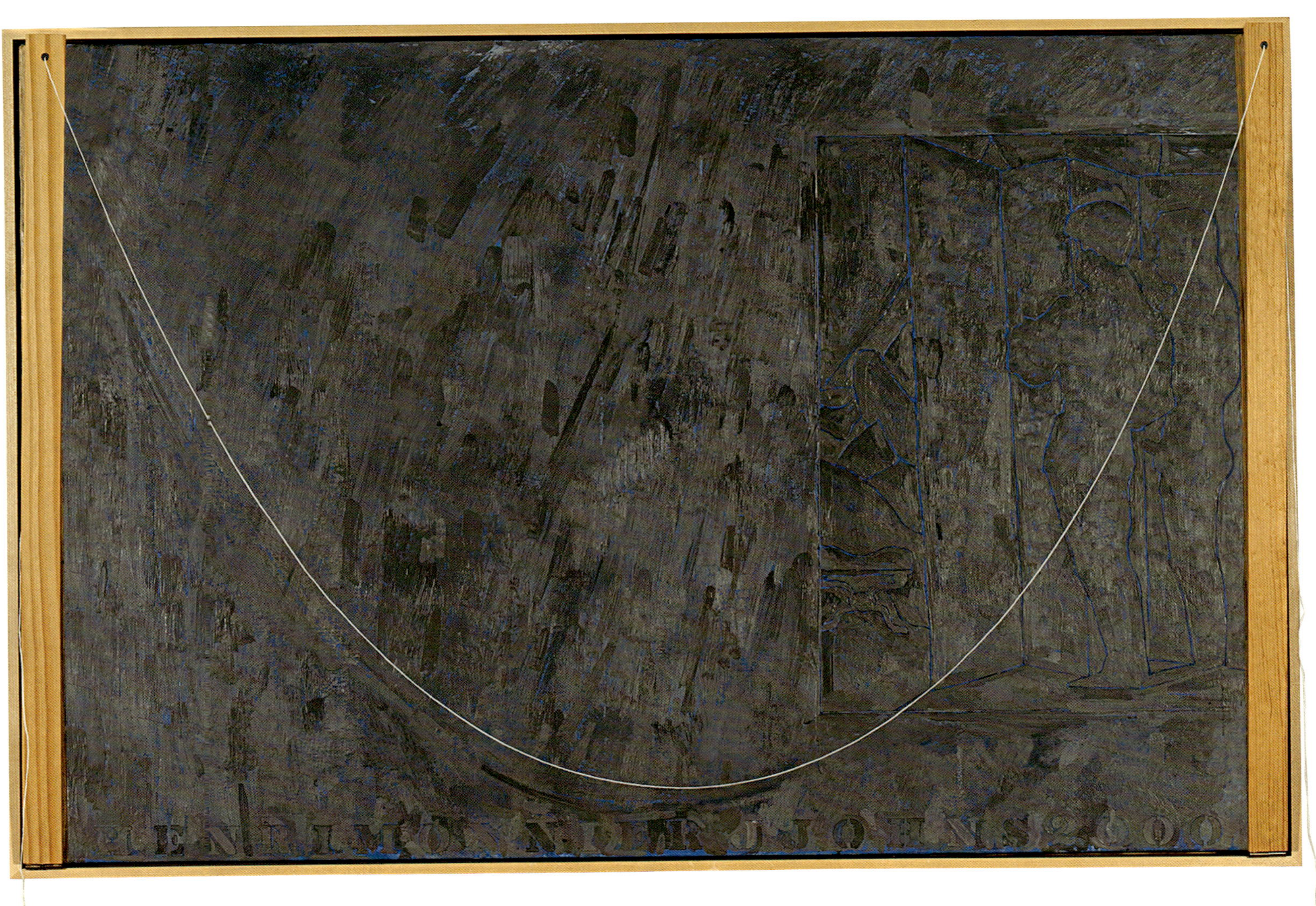

130. *Catenary (Henri Monnier)*, 2000
Encaustic on canvas with objects
71.4 × 107 × 8.9 cm (28 ⅛ × 42 ⅛ × 3 ½ in.)
Private collection, London

131. *Study for a Painting*, 2002
Encaustic on canvas and wood with objects
160.3 × 198.8 × 15.2 cm (63 ⅛ × 78 ¼ × 6 in.)
Collection of Michael Crichton

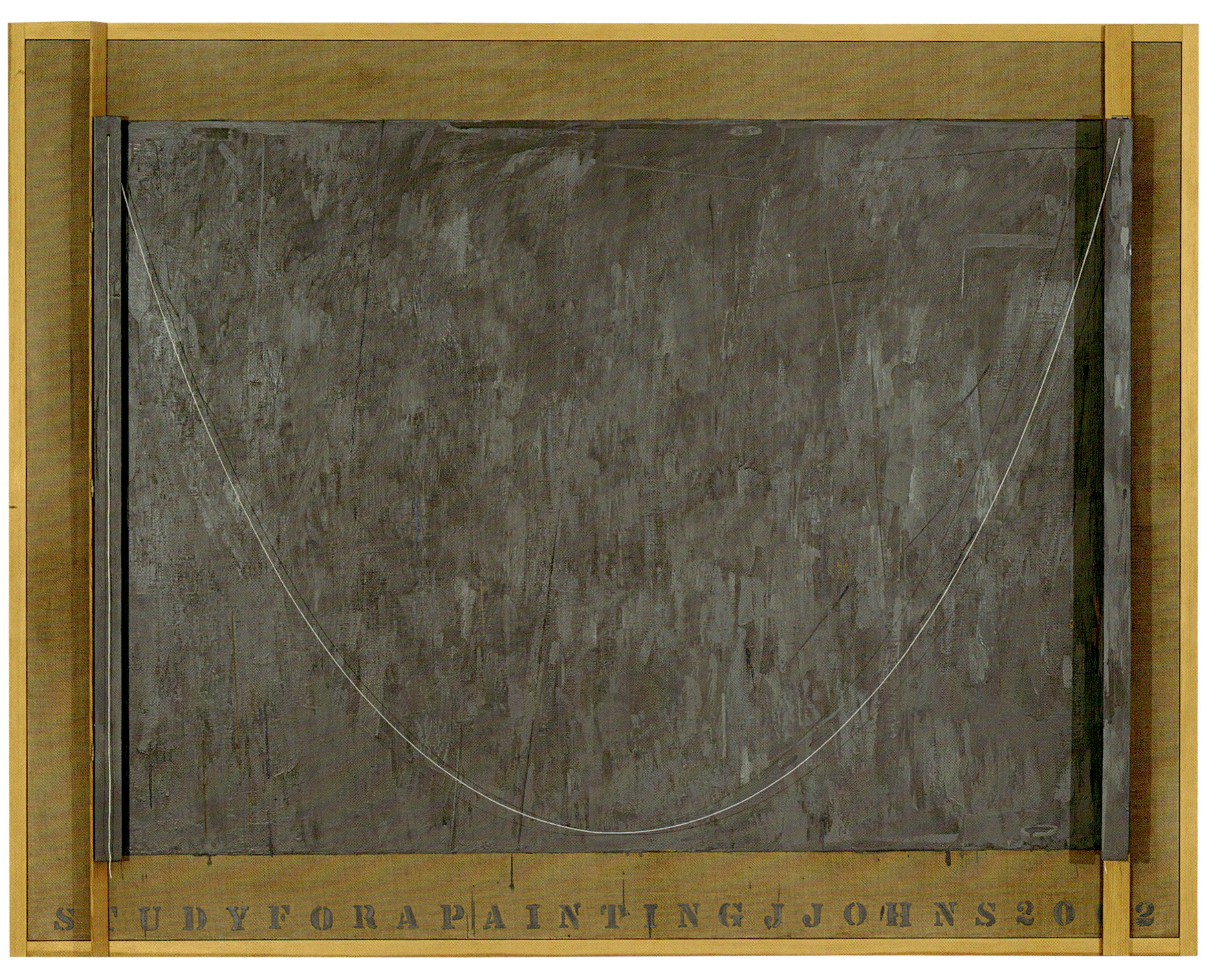
STUDY FOR A PAINTING J JOHNS 20 2

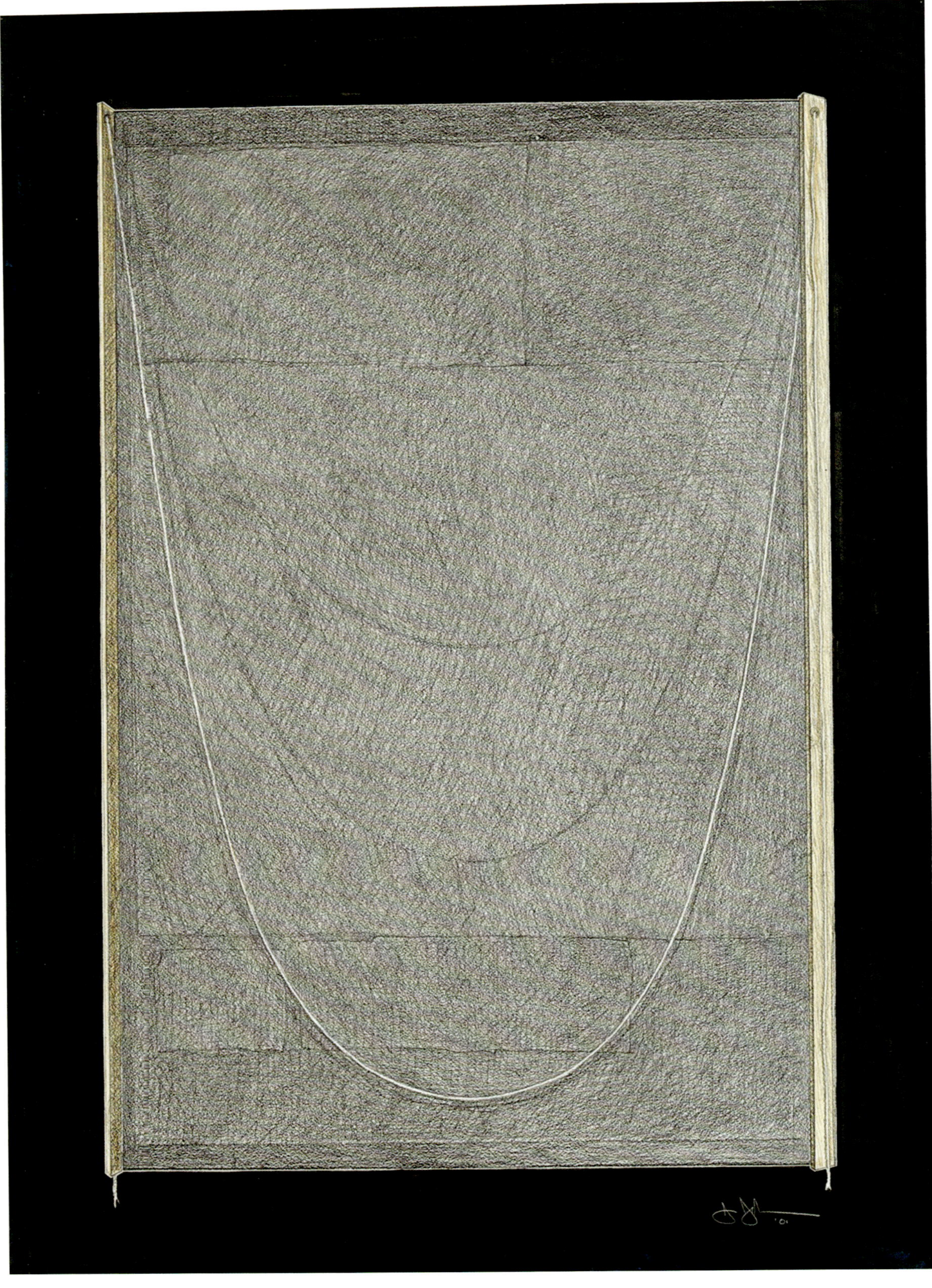

132. *Untitled*, 2001
Graphite, acrylic, and watercolor on ivory wove paper
91.5 × 65.1 cm (36 × 25 5/8 in.)
The Art Institute of Chicago, Margaret Fisher Endowment, 2003.7

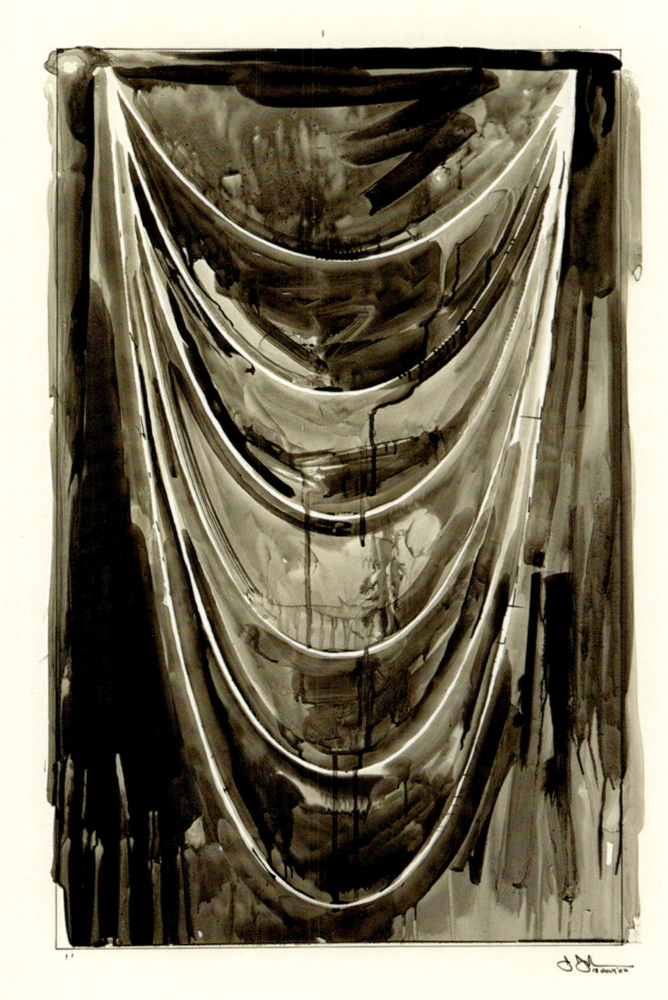

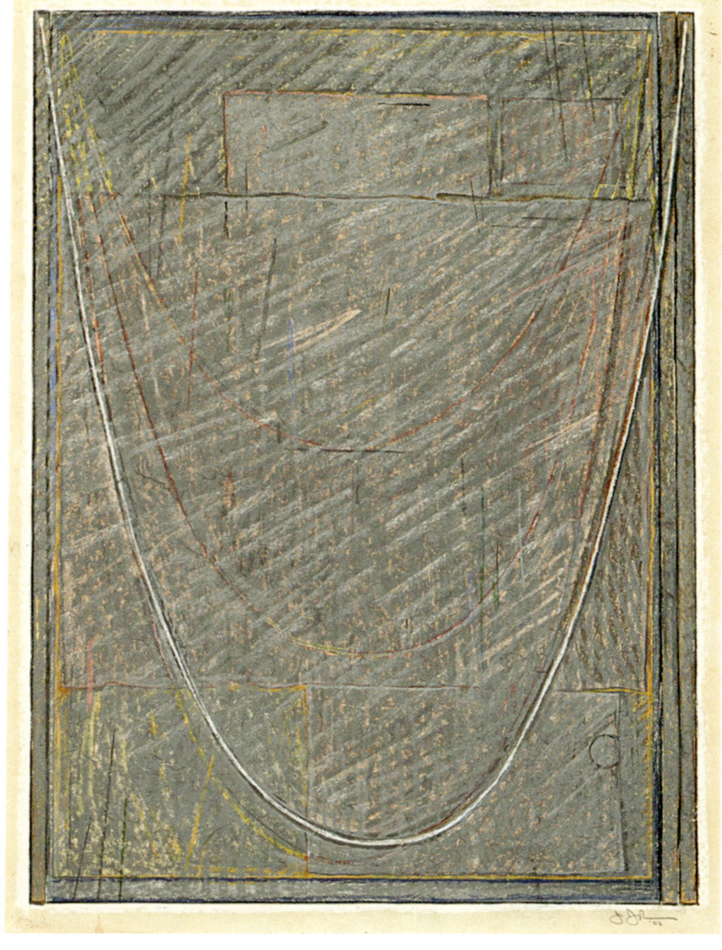

133. *Untitled*, 2002
Ink on plastic
97.2 × 63.5 cm (38 ¼ × 25 in.)
Collection of Kate Ganz

134. *Near the Lagoon*, 2002
Pastel, watercolor, and graphite on
cream wove paper
80 × 62.9 cm (31 ½ × 24 ¾ in.)
Private collection

135. *Near the Lagoon*, 2002–03
Encaustic on canvas and wood with objects
301.9 × 200 × 10.2 cm (118 7⁄8 × 78 3⁄4 × 4 in.)
The Art Institute of Chicago, through prior gift
of Muriel Kallis Newman in memory of Albert
Hardy Newman, 2004.146

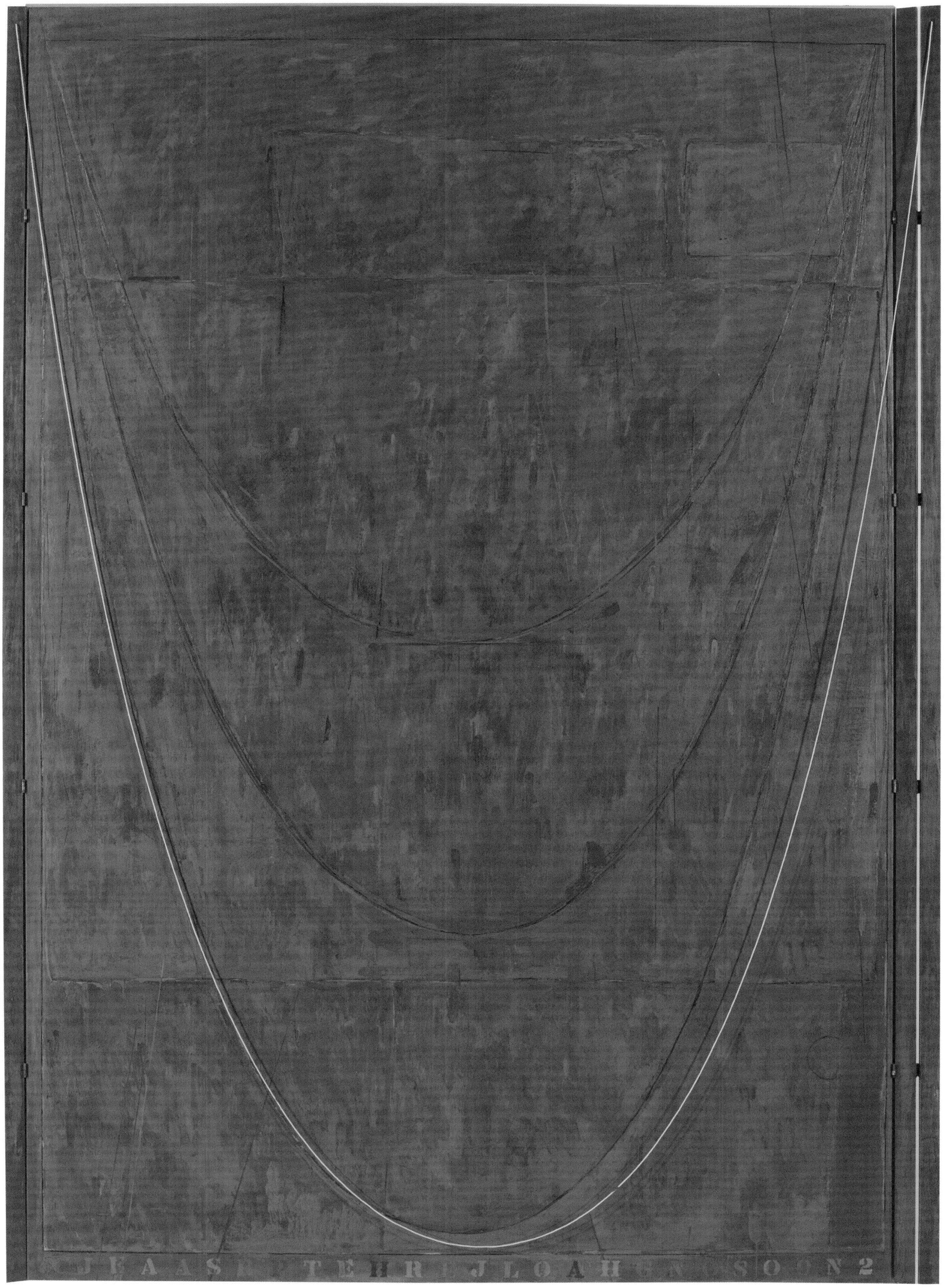

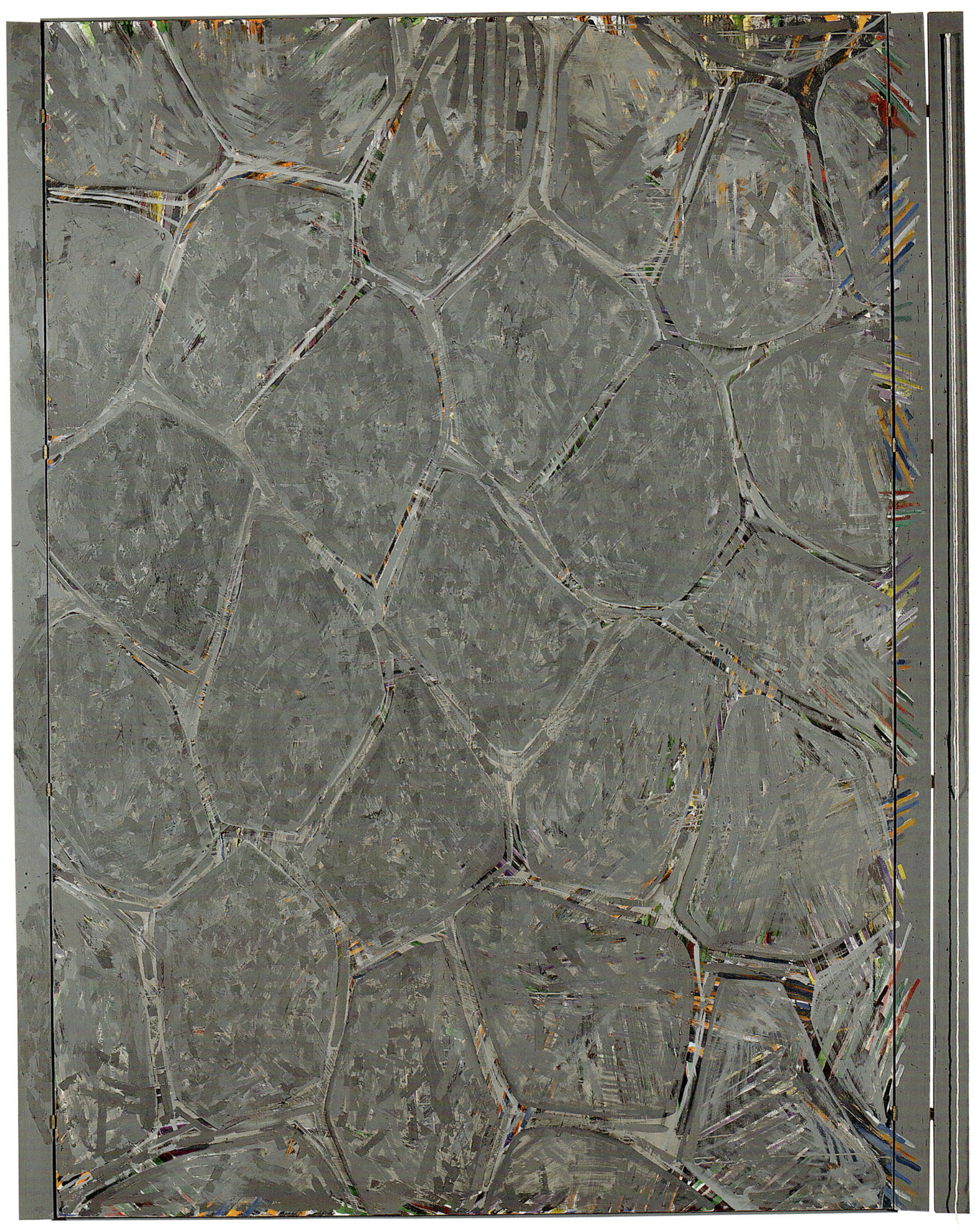

136. *Within*, 1983 and 2005
Oil on canvas and wood with objects
257.8 × 184.2 × 7.6 cm (101 ½ × 72 ½ × 3 in.)
Collection of the artist

137. *Within*, 2007
ULAE, 2007
Intaglio from six copper plates on ivory wove paper (Hahnemühle)
image: 84.5 × 62.9 cm (33 ¼ × 24 ¾ in.)
sheet: 108 × 82.6 cm (42 ½ × 32 ½ in.)
The Art Institute of Chicago, partial and promised gift of Judith Racht and Irving Stenn, Jr.

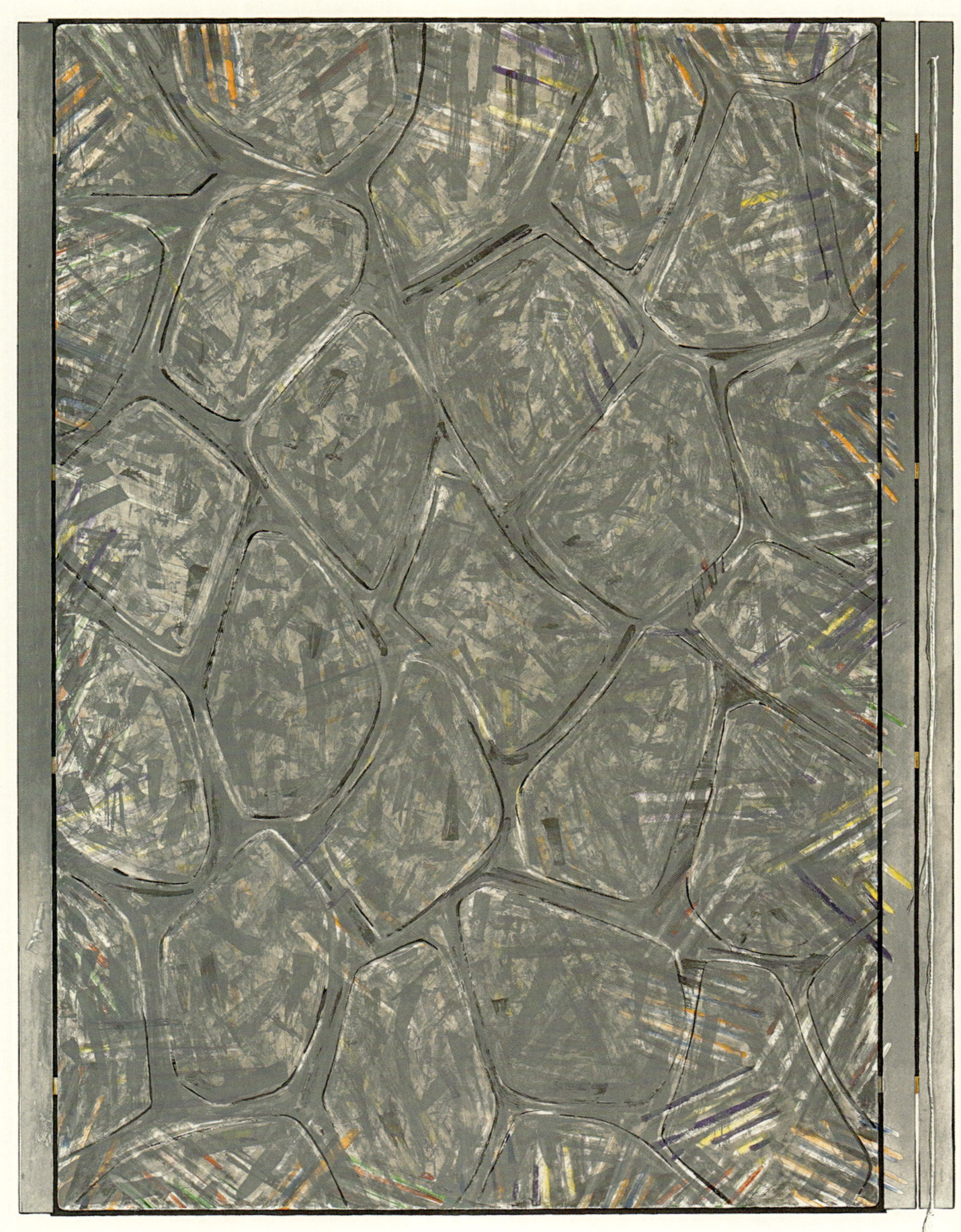

138. *Beckett*, 2005
Oil and encaustic on canvas and wood
with objects (two panels)
171.5 × 128.4 × 16.7 cm (67 1/2 × 50 9/16 × 6 9/16 in.)
Private collection

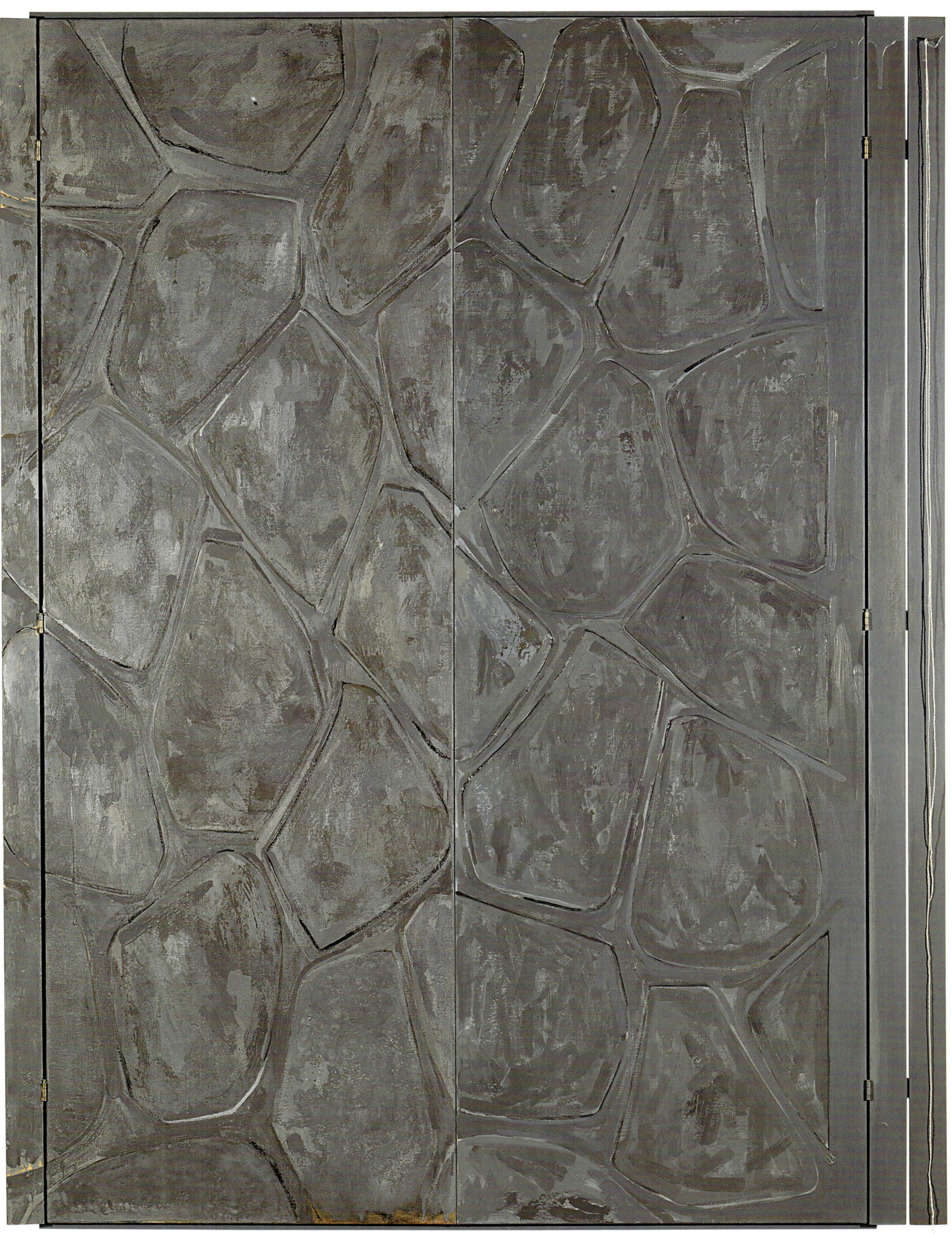

SELECTED BIBLIOGRAPHY

Anonymous. 1958. Leo Castelli at 4 E. 77 St. *East of Fifth* (January). Photocopy provided by the library of the Museum of Modern Art, New York.

——. 1959. His Heart Belongs to Dada. *Time* 73, 59 (May 4), p. 58. Reprinted in *Writings* 1996, pp. 81–82.

——. 1965. Pop's Dada. *Time* 85, 6 (February 5), p. 85.

——. 1974. *Jasper Johns Drawings*. Exh. cat. Arts Council of Great Britain, London.

Ashbery, John. 1961. Art and Artists. *New York Herald Tribune* (European edition), June 28, p. 7.

——. 1962. Paris Notes. *Art International* 6, 10 (December 20), pp. 48–52.

Ashton, Dore. 1963. Jasper Johns. *Arts and Architecture* 80, 3 (March), pp. 6–7.

——. 1964. Acceleration in Discovery and Consumption. *Studio International* 167, 853 (May), pp. 212–14.

Bernard, April, and Mimi Thompson. 1984. Johns on . . . *Vanity Fair* 47, 2 (February), p. 65. Reprinted in *Writings* 1996, pp. 214–17.

Bernstein, Roberta. 1975. Things the Mind Already Knows: Jasper Johns' Paintings and Sculptures 1954–1974. Ph.D. diss., Columbia University.

——. 1977. Jasper Johns and the Figure: Part One: Body Imprints. *Arts* 52, 2 (October), pp. 142–44.

——. 1981. An Interview with Jasper Johns, in *Fragments: Incompletion and Discontinuity*, edited by Lawrence D. Kritzman. *New York Literary Forum*, vol. 8–9 (1981), pp. 279–90. Interview originally conducted on Jan. 18, 1980. Reprinted in *Writings* 1996, pp. 200–04.

——. 1985. *Jasper Johns' Paintings and Sculptures 1954–1974: The Changing Focus of the Eye*. UMI Research Press.

——. 1991. *Jasper Johns: The Seasons*. Exh. cat. Brooke Alexander Editions.

——. 1996. Seeing a Thing Can Sometimes Trigger the Mind to Make Another Thing. In Varnedoe 1996, pp. 39–91.

Bourdon, David. 1977. Interview with Jasper Johns, October 11, 1977. Reprinted in *Writings* 1996, pp. 155–62.

Brundage, Susan, ed. 1993. *Jasper Johns: 35 Years, Leo Castelli*. Leo Castelli Gallery.

Cage, John. 1964. Stories and Ideas. In Solomon 1964, pp. 21–26.

Carpenter, Joan. 1977. The Infra-Iconography of Jasper Johns. *Art Journal* 36, 3 (Spring), pp. 221–27.

Clements, Paul. 1990. The Artist Speaks. *Museum and Arts Washington* 6, 3 (May–June), pp. 76–81, 116–17. Reprinted in *Writings* 1996, pp. 242–44.

Coplans, John. 1972. Fragments According to Johns, an Interview with Jasper Johns. *Print Collector's Newsletter* 3, 2 (May–June), pp. 29–32. Reprinted in *Writings* 1996, pp. 138–41.

Cork, Richard. 1990. The Liberated Millionaire Is Not Flagging. *Times* (London), November 30, p. 21. Reprinted in *Writings* 1996, pp. 257–58.

Cotter, Holland. 2007. Bull's-Eyes and Body Parts: It's Theater, From Jasper Johns. *New York Times*, February 2, section B, pp. 29, 35.

Craft, Catherine. 2000. New Haven and Dallas: Recent Works by Jasper Johns. *Burlington Magazine* 142, 1166 (May), pp. 329–30.

Crichton, Michael. 1977. *Jasper Johns*. Exh. cat. Whitney Museum of American Art/ Harry N. Abrams.

——. 1994. *Jasper Johns*. Harry N. Abrams. Revised and expanded edition of 1977 original published by the Whitney Museum of American Art, New York.

Cuno, James. 1987a. Voices and Mirrors/ Echoes and Allusions, Jasper Johns's *Untitled*, 1972. In Cuno 1987b, pp. 201–34.

——, ed. 1987b. *Foirades/Fizzles: Echo and Allusion in the Art of Jasper Johns*. Exh. cat. The Grunwald Center for the Graphic Arts/ Wight Art Gallery, University of California, Los Angeles.

Dannatt, Adrian. 2007. Artist Interview: Jasper Johns. *Art Newspaper* 16, 176 (January), pp. 34–35.

Davvetas, Demosthène. 1984. Jasper Johns et sa famille d'objets. *Art Press* (Paris) 80 (April), pp. 11–12. Reprinted in *Writings* 1996, pp. 217–19.

de Antonio, Emile. 1984. *Painters Painting*. Abbeville Press.

Diamonstein Spielvogel, Barbaralee. 1994. *Inside the Art World: Conversations with Barbaralee Diamonstein*, pp. 114–20. Rizzoli. Reprinted in *Writings* 1996, pp. 290–99.

Elderfield, John. 2007. *Diver*: A Delay. In Weiss 2007b, pp. 190–205.

Esterow, Milton. 1993. The Second Time Around. *Artnews* 92, 6 (Summer), pp. 148–53.

Fenton, James. 1996. A Banner with a Strange Device. *New York Review of Books* 43, 20 (December 19), pp. 61–67.

Field, Richard S. 1970. *Jasper Johns: Prints 1960–1970.* Exh. cat. Philadelphia Museum of Art/Praeger.

——. 1978. *Jasper Johns: Prints 1970–1977.* Exh. cat. Center for the Arts, Wesleyan University.

——. 1999. Chains of Meaning: Jasper Johns's Bridge Paintings. In Garrels et al. 1999, pp. 15–36.

Fine, Ruth. 1990. Making Marks. In Rosenthal and Fine 1990, pp. 46–67.

Fine, Ruth, and Nan Rosenthal. 1990. Interview with Jasper Johns. In Rosenthal and Fine 1990, pp. 69–83.

Fisher, Philip. 1990. Jasper Johns: Strategies for Making and Effacing Art. *Critical Inquiry* 16, 2 (Winter), pp. 313–54.

Francis, Richard. 1984. *Jasper Johns*. Abbeville Press.

Fuller, Peter. 1978a. Jasper Johns Interviewed I. *Art Monthly* (London), 18 (July–August), pp. 6–12. Reprinted in *Writings* 1996, pp. 173–82.

——. 1978b. Jasper Johns Interviewed Part II. *Art Monthly* (London), 19 (September), pp. 5–7. Reprinted in *Writings* 1996, pp. 182–88.

Garrels, Gary, et al. 1999. *Jasper Johns: New Paintings and Works on Paper*. Exh. cat. San Francisco Museum of Modern Art.

Geelhaar, Christian. 1980a. Interview with Jasper Johns. In Geelhaar 1980b, pp. 37–56. Reprinted in *Writings* 1996, pp. 188–97.

——, ed. 1980b. *Jasper Johns Working Proofs*. Exh. cat. Petersburg Press.

Glueck, Grace. 1966. No Business like No Business. *New York Times*, January 16, section 2, p. 26. Reprinted in *Writings* 1996, p. 128.

——. 1977. The 20th-Century Artists Most Admired by Other Artists. *Artnews* 76, 9 (November), pp. 78–103. Portions reprinted in *Writings* 1996, pp. 162–64.

Goldman, Judith. 1981. *Jasper Johns: Prints, 1977–1981*. Exh. cat. Thomas Segal Gallery, Boston.

——. 1982. *17 Monotypes*. Universal Limited Art Editions.

——. 1987. *Jasper Johns: The Seasons.* Exh. cat. Leo Castelli.

Gratz, Roberta Brandes. 1970. Daily Closeup: After the Flag. *New York Post* (December 30), p. 25. Reprinted in *Writings* 1996, pp. 137–38.

Greenberg, Clement. 1962. After Abstract Expressionism. *Art International* 6, 8 (October), pp. 24–32.

Higginson, Peter. 1974. Jasper Johns and the Influence of Ludwig Wittgenstein. M.A. thesis, University of British Columbia.

——. 1976. Jasper's Non-Dilemma: A Wittgensteinian Approach. *New Lugano Review* 10, pp. 53–60.

Hindry, Ann. 1989. Conversation with Jasper Johns/Conversation avec Jasper Johns. *Artstudio* 12 (Spring), pp. 6–25. Reprinted in *Writings* 1996, pp. 227–34.

Hopps, Walter. 1965. An Interview with Jasper Johns. *Artforum* 3, 6 (March), pp. 32–36. Reprinted in *Writings* 1996, pp. 106–13.

Jespersen, Gunnar. 1969. Møde med Jasper Johns. *Berlingske Tidende* (Copenhagen) (February 23), p. 14. Excerpted in *Writings* 1996, pp. 134–37.

Johns, Jasper. 1959. Artist's statement. In *Sixteen Americans*, edited by Dorothy C. Miller, p. 22. Exh. cat. Museum of Modern Art, New York. Reprinted in *Writings* 1996, pp. 19–20.

——. 1966. "This Week's Cover": *White Flag*, Tokyo, 25 Oct. '66. *Asahi Magazine* (Tokyo) 8, 46 (November 6), p. 110. Reprinted in *Writings* 1996, pp. 21–22.

——. 1968. Marcel Duchamp (1887–1968). *Artforum* 7, 3 (November), p. 6. Reprinted in *Writings* 1996, p. 22.

Johnson, Ellen. 1974. For Jasper Johns. Brochure produced by the Arts Council of Great Britain.

Katz, Jonathan. 1998. Jasper Johns' Alley Oop: On Comics and Camouflage. http://www.queerculturalcenter.org/Pages/KatzPages/Katzoops.html.

Kent, Sarah. 1990. Jasper Johns: Strokes of Genius. *Time Out* (London) (December 5–12), pp. 14–15. Reprinted in *Writings* 1996, pp. 258–59.

Kimmelman, Michael. 1996. Sifting Among the Icons for the Key to Johns. *New York Times*, October 18, pp. C1, C32.

——. 2005. Jasper Johns: "Catenary." *New York Times,* May 27, p. B32.

Klüver, Billy. 1963. Interview with Jasper Johns, March 1963. Reprinted in *Writings* 1996, pp. 84–91.

Kozloff, Max. 1964. The Many Colorations of Black and White. *Artforum* 2, 8 (February), pp. 22–25.

——. 1967. The "Colors"; The "Maps"; The "Devices." *Artforum* 6, 3 (November), pp. 26–31.

——. 1968. *Jasper Johns*. Harry N. Abrams.

Krauss, Rosalind. 1965. Jasper Johns. *Lugano Review* 1, 2, pp. 84–113.

——. 1976. Jasper Johns: The Functions of Irony. *October* 2 (Summer), pp. 91–99.

Lewis, Jo Ann. 1990. Jasper Johns, Personally Speaking. *Washington Post*, May 16, pp. F1, F6. Reprinted in *Writings* 1996, pp. 240–42.

Livingstone, Marco. 2000. Jasper Johns. In *Encounters: New Art from Old*, edited by Richard Morphet, pp. 177–89. Exh. cat. National Gallery, London/National Gallery Company Limited.

Mancusi-Ungaro, Carol. 2007. A Sum of Corrections. In Weiss 2007b, pp. 236–60.

Marden, Brice. 1971. Three Deliberate Greys for Jasper Johns. *Art Now: New York* 3, 1 (March), n.pag.

McKenzie, Sylvia L. 1965. Allendale Native: Jasper Johns Art Hailed Worldwide. *Charleston News and Courier* (South Carolina), October 10, p. 13B. Reprinted in *Writings* 1996, p. 122.

Meyer, James. 2006. Hodgkin's Body. In *Howard Hodgkin*, pp. 19–60. Exh. cat. Tate Britain/Tate Publishing.

Morris, Robert. 2007. Jasper Johns: The First Decade. In Weiss 2007b, pp. 208–33.

Nash, Jay, and James Holmstrand. 1964. Zeroing in on Jasper Johns. *Literary Times* 3, 7 (September), pp. 1, 9, 14. Reprinted in *Writings* 1996, pp. 104–06.

Olson, Roberta J. M. 1977. Jasper Johns: Getting Rid of Ideas. *SoHo Weekly News* 5, 5 (November 3), pp. 24–25. Reprinted in *Writings* 1996, pp. 166–69.

Orton, Fred. 1994. *Figuring Jasper Johns*. Reaktion Books.

——. 1996. *Jasper Johns: The Sculptures*. Exh. cat. The Centre for the Study of Sculpture at the Henry Moore Institute, Leeds, England.

Pissarro, Joachim. 1999. Jasper Johns's *Bridge* Paintings under Construction. In Garrels et al. 1999, pp. 37–55.

Pohlen, Annelie. 1978. Interview mit Jasper Johns. *Heute Kunst* (Milan) 22 (May–June), pp. 21–22. Translated in *Writings* 1996, pp. 170–73.

Porter, Fairfield. 1964. The Education of Jasper Johns. *Artnews* 62, 10 (February), pp. 44–45, 61–62.

Powers, John. 1966. Twelve Paintings from the Powers' Collection. *Aspen* 3, item 8. http://www.ubu.com/aspen/aspen3/powers.html.

Prather, Marla. 2000. Jasper Johns. In *The Ebsworth Collection: Twentieth-century American Art*, edited by Bruce Robertson and Charles Brock, pp. 147–50. Exh. cat. National Gallery of Art, Washington.

Pye, Michael. 1990. Behind Veils, the Elusive Heart. *Independent on Sunday* (London), November 18, pp. 21–22. Reprinted in *Writings* 1996, pp. 254–56.

Raynor, Vivien. 1973. Jasper Johns: "I have attempted to develop my thinking in such a way that the work I've done is not me." *Artnews* 72, 3 (March), pp. 20–22. Reprinted in *Writings* 1996, pp. 142–46.

Robertson, Bryan. 1978. *Jasper Johns*. Exh. cat. Hayward Gallery, London.

Robertson, Bryan, and Tim Marlow. 1993. Jasper Johns. *Tate: The Art Magazine* (London) 1 (Winter), pp. 40–47. Reprinted in *Writings* 1996, pp. 285–90.

Rose, Barbara. 1964. New York Letter. *Art International* 8, 1 (February), pp. 40–41.

——. 1965a. The Second Generation: Academy and Breakthrough. *Artforum* 4, 1 (September), pp. 53–63.

——. 1965b. ABC Art. *Art in America* 53, 5 (October–November), pp. 57–69.

——. 1970a. The Graphic Work of Jasper Johns. *Artforum* 8, 7 (March), pp. 39–45.

——. 1970b. The Graphic Work of Jasper Johns, Part II. *Artforum* 9, 1 (September), pp. 65–74.

——. 1977. Jasper Johns: Pictures and Concepts. *Arts Magazine* 52, 3 (November), pp. 148–53.

——. 1987. Jasper Johns: The Seasons. *Vogue* (New York) 177, 1 (January), pp. 192–94, 199, 259–60.

——. 1993. Jasper Johns: *The Tantric Details*. *American Art* 7, 4 (Fall), pp. 46–71.

Rosenberg, Harold. 1977. The Art World: Twenty Years of Jasper Johns. *New Yorker* 54, 45 (December 26), pp. 42–45.

Rosenblum, Robert. 1960. Jasper Johns. *Art International* 4, 7 (September), pp. 74–77.

Rosenthal, Mark. 1993. Jasper Johns. In *Artists at Gemini G.E.L.: Celebrating the 25th Year*, pp. 58–67. Harry N. Abrams. Reprinted in *Writings* 1996, pp. 281–84.

Rosenthal, Nan. 1990. Drawing as Rereading. In Rosenthal and Fine 1990, pp. 13–45.

Rosenthal, Nan, and Ruth E. Fine. 1990. *The Drawings of Jasper Johns*. Exh. cat. National Gallery of Art, Washington.

Rothfuss, Joan. 1993. "Foirades/Fizzles": Jasper Johns's Ambiguous Objects. *Burlington Magazine* 135, 1081 (April), pp. 269–75.

——. 2003a. What Do You See: Jasper Johns' Green Angel. In Rothfuss 2003b, pp. 28–39.

——, ed. 2003b. *Past Things and Present: Jasper Johns Since 1983*. Exh. cat. Walker Art Center.

Rothkopf, Scott. 2005. *Jasper Johns: Catenary*. Exh. cat. Steidl/Matthew Marks Gallery.

Schjeldahl, Peter. 2005. String Theory. *New Yorker* (May 30), pp. 96–97.

Shapiro, David. 1971. Imago Mundi. *Artnews* 70, 6 (October), pp. 40–41, 66–68.

——. 1984. *Jasper Johns, Drawings: 1954–1984*. Harry N. Abrams.

Shiff, Richard. 1987. Anamorphosis: Jasper Johns. In Cuno 1987b, pp. 147–66.

——. 2003. Preference without a Cause. In Rothfuss 2003b, pp. 12–27.

——. 2006. Flicker in the Work: Jasper Johns in Conversation with Richard Shiff. *Master Drawings* 44, 3 (Autumn), pp. 275–98.

Slavin, Kathleen, et al. 1991. *Jasper Johns: Prints from the Leo Castelli Collection*. Exh. cat. Galerie Isy Brachot, Brussels.

Solomon, Alan R. 1964. *Jasper Johns*. Exh. cat. Jewish Museum, New York.

Solomon, Deborah. 1988. The Unflagging Artistry of Jasper Johns. *New York Times Magazine* (June 19), pp. 20–23, 63–64, 66. Reprinted in *Writings* 1996, pp. 220–21.

Sozanski, Edward. 1988. The Lure of the Impossible. *Philadelphia Inquirer Magazine* (October 23), pp. 25–31. Excerpted in *Writings* 1996, pp. 224–26.

Sparks, Esther. 1990. *Universal Limited Art Editions: A History and Catalogue: The First Twenty-Five Years*. The Art Institute of Chicago/Harry N. Abrams.

Steinberg, Leo. 1962/1972. Jasper Johns: The First Seven Years of His Art. *Metro* (New York) 4/5 (May 1962); revised and reprinted in *Other Criteria: Confrontations with Twentieth-Century Art*. Oxford University Press, 1972, pp. 17–54. Excerpted in *Writings* 1996, pp. 83–84.

Stevens, Mark, and Cathleen McGuigan. 1977. Super Artist: Jasper Johns, Today's Master. *Newsweek* 90, 17 (October 24), pp. 66–79. Excerpted in *Writings* 1996, pp. 164–66.

Stuckey, Charles. 1976. Letters: Johns: Yet Waving? *Art in America* 64, 3 (May–June), p. 5.

Swenson, Gene R. 1964. What is Pop Art? Part II. *Artnews* 62, 10 (February), pp. 40–43, 62–67. Reprinted in *Writings* 1996, pp. 92–96.

Sylvester, David. 1965. Interview with Jasper Johns recorded for the BBC in June 1965, broadcast the following October. Excerpted in *Writings* 1996, pp. 113–21.

——. 1996. *Jasper Johns Flags: 1955–1994*. Anthony d'Offay Gallery, London.

——. 1997a. Johns–II. In *About Modern Art: Critical Essays 1948–1997*, pp. 463–76. Henry Holt.

——. 1997b. Shots at a Moving Target. *Art in America* 85, 4 (April), pp. 90–97, 127.
Taylor, Paul. 1990. Jasper Johns. *Interview* 20, 7 (July), pp. 96–100, 122–23. Reprinted in *Writings* 1996, pp. 244–53.

——. 2001. "Jasper Johns 1965." In *Interviews with American Artists*, pp. 145–170. Chatto and Windus.

Tomkins, Calvin. 1980. *Off the Wall: Robert Rauschenberg and the Art World of Our Time*. Doubleday and Company.

——. 2006. The Mind's Eye. *New Yorker* (December 11), pp. 76–85.

Tone, Lilian. 1996. Chronology. In Varnedoe 1996, pp. 119–336, passim.

Tono, Yoshiaki. 1964. I Want Images to Free Themselves from Me. *Geijutsu Shincho* (Tokyo) 15, 8 (August), pp. 54–57. Translated in *Writings* 1996, pp. 96–101.

Tuma, Kathryn A. 2007. The Color and Compass of Things: Paul Cézanne and the Early Work of Jasper Johns. In Weiss 2007b, pp. 170–87.

U.S.A. Artists 8: Jasper Johns. 1966. 16mm film produced and directed by Lane Slate, written by Alan R. Solomon. N.E.T. (National Educational Television Network) and Radio Center. Transcribed in *Writings* 1996, pp. 123–28.

Varnedoe, Kirk, ed. 1996. *Jasper Johns: A Retrospective*. Exh. cat. Museum of Modern Art, New York/Harry N. Abrams.

Vaughan, David. 1990. *Dancers on a Plane: Cage, Cunningham, Johns*. Anthony d'Offay Gallery, London.

Wallach, Amei. 1977. Jasper Johns, Enigma. *New York Newsday,* October 2, part 2, pp. 4–5, 14. Reprinted in *Writings* 1996, p. 155.

——. 1988. Jasper Johns at the Top of His Form. *New York Newsday,* October 30, part 2, pp. 4, 33. Reprinted in *Writings* 1996, pp. 226–27.

——. 1999. A Master of Silence Who Speaks in Grays. *New York Times*, September 5, pp. AR29, 31.

Weatherby, W. J. 1990. The Enigma of Jasper Johns. *Guardian* (London), November 29, p. 29. Reprinted in *Writings* 1996, pp. 256–57.

Weinberg, Jonathan. 1988. It's in the Can: Jasper Johns and the Anal Society. *Genders* 1 (Spring), pp. 40–56.

Weiss, Jeffrey. 2007a. Painting Bitten by a Man. In Weiss 2007b, pp. 2–56.

——, ed. 2007b. *Jasper Johns: An Allegory of Painting, 1955–1965*. Exh. cat. National Gallery of Art, Washington/Yale University Press.
Welish, Marjorie. 1999. *Signifying Art: Essays on Art after 1960*. Cambridge University Press.

White, Edmund. 1977. Jasper Johns and Samuel Beckett. *Christopher Street* 2, 4 (October), pp. 20–24. Reprinted in *Writings* 1996, pp. 153–55.

Willard, Charlotte. 1966. Eye to I. *Art in America* 54, 2 (March–April), pp. 49–59.

Winkfield, Trevor. 1996. The Artists' Artist. *Modern Painters* 9, 4 (Winter), pp. 22–25.

Writings. 1996. *Jasper Johns: Writings, Sketchbook Notes, Interviews.* Edited by Kirk Varnedoe. Compiled by Christel Hollevoet. Museum of Modern Art, New York/Harry N. Abrams.

Yau, John. 1996. *The United States of Jasper Johns*. Zoland Books.

——. 2007. Jasper Johns with John Yau. *Brooklyn Rail* (February), pp. 20–22.

Young, Joseph E. 1969. Jasper Johns: An Appraisal. *Art International* 13, 7 (September), pp. 50–56. Reprinted in *Writings* 1996, pp. 129–34.

PHOTOGRAPHY CREDITS

Photographs of catalogue numbers 1–22, 24–87, and 89–138 were taken by Jamie Stukenberg of Professional Graphics, Inc., Rockford, Illinois.

Photographs of catalogue numbers 23 and 88 were taken by Taku Saiki, Tokyo.

The following credits apply to all images in this catalogue for which separate acknowledgment is due.

Rondeau Essay

2: Photograph by Colette Masson. 5: Digital Image © The Museum of Modern Art / Licensed by SCALA / Art Resource, NY. 8: Art © Estate of Aleksandr Rodchenko / RAO, Moscow / Licensed by VAGA, New York, NY. Digital Image © The Museum of Modern Art / Licensed by SCALA / Art Resource, NY. 9: Digital Image © The Museum of Modern Art / Licensed by SCALA / Art Resource, NY. 10: The Museum of Modern Art, New York, gift of the Advisory Committee. Digital Image © The Museum of Modern Art / Licensed by SCALA / Art Resource, NY. 11: Art © 2007 The Willem de Kooning Foundation / Artists Rights Society (ARS), New York. 12: © The Clyfford Still Estate. 13: Art © The Barnett Newman Foundation, New York / Artists Rights Society (ARS), New York. Digital Image © The Museum of Modern Art / Licensed by SCALA / Art Resource, NY. 15: Art © Robert Rauschenberg / Licensed by VAGA, New York, NY. 17: Kunstmuseum Basel, Gift of Marguerite Arp-Hagenbach 1968. 18: Art © The Pollock-Krasner Foundation / Artists Rights Society (ARS), New York. 19: Art © 2007 Estate of Ad Reinhardt / Artists Rights Society (ARS), New York. Photograph © The Metropolitan Museum of Art, New York. 20: Art © C. Herscovici, Brussels / Artists Rights Society (ARS), New York. Photograph © Photothèque R. Magritte-ADAGP / Art Resource, NY. 21: Art © 2007 Artists Rights Society (ARS), New York / ADAGP, Paris. 22: Art © 2007 Estate of Pablo Picasso / Artists Rights Society (ARS), New York. 23: Art © 2007 Artists Rights Society (ARS), New York. Photograph © Tate, London / Art Resource, NY. 24: Art © Artists Rights Society (ARS), New York / SIAE, Rome. 25: Photograph by Gordon Riley Christmas, courtesy PaceWildenstein, New York. © Robert Ryman, courtesy PaceWildenstein, New York. 27: Art © Robert Rauschenberg / Licensed by VAGA, New York, NY. Digital Image © The Museum of Modern Art / Licensed by SCALA / Art Resource, NY. 28–29: Photographs © 2007 Estate of Rudy Burckhardt / Artists Rights Society (ARS), New York. 42: Art © Robert Rauschenberg / Licensed by VAGA, New York, NY. 47: Art © Brice Marden / Artists Rights Society (ARS), New York. Digital Image © National Gallery of Canada. 48: Photograph by Friedrich Rosenstiel, Cologne.

Druick Essay

2: Photograph by Richard Carafelli, National Gallery of Art, Washington, D.C. 4: Art © 2007 The Josef and Anni Albers Foundation / Artists Rights Society (ARS), New York. 7–9: Picture Collection, The Branch Libraries, The New York Public Library, Astor, Lenox and Tilden Foundations. 11: Photograph © The Metropolitan Museum of Art, New York. 12: Digital Image © The Museum of Modern Art / Licensed by SCALA / Art Resource, NY. 23 Photograph by Lee Stalsworth. 25: Art © 2007 The Munch Museum / The Munch-Ellingsen Group / Artists Rights Society (ARS), New York. 26: © English Heritage Photo Library.

Pascale Essay

2, 4: Photographs courtesy Universal Limited Art Editions. 8: Art © 2007 Artists Rights Society (ARS), New York / ADAGP, Paris. 10: Art © 2007 Georgia O'Keeffe Museum / Artists Rights Society (ARS), New York.

Shiff Essay

1: Art © 2007 The Barnett Newman Foundation, New York / Artists Rights Society (ARS), New York. 2: Photograph by Jamie Stukenberg. 3–4: Erich Lessing / Art Resource, NY. 5, 12–13: Photographs by Dorothy Zeidman. 8: Digital Image © The Museum of Modern Art / Licensed by SCALA / Art Resource, NY. 9: Photograph by Michael Fredericks. 10: Photograph by Efraim Le-ver. 11: Art © 2007 Estate of Pablo Picasso / Artists Rights Society (ARS), New York. Photograph © Réunion des Musées Nationaux / Art Resource, NY.

Rose Essay

1: Digital Image © The Museum of Modern Art / Licensed by SCALA / Art Resource, NY. 2: Art © Robert Rauschenberg / Licensed by VAGA, New York, NY. 4: Photograph by Jim Strong, Inc., New York. 6: Art © 2007 Frank Stella / Artists Rights Society (ARS), New York. 8: Brian Forrest.

Keegan & Lister Essay

6: Photograph © The National Gallery, London.

INDEX OF WORKS

For ease of identification, works of art by Jasper Johns are identified as drawing (d), painting (p), print (pr), or sculpture (s); the abbreviation d/pr has been used to indicate a drawing over a print. Numbers in **bold** refer to pages with illustrations.